Counseling
California
Corporations

Counseling California Corporations

AUTHORS
Hilary Huebsch Cohen
William T. Manierre
William M. McKenzie, Jr.
Jerry W. Monroe
Stephen P. Pezzola
Doron M. Tisser
Alan L. Zimmerman

EDITED BY CEB ATTORNEYS
Margaret Shulenberger, Project Supervisor
Edward D. Giacomini

CONTINUING EDUCATION OF THE BAR ▪ CALIFORNIA

Berkeley, California
For supplement information, call (415) 642-8000

Library of Congress Catalog Card No. 90–080013

©1990 by The Regents of the University of California
Printed in the United States of America
ISBN 0-88124-264-0

5 4 3 2

BU–39230

CONTINUING EDUCATION OF THE BAR ▪ CALIFORNIA

By agreement between the Board of Governors of the State Bar of California and The Regents of the University of California, California Continuing Education of the Bar offers an educational program for the benefit of practicing lawyers. The program is administered by a Governing Committee through the University of California in cooperation with local bar associations and the Joint Advisory Committee made up of the State Bar Committee on Continuing Education of the Bar and the Deans of accredited law schools.

Practice books are published as part of the educational program. Authors are given full opportunity to express their individual legal interpretations and opinions, and these obviously are not intended to reflect any position of the State Bar of California or of the University of California. Chapters written by employees of state or federal agencies are not to be considered statements of governmental policies.

California Continuing Education of the Bar publications and oral programs are intended to provide current and accurate information about the subject matter covered and are designed to help attorneys maintain their professional competence. Publications are distributed and oral programs presented with the understanding that CEB does not render any legal, accounting, or other professional service. Attorneys using CEB publications or orally conveyed information in dealing with a specific client's or their own legal matters should also research original sources of authority.

CEB considers that the publication of any CEB practice book is the beginning of a dialogue with our readers. The periodic supplements to this book will give us the opportunity to make corrections or additions you suggest. If you know something we did not include, or if we erred, please share your knowledge with other California lawyers. Send your comments to:

Supplement Editor
California Continuing Education of the Bar
2300 Shattuck Avenue
Berkeley, California 94704

EDUCATION OF THE BAR

Richard Pearl, San Francisco
Bruce E. Ramsey, Modesto
James J. Scherer, Oakland
Richard L. Schwartzberg, Santa Ana
Anthony F. Sgherzi, Los Angeles
Suzelle M. Smith, Los Angeles
Richard Neil Snyder, San Francisco
Gary L. Waldron, Fresno
David M. Zeligs, Fair Oaks

Law School Dean Members
Dean Florian Bartosic, University of California (Davis)
Dean Scott H. Bice, University of Southern California Law Center
Dean Paul A. Brest, Stanford University
Dean Benjamin Bycel, Ventura/Santa Barbara Colleges of Law
Dean Jesse H. Choper, University of California (Berkeley)
Dean Charles E. D'Arcy, Lincoln Law School of Sacramento
Dean Michael H. Dessent, California Western School of Law
Dean Barbara S. Evans, Monterey College of Law
Dean John A. FitzRandolph, Whittier College School of Law
Dean H. Jay Folberg, University of San Francisco School of Law
Dean Arthur N. Frakt, Loyola Law School
Dean Nels B. Fransen, Humphreys College of Law
Dean Seymour Greitzer, Glendale University College of Law
Dean Kenneth Held, University of LaVerne/University of LaVerne at
San Fernando Valley Colleges of Law
Dean Chris Kanios, New College of California School of Law
Acting Dean George Kraft, Western State University College of Law of
San Diego
Dean Jeffrey Kupers, John F. Kennedy University School of Law
Dean Robert Leahy, Empire College School of Law
Dean Mark Owens, Jr., San Francisco Law School
Dean Anthony J. Pagano, Golden Gate University School of Law
Dean Janice L. Pearson, San Joaquin College of Law
Dean Ronald F. Phillips, Pepperdine University School of Law
Dean Perry Polski, University of West Los Angeles School of Law
Dean Susan Westerberg Prager, University of California (Los Angeles)
Dean Franklin Thompson Read, Hastings College of Law
Dean Gordon D. Schaber, McGeorge School of Law,
University of the Pacific
Dean Wade V. Shang, Northrop University Law Center
Dean Kristine Strachan, University of San Diego School of Law
Dean Leigh H. Taylor, Southwestern University School of Law
Dean William H. J. Tiernan, National University School of Law
Dean Gerald F. Uelmen, University of Santa Clara School of Law
Dean Marcia B. Wilbur, Western State University College of Law of
Orange County

Preface

This book is a companion volume to *Organizing Corporations in California* (2d edition), which provides the California business lawyer with the necessary tools for forming a new corporation. *Counseling California Corporations* covers the most commonly met situations during a corporation's lifetime that ordinarily call for an attorney's services. It replaces the 1978 volume entitled *Operating Problems of California Corporations*.

In the period since the earlier volume was published, there have been many new developments in corporate law practice. Directors and officers have become increasingly subject to personal liability arising out of the performance of their duties, and as a result, California has passed legislation enabling corporations to limit or eliminate directors' personal liability for negligence, and to indemnify directors, officers, or other agents if they are held personally liable. Mergers and acquisitions of other corporations have become almost commonplace in the corporate world. And a series of major legislative enactments in the field of taxation have seriously affected considerations in paying dividends or making other corporate distributions. These and other developments are dealt with extensively in *Counseling California Corporations*. In some instances, however, where the authors have determined that material from the earlier book is an accurate statement of present law and practice, that material has been incorporated into the present volume.

The business law practitioners who are authors of the chapters of this book have been most generous of their time and effort. Their names are listed on the title page of the book and at the beginning of their respective chapters. To each of them CEB expresses its sincere appreciation. We are also deeply grateful to the lawyers who served as consultants; their names are listed on the acknowledgements page.

Margaret Shulenberger was the managing attorney of this project, and the legal editor of chapters 1, 2, 3, 4, 6, and 7. Edward D. Giacomini was legal editor of chapter 5. Senior Editors Mary Fenneman and Sheila Millais were the copy and production editors. Additional editorial assistance was provided by Nancy Malen, April

Nelson, Lane Parker, Mary Bruce Reid, Mindy Spatt, Janette Tom, Patricia Van Loon, and Helene Walton. The index was prepared by Ted Francis. Ann Becker, Jean Hohenthal, Kathryn Murphy, Sue Weaver, and Myra Wysinger were the compositors. Graphics were by Jim Predny. The cover and title page were designed by Alan M. Bond. Carine Archer, head of CEB's book department, provided advice.

The general cutoff date for this book is October 1, 1989, but California legislation taking effect January 1, 1990, and some other later developments have been included. CEB plans to supplement this book on a regular basis. We solicit your comments and suggestions to help us keep it accurate and up to date.

William A. Carroll
Director

Acknowledgments

The following attorneys served as consultants on this book, reviewing and commenting on one or more chapters. Their suggestions have made the book more accurate, more practical, and more reflective of actual practice. To each of them, we express our special thanks.

Robert M. Arhelger, Senior Corporations Counsel, Department of Corporations, Sacramento

Jerry L. Baker, Senior Corporations Counsel, Department of Corporations, Los Angeles

Janyce Keiko Imata Blair, Gardena

D. Steven Blake, of Downey, Brand, Seymour & Rohwer, Sacramento

William R. Braun, of Rowe, McEwen, Braun & Rowe, San Diego

Ronald C. Carruth, Senior Corporations Counsel, Department of Corporations, San Francisco

George J. B. Cote, Newport Beach

Jeffrey W. Curcio, of Wagner & Kirkman, Sacramento

Donna M. Dell, Walnut Creek

Twila L. Foster, of Jackson, Tufts, Cole & Black, San Francisco

Paul D. Freeman, San Diego

Paul A. Graziano, of Allen & Kimbell, Santa Barbara

Bill Holden, Staff Counsel, Office of the Secretary of State, Sacramento

Thomas W. Kellerman, of Brobeck, Phleger & Harrison, San Francisco

Albin C. Koch, of Morrison & Foerster, Los Angeles

Robert Kovsky, Oakland

David V. Otterson, of Crosby, Heafey, Roach & May, Oakland

Robert C. Pearman, Jr., of Robinson & Pearman, Los Angeles

Lisa Greer Quateman, Los Angeles

Donald C. Reinke, of Zimmerman, Pezzola & Reinke, Oakland

Helen Rowe, of Rowe, McEwen, Braun & Rowe, San Diego

Charles Schug, of Bronson, Bronson & McKinnon, San Francisco

Harvey W. Stein, Oakland

Doron M. Tisser, Woodland Hills

Robin Tucker, of Weissburg & Aronson, San Francisco

Virginia L. Weber, San Diego

Fred B. Weil, of Broad, Schulz, Larson & Weinberg

Wallace M. Wong, Senior Corporations Counsel, Department of Corporations, Los Angeles

Barbara H. Yonemura, Senior Corporations Counsel, Department of Corporations, Sacramento

Contents

1

Corporate Housekeeping

Alan L. Zimmerman
Stephen P. Pezzola

ALAN L. ZIMMERMAN, B.S., 1964, Miami University (Ohio); J.D., 1967, New York University.
STEPHEN P. PEZZOLA, B.A., 1978, University of California (Berkeley); J.D., 1981, Boalt Hall School of Law, University of California (Berkeley).
The authors, both of the firm of Zimmerman, Pezzola & Reinke, practice in Oakland.

I. ROLE OF COUNSEL IN CORPORATE ACTIVITIES

§1.1   **A. In General**

Corporations routinely require the advice and assistance of counsel in connection with a variety of business problems, governmental regulations, and certain actions necessary to keep their internal affairs in order. This chapter is intended to help attorneys guide and advise small and medium-sized California corporate clients in routine corporate housekeeping and other commonly occurring activities and transactions.

The degree of responsibility for routine activities and transactions assumed by counsel may vary substantially from one corporate client to another, and from time to time. Sometimes the attorney will be requested to assume the role of "general counsel," representing and counseling the corporation in connection with routine corporate business matters in addition to the traditional housekeeping functions. These activities may include regularly advising management with regard to proposed actions, preparing business forms, negotiating business agreements, and assisting in debt collection and tax planning, as well as handling internal corporate procedures, securities, and legal affairs. In other cases, the attorney will participate only in activities or transactions that affect corporate ownership, control, or existence.

The scope and the character of the attorney's representation will be affected by the corporation's economic situation, the nature of its business, and the extent to which other professionals provide outside assistance to corporate officials. At the outset, the client and the attorney should discuss and clearly understand the nature and extent of the attorney's role, the degree to which the attorney is to participate in corporate affairs, and the degree of responsibility the attorney is to assume in providing legal services.

It is ordinarily desirable, and often necessary, for the attorney to establish communication with others who provide specialized advice or services to the client, including accountants, insurance brokers and advisers, pension and other benefit plan consultants, and financial and investment consultants or brokers. Contacting these other professionals and specialists at an early stage in the attorney-client relationship helps ensure that matters requiring assistance of counsel are brought to the attorney's attention at the appropriate time.

The attorney should be thoroughly familiar with the State Bar of California's Rules of Professional Conduct, effective May 27, 1989. This complete revision of the disciplinary rules is divided into five chapters, as follows: Chapter 1, Professional Integrity in General; Chapter 2, Relationship Among Members; Chapter 3, Professional Relationship with Clients; Chapter 4, Financial Relationship with Clients; and Chapter 5, Advocacy and Representation. See §§2.3–2.14 for discussion of conflict of interest problems in representing corporations and their principals. See also 10 CEB Cal Bus L Rep 170 (Jan. 1989) for summary of changes that are of interest to business attorneys.

§1.2   B. Attorney Fees

Fee arrangements and billing procedures should be discussed at the outset, to minimize the risk of misunderstandings that could later result in disputes. See Bus & P C §6148. It may be useful to summarize these discussions in a letter or, in special circumstances (*e.g.,* collections, securities, or litigation), in a formal agreement, to be certain that the attorney's role, fee arrangements, and any other significant matters are clearly defined.

Section 6148 of the Business and Professions Code states that if it is reasonably foreseeable that total expense to a client, including attorney's fees, will exceed $1000, the contract for services shall be in writing and contain the following:

(1) The hourly rate and other standard rates, fees, and charges applicable to the case;

(2) The general nature of the legal services to be provided to the client; and

(3) The respective responsibilities of the attorney and the client as to the performance of the contract.

Additionally, all attorneys' bills must clearly state the work performed and the method of determining the attorney's fees. Although this is not a mandatory requirement if the client is a corporation, it is nonetheless advisable to have a fee agreement even if the client is a corporation. See Bus & P C §§6146–6149. See also the sample written fee agreement forms approved by the State Bar of California Board of Governors on June 20, 1987. A copy of these forms can be obtained by sending a written request and a check or money order for $3.50 payable to the State Bar of California, addressed as follows: Fee Agreements, P.O. Box 24527, San Francisco, CA 94124–9959.

The attorney should also be familiar with the State Bar of California's Rules of Professional Conduct (effective May 27, 1989), chap 4, Financial Relationship with Clients.

§1.3   II. DETERMINING APPLICABLE LAW

The General Corporation Law (Corp C §§100–2319), effective January 1, 1977, made substantial changes in many requirements and procedures for most types of corporations. (For coverage and exclusions, see Corp C §102.) Corporations in existence before that date may still be subject to certain provisions of the prior law unless they have formally elected, by amending their articles of incorporation, to be governed entirely by the new law. Corp C §2302; see §§5.132–5.133. Counsel for such corporations should refer to Corp C §§2300–2319 to determine which law applies to a particular corporate activity. Except as otherwise noted, the former law will not be discussed in this chapter.

Many of the statutory requirements discussed in this chapter may be modified by provisions in a corporation's articles of incorporation, its bylaws, or in a shareholders' agreement. However, certain provisions are not effective unless expressly set forth in the articles; see Corp C §204(a).

Professional corporations are subject to a number of restrictions and requirements that vary from the provisions of the General Corporation Law. These are imposed by the Moscone-Knox Professional Corporation Act (Corp C §§13400–13410) and the statutes and regulatory provisions applicable to the particular profession. Discussion of these restrictions and requirements is beyond the scope of this chapter; see generally ATTORNEY'S GUIDE TO CALIFORNIA PROFESSIONAL CORPORATIONS (4th ed Cal CEB 1987).

Nonprofit corporations are governed by the Nonprofit Corporation Law (Corp C §§5000–10841) rather than the General Corporation Law, and are not within the scope of this book. For treatment, see ADVISING CALIFORNIA NONPROFIT CORPORATIONS (Cal CEB 1984).

§1.4   III. TABLE: COMMON TRANSACTIONS OF CONCERN TO COUNSEL

Activity	Action Required or Recommended	Basic Statutory Provisions	Reminders for Attorney
(A) Corporate directors			
(1) Annual election	Election by vote at annual shareholders' meeting, or by written consent without a meeting.	Corp C §§301, 600–604, 700–709.	For general rules, see §§1.31–1.63. Review articles of incorporation, bylaws, shareholders' agreements, and corporate contracts for special procedures, restrictions, or limitations. Make sure all notice requirements are set. See §§1.40–1.45. Cumulative voting may be required by any shareholder. See §1.51. Election of directors without a meeting requires unanimous written consent of all shares entitled to vote for directors.

Activity	Action Required or Recommended	Basic Statutory Provisions	Reminders for Attorney
(2) Removing directors			
(a) By board of directors	Removal by board action at a meeting or by unanimous written consent without a meeting, if director is judicially declared of unsound mind or convicted of a felony.	Corp C §§302, 303(c), 307.	Review articles of incorporation, bylaws, and shareholder agreements. See §§1.5–1.30 for general procedure for board action.
(b) By shareholders	Without cause at a meeting or by written consent without a meeting.	Corp C §§152, 303, 600–605.	Review articles of incorporation, bylaws, and shareholder agreements. See §§1.31–1.63 for general procedures for shareholder action.
(c) By court order	On petition of 10 percent of outstanding shares of any class, on grounds of fraud, dishonest acts, or gross abuse of discretion with respect to the corporation.	Corp C §§304, 309, 317.	Consider ethical implications if counsel for corporation also represents director. Consider whether director can be reimbursed for expenses.
(3) Filling vacancy on board			
(a) By board of directors	Board may elect director to fill vacancy (unless vacancy created by removal of director) at a meeting or by unanimous written consent.	Corp C §§192, 305, 307.	Review articles of incorporation, bylaws, and shareholder agreements. For general procedure for board action, see §§1.5–1.30.

Activity	Action Required or Recommended	Basic Statutory Provisions	Reminders for Attorney
(b) By share-holders	Shareholders may elect director to fill vacancy at a shareholders' meeting or by written consent.	Corp C §§305, 603.	Review articles of incorporation, bylaws, and shareholder agreements. For general procedure for shareholders' action, see §§1.31–1.63.
(4) Appointing committees of board	Committees may be created, and members and alternate members appointed, by board resolution adopted at meeting or by unanimous written consent without a meeting.	Corp C §§151, 307, 311.	See §§1.7, 1.23. Review bylaws. The board may delegate substantial authority to bind the corporation.
(B) Corporate officers			
(1) Appointment and removal	Officers may be appointed and removed by the board at a meeting or by unanimous written consent without a meeting. Officers ordinarily are chosen at annual organization meeting of board following annual shareholders' meeting at which directors are elected.	Corp C §§212(b)(6), 307, 312.	Review articles of incorporation, bylaws, and shareholder agreements for special procedures and types and numbers of officers. Officers serve at pleasure of the board. See §1.22. Same person may hold any number of offices.

Activity	Action Required or Recommended	Basic Statutory Provisions	Reminders for Attorney
(2) Execution of corporate documents	Documents executed by (a) the chairman of the board, president, or vice president, and (b) the secretary, assistant secretary, chief financial officer, or assistant treasurer are presumed authorized. Special signature requirements apply to officers' certificates (Corp C §173), certifications of corporate records (Corp C §314), share certificates (Corp C §416(a)), merger agreements (Corp C §1102), certificates of reorganization (Corp C §1401), and dissolution documentation (Corp C §§1901–1902). Documents generally may be executed by any official with proper authority to do so.	Corp C §§173, 208, 313–314, 416(a), 1102, 1401, 1901–1902.	Signature should be in name of corporation by officer signing; be sure officer has appropriate authority to sign, by checking bylaws and prior actions of the board.

Activity	Action Required or Recommended	Basic Statutory Provisions	Reminders for Attorney
(C) Transactions between corporation and directors, officers, or shareholders			
(1) Indemnification of official or agent	Corporation may, by board action, shareholder approval, or court order, generally indemnify corporate officials and agents who acted reasonably and in good faith on its behalf, and who, in criminal cases, had no reason to believe their conduct was unlawful. Corporation may indemnify agents beyond express terms of Corp C §317.	Corp C §§204(a)(10)–(11), 317, 1501(b)(2).	Review facts of case carefully; review articles, bylaws, and shareholder agreements for restrictions. Disclosure in annual report may be required. See also §§2.62–2.73.
(2) Loans			
(a) Loans to corporate officers, or parent or subsidiary corporations	May be made only by majority vote of shares of all classes other than shares held by borrower, except proper advances for expenses, or loans to officers or employees under employee benefit plan when board finds corporate benefit, and, in some cases, shareholders approve.	Corp C §§175, 189, 315, 316(a)(3), 1501(b); IRC §§301, 316.	See §§1.78–1.80. Disclosure in annual report may be required. Loans should be on reasonable terms and formally documented to avoid possible interpretation as dividend or compensation. Loans made without proper approval may subject directors to personal liability. See also §2.24.

Activity	Action Required or Recommended	Basic Statutory Provisions	Reminders for Attorney
(b) Loans secured by corporation's stock	Unless otherwise adequately secured, loans are subject to restrictions and considerations similar to those for loans to corporate officers ((C)(1), above).	Corp C §§315, 316(a)(3), 1501(b); IRC §§301, 316.	See loans to corporate officers ((C)(2)(a), above).
(c) Loans to corporation by shareholders	May be made; should be carefully documented.	IRC §1361(b)(1).	If loan is not properly documented, creditors or taxing authorities may claim that it is a contribution to equity rather than a corporate debt. See §1.78. Loans by shareholders of S corporations, if not properly documented or terms not observed, entail risk of claim that shareholder's advance creates a second class of stock, disqualifying corporation for S tax treatment.
(3) Employing shareholders	Formal employment agreement often desirable to define compensation and duties.		Payments to shareholder-employees may be construed as compensation or as dividends for tax purposes.

Activity	Action Required or Recommended	Basic Statutory Provisions	Reminders for Attorney
(4) Transactions between corporation and director	Transaction in which director has a material financial interest may be protected against an attack based on the interest or on director's presence at meeting, if (a) the transaction is approved by the shareholders (excluding shares held by the director) after full disclosure, or (b) the transaction is approved by the other directors after disclosure, and is just and reasonable as to the corporation. Formal resolution is desirable. Director's liability for monetary damages may be limited by articles of incorporation. Corp C §204(a)(10).	Corp C §§153, 309–310, 1501(b)(1), 204(a)(10).	Directors approving such a transaction should determine that it is in the best interest of the corporation and its shareholders, and the resolution should reflect this determination. See §§1.78–1.80. Disclosure of transaction in annual report may be required. See also §1.88.
(D) Records and reports			
(1) Preparing and disclosing financial records and reports	Corporation must keep adequate and correct records of accounts in writing or in a form that can be converted to writing. Shareholders have the right to inspect financial records, and to inspect or receive copies of financial reports on request.	Corp C §§1500–1501, 1507–1508, 1601–1605, 2200, 2202, 2254–2256.	See §§1.92–1.97, 3.2–3.20. Corporation and individuals may be liable for failure to comply with these requirements.

Activity	Action Required or Recommended	Basic Statutory Provisions	Reminders for Attorney
(2) Preparing and disclosing minutes	Corporation must keep written minutes of proceedings of board of directors, committees of board, and shareholders. Shareholders have the right to inspect on request.	Corp C §§1500, 1507–1508, 1601–1604, 2255–2256.	See §§1.16–1.30, 1.52–1.63, 1.84. See also §§3.15–3.16.
(3) Maintaining and disclosing record of shareholders	Corporation must maintain record of shareholders in writing or in a form that can be converted to writing. Shareholders have rights to inspect and obtain copies.	Corp C §§1500, 1507–1508, 1600, 1602–1605, 2200–2202, 2254–2256.	See §1.85. See also §§3.9–3.12.
(4) Making annual report to shareholders	Except when expressly waived in bylaws of a corporation with less than 100 shareholders, an annual report (contents specified by statute) to shareholders must be sent within 120 days after close of fiscal year and at least 15 days before annual meeting of shareholders.	Corp C §§1501, 1507.	See §§1.88–1.89; see also §§3.3–3.8. Attorney should review report before it is distributed, to determine that it complies with statutory requirements.

Activity	Action Required or Recommended	Basic Statutory Provisions	Reminders for Attorney
(5) Filing Statement of Domestic Corporation	Must be filed at least annually with Secretary of State	Corp C §§1502–1504, 2204; Rev & T C §25936.	See §§1.86–1.87. Penalty imposed for failure to comply. Revised statement may be filed when information changes. New statement must be filed to change agent for service of process.
(E) Shares and other securities			
(1) Transferring shares	Unless there are restrictions on transfer in articles, bylaws, shareholders' agreements, or other agreements, the corporation's action consists of canceling and issuing share certificates and recording shareholder information.	Corp C §§411–412, 416–418, 420–421; Com C §§8301–8302, 8308–8309, 8313, 8401–8408.	See §§1.64–1.75. Review articles, bylaws, and agreements. Determine whether Commissioner of Corporations' consent is needed (§§1.66–1.69). Determine whether number or type of transferees will jeopardize status as S corporation for tax purposes (see §1.65) or as close corporation (see §1.91). Ensure that necessary legends are on certificate and that it is delivered with any required notices or copies of regulations (§§1.71–1.75).

Activity	Action Required or Recommended	Basic Statutory Provisions	Reminders for Attorney
(2) Selling additional shares	If additional shares are authorized by articles, board of directors must adopt resolutions (at a meeting or by unanimous written consent without a meeting) authorizing issuance of stated number of shares, stating consideration or price per share, and authorizing officers to cause preparation of necessary documents for qualification of offer and sale with Department of Corporations, or notice of issuance under Corp C §25102(f) or §25102(h), and federal registration if required.	Corp C §§400–403, 406, 409–414, 416–418, 1500, 25102(f), 25102(h). IRC §1244.	Review articles and share records to be certain that shares to be issued are authorized and unissued; check whether shares must be offered to existing shareholders under preemptive or preferential rights; review articles and shareholders' agreement for any requirement that shareholders approve sale; review requirements of California corporate securities law and federal securities laws. See IRC §1244 for tax planning ideas; see also chap 4.

Activity	Action Required or Recommended	Basic Statutory Provisions	Reminders for Attorney
(3) Replacing lost, stolen, or destroyed securities	Corporation should obtain statement or declaration from shareholder that certificate has been lost, stolen, or destroyed, requesting new certificate, and agreement to indemnify corporation against claim against it because of alleged loss, theft, or destruction. Corporation may require bond or security. New certificate should then be issued.	Corp C §§419, 416–418, 421, 1500; Com C §8405.	Ensure that proper stock record entries reflect cancellation of lost, stolen, or destroyed certificate.
(F) Declaring and paying dividends; redeeming shares	Declaration and payment of dividends (in cash, shares, or other property) must be approved by resolution of board of directors adopted at a meeting or by unanimous written consent without a meeting. Notice of redemption given by mail and publication; redemption funds may be deposited as trust fund.	Corp C §§207(d), 316, 500–511.	Review articles, bylaws, shareholders agreements, corporate agreements (e.g., loan and investment agreements), and securities for restrictions or special requirements. Review statutory financial requirements. See §§4.8–4.22. Directors and shareholders may be liable for illegally declared dividend. See §§2.32–2.35. Redeemed shares become authorized, but unissued, shares. Review tax effect of transaction. See §§4.23–4.59.

Activity	Action Required or Recommended	Basic Statutory Provisions	Reminders for Attorney
(G) Employee benefits			
(1) Adopting benefit plan involving securities	Board of directors adopt written plan by resolution adopted at a meeting or adopted by unanimous written consent without a meeting. Shareholder approval of some plans may be required.	Corp C §§315, 408, 500–511.	Review articles to determine whether shareholder approval is required (including effect of preemptive or preferential rights). Review articles and share records to determine whether shares subject to plan are authorized and unissued. Reserve appropriate number of shares by board resolution. Review tax consequences to corporation and to employees. Qualify with Commissioner of Corporations, and register under federal securities laws, if required. If plan requires repurchase by corporation, consider restrictions on repurchases. See pension, profit-sharing, and similar retirement plans ((G)(2), below).

Activity	Action Required or Recommended	Basic Statutory Provisions	Reminders for Attorney
(2) Pension, profit-sharing, and similar retirement plans	Board of directors adopts resolutions at a meeting or by unanimous written consent without a meeting, to adopt plan and to determine amount of contribution (if amount not fixed in plan), before end of fiscal year. Shareholder approval of some plans may be required.	Corp C §§207(f), 315; numerous IRC provisions (see *Reminders for Attorney* column).	For detailed discussion, tax references, and procedure, see ATTORNEY'S GUIDE TO PENSION AND PROFIT-SHARING PLANS (3d ed Cal CEB 1985). Ensure that resolutions and minutes are properly prepared. Submit application for qualification of plan to IRS and Franchise Tax Board. To qualify for deduction, corporate contributions must be paid before time for filing corporate tax return. Consult administrator of plan to assure that required governmental reports and tax returns are filed. Comply with fiduciary bonding requirements. Annual premium may be payable to Federal Pension Guarantee Corporation. If securities are to be issued or delivered under plan, see (G)(1) above.

Activity	Action Required or Recommended	Basic Statutory Provisions	Reminders for Attorney
(H) **Amending articles of incorporation**	Amendment ordinarily must be approved by resolutions adopted by board of directors and shareholder vote. Officer's certificate of amendment must be filed with Secretary of State.	Corp C §§152, 173–174, 900–911, 2302.	See chap 5. Check articles, shareholders' agreements, and statute for specific voting requirements.
(I) **Adopting fictitious business name (name other than that set forth in articles of incorporation)**	Fictitious business name statement must be executed by appropriate corporate official, filed by county clerk in county of principal place of business, and, within 30 days of filing, published once a week for 4 weeks. Declaration of publication is filed with county clerk.	Bus & P C §§17900–17930; Govt C §6064.	Some counties require use of local printed form. Check with county clerk and local legal newspaper for information and assistance. Statement is effective for 5 years. For discussion, see ADVISING CALIFORNIA PARTNERSHIPS §§3.20–3.27 (2d ed CEB 1988).
(J) **Protecting trademarks**			
(1) California registration	Corporation may register trademark with Secretary of State.	Bus & P C §§14200–14342.	Provides protection within state; registration establishes prima facie ownership. For forms and instructions, write to Secretary of State, 111 Capitol Mall, Sacramento, CA 95814.

Activity	Action Required or Recommended	Basic Statutory Provisions	Reminders for Attorney
(2) Federal registration	Corporation may register trademark with United States Patent Office.	15 USC §§1051–1127.	Federal registration may be desirable when corporation does business in other states. See U.S. Patent and Trademark Office publication, GENERAL INFORMATION CONCERNING TRADEMARKS (rev 1984).
(K) Qualifying to do business in other states	Corporation doing business in other states may be required to qualify with appropriate officials in those states.		Qualification ordinarily will protect use of corporate name in other state. For summaries of various state requirements and penalties for failure to qualify, see CT Corporation System, WHAT CONSTITUTES DOING BUSINESS (1981). Corporation service companies can help determine requirements and file documents.

IV. ACTION BY DIRECTORS

§1.5   A. Necessity for Directors' Action

The corporation's business and affairs generally are managed and corporate powers are exercised by the board of directors or under its direction. Corp C §300(a). (Statutory close corporations, however, through appropriate provisions in their shareholders' agreement, may modify this general principle and assign corporate responsibilities customarily exercised by the board to other corporate officials; see §§1.91–1.99.)

Actions that generally require approval of, or that may be taken by, the board of directors include the following:

(1) Electing officers of the corporation (Corp C §312);

(2) Adopting, amending, or repealing bylaws (Corp C §211);

(3) Electing directors to fill vacancies on the board (Corp C §305(a));

(4) Adopting business policies and plans (see Corp C §300(a));

(5) Designating committees of the board and allocating authority to the committees (Corp C §§307, 311);

(6) Approving indemnification of corporate directors, officers, and agents (Corp C §317(e));

(7) Approving issuance and sale of corporate securities (Corp C §409);

(8) Calling shareholder meetings (Corp C §600);

(9) Declaring dividends and other shareholder distributions, and share redemptions (Corp C §§166, 300, 311(f));

(10) Amending the articles of incorporation in certain cases (Corp C §§212(a), 901–902, 2302, 2304);

(11) Approving the sale, lease, conveyance, exchange, transfer, or other disposition of corporate property and assets (Corp C §§300, 1001; but see Corp C §313 regarding documents signed without authority);

(12) Approving mergers and reorganizations (Corp C §§1101, 1200);

(13) Approving the adoption of pension, profit-sharing, and other employee benefit plans (Corp C §§207(f), 300, 315(b), 408);

(14) Approving corporate borrowing and loans (Corp C §§207(g), 300; see Corp C §§310, 315–316, 1501 regarding loans to insiders or secured by the corporation's shares);

(15) Designating corporate depository bank and authorized signatories; and

(16) Removing directors in some instances (Corp C §§302, 305).

NOTE: The above list is not exhaustive, and some of the actions listed may require shareholder consent or approval (see §§1.31–1.34).

B. Procedure

§1.6   1. Types of Action

Action by directors is customarily taken at regular or special meetings of the board of directors or of a committee of the board. Corp C §§307, 311. See §§1.8–1.28. The board of directors may act without a meeting by unanimous written consent of the members. Corp C §§195, 307(b). See §§1.29–1.30. Many provisions of the Corporations Code permit the statutory requirements to be modified by provisions in the articles of incorporation or bylaws. See discussion of this point in §1.33.

§1.7   2. Committees

The board of directors may ordinarily establish committees of the board made up of board members, and may delegate to those committees the authority to act on behalf of the full board. Corp C §§151, 311. Authority to take the following actions, however, may not be delegated to committees of the board:

(a) Actions for which shareholder approval is also required;

(b) Filling vacancies on the board of directors or committees;

(c) Fixing the compensation of directors;

(d) Adopting, repealing, or amending bylaws;

(e) Amending or repealing any resolution of the board that expressly provides that it is not amendable or repealable by a committee;

(f) Approving a distribution to shareholders, unless the board has established appropriate guidelines for shareholder distributions by committee; or

(g) Establishing other committees of the board or appointing or removing members of committees. Corp C §311.

Committees of the board must consist of two or more directors who serve on the committee at the pleasure of the board. The board may also designate directors as alternate members of any committee, with the authority to replace any absent member at any committee meeting. Committees of the board are established by an appropriate bylaw or a resolution adopted by a majority of the authorized number of directors, defining the committee's authority, responsibility, and number of members. See Corp C §311. For a form of resolution for this purpose, see §1.23. The appointment of committee members or alternate members requires the vote of a majority of the authorized number of directors. Corp C §311.

3. Meetings

§1.8   **a. Frequency**

The number and frequency of meetings of the board of directors or its committees will depend largely on the nature and extent of the corporation's business and activities, whether it has outside directors, and whether it is closely held. An organizational meeting of the board customarily is held following the annual meeting of shareholders at which new directors are elected. A primary purpose of the organizational meeting is to elect officers of the corporation to serve in the coming year. The board or its committees may hold regular meetings throughout the year or call special meetings when necessitated by corporate business.

§1.9   b. Form: Call of Meeting

Form 1.9–1

CALL OF [*BOARD OF DIRECTORS/_ _ _ _ _ _ COMMITTEE*] **MEETING OF** [*NAME OF CORPORATION*]

I call a [*regular/special*] **meeting of the** [_ _ _ _ _ _ _ *committee of the*] **board of directors of this corporation, to be held at** [*address and city*], **California, at** [*time*] **on** [*date*].

[*Add, if desired*]

The purpose of this meeting will be to consider and act on

[*list topics*] **and such other business as may properly come before the** [*board/committee*].

[*Continue*]

Dated: _ _ _ _ _ _ _

[*Signature*]
[*Typed name and title*]

Comment: Although the statute does not require a written call of the meeting, it is sometimes useful to provide a record. If used, it should be filed with the notice of the meeting. Unless the articles or bylaws provide otherwise, board meetings may be called by the chairman of the board, the president, any vice president, the secretary, or any two directors. Corp C §307(a)(1).

c. Notice of Meeting

§1.10   (1) Form: Notice of Board or Committee Meeting

Form 1.10–1

NOTICE OF [*BOARD OF DIRECTORS/_ _ _ _ _ _ _ COMMITTEE*] **MEETING OF** [*NAME OF CORPORATION*]

Notice is given that a [*regular/special*] **meeting of the** [_ _ _ _ _ _ _ *committee of the*] **board of directors of this corporation has been called by the** [*president/chairman /specify others*] **to be held at** [*address and city*], **California, at** [*time*] **on** [*date*].

[*Add, if desired*]

The purpose of the meeting is to consider and act on [*list topics*] **and such other business as may properly come before the** [*board/committee*].

[*Continue*]

Dated: _ _ _ _ _ _ _

[*Signature*]
Secretary

Comment: Unless otherwise provided in the articles or bylaws, board meetings may be called by the chairman of the board, president, vice president, secretary, or any two directors. Corp C §307(a)(1). Special meetings of the board may be held on four days' notice by mail or 48 hours' notice delivered personally or by telephone or telegraph. Corp C §307(a)(2). Notice of board meetings cannot be dispensed with in the articles or bylaws, but regular meetings may be held without notice if the time and place are fixed by the bylaws or the board. Corp C §307(a)(2). Notice need not be given to any director who, either before or after the meeting, signs a waiver of notice or a consent to holding the meeting or an approval of the minutes of the meeting, or who attends the meeting without protesting the lack of notice, before or at the beginning of the meeting. Corp C §307(a)(3).

The notice need not specify the purpose of the meeting. Corp C §307(a)(2).

Meetings of committees of the board are governed by the rules that apply to board meetings. For notice requirements applicable to adjourned meetings, see Corp C §307(a)(4).

§1.11 (2) Form: Agenda, Board of Directors' Meeting

Form 1.11–1

AGENDA FOR [*REGULAR/SPECIAL*] MEETING
OF
BOARD OF DIRECTORS OF
[*NAME OF CORPORATION*]

1. **Calling the meeting to order.**

2. **Taking attendance.**

3. **Considering minutes of last meeting.**

4. [*Election of officers*].

5. [*Business continued from previous meetings, if any*].

6. [*Specify new business, if desired*].

[7.] **Other business.**

[8.] **Adjournment.**

Comment: Although business to be conducted need not be specified in the notice (Corp C §307(a)(2)), an agenda often is included for convenience.

§1.12   (3) Form: Waiver of Notice and Consent to Meeting

Form 1.12–1

**WAIVER OF NOTICE AND CONSENT
TO HOLDING [*REGULAR/SPECIAL*] MEETING
OF
[_ _ _ _ _ _ _ _ *COMMITTEE OF THE*] BOARD OF
DIRECTORS OF [*NAME OF CORPORATION*]**

The undersigned, [*all of the*] members of the [_ _ _ _ _ _ _ *committee of the*] **board of directors of this corporation, waive notice and consent to the holding of a [***regular/special***] meeting of [***the board/this committee***] at [***address and city***], California, on [***date***] at [***time***], and agree that any business transacted at this meeting shall be as valid and legal and have the same force and effect as though it were held after notice duly given.**

Dated: _ _ _ _ _ _ _
                             [*Signatures*]

Comment: Waivers of notice are often used as an alternative to formal notices of meetings, particularly in small- and medium-sized corporations. See Comment to Form 1.10–1, in §1.10. Waivers, consents, and approvals of the minutes must be filed with the corporate records or made a part of the minutes of the meeting. Corp C §307(a)(3).

d. Meeting Procedure

§1.13   (1) Attendance and Quorum

Directors may participate in meetings either in person or by conference telephone or similar communications equipment, as long as all directors participating in the meeting can hear each other. Directors so participating by telephone or use of similar equipment are considered present at the meeting. Corp C §307(a)(6).

A quorum is a majority of the authorized number of directors, unless a different number is provided in the articles (see Corp C §204(a)(5)); except in one-director corporations, the quorum number cannot be less than one third of the authorized number of directors or two directors, whichever is larger. Corp C §307(a)(7). If a quorum is initially present at a meeting but some directors leave, business may still be transacted by the approval of a majority of the quorum required for the meeting. Corp C §307(a)(8).

§1.14 (2) Conducting the Meeting

The chairman of the board of directors, if there is such an officer, ordinarily presides at board meetings; if there is no chairman of the board, the president presides. The presiding officer often relies on the attorney's guidance and assistance in conducting the meeting, particularly in small, closely held corporations. It is usually desirable for the attorney to go over the agenda with the presiding officer, discussing the manner in which the meeting will be conducted and the number of votes necessary to take various actions.

§1.15 (3) Voting at Meetings

The vote of a majority of the directors present ("directors present" includes those participating by conference telephone or similar arrangement; see Corp C §307(a)(6)) at a meeting at which there is a quorum, ordinarily is required for board action. Corp C §307(a)(8). This requirement cannot be relaxed by the articles or bylaws. If a quorum is initially present and then lost because some directors leave the meeting, action may still be taken by vote of a majority of the quorum required for the meeting (see §1.13). However, only the vote of a majority of those *present* (even if there is not a quorum) is necessary to adjourn the meeting to another time and place. Corp C §307(a)(4). (Note that notice of the adjournment may have to be given to directors not present. Corp C §307(a)(4).)

e. Recording the Proceedings

§1.16   (1) Checklist for Preparation of Minutes

Form 1.16–1

MINUTES PREPARATION CHECKLIST
Board of Directors or Committee Meeting
[ ] Board of Directors   [ ] Committee

1. Name of corporation: _____

2. Date and time of meeting: _____

3. Place of meeting: _____

4. Type of meeting: ___ Regular ___ Special

5. Meeting held pursuant to: ___ Waiver ___ Notice (attach notice)

6. Number of directors required for quorum: _____

7. Directors present: _____

   _____

8. Directors absent: _____

   _____

9. Others present: _____

   _____

10. Minutes of previous meeting approved? ___ Yes ___ No

11. Financial report presented: ___ Oral ___ Written

    Date of report: _____ Copy attached

12. Election of officers (after annual meeting of shareholders or as required by resignation or removal of officers):

President [*and Chief Executive Officer*]:

_____

Vice president: _____

Secretary: _____

Chief Financial Officer:

Comment: The president (or, if there is no president, the chairman of the board) is general manager and chief executive officer unless the articles or bylaws provide otherwise. Corp C §312(a). Corporations need not have a vice president or a treasurer, but must have a chief financial officer. Corp C §312(a). In corporations existing on January 1, 1977, the treasurer is the chief financial officer. Corp C §2305.

13. Designation of agent for service of process: _____

_____

14. Other business:

A. Amendment to articles

Article Number: _____
Change: _____

_____

B. Amendment to bylaws

Article and Paragraph Number: _____

Change: _____

_____

Comment: A checklist such as this may help counsel or corporate officials take notes of the proceedings of board or committee meetings, and may be used as a basis for preparing formal meeting minutes. Tape recordings and other aids may also be helpful. If a meeting is to be taped, the consent of all parties who participate should be obtained.

§1.17   (2) Use of Minutes

A written record of the proceedings of the board of directors and its committees must be kept. Corp C §1500. See also Corp C §§300(e) (informal proceedings of close corporations), 1507 (liability for false entries and changes). The original or a copy of the minutes, certified by the secretary or assistant secretary, is prima facie evidence that the meeting was held and that the matters stated are true. Corp C §314.

The corporation's attorney frequently assumes responsibility for preparing formal minutes of meetings of the board of directors or committees. A carefully drafted set of formal minutes establishing a written record of corporate action and proceedings is particularly desirable if an action by the board (a) makes a major change in corporate structure, management structure, or business operations, or is generally outside the ordinary course of business; (b) authorizes a distribution to shareholders; (c) involves amendments to corporate charter documents; (d) affects the purchase, sale, or transfer of the corporation's securities; or (e) may have significant tax consequences to the corporation, its employees, or its shareholders.

The attorney or other person preparing the minutes should be aware that he or she is establishing a written record for future reference, which may be used to determine the nature of the corporate action, the time and circumstances under which it was taken, and the basis for that action. Sufficient information should be included in the minutes and in the resolutions as adopted to pinpoint the actions taken and the surrounding circumstances and facts that led to the board's actions.

(3) Forms: Minutes of Directors' Meeting

§1.18   (a) Introduction

Form 1.18–1

MINUTES OF [*REGULAR/SPECIAL*] MEETING
OF
BOARD OF DIRECTORS OF
[*NAME OF CORPORATION*]

A [*regular/special*] meeting of the board of directors of this corporation was held at [*time*] on [*date*] at [*address and city*].

§1.19   (b) Persons Present

Form 1.19–1

The following directors were present at the meeting:

[*List names*]

The following directors were absent from the meeting:

[*None/List names*]

The following individuals also were present at the meeting:

[*List names*]

§1.20   (c) Notice

Form 1.20–1 (Notice Given)

The chairman called the meeting to order and announced that the meeting was held pursuant to a written notice of meeting which was given to all directors of the corporation. A copy of this notice was ordered inserted in the minute book immediately preceding the minutes of this meeting.

Comment: For notice requirements and form, see §1.10.

Form 1.20–2 (Notice Waived)

The chairman called the meeting to order and announced that the meeting was held pursuant to written waiver of notice and consent to the holding of the meeting. The waiver and consent was presented to the meeting and, on a motion duly made, seconded, and [*unanimously*] carried, was made a part of the records and ordered inserted in the minute book immediately preceding the records of this meeting.

Comment: For waiver of notice procedure and form, see §1.12.

§1.21   (d) Minutes of Last Meeting

Form 1.21–1 (Minutes Read)

The minutes of the last meeting of directors were then read and approved.

Form 1.21–2 (Reading Dispensed With)

It was then moved, seconded, and [*unanimously*] resolved to dispense with the reading of the minutes of the last meeting.

§1.22   (e) Election of Officers

Form 1.22–1

The chairman stated that the election of new officers was in order. The board then proceeded to elect new officers of the corporation. The following nominations were made and seconded:

Name   **Office**

_ _ _ _ _ _ _ _ _ _ _ _ _ _ _   _ _ _ _ _ _ _ _ _ _ _ _ _ _ _

_ _ _ _ _ _ _ _ _ _ _ _ _ _ _   _ _ _ _ _ _ _ _ _ _ _ _ _ _ _

[*If election uncontested, insert*]

No further nominations were made, and the persons named above were [*duly/unanimously*] elected to the offices set forth opposite their respective names.

[*If election contested, insert*]

No further nominations were made, and the following persons were duly elected to the offices set forth opposite their respective names:

Name   Office

_____   _____
_____   _____

§1.23   (f) Establishment of Committee

Form 1.23–1

The chairman suggested that a committee be set up by the board to [*e.g., investigate the kinds of additional financing the corporation would require in the future and the financial arrangements that would be suitable to meet those requirements, and to report to the board of directors regarding the various possibilities*]. After discussion and motion duly made, seconded, and [*unanimously*] carried, the following resolutions were adopted:

RESOLVED that the board of directors establish [*e.g., a finance*] committee consisting of [*name*] as chairman, [*names*] as members, and [*name*] as alternate.

RESOLVED FURTHER that the [*e.g., finance*] committee shall [*e.g., study future financial needs of the corporation and report to the board from time to time on the results of its study, alternative methods of obtaining financing, and its recommendations for obtaining financing*], and shall meet and act at the call of its chairman at such times as circumstances require.

Comment: For requirements for committee membership, functions, and procedures, see Corp C §§307(c), 311. See also §1.7.

§1.24   (g) Adoption of Share Purchase Agreement

Form 1.24–1

The board next reviewed the proposed share purchase agreement. This agreement provides for the purchase and sale of the shares of a shareholder in the event of the shareholder's [*death/ disability/termination of employment by the corporation/state other*]. **On motion duly made, seconded, and** [*unanimously*] **carried, the board approved the share purchase agreement and authorized its execution by the president and secretary of the corporation. The board then ordered that a copy of the agreement be placed in the minute book following the minutes of this meeting.**

§1.25   (h) Adoption of Medical Reimbursement Plan

Form 1.25–1

The board then discussed the merits of having a medical and dental reimbursement plan for qualified employees. On motion duly made, seconded, and [*unanimously*] **carried, the board of directors adopted the following resolution:**

RESOLVED that the board of directors approve and adopt the medical and dental reimbursement plan, attached to this resolution as Exhibit A, and by this reference incorporated into this resolution, and the proper officers are authorized and directed to take such steps as may be necessary or convenient to cause that plan to become effective as of [*date*].

§1.26   (i) Approval of Employment Agreement

Form 1.26–1

The chairman then introduced the matter of an employment agreement between the corporation and its [*title of employee*]. **A proposed draft of an employment agreement between the corporation and** [*name*] **was reviewed and discussed. On motion duly made, seconded, and** [*unanimously*] **carried, the board adopted the following resolutions:**

WHEREAS the board has reviewed and considered the terms and conditions of the proposed employment by corporation of [*name*] **to provide** [*describe*] **services beginning on** [*date*] **and the proposed terms and conditions of employment of** [*name*] have been reduced to writing in the form of a draft employment agreement; and

WHEREAS the board believes that the approval of the proposed employment agreement is in the best interests of the corporation, and that the salary and other benefits provided for are reasonable in relationship to the anticipated value to the corporation of such [describe] services, and in relation to salaries received by other [title of position].

In view of the above, it is

RESOLVED that the terms and conditions of employment by the corporation of [name], as set forth in the proposed employment agreement, are approved.

RESOLVED FURTHER that the officers of the corporation are authorized to execute that agreement on behalf of the corporation and are directed to file a copy of the executed employment agreement in the minute book of the corporation immediately following the minutes of this meeting.

Comment: It may also be desirable to grant to specified officers the power to make nonmaterial changes in the draft agreement.

§1.27 (j) Corporate Consent to Stock Transfer

Form 1.27–1

The board discussed the proposed transfer of shares of stock from [name] to [name] for a purchase price of $_ _ _ _ _ _ per share. Noting that the corporation's bylaws contain certain restrictions on the transfer of shares, on a motion duly made, seconded, and [unanimously] carried, the board adopted the following resolution:

RESOLVED that the board of directors waives the right of the corporation to purchase [number] shares of stock from [name] and [unanimously] authorizes and consents to the sale and transfer of those [number] shares of the common stock of the corporation by [transferor's name] to [transferee's name].

§1.28　　　(k) Adjournment

Form 1.28–1

There being no further business to come before the meeting, the meeting was duly adjourned.

> [*Signature*]
> **Secretary**

C. Directors' Action Without Meeting

§1.29　　　1. Requirements for Action

Directors may act by written consent without a meeting. Unlike actions taken at meetings, however, an action by written consent without a meeting requires consent of all the directors and has the effect of a unanimous vote. Corp C §307(b). The writing may be in the form of one or more documents signed by the directors, facsimiles of those documents, or telegraphic communication. See Corp C §195. Consents must be filed with the minutes of board proceedings. Corp C §307(b).

§1.30　　　2. Form: Written Consent to Action Without Meeting

Form 1.30–1

[*NAME OF CORPORATION*]
CONSENT TO ACTION
BY BOARD OF DIRECTORS WITHOUT A MEETING

The undersigned director(s) of [*name of corporation*]**, a California corporation, consent(s) to the following action of the board of directors without a meeting by unanimous consent of all of the directors:**

[*Insert, as appropriate*]

Adoption of the following resolution of the board of directors: [*text of resolution*].

The election of the following persons as officers of the corporation: [*names and titles*].

[Continue]

This action is taken under section 307(b) of the California Corporations Code.

Dated: _ _ _ _ _ _ _ _

[Signature(s)]

Comment: See §1.29. Consents executed by all directors must be filed with the minutes of board meetings. Corp C §307(b).

V. SHAREHOLDERS' APPROVAL, CONSENT, OR OTHER VOTE

A. Statutory Requirements

§1.31   1. General Rule: Two Types of Approval

Shareholder approval of corporate transactions is necessary or desirable in a variety of circumstances. For certain corporate acts, shareholder approval is required, and for others it is permitted, *e.g.,* as an alternative to approval by the board of directors.

NOTE: Special rules apply to statutory close corporations; see §§1.92–1.99.

The Corporations Code defines two different types of shareholder approval: approval "by the shareholders" (Corp C §153), and approval "by the outstanding shares" (Corp C §152). To determine which type of approval is required in a given instance, counsel should consult the Code section dealing with the particular matter being voted on. See §1.32 for a list of some particular matters and the type of approval required by statute.

Actions that must be approved "by the shareholders" (Corp C §153) must receive the affirmative vote of a majority (or any greater proportion required by the articles or statute) of the *shares represented and voting* at a duly held meeting at which a quorum is present (which shares, voting affirmatively, must also constitute at least a majority of the required quorum), or by written consent of the shareholders under Corp C §603. Corp C §153. Shares may be present and voting by proxy as well as in person; see §1.46 below.

Actions that must be approved by "the outstanding shares" (Corp

C §152) must receive the affirmative vote of a majority (or any greater proportion required by the articles or statute) of *all the outstanding shares entitled to vote.* Since abstention is in effect a negative vote, this requirement is much more stringent than mere approval of "the shareholders."

Some Code sections permit a corporation to vary the statutory type of approval by a provision to the contrary in the articles or bylaws; see §1.33.

NOTE: Both approval "by the shareholders" and approval "by the outstanding shares" require the affirmative vote of the required proportion of the outstanding shares of any *class or series* of shares entitled to vote as a class or series on the subject at issue. See Corp C §§117, 152–153.

Shareholder action by written consent without a meeting (see §§1.61–1.63) generally requires consent of the same number of shares that would be necessary to take the action at a meeting at which all shares entitled to vote were present and voting. Corp C §603.

§1.32   2. List of Common Transactions and Type of Approval Required

Statutes relating to specific matters may impose special voting requirements, which may in some cases include a vote by shares whose voting rights otherwise would be limited or restricted. See, *e.g.,* Corp C §158(b)–(c) (status as a close corporation); Corp C §315 (loans or guaranties to directors or officers); Corp C §§903–904 (certain amendments to articles); Corp C §1111 (merger of a close corporation); Corp C §1201 (certain reorganizations); Corp C §2007 (certain distributions on dissolution).

Common matters on which the Corporations Code requires or provides for shareholder approval and the vote required (subject to detailed provisions of individual statutes) include the following:

• **Election of directors.** Plurality of the shares represented at meeting (cumulative voting possible (see §1.51)); unanimous vote if by written consent without meeting. Corp C §§600(b), 602(a), 603(d), 708. If election is to fill a vacancy, see Corp C §305 for requirements.

- **Removal of directors.** Approval of the outstanding shares (Corp C §152) subject to specified limitations. Corp C §303.
- **Amendment of the articles of incorporation, in general.** Approval of the outstanding shares (Corp C §152); additional requirements apply to certain types of amendments. Corp C §§902–904. See chap 5.
- **Adoption, amendment, or repeal of bylaws, in general.** Approval of the outstanding shares (Corp C §152). Corp C §211.
- **Adoption of bylaw specifying or changing fixed number, or limits of variable number, of directors.** Approval of the outstanding shares (Corp C §152); special vote requirement applies if number reduced to less than five. Corp C §212(a).
- **Indemnification of director, officer, employee, or other agent.** Approval of the shareholders (Corp C §153), excluding shares owned by the indemnified party. Corp C §317(e)(3).
- **Transactions between corporation and director.** Approval of the shareholders (Corp C §153), excluding shares owned by the interested director. Corp C §§310, 1501(b).
- **Loans or guaranties of loans to insiders, in general.** Vote of the majority of outstanding shares (other than shares held by the benefited party) of all classes, regardless of limitations on voting rights. Corp C §§315, 316(a)(3). See chap 2.
- **Adoption of a corporate stock purchase plan, stock option plan, or employee benefit plan that includes officers or directors.** Approval of the shareholders (Corp C §153). Corp C §§315(b), 408.
- **Sale or transfer of substantially all of the assets.** Approval of the outstanding shares (Corp C §152). Corp C §1001. See chaps 6–7.
- **Some corporate reorganizations.** Approval of the outstanding shares (Corp C §152) of each class. Corp C §1201. See chap 6.
- **Most corporate dissolutions.** Vote of the shareholders holding 50 percent of the voting power. Corp C §1900.
- **Transactions affecting shareholder rights or obligations, in general.** Requirements vary; consult the particular statute. See also chap 3.

For further discussion of shareholder voting requirements, see §§1.49–1.51; see also 2 MARSH'S CALIFORNIA CORPORATION LAW §11.4 (2d ed).

§1.33 3. Variations Based on Provisions in Articles or Bylaws

Some Corporations Code sections specifying shareholder actions or procedures for particular corporate activities also permit a corporation to vary the statutory type of approval by appropriate provisions in its articles of incorporation or bylaws. On a given matter, to determine whether the controlling rule is the one set forth in the statute or a modification set forth in the articles or bylaws, counsel should search the appropriate statute for the phrase "unless otherwise provided in the articles [or bylaws]." If modification is permitted, counsel should then consult the articles or bylaws to see if the corporation has adopted a variant rule.

The procedures described in this chapter are those applicable to corporations whose articles and bylaws are standard rather than modified.

§1.34 4. Variations for Close Corporations

Many requirements applicable to corporations generally may be relaxed for statutory "close corporations." See §§1.91–1.99.

§1.35 B. Shareholder Meetings

Action by shareholders may be taken at annual or special meetings of shareholders (see §§1.36–1.60), or by written consent of shareholders without a meeting (see §§1.61–1.63). Corp C §§600, 603. The percentage of affirmative votes required depends on the subject matter and the voting procedure being used; see §§1.50–1.51.

1. Preliminary Procedures

a. Annual Meeting

§1.36 (1) Form: Counsel's Reminder Letter to Client

Form 1.36–1

[*Name and address of corporation*]
Attn: [*Name and title of appropriate officer*]

Re: Annual Meeting of Shareholders

Dear [*name*]:

Under the bylaws of your corporation, the annual meeting of shareholders should be scheduled for [*date or period*]. [*The annual report to shareholders must be sent at least 15 days before the annual meeting.*] The shareholders' meeting should be followed by the regular meeting of the board of directors.

The matters generally brought before the annual meeting of shareholders are the election of directors and an annual report regarding the corporation's operations and financial condition. There may also be other matters requiring shareholder approval that should be included on the agenda. For your information, I am enclosing a suggested agenda that can serve as a starting point.

Please contact me so we can discuss the date, necessary procedures, and what other items should be included on the agenda.

Very truly yours,

[*Signature of attorney*]
[*Typed name*]
enclosure: Agenda

Comment: Each California corporation must hold an annual shareholders' meeting to elect directors, and at that meeting the shareholders may consider and take action on such other business as may properly be brought to their attention. Corp C §600(b). The date and time of the annual meeting ordinarily are set forth or otherwise provided for in the corporation's bylaws. See Corp C §212(b)(2); see also ORGANIZING CORPORATIONS IN CALIFORNIA §§2.51–2.53 (2d ed Cal CEB 1983).

If no date is specified, or if the annual meeting is not held within 60 days after the date specified, a shareholder may apply to the court, within 15 months after the date of incorporation or the date of the corporation's last annual meeting, for a court order compelling a meeting. Corp C §600(c). The statutory provision that an annual report be sent to shareholders at least 15 days before the annual meeting does not limit the requirement for holding the meeting. Corp C §1501(a). It is good practice for the attorney providing general legal counsel to calendar a reminder to the appropriate corporate officers from 40 to 60 days before the meeting date.

NOTE: Mailing of annual reports by third-class mail is now permitted, but if sent third class, reports must be mailed at least 35 days (rather than 15 days as for first-class mail) before the annual meeting. Corp C §1501(a). For annual report requirements and conditions under which they may be waived, see §§1.88–1.89.

§1.37 (2) Form: Agenda, Annual Shareholders' Meeting

Form 1.37–1

**AGENDA FOR ANNUAL MEETING
OF
SHAREHOLDERS OF
[*NAME OF CORPORATION*]**

1. Calling meeting to order.

2. Taking attendance.

3. Considering minutes of last meeting.

4. Electing directors.

5. Presentation of the corporation's operations and financial condition.

6. Special business: [*Describe*].

7. Other business.

8. Adjournment.

Comment: Election of directors is a required agenda item; any other proper business may be transacted. Corp C §600(b). In some situations it may be desirable to prepare a more detailed written plan for the meeting.

b. Special Meeting

§1.38 (1) Forms: Letters to Client re Need or Demand for Special Meeting

Form 1.38–1 (Letter re Proposed Action Requiring Special Meeting)

[*Date*]

[*Name and address of corporation*]
Att'n: [*Name and title of appropriate officer*]

Re: Proposed Action Requiring Special Meeting of Shareholders

Dear [*name*]:

It is my understanding that the corporation wishes to [*describe proposed action*]**, which will require formal shareholder approval by the vote of** [*proportion required for approval of proposed action*]**. I recommend that a special meeting of shareholders to approve the proposed action be called for sometime before** [*date*]**.**

Please call me at your earliest convenience so that we can go over the procedure for calling and holding this special meeting.

Sincerely,

[*Signature of attorney*]
[*Typed name*]

Comment: Special meetings of shareholders may be called any time shareholder discussion or action is required or appropriate. They may be called by a vote of the board of directors, the chairman of the board of directors, the president of the corporation, the holders of shares entitled to cast at least 10 percent of the votes at the meeting (see following form), or other persons authorized in the articles, bylaws, or shareholders' agreement. Corp C §§600(d), 601(c).

Form 1.38–2 (Letter re Shareholder Demand for Special Meeting)

[*Date*]

[*Name and address of corporation*]
Att'n: [*Name and title of appropriate officer*]

Re: Shareholder Demand for Special Meeting of Shareholders

Dear [*name*]:

As you know, the corporation has received a written demand from [*name(s) of shareholder(s)*], **shareholders representing at least 10 percent of its shares, calling for a special meeting of the shareholders to deal with the subject of** [*describe*].

The corporation is required by its bylaws and the California Corporations Code to hold such a meeting at least 35 but not more than 60 days after the date of the request. Failure to give notice of the meeting within 20 days after the request was received will allow the requesting shareholders or the superior court to call the meeting. In your case the pertinent dates are as follows:

        Date demand was received: _ _ _ _ _ _ _ _ _
        Earliest date for meeting: _ _ _ _ _ _ _ _ _
        Latest date for meeting: _ _ _ _ _ _ _ _ _
        Notice must be sent out by: _ _ _ _ _ _ _ _ _

Please call me at your earliest convenience so that we can go over the procedure for calling and holding this special meeting.

                      Sincerely,

                      [*Signature of attorney*]
                      [*Typed name*]

Comment: See Comment to previous form. Holders of 5 percent of the outstanding shares have a right to call a special meeting to elect new directors if a majority of the directors were appointed by the board; see Corp C §305(c). For discussion and forms for shareholder demands for a meeting, see §§3.22–3.26.

§1.39 (2) Form: Agenda, Special Shareholders' Meeting

Form 1.39–1

AGENDA FOR SPECIAL MEETING
OF
SHAREHOLDERS OF
[NAME OF CORPORATION]

1. Calling the meeting to order.

2. Establishing due notice.

3. Taking attendance.

4. Considering minutes of last meeting.

5. *[Proposed action to be taken by shareholders.]*

6. Other business.

7. Adjournment.

Comment: In the absence of appropriate waivers and consents (see Corp C §601(e)), business may be transacted at a special meeting only if its general nature is set forth in the notice of the meeting (see §§1.41–1.43). Corp C §601(a), (f).

2. Notification to Shareholders

§1.40 a. Record Date for Identifying Shareholders Entitled To Vote

The identity and shareholdings of the shareholders who are entitled to vote at a meeting and must be given notice of the meeting are determined from the corporate records as of a date certain, called the "record date." The record date is a date fixed (1) by the board resolution calling the shareholder meeting, (2) by a bylaw provision, or (3) if neither of the above, by statute. A record date fixed by a bylaw provision or by board resolution may not be more than 60 days or less than ten days before the meeting date. Corp C §701.

Unless otherwise fixed, the statutory record date for determining shareholders entitled to receive notice of and vote at a meeting is at the close of business on the business day preceding the day notice is given (see Corp C §118 for definition), or, if notice is waived (see §§1.44–1.45), at the close of business on the business day preceding the day the meeting is held. Corp C §701(b)(1). (For purposes of obtaining shareholder written consent to action without a meeting, if no prior board action has been taken, the record date, unless otherwise fixed, is the day on which the first written consent is given. Corp C §701(b)(2). See §§1.61–1.63. The record date for determining shareholders for any other purpose (*e.g.*, receiving a dividend), unless otherwise fixed, is at the close of business on the day on which the board adopts the resolution relating to the particular matter. Corp C §701(b)(3).)

If a shareholder meeting is adjourned, the record date for the adjourned meeting applies for purposes of notice and voting, unless the board fixes a new date for the adjourned meeting or the meeting is adjourned for more than 45 days. Corp C §701(c).

§1.41   b. Notice of Meeting

The primary procedure for initiating a shareholders' meeting is to give formal written notice to shareholders entitled to vote at the meeting (see §1.40). See Corp C §601.

For discussion of required contents of the notice, see Comment to Form 1.42–1 in §1.42.

In practice, meetings of small or medium-sized corporations and other closely held corporations are often called by informal notice to the shareholders, with a waiver of notice and consent to holding the meeting (see §1.45) or a written approval of the minutes of the meeting signed by any shareholders not present, which is then filed in the minute book. Corp C §601(e). Shareholder action also may be taken without a meeting by written consent of the shareholders under Corp C §603. See §§1.61–1.63.

§1.42   (1) Form: Notice of Shareholders' Meeting

Form 1.42–1

NOTICE OF [*ANNUAL/SPECIAL*] MEETING
OF
SHAREHOLDERS OF
[*NAME OF CORPORATION*]

Notice is given that [*the annual/a special*] meeting of the shareholders of [*name of corporation*] will be held at [*address and city*], California, on [*date*], at _ _.m., to consider and act on:

[*If annual meeting*]

1. Election of directors. The board of directors intends at this time to present the following nominees for election:

[*List names*]

[2.] [*E.g., annual report to shareholders.*]

[3.] [*Other business; state its general nature.*]

[4.] [*E.g., such other business as may be properly brought up at the meeting.*]

[*If special meeting*]

[*Describe action proposed to be taken*]

[*For either annual or special meeting,
add if desired (and enclose proxy form)*]

If you do not expect to be present at the meeting and wish your shares to be voted, you may complete the attached form of proxy and mail it in the enclosed addressed envelope.

[*Continue*]

Dated: _ _ _ _ _

[*Signature*]
[*Typed name and title*]

Comment: The notice must state the date, hour, and place of the meeting. The date must be at least ten days but not more than 60 days after the notice is given. Corp C §601(a). The place of the meeting may be specified in or fixed in accordance with the bylaws. See Corp C §212(b)(2). If it is not so specified or fixed, the meeting must be held at the corporation's principal executive office. Corp C §600(a).

- **Election of directors.** The notice of any meeting, annual or special, at which directors are to be elected must include the names of any nominees that the board, at the time of the notice, intends to present for election. Corp C §601(a). Shareholders, however, may nominate directors at the meeting.
- **Special meetings.** The notice of a special meeting must state the general nature of the business to be transacted; no business other than that specified in the notice may be transacted. Corp C §601(a).
- **Annual meetings.** The notice of an annual meeting must state the general nature of matters that the board, at the time of the notice, intends to present for shareholder action. However, subject to the limitations of Corp C §601(f) (see following paragraph), at the annual meeting any proper matter may be presented for shareholder action, whether or not it was described in the notice.
- **Unanimous approval needed.** Under Corp C §601(f), unanimous approval by all shareholders entitled to vote is required for the following items, if the general nature of the proposal was not stated in the notice of the meeting or any written waiver:
  - Approval or ratification of a contract or transaction between the corporation and one or more of its directors, or between the corporation and another entity in which one or more of the directors has a material financial interest (see Corp C §310);
  - Amendments of the articles of incorporation that require approval of the outstanding shares (Corp C §152) under Corp C §902;
  - Approval of the principal terms of reorganization by the outstanding shares (Corp C §152) under Corp C §1201;
  - Election to voluntarily wind up and dissolve the corporation (see Corp C §1900); or
  - Approval of a plan of liquidation of corporations having two classes of shares, in certain situations (see Corp C §2007).
- **Procedural requirements.** Notice must be given at least ten days and not more than 60 days before the meeting. Corp C §601(a). Notice of the annual shareholders' meeting must be given either personally or by first-class mail, except that corporations with 500 or more shareholders of record may send notice by third-class

mail (Corp C §601(b)), provided the notice is sent not less than 30 days nor more than 60 days before the meeting date. Corp C §601(a). The notice must be addressed to the shareholder's address appearing on the corporation's books or the address given by the shareholder for the purpose of notice. If there is no such address, the notice may be addressed to the shareholder at the place where the corporation's principal executive office is located, or may be given by publication. If the notice is returned undelivered by the post office, requirements for future notices to the shareholder are modified. See Corp C §601(b).

• **Adjourned meetings.** For notice requirements if a meeting is adjourned to a later date, see Corp C §601(d).

§1.43   (2) Form: Declaration of Mailing

Form 1.43–1

DECLARATION OF MAILING NOTICE
OF
MEETING OF SHAREHOLDERS

I, [*name*], am, and at all times mentioned in this declaration was, the [*secretary/assistant secretary/transfer agent*] of [*name of corporation*]. On [*date*], I caused a notice of the [*annual/special*] meeting of shareholders of the corporation, a copy of which is attached to and incorporated in this declaration, to be deposited in the United States mail at [*city and state*], first-class postage prepaid, addressed to each shareholder entitled to vote at the meeting at the address of that shareholder appearing on the books of the corporation or given by the shareholder to the corporation for the purpose of notice. I declare under penalty of perjury under the laws of the state of California that the foregoing is true and correct.

[*Signature*]
[*Typed name and title*]

Comment: An affidavit of mailing of the notice signed by the secretary, assistant secretary, or transfer agent is prima facie evidence that notice was given. Corp C §601(b). A declaration under penalty of perjury, as in the form above, may be used in place of an affidavit. CCP §2015.5. If third-class mail is used to mail the notice, the reference to "first-class postage" in Form 1.43–1 should be appropriately modified.

c. Informally Noticed Meetings

§1.44 (1) Statutory Requirements

Shareholder meetings may be held and valid actions taken without formal notice. See Corp C §601(e). This is the procedure most commonly used by closely held corporations, when compliance with the requirements of formal notice serves little purpose. It may cause problems, however, if shareholders are not available to sign the necessary documentation when it is needed. To hold a valid, informally noticed meeting under Corp C §601(e), the following conditions must be met:

(1) A quorum must be present at the meeting, either in person or by proxy; and

(2) Each person not present in person or by proxy but entitled to vote must sign, before or after the meeting, either (a) a written waiver of notice, or (b) a consent to the holding of the meeting, or (c) an approval of the minutes; these must be filed with or incorporated in the corporation's minutes.

A shareholder who attends a meeting waives notice of the meeting unless a proper objection is made at the beginning of the meeting. Attendance, however, is not a waiver of any right to object at the meeting to consideration of matters required to be included in the notice that were not so included. Corp C §601(e).

§1.45 (2) Form: Waiver of Notice and Consent

Form 1.45–1

**WAIVER OF NOTICE AND CONSENT
TO HOLDING [*ANNUAL/SPECIAL*] MEETING
OF
SHAREHOLDERS OF
[*NAME OF CORPORATION*]**

The undersigned shareholder(s) of [*name of corporation*]**, a California corporation, desiring to hold a(n)** [*annual/special*] **meeting of the shareholders of that corporation at _ _ _ _ _ _ _, California, at _ _.m., on** [*date*]**, waive notice and consent to the**

holding of that meeting, and agree that any business transacted at that meeting shall be as valid and legal and have the same force and effect as though that meeting were held after notice was duly given.

[*Add, if required by Corp C §601(f)*]

The business conducted or to be conducted at that meeting includes [*describe in general terms proposals that must be specified*].

[*Continue*]

Dated: _ _ _ _ _ _ _

[*Signature(s)*]
[*Shareholder(s)*]

Comment: Unless otherwise required by the articles or bylaws, the waiver need not set forth the nature of the business conducted at the meeting, except those actions specified in Corp C §601(f) (see Comment, §1.42, for list). The waiver and consent must be filed with the corporate records or made a part of the minutes of the meeting. Corp C §601(e).

3. Proxies

§1.46   a. Use of Proxies

Every person entitled to vote shares may authorize others, by a proxy, to vote the shares on his or her behalf. Corp C §705(a); see Corp C §§178–179. A proxy purporting to be executed in accordance with the General Corporation Law is presumptively valid. Corp C §705(a).

As a general rule, a proxy is valid only for 11 months from its date, unless a later expiration date is provided for in the proxy. Corp C §705(b). Proxies may be revoked by (1) a written notice to the corporation, or (2) execution and presentation to the meeting of a later proxy. Corp C §705(b). If more than one proxy has been executed, the dates on the proxy forms presumptively govern the order of execution, not the postmark dates. Corp C §705(b). Attendance at a meeting and voting in person by the person executing the proxy revokes a proxy for that meeting only; an otherwise unexpired proxy will continue in effect for all meetings not attended by the person executing the proxy. Corp C §705(b).

Subject to statutory limitations, a proxy may in some instances be made irrevocable for certain periods by so stating in the proxy. This may be done (1) if the proxy is given to secure performance or to protect a legal or equitable title until the happening of events which, by the proxy's terms, discharge the obligation secured, or (2) if the proxy is held by any of the following or a nominee of any of the following (Corp C §705(e)):

(a) A pledgee of the shares;

(b) A person who has purchased, has agreed to purchase, or holds an option to purchase the shares, or a person who has sold a portion of his or her shares to the maker of the proxy;

(c) A creditor of the corporation or of the shareholder who gives the proxy in consideration of the extension or continuation of credit to the corporation or the shareholder;

(d) An employee of the corporation if the proxy is given as required consideration in connection with his or her employment contract;

(e) A person designated by or under a voting trust or a close corporation's shareholders' agreement; or

(f) A beneficiary of a trust with respect to shares held by the trust. Proxies held under Corp C §705(e) may be revoked by events making them no longer applicable; see Corp C §705(e), last paragraph. For further discussion, see §§3.30–3.35.

Unless the existence of an irrevocable proxy and its irrevocability are noted on the share certificate, a transferee of the shares without knowledge can revoke the proxy. Corp C §705(f). The maker's death or incapacity does not revoke the proxy unless the corporation receives written notice of death or incapacity before the vote is counted. Corp C §705(c).

Detailed requirements for and limitations on irrevocable proxies are set forth in Corp C §§705(d)–(f), 706. See also Corp C §604; §3.31

Proxies of corporations subject to federal securities reporting requirements are regulated in considerable detail. See Securities Exchange Act of 1934 §14 (15 USC §78n); Securities and Exchange Commission Reg 14A (17 CFR §§240.14a). Discussion of these federal regulations is beyond the scope of this chapter. See 11A Gadsby, BUSINESS ORGANIZATIONS—SECURITIES REGULATION chap 7 (1977).

§1.47   b. Forms: Proxy for Corporations Not Subject to Federal Securities Laws

Form 1.47–1 (Corporations With Fewer Than 100 Shareholders)

PROXY
[NAME OF CORPORATION]

The undersigned, owner of shares of corporate stock the number and description of which are set forth below, appoints the person named below to act as the undersigned's proxyholder at the meeting specified, and any adjournment of that meeting.

Type of meeting: *[Annual/Special]*
Date of meeting: _ _ _ _ _ _, 19 _ _
Place of meeting: _ _ _ _ _ _ _ _, California
Name of proxy holder: _ _ _ _ _ _ _ _ _ _ _ _ _ _ _ _ _ _
[To be filled in by shareholder]

The proxy holder shall be entitled to cast the number of votes the undersigned would be entitled to cast if personally present, for or against any proposal, including the election of members of the board of directors, and any and all other business that may come before the meeting.

Dated: _ _ _ _ _ _ _   Signed:

_ _ _ _ _ _ _ _ _ _ _ _ _ _ _ _ _ _
(Shareholder)

_ _ _ _ _ _ _ _ _ _ _ _ _ _ _ _ _ _
(Shareholder)

Number and class of shares held:

_ _ _ _ _ _ _ _ _ _ _ _ _ _ _ _ _ _

INSTRUCTIONS TO SHAREHOLDER: PLEASE SIGN EXACTLY AS YOUR NAME APPEARS ON YOUR STOCK CERTIFICATE. JOINT SHAREHOLDERS SHOULD EACH SIGN PERSONALLY. IF SIGNED BY AN ATTORNEY-IN-FACT, ATTACH THE POWER OF ATTORNEY.

[Add, if desired]

IF YOU ARE UNABLE TO ATTEND THE MEETING,

MANAGEMENT OF THE CORPORATION RECOMMENDS THAT YOU APPOINT [*NAME*] AS YOUR PROXY.

Comment: This form may be used by corporations with fewer than 100 shareholders that are not subject to either Corp C §604 (more than 100 shareholders; see Comment to Form 1.47–2 below) or to federal securities law requirements.

Form 1.47–2 (Corporations With 100 or More Shareholders If Proxy Distributed to Ten or More Shareholders)

PROXY
[*NAME OF CORPORATION*]

The undersigned shareholder(s) of [*name of corporation*], a California corporation (the Company), appoint(s) [*name of proxy holder*] as proxy and attorney-in-fact, with full power of substitution, to represent the undersigned at the [*annual/special*] meeting of shareholders to be held on [*date*] at [*time*], at the Company's principal offices located at [*address*], and at any adjournment of that meeting, and to vote all shares of common stock which the undersigned would be entitled to vote if personally present, on the matters and in accordance with any instructions set forth below.

The proxy holder shall be entitled to cast the number of votes the undersigned would be entitled to cast if personally present, for or against any proposal, including the election of members of the board of directors, and any and all other business that may come before the meeting.

SHAREHOLDER: IF YOU WISH TO INSTRUCT THE PROXY HOLDER REGARDING THE VOTING OF YOUR SHARES, PLEASE CHECK THE APPROPRIATE BOXES BELOW AND COMPLETE THIS FORM. WITH RESPECT TO ELECTION OF DIRECTORS, IF YOU WISH TO WITHHOLD AUTHORITY TO VOTE FOR ANY INDIVIDUAL NOMINEE, DRAW A LINE THROUGH THAT NOMINEE'S NAME. YOUR SHARES WILL BE VOTED IN ACCORDANCE WITH YOUR INSTRUCTIONS.

ANY SHAREHOLDER COMPLETING THIS PROXY WHO FAILS TO CHECK ANY BOXES OR OTHERWISE MARK THE PROXY FORM WILL BE DEEMED TO HAVE GIVEN THE PROXY HOLDER

COMPLETE DISCRETION IN VOTING WITH RESPECT TO THE MATTERS LISTED BELOW.

1. Election of Directors:

FOR all nominees listed below except as indicated [ ]   WITHHOLD authority to vote for all nominees listed [ ]

NOMINEES
[List names]

2. **Proposal to** *[insert description of proposed action]*:

Approve [ ]   **Disapprove** [ ]   **Abstain** [ ]

3. **Proposal to** *[insert description of proposed action]*:

Approve [ ]   **Disapprove** [ ]   **Abstain** [ ]

_____
[Typed or printed name]

_____
[Signature]

_____
[Signature]

_____
[Title, if applicable]

Dated: _____

I plan to attend this meeting. [ ] **Yes**   [ ] **No**

SHAREHOLDER: THIS PROXY SHOULD BE MARKED, DATED, AND SIGNED BY THE SHAREHOLDER(S) EXACTLY AS HIS OR HER NAME APPEARS ON THE SHARE CERTIFICATE(S), AND RETURNED PROMPTLY IN THE ENCLOSED ENVELOPE. A CORPORATION SHOULD SIGN ITS NAME BY ITS PRESIDENT OR OTHER AUTHORIZED OFFICER, DESIGNATING THE OFFICE HELD. IF SHARES ARE HELD IN TWO NAMES, BOTH PERSONS SHOULD SIGN.

Comment: The proxy must be signed by the shareholder or his or her attorney-in-fact, by placing the shareholder's name on the proxy by manual signature, typewriting, telegraphic transmission, or otherwise. Corp C §178. Any proxy form distributed to ten or more shareholders of a corporation that has 100 or more shareholders as determined under Corp C §605 (other than certain corporations with securities registered or exempted from registration under Section 12 of the Securities Exchange Act of 1934) must offer the shareholder an opportunity to specify a choice between approval and disapproval of each matter or group of related matters intended to be acted upon at the meeting. Corp C §604(a), (d). In an election of directors naming the nominees, any proxy marked by the shareholder "withhold" shall not be voted for the election of a director. Corp C §604(b).

NOTE: Under California law a negative or withheld vote in an election of directors does not have any effect; the candidates receiving the highest number of affirmative votes are elected. Corp C §708(c).

Requirements for proxies under federal securities laws and regulations are beyond the scope of this chapter.

4. Meeting Procedure

§1.48   a. Conducting the Meeting

The president of the corporation ordinarily presides at shareholders' meetings. However, if authorized by the bylaws, some other person may preside. Corp C §212(b)(2); see bylaw provision in ORGANIZING CORPORATIONS IN CALIFORNIA §2.76 (Cal CEB 2d ed 1983). Particularly in small closely held corporations, the presiding officer often relies on the guidance and assistance of the attorney in conducting the meeting. It is generally desirable for the attorney to go over the agenda with the presiding officer and discuss the manner in which the meeting will be conducted and votes taken, and the required proportion of shares for approval (see §§1.31, 1.50–1.51). The degree of formality depends to a great extent on the number of and relationship among the shareholders.

The first order of business after the meeting is called to order should be to determine whether a required quorum is present or represented at the meeting (see §1.49) and the number of shares that each shareholder is entitled to vote. This may be a simple matter in closely held corporations, but corporations with many shareholders may require formal shareholder certification procedures. See Corp C §707 for these procedures. Further proceedings depend on the type of business to be transacted.

For procedures related to shareholder proposals, see §3.27.

§1.49   b. Quorum

Unless otherwise provided in the articles, a majority of the shares entitled to vote, represented at the meeting in person or by proxy, constitutes a quorum, but in no event may a quorum consist of less than one third of or more than a majority of the shares entitled to vote. (Certain exceptions are provided for close corporations and mutual water companies.) Corp C §602(a). Shares disqualified from voting on a particular matter are not considered outstanding for the determination of a quorum at a meeting to act on that matter. Corp C §112. If a quorum is initially present at a meeting, but enough shareholders withdraw to reduce the number remaining to less than a quorum, business may nevertheless be transacted, subject to a minimum vote requirement. Corp C §602(b). If a quorum is lost, the meeting may be adjourned by a vote of a majority of the shares represented. Corp C §602(c).

Special quorum requirements apply to shareholder meetings ordered by a court after the corporation has failed to hold a required annual meeting. Corp C §600(c).

For a more detailed discussion of quorum provisions, see 2 MARSH'S CALIFORNIA CORPORATION LAW §11.12 (2d ed).

c. Voting

§1.50   (1) Voting Procedure; Form of Written Ballot (Noncumulative Voting)

Shareholder votes are generally cast by voice vote or show of hands, particularly in corporations having relatively few shareholders. Elections for directors need not be by ballot unless a shareholder demands election by ballot at the meeting and before the voting begins, or unless the bylaws so require. Corp C §708(e). Except for cumulative voting on directors (see §1.51) and except as otherwise provided in the articles, each outstanding share, regardless of class, is entitled to one vote on each matter submitted to a vote of shareholders. Corp C §700(a). A holder of shares entitled to vote on any matter may vote part of those shares in favor of the proposal and refrain from voting the remaining shares or vote them against the proposal (other than elections to office), but if the shareholder fails to specify the number of shares he or she is voting affirmatively, it is conclusively presumed that the shareholder's approving vote is with respect to all shares he or she is entitled to vote. Corp C §700(b).

Special rules are provided for particular types of shareholders. See Corp C §702 (representatives, fiduciaries, receivers, and pledgees); Corp C §703 (shares held by corporations); Corp C §§189(b), 703(b) (shares held by 25 percent subsidiary); Corp C §704 (joint tenancies and other joint holdings).

If a written ballot is required, the following form may be used:

Form 1.50–1 (Written Ballot for Noncumulative Voting)

BALLOT
[*NAME OF CORPORATION*]
ANNUAL MEETING OF SHAREHOLDERS
[*DATE*]

A. Name of Shareholder(s): (Please print name(s) exactly as they appear on your certificate)

_____
[*Printed name(s)*]

B. If voting party is other than the owner of the shares, state capacity in which voting party is acting (e.g., proxy holder, trustee):

_____
[*Capacity*]

C. Number of shares being voted: _____

UNLESS OTHERWISE DESIGNATED, THIS BALLOT SHALL BE CONSIDERED TO BE A VOTE OF ALL OF THE SHARES THAT THE UNDERSIGNED IS ENTITLED TO VOTE. A VOTE TO ABSTAIN SHALL BE CONSIDERED A VOTE AGAINST.

WRITTEN BALLOT

1. Election of directors for the coming year:
(Vote only for [number of directors to be elected])

Nominee	For	Against	Abstain
[name]	____ [no. of shares]	____ [no. of shares]	____ [no. of shares]
[name]	____ [no. of shares]	____ [no. of shares]	____ [no. of shares]

2. Approval of amendment to the articles of incorporation that would [describe purpose or effect of amendment].

FOR	AGAINST	ABSTAIN
____ [no. of shares]	____ [no. of shares]	____ [no. of shares]

3. Approval of proposed action by the board of directors that would [describe purpose or effect of proposed action].

FOR	AGAINST	ABSTAIN
____ [no. of shares]	____ [no. of shares]	____ [no. of shares]

4. Ratification of the appointment of [name of firm] **as** [e.g., independent public accountants].

For	Against	Abstain
____ [no. of shares]	____ [no. of shares]	____ [no. of shares]

ALL BALLOTS MUST BE SIGNED.

**For Shareholders
Voting in Person:**

_____
Signature(s)

_____
[*Printed name(s) exactly
as on certificate*]

**For Shares Being
Voted by Proxy
(attach proxy):**

_____
[*Printed name of proxy holder*]

_____
[*Printed name(s) of holder of record*]

By: _____
[*Signature of proxy holder*]

Comment: In this form of written ballot, blanks to be completed by management are indicated by broken lines, and blanks to be left for completion by the voter are indicated by solid lines.

§1.51   (2) Cumulative Voting for Directors

Except as otherwise provided in the shareholder agreement of a statutory close corporation (see §1.94) or in the articles of a "listed" corporation (see Corp C §301.5), shareholders are entitled to cumulate their votes for the election of directors. Corp C §708. If candidates' names have been placed in nomination before the voting, and if any shareholder has given notice at the meeting, before the voting, of the intention to cumulate votes, all shareholders may cumulate their votes for candidates in nomination. Corp C §708(b).

In cumulative voting a shareholder may cast a number of votes equal to the number his or her shares would otherwise be entitled to, multiplied by the number of directors to be elected. See Corp C §708(a). For example, if five directors are to be elected, a shareholder who holds 100 shares may cast 500 votes, which need not be spread equally over the five vacancies. By casting all their "cumulated" votes for one candidate, minority shareholders or groups may obtain representation on the board.

For detailed discussion, as well as formulas for determining the number of shares needed to elect a specified number of directors and the number of directors that may be elected by a specified number of shares, see 2 MARSH'S CALIFORNIA CORPORATION LAW §11.2 (2d ed).

If a written ballot is desired, the following form may be used.

Form 1.51–1 (Ballot for Cumulative Voting for Directors)

BALLOT
[*NAME OF CORPORATION*]
ANNUAL MEETING OF SHAREHOLDERS
[*DATE*]

A. Name of Shareholder(s):
(Please print name(s) exactly as they appear on your certificate)

_____
[*Printed name(s)*]

B. If voting party is other than the owner of the shares, state capacity in which voting party is acting (*e.g.*, proxy holder, trustee):

_____
[*Capacity*]

C. Number of shares being voted: _____

D. Number of directors to be elected: [*management to fill in*]

ELECTION OF DIRECTORS

Notice of cumulative voting having been given, you are entitled to vote the number of shares set forth in paragraph C above, multiplied by number of directors to be elected, set forth in paragraph D above. You may cast all your votes for one nominee, or you may allocate the total among some or all of the nominees in any manner you desire. A VOTE TO ABSTAIN IS CONSIDERED A VOTE AGAINST.

NOMINEE	FOR	AGAINST	ABSTAIN
[Name]	____ [no. of votes]	____ [no. of votes]	____ [no. of votes]
[Name]	____ [no. of votes]	____ [no. of votes]	____ [no. of votes]

ALL BALLOTS MUST BE SIGNED.

**For Shareholders
Voting in Person:**
_____
Signature(s)

_____
[Printed name(s) exactly
as on certificate]

**For Shares Being
Voted by Proxy
(attach proxy):**
_____
[Printed name of proxy holder]

_____
[Printed name(s) of holder of record]

By: _____
[Signature of proxy holder]

Comment: In this form of written ballot, blanks to be completed by management are indicated by broken lines, and blanks to be left for completion by the voter are indicated by solid lines.

§1.52   d. Recording the Proceedings

Each corporation must keep minutes of the proceedings of its shareholders. Corp C §1500. See also Corp C §1507(b) (liability for false entries). To meet this requirement, minutes of each shareholders' meeting, or written consents of shareholders to action taken without a meeting, are filed in the corporation's minute book. Copies of notices and waivers of notice of shareholders' meetings should also be filed in the minute book.

The original or a copy of the minutes of a meeting, certified by the secretary or assistant secretary, is prima facie evidence that the meeting was held and that the matters stated are true. Corp C §314.

§1.53 (1) Form: Checklist for Preparation of Minutes

Form 1.53–1

MINUTES PREPARATION CHECKLIST
SHAREHOLDER MEETING

1. Name of corporation: _____

2. Date and time of meeting: _____

3. Place of meeting: _____

4. Type of meeting: ___ Annual ___ Special

5. Meeting held pursuant to: ___ Waiver ___ Notice (attach notice)

6. Shareholders present:

    Shareholder   No. of shares held

    _____   _____

    _____   _____

7. Proxies presented:

    | | Name of proxy | |
    | Shareholder represented | holder present | No. of shares |
    | _____ | _____ | _____ |
    | _____ | _____ | _____ |

8. Total shares outstanding: _____

9. Number of shares constituting quorum: _____

10. Other persons present: _____

11. Minutes of previous meeting approved? _ _ _ Yes _ _ _ No

12. Reports presented:

   a. Operations

      Person making report: _ _ _ _ _ _ _

   b. Financial condition

      Person making report: _ _ _ _ _ _ _

   c. Written financial report also presented? _ _ _ Yes _ _ _ No

      Date of written report: _ _ _ _ _ _ _

13. Directors nominated:

Nominee	No. of shares voted for (if elected, indicate with X)
_ _ _ _ _ _ _ _ _ _ _ _ _ _	_ _ _ _ _ _ _ _ _ _ _ _ _ _ _ _ _ _

14. Other business:

   a. Amendment to articles

      Number of shares voting for amendment: _ _ _ _ _ _ _

      Article no.: _ _ _ _ _ _ _

      Change: _ _ _ _ _ _ _

   b. Amendment to bylaws

      Number of shares voting for amendment: _ _ _ _ _ _ _

      Article and paragraph no.: _ _ _ _ _ _ _

      Change: _ _ _ _ _ _ _

[*Add other business as appropriate*]

Comment: The proceedings of shareholders' meetings may be taken and transcribed by a court reporter or recorded on a tape recorder or similar device as an aid in preparing minutes. Such elaborate recording procedures are usually unnecessary, however, except at meetings of publicly held corporations or meetings at which the actions to be taken are likely to be contested. Handwritten notes of the proceedings ordinarily will provide sufficient detail for preparation of minutes. The use of a form such as this helps organize the notes and ensure that all actions are recorded.

(2) Forms: Minutes of Shareholders' Meeting
§1.54　(a) Introduction

Form 1.54–1

**MINUTES OF [*ANNUAL/SPECIAL*] MEETING
OF
SHAREHOLDERS OF
[*NAME OF CORPORATION*]**

[*The annual/A special*] **meeting of the shareholders of** [*name of corporation*]**, a California corporation, was held on** [*date*]**, at** [*address and city*]**, California.**

§1.55　(b) Persons Present

Form 1.55–1

The following shareholders were present at the meeting, in person or by proxy, representing shares as indicated:

Shareholder	No. of shares held
_____	_____
_____	_____

The following persons also were present:

[*List names*]

_____	_____
_____	_____

§1.56   (c) Notice of Meeting

Form 1.56–1 (Meeting Held Pursuant to Notice)

The president of the corporation called the meeting to order and announced that a quorum was present and that the meeting was held pursuant to a written notice of meeting given to all shareholders of the corporation. A copy of this notice was ordered inserted in the minute book immediately preceding the minutes of this meeting.

Comment: For form of notice, see §1.42.

Form 1.56–2 (Notice Waived)

The president of the corporation called the meeting to order, and announced that the meeting was held pursuant to waiver of notice and written consent to the holding of the meeting. The waiver and consent was presented to the meeting and, on a motion duly made, seconded, and unanimously carried, was made a part of the records and ordered inserted in the minute book immediately preceding the records of this meeting.

Comment: For form of waiver and consent, see §1.45.

§1.57   (d) Reading of Previous Minutes

Form 1.57–1 (Minutes Read and Approved)

The minutes of the previous meeting of shareholders were then read and approved.

Form 1.57–2 (Reading of Minutes Dispensed With)

It was then moved, seconded, and unanimously resolved to dispense with the reading of the minutes of the last meeting.

§1.58   (e) Election of Directors

Form 1.58–1

The president announced that the next order of business

was the election of directors, to serve until the next annual meeting of stockholders, and until their successors have been duly elected and qualified. The following nominations were made and seconded:

[*List names*]

_____   _____
_____   _____

[*If election uncontested, conclude*]

No further nominations were made, and the persons named above were [*duly/unanimously*] elected as directors of the corporation.

[*If election contested, conclude*]

No further nominations were made, and the following persons were duly elected as directors of the corporation:

[*List names*]

_____   _____
_____   _____

§1.59   (f) Other Business

Form 1.59–1

The president then announced that the next order of business was approval by the shareholders of [*describe matter to be approved*]. After discussion, the matter was [*approved/ disapproved*] by the shareholders by the following vote: [*describe or tabulate*].

§1.60   (g) Adjournment

Form 1.60–1

There being no further business to come before the meeting, on motion duly made, seconded, and adopted, the meeting was adjourned.

[*Signature*]
Secretary

Comment: The minutes should be filed in the corporate minute book, along with appropriate notices, consents, and waivers.

§1.61   C. Shareholders' Action or Consent Without Meeting

Subject to restrictions in the articles of incorporation, any action that may be taken by shareholders at an annual or special meeting may also be taken by the shareholders' written consent without a meeting. Corp C §§195, 603(a). Election of directors by this method requires the unanimous consent of all shares entitled to vote for directors, unless the election is to fill a vacancy under Corp C §305(b), in which case the consent of a majority of the outstanding shares entitled to vote (Corp C §152) is necessary. Corp C §603(d).

Actions other than the election of directors may be taken by written consent without a meeting, requiring the consent of the same proportion of the outstanding shares as would be necessary to take the action at a meeting at which all shares entitled to vote were present and voting. Corp C §603(a). If the consent of all shareholders entitled to vote has not been solicited in writing, a special notice of the action must be given to those who have not consented. Corp C §603(b).

A consent may be revoked if the corporation receives written revocation before the number of consents necessary to authorize the action have been filed with the secretary. Corp C §603(c).

§1.62   1. Form: Solicitation of Written Consent

Form 1.62–1

[*Date*]

[*Name and address of shareholder*]

Re: Written Consent by Shareholders of [*name of corporation*] **to Action Without a Meeting**

Dear Shareholder:

The board of directors of [*name of corporation*] **has approved**

[*describe action to be taken*]. **The board believes this is necessary because** [*simple statement of reason for action*].

Under California law, this proposed action requires the consent of shareholders. In the interests of time and economy, we are soliciting your written consent. If you consent, please complete, date, and sign the enclosed form and return it in the envelope provided for your convenience no later than [*date*].

[*Insert, if desired*]

Also enclosed is a memorandum that more fully explains the reasons and necessity for the proposed action.

[*Continue*]

Should you have any further questions about this, please write or telephone me immediately. Thank you for your prompt attention to this important matter.

Very truly yours,

[*Signature*]
President

§1.63   2. Form: Shareholders' Consent

Form 1.63–1 (Corporation With Fewer Than 100 Shareholders)

[*NAME OF CORPORATION*]
ACTION BY SHAREHOLDERS
WITHOUT A MEETING

The undersigned, shareholder(s) of [*name of corporation*], **a California corporation, consent to the following actions of the corporation:**

1. Adoption of the following resolutions by the shareholders: [*Full text of resolutions*].

2. Election of the following persons as directors of the corporation: [*Names of directors*].

This consent is granted under section 603 of the California

Corporations Code with respect to all shares held by the undersigned that are entitled to vote on these matters.

Dated: _ _ _ _ _ _ _

[Signature(s) of shareholder(s)]
[Typed name(s)]

Comment: See Comment to Form 1.63–2.

Form 1.63–2 (Corporations With 100 or More Shareholders If Consent Distributed to Ten or More Shareholders)

[NAME OF CORPORATION]
**ACTION BY SHAREHOLDERS
WITHOUT A MEETING**

Pursuant to section 603 of the California Corporations Code, the undersigned shareholder(s), with respect to all shares held by the undersigned,

(Check one):

[ ] Approve of

[ ] Disapprove of

[ ] Abstain from voting on

the adoption of the following resolution:

[Full text of resolution]

Dated: _ _ _ _ _ _ _ _ _ _ _

[Signature(s) of shareholder(s)]
[Typed or printed name(s)]

Comment: Any form of written consent distributed to ten or more shareholders of a corporation with shares held of record by 100 or more persons must afford an opportunity on the form for the shareholder to specify a choice between approval or disapproval of each matter or group of related matters intended to be acted on. Corp C §604(a). The executed consents should be filed in the corporation's minute book. Written consent may also be given by facsimile or telegraphic communication. Corp C §195.

VI. TRANSFERRING SHARES

§1.64   A. Introduction

The corporation's attorney often is responsible for assisting the small and medium-sized corporation and its shareholders in transferring shares. The discussion in §§1.65–1.75 is intended to assist the attorney for corporations whose shares are regulated by California securities law. Discussion of federal securities law is beyond the scope of this chapter.

Transfers ordinarily involve both the transfer between the parties (see Com C §§8301–8302, 8308–8309, 8313) and registration of the transfer on the company's books (see Com C §§8401–8406). They may be subject to requirements of the Commissioner of Corporations. See §§1.66–1.71. In addition to its direct effect on the parties, a transfer of shares may also have a profound effect on the status of the corporation itself. For example, its status as an S corporation for tax purposes (IRC §§1361–1378, Rev & T C §§23800–23811) or as a California close corporation (Corp C §158) may be lost if the transfer makes certain changes in the number or type of shareholders (see §1.65).

§1.65   B. Pretransfer Checklist

Before beginning the actual transfer of any of the corporation's shares, the attorney should look for factors concerning the feasibility, the form, and the ultimate effect of the proposed transfer. Steps to be taken include the following:

(1) Review articles of incorporation for restrictions on transfers.

(2) Review bylaws for restrictions on transfers and for any required internal transfer procedures.

(3) Review existing shareholder buy-out agreements, share pledge agreements, corporate financing agreements, and other agreements that may restrict the transfer of shares.

(4) If the corporation is a California statutory close corporation (Corp C §158; see §§1.91–1.99), review the shareholders' agreement for restrictions or limitations on share transfers; consider the necessity

of having transferees of shares execute a shareholders' agreement, and consider whether the number of new shareholders will disqualify it as a close corporation.

(5) If the corporation is an S corporation (IRC §§1361–1378), consider whether the prospective shareholder is of a type permitted by statute, and whether the total number of shareholders will exceed the statutory limit of 35 shareholders. Note that new shareholders are bound by the corporation's initial election of S corporation status. See IRC §1362(c), (d)(1)(B).

(6) Review the need to obtain consent of the Commissioner of Corporations before transfer (see §§1.66–1.69; Corp C §§25131–25133; 10 Cal Code Regs §§260.102.6, 260.131, 260.141.11, 260.151)), or the need for qualification of the transaction (see §1.70).

C. Compliance With California Securities Law

§1.66   **1. Commissioner of Corporations' Consent to Transfer**

For corporations whose securities are exempt from qualification, the question of whether the Commissioner of Corporations' consent to a transfer of issued share is required may depend on whether the shares were issued under the traditional "small offering" exemption of Corp C §25102(h) or the more recent "limited offering" exemption of Corp C §25102(f). See ORGANIZING CORPORATIONS IN CALIFORNIA §§4.47–4.70 (2d ed Cal CEB 1983) for discussion of these two exemptions.

Securities Under §25102(h) Exemption; "Legended" Stock: For securities issued under the "small offering" exemption from qualification of Corp C §25102(h), or securities on which the Commissioner of Corporations has imposed a legend condition (see Corp C §§25133, 25151), it may be necessary to obtain the Commissioner's consent to a transfer. See 10 Cal Code Regs §§260.102.4–260.102.9; see also 10 Cal Code Regs §§260.141.1, 260.141.10–260.141.11, 260.534. To obtain the Commissioner's consent, an application form and statements of the prospective transferees should be submitted. See §§1.67–1.69.

Exceptions to the Requirement: However, consent is not required for many specified transactions, including transfers to persons who are already holders of the same class of securities and transfers to certain specified relatives of the transferor. Many transfers of shares of small and medium-sized corporations fall in those categories. Other transfers that do not require the Commissioner's consent include transfers to the issuer, or between a corporation and its wholly owned subsidiary or sole parent corporation; transfers under court order or process; transfers to certain specified public agencies, institutions, corporations, trustees, or custodians; gifts or donations on death; certain pledges and liens; and certain transactions involving broker-dealers. Regardless of whether an exception applies, the new certificates must bear specified legends, and copies of the applicable rules must be delivered to the transferee. 10 Cal Code Regs §§260.102.6, 260.141.11; see §1.71.

No Consent Required for §25102(f) Securities: The transfer of shares exempted from qualification under Corp C §25102(f) (the "limited offering" or "private placement" exemption) does not require the Commissioner's consent. That is, Corp C §25102(f) does *not* require as a condition to its use that subsequent transfers be subject to the Commissioner's consent and that the shares bear the legend set forth in Rule 260.131.11(c).

§1.67   a. Official Form: Application for Consent to Transfer (Corp C §25102(h) Shares)

Form 1.67-1

```
(Dept. of Corporations Use Only)        Dept. of Corporations File No.
Fee Paid    $_____ _____
Receipt No. _____    _____
_____ ___    (Insert file no. of previous
                                        filings before the Dept. if any)

                                        FEE: $_____
                                        (To be completed by appli-
                                        cant.  The required fee is
Date of Application:                    $10 per transferor (Sec.
                                        25608(m), Corp. Code).)
_____ ____
```

**DEPARTMENT OF CORPORATIONS
STATE OF CALIFORNIA**

**APPLICATION FOR CONSENT TO TRANSFER SECURITIES PURSUANT TO
SECTION 25151 OF THE CORPORATE SECURITIES LAW OF 1968**

```
This represents (check appropriate box):
  [ ] The initial filing.  [ ] An amendment to application dated _____.
THE SECURITIES PROPOSED TO BE TRANSFERRED ARE SUBJECT TO (CHECK APPROPRIATE BOX)
  [ ] LEGEND CONDITION.     [ ] ESCROW CONDITION.
```

1.   (a) Name of Issuer:
     (b) Former Name, if any:

2.   Description of securities proposed to be transferred: (State title of each
     class of securities (e.g., Class A Common Stock). If rights, warrants and
     options are listed, also specify the securities to be transferred upon
     exercise thereof. If securities are to be pledged, so state.)

     _____
     _____
     _____

3.   Name and address of each transferor (if space is insufficient, incorporate
     and attach additional sheets):

```
                                             Aggregate number or amount
                                             of securities proposed to
                                             be transferred by each
     Name              Address               transferor:
     _____
     _____
     _____
                                             Total: _____
```

4.   Name and address of each proposed transferee (if space is insufficient,
     incorporate and attach additional sheets):

```
                                             Aggregate number or amount
                                             of securities proposed to
                                             be transferred to each
     Name              Address               transferee:
     _____
     _____
     _____
                                             Total: _____
```

260.151 (3/83)

5. Address of principal executive office of Issuer:

| (Number and Street) | (City) | (State) | (Zip Code) |

6. Name and address of person to whom correspondence regarding this application should be directed:

7. There are attached hereto as exhibits statements by each of the proposed transferees in the form required by Section 260.151 of Title 10 of the California Administrative Code. (Note: Upon request, such statements will be treated as confidential by the Commissioner, subject to the provisions of Section 250.10, Title 10, California Administrative Code.)

8. (Check appropriate box)

☐ (a) There are no restrictions upon the transfer of the securities proposed to be transferred other than the legend or escrow condition imposed by the Commissioner of Corporations.

☐ (b) There are restrictions upon the transfer of the securities proposed to be transferred other than the legend or escrow condition imposed by the Commissioner of Corporations which are described in an exhibit attached hereto and incorporated herein by reference. Such restrictions have been complied with so as to make the transfer to the proposed transferees valid and are known to the proposed transferees.

9. No portion of the consideration to be given by the transferees of the securities will be for the direct or indirect benefit of the Issuer identified in Item 1. (If the Issuer is to benefit from proposed transfer, see Section 25011 of the Corporate Securities Law and 1968 and Section 260.011 of Title 10 of the California Administrative Code. Qualification of the transaction may be required.)

10. Execution Instructions:

If a transferor is other than an individual, the name of the entity should be typed or printed above the signature line exactly as shown in Item 3. The signature should show the name and title of the person authorized to sign for such transferor.

I/We certify (or declare) under penalty of perjury under the laws of the State of California that I/we have read this application and know the contents thereof, and that the statements therein are true and correct. Executed at _____ , _____ , 19____ .
                          (Place)   (Date)
(If the transferor is other than an individual, give the name of the entity and the name and title of the person executing the application on behalf of such entity.)

| (Signature of Transferor) | (Signature of Transferor) |

| (Signature of Transferor) | (Signature of Transferor) |

| (Signature of Transferor) | (Signature of Transferor) |

Comment: This form is prescribed by 10 Cal Code Regs §260.151(a). Copies may be obtained from the Department of Corporations. See 10 Cal Code Regs §260.608(b). This form must be accompanied by a statement by each proposed transferee (see §1.68). For procedure and sample transmittal letter, see §1.69.

§1.68 b. Official Form: Transferee's Statement

Form 1.68–1

**TO THE COMMISSIONER OF CORPORATIONS OF
THE STATE OF CALIFORNIA**

**STATEMENT OF TRANSFEREE TO ACCOMPANY APPLICATION FOR
CONSENT TO TRANSFER SECURITIES SUBJECT TO
LEGEND OR ESCROW CONDITION**

(If securities are to be received in pledge, so state.)

The undersigned intends to purchase* _____ shares or units
(Number)

of _____
(Description of security, e.g., $10 common, Class A common)

issued by _____
(Name of Issuer)

from _____ and makes the following statements:

1. I have received from the issuer and/or the transferor a recent financial statement of the issuer and such additional information with respect to the issuer as I have deemed necessary to make an independent evaluation of the business prospects of the issuer and the fairness of the investment. (If answered in the negative, explain fully.) . . . . Yes ☐ No ☐

2. I am a director and/or an officer of issuer . . . . Yes ☐ No ☐

3. (a) I will actively participate in the operation of issuer's business and devote my full time or a substantial portion of my time thereto, with an opportunity to be fully aware of all of issuer's affairs . . . . Yes ☐ No ☐

   (b) I will be compensated for such services . . . . Yes ☐ No ☐

4. Are the securities being purchased promotional shares subject to waivers of assets and dividends? (See Sections 260.141 and 260.141.1 of the rules.) . . . . Yes ☐ No ☐

5. If the issuer is not a partnership and all parts of questions 2 and 3 above are answered in the negative, attach a separate *signed* statement elaborating on the items shown below.
   (a) The length of time officers and directors of issuer have been known, and the nature of prior business dealings with any officer or director of issuer or with the issuer.
   (b) Any prior investment experience in a business of similar size and nature.
   (c) Whether the amount of the proposed investment in issuer is in excess of 10% of either the net worth or the annual income of the transferee.
   (d) Whether the transferee has received advice from any attorney, accountant or other professional adviser independent of the issuer.
   (e) How transferee became aware of proposed investment.

6. If the issuer is a partnership, complete the following:
   (a) My annual income is in excess of $_____

   (b) My net worth (exclusive of my home, its furnishings and my automobiles) is in excess of $_____

7. (a) I am acquiring the securities as record and beneficial owner . . . . Yes ☐ No ☐

   (b) I am acquiring the securities as beneficial owner and not as record owner . . . Yes ☐ No ☐
   The record owner is_____

   (c) I am acquiring the securities as record owner and have no beneficial interest therein . . . . Yes ☐ No ☐

   The beneficial owner is _____

*Include rights, warrants, and options and the securities to be transferred upon exercise thereof.

If the transferee is other than an individual, the name of the entity should be typed or printed beside the signature line exactly as shown in Item 4 of the Transferor's Application (Form 260.151). The signature should show the name and title of the person authorized to sign for the transferee.

I certify (or declare) under penalty of perjury under the laws of the State of California that I have read this Statement of Transferee and know the contents thereof, and that the statements therein are true and correct.

Executed at_____ , _____ , 19 _____ .
              (Place)   (Date)

_____   _____
       (Name of Entity)   (Signature of Transferee)

                                         _____
                                                   (Title)

Comment: This form is prescribed by 10 Cal Code Regs §260.151(b). Copies may be obtained from the Department of Corporations. See 10 Cal Code Regs §260.608(b). A copy of this form executed by each proposed transferee must accompany the application for consent to the transfer (see §1.67). For transmittal letter and procedure, see §1.69.

§1.69　　c. Form: Transmittal Letter

Form 1.69–1

Department of Corporations
State of California
[*Address*], California

Re: Application for Consent To Transfer Legended Securities
Under Corporations Code section 25151
Name of corporation: _ _ _ _ _ _ _
Department of Corporations File No.: _ _ _ _ _ _ _

Dear Sir or Madam:

Enclosed for filing on behalf of [*name(s) of transferor(s)*] are an original and a copy of (1) an application to transfer legended securities of the corporation named above and (2) the transferee's statements indicated in the application. Also enclosed is a check for $_ _ _ _ _ _ in payment of the application fee. Please file-stamp the copies and return in the self-addressed envelope provided.

If you have any questions concerning the application, please call me at [*telephone number*].

Very truly yours,

[*Signature of attorney*]
[*Typed name*]

Comment: The completed application form (see §1.67) signed by all transferors, along with a transferee's statement (see §1.68) executed by each proposed transferee, should be submitted by mail or in person to the nearest office of the Department of Corporations. Offices are located at:

1115 11th Street
Sacramento, California 95814
Telephone: (916) 445–7205

1390 Market Street, Suite 810
San Francisco, California 94102
Telephone: (415) 557–3787

600 S. Commonwealth Avenue, 16th Floor
Los Angeles, California 90005
Telephone: (213) 736–2741

1350 Front Street, Room 2034
San Diego, California 92101
Telephone: (619) 237–7341

The application fee is $10 for each transferor. Corp C §25608(m).

NOTE: A trial program of expediting Applications for Consent to Transfer for shares of stock issued under Corp C §25102(a) was begun in 1987. Attorneys who are interested in the expedited procedure should contact their local office of the Department of Corporations.

§1.70   2. Qualification and Exemptions From Qualification of Nonissuer Offers and Sales

Although the Corporation Code requires qualification of nonissuer offers and sales of shares (Corp C §25130), most offers and sales by shareholders of small or medium-sized corporations fall within one or more of the numerous exemptions from this requirement. For example, nonissuer offers and sales of certain securities subject to federal regulation are exempt from qualification; see Corp C §25101. Other exempted nonissuer transactions include:

• Private unadvertised sale by owner (Corp C §25104(a));
• Certain unsolicited sales by broker-dealers (Corp C §25104(b));
• Sales to certain institutional investors (Corp C §25104(c));
• Certain transactions involving underwriters (Corp C §25104(d));
• Transfers in liquidation of a secured debt (Corp C §25104(e));
• Transfers by an executor, administrator, sheriff, marshal, trustee in bankruptcy, guardian, or conservator (Corp C §25104(f));
• Offers (but not sales) when federal registration is pending (Corp C §25104(g)); and
• Certain sales soon after an issuer qualification (Corp C §25104(h)).

For other exemptions for specific types of transfers or securities, see 10 Cal Code Regs §§260.105, 260.105.2, 260.105.7, 260.105.11, 260.105.14, 260.105.17. See also Corp C §25101(b). For detailed discussion of qualification requirements and exemptions, see 1 Marsh

& Volk, Practice Under the California Securities Laws §§10.01–10.03 (rev ed).

If qualification of a nonissuer transaction is required, it is ordinarily accomplished by notification. See Corp C §25131(a). For notification procedure, see Corp C §25131(b)–(d); 10 Cal Code Regs §260.131; 1 Marsh & Volk §§10.05–10.06. See also 10 Cal Code Regs §§260.140.135– 260.140.139.

Note: The attorney should understand that the requirement of the Commissioner's consent to the transfer of a security (see §§1.66–1.69) and the requirement of qualification of a nonissuer offer and sale of the same security are independent requirements.

§1.71   3. Legend and Notice Requirements

For legended securities (regardless of whether the Commissioner's consent to the transfer is required), each new certificate issued to a transferee must bear on its face the prescribed legend (see 10 Cal Code Regs §260.141.11(c)), and a copy of 10 Cal Code Regs §260.141.11 must be delivered to the transferee. See 10 Cal Code Regs §260.141.11 (general legend and delivery requirements). See also 10 Cal Code Regs §260.141.10 (basis for imposition of legend condition); 10 Cal Code Regs §260.102.6 (shares issued under the exemption of Corp C §25102(h)); 10 Cal Code Regs §260.534 (shares issued in violation of qualification requirements).

D. Procedure for Transferring Shares
§1.72   1. Share Transfer Checklist

- Obtain the transferor's share certificates with proper endorsement or assignment (see §1.73), and transferor and transferee statements, if needed (see §§1.67–1.68).
- Check the certificate against the corporation's share books, share journal, or share ledger for number of shares, class, name of shareholder, and date of issuance.
- Review the shareholder records to be certain all consideration due the corporation has been paid. See Corp C §§411–412.
- Obtain Commissioner of Corporations' consent or qualification, if required. See §§1.66–1.71.
- Mark the transferor's certificates "CANCELLED." The cancelled

certificates should be put back into the share book, with the original stubs attached. Make share-record entries documenting the transfer. See Corp C §1500; for sample forms, see §1.74. For issuer's rights and duties in registering transfers, see Com C §§8401–8405; Corp C §420.

- Prepare new share certificate for issuance to transferee. Corp C §§407, 416–418. For detailed discussion of forms of securities, see FINANCING CALIFORNIA BUSINESSES chap 4 (Cal CEB 1976). Add any required legends and notices (see §1.71), which may include the following:

  - Legend on certificate for shares issued under exemption of Corp C §25102(h). For requirement and form, see 10 Cal Code Regs §§260.102.6, 260.141.11. The legend may be easily applied by a rubber stamp.

  - Legend on certificate for shares issued in violation of qualification requirements (Corp C §25534). For requirement and form, see 10 Cal Code Regs §§260.534, 260.141.11.

  - Legend on certificates for other shares subject to legend condition imposed by Commissioner of Corporations. See Corp C §25141. For requirement and form, see 10 Cal Code Regs §§260.141.10– 260.141.11.

  - If a statutory close corporation (Corp C §158), the legend specified in Corp C §418(c). See Corp C §§418(d), 421, 2307.

  - Any legend required or desirable under federal securities laws. See FINANCING CAL BUS §§4.9–4.11.

  - Notices or legends required by shareholder agreements, pledge agreements, or buy-out agreements. See, *e.g.,* FINANCING CAL BUS §§4.5–4.6, 4.12. For notice requirement if shares are subject to an irrevocable proxy, see Corp C §705(f).

  - If the corporation has more than one class of shares or two or more series of any class of shares, the statement specified in Corp C §417. See Corp C §174 for definition of "on the certificate"; see also Corp C §2307.

  - If the shares are redeemable, convertible, assessable, not fully paid, subject to restrictions on transfer, or subject to a voting agreement, irrevocable proxy, or restrictions on voting rights contractually imposed by the corporation, the statements specified in Corp C §418. See Corp C §174 for definition of "on the certificate"; see also Corp C §2307.

- Two signatures (manual or facsimile) are required on the share certificate: (1) that of the president, vice president, chairman, or vice chairman of the board; and (2) that of the chief financial officer, an assistant treasurer, the secretary, or any assistant secretary. Corp C §416(a). The signatures of the president and secretary are customarily used.
- Send new share certificate to the transferee (see §1.75), with any required copies of the applicable securities rules. See 10 Cal Code Regs §§260.102.6, 260.141.10–260.141.11, 260.534.

§1.73   2. Form: Assignment Separate From Certificate

Form 1.73–1

ASSIGNMENT OF CORPORATE SHARES SEPARATE FROM CERTIFICATE

FOR VALUE RECEIVED, I, [*name of transferor*], **sell, assign, and transfer to** [*name of transferee*] [*number*] **shares of the** [*common/preferred*] **stock of** [*name of corporation*] **standing in my name on the books of that corporation, represented by Certificate No. _ _ _ delivered with this assignment, and I hereby** [*irrevocably constitute and appoint _ _ _ _ _ _ as my attorney-in-fact with full power of substitution/instruct and appoint the custodian of that corporation's stock books*] **to so transfer those shares on the books of that corporation.**

Dated: _ _ _ _ _ _ _

[*Signature of shareholder*]
[*Typed name and address*]

Comment: Most standard printed share certificates have endorsement forms on the back. If transfers are to be made to a number of transferees, a separate assignment form such as this may be executed for each proposed transferee. See Com C §8308(5). The separate assignment constitutes an endorsement of the security. Com C §8308(1). See also Com C §§8307–8406.

The space for appointing an attorney-in-fact, although ordinarily provided, is usually left blank. See 1A Ballantine & Sterling, CALIFORNIA CORPORATION LAWS §211[7][a] (4th ed).

§1.74 3. Sample Forms: Share Journal and Ledger Entries

Form 1.74–1 (Share Journal Pages)

ORIGINAL REGISTER COMMON SHARES						
CERTIFICATE NUMBER		DATE	SHAREHOLDER'S NAME	NO. OF SHARES	LEDGER PAGE	
ORIGINAL	REISSUE					
1		1/15/89	J. Q. SMITH	500	1	
			215 A St.			
			Hightown, California			
2		1/15/89	R. V. JONES	500	1	transferred
			51 B St.			
			Lowtown, California			
3		5/1/89	J. Q. SMITH	500	1	
			215 A St.			
			Hightown, California			

TRANSFERRED SHARE CERTIFICATES COMMON SHARES						
DATE	IN WHOSE FAVOR	NEW CERTIFICATE		SURRENDERED CERTIFICATE		LEDGER PAGE
		NUMBER	NO. OF SHARES	NUMBER	NO. OF SHARES	
5/1/89	J. Q. SMITH	3	500	2	500	1
	215 A St.					
	Hightown, California					

Form 1.74–2 (Share Ledger Page)

COMMON SHARES							
CERTIFICATES CANCELLED				CERTIFICATES ISSUED			
DATE	JOURNAL PAGE	CERTIFICATE NUMBER	NO. OF SHARES	DATE	JOURNAL PAGE	CERTIFICATE NUMBER	NO. OF SHARES
				1/15/89	1	1	500
5/1/89	1	2	500	1/15/89	1	2	500
				5/1/89	1	3	500

Comment: Each corporation is required to keep a record of its shareholders, giving the names and addresses of all shareholders and the number and class of shares held by each, either in written form or in any other form capable of being converted into written form. Corp C §1500. The sample entries in this form show the initial issuance of 500 shares of common stock each to Smith and Jones on January 15, 1989, and Jones' transfer of his 500 shares to Smith on May 1, 1989.

§1.75　　4. Form: Transmittal Letter

Form 1.75–1

[*Transferee's name and address*]

[*CERTIFIED/REGISTERED*]
**MAIL RETURN RECEIPT
REQUESTED**

Re: Delivery of Stock Certificate

Dear [*name*]**:**

Enclosed is Stock Certificate No. ____, representing [*number*] **shares of** [*common/preferred*] **stock of** [*name of corporation*], **which have been transferred to your name. It is recommended that you store this certificate in a safe or safe deposit box.**

[*Add, if delivery of rule is required*]

Also enclosed is a copy of section 260.141.11 of the Corporate Securities Rules of the California Commissioner of Corporations, which we are required to send you.

[*Continue*]

Please sign the acknowledgment of receipt on the copy of this letter and return it to me in the enclosed envelope.

Very truly yours,

[*Signature*]
[*Typed name*]

I acknowledge receipt of the share certificate [*and copy of section of Corporate Securities Rules*] **mentioned above.**

Dated: _____　　Signed:

_____
[*Leave blank for shareholder's signature*]

Comment: For requirement that a copy of the applicable Commissioner's rule be delivered with the certificate in certain situations, see 10 Cal Code Regs §260.141.11(a) and discussion in §1.71. Use of registered or certified mail, return receipt requested, along with the transferee's acknowledgment, provides evidence of delivery of the certificate and any copies of rules.

VII. CORPORATE BORROWING AND LENDING

A. Borrowing From Outsiders

§1.76   1. Procedure

To avoid jeopardizing the investors' limited liability status resulting from use of the corporate form, all corporate borrowing and lending transactions should be carefully documented as the action of the corporation. If allowed to look like the action of an individual, the transaction may invite an attempt to pierce the corporate veil. See Corp C §207(g) (corporation's power to borrow and lend); Corp C §313 (apparent authority of signing officers). See also Corp C §300(e) (failure of close corporation to observe certain formalities).

If the amount to be borrowed is large in relation to the size of the corporation, it is ordinarily preferable to authorize the transaction by a resolution of the board of directors or the appropriate committee of the board. See §1.77 for a form of resolution. If the corporation's business requires routine borrowings, the board or committee will often delegate to one or more corporate officers the authority to borrow money within specified limits without the necessity of board approval of each transaction. See Corp C §300(a). In preparing the minutes of the board or committee meeting at which loan transactions are approved or ratified, a brief statement of the circumstances surrounding the decision to borrow and a description of any corporate property securing the loan may be desirable. See Corp C §314.

For a discussion of loan financing, primarily through banks, and a form of bank loan agreement, see FINANCING CALIFORNIA BUSINESSES chap 5 (Cal CEB 1976).

§1.77   2. Form: Resolution Authorizing Borrowing

Form 1.77–1

WHEREAS it is desirable, in order to accomplish the corporation's business objectives, that the corporation borrow [*the sum of/a sum not to exceed*] **$_ _ _ _ _ _; and**

WHEREAS the officers of the corporation have arranged a loan commitment from [*name of lender*] **on** [*substantially*] **the following** [*principal*] **terms:**

[*Set forth terms*]

In view of the above, it is

RESOLVED that the corporation is authorized to borrow from [*name of lender*] [*the sum of/a sum not to exceed*] **$_ _ _ _ _ _ on the terms of the commitment received by the corporation.**

RESOLVED FURTHER that the president and secretary of the corporation are authorized to execute such documents and notes on behalf of the corporation as they shall deem necessary and prudent to effect that loan.

Comment: Most banks and other lending institutions furnish a particular form of resolution that they require their borrowers to use. If the lender does not require a particular form, this one may be used.

B. Transactions With Insiders and Affiliates

§1.78   1. Borrowing

Observing the corporate formalities is even more important when the corporation is borrowing from shareholders, directors, or officers than when it is borrowing from outsiders.

- **Borrowing From Shareholders:** Proper documentation and observation of formalities are essential in borrowing from shareholders, to minimize the risk that the loans may be construed as equity contributions. Such an interpretation could be advanced by a creditor with a competing claim, or by taxing authorities seeking to treat loan payments as dividends rather than repayment of principal and payment of interest. Proper documentation would in most cases include a promissory note and board approval or ratification of the transaction. See also Corp C §1501(b)(1) (disclosure of insider transactions in annual report).
- **Borrowing From Directors:** If the lender is a director or an entity in which a director has a material financial interest, there is a risk that the transaction may be void or voidable if the director

or other person asserting the validity of the transaction does not sustain the burden of showing that the transaction was just and reasonable as to the corporation at the time it was authorized, approved, or ratified. Corp C §310(a)(3).

• **"Safe Harbor" for Interested Director Transactions:** The same statute, however, provides a "safe harbor" rule. A transaction is not void or voidable because of the director's or other entity's interest or because of the interested director's presence at the meeting at which it was authorized, if the transaction was either: (1) approved in good faith by a majority of the shareholders entitled to vote thereon, on the basis of full disclosure to or knowledge by the shareholders of the material facts of the transaction and the director's interest in it; or (2) approved, authorized, or ratified in good faith by the board of directors or a committee of the board without counting the vote of the interested director, on the basis of full disclosure to or knowledge by the board or committee of the material facts of the transaction and the director's interest in it, and if, in addition, it was just and reasonable to the corporation at the time it was so authorized, approved, or ratified. Corp C §310(a). For further discussion, see §§2.19–2.23. The provisions for validating transactions between corporations with a common director are less stringent. See Corp C §310(b).

2. Loans, Guaranties, and Use of Shares as Security

§1.79   ### a. Restrictions

• **Loans to Directors and Officers—General Rule and Exceptions.** Corporations are generally prohibited from making loans of money or property to, or guaranteeing the obligations of, any director or officer of the corporation or of its parent, unless the transaction is approved by a majority of shareholders entitled to act on the matter. Corp C §315(a). See §2.24. An exception is provided for corporations with 100 or more shareholders, if the corporation has a bylaw approved by the outstanding shares that authorizes the board alone to approve such transactions, and if the board determines that the particular transaction may reasonably be expected to benefit the corporation. Corp C §315(b).

For other exceptions see Corp C §315(d)–(f). For definition of "approval by a majority of the shareholders entitled to act," see Corp C §315(g).

- **Loans Secured by Shares.** Corporations are generally prohibited from making any loans of money or property to anyone, or guaranteeing anyone's obligations, upon the sole security of shares of the corporation or its parent, unless the loan or guaranty is approved by a majority of the shareholders entitled to act thereon. Corp C §315(c),(g).
- **Directors' Liability for Violations.** Subject to the provisions of Corp C §309 (discussed in §2.17), directors of a corporation who approve the making of any loan or guaranty contrary to Corp C §315 may be jointly and severally liable to the corporation for the benefit of its creditors or shareholders, up to the amount of the loss suffered by the corporation as a result of the illegal loan or guaranty. Corp C §315(a)(3), (d).
- **Other Problems re Insider Loans.** In addition to the statutory strictures stated above there is a risk that creditors or taxing authorities may contend that a loan or guaranty to a corporate insider is compensation or a dividend, particularly if the loan or guaranty is not an arm's length transaction and the terms are more favorable than those available from independent commercial sources.

§1.80   b. Form: Shareholders' Resolution Consenting to Loan

Form 1.80–1

The corporation has sufficient cash and other assets to meet its existing obligations.

It is in the best interests of the corporation to lend the sum of $_ _ _ to [*name*], **who is** [*describe relationship, e.g., a director*] **of the corporation.**

[*For loans secured by shares, add*]

This loan is to be secured by a security interest in [*number*] **of the corporation's issued and outstanding** [*e.g., common*] **shares standing in the name of _ _ _ _ _ _ _.**

[Continue]

The terms and conditions of the loan are just and commercially reasonable to the corporation.

In view of the above, it is

RESOLVED that the shareholders of *[name of corporation]* approve the loan by the corporation to *[name]* in the amount of $_ _ _,

[For loans secured by shares, add]

secured by *[number]* of the corporation's *[e.g., common]* shares standing in the name of _ _ _ _ _ _ _,

[Continue]

on the following terms:

[Set forth interest rate, terms of repayment, description of other security, and any other significant terms]

RESOLVED FURTHER that the president and secretary of the corporation are authorized to take such action and to execute such documents as shall be necessary and appropriate to cause the loan to be made and its terms enforced.

Comment: If the transaction being approved comes within Corp C §315(a) or §315(c) (see §1.79) and thus requires "approval by a majority of the shareholders entitled to act," the vote required for approval depends in part on whether the approval is being sought by written consent or by vote at a duly held meeting. Approval by written consent of the shareholders requires approval by a majority of the *outstanding* shares, without counting as outstanding or as voting any shares owned by any officer or director eligible to participate in the plan or transaction that is subject to the approval. Approval at a meeting requires the affirmative vote of a majority of the shares *present and voting* at a duly held meeting at which a quorum is otherwise present, without counting for purposes of the vote as either present or voting any shares owned by any officer or director eligible to participate in the plan or transaction that is subject to the approval. Corp C §315(g). A third alternative provides simply for approval by the *unanimous* written consent or vote of the shareholders. Corp C §315(g).

VIII. RECORDS AND REPORTS

§1.81   A. Role of the Attorney

Although the attorney for a corporation is usually not actively involved in the keeping of its financial and other corporate records or the preparation and dissemination of financial reports, the attorney should be aware of the general requirements and of the areas in which legal assistance may be needed. The attorney should be acquainted with and have access to the corporation's accountant.

The choice of accounting method and taxable year are discussed in §1.82, and the records and reports required by the General Corporation Law (Corp C §§100–2319) are discussed in §§1.83–1.87.

A particular corporation may be subject to other reporting and record-keeping requirements not covered by the General Corporation Law, such as requirements resulting from the particular business conducted by the corporation, tax and labor law requirements, requirements imposed by regulatory or licensing agencies, and reporting requirements under federal and state securities laws. These matters are not within the scope of this chapter; counsel, however, should be alert for legal problems arising in any of these areas.

§1.82   B. Taxable Year and Accounting Method Under the IRC

- **Taxable Year.** Internal Revenue Code §1378 provides that S corporations must use a calendar year for federal income tax purposes unless a satisfactory business purpose for a different accounting year can be established. A similar rule is stated for personal service corporations; see IRC §441. However, under IRC §444, S corporations and personal service corporations are permitted to elect a fiscal year (IRC §444(a)) if the corporation is not part of a tiered structure (IRC §444(d)(3)) and if the deferral period of the taxable year elected is generally not longer than three months (IRC §444(b)). S corporations that make a section 444 election must satisfy the required payment rules of IRC §7519, and personal service corporations making the election are subject to the deduction limitations set forth in IRC §280H. IRC §444(c).
- **Accounting Method.** C corporations (*i.e.*, corporations that are not S corporations) and partnerships that have a C corporation as a partner are prohibited from using the cash method of

accounting, unless the entity is a personal service corporation, is a farming business, or has average annual gross receipts not exceeding $5 million. IRC §448.

C. Maintaining and Inspecting Records

§1.83   1. Accounting Records

All corporations must maintain "adequate and correct books and records of account," which must be in writing or be capable of being converted into writing. Corp C §1500. Directors have an absolute right to inspect and copy these financial records of the corporation and its subsidiaries at any reasonable time, in person or by agent or attorney. Corp C §1602.

Upon written demand and "for a purpose reasonably related to such holder's interests as a shareholder or as the holder of such voting trust certificate," any shareholder or holder of a voting trust certificate may inspect and copy these records, in person or by agent or attorney. Corp C §1601. If inspection is demanded, any records not maintained in writing must be made available in written form, at the corporation's expense. Corp C §1605. See §§3.2–3.19.

The right to inspect may be enforced by court action, and if the corporation's failure to comply with a demand for inspection was without justification, the shareholder may be awarded expenses, including attorneys' fees. Corp C §§1603–1604. A penalty may be imposed on the corporation for failure to maintain the books of account (see Corp C §§2200, 2202), and refusal to make a book entry required by law is a felony (Corp C §2254). In addition, the attorney general may take action to enforce the corporation's obligations. See Corp C §1508. For general penalty provisions, including those applicable to false or fraudulent acts, see Corp C §§1507, 2200–2260. See also discussion in §3.20.

The shareholders' right of inspection cannot be limited in the articles or bylaws (Corp C §1601(b)), or waived in a close corporation shareholders' agreement (Corp C §300(c)).

§1.84   2. Minutes

Each corporation must keep written minutes of proceedings of its shareholders, board of directors, and committees of the board. Corp C §1500; see §§1.53–1.60, 1.16–1.28 for forms and procedure.

Rights of inspection, enforcement, and prohibition of limitations on those rights are the same with respect to the minutes as with respect to accounting records (see §1.83), except that minutes are not included in the penalty provisions of Corp C §2200, and the criminal sanctions of Corp C §2254 do not apply to failure to make entries in the minutes.

§1.85   3. Record of Shareholders

The corporation must keep a record of shareholders (formerly called a share register) at its principal executive office or at the office of its transfer agent or registrar. The record may be either in writing or in another form capable of being converted to writing, and if the latter, must be converted to writing when inspection is requested. See Corp C §1605. It must include each shareholder's name, address, and the number and class of shares held. Corp C §1500. For an example, see §1.74.

Directors have an absolute right to inspect the record of shareholders and make copies, in person or by agent or attorney. Corp C §1602.

The right of shareholders to inspect and copy the record of shareholders depends on the percentage of shares held and the purpose of the inspection or copying. Any shareholder or holder of a voting trust certificate, in person or by agent or attorney, may inspect and copy the record of shareholders during usual business hours, on written demand, "for a purpose reasonably related to such holder's interests as a shareholder or holder of a voting trust certificate." Corp C §1600(c). A shareholder or group of shareholders that holds 5 percent of the outstanding voting shares (or 1 percent for certain stocks subject to federal regulation) need not state a purpose but may inspect and copy the record of shareholders during usual business hours on five days' written demand, or may obtain from the transfer agent a list of shareholders' names, addresses, and holdings on five days' written demand and tender of the transfer agent's usual charges. Corp C §1600(a). For discussion and demand forms, see §§3.9–3.12.

If the corporation or transfer agent fails to respond or delays in responding to a shareholder request, the statutes provide various means of enforcement, including (a) a court order, available to the shareholder, postponing a noticed shareholders' meeting for a period equal to the delay (Corp C §1600(b)); (b) court orders enforcing inspection or auditing (Corp C §1603(a)); (c) reimbursement of the shareholder's reasonable expenses, including attorney fees, in some situations (Corp C §1604); (d) a penalty of $25 per day, beginning 30 days after the request is received, up to a maximum of $1500, to be paid to the complaining shareholders (Corp C §2200); and (e) enforcement by the Attorney General (Corp C §1508).

The shareholder's rights provided by Corp C §1600 cannot be limited by the articles or bylaws (Corp C §1600(d)), or waived in a close corporation shareholders' agreement (Corp C §300(c)).

D. Annual Statement Filed With Secretary of State

§1.86   1. Procedure

Every year, each corporation must file a Statement by Domestic Stock Corporation with the California Secretary of State. Corp C §1502. This statement gives current information about the corporation's directors, officers, and place of business, and designates an agent for service of process. Corp C §1502. For copy of the official form, see §1.87.

The Statement by Domestic Stock Corporation is due within 90 days after filing of a corporation's original articles of incorporation, and annually thereafter. Corp C §1502(a). The annual filing period includes the calendar month during which the original articles were filed and the immediately preceding five calendar months. Corp C §1502(d). The Secretary of State mails blank forms to each corporation approximately three months before the close of the applicable filing period, but failure of a corporation to receive the form is not an excuse for failure to file. Corp C §1502(d).

If there has been no change since the last filed statement, the corporation may instead inform the Secretary of State, on a form supplied by the Secretary, that no changes in the required information have occurred during the applicable period. Corp C §1502(c).

If a statement is not filed within 60 days after the Secretary of State mails a notice of delinquency to the corporation, the Franchise Tax Board will assess a $250 penalty against the corporation. Corp C §2204; Rev & T C §25936. The Secretary of State has discretion to excuse the nonfiling of an annual report and to prevent imposition of the $250 penalty. Corp C §2204. The Secretary may also suspend the corporate franchise of a corporation that has failed to file the required statement for two years. Corp C §2205.

§1.87   2. Official Form: Statement by Domestic Stock Corporation

Form 1.87–1

State of California
March Fong Eu
Secretary of State

P.O. Box 944230
Sacramento, CA   94244-0230
Phone: (916) 445-2020

STATEMENT BY DOMESTIC STOCK CORPORATION

THIS STATEMENT MUST BE FILED WITH CALIFORNIA SECRETARY OF STATE (SEC. 1502, CORPORATIONS CODE)

A $5 FILING FEE MUST ACCOMPANY THIS STATEMENT.

WHEN COMPLETING FORM, PLEASE USE BLACK TYPEWRITER RIBBON OR BLACK INK

IMPORTANT—Please Read Instructions On Back Of Form

1.

DO NOT ALTER PREPRINTED NAME. IF ITEM NO. 1 IS BLANK, PLEASE ENTER CORPORATE NAME

DO NOT WRITE IN THIS SPACE

THE CALIFORNIA CORPORATION NAMED HEREIN, MAKES THE FOLLOWING STATEMENT

2. STREET ADDRESS OF PRINCIPAL EXECUTIVE OFFICE	ROOM NO.	2A. CITY AND STATE	2B. ZIP CODE
3. STREET ADDRESS OF PRINCIPAL BUSINESS OFFICE IN CALIFORNIA (IF ANY)	ROOM NO.	3A. CITY CA	3B. ZIP CODE
4. MAILING ADDRESS	ROOM NO.	4A. CITY AND STATE	4B. ZIP CODE

THE NAMES OF THE FOLLOWING OFFICERS ARE:

5. CHIEF EXECUTIVE OFFICER	5A. STREET ADDRESS (SEE REVERSE SIDE)	5B. CITY AND STATE	5C. ZIP CODE
6. SECRETARY	6A. STREET ADDRESS (SEE REVERSE SIDE)	6B. CITY AND STATE	6C. ZIP CODE
7. CHIEF FINANCIAL OFFICER	7A. STREET ADDRESS (SEE REVERSE SIDE)	7B. CITY AND STATE	7C. ZIP CODE

INCUMBENT DIRECTORS, INCLUDING DIRECTORS WHO ARE ALSO OFFICERS (Attach supplemental list if necessary)

8. NAME	8A. STREET ADDRESS (SEE REVERSE SIDE)	8B. CITY AND STATE	8C. ZIP CODE
9. NAME	9A. STREET ADDRESS (SEE REVERSE SIDE)	9B. CITY AND STATE	9C. ZIP CODE
10. NAME	10A. STREET ADDRESS (SEE REVERSE SIDE)	10B. CITY AND STATE	10C. ZIP CODE

11. THE NUMBER OF VACANCIES ON THE BOARD OF DIRECTORS, IF ANY: _____

DESIGNATED AGENT FOR SERVICE OF PROCESS   (Only one agent may be named)

12. NAME

13. CALIFORNIA STREET ADDRESS IF AGENT IS AN INDIVIDUAL. (DO NOT USE P.O. BOX) DO NOT INCLUDE ADDRESS IF AGENT IS A CORPORATION.

14. DESCRIBE TYPE OF BUSINESS OF THE CORPORATION NAMED IN ITEM 1.

15. I DECLARE THAT I HAVE EXAMINED THIS STATEMENT AND TO THE BEST OF MY KNOWLEDGE AND BELIEF, IT IS TRUE, CORRECT AND COMPLETE.

| TYPE OR PRINT NAME OF SIGNING OFFICER OR AGENT | SIGNATURE | TITLE | DATE |

16. I DECLARE THERE HAS BEEN NO CHANGE IN THE INFORMATION CONTAINED IN THE LAST STATEMENT OF THE CORPORATION WHICH IS ON FILE IN THE SECRETARY OF STATE'S OFFICE. DOES NOT APPLY ON INITIAL FILING. (READ INSTRUCTIONS BEFORE COMPLETING THIS ITEM)

| (CHECK HERE) TYPE OR PRINT NAME OF SIGNING OFFICER OR AGENT | SIGNATURE | TITLE | DATE |

SO-200 (REV. 6/88)   88 49084

SECRETARY OF STATE
P.O. BOX 944230, SACRAMENTO, CA 94244-0230

INSTRUCTIONS FOR COMPLETING STATEMENT BY DOMESTIC STOCK CORPORATION

IMPORTANT NOTICE — If there has been no change in the corporation's last statement on file in the Secretary of State's Office, fully complete items 1 and 16. Please submit signed statement, with $5.00 filing fee. **IF THERE HAS BEEN A CHANGE IN ANY OF THE INFORMATION, ALL ITEMS, 1 THROUGH 15, MUST BE COMPLETED.**

FILING PERIOD: All corporations must file within 90 days after filing articles of incorporation. Thereafter, corporations must file annually by the end of the calendar month of the anniversary date of its incorporation, and when the agent for service of process or his/her address is changed. CORPORATIONS FILING FOR THE FIRST TIME MUST COMPLETE ITEMS 1 THROUGH 15 ONLY.

FILING FEE: All corporations must submit a five dollar ($5.00) filing fee with this statement. (Section 12210, Government Code.) Check or money order should be made payable to Secretary of State. Please do not send cash. Your canceled check will be your receipt.

ITEM 1: Do not alter the preprinted corporate name. If corporation name has been changed and is not correct, please attach statement indicating the correct name and the date the name change amendment was filed with the Secretary of State. If space is blank enter exact corporate name and number. Do not include your DBA name.

ITEMS 2–2B: The address to be entered is the STREET address of the corporation's principal executive office. Enter room or suite number and ZIP code. (DO NOT USE POST OFFICE BOX NUMBER.) Do not abbreviate city name.

ITEMS 3–3B: Complete this item only if the address in Item 2 is outside California. The address to be entered is the STREET address of the corporation's principal office in CALIFORNIA, if any. (DO NOT USE POST OFFICE BOX NUMBER.)

ITEMS 4–4B: The address to be entered is the MAILING ADDRESS for the corporation.

ITEMS 5–7C: Enter the names and complete business or residence addresses of the corporation's chief executive officer (i.e. president), secretary, and chief financial officer (i.e. treasurer). The corporation must have these three officers in accordance with section 312, Corporations Code. Any of the offices may be held by the same person unless the articles of incorporation or bylaws provide otherwise. Names of additional officers should not be submitted. DO NOT USE POST OFFICE BOX NUMBERS. (IF THERE IS NOT A NUMBERED STREET ADDRESS, GIVE PHYSICAL LOCATION ADDRESS. (e.g.: NW Corner of Hammer Lane and Road 113.)*

ITEMS 8–10C: Enter the names and complete STREET addresses of the incumbent directors. DO NOT USE POST OFFICE BOX NUMBERS. If there are more than 3 directors, please attach supplemental listing.

ITEM 11: Enter the number of vacancies on the board of directors, if any.

ITEMS 12–13: Section 1502(b), Corporations Code, requires that domestic corporations designate an agent for service of process. An agent for service of process is one who may accept papers in case of a lawsuit against the corporation. The agent may be an individual who is an officer or director of the corporation, or any other person. The person named as agent must be a resident of California. ONLY ONE INDIVIDUAL MAY BE NAMED AS AGENT FOR SERVICE OF PROCESS. Or, the agent may be another corporation. However, a corporation named as agent for service of process for another corporation must have on file in the Secretary of State's Office a certificate pursuant to section 1505, Corporations Code. This certificate is required ONLY if a corporation is named as agent for service of process for other corporations. A CORPORATION CANNOT BE NAMED AS AGENT FOR SERVICE OF PROCESS FOR ITSELF. (For example, ABC Corporation cannot name ABC Corporation as its agent for service of process.)

If the agent is a person, enter that person's name and complete STREET address. If the agent is another corporation, enter the name of corporation only. Do not complete address section. Only one agent for service of process is to be named.

You must have advance approval from the agent that the designated agent has agreed to act as agent for service of process.

ITEM 14: Complete by entering a statement of the general type of business which constitutes the principal business activity of the corporation named in Item 1. Explanation must be brief. (Examples: Manufacturer of aircraft, auto parts distributor, retail department store.)

ITEM 15: Type or print name of signing officer or agent. Signature and title of corporate officer or agent is required to complete the form. Enter date if the form is signed.

ITEM 16: (See **IMPORTANT NOTICE** above)

SPECIAL NOTES

* THE STATEMENT WILL NOT BE FILED IF A POST OFFICE BOX ADDRESS APPEARS IN ITEM 2, 3, 5A–7A, 8A–10A, OR 13.

IT IS REQUIRED THAT A CORPORATION FILE A STATEMENT EVEN THOUGH IT MAY NOT BE ACTIVELY ENGAGED IN BUSINESS AT THE TIME THIS STATEMENT IS DUE.

FAILURE TO FILE THIS COMPLETED FORM BY THE PREPRINTED DUE DATE IN ITEM 1 OR WITHIN 90 DAYS OF INCORPORATION WILL RESULT IN THE ASSESSMENT OF A $250 PENALTY. (Section 2204, Corporations Code, and Section 25936, Revenue & Taxation Code.)

PLEASE MAKE A COPY OF THE COMPLETED FORM IF YOU WISH A COPY FOR YOUR FILES.

E. Reports to Shareholders

1. Annual Report

§1.88 a. Contents

The corporation must send its shareholders an annual report, unless it has fewer than 100 shareholders and a bylaw expressly waives the requirement. Corp C §1501. See §3.3. This requirement cannot be waived in a close corporation shareholders' agreement. Corp C §300(c).

The requirements of the annual report are spelled out in detail in Corp C §1501. It must include a balance sheet as of the end of the fiscal year and an income statement and statement of changes in financial position for that fiscal year. Corp C §1501(a). The statements must be accompanied by a report of independent accountants (defined in Corp C §115) or by the certificate of an authorized corporate officer that they were prepared without audit. Corp C §1501(a). Financial statements of corporations with fewer than 100 shareholders of record need not be prepared in conformity with generally accepted accounting principles if they reasonably set forth the assets and liabilities and the income and expense of the corporation and disclose the accounting basis used in their preparation. Corp C §1501(a).

In addition, corporations with 100 or more shareholders of record that are not subject to federal regulation must describe insider transactions larger than $40,000 and indemnifications of or advances to officers or directors larger than $10,000, unless the transaction was approved by the shareholders. Corp C §1501(b).

§1.89 b. Timing of Annual Report

The annual report must be sent to shareholders not later than 120 days after the close of the fiscal year, except for corporations with fewer than 100 shareholders whose bylaws expressly waive this requirement. Corp C §1501(a). Unless so waived, the report must be sent at least 15 days before the annual shareholders' meeting if sent by first-class mail or 35 days before the meeting if sent by third-class mail. Corp C §1501(a).

§1.90   2. Quarterly Reports Requested by Shareholders

A shareholder or group of shareholders holding 5 percent or more of the outstanding shares of any class is entitled to receive, on written request, a balance sheet and an income statement for the three-month, six-month, or nine-month period of the current fiscal year ended more than 30 days before the request. Corp C §1501(c)–(d). In addition, if no annual report for the last fiscal year has been sent to the shareholders (see §§1.88–1.89), the corporation must provide the financial statements required in annual reports upon any shareholder's written request made more than 120 days after the close of the fiscal year. Corp C §1501(c). See §3.5. The requested financial information must be delivered or mailed to the person requesting it within 30 days. Corp C §1501(c).

Each corporation must keep a copy of its quarterly financial statements at its principal office for 12 months, and these must be exhibited at all reasonable times (or a copy mailed) to any shareholder on demand. Corp C §1501(c)–(d).

The shareholders' right to financial statements may be enforced by suit. If good cause is shown, the court may extend the time for providing the reports. Corp C §1501(e). If, however, the corporation's failure is without justification, the court may award reasonable expenses, including attorney's fees, to the shareholder. Corp C §1501(f). In addition, the corporation may be liable for statutory penalties. See Corp C §2200.

IX. SPECIAL RULES FOR CLOSE CORPORATIONS (CORP C §158)

§1.91   A. "Close Corporation" Defined

The "close corporation" or "statutory close corporation" is a form of closely held corporation established by California statute. See Corp C §158. It was designed to give small companies the benefits of incorporation but allow them the freedom to disregard corporate formalities and manage the corporate business with the flexibility of a partnership, if so provided in a shareholders' agreement.

A close corporation is statutorily defined as a corporation whose articles contain (1) a provision that all issued shares of all classes be held of record by not more than a specified number of persons, not exceeding 35, and (2) the statement, "This corporation is a close corporation." Corp C §158(a). In addition, the corporate name must contain the word "corporation," "incorporated," "limited," or an appropriate abbreviation. Corp C §202(a). Special rules apply for counting the shareholders for this purpose (*e.g.*, husband and wife count as one shareholder). See Corp C §158(d). All close corporation share certificates must contain a legend concerning the form of the corporation. Corp C §418(c).

§1.92   B. Advantages and Disadvantages

A lengthy discussion of the advantages and disadvantages of the statutory close corporation is beyond the scope of this chapter. See 1 Ballantine & Sterling, CALIFORNIA CORPORATION LAWS §60.02[2] (4th ed). See also Berger, *California's New General Corporation Law: Close and Closely-Held Corporations,* 7 Pac LJ 585 (1976); Jordan, *The Close Corporation Provisions of the New California General Corporation Law,* 23 UCLA L Rev 1094 (1976); O'Neal & Magill, *California's New Close Corporation Legislation,* 23 UCLA L Rev 1155 (1976).

In general, close corporations have broad latitude to define and allocate management responsibilities in a shareholders' agreement. Corp C §§186, 300. If a corporation is acting within the provisions set forth in such an agreement, the failure to observe corporate formalities relating to meetings of shareholders or directors in connection with the management of its affairs "shall not be considered a factor tending to establish that the shareholders have personal liability for corporate obligations." Corp C §300(e). Thus, a close corporation may presumably be managed in an informal manner, using procedures established in the shareholders' agreement, without the necessity of compliance with certain provisions of the Corporations Code that otherwise might require formal action by the board or the shareholders.

Although Corp C §300 is very permissive, counsel should bear in mind that other factors may make it necessary or desirable for a close corporation to observe and document certain of the corporate formalities. This is particularly true with respect to the election of directors and officers, securities matters, changes in corporate charter documents, and acquisitions, mergers, or dissolutions. Observation of corporate formalities may also be desirable in connection with employing and compensating shareholder-employees, extending credit to shareholders, directors, or officers, and matters related to taxes or potential liabilities. After considering the possible consequences, the attorney may find that instances in which corporate formalities should or may reasonably be disregarded are the exception rather than the rule.

Many practitioners do not recommend using the statutory close corporation because they feel its disadvantages outweigh its advantages. For a discussion of the pitfalls in electing close corporation status, including the risk of adverse tax consequences from unanticipated dividends, and possible problems under the California Corporate Securities Law, see Wang, *The California Statutory Close Corporation: Gateway to Flexibility or Trap for the Unwary?* 15 San Diego L Rev 687 (1978).

C. Special Procedures, Rules, and Forms

§1.93   1. Electing Close Corporation Status

Election to be a statutory close corporation must be made either in the original articles (Corp C §158(a)) or by amendment to the articles unanimously approved by the outstanding shares (Corp C §158(b)). See ORGANIZING CORPORATIONS IN CALIFORNIA §§1.54, 2.8, 2.32 (2d ed Cal CEB 1983); see also 3 MARSH'S CALIFORNIA CORPORATION LAW §21 (2d ed). The number of shareholders may not exceed 35. Corp C §158(a).

NOTE: The requirements for close corporation status under the General Corporation Law are not the same as the requirements for S corporation tax treatment (IRC §§1361–1379; Rev & T C §§23800–23811) or the requirements for exemption from qualification of corporate securities as a small or limited offering under Corp C §25102(f) or (h)); see Corp C §116. Because securities law exemptions do not exactly match the requirements for a close corporation, some close corporations may not come within the small offering exemption of Corp C §25102(h), but the limited offering exemption of Corp C §25102(f) should ordinarily apply. See ORGANIZING CORPS §§4.48–4.70.

§1.94 2. Shareholders' Agreement

The most important statutory provisions regarding close corporations are those that authorize a close corporation to regulate its management and control by provisions contained in a "shareholders' agreement." See Corp C §§186, 204, 300. See also ORGANIZING CORPORATIONS IN CALIFORNIA §2.4 (2d ed Cal CEB 1983); 1 Ballantine & Sterling, CALIFORNIA CORPORATION LAWS §§62.01–62.03 (4th ed); 3 MARSH'S CALIFORNIA CORPORATION LAW §21.7 (2d ed). The shareholders' agreement may alter traditional corporate management procedures and provide for other modes of managing the corporation's affairs. It may regulate division of the corporation's profits, distribution of its assets upon liquidation, and other matters of concern to the shareholders. Corp C §300(b). A shareholders' agreement may be wide ranging or narrow in scope. See generally Jordan, *The Close Corporation Provisions of the New California General Corporation Law,* 23 UCLA L Rev 1094, 1114 (1976); O'Neal & Magill, *California's New Close Corporation Legislation,* 23 UCLA L Rev 1155, 1160 (1976).

CAVEAT: The shareholder's agreement cannot waive or alter specific statutory provisions relating to (a) the election, revocation, and loss of close corporation status (see Corp C §158); (b) required filings with the Secretary of State (see Corp C §300(b), (c)); (c) transfer restrictions that must appear on stock certificates (Corp C §300(c)); (d) distributions to shareholders (see Corp C §§500–501); (5) shareholders' vote on mergers and reorganizations (see Corp C §§1111, 1201(e)); (f) records, reports, and rights of inspection (see Corp C §§1500–1605); (g) certain aspects of dissolution, including involuntary dissolution (see Corp C §§1800–1809, 2009–2011); or (h) crimes and penalties (see Corp C §§2200–2260).

§1.95 3. Articles and Bylaws of Close Corporations

A close corporation's articles of incorporation must contain a provision establishing the corporation as a close corporation. If this provision is included in the articles by amendment after the issuance of shares, it requires the affirmative vote of all of the issued and outstanding shares of all classes. Corp C §158(b). This provision may be changed by amendment, but such an amendment, unless the articles provide for a lesser vote, requires the affirmative vote of at least two thirds of each class of the outstanding shares. Corp C §158(c).

Although a close corporation is not required to have bylaws, it is generally advisable that bylaws be adopted, because the Corporations Code is structured for bylaws. A close corporation's bylaws should contain provisions to preserve management flexibility and prevent loss of close corporation status. Counsel should be alert for any potential conflicts between the shareholders' agreement and the bylaws. Standard form bylaws, if used, may require amendment to give effect to the shareholders' agreement.

§1.96　　　　4. Form: Bylaw Expanding Directors' Powers

Form 1.96–1

Section _ _. Powers. Subject to the applicable provisions of the California General Corporation Law, and to any limitations in the articles of incorporation and these bylaws relating to actions required to be approved by the shareholders or the outstanding shares, and further subject to the provisions of any shareholders' agreement relating to any of the affairs of this corporation as long as it remains a close corporation under the California General Corporation Law, the business and affairs of the corporation shall be managed and all corporate powers shall be exercised by or under the direction of the board of directors. The board of directors may delegate management of the day-to-day operation of the corporation's affairs to a management company or other person, provided that, subject to any shareholders' agreement, such management shall remain under the ultimate direction of the board of directors.

§1.97　　　　5. Form: Bylaw Requiring Share Certificate Legend

Form 1.97–1

Section _ _. Legend. Every certificate representing shares of the corporation shall contain the following legend conspicuously on its face:

THIS CORPORATION IS A CLOSE CORPORATION. THE NUMBER OF HOLDERS OF RECORD OF ITS SHARES OF ALL

CLASSES CANNOT EXCEED [*number not larger than 35*]. ANY ATTEMPTED VOLUNTARY INTER VIVOS TRANSFER THAT WOULD VIOLATE THIS REQUIREMENT IS VOID. REFER TO THE ARTICLES, BYLAWS, AND ANY AGREEMENTS ON FILE WITH THE SECRETARY OF THE CORPORATION FOR FURTHER RESTRICTIONS.

Comment: This legend is required by Corp C §418(c), (d). Any other restrictions on transfer, redemption rights, or voting (including voting agreements and irrevocable proxies) must also be stated on the share certificates; otherwise such restrictions are not enforceable against a transferee without actual knowledge of them. See Corp C §418(a), (b).

§1.98   6. Other Statutory Provisions Relating to Close Corporations

In addition to the statutory provisions already discussed, Corporations Code provisions relating specifically to close corporations include the following: election, revocation, and loss of close corporation status (Corp C §158); definition of shareholders' agreement (Corp C §186); corporate name (Corp C §202(a)); shareholders' agreement as controlling allocation of management powers, liability, corporate formalities (Corp C §300); share certificates and their transfer (Corp C §418); constructive notice of restrictions on transfers of shares (Corp C §421); exemption from certain quorum requirements (Corp C §602); voting agreements between shareholders (Corp C §706(a)); shareholder approval of merger in which disappearing corporation is a close corporation and surviving corporation is not (Corp C §1111); shareholder approval of reorganization that would result in receipt of shares of a corporation that is not a close corporation (Corp C §1201(e)); shareholders' right to file for involuntary dissolution (Corp C §1800(a)(2)); and shareholders' right to file for judicial supervision of voluntary dissolution (Corp C §1904).

§1.99   7. Terminating Close Corporation Status

Close corporation status may be terminated voluntarily or involuntarily. See Corp C §158(e). For discussion of termination procedures generally, see chap 7. See also 1 Ballantine & Sterling,

CALIFORNIA CORPORATION LAWS §§64–64.03 (4th ed); 3 MARSH'S
CALIFORNIA CORPORATION LAW §21.5 (2d ed).

X. OPINION AND AUDIT LETTERS

§1.100   A. Opinion Letters

Corporate clients may request their attorney to give legal opinions
for many purposes. Such an opinion may be sought as guidance
for a proposed course of business activity, as a condition to execution
of corporate instruments and agreements, in connection with offering
or selling securities, or to aid in evaluating the merits of claims
or controversies. Typically, it is a writing prepared by the attorney
expressing his or her informed opinion of the legal principles
generally applicable to a specific business transaction. Its contents
will vary according to the type of business transaction involved,
but usually its most important aspect will be the attorney's express
opinion that the written agreements memorializing the transaction
are valid and legally enforceable. It is usually provided in the form
of a letter delivered to one or more parties involved in the transaction,
although it may be delivered to the client or to another attorney.

For general discussion of legal opinions and practical instructions
on how to prepare an opinion letter, see Freeman, *Legal Opinions
in Business Transactions,* 3 CEB Cal Bus L Practitioner 1 (Winter
1988).

• **Preliminary Considerations:** Before beginning to prepare an
  opinion letter, counsel should consider the following general
  questions:

  (1) Have the purpose, nature, and scope of the requested opinion
been made clear? These should be set forth in writing before you
proceed.

  (2) Have the people who will receive or have access to the opinion
letter been identified?

  (3) Is the opinion to be based on hypothetical facts or assumptions?
If so, have they been made clear?

  (4) If the opinion is to be based on an actual situation, do you
have sufficient factual information to render the opinion? Is the source
of this information sufficiently reliable?

  (5) Have all attorneys who have knowledge of facts or information
about the client been informed of the request for an opinion? Should
they participate in preparing it?

(6) Have the time and expense necessary to render the opinion been discussed with the client?

(7) Are you aware of any factors that would make it difficult to be independent in rendering the opinion?

(8) Are you sufficiently knowledgeable about the subject matter? If not, whose assistance may you enlist?

(9) Will the existence of the opinion letter have an impact on any unrelated transactions, claims, or controversies? If so, will appropriate confidentiality be maintained, and will the attorney-client privilege be preserved?

(10) Will the opinion letter be discoverable in any pending or future action or proceeding?

- **Checklist for Preparing the Opinion:** Because of the variety of the types of opinions that may be requested and the contexts in which requests are made, there is no general form appropriate to all situations. The following checklist is provided as a guide for including the appropriate items:

(1) Identify the date as of which the opinion is rendered.

(2) Identify your client and the basis of your authorization to issue the opinion letter if it is to be delivered to someone other than the client.

(3) Identify the person to whom the letter is directed, the purpose for which it is intended, and any appropriate caveats limiting the scope of the recipient's reliance on the opinion.

(4) Recite as hypothetical any hypothetical facts on which the opinion is based.

(5) Identify the sources of information relied on and any assumptions made about their reliability.

(6) If you have not examined a particular source of relevant information, describe what you have not done (and consider whether further investigation is necessary).

(7) If you are relying on or giving an opinion under the law of a particular jurisdiction but there is a possibility that the law of another jurisdiction might apply, identify the jurisdiction on whose law the opinion is based. Because of potential problems in rendering an opinion under the law of a state in which the attorney is not licensed to practice, a caveat such as the following is sometimes included:

It is noted that the agreement provides that it shall be governed by the law of the State of New York. In this

connection and with your approval, we are not expressing an opinion on the applicability of New York law to this transaction, and you are not relying on us as to New York law. Our opinion expressed herein is limited to California law in the event and to the extent California law is or may be applicable.

(8) State the opinion as carefully and precisely as possible. Define terms if necessary for a clear understanding.

(9) If appropriate, state whether you will, without specific requests, advise the addressee of changes in relevant facts or law that might affect the opinion.

(10) If appropriate, state any reasonably likely later events that might affect the opinion.

(11) State any appropriate limitations on the addressee's use or dissemination of all or part of the opinion. Counsel rendering an opinion can rarely be certain who may see the opinion, and for what purposes, other than that intended, it may later be relied on. Restrictive language such as the following is sometimes included:

This opinion is delivered to you under [*e.g., description of agreement provision*], and is intended for your use only in connection with [*e.g., the consummation of the transaction contemplated by that agreement*]. You should not rely on this opinion for any other purpose, and others should not rely on this opinion for any purpose. This opinion should not be quoted in whole or in part or distributed in any other way to any person other than yourself.

Before issuing an opinion letter it is good practice, when possible, to have another attorney carefully review it.

For further guidance, see Groh, A Checklist for Preparing Opinion Letters in Standard Corporate Transactions, 4 CEB Cal Bus L Practitioner 137 (Fall 1989).

B. Counsel's Response to Accountants' Inquiries

§1.101   1. Need To Proceed With Caution

Corporate clients often engage independent accountants to prepare or audit financial statements for various purposes, such as complying with securities law requirements, establishing or maintaining satisfactory relationships with creditors, providing information for shareholders who do not participate in management, providing information in connection with corporate acquisitions or reorganizations, or complying with regulatory requirements imposed on the corporation because of the nature of its business.

Attorneys often receive "audit inquiry" letters from their corporate clients, requesting that information be sent to the independent accountants auditing the company's financial records. Although the request to supply client information may seem simple and straightforward on its face, the attorney should proceed cautiously whenever such a request is received.

It has been frequently noted that a fundamental conflict of interests exists between the client's auditor and its attorney regarding information that may be protected by the attorney-client privilege, *e.g.,* threatened or potential litigation and other contingent liabilities. The auditor seeks maximum disclosure on such matters, whereas the attorney seeks to preserve the attorney-client privilege. The client is often unaware that the information sought is privileged and that if disclosed by the attorney, the privilege might be waived.

Because of their conflicting interests, lawyers and accountants have traditionally clashed over the proper disclosure standards for legal claims. This conflict was apparently resolved in 1976 when the American Bar Association issued its Statement of Policy Regarding Lawyers' Responses to Auditors' Requests for Information (see next paragraph) and the American Institute of Certified Public Accountants (AICPA) issued its corresponding Statement on Auditing Standards No. 12. These two statements, taken together, represent an official "settlement agreement" between the two professions, permitting each profession to fulfill its respective duties to its clients without violating professional ethics.

The ABA Statement of Policy and accompanying materials are set forth in 31 Bus Lawyer 1709 (1976), and are also available in the Auditor's Letter Handbook (price $6.00) from the Section of Corporation, Banking and Business Law, American Bar Association, 750 North Lakeshore, Chicago, Illinois 60611 (telephone (312) 988–5555).

Responding to an audit inquiry letter absolutely requires that the attorney be familiar with the ABA Statement and its illustrative forms. See Martin, *How To Respond To An Auditor's Inquiry Letter,* 3 CEB

Cal Bus L Practitioner 125 (Summer 1988), which reprints the ABA Statement and illustrative forms at 130–143. See also Fuld, *Lawyers' Responses to Auditors—Some Practical Aspects,* 44 Bus Lawyer 159 (Nov. 1988). Once familiarity with the ABA Statement of Policy is achieved, drafting the response is not difficult. In most instances, the only matters that will be identified and discussed will be pending litigation.

§1.102   2. Checklist: "Do's and Don'ts" of Responding to an Audit Inquiry Letter

The following checklist is taken from Martin, *How To Respond to an Auditor's Inquiry Letter,* 3 CEB Bus Law Practitioner 125, 129 (Summer 1988):

Generally, the attorney's response *may disclose* the following:

1. The existence of, and nonprivileged information regarding, all overtly threatened or pending litigation.

2. The existence of, and nonprivileged information regarding, contractual obligations that your client has specifically identified and on which the client has requested comment.

3. The existence of, and nonprivileged information regarding, possible unasserted claims that your client has specifically identified and on which the client has requested comment.

Generally, the attorney's response *should not* do any of the following:

1. Evaluate or express judgments as to the outcome of pending or threatened litigation except in the relatively few cases where it appears that an unfavorable outcome is "probable" or "remote" and the resulting liability would be "material."

2. Disclose to the auditor the existence or nonexistence of a possible unasserted claim or contractual obligation except those that the client has specifically identified and on which the client has requested comment.

3. Confirm to the auditor the completeness of management's list of possible unasserted claims, or the accuracy of management's advice to the auditor.

4. Respond to a "general inquiry" or a request for "all information" about all possible unasserted claims or other matters without reference to the standards of materiality set forth in Paragraph [3] of the ABA Statement.

2

Directors and Officers

William M. McKenzie, Jr.

WILLIAM M. MCKENZIE, Jr., B.A., 1953, Yale University; LL.B., 1959, University of Michigan. Mr. McKenzie, of the firm of Luce, Forward, Hamilton & Scripps, practices in San Diego.

§2.1 I. INTRODUCTION; SCOPE OF CHAPTER

In recent years, much attention has been focused on the increasing number of shareholder suits filed against directors and officers (particularly for their decisions in merger or takeover situations), on the difficulty of obtaining insurance to protect members of management from personal liability for their acts on behalf of the corporation, and on the resultant problems many companies have faced in attracting qualified directors. The California legislature, following Delaware's lead, has adopted amendments to its corporations laws permitting corporations to limit directors' liability and indemnify directors and other corporate agents for expenses if they are sued. See §§2.57–2.73.

Despite this recent emphasis on limiting management's liability, the corporation's lawyer should be concerned primarily with counseling directors and officers on the proper performance of their duties. See §§2.16–2.24. The lawyer must also be aware of the possible ambivalence of his or her own role because of the various constituencies that corporate counsel is often asked to serve or advise. Common situations in which corporate counsel may encounter conflicts of interest, and the lawyer's ethical responsibilities under the new Rules of Professional Conduct, are discussed in §§2.2–2.15. Common areas in which the corporation and its management may need preventive counseling to avoid liability are discussed in §§2.25–2.50; compensation of officers and employment agreements are discussed in §§2.51–2.56. This chapter is not an exhaustive analysis of the many areas of substantive law where corporate management may encounter problems. It is intended to serve as a checklist of major pitfalls and a starting point for counsel in advising management.

II. ROLE OF COUNSEL: POSSIBLE CONFLICTS OF INTEREST

§2.2 A. Applicable Rules of Professional Conduct

On matters of professional conduct, California attorneys are governed by the Rules of Professional Conduct of the State Bar of California (Cal Rules of Prof Cond), as well as applicable law, which includes the State Bar Act (Bus & P C §§6000–6228), and opinions of California courts. A completely revised version of the

Rules of Professional Conduct became effective May 27, 1989. For a willful breach of any of these rules, the Board of Governors of the State Bar has the power to discipline an attorney as provided by law. Bus & P C §§6076–6077; Cal Rules of Prof Cond 1–100. If the California rules are silent on a particular matter, the courts may use the American Bar Association's Model Rules of Professional Conduct in considering the ethical issues involved. See *Altschul v Sayble* (1978) 83 CA3d 153, 147 CR 716.

NOTE: Attorneys with a pressing ethical problem may wish to call the State Bar's ethics "hotline," at 800–2–ETHICS (800–238–4427).

California Rules of Professional Conduct 3–300, 3–310, and 3–600 are of particular importance to attorneys with corporate clients, and are reprinted in full here, for easy reference. In the Rules, the word "member" refers to counsel, and the word "constituents" refers to the individuals who manage, own, or control a corporation, including its directors, officers, and controlling shareholders.

Rule 3–300 reads as follows:

> Rule 3–300. Avoiding Adverse Interests.
> A member shall not enter into a business transaction with a client; or knowingly acquire an ownership, possessory, security, or other pecuniary interest adverse to a client, unless each of the following requirements has been satisfied:
> (A) The transaction or acquisition and its terms are fair and reasonable to the client and are fully disclosed and transmitted in writing to the client in a manner which should reasonably have been understood by the client; and
> (B) The client is advised in writing that the client may seek the advice of an independent lawyer of the client's choice and is given a reasonable opportunity to seek that advice; and
> (C) The client thereafter consents in writing to the terms of the transaction or the terms of the acquisition.

> Discussion:
> Rule 3–300 is not intended to apply to the agreement by which the member is retained by the client, unless the agreement confers on the member an ownership, possessory, security, or other pecuniary interest adverse to the client. Such an agreement is governed, in part, by rule 4–200.
> Rule 3–300 is not intended to apply where the member and client each make an investment on terms offered to the general public or a significant portion thereof. For example, rule 3–300 is not intended to apply where A, a member, invests in a limited partnership syndicated by a third party. B, A's client, makes

the same investment. Although A and B are each investing in the same business, A did not enter into the transaction "with" B for the purposes of the rule.

Rule 3–300 is intended to apply where the member wishes to obtain an interest in client's property in order to secure the amount of the member's past due or future fees.

Comment: Counsel for a corporation should generally avoid entering into business transactions with a corporate client or acquiring an ownership interest in the client, not only to conform with the Rules and avoid conflicts of interest, but also to maintain objectivity in advising the client. Whenever a lawyer has a personal financial interest in the client's affairs, his judgment may cease to be impartial.

Rule 3–310 reads as follows:

Rule 3–310. Avoiding the Representation of Adverse Interests. (A) If a member has or had a relationship with another party interested in the representation, or has an interest in its subject matter, the member shall not accept or continue such representation without all affected clients' informed written consent.

(B) A member shall not concurrently represent clients whose interests conflict, except with their informed written consent.

(C) A member who represents two or more clients shall not enter into an aggregate settlement of the claims of or against the clients, except with their informed written consent.

(D) A member shall not accept employment adverse to a client or former client where, by reason of the representation of the client or former client, the member has obtained confidential information material to the employment except with the informed written consent of the client or former client.

(E) A member shall not accept compensation for representing a client from one other than the client unless:

(1) There is no interference with the member's independence of professional judgment or with the client-lawyer relationship; and

(2) Information relating to representation of a client is protected as required by Business and Professions Code section 6068, subdivision (e); and

(3) The client consents after disclosure, provided that no disclosure is required if;

(a) such nondisclosure is otherwise authorized by law, or

(b) the member is rendering legal services on behalf of any public agency which provides legal services to other public agencies or members of the public.

(F) As used in this rule "informed" means full disclosure to the client of the circumstances and advice to the client of any actual or reasonably foreseeable adverse effects of those circumstances upon the representation.

Discussion:

Rule 3–310 is not intended to prohibit a member from representing parties having antagonistic positions on the same legal question that has arisen in different cases, unless representation of either client would be adversely affected.

Paragraph (A) is intended to apply to all types of legal employment, including the representation of multiple parties in litigation or in a single transaction or other common enterprise or legal relationship. Examples of the latter include the formation of a partnership for several partners or a corporation for several shareholders; the preparation of an ante-nuptial agreement, or joint or reciprocal wills for a husband and wife, or the resolution of an "uncontested" marital dissolution. In such situations, for the sake of convenience or economy, the parties may well prefer to employ a single counsel, but a member must disclose the potential adverse aspects of such multiple representation (e.g., Evid. Code, §962) and must obtain the consent of the clients thereto. Moreover, if the potential adversity should become actual, the member must obtain the further consent of the clients pursuant to paragraph (B).

Paragraph (E) is not intended to abrogate existing relationships between insurers and insureds whereby the insurer has the contractual right to unilaterally select counsel for the insured, where there is no conflict of interest. (See *San Diego Navy Federal Credit Union v. Cumis Insurance Society* (1984) 162 Cal.App.3d 358 [208 Cal.Rptr.494].)

Rule 3–600 reads as follows:

Rule 3–600. Organization as Client.

(A) In representing an organization, a member shall conform his or her representation to the concept that the client is the organization itself, acting through its highest authorized officer, employee, body, or constituent overseeing the particular engagement.

(B) If a member acting on behalf of an organization knows that an actual or apparent agent of the organization acts or intends or refuses to act in a manner that is or may be a violation of law reasonably imputable to the organization, or in a manner which is likely to result in substantial injury to the organization, the member shall not violate his or her duty of protecting all confidential information as provided in Business and Professions Code section 6068, subdivision (e). Subject to Business and Professions Code section 6068, subdivision (e), the member may take such actions as appear to the member to be in the best lawful interest of the organization. Such actions may include among others:

(1) Urging reconsideration of the matter while explaining its likely consequences to the organization; or

(2) Referring the matter to the next higher authority in the organization, including, if warranted by the seriousness of the matter, referral to the highest internal authority that can act on behalf of the organization.

(C) If, despite the member's actions in accordance with paragraph (B), the highest authority that can act on behalf of the organization insists upon action or a refusal to act that is a violation of law and is likely to result in substantial injury to the organization, the member's response is limited to the member's right, and, where appropriate, duty to resign in accordance with rule 3–700.

(D) In dealing with an organization's directors, officers, employees, members, shareholders, or other constituents, a member shall explain the identity of the client for whom the member acts, whenever it is or becomes apparent that the organization's interests are or may become adverse to those of the constituent(s) with whom the member is dealing. The member shall not mislead such a constituent into believing that the constituent may communicate confidential information to the member in a way that will not be used in the organization's interest if that is or becomes adverse to the constituent.

(E) A member representing an organization may also represent any of its directors, officers, employees, members, shareholders, or other constituents, subject to the provisions of rule 3–310. If the organization's consent to the dual representation is required by rule 3–310, the consent shall be given by an appropriate constituent of the organization other than the individual or constituent who is to be represented, or by the shareholder(s) or organization members.

Discussion:

Rule 3–600 is not intended to enmesh members in the intricacies of the entity and aggregate theories of partnership.

Rule 3–600 is not intended to prohibit members from representing both an organization and other parties connected with it, as for instance (as simply one example) in establishing employee benefit packages for closely held corporations or professional partnerships.

Rule 3–600 is not intended to create or to validate artificial distinctions between entities and their officers, employees, or members, nor is it the purpose of the rule to deny the existence or importance of such formal distinctions. In dealing with a close corporation or small association, members commonly perform professional engagements for both the organization and its major constituents. When a change in control occurs or is threatened, members are faced with complex decisions involving personal and institutional relationships and loyalties and have frequently had difficulty in perceiving their correct duty. (See *People ex rel Deukmejian v. Brown* (1981) 29 Cal.3d 150 [172 Cal.Rptr. 478]; *Goldstein v. Lees* (1975) 46 Cal.App.3d 614 [120 Cal.Rptr. 253]; *Woods v. Superior Court* (1983) 149 Cal.App.3d. 931 [197 Cal.Rptr. 185]; *In re Banks* (1978) 283 Ore. 459 [584 P.2d 284]; 1 A.L.R.4th 1105.) In resolving such multiple relationships, members must rely on case law.

B. Identifying the Client

§2.3   ## 1. General Rule: Corporation as Client

When counseling corporations, an attorney is frequently faced with the preliminary problem of determining who is the client, particularly in situations where both the corporation itself and individual directors, officers, or shareholders are involved. The attorney must be aware of, and maintain, the distinction between the corporation and its individual officers and directors as individuals, and its shareholders.

This issue is dealt with in Cal Rules of Prof Cond 3–600, which, at the outset, states that a lawyer representing an organization "shall conform his or her representation to the concept that the client is the organization itself, acting through its highest authorized officer, employee, body, or constituent overseeing the particular engagement." Cal Rules of Prof Cond 3–600(A).

In addition, Rule 3–600(D) provides that in dealing with a corporation's "directors, officers, employees, members, shareholders, or other constituents," the lawyer should explain the identity of the client for whom the lawyer is acting, "whenever it is or becomes apparent that the organization's interests are or may be adverse to those of the constituent(s) with whom the [lawyer] is dealing." The Rule also requires that counsel "not mislead" such a person or group concerning the use of confidential information communicated to counsel in the organization's interest if that information is or becomes adverse to the individual. That individual should be advised to obtain independent counsel and that any communications with the corporate counsel may not be privileged.

This principle, although quite simple as stated, may be difficult to put into practice. Since the corporate entity is a fictitious being, the attorney must deal with the corporation through individuals, usually its officers, directors, or controlling shareholders. One or more of these individuals may have initially consulted or hired the attorney. It is only through individuals that the attorney receives information, gives advice, or recommends actions on the corporation's behalf. As a result, the distinction between the corporate entity and the individuals who own or are employed by it often becomes blurred. Nevertheless, an attorney who fails to recognize and maintain this distinction may end up representing adverse interests or inadequately representing the corporate client.

In the corporate context, particularly when control of a corporation changes or is challenged, attorneys may be "faced with complex decisions involving personal and institutional relationships and loyalties, and have frequently had difficulty in perceiving their correct duty." See discussion following Cal Rules of Prof Cond 3–600. In resolving such multiple relationships, counsel must rely on case law. See Martin, *When Corporate Counsel Get Caught in the Middle,* Cal Law 75 (Dec. 1989).

2. Dual Representation

§2.4   a. Written Consent Required

In many conflicts situations, corporate counsel's motives may be misunderstood if he or she either refuses to represent an individual member of management or requires that the corporation hire another lawyer to represent the corporation. In fact, the practical result might well be the loss of both clients. Recognizing this reality, the Rules of Professional Conduct permit dual representation of a corporation and one or more of its "constituents" if all of the parties give their informed written consent as provided in Rule 3–310(A). Cal Rules of Prof Cond 3–600(E). The corporation's consent, if required by Rule 3–310, must be given either by the shareholders or by an appropriate constituent of the corporation other than the party who is to be represented. Rule 3–600(E). In this context, "informed" consent requires "full disclosure to the client of the circumstances and advice to the client of any actual or reasonably foreseeable adverse effects of those circumstances upon the representation." Rule 3–310(F).

Both the corporation and the individual must give their informed written consent; if either is lacking, dual representation is prohibited. See San Diego Ethics Opinion 1974–13.

§2.5   b. Previous Clients; "Start-Up" Corporations

The attorney representing a "start-up" corporation should be particularly aware of possible conflicts. The individual forming the corporation may already be a client of the attorney, or one of a group of individuals who are planning to form and invest in a corporation may be a former client. If the parties, for the sake of convenience or economy, prefer to employ a single attorney as counsel, the lawyer must disclose the circumstances of the prior representation and the potential adverse aspects of multiple representation, and must obtain the informed written consent of the parties before accepting the employment. Cal Rules of Prof Cond 3–310. Note also that disclosure to and consent by the former client may be required under Rule 3–310(D) if the attorney has obtained confidential information during the prior representation. See *Woods v Superior Court* (1983) 149 CA3d 931, 197 CR 185.

Corporate counsel should also recognize the potential conflicts of interest between individual investors or incorporators and the corporation itself once it has been formed. See ORGANIZING CORPORATIONS IN CALIFORNIA §1.3 (2d ed Cal CEB 1983). Even with the appropriate consents, dual representation may promote the interests of one client at the expense of the other. Ideally, dual representation should be avoided and separate counsel obtained to represent either the incorporators or the corporation. As a practical matter, the lawyer will often undertake the dual representation, but in such instances should be scrupulous about obtaining the necessary consents and adhering to their terms and conditions.

§2.6   c. Handling Transactions Between the Corporation and Its Officers or Directors

Corporate counsel may expect acute conflicts problems when handling business deals between the corporation and a member of management, particularly if there are minority shareholders who are not represented by management. For example, the president and principal shareholder of a client corporation may ask counsel to review a lease between the corporation and the president. The president is not represented by a separate attorney. Corporate counsel would normally be acting as the corporation's attorney rather than the president's. See Cal Rules of Prof Cond 3–600(A). However, counsel may have represented the president individually in matters over a period of time, perhaps longer than he or she has represented the corporation. Further, counsel may be dependent on the president's goodwill for continued employment as corporate counsel. Under these circumstances, the risk is that the corporation, not the president, will be the unrepresented party.

The fact that the officer consents to the dual representation does not eliminate the appearance of a conflict of interest. One obvious solution, and the one that most clearly satisfies the Rules of Professional Conduct set forth above, is for the individual to hire separate counsel. The cost, however, may be excessive in small matters.

If corporate counsel agrees to act for both parties, full written disclosure of the dual representation and its possible adverse effects on the corporation should be made when the transaction is submitted for approval of the shareholders or disinterested directors. See §§2.19–2.23.

§2.7   3. Drafting Buy-Out Agreements

When drafting buy-out agreements, corporate counsel will be faced with a conflict of interest if asked to represent both the corporation and one or more shareholders. Dual representation in this situation is not uncommon, because it serves to shift at least some of the legal costs from the shareholder to the corporation; it is permissible, upon full written disclosure to both parties of any actual or reasonably foreseeable adverse agreement, followed by their informed written consent.

Separate counsel for the shareholders is always preferable when negotiating and drafting buy-out agreements or other agreements that establish what will occur if the shareholder and corporation disagree or if one of the parties dies. Separate counsel, if not feasible during the negotiations stage, should at least be engaged to review and explain the legal impact of the document to the shareholders. Otherwise, the validity of the agreement may eventually be challenged (particularly when a court is considering the impact of the agreement on a widow or an unrepresented spouse) on grounds that (a) the shareholders did not have independent counsel, (b) undue influence was used, or (c) counsel took advantage of unrepresented individuals.

NOTE: To avoid the risk of a challenge to the validity of the argument, drafting attorney should write a letter to the shareholders advising them of the need to have the document reviewed by independent counsel. Corporations, upon request, frequently reimburse the shareholder's reasonable legal expense (up to $200 or $300) for the review.

Attorneys drafting a buy-out agreement should never regard themselves as mere legal scriveners, especially in view of the critical legal and tax considerations that will influence its provisions. See generally BUSINESS BUY-OUT AGREEMENTS (Cal CEB 1976).

4. Counsel's Conflicts During Litigation

§2.8 **a. Shareholder Derivative Suits**

In a shareholder's derivative suit, one or more shareholders sue one or more directors on behalf of the corporation. Since the corporation is in effect a plaintiff, counsel for the corporation cannot represent any of the directors being sued. In this situation, corporate counsel should insist that the corporation engage another attorney to evaluate the merits of the shareholders' complaint. Furthermore, the attorney who reviews the shareholders' complaint to determine whether the corporation should join in the suit should not be personal counsel for any of the defendant directors, particularly if the relationship is so close that the attorney cannot exercise independent judgment.

Shareholder derivative suits can arise in many different contexts. Some transactions are especially vulnerable to shareholder derivative action, *e.g.,* the corporation's purchase of property from, or the sale of property to, a member of management; lending money to a member of management; the adoption of particularly lucrative compensation plans for executives; or the approval or rejection of a merger or tender offer. In high-risk situations, counsel should remind management that he or she represents the corporation, not the individual directors or officers. Although such a warning may be quite difficult to give, particularly if counsel has previously represented the directors or officers as individuals, it is nonetheless essential.

In unusual situations, corporate counsel may wish to represent the individual director rather than the corporation. In order to do so, the attorney must first obtain the informed written consent of both the individual directors and the corporation. Cal Rules of Prof Cond 3–310. In responding to a request for such a consent, the corporation should have the advice of independent counsel; otherwise its consent to this arrangement may not be effective.

§2.9   b. Third Party's Suit Against Corporation and Individual Directors or Officers

A variety of claims may be brought by outsiders against the corporation and individual members of management. For example, in an action on a contract, the plaintiff may contend that the corporation is merely the alter ego of the individual officers or directors, who should be held personally responsible along with the corporation. See 1A Ballantine & Sterling, CALIFORNIA CORPORATION LAWS §§295–300 (4th ed). If either the corporation or the individuals could avoid liability by thrusting it onto one or more of their co-defendants, counsel should not attempt to represent both clients. Or in a suit against the corporation and its directors alleging that a dividend was erroneously paid, some of the directors may wish to defend on the ground that they relied in good faith on reports prepared by other directors or officers. Again, counsel cannot represent all of the defendants in such a case. Nor can the attorney represent individual officers or directors who are co-defendants if the corporation's defense is that such individuals were acting beyond the scope of their authority.

Another problem arises if the co-defendant is a director and also president of the corporation. To whom can counsel make disclosure in order to obtain the corporation's informed consent to the multiple representation? The problem may be complicated further if the president and director is also the controlling shareholder, with interests largely identical to those of the corporation. In such a situation, counsel must disclose all the circumstances to the full board of directors so that they can make an informed decision through a committee of independent directors. Counsel should avoid the position of being ethically unable to make disclosure to the corporation by declining to act in a confidential capacity to individual members of management.

If corporate counsel discovers that officers or directors have acted outside the scope of their authority and that the corporation needs to use this as a defense, counsel should clearly withdraw as counsel for the individuals. The attorney may even have to withdraw as counsel for the corporation, if he or she has previously worked closely with the officer or director and will have difficulty exercising independent professional judgment on behalf of the corporation.

NOTE: Individual members of management frequently wish to have corporate counsel defend them so that the corporation will pay their legal fees. Management's risk of personal liability for large legal fees will be ameliorated if the corporation has adopted the indemnification provisions permitted by the Corporations Code. See §§2.62–2.73.

§2.10   c. Failure To Indemnify

In the unlikely event that the corporation plans not to indemnify its officers or directors for liability incurred in performing their duties, counsel may not be able to represent the officers or directors and continue to represent the corporations, because the individuals may later sue the corporation for failure to indemnify. See Schwab & Titelbaum, *Indemnifying and Insuring Officers and Directors,* 7 Cal Lawyer 46 (Mar. 1987). See also §§2.62–2.73.

§2.11   d. Criminal Proceedings

Sometimes a corporation and individual officers or directors are named as defendants in an action that could involve criminal penalties, *e.g.,* an action under the federal Racketeer Influenced and Corrupt Organizations Act (RICO), 18 USC §§1961–1968. See *United Energy Owners Committee, Inc. v United States Energy Mgmt. Sys., Inc.* (9th Cir 1988) 837 F2d 356. For general discussion, see Brickey, CORPORATE CRIMINAL LIABILITY (1984).

Direct conflicts between corporate interests and individual interests are less likely to occur in criminal proceedings than in civil suits, because in criminal matters the corporation's guilt or innocence will ordinarily depend on the existence of specified facts but the officers' guilt or innocence will depend on their responsibility for and personal knowledge of the fact situation. Dual representation may still be improper if defense tactics or settlement considerations are different for the corporate and individual defendants. See *U.S. v Castellano* (SD NY 1985) 610 F Supp 1151 (counsel could represent both corporation and individuals during pretrial proceedings but not during trial). As a minimum, the individual defendants should have separate counsel for advice on plea bargaining or settlement.

§2.12   e. Corporate Counsel as Witness

At times, corporate counsel may find it necessary or desirable to be a witness for the corporation. For example, counsel may have been present at board meetings at which management made key decisions, which later become relevant in a lawsuit. More and more in recent years, disqualification of an opponent's counsel by calling him or her as a witness is being used as a trial tactic to disrupt the preparation of the case. In another situation, counsel who participated in negotiating an agreement may be a key witness regarding the parties' intent, or may be the only person who has retained copies of early drafts of the agreement that provide a record of how the document evolved.

In these situations counsel's appearance as a witness does not come within the exception to the prohibition of Cal Rules of Prof Cond 5–210, which provides:

> A member [of the California State Bar] shall not act as an advocate before a jury which will hear testimony from the member, unless
> (A) The testimony relates to an uncontested matter; or
> (B) The testimony relates to the nature and value of legal services rendered in the case; or
> (C) The member has the informed written consent of the client.

Rule 5–210 does not apply to (1) testimony before a judge without a jury; (2) nonadversarial proceedings, *e.g.,* testimony on behalf of the client before a legislative body; or (3) situations in which the attorney's partner or associate will be a witness. See Discussion, Cal Rules of Prof Cond 5–210.

For further guidance, see ABA Model Rule 3.7(a)(3), which allows counsel to testify and still continue representation if "disqualification of the lawyer would work substantial hardship on the client." See also LA Bar Comm'n on Legal Ethics, Opinion No. 312 (1969), and ABA, Opinions On Professional Ethics, Opinion 220, p. 508 (1967). This exception for substantial hardship would arguably apply to complex litigation dealing with many facts arising over a long period of time, on the basis that new counsel would have to spend much time familiarizing themselves with the facts and then might miss a critical nuance that the corporation's regular counsel would perceive.

If counsel's testimony is required, the matter should be fully discussed with the client, including the fact that counsel's credibility as a witness may be more easily attacked if he or she is also the corporation's counsel in the litigation. If the corporation still elects not to retain other counsel, the attorney may continue as counsel and also appear as a witness, unless the testimony would violate the confidential attorney/client relationship. See *Goldstein v Lees* (1975) 46 CA3d 614, 120 CR 253. Consequently, counsel's testimony should not be adverse to the corporation, and the information to which he or she will testify should not have been obtained in the course of representing the client, unless the client decides on independent advice to waive the attorney-client privilege, or unless the testimony falls within one of Rule 5–210's special exceptions.

If none of these exceptions apply, the testifying attorney should withdraw as corporate counsel. However, under ABA Model Rule 3.7, a disqualified attorney's firm may continue the representation unless it is precluded from doing so under some other rule. See, *e.g.,* ABA Model Rules Rules 1.7, 1.9. See also *U.S. v Castellano* (SD NY 1985) 610 F Supp 1151, in which the court, ruling on the issue of disqualification of counsel, permitted the attorney to represent the client through pretrial proceedings, but not at the trial.

§2.13   5. Counsel's Conflicts in Proxy Contests

If a proxy fight develops between minority and majority directors, corporate counsel probably should not attempt to represent either side, because the interests of either group of directors may well conflict with those of the corporation. See Cal Rules of Prof Cond 3–310(B) (reprinted at §2.2), which forbids representing parties with adverse interests. Former counsel for the corporation should also avoid representing either group, because of the confidential corporate information that may have been received during the earlier representation. See Cal Rules of Prof Cond 3–310(D).

§2.14   6. Giving Personal Advice to Members of Management

Corporate counsel is often asked to give advice on personal matters such as estate planning or taxes to the principal executive officers. Unless the corporation's interests are somehow involved (*e.g.,* regarding provisions of a buy-out agreement; see §2.7), counsel may ordinarily continue to represent the corporation while advising the individual officer in areas unrelated to the business of the corporation (*e.g.,* the individual's personal taxes, real estate investments, or probate matters). The individual, not the corporation, should be billed for such services, absent a special arrangement under which such legal services are a corporate fringe benefit to the executive.

§2.15   C. Protecting Confidential Communications

The communications between attorney and client are privileged, whether or not the client is a corporation. In the corporate context, however, the privilege is complicated by the nature of corporations. As artificial persons, they can communicate with counsel only through natural persons—ordinarily the corporation's directors, officers, or key employees. Exactly which corporate officials' communications with counsel will be protected by the attorney-client privilege is a matter for decision by the courts.

Formerly, federal courts used a "control group" test, under which only communications made by individuals who controlled or significantly participated in corporate decisions were protected. This test was rejected by the United States Supreme Court in *Upjohn Co. v U.S.* (1981) 449 US 383, on the basis that it unduly hampered the free flow of communication between counsel and many corporate employees. Without formulating a specific rule, the court broadened the privilege to include all communications between counsel and corporate employees necessary for carrying out counsel's advisory, investigatory, and litigating functions. In *Upjohn,* this holding prevented the IRS from obtaining specific attorney-client communications. However, the rule in *Upjohn* does not protect the underlying facts of the communications. A fact does not become privileged by virtue of its having been communicated to an attorney. Presumably the IRS could still directly interview Upjohn's employees to obtain the otherwise confidential information.

The rule stated in *Upjohn* applies to federal actions. In actions based on state substantive law, the state's law of privileges applies. *Connolly Data Sys., Inc. v Victor Technologies, Inc.* (SD Cal 1987) 114 FRD 89. See *D.I. Chadbourne, Inc. v Superior Court* (1964) 60 C2d 723, 36 CR 468, in which the California Supreme Court set forth a number of principles to guide the courts in determining whether communications between a corporation's counsel and its employees are privileged. See also Evid C §954.

The attorney-corporate client privilege may be waived, but only by an individual with power to act for the corporation. Ordinarily, this power rests with corporate management and is exercised by an officer or director. New management may waive the attorney-corporate client privilege for communications made by former officers and directors. A trustee in bankruptcy ordinarily has the power to waive the corporation's attorney-client privilege. *Commodity Futures Trading Comm'n v Weintraub* (1985) 471 US 343. But see *In re Carter* (Danning v Donovan) (1986 Bankr CD Cal) 62 Bankr 1007, in which the principal shareholder of a corporation in bankruptcy was ruled the holder of the attorney-client privilege, and the trustee was prevented from waiving the privilege.

In dealing with individual members of management, counsel must remember to clarify the identity of the client for whom he or she is acting whenever it appears that the corporation's interests are or may become adverse to the interests of the individual. The attorney should not mislead the individual into believing that the communication of confidential information to the attorney can be made in such a way as to prevent its being used in the corporation's interest if that interest becomes adverse to the individual's interest. Cal Rules of Prof Cond 3–600(D).

III. DIRECTORS' DUTIES AND OBLIGATIONS

§2.16   A. General Responsibilities of the Board

The board of directors is generally responsible for managing the corporation's business and affairs, and, subject to any requirements for shareholder approval, all corporate powers must be exercised by or under the direction of the board. Corp C §300(a). The directors need not fulfill this responsibility personally, but may delegate the management of day-to-day operations to a management company or other persons (*e.g.*, officers), as long as the corporation's business and affairs are managed and its powers are exercised "under the ultimate direction of the board." Corp C §300(a).

§2.17　　　B. Directors' Duties of Loyalty and Care

Duty of Loyalty. A director's duties as a director or as member of a committee of the board must be performed "in good faith [and] in a manner such director believes to be in the best interests of the corporation and its shareholders." Corp C §309(a). This statute codifies the rule expressed in *Remillard Brick Co. v Remillard-Dandini* (1952) 109 CA2d 405, 241 P2d 66, where the court, after noting that directors are fiduciaries and bear a fiduciary relationship to the corporation and its shareholders, stated: "Directors owe a duty of highest good faith to the corporation and to its stockholders." 109 CA2d at 419, 241 P2d at 74.

Duty of Care. A director's duties must be performed "with such care, including reasonable inquiry, as an ordinarily prudent person in a like position would use under similar circumstances." Corp C §309(a). This statutory enactment codifies the traditional directors' duty of care, and establishes the "prudent person" standard for evaluating the degree of care exercised by a director in a given situation.

Effect of Exculpation Clause. If the corporation adopts an exculpation provision in its articles limiting or eliminating directors' personal liability (see §§2.57–2.61), such exculpation applies only to a director's violation of the duty of care (*i.e.*, negligence). Exculpation clauses do not apply to violations of the directors' duty of loyalty.

Right To Rely on Information From Others. In performing their duties, directors are entitled to rely on information (including opinions, reports, statements, and financial data) prepared or presented by corporate officers or employees, legal counsel, independent accountants and other professionals or experts, and committees of the board on which the director does not serve. The director must believe in the presenter's reliability, competence, or expertise in the matters presented. In so relying, the director must act in good faith, after reasonable inquiry (if called for by the circumstances), and without knowledge that would cause reliance to be unwarranted. Corp C §309(b).

Effect of Compliance With Standards. Directors who perform their duties within the above standards (Corp C §309(a)–(b)) "shall have no liability based upon any alleged failure to discharge the person's obligations as a director." Corp C §309(c).

§2.18   C. Corporate Opportunities

Directors violate their duty of loyalty to the corporation if they usurp for themselves business opportunities that are within the corporation's line of activities. For example, the corporation may be in the business of developing real estate, and the director on his own time may find an excellent parcel of real property and purchase it for himself, rather than having the corporation purchase and develop it. Or the director may receive consulting fees or interests in other businesses in exchange for advice or services. In either instance, a breach of fiduciary duty may occur if (1) the director does not first disclose the opportunity to the corporation, and (2) the nondisclosure has a detrimental effect on the corporation. A shareholder may bring a derivative action under Corp C §800 to force the director to transfer to the corporation the property or other benefits from the disloyal transaction. *Thompson v Price* (1967) 251 CA2d 182, 59 CR 174.

The director may defend by showing that his or her conduct was just and reasonable to the corporation. See *Industrial Indem. Co. v Golden State Co.* (1953) 117 CA2d 519, 256 P2d 677. If a director is held accountable for abuse of a corporate opportunity, the trier of fact considers the director's good faith, loyalty, and ethical conduct. *Mueller v MacBan* (1976) 62 CA3d 258, 132 CR 222.

Members of management can, of course, make investments that are unrelated to the corporation's activities. Many investment opportunities fall within a gray area between absolute fairness to the corporation and clear violation of fiduciary duty. In determining whether a corporate opportunity existed in any given situation, the trier of fact must find what areas are within the corporation's "line of activities." This turns on various factors, including the needs of the corporation, its financial ability to undertake the opportunity, the adaptability of the opportunity to the corporation's business, the corporation's practical experience with regard to the business opportunity, and its interest and expectations under the circumstances. The decision in each case depends on the particular facts.

See, *e.g.*, *New v New* (1957) 148 CA2d 372, 306 P2d 987, in which a director of two companies that were engaged in the business of drilling and operating oil wells leased a parcel of property adjacent to the companies' drilling area, after being informed by city officials that under no circumstances would the parcel be leased to the two companies. The director, who also wished to prevent competitors from leasing the property, was exonerated by the court on the basis that the companies were organized solely for the purpose of extracting and removing oil, and that they were precluded from pursuing the opportunity in any event.

No corporate opportunity exists if the corporation is financially unable to take advantage of an opportunity that the director contracted for. *Rankin v Frebank Co.* (1975) 47 CA3d 75, 121 CR 348. Likewise, directors are exonerated if they offer the opportunity to the corporation, with full disclosure, and the corporation refuses to accept the opportunity.

For general discussion, see 1A Ballantine & Sterling, CALIFORNIA CORPORATION LAWS §104.01 (4th ed); 1 MARSH'S CALIFORNIA CORPORATION LAW §10.21 (2d ed). See also Wallach, *Application of the Doctrine of Corporate Opportunity to the Investment Company Director,* 45 Calif L Rev 183 (1957).

D. Transactions Between the Corporation and Its Directors ("Insider" Transactions)

§2.19 1. General Rule

Generally speaking, transactions between a corporation and a director are permitted in California if, after full disclosure, the transaction is approved by either the shareholders or a disinterested majority of the board. Corp C §310(a) (which codifies *Remillard Brick Co. v Remillard-Dandini* (1952) 109 CA2d 405, 241 P2d 66). Even if not properly approved, the transaction is not voidable if the interested director can prove that it was fair and reasonable to the corporation. *Tenzer v Superscope, Inc.* (1985) 39 C3d 18, 216 CR 130. Similar requirements must be met with respect to transactions between corporations with common directors. Corp C §310(b). For more detailed discussion of Corp C §310, see §2.20.

"Insider" transactions commonly occur in sales or leases of property between a corporation and a director, or in business dealings over a period of time between related companies, *e.g.*, subcontracting by a corporation to another company in which a director has a substantial interest. In pursuing such transactions, directors may not assume a position adverse to the corporation. *Abbot Kinney Co. v Harrah* (1948) 84 CA2d 728, 191 P2d 761. See also *Efron v Kalmanovitz* (1967) 249 CA2d 187, 57 CR 248 (invalidating a contract transferring substantial assets of a brewery corporation to another company wholly owned by the brewery corporation's majority shareholder and director).

In most instances, it would be wise to obtain the approval of either the board or the shareholders rather than waiting for a court to determine the transaction's fairness (see §2.21). The simplest procedure is usually for the interested director to present the matter to the board of directors, to explain it fully, and to abstain from voting. If several directors are involved in the transaction, all of them must refrain from voting on it. If it is a complex matter, information should be supplied to the board for review in advance of the meeting. If the transaction is submitted to the shareholders rather than the board, shares held by interested directors are disqualified from voting.

§2.20   a. Statutory Requirements

Transactions between a corporation and one or more of its directors, or between a corporation and another entity in which a director has a "material financial interest" may be void or voidable if the requirements set forth in Corp C §310 are not complied with.

This statute, however, is stated in the negative. It provides that such "insider" contracts or transactions are not void or voidable if the material facts about the transaction and the director's interest are either (1) fully disclosed or known to the shareholders, who approve the transaction in good faith, with the shares owned by the interested director not being entitled to vote; or (2) fully disclosed or known to the board or a committee of the board, who authorize, approve, or ratify the transaction by a sufficient vote without counting the vote of the interested director; provided that the transaction is just and reasonable to the corporation at the time it is authorized, approved, or ratified. Corp C §310(a)(1)–(2). A contract or transaction not meeting these requirements is still neither void nor voidable if the person asserting its validity sustains the burden of proving that it was just and reasonable to the corporation at the time it was authorized, approved, or ratified. Corp C §310(a)(3).

A mere common directorship in corporations dealing with each other does not constitute a "material financial interest" within the meaning of Corp C §310, and the mere presence of the interested or common director at a board or committee meeting where the transaction was approved does not make the transaction void or voidable. Corp C §310(a)–(b). Interested directors may be counted in determining the presence of a quorum at a board or committee meeting in which an "insider" transaction is authorized, approved, or ratified. Corp C §310(c).

For a discussion of the meaning of "material financial interest," see 1 Ballantine & Sterling, CALIFORNIA CORPORATION LAWS §103.01 n8 (4th ed).

§2.21 b. Fairness Test

Dealings of management members with the corporation are subject to rigorous scrutiny by the courts, and the burden lies with the interested director to prove his or her good faith and the inherent fairness of the transaction to the corporation. In applying the test of fairness, the trier of fact considers whether the transaction was conducted at arm's length. *Mueller v MacBen* (1967) 62 CA3d 258, 132 CR 222.

The California Supreme Court applied the fairness test in *Tenzer v Superscope, Inc.* (1985) 39 C3d 18, 216 CR 130 (citing *Pepper v Litton* (1939) 308 US 295, 307). *Tenzer* involved a real estate corporation and a director who was a real estate finder. The court held that the director was charged with the knowledge that any commission contract he entered into with his own corporation, even if valid and enforceable in all other respects, could be voided at the corporation's option if it were determined to be unfair or unreasonable to the corporation, and that the director was required to prove its fairness and reasonableness. The court stated that corporate directors should be required to pass on information vital to the survival of their corporation whenever such information is either incidental to the director's usual mode of earning a living or is casually acquired. The court, noting that the determination of fairness to the corporation involves evaluation of the specific facts surrounding the transaction, said that some considerations here included whether the director was dependent on the questioned transactions for his livelihood, whether the facts were known to the president, and how the director became aware of the information. 39 C3d at 33, 216 CR at 138.

§2.22 c. Disclosure of Material Facts

All "material facts" regarding the transaction with the corporation and the director's interest in it must have been disclosed when the director submits the transaction for approval by either the shareholders or the disinterested directors. Corp C §310(a)(1)–(2).

§2.23 d. Approval by Disinterested Directors

In insider transactions, the authorization, approval, or ratification by the disinterested directors protects the transaction from voidability. Corp C §310(a)(2). The disinterested directors should be advised that they should not act as mere rubber stamps for the interested directors, because their approval must be in good faith. Corp C §310(a)(2). Disinterested directors have a statutory responsibility to make reasonable inquiry to determine if the terms of a proposed transaction are in the best interests of the corporation. Corp C §309(a).

Often this determination can be easily made. For example, suppose that a director wishes to lease a factory building to the corporation. If the board has access to accurate information about average rentals for similar properties, it should be easy for them to determine the dollar amount of rent within an acceptable range. Much more difficult are evaluations of a series of business dealings over a period of time, *e.g.,* a subcontract in which there may be many individual transactions, each of which may require a determination as to whether the corporation is being overcharged.

Counsel should advise a disinterested director who is uncertain about the fairness of a transaction between a director and the corporation to either vote against the transaction or insist that it be submitted to the shareholders for their approval. Either action will minimize the very real risk of a shareholder derivative suit in which minority shareholders may seek to prove that the contract was unfair to the corporation. Directors who approve a questionable transaction may be suspected of having done so in violation of their duty of loyalty and may be sued along with the interested directors. See Corp C §§309(a), 800.

Directors who vote to approve the transaction should be advised to ensure that the minutes of the meeting reflect the disclosures made and the reports relied on, so that their good faith, as required by Corp C §§309(a) and 310(a)(2), can be proved.

NOTE: Although Corp C §309(a) creates a standard by which a director's conduct may be judged, it is not intended to place liability on a director for an honest mistake of business judgment. See Small, *The Evolving Role of the Director in Corporate Governance,* 30 Hastings LJ 1353 (1979); Stern, *General Standard of Care Imposed on Directors under the New California Corporations Law,* 23 UCLA L Rev 1269 (1976). See also 1 Ballantine & Sterling, CALIFORNIA CORPORATION LAWS §103.01 (4th ed); 1 MARSH'S CALIFORNIA CORPORATION LAW §§10.7–10.12 (2d ed).

§2.24   2. Loans and Guaranties of Obligations

A corporation is not permitted to loan money to or guarantee the obligation of any director or officer of the corporation unless either (1) the transaction is approved by a majority of the shareholders entitled to vote or (2) the transaction comes within an employee benefit plan authorizing such loans or guaranties. If the transaction is entered into under an employee benefit plan, the plan must disclose that it may include officers or directors, and it must have been approved by a majority of the shareholders entitled to vote.

However, if the corporation has outstanding shares held of record by at least 100 persons, and if it has a bylaw approved by the outstanding shares that authorizes the board to approve loans or guaranties to officers or directors, the loan or guaranty may be approved by the board alone (without counting the vote of any interested directors), upon a determination that the loan or guaranty may reasonably be expected to benefit the corporation. The minutes adopting the resolution should specify the anticipated benefit to the corporation.

A corporation may not make any loan or guaranty upon the security of shares of the corporation's stock unless the loan or guaranty is

(1) adequately secured beyond the shares, or (2) approved by a majority of the shareholders. Corp C §315(c).

Exemptions From the Prohibition. A corporation is permitted to advance money to directors or officers for expenses reasonably anticipated to be incurred in the course of their duties. Corp C §315(c). The prohibition against loans and guaranties does not apply to transactions under Corp C §408 (employee stock option plans), nor does it apply to loans or guaranties by a corporation that makes such loans in the ordinary course of its business. Corp C §315(f); *Englert v IVAC Corp.* (1979) 92 CA3d 178, 154 CR 804. The prohibition also does not apply to the payment of premiums by a corporation on a life insurance policy insuring the life of a director or officer, if the repayment to the corporation of the amount of the premiums paid by it is secured by the policy proceeds and its cash surrender value. Corp C §315(e).

Liability of Approving Directors. Directors who approve improper loans or guaranties become jointly and severally liable to the corporation for any loss incurred as a result of the prohibited loan or guaranty. Corp C §316(a)(3), (d); *Wulffjen v Dolton* (1944) 24 C2d 878, 151 P2d 840. Directors abstaining from voting on the improper loan or guaranty are deemed to have approved it. Corp C §316(b).

IV. PREVENTIVE COUNSELING; AVOIDING MANAGEMENT LIABILITY

§2.25   **A. Table: Common Areas of Management Exposure**

NOTE: The potential liability of directors is a developing area. Matters such as the application of the business judgment rule and the reasonableness of directors' reliance on information supplied by others may be called into question at a later date. In addition, issues of director liability may arise in the context of laws relating to securities, antitrust, the environment, labor, tax, or other specific subjects. Therefore, while the following table identifies a number of areas of management exposure, it is not comprehensive in scope or in its identification of relevant statutes. Caution should be exercised in its use.

Area of Risk	Conduct Causing Management Liability	Possible Results
(1) Issuing corporate securities	Material misstatements or omissions in SEC registration statements (§2.26) or California permit applications (§2.27); violation of state blue sky laws (§2.27). See also §2.37.	Corporate and individual liability for damages; rescission; criminal sanctions for fraud or other intentional violations. See §§2.26–2.27, 2.37.
(2) Trading in corporate securities	(a) Realizing "short-swing" profits on the shares (Exchange Act §16(b), 15 USC §78p(b); see §2.29). (b) Using knowledge about securities values acquired as "insider" (SEC Rule 10b–5; see §§2.30, 2.37).	(a) Recovery of such profits by the corporation, *e.g.,* in a shareholder's derivative suit. See §2.29. (b) Violator and "controlling person" subject to treble damages. See §2.37.
(3) Dividends	Payment of dividends (cash or stock) in violation of Corp C §500 or other legal limitations. See §§2.32–2.34.	Individual civil liability, fine, or imprisonment. Corp C §§316(a)(1), 2253. See §§2.32–2.34, 4.57.
(4) Stock repurchases or redemptions	A distribution of corporate assets or stock in violation of Corp C §500 or other legal limitations. See §2.35.	Individual civil liability, fine, or imprisonment. Corp C §§316(a), 2253. See §2.35.
(5) Publication of false information	Intentional material misrepresentations or nondisclosures regarding corporation's shares, assets, earnings, accounts, etc. See Corp C §1507. See also (1) above.	Individual civil liability for damages. Corp C §§1507–1508. Erroneous statement made in a proxy fight may result in invalidation of the election. See SEC Rule 14a–9.
(6) Directors' or officers' transactions with the corporation	Breach of fiduciary duties to corporation or shareholders, or lack of fairness in the transaction. Protection is offered by full disclosure and approval by "disinterested directors" or shareholders. Corp C §310. See §§2.19–2.23.	Contracts may be void or voidable. the management party may be forced to repay proceeds of the transaction, plus interest. See §§2.19–2.20.

Area of Risk	Conduct Causing Management Liability	Possible Results
(7) Loans to officers or directors	Loans to an officer, director, or any other person solely on the security of shares of the corporation's stock, unless the transaction has been approved by a majority of shares (excluding those of the borrower). Corp C §315. See §2.24.	The directors who approve the loan may be individually liable for repayment. Corp C §§315, 316(a)(3). There may also be liability for breach of fiduciary duties. See §2.17.
(8) Corporate opportunities	Officer or director usurps potential corporate investment or other opportunity for himself, or profits personally by virtue of his corporate office, e.g., from consulting fees. See §2.18.	Officer or director may be forced, perhaps by shareholder derivative suit, to give up the profits, plus interest, and to pay damages to the corporation. See Corp C §800.
(9) Acquiring or selling a business	(a) Violation of SEC registration or proxy requirements (e.g., SEC Rule 145(a)) by either the acquired or the acquiring entity. See §§2.26, 2.28–2.30, 2.37. (b) Misrepresentation or breach of warranties in the acquisition agreement. See §2.39.	(a) Individual liability for damages; criminal sanctions for fraud and other intentional violations. See §2.37. (b) Damages for individual officer's or director's representations or warranties made in connection with the acquisition. See §2.39.
(10) Antitrust problems	Monopolistic practices, price fixing, discriminatory pricing, illegal licensing arrangements, or other violations of antitrust laws. See §§2.40–2.44.	Individual civil liability and criminal sanctions including imprisonment (an actual risk in the antitrust area). See §§2.40, 2.42.

Area of Risk	Conduct Causing Management Liability	Possible Results
(11) Employment practices	(a) Violation of strict requirements regarding payment of workers. Lab C §§200–240. See §2.45. (b) Violation of state or federal health or safety requirements. Lab C §§6400–6413.5; Occupational Safety & Health Act of 1970 (OSHA); 29 USC §§651–678. See §2.47. (c) Unfair labor practices in violation of Labor Management Relations Act, 29 USC §§141–187. See §2.48. (d) Violation of federal or state antidiscrimination laws, 42 USC §2000e; Govt C §§12940–12948. See §2.49. (e) Wrongful termination. See §2.50.	(a) Criminal prosecution of the corporate officer responsible for the violation. Lab C §§212, 215–216. See §2.45. (b) Possible shutdown of the business until the violation is remedied. 29 USC §662. Criminal prosecution of the responsible officers. Lab C §6425. See §2.47. (c) Corporate liability from NLRB proceedings; monetary awards are enforceable by contempt proceedings. If business suffers, possible shareholder derivative suit against directors or officers. See §2.18. (d) Corporation may be liable for back pay, reinstatement, compensatory and punitive damages. See §2.49. (e) Corporation may be liable for compensatory and punitive damages. See §2.50.
(12) Nonpayment of withheld taxes	Failure to pay over to the IRS or other appropriate taxing authority any federal or state income taxes, or social security tax, withheld from employees' compensation. See §2.46.	Individuals responsible are each subject to 100% penalty by IRS; possible criminal liability. IRC §§6672, 7215. See §2.46.
(13) Administration of pension or profit-sharing plans	Intentional violation of fiduciary rules, reporting and disclosure requirements, or other provisions of Employment Retirement Security Act of 1974 (ERISA), 29 USC §§1001–1461. See, e.g., 29 USC §§1104–1106.	Fiduciaries of ERISA plans are personally liable to make good any losses to the plan (29 USC §1109); may also incur civil penalties (29 USC §1132) as well as fine or criminal penalties (18 USC §1027).

B. Corporate Securities Transactions

1. Issuing Securities

§2.26   a. Federal Regulation

In a public offering subject to federal regulation (see FINANCING CALIFORNIA BUSINESSES §7.85 (Cal CEB 1975)), the sale of securities to an outsider, *i.e.,* to a person who does not participate in the corporation's business and is unfamiliar with it, creates certain risks and responsibilities for the corporation's management. The Securities Act of 1933, 15 USC §§77a–77aa, imposes liability on the corporation to return the proceeds of sales in the event of any material misstatement or the omission of any material fact in either a registration statement filed with the Securities and Exchange Commission (SEC) or a prospectus delivered to purchasers of the stock. 15 USC §§77k–77*l*. See Sowards, THE FEDERAL SECURITIES ACT AND TRUST INDENTURE ACT OF 1939 §§7.01[3], 9.02[5] (rev ed). The corporation's directors and officers may be personally responsible and liable for consequences of the misstatement or omission unless they can prove that they acted in good faith in preparing the registration statement or prospectus.

In general, a securities issuance must be registered unless an exemption from registration applies. Securities Act of 1933 §§4–5 (15 USC §§77d–77e). The more commonly used methods to effect a registration or an exemption for the issuance of securities in the purchase of a business include the following:

- In transactions under Rule 145 (17 CFR §230.145), which includes mergers, consolidations, and sales of assets, but not stock-for-stock exchanges, the acquiring corporation may use a short form of registration, together with the proxy statement to be used in the transaction.

- The private offering exemption of Securities Act §4(2), which exempts transactions by an issuer not involving any public offering. 15 USC §77d(2). Rule 506 (17 CFR §230.506) in Regulation D (discussed next) provides a safe harbor for this exemption.

- Rules 504–506 under Regulation D (17 CFR §§230.504–230.506) contain three separate levels of exemptions. Rule 504 (17 CFR §230.504) exempts offerings up to $1 million if no more than $500,000 is sold without registration under state securities laws), without limitation on the number or the nature of the purchasers or the information disclosure required. Rule 505 (17 CFR §230.505) exempts offerings up to $5 million, but there can be no more than 35 unaccredited investors (the number of accredited investors is unlimited) and, if any investor is unaccredited, strict information disclosures apply. Rule 506 (17 CFR §230.506) provides an exemption similar to that of Rule 505, except that it has no dollar limit and unaccredited investors must meet certain sophistication requirements. For a brief summary of additional requirements under Regulation D, see SALE OF BUSINESSES §2.55 (2d ed Cal CEB 1988).

- A fairness hearing exemption in Securities Act §3(a)(10) (15 USC §§77c(a)(10)) exempts securities in certain exchanges of securities for outstanding securities, claims, or property interests, or partly in such exchange and partly for cash, if the transaction is approved after a hearing on its fairness by a court of a governmental authority such as the California Commissioner of Corporations. See Corp C §25142; 10 Cal Code Regs §§260.140.62, 260.142. See Ash, *Reorganizations and Other Exchanges Under Section 3(a)(10) of the Securities Act of 1933*, 75 NW U L Rev 1 (1980).

- The intrastate offering exemption in Securities Act §3(a)(11) (15 USC §77c(a)(11)) exempts securities offered and issued solely to California residents by a California corporation doing business in California (or similarly for any other single state). Both the offering and the sale of the securities must be made in this state. Rule 147 (17 CFR 230.147) provides a safe harbor for this exemption, requiring among other things that no resales of the securities be made to non-California residents within nine months after the offering has been completed.

- Regulation A (17 CFR §230.254(a)(1)(i)), for offerings of $1.5 million or less, involves a slightly less onerous form of registration. It is also available to an acquiring corporation that issues its securities in the transaction.

- Securities issued in a Rule 145(a) (17 CFR §230.145(a)) transaction (see (1) above), and securities issued in certain mergers and exchange offers may be sold in a transaction registered with the SEC on Form S–4 (17 CFR §239.25).

Defense of Nonmateriality. One defense to management's personal liability for failure to disclose all information in connection with a public offering is that the undisclosed item was not material.

77 USC §77k(a). This defense, however, is seldom reliable, because management's good faith decision about an item's materiality will be judged by someone else's hindsight. See Sowards §9.02[5].

Defense of Due Diligence. The courts impose a heavy burden on directors asserting a due diligence defense. See *Escott v Barchris Constr. Corp.* (SD NY 1968) 283 F Supp 643, 682. The extent of responsibility of any director or member of management is difficult to determine in a particular case. Directors who are also officers of the corporation or its general counsel or attorneys are generally held to a higher standard than that applied to "outside directors." See Caplin, *Outside Directors and Their Responsibilities: A Program For the Exercise of Due Care,* 1 J Corp Law 57 (1975). Outside directors, however, are not fully insulated from liability. The standard of due diligence applied to outside directors probably requires that they attend meetings, ask questions, and understand why items have been included in or omitted from the prospectus or registration statement. It is no defense for management to assert that an attorney was responsible for writing the prospectus. Members of management may be held liable if the attorney who prepared the registration statement failed to disclose something that should have appeared in the statement or misdescribed an item, or if information was deliberately withheld from the attorney. See Sowards §9.02[5][c].

Reliance on Opinions of Accountants. Officers and directors may rely on the opinion of their accounting firm and its certification of the financial statements unless they know or should know that the financial statements are in error. See Sowards §9.02[3]. Directors should insist on an explanation of anything they cannot understand; otherwise they may be held personally liable. 15 USC §77k.

Further Reference. For further discussions of the federal securities laws there are innumerable articles and treatises. Leading treatises include Loss & Seligman, SECURITIES REGULATION (3d ed 1989); Sowards, BUSINESS ORGANIZATIONS (1989); Clark Boardman's SECURITIES LAW SERIES (1989); and SECURITIES LAW TECHNIQUES (1989).

§2.27   b. State Regulation

California Securities Regulation. In general, an issuance of securities in California must be qualified with the Commissioner of Corporations unless an exemption applies. Corp C §§25100. The most commonly invoked exemptions are the small offering exemption (35 potential shareholders or less) of Corp C §25102(h), and the limited offering exemption (no more that 35 non-excluded purchasers of Corp C §25102(f). See 10 Cal Code Regs §§260.102.4–260.102.9, 260.102.12–260.102.14. For general overview of the California securities law regulatory structure, see ORGANIZING CORPORATIONS IN CALIFORNIA §§4.27–4.168 (2d ed Cal CEB 1983); the common exemptions are discussed in ORGANIZING CORPS §§4.36–4.79.

Liability for Securities Law Violations. The California Corporations Code imposes liability on corporations for misstatements made in any permit application filed in connection with issuing its securities, as well as for failing to obtain a permit for issuance when required. Corp C §§25501–25503; see ORGANIZING CORPS §§4.152–4.157. Any corporation that incurs a liability to a purchaser of its securities has a right to be indemnified by its principal officers, directors, and controlling persons in the event that they willfully violated the law. Corp C §§25505. Consequently, management must exercise care in preparing, reviewing, and signing documents in connection with issuing shares.

Inadequate Consideration. Management may also be liable to the corporation if shares are issued for inadequate consideration: This will not be a difficult task in the normal situation where stock is issued for cash or property. The principal concern in that situation will be not to overvalue the property. The board of directors has considerable latitude in determining the value of property or services given as consideration for corporation stock. In the absence of fraud, the directors' determination of the value of such items will ordinarily be conclusive. See Corp C §409; 1 Ballantine & Sterling, CALIFORNIA CORPORATION LAWS §126.02(2)(a) (4th ed). However, the directors should be aware that issuing shares for inadequate consideration can subject them to civil liability (see Corp C §415), and, in the case of willful violations, criminal penalties (see Corp C §2251).

Overissues. The directors should be aware of the possibility of an overissue of stock. A corporation cannot lawfully issue more shares than are authorized in its articles of incorporation (see Corp C §202(d)–(e)), and the officers and directors can be subject to both civil liabilities and criminal penalties for doing so. See Corp C §§415, 2251. In order to avoid an overissue, they must, before the proposed issuance, determine (1) how many shares are outstanding, (2) how many shares are reserved to cover the exercise of warrants or options or conversions of convertible securities, and (3) how many shares are authorized. Computation of stock available for the issue may be somewhat complicated if the corporation has convertible or other securities outstanding that contain antidilution provisions. If reasonable care is taken, however, an overissue is a slight risk. Special precautions will be required if the corporation is close to its authorized limit, perhaps because it has just made a number of acquisitions for stock. In that situation, it may be necessary to increase the authorized number of shares by amending the articles of incorporation.

State Blue Sky Laws. Counsel must review the facts to see whether the securities laws of any other states apply. This review is especially important if any shareholders reside in other states. If so, it is essential to work with sources in those states to ensure compliance. Violation of such laws can be grounds for rescinding the sale, and may also result in suspension of trading in the stock in that state and possible criminal action. See generally Loss & Seligman, SECURITIES REGULATION 29–152 (3d ed 1989). In addition, most state securities laws, like the federal, provide that if there is a material misstatement or omission, any purchasers of the stock can rescind and recover their money plus interest.

§2.28　2. Trading in Corporate Stock

In corporations whose securities are publicly traded, two critical questions of interest to directors and officers are: (1) When and under what circumstances may an individual director or officer buy or sell its securities? (2) What can such individuals do to protect themselves against potential liability to the corporation and its shareholders under the securities laws?

Management needs to be particularly aware of the possibility of section 16(b) liability (see §2.29) and Rule 10b–5 liability (see §2.30).

§2.29　a. Section 16(b) Liability

Counsel for any corporation with publicly traded securities should provide all officers and directors with a memorandum briefly summarizing their potential exposure under the federal securities laws. Under section 16(b) of the Securities Exchange Act of 1934 (the Exchange Act), 15 USC §78p(b), an officer, director, or beneficial owner of 10 percent or more of any class of equity securities who engages in a purchase and sale (or a sale and purchase) of such securities within a six-month period may be liable for any profit realized from the transactions, including profits from the exercise of stock options. Such "short-swing" profits are the property of the corporation, and may be recovered by either the corporation itself or by any shareholder suing on the corporation's behalf. See *Kern County Land Co. v Occidental Petroleum Corp.* (1973) 411 US 582; *Lewis v McAdam* (9th Cir 1985) 762 F2d 800.

For further discussion of Rule 16(b), see Gadsby, THE FEDERAL SECURITIES EXCHANGE ACT OF 1934 §8.04 (rev ed).

§2.30   b. SEC Rule 10b–5 Liability

Counsel should make sure management is informed of the content of SEC Rule 10b–5, 17 CFR §240.10b–5, which generally forbids manipulative or deceptive devices in the purchase or sale of publicly traded securities. Rule 10b–5 has been broadly applied by the courts, and a discussion of it is beyond the scope of this chapter. For discussion, see Gadsby, THE FEDERAL SECURITIES EXCHANGE ACT OF 1934 §5.05 (rev ed). Management of public corporations should be advised that although trading in the corporation's stock is never entirely free of risk under Rule 10b–5, risks can be minimized by adhering strictly to the following principle: No member of management should buy or sell any securities of the corporation if management is aware of material information affecting the corporation that is not publicly known. In applying this principle, many attorneys believe that the safest time for management to buy or sell securities of the corporation is during the two- or three-week period immediately following the time that the corporation's shareholders receive its annual report. If the transaction is close in time to a material change in the corporation's affairs but before the information has been made public, the corporate insider who purchases or sells the stock may well become a defendant in a lawsuit brought under Rule 10b–5. For an important decision addressing the materiality question, see *Basic, Inc. v Levinson* (1988) 485 US 224. See also *TSC Indus., Inc. v Northways* (1976) 42 US 438.

Another practice that will help protect corporate management is to make material information regarding the corporation, whether favorable or unfavorable, known to the public as soon as it is practicable to do so without damaging the corporation.

Privately held corporations do not ordinarily need to be as concerned as public corporations with the aspects of Rule 10b–5 requiring public disclosure of information, because private corporations will seldom have an active market for their securities, and few people, if any, will be relying on public statements of management in buying or selling their stock. However, the management of private corporations must be advised that Rule 10b–5 may still apply to them, and that they should not directly or indirectly buy or sell the shares of minority shareholders (who are not as well informed about the corporation's affairs) without first disclosing to such shareholders all good or bad news about the corporation that the minority shareholders might not know.

§2.31   3. Tender Offers

A tender offer is an attempt by one corporation to acquire a controlling interest in another corporation by means of an open-market purchase. If a group is formed to acquire control of a corporation, certain information must be filed with the SEC under the Williams Act (15 USC §§78m(d)–(e), 78n(d)–(f)), and if any member of that group becomes the owner of more than 5 percent of the stock of the target corporation, another filing is required after the acquisition. A possible pitfall is that, unknown to management, some of its directors or officers may own stock in the target corporation. Although the number of such shares may be small, if it is possible that when they are added to those the corporation already owns, management liability may be triggered under the Williams Act.

For discussion of tender offers and takeovers, see Bradley & Rosenzweig, *Defensive Stock Repurchase,* 99 Harv L Rev 1377 (1986); Bagley, *Recent Corporate Takeover Developments and the Business Judgment Rule,* 7 CEB Cal Bus L Rep 22 (May 1986); Lipton & Steinberger, TAKEOVERS AND FREEZEOUTS (2d ed).

Tender offers may also subject management to liability under SEC Rule 10b–5 (discussed in §2.30). See *Shapiro v Merrill Lynch, Pierce, Fenner & Smith, Inc.* (2d Cir 1974) 495 F2d 228.

C. Distributions and Dividends

§2.32   1. Distributions Generally

Under California law, before a corporation may make any distribution to its shareholders, the corporation's debts must be paid or adequately provided for. Corp C §501. Directors and shareholders may have personal liability, on a joint and several basis, to the corporation for the benefit of creditors for illegal distributions. Any director who is present at a board of directors' meeting and who does not vote against the unlawful distribution is liable. Corp C §316(a). This liability extends to members of the board who are present at the meeting and abstain from voting. Corp C §316(b).

Directors who rely on information supplied by others, *e.g.,* corporate accountants, are not liable if their reliance was in good faith and was reasonable under the circumstances. Corp C §309(b)–(c); see *England v Christensen* (1966) 243 CA2d 413, 435, 52 CR 402, 416.

Creditors and preferred shareholders whose rights have been adversely affected by an unlawful distribution may sue the directors in the name of the corporation. Corp C §§316(c), 506(b). Directors are liable for damages caused by an unlawful distribution, *e.g.,* the resultant unpaid debts or unpaid dividends to preferred shareholders. Directors who are held liable and pay more than their pro rata share of damages are entitled to contribution from other directors. Corp C §316(e). Such directors are also subrogated to the rights of the corporation to recover the unlawful distribution from the shareholders who received it. Corp C §316(f).

The defense of good faith reliance on others is an inadequate substitute for avoiding the liability by thoroughly investigating the distribution beforehand to make certain that it is legal. Directors should be especially cautious in making liquidation distributions because of the danger that contingent claims may arise after the corporation's assets have been distributed. If a post-distribution claimant is successful, the directors may have to pay the judgment themselves. As a matter of minimum self-protection, directors should satisfy themselves that notices of liquidation have been sent to all of the corporation's known creditors and that all the dissolution formalities have been observed. See Corp C §1903. See also chap 7.

§2.33   2. Dividends in Cash or Property

Declaring dividends is a common corporate event with many legal and practical ramifications of which management should be aware. The corporation may be under pressure to maintain a certain dividend rate, particularly in a falling stock market, when dividends will tend to support the market price of the corporation's stock.

Dividends may be paid only if the corporation meets one of the alternative financial requirements set forth in Corp C §500. Basically, a corporation may pay dividends and make other distributions to shareholders out of retained earnings, or if retained earnings are insufficient, the dividend may still be paid if (1) it does not reduce the corporation's assets below an amount equal to one and one quarter times its liabilities generally, and (2) current assets after the distribution are at least equal to current liabilities. See Corp C §501. For fuller discussion, see §§4.8–4.15.

Directors who willfully violate the prohibitions against improper distributions are subject to civil and criminal liabilities. See Corp C §§316(a)(1), 2253. For directors who approve an improper dividend or distribution, the general rules regarding a director's reliance in good faith on reports prepared by others, and the need to make reasonable inquiries when circumstances indicate the need to do so (see §2.17), are applicable.

§2.34   3. Stock Dividends

Stock dividends (share dividends) are authorized by Corp C §409(a)(2). They are expressly exempted from the general financial requirements of Corp C §§500–501 that apply to other corporate distributions. Corp C §166. However, share dividends may entail certain tax risks. See §§4.37–4.46, 5.22.

An amendment to the articles will be necessary if the authorized number of shares is not great enough to permit the share dividend. See Corp C §202(d)–(e). For discussion of amendments, see §§5.15– 5.21.

§2.35   4. Share Repurchases and Redemptions

A corporation may wish to repurchase some of its shares for a variety of reasons. (The term repurchase is used here to include a redemption. See Corp C §509.) Some examples of such reasons are to settle a shareholders' dispute, to purchase a deceased shareholder's interest under a buy-out agreement, or simply to provide a form of return to the shareholders. The financial requirements of the Corporations Code for share repurchases are the same as those for other corporate distributions, *e.g.*, dividends. See Corp C §§500–501. See also §2.33. Repurchases may be made out of retained earnings or out of other funds if the asset-to-liability ratios of Corp C §500 are maintained. The repurchase must not, however, violate the solvency test of Corp C §501. Violation of these provisions may subject the directors to liability under Corp C §316(a)(1). See §2.33.

The determination as to whether a corporation meets the financial requirements of Corp C §500 is ordinarily made at the time of the repurchase. If the standards are met at that time, they do not have to be reviewed when each payment is made. See Corp C §§166, 500.

D. Acquiring or Selling a Business

§2.36   1. General Rules

Management's exposure to civil liability in the acquisition of another business is largely dependent on the form of the acquisition. Generally speaking there are two major categories of acquisitions: cash buy-outs and corporate reorganizations.

In a buy-out acquisition, two or more business entities combine into a single entity, after which the shareholders of one of the entities no longer retain any interest in the combined enterprise. Such a transaction normally involves the cash purchase of the acquired corporation's shares. In this type of transaction, the liability of the selling corporation's management is minimal. Once the sale is completed, their shareholders will have been paid in full and will have no reason to be concerned about the long-term financial strength of the buyer or the future operations of the business.

In a corporate reorganization, two or more corporations are combined into a single business entity in which the shareholders of both corporations maintain some continuing interest in the business. The Internal Revenue Service recognizes three main types of corporate reorganizations:

(1) a statutory merger, in which the acquired company is merged into the acquiring company or one of its subsidiaries (see IRC §368(a)(1)(A));

(2) a transaction in which the stock of the acquired company is acquired through an exchange of stock (see IRC §368(a)(1)(B)); and

(3) a transaction in which the assets of the acquired company are exchanged for stock in the acquiring company (see IRC §368(a)(1)(C)).

Each of these three types of corporate reorganizations can be reversed, *i.e.,* structured to make it appear that a smaller corporation is acquiring a larger corporation, when in fact the reverse has happened. For a basic treatment of mergers, acquisitions, and reorganizations, see chap 6. See also SALE OF BUSINESSES chap 6 (2d ed Cal CEB 1988).

Directors and officers of both corporations in an acquisition have many responsibilities to consider, including their duties to their shareholders, to the other corporation and its shareholders, and to creditors of both entities. These duties can arise not only under the California General Corporation Law but also under federal or state securities laws, or under the language of the acquisition agreement itself.

§2.37   2. Federal Securities Laws

If a publicly held corporation acquires another corporation (whether publicly or privately held) in exchange for stock of the acquiring corporation, and the issuance of that stock cannot qualify for an exemption under the Securities Act of 1933, then federal registration of the acquiring corporation's stock to be issued is required, and a registration statement must be filed with the SEC. See 15 USC §77e(c). Willful noncompliance with registration requirements is a crime punishable by fine and imprisonment. 15 USC §77x.

Most corporations therefore will make every effort to fit the transaction within one or more of the federal exemptions from registration. See summary of federal exemptions in §2.26. See also ORGANIZING CORPORATIONS IN CALIFORNIA §§4.3–4.26 (2d ed Cal CEB 1983). For a more detailed discussion, see 7 Hicks, EXEMPTED TRANSACTIONS UNDER THE SECURITIES ACT OF 1933 (rev ed 1989).

Preparing a registration statement under the Securities Act is a time-consuming and expensive process. See discussion in 1 Sowards, THE FEDERAL SECURITIES ACT AND TRUST INDENTURE ACT OF 1939 (rev ed) chap 7. The acquiring corporation must issue a prospectus setting forth all material information that will enable the prospective investors (*i.e.,* the acquired corporation's shareholders who will receive shares in the acquiring corporation) to make an informed judgment. A prospectus may be carefully reviewed by the SEC, or it may be not reviewed at all; in either event, the corporation and its directors and officers are responsible for its accuracy. In addition, proxies will probably be solicited from the acquired corporation's shareholders to obtain their approval of the transaction. The prospectus is customarily used as the proxy statement of the acquired corporation.

Producing a document that will serve as both a prospectus and a proxy statement places a heavy responsibility on the management of the acquiring corporation. If the description of the acquired corporation is inaccurate in some respect, a shareholder of the acquired corporation may have a cause of action against the acquiring corporation and its management under the 1933 Act, 15 USC §77k. The burden on a small corporation's management will be still more onerous if the transaction is structured so that the smaller corporation appears to be the acquiring rather than the acquired corporation. See §2.36. A small corporation may not have the capacity to make an adequate investigation of the other corporation and all its books and records, even if full access is granted. Consequently, the management of the smaller entity can only investigate to the best of its ability and seek expert legal advice in drafting the descriptions that must be set forth in the registration statement.

Another effect of an acquisition may be to bring the acquiring company within the ambit of the 1934 Act (if this is not already the case), which will require disclosure on a continuing basis. See Bloomenthal, SECURITIES LAW HANDBOOK §5.02 (1987–1988).

NOTE: Trading in the stock of a publicly held corporation that is a party to a merger or other acquisition before its public announcement may create serious problems of civil and criminal liability. This possibility should be made clear to corporate insiders and their "tipees." Under the Insider Trading Sanctions Act of 1984 (15 USC §§78u–1(a)(2)–(3)), treble damages may be awarded against anyone who violates insider trading rules. See Phillips & Kutz, *The Insider Trading Doctrine: A Need for Legislative Repair,* 28 Corp Prac Comm'n 423 (1986); Wimberly, *Corporate Recovery of Insider Trading Profits at Common Law,* 8 Corp L Rev 197 (1985); Farley,

A Current Look at the Law of Insider Trading, 39 Bus Lawyer 1771 (1984).

Note also that the United States Supreme Court, in considering whether the sale of a business is subject to the federal securities laws, ruled in *Landreth Timber Co. v Landreth* (1985) 471 US 681, and *Gould v Ruefenacht* (1985) 471 US 701, two cases concerning change in corporate control, that privately negotiated stock sales in closely held corporations are subject to the anti-fraud provisions of the federal securities laws.

For discussion of civil liabilities under both the 1933 and the 1934 Act, see Gadsby, THE FEDERAL SECURITIES EXCHANGE ACT OF 1934 chap 5.

§2.38   3. California Corporate Securities Laws

In a merger, consolidation, or purchase of assets, the acquiring corporation's issuance of its securities as consideration in the transaction must be qualified by obtaining a permit from the Commissioner of Corporations, unless an exemption from qualification applies. Corp C §§25120–25122.

Normally, a negotiating permit is not necessary before a general solicitation of the shareholders. The application for a definitive permit should be filed and the permit issued before a general solicitation of the shareholders is made through distribution of proxy materials. Corp C §25103(a); 10 Cal Code Regs §260.140.63. But if negotiations are conducted without a permit even though a permit is required, the issuance of a permit later (before the securities are issued or the consideration received) will prevent civil liability for the unqualified negotiations. Corp C §25503.

See discussion of California corporate securities regulation in §2.27.

§2.39   4. Representations and Warranties Made in Acquisition Agreement

Management liability in a corporate acquisition may arise from the representations and warranties that officers or directors are usually required to make about their corporation as part of an acquisition agreement. For example, the chief financial officer and the chief executive officer of the acquired corporation are often required to make representations concerning their company's financial condition. The extent of the individual's liability will depend on the scope of the representations made. Obviously, to avoid liability, each party to the transaction should be advised to make as few representations and warranties as possible. Counsel should advise members of management that they may be held liable for representations and warranties they have made even though the particular individual has not signed the acquisition agreement.

An individual's liability may be limited somewhat by including a statement that the information represented is true and correct to the best of the individual's knowledge. This, however, will not insulate from liability anyone who has no reasonable basis upon which to make the representation or one who is aware of contradictory information. See *Campbell v McClure* (1986) 182 CA3d 806, 227 CR 450. See also SALE OF BUSINESSES §4.23 (2d ed Cal CEB 1988).

§2.40 E. Antitrust Violations

Antitrust violations may arise under a wide variety of laws, including but not limited to the Sherman Act, 15 USC §§1–7; the Clayton Act, 15 USC §§12–27; the Hart-Scott-Rodino Act, 15 USC §18a; the Robinson-Patman Act, 15 USC §13a; and the Federal Trade Commission Act, 15 USC §§41–51. Violations of the antitrust laws may lead not only to civil liability of individual officers and directors, but also to criminal penalties. See, *e.g.,* 15 USC §1 (conspiracy to restrain trade).

A full discussion of the federal and state antitrust laws and their impact on individual officers and directors is beyond the scope of this chapter, which offers merely an overview of factors that management should be aware of. For a fuller treatment, see Hills, ANTITRUST ADVISER (3d ed 1985). See also ATTORNEY'S GUIDE TO THE LAW OF COMPETITIVE BUSINESS PRACTICES chap 5 (Cal CEB 1981).

The restraints imposed by the antitrust laws fall into three general categories: (1) monopolizing or attempting to monopolize an area, (2) price fixing by competitors, and (3) marketing practices other than price fixing that are subject to regulation ("unfair practices").

NOTE: Practitioners who do not ordinarily work in the antitrust area should be aware of the Federal Trade Commission (FTC) guidelines, which are not commonly thought of as "antitrust laws." Certain practices that may not constitute violations of the Sherman or Clayton Acts may nonetheless be found to constitute "unfair methods of competition" under §5 of the Federal Trade Commission Act, 15 USC §45. Thus, the FTC Act supplements and bolsters other antitrust laws. See Hills §5.04. However, the FTC has held that to constitute a violation of §5, a practice must have anti-competitive effects similar to those prohibited by the Clayton Act. See *General Motors Corp.* (FTC 1984) [1983–1987, Transfer Binder] 3 CCH Trade Reg §22165.

§2.41   1. Monopolistic Practices

Monopoly problems usually arise from predatory pricing practices, the acquisition of one firm by another, or the misuse of patents. Although §2 of the Sherman Act (15 USC §2), which prohibits monopolization, generally requires an intent to control prices or eliminate competition, other deliberate acts that may not strictly constitute an attempt to monopolize may be found to be illegal practices. See *e.g., Aspen Skiing Co. v Aspen Highlands Skiing Corp.* (1985) 472 US 585 (refusal by a monopoly holder to cooperate with a competitor diminished the competitor's ability to compete, was not justified by normal business purposes, and therefore constituted an antitrust violation). Although the courts generally try to distinguish between simple aggressive competitive behavior and predatory conduct, the vigor with which the corporation promotes its products and the amount of debate between the firm's counsel and its marketing personnel may be critical factors in antitrust cases. Management should be certain that under its internal operating procedures antitrust counsel has an opportunity to express itself before marketing decisions are made and implemented. See ABA, ANTITRUST LAW DEVELOPMENTS (1984).

§2.42   2. Price Fixing

One of the basic premises of the antitrust laws is that price fixing among competitors is per se illegal. Counsel should advise the corporation that it cannot enter into agreements with its competitors as to what prices to charge, even if those prices are reasonable. To avoid the appearance of such agreements, management should beware of large meetings that competitors' personnel will attend. If management members attend a trade association meeting and the subject of prices comes up, they should immediately leave. Management should also be advised that price fixing or other antitrust violations can also arise from reciprocal arrangements with competitors, customers, or suppliers; or from cooperation between competitors in the sharing of price information, discussions of marketing strategy, or agreements with competitors not to compete in a given area. Price fixing is regarded as a "hard-core" antitrust violation for which the Antitrust Division typically urges imprisonment. See Hills, ANTITRUST ADVISER §8.02 (3d ed 1985).

Counsel should also make sure management understands that the offense of price fixing does not necessarily involve an agreement to fix ultimate prices; it is enough that there is a conspiracy to fix an element of the price. *Catalano, Inc. v Target Sales, Inc.* (1980) 446 US 643.

§2.43   3. Price Discrimination Under Robinson-Patman Act and California Law

Almost any California corporation with products to market must sooner or later concern itself with the Robinson-Patman Act, 15 USC 13–13b, 21a, or with California Bus & P C §§17040–17051, both of which prohibit discriminatory pricing practices. See the discussion of the Robinson-Patman Act in Hills, ANTITRUST ADVISER chap 4 (3d ed 1985). Discriminatory pricing may also be within the ambit of other antitrust regulations, including §5 of the FTC Act, 15 USC §45. These statutes may seriously affect the marketing of the company's products.

Counsel should be alert to various management attitudes and policies that could create risks under the Robinson-Patman Act. Under certain sections of the Act, injury to competition is not necessarily an element of a violation. For example, management may believe that to maximize profits they must sell their product at the highest price obtainable, and if they can obtain a higher price for their product in certain geographic areas, and less in others, they will vary their prices accordingly. This practice may be a violation of either the Robinson-Patman Act or the California law. See Hills §4.24; Bus & P C §§17040–17042.

Violations may also arise from selling to a highly effective distributor at a lower price than to one who sells small quantities of the company's products, or from giving a more favorable price to large chain stores than to smaller stores. Quantity discounts must be based on real cost savings and should not be given to larger customers merely because they seem to have more "clout." See Hills §4.03.

NOTE: Because many of the major questions concerning interpretation of the Robinson-Patman Act have been answered, it is more predictable now than formerly whether a particular set of facts will be held to constitute a violation of the Act. Corporate counsel should insist that outside counsel with expertise in antitrust matters be consulted whenever the corporation or management intends to embark on a questionable line of conduct.

§2.44   4. Acquisition of Patents

In deciding whether the acquisition of a patent may violate antitrust laws, counsel must consider several statutes. Sections 1 and 2 of the Sherman Act (15 USC §§1–2), §§3 and 7 of the Clayton Act (15 USC §§14, 18), and §5 of the Federal Trade Commission Act (15 USC §45) are the most important statutes in this area. For discussion, see Hills, ANTITRUST ADVISER §6.08 (3d ed 1985).

In any transaction involving the acquisition of a patent, three different antitrust violations must be considered: (1) A patent acquisition agreement may be considered an agreement to restrict trade in violation of §1 of the Sherman Act (15 USC §1); (2) any acquisition, including a patent acquisition, that enables a company to dominate an industry may violate §2 of the Sherman Act (15 USC §2); and (3) if the effect of the acquisition is to substantially lessen competition, the acquisition may violate §7 of the Clayton Act (15 USC §18). See Hills §6.14.

Problems may also arise if the patent holder does not itself exploit its patent but instead licenses others to do so. No patent licensing arrangement should be entered into without the guidance of antitrust counsel.

F. Employment Practices

§2.45   1. Payment of Workers

California law imposes rigid requirements as to the payment of workers, including how often and how much they must be paid. See Lab C §§200–240. With some exceptions, workers must be paid at least twice a month and within a specified time (about ten days) after the completion of each pay period. Lab C §204. Paying wages with a bad check is a crime, as are some other violations of the payment provisions, and the corporate officer or employee who is responsible for the violation may be prosecuted. Lab C §§212, 215–216.

Most employers must comply with the federal Fair Labor Standards Act, 29 USC §§201–219, which was formulated to promote the health, well-being, and efficiency of workers by regulating wages, hours, and working conditions. For discussion, see ADVISING CALIFORNIA EMPLOYERS §§4.2–4.40 (Cal CEB 1981). In addition, California has its own labor standards laws. See Lab C §§1171–1204; 8 Cal Code of Regs §§11010–11150. These statutes impose specific requirements on certain industries and spell out particular working conditions that are required. If state and federal statutes overlap, the employer must meet the more stringent requirements. For discussion of the California wage and hour laws, see ADVISING CAL EMPL §§4.41–4.60.

Under California law, unless otherwise provided in their collective bargaining agreement, employees have a right to accumulate vacation time as their labor is rendered, and vested vacation time cannot be forfeited upon termination of employment. Lab C §227.3. Vacation is really considered to be part of an employee's earnings. Terminated employees must be paid for accrued vacation time in their last paycheck. *Suastez v Plastic Dress-Up Co.* (1982) 31 C3d 774, 183 CR 846.

§2.46   2. Withholding Taxes

All employers must comply with federal, state, and local payroll tax and withholding tax laws. See ADVISING CALIFORNIA EMPLOYERS §§1.57–1.62 (Cal CEB 1981). Individual management members may be liable for severe penalties if taxes withheld from employees' compensation are not paid. Failure to pay tax withholdings to the state or federal government will cause imposition of a penalty equal to the amount of the taxes not paid. IRC §6672. The Internal Revenue Service aggressively asserts the 100 percent penalty against corporate officers responsible for the payment, and the entire 100 percent penalty may be assessed against each such person. See IRC §6672. Criminal sanctions may also be imposed. IRC §7215.

§2.47   3. Safety Violations

California employers must comply with the federal Occupational Safety and Health Act (OSHA), 29 USC §§651–678), and its California counterpart (CAL-OSHA), principally Lab C §§140–147.2, 6300–6711; Health & S C §17022. For discussion, see ADVISING CALIFORNIA EMPLOYERS §§4.61–4.78 (Cal CEB 1981).

Corporations violating health or safety regulations can be required to close their doors until the violations are remedied. See 29 USC §662. Also, if serious injury or death results from a willful safety violation, the corporation and individual members of management may be heavily fined and the managers subjected to imprisonment. See Lab C §6425. See also *Granite Constr. Co. v Superior Court* (1983) 149 CA3d 465, 197 CR 3 (corporation could properly be prosecuted for manslaughter as a result of the death of seven workers on a construction project).

Failure to adequately stress safety in the workplace could lead to liability on the part of the corporation and its officers. Corporate counsel should encourage management to implement a safety program to detect safety violations, which may be difficult to discover, especially in larger companies. Although maintaining safety programs and safe equipment may appear to be unprofitable, cutting back on safety to save money will be more unprofitable in the long run.

§2.48   4. Union Activity; Unfair Labor Practices

As soon as management becomes aware that a union organizing drive has begun, it should consult with counsel regarding what it can and cannot do (either to resist or to encourage unionization) without committing an unfair labor practice under the Labor Management Relations Act (29 USC §§141–187). This complex subject is discussed in Gorman, BASIC TEXT ON LABOR LAW chaps VII–IX (1976). For an overview, see ADVISING CALIFORNIA EMPLOYERS chap 7 (Cal CEB 1981).

If a serious unionization campaign is underway, corporate counsel may find it necessary to associate counsel who specialize in labor law, to provide guidance in avoiding actions that could result in possible unfair labor practice proceedings before the National Labor Relations Board (NLRB). A seemingly harmless act, *e.g.,* announcing a pay raise near the time of a union election, may constitute a punishable unfair labor practice. The NLRB has broad authority to issue orders, including monetary awards, that are enforceable by contempt proceedings against individual corporate officers. See Gorman chap II §2. In addition, if the corporation's business suffers injury as a result of the unfair labor practice, that injury may ultimately be grounds for a shareholder derivative suit against management.

§2.49   5. Discriminatory Practices

Employment discrimination on the basis of race, color, religion, national origin, sex, age, handicap, marital status, pregnancy, or medical condition is prohibited by federal and state statutes. See 42 USC §2000e–2; 29 USC §623(a); Govt C §§12940–12948. See also ADVISING CALIFORNIA EMPLOYEES chaps 2–3 (Cal CEB 1981). In California, sexual harassment on the job constitutes an unfair employment practice. Govt C §12940(h). The California Fair Employment and Housing Commission recently ruled that AIDS is a handicap. See *DFEH v Raytheon Co.* (1987) FEHC Decision No. 87–04.

Employment discrimination prohibitions apply not only to hiring and firing, but also to promotions, compensation, and other terms, conditions, and privileges of employment. California employers cannot deny equal pay for equal work, and in addition they are required to grant up to six weeks pregnancy disability leave and up to four months pregnancy leave and to allow female employees to use accrued vacation and sick time during that time. See Govt C §12945. Employers who violate the anti-discrimination laws may be required to reinstate aggrieved employees, pay back wages, or comply with other orders that may be quite burdensome. See, *e.g.,* 42 USC §2000e–5. In California, both compensatory and punitive damages may be recovered in employment discrimination lawsuits.

Commodore Home Sys., Inc. v Superior Court (1982) 32 C3d 211, 185 CR 270.

Corporations should be advised to document their employment actions to confirm that anti-discrimination laws are being complied with, and corporate counsel should periodically review the corporation's employment practices with this in mind.

§2.50   6. Wrongful Termination

Under California law, employees hired for an unspecified period are presumed to be terminable at will. Lab C §2922. At-will employees may be terminated or may quit, with or without cause, at any time. However, California courts have created three far-reaching exceptions to this general rule. If

- the reason for terminating an at-will employee violates public policy,
- terminating the employee violates the implied covenant of good faith and fair dealing, or
- the company's policy manuals or other representations have created in the employee an expectation of continued employment,

California courts are likely to find a wrongful termination. See *Tameny v Atlantic Richfield Co.* (1980) 27 C3d 167, 164 CR 839; *Koehrer v Superior Court* (1986) 181 CA3d 1155, 226 CR 820; *Pugh v See's Candies, Inc.,* (1981) 116 CA3d 311, 171 CR 917; *Cleary v American Airlines* (1980) 111 CA3d 443, 168 CR 772. But see *Foley v Interactive Data Corp.* (1988) 47 C3d 654, 254 CR 211 (public policy does not prohibit terminating employee who informed employer of another employee's embezzlement; however, implied covenant may exist that prohibits termination except for good cause).

Punitive damages have been awarded for wrongful termination in California. See, *e.g., Stephens v Coldwell Banker Commercial Group* (1988) 199 CA3d 1394, 245 CR 606; *Smith v Brown-Forman Distillers Corp.* (1987) 196 CA3d 503, 241 CR 916.

Corporate counsel should keep management aware of the developments in this area, and should not hesitate to recommend that they seek advice from a labor law specialist to prevent liability for wrongful termination. See generally WRONGFUL EMPLOYMENT TERMINATION PRACTICE (Cal CEB 1987).

V. COMPENSATION OF OFFICERS

§2.51   A. Limitation by Commissioner of Corporations

The Commissioner of Corporations is authorized to impose a limit on salaries paid when it grants the corporation a permit to issue stock. See Corp C §25141. The limitation might possibly be applied to new, small corporations where there may be a danger that the principals will take such high salaries that the corporation will not generate enough surplus to pay the investors a return.

§2.52   B. Tax Considerations: Reasonableness of Compensation

For federal income tax purposes, corporations may claim "a reasonable allowance for salaries or other compensation for personal services actually rendered" as a business expense deduction. IRC §162(a)(1). California law regarding allowable corporate business expense deductions is the same as federal law. See 2 Ballantine & Sterling, CALIFORNIA CORPORATION LAWS §471.02 (4th ed); see also CALIFORNIA TAXES §§4.38–4.46 (Cal CEB 1989). To the extent that such compensation exceeds a reasonable amount, it is treated as a distribution of earnings, a taxable dividend, and the corporation is not entitled to a deduction for the excess amounts. See Treas Reg §1.162–7(b)(1). See also Bond, *The Reasonable Compensation Issue*, 18 Tax Adviser 897 (1987). The impact on the corporation of such a disallowance can be substantial.

The reasonableness of compensation depends on the circumstances of each case. Treas Reg §1.162–7(b)(3). The Internal Revenue Service takes into account all forms of compensation paid to the individual for personal services, including but not limited to deferred compensation (*e.g.,* corporate contributions to pension or profit-sharing plans), stock options, insurance programs, and automobiles furnished to employees. See 1 Mertens, THE LAW OF FEDERAL INCOME TAXATION §6.05 (1987). In determining the reasonableness of the total amount of compensation, the IRS considers such factors as the corporation's earnings history, salaries paid to individuals in similar posts in similar businesses, the service that the individual performs for the business, the corporation's dividend record, and the size of the business. See Treas Reg §1.162–7(b)(3). See also the discussion of significant factors in Bond, *supra.*

NOTE: S corporations do not need to grapple with the reasonable compensation issue with respect to officers who are also shareholders. Because S corporations are taxed in a manner similar to partnerships, there is no danger that distributions of corporate earnings will be disguised as compensation to avoid taxation: all corporate income is taxed to the shareholders, whether it is distributed or not.

C. Employment Agreements

§2.53   1. Generally

The practice of giving executives long term employment agreements varies widely among corporations—some never use such agreements, while other corporations enter into agreements with almost all members of top management.

From the corporation's standpoint, an employment agreement should set forth, at a minimum, the employee's compensation and duties, the agreement's duration, and all grounds for terminating the employee. The statement of such grounds is very important because it defines the limits of the corporation's power to terminate the employee without incurring a suit for breach of contract. (The corporation may still terminate for serious misconduct commonly known as "cause" (*e.g.,* stealing), but this ground is rarely asserted against management personnel).

See generally ADVISING CALIFORNIA EMPLOYERS chap 5 (Cal CEB 1981). This chapter, entitled Executive and Managerial Contracts, contains both discussion and forms. See also WRONGFUL EMPLOYMENT TERMINATION PRACTICE §§2.36–2.39 (Cal CEB 1987).

§2.54   2. Clause Requiring Repayment of Excess Compensation

The employment agreement may provide that the employee repay to the corporation any portion of his or her compensation that is disallowed as a deduction by the Internal Revenue Service or the California Franchise Tax Board. See the discussion of reasonable compensation at §2.52. Without such a provision, the corporation may be in the predicament of having paid out the salary under the agreement and also having lost a portion of the deduction. However, inclusion of a repayment clause may lead the IRS and the courts to conclude that the compensation is excessive. See *Saia Elec., Inc.* 33 TC Memo 1357, aff'd in unpublishable op (5th Cir 1976) 536 F2d 388, cert den 429 US 979. At least one case has also suggested that the *absence* of a repayment provision was implied evidence of the parties' understanding that the compensation arrangement was reasonable. See *Steel Constructors, Inc.* 37 TC Memo 1851. The IRS does not issue advance rulings on the consequences of repayment clauses. Rev Proc 89–3, 1989–1 Int Rev Bull 29. The decision whether to include such a clause should be made only after evaluating the risks, perhaps with the aid of tax counsel.

For discussion and form, see ADVISING CALIFORNIA EMPLOYERS §5.18 (Cal CEB 1981).

§2.55   3. "Golden Parachute" Provisions

Many corporate employment agreements established or amended in the past provided for "golden parachute" arrangements as a defense against a possible hostile takeover. Under such agreements, individual members of management would receive lavish severance payments in the event of a successful takeover. The Tax Reform Act of 1984, however, reduced the flexibility and usefulness of golden parachute arrangements by providing, in general, that if an individual receives excess parachute payments, the corporate employer loses the right to deduct such payments and the individual becomes subject to a non-deductible 20 percent excise tax penalty in addition to the ordinary income taxes levied on such benefits. Excess parachute payments are those that exceed three times the individual's base amount, which is the individual's average annual taxable compensation over the five-year period preceding the takeover. See generally IRC §§280G, 275(a).

In 1986, the golden parachute rules were liberalized to some extent. "Small business corporations," *i.e.,* those eligible to make an S corporation election under IRC §1361(b), are exempt from the golden parachute rules entirely. IRC §280G(b)(5)(A)(i). Also excluded from the rules are corporations whose stock is not readily traded on an established securities market or otherwise, if shareholder approval is obtained. IRC §280G(b)(5)(A)(ii). The 1986 Act also made some important technical modifications in the determination of "excess payments." See IRC §280G(b)(4), (6).

§2.56 D. Compensation Planning

Planning for executive compensation, current and deferred, is a complex area, and a detailed discussion is beyond the scope of this chapter. For a general discussion of fringe benefits for employees, see ADVISING CALIFORNIA EMPLOYERS §§1.23–1.56 (Cal CEB 1981). See also ATTORNEY'S GUIDE TO PENSION AND PROFIT-SHARING PLANS (3d ed Cal CEB 1985).

Effective compensation planning requires careful attention to the impact of federal and state income taxes on both the employer and the employee. Expert assistance in this area will probably be required by most corporations.

VI. LIMITING OR ELIMINATING DIRECTORS' LIABILITY

§2.57 A. Exculpation Requires a Provision in the Articles of Incorporation

Under Corp C §204(a)(10), which was enacted in 1987, a corporation is permitted to eliminate or limit "the personal liability of a director for monetary damages in an action brought by or in the right of the corporation for breach of a director's duties to the corporation and its shareholders," if a provision to that effect is included in the corporation's articles of incorporation. For existing corporations, this means that there be an amendment to the articles, which must be approved by the shareholders. Corp C §903. See also §5.68. Inasmuch as the limitation is a curtailment of the right of shareholders to bring derivative actions, approval by the shareholders may not be automatically forthcoming.

The language of the provision in the articles should be substantially as follows: "The liability of the directors of the corporation for monetary damages shall be eliminated to the fullest extent permissible under California law." Corp C §204(a). See also §5.134 (form and comment). Full and fair disclosure must be made to the shareholders when approval of such a provision is sought. This will usually involve the preparation of a proxy statement fully explaining the effect of the amendment to the shareholders.

B. Restrictions on Corporation's Right To Exculpate

§2.58   ### 1. Not Applicable to Violations of Duty of Loyalty

Exculpation provisions in the articles apply only to breaches of a director's duty of care (*i.e.,* negligence), not to violations of the duty of loyalty to the corporation and its shareholders (*i.e.,* self-dealing and the like). See 1987 Legislative Note to Corp C §204(a)(10)–(11): "It is not the intent of the Legislature by this act to change case law or statutory law regarding the duty of loyalty of a director." Stats 1987, ch 1203 §4.

§2.59   ### 2. Applicable Only to Directors Acting as Directors

Exculpation of directors from liability under Corp C §204(a)(10) extends only to liability resulting from their acts as directors. The statute specifically states that "no such provision shall eliminate or limit the liability of an officer for any act or omission as an officer, notwithstanding that the officer is also a director or that his or her actions, if negligent or improper, have been ratified by the directors." Corp C §204(a)(10)(C).

§2.60   ### 3. Applicable Only to Monetary Damages in Derivative Actions

Provisions in the articles exculpating directors from liability extend only to monetary damages, and those damages must be incurred in a derivative action ("an action brought by or in the right of the corporation for breach of a director's duties to the corporation"). Corp C §204(a)(10). A director may still be personally liable for monetary damages in a third party suit. Likewise, Corp C §204(a)(10) does not impair shareholder rights to seek equitable remedies, *e.g.,* bringing an action to enjoin a transaction.

§2.61   ### 4. Not Applicable to Certain Specified Acts (The "Seven Deadly Sins")

An exculpation provision permitted by Corp C §204(a)(10) may not eliminate or limit directors' liability:

(i) for acts or omissions that involve intentional misconduct or a knowing and culpable violation of law,

(ii) for acts or omissions that a director believes to be contrary to the best interests of the corporation or its shareholders or that involve the absence of good faith on the part of the director,

(iii) for any transaction from which a director derived an improper personal benefit,

(iv) for acts or omissions that show a reckless disregard for the director's duty to the corporation or its shareholders in circumstances in which the director was aware, or should have been aware, in the ordinary course of performing a director's duties, of a risk of serious injury to the corporation or its shareholders,

(v) for acts or omissions that constitute an unexcused pattern of inattention that amounts to an abdication of the director's duty to the corporation or its shareholders,

(vi) under [Corp C] Section 310 [regarding transactions between corporations and directors], or

(vii) under [Corp C] Section 316 [regarding directors' liability for distributions, loans, and guaranties].

Corp C §204(a)(10)(A). The acts listed in this statute have been humorously referred to as the "seven deadly sins," for which directors remain personally liable.

VII. INDEMNIFICATION OF DIRECTORS, OFFICERS, AND OTHER AGENTS

A. Under Corporations Code §317

§2.62   **1. Current and Prior Law; Definitions**

Three key sections of the Corporations Code currently determine whether and to what extent corporate agents (*e.g.,* directors, officers, employees) may be indemnified for acts performed in the course of their duties: Corp C §§204(a)(10), 204(a)(11), and 317. Prior to 1987, when a major revision in the statutory law in this area was enacted, only indemnifications that met the complex requirements of Corp C §317 were permitted.

For purposes of indemnification under Corp C §317, "agent" means any person who is or was a director, officer, employee, or other agent of the corporation; "proceeding" means any threatened, pending, or completed action or proceeding, whether civil, criminal, administrative, or investigative; and "expenses" includes without limitation attorneys' fees and any expenses of establishing a right to indemnification under this section. Corp C §317(a). These definitions were not changed by the 1987 revisions.

§2.63   2. Successful Defense on the Merits

If a corporate agent is successful on the merits in defense of a third party action, a derivative action, or in defense of any claim, issue, or matter in such an action, the agent must be indemnified by the corporation for expenses actually and reasonably incurred by the agent in connection with the action. Corp C §317(d).

§2.64   3. Authorization of Indemnification: Traditional Requirements

Prior to the 1987 revisions, Corp C §317 defined the limits of allowable indemnification and did not permit any expansion of indemnification beyond the limits set out in §317. See former Corp C §317(g). There were only three methods of authorizing indemnification under the former law: (1) by a majority vote of the disinterested directors; (2) by approval of a majority (or more if required by the articles or bylaws) of disinterested shares; or (3) by court order. (These three methods are still available, in addition to others added in 1987.)

Under pre-1987 law, authorization by any method required a determination that the agent had met the applicable standard of conduct. This requirement by necessary implication prohibited authorization of indemnification in advance. Under the prior law, the requirements for indemnification in third party actions differed from the requirements for derivative actions: an agent needed to meet a duty of care standard in a derivative action, but not in a third party suit. A corporation could advance expenses incurred in defending a proceeding, but only if the agent agreed to reimburse the corporation unless it was ultimately determined that the agent was entitled to indemnification under Corp C §317. In all cases, the potential monetary exposure of an agent was limited only by the damages proved in the litigation and any considerations of fairness by the judge or jury.

§2.65   4. New Alternative: Opinion of Legal Counsel

Before 1987, indemnification could be authorized only by the disinterested directors, the disinterested shareholders, or a court order. See §2.64. Since the 1987 revisions, if a quorum of disinterested directors is not obtainable, the determination that indemnification is proper because the agent has met the applicable standard of conduct can be made by independent legal counsel in a written opinion. Corp C §317(e)(2).

NOTE: Before providing such opinion, counsel should consider asking the corporation for the same indemnification protection afforded to other agents.

§2.66   5. Agent's Required Standard of Conduct

Any indemnification under §317 must be authorized by the corporation in the specific case, upon a determination that indemnification is proper in the circumstances "because the agent has met the applicable standard of conduct" set forth in §317(b) or (c). Corp C §317(e).

Under Corp C §317(b) and (c), if an appropriate article is adopted (see §2.69), the agent or other person whom the corporation may now indemnify must have acted "in good faith, in a manner the person believed to be in the best interests of the corporation and its shareholders."

NOTE: This language is not repeated in Corp C §204(a)(11), which does not explicitly require that the agent meet any standard of conduct. The failure of Corp C §204(a)(11) to set forth a standard of conduct for "excess" indemnification may permit potential abuses with respect to the standard of conduct required for an agent to be indemnified under an indemnification agreement. There has been concern expressed over this omission, and it is likely that the legislature will remedy this oversight at a future date.

§2.67   6. Third Party or Derivative Action

Indemnification in third party actions is treated in Corp C §317(b), and indemnification in derivative actions (actions "by or in the right of the corporation to procure a judgment in its favor") is treated in Corp C §317(c). Under prior law, there were different standards in the two different types of actions, but the 1987 revisions to Corp C §317 have made the standard of conduct for indemnification in third party actions similar to that required for indemnification in derivative actions.

The revisions removed the duty of care standard previously contained in Corp C §317(c). Formerly, the agent had to act as an "ordinarily prudent person" before the corporation could indemnify the agent for expenses in a derivative action. With the deletion of the duty of due care standard, a California corporation can indemnify an agent for expenses in a derivative action even though the agent may have acted in a negligent fashion.

In a derivative action, an agent who is adjudged liable to the corporation for breach of the agent's duty to the corporation or its shareholders can be indemnified only if the court in which the proceeding is or was pending determines that the agent is fairly and reasonably entitled to indemnity, and then only to the extent that the court determines. Corp C §317(c)(1).

There can be no indemnification of amounts paid in settling or otherwise disposing of a pending derivative action without court approval, or of expenses incurred in defending such a pending action that is settled or otherwise disposed of without court approval. Corp C §317(c)(2)–(3). (This is a liberalization of the former law, which prohibited indemnification in settled derivative actions regardless of whether or not the court approved the settlement.)

§2.68   7. Advancement of Expenses

Expenses incurred in defending any proceeding may be advanced by the corporation upon receipt of an undertaking by or on behalf of the agent to repay the advances if it is ultimately determined that the agent is not entitled to be indemnified. Corp C§317(f).

§2.69   B. "Excess" Indemnification Under Corp C §204(a)(11)

Since 1987, Corp C §317 is no longer the exclusive statute authorizing the indemnification of agents. See Corp C §317(g), which now states that the indemnification allowed under Corp C §317 "shall not be deemed exclusive of any other rights to which those seeking indemnification may be entitled under any bylaw, agreement, vote of shareholders or disinterested directors, or otherwise." California corporations are allowed to grant indemnification in excess of the indemnity permitted by Corp C §317, "to the extent such additional rights to indemnification are authorized in the articles of incorporation." Corp C §317(g). The articles provision itself is the subject of Corp C §204(a)(11).

The extent to which a corporation may go in granting excess indemnification remains to be determined by case law.

§2.70   1. Requirement: Provision in the Articles

Subsection §204(a)(11) (a part of the Corporations Code section on provisions effective only if expressly set forth in the articles of incorporation) allows a corporation to include in its articles a provision authorizing indemnification of agents in excess of that permitted by Corp C §317. For sample forms, see §5.135. Although Corp C §204(a)(11) does not distinguish between derivative actions and third party actions, it does impose certain restrictions on the indemnification that a corporation can authorize.

§2.71   2. Statutory Restrictions

A corporation "may not provide for indemnification of any agent for any acts or omissions or transactions from which a director may not be relieved of liability as set forth in the exception to paragraph (10)" of Corp C §204(a). Corp C §204(a)(11). This is a reference to the "seven deadly sins" set forth in §2.61. If a director cannot be exculpated from liability for a particular act or course of conduct, neither can an agent be indemnified for such acts or conduct.

Corporations Code §204(a)(11) also prohibits a California corporation from authorizing indemnification of agents "as to circumstances in which indemnity is expressly prohibited by Corp C §317." Although this prohibition may ultimately be given a broader interpretation, it seems at the very least to prohibit indemnification in a derivative action with regard to any matter for which the agent was adjudged liable for breach of duty to the corporation and its shareholders, unless a court permits such indemnification. This clause presents an internal statutory conflict.

On the one hand, Corp C §317(g) states that the indemnification authorized by Corp C §317 "shall not be deemed exclusive of any other rights to which those seeking indemnification may be entitled under any bylaw, agreement, vote of shareholders or disinterested directors, or otherwise." This language clearly allows corporations to provide agents with indemnification above and beyond that permitted under Corp C §317(b)–(f), (h). The extent of excess indemnification appears to be limited only by the arrangements reached between the corporation and its agent and by the restrictions set forth in Corp C §204(a)(11).

On the other hand, the restrictive clause of Corp C §204(a)(11) seems to impose the same prohibitions and standards of indemnification of Corp C §317 on any "excess" indemnification arrangement. Such a reading of Corp C §204(a)(11) would make an indemnification agreement merely a contractual reaffirmation of the statutory indemnification scheme of Corp C §317, and would make nonsense of the 1987 statutory revisions in this area. The courts will ultimately need to determine the extent to which a corporation can expand upon the indemnification provided under Corp C §317.

§2.72   C. Indemnification Agreements

The California courts have not yet had the opportunity to provide any guidance as to the extent to which California corporations can expand the indemnification of agents as permitted under Corp C §317(g). Indemnification agreements drafted by California corporations can vary, based on whether the corporation has adopted a conservative, a moderate, or an aggressive interpretation of the new law. Corporations, with the advice of their counsel, will need to decide which of these stances they will adopt in their indemnification agreements. Despite the usual severability clause, the adoption of aggressive provisions may risk putting into question the enforceability of key indemnification provisions, or having the courts declare the entire agreement in violation of public policy. On the other hand, the selection of extremely conservative provisions will preclude corporate agents from taking full advantage of the indemnity to which they are entitled under Corp C §317.

A moderate perspective in drafting indemnification agreements would generally track the scheme of Corp C §317, but would probably also include some or all of the following provisions:

- A provision that would establish the presumption that the agent had met the applicable standard of conduct required for indemnification;
- A provision that the agent may bring suit to have the corporation meet its obligations under the indemnification agreement and that the corporation will pay the expenses of that suit;
- A provision that the indemnification agreement applies to claims relating to events that occurred before the effective date of the indemnification agreement;
- A provision indemnifying agents for amounts paid in settling derivative actions even though court approval has not been obtained;
- A provision that limits the benefits to those allowable under the then-effective law in force at the time the indemnification is sought and also automatically incorporates future changes in the law increasing the protection available to agents.

A more aggressive stance in the preparation of its indemnification agreement might include a provision eliminating the requirement that any applicable standard of conduct be met for providing indemnity in connection with third party actions or derivative actions, and a provision allowing for indemnification in third party actions even if such indemnification is for one of the "seven deadly sins" set forth in Corp C §204(a)(10)(A).

For a sample form of indemnification agreement, see §5.137.

Although shareholder approval may not be legally required to authorize indemnification agreements, it would be prudent to submit the form of indemnification agreement to shareholders for their approval. Since each of the directors who approves the form of indemnification agreement will be a party to the indemnification agreement and therefore will potentially benefit by it, approval of the form of indemnification agreement by shareholders will insulate the indemnification agreement against challenges to its legality. See Corp C §310, which provides generally that a contract between a corporation and one or more of its directors cannot be considered void or voidable if the material facts as to the transaction between the corporation and its director or directors are disclosed or known to the shareholders and such contract is approved by affirmative vote of the majority of disinterested shareholders.

§2.73   D. Insurance ("D & O" Insurance)

In recent years the cost of directors' and officers' liability insurance ("D & O" insurance) has increased dramatically and availability of D & O Insurance has decreased. By amending Corp C §204 to permit a corporation to eliminate or limit the personal liability of directors for monetary damages in derivative actions and to expand its ability to indemnify them, the California legislature has reduced the breadth of insurance coverage required for a corporation to protect its directors. Gaps in protection, however, remain.

Insurance is still needed to offer protection in circumstances in which indemnification is legally unavailable or, although legally permissible, is otherwise unavailable because a corporation is either unable or unwilling to indemnify its officers and directors. For example, the insolvency of a corporation may make indemnification unavailable, or a hostile takeover of a corporation may make the new board unwilling to grant indemnification.

Such gaps have led corporations that cannot afford D & O insurance to self-insure. Some corporations have designed self-funded insurance arrangements or have established subsidiaries to provide D & O insurance coverage. Other corporations have designed mutual or consortium insurance companies to provide needed coverage.

Corporations Code §317(i), as amended in 1987, addresses self-insurance, as follows:

> A corporation shall have power to purchase and maintain insurance on behalf of any agent of the corporation against any liability asserted against or incurred by the agent in such capacity or arising out of the agent's status as such whether or not the corporation would have the power to indemnify the agent against that liability under this section. The fact that a corporation owns all or a portion of the shares of the company issuing a policy of insurance shall not render this subdivision inapplicable if either of the following conditions are satisfied: (1) if the articles authorize indemnification in excess of that authorized in this section and the insurance provided by this subdivision is limited as indemnification is required to be limited by paragraph (11) of subdivision (a) of Section 204; or (2) (A) the company issuing the insurance policy is organized, licensed, and operated in a

manner that complies with the insurance laws and regulations applicable to its jurisdiction of organization, (B) the company issuing the policy provides procedures for processing claims that do not permit the company to be subject to the direct control of the corporation that purchased that policy, and (C) the policy issued provides for some manner of risk sharing between the issuer and purchaser of the policy, on one hand, and some unaffiliated person or persons, on the other, such as by providing for more than one unaffiliated owner of the company issuing the policy or by providing that a portion of the coverage furnished will be obtained from some unaffiliated insurer or reinsurer.

This language indicates that self-insurance programs whereby a corporation owns all or a portion of the shares of the company issuing D & O insurance are permitted if such self-insurance programs are either (1) limited to provide protection to the extent indemnification would otherwise be permitted, (2) structured to assure that the processing of claims will not be subject to the direct control of the corporation that purchases the policy, or (3) subject to some manner of risk sharing between the issuer and the purchaser of the policy.

Shareholders' Rights and Liabilities

William M. McKenzie, Jr.

WILLIAM M. MCKENZIE, Jr., B.A., 1953, Yale University; LL.B., 1959, University of Michigan. Mr. McKenzie, of the firm of Luce, Forward, Hamilton & Scripps, practices in San Diego.

I. SHAREHOLDERS' RIGHTS

§3.1   **A. Introduction**

The law surrounding shareholders' rights and responsibilities has changed considerably in recent years. Both state and federal laws have changed through the enactment of substantive new legislation and through judicial decisions. Judicial scrutiny of the actions taken by a board of directors has increased, and the courts have become quicker to question the decisions reached by the board. An adequate evaluation of shareholder rights often requires consideration of the duties, responsibilities, and liabilities of a corporation's directors and officers. See chap 2.

This chapter discusses the right of shareholders to receive and obtain information about the corporation (§§3.2–3.20); their right to participate in corporate management (§§3.21–3.43); their ownership rights in the corporation (§§3.44–3.49); and their right to bring suit (§§3.50–3.53). Shareholders' liabilities and obligations are discussed in §§3.54–3.62.

B. Right To Obtain Information About the Corporation

§3.2   1. General Rules

All shareholders are entitled to receive certain information about the corporation in which they have invested, but their rights in this respect may vary considerably, depending on factors such as the size of the corporation or the size of the particular shareholder's holding in the corporation. In some instances, the shareholder must state a purpose that is reasonably related to his or her interest in the corporation.

Rights of All Shareholders, Without Stating a Purpose. All shareholders, regardless of the size of their holding, are entitled to receive an annual report. Corp C §1501(a); see §3.3. However, in a corporation of fewer than 100 shareholders of record (see Corp C §605), the annual report requirement may be waived by an express provision in the bylaws, in which case the shareholder may demand financial information similar to that required in the annual report. Corp C §1501(c); see §3.5. Any shareholder may also inspect or obtain a copy of the bylaws (Corp C §213; see §3.17), and may obtain the results of any shareholder vote at an annual, regular, or special meeting (Corp C §§1509–1511; see §3.18).

Rights of Specified Percentage Shareholders, Without Stating a Purpose. Shareholders who individually or in the aggregate own a specified percentage of a corporation's shares (usually 5 percent) have an *absolute right* to inspect and copy (or be sent a copy of) shareholder lists and records (Corp C §1600(a); see §3.11); and may obtain quarterly financial information (Corp C §1501(c)–(d); see §3.7) without the necessity of stating or establishing any purpose.

Rights of All Shareholders, for Reasonably Related Purpose. In addition, all shareholders are entitled, *for purposes reasonably related to their interests as shareholders,* to inspect and copy the following: shareholder lists and records (Corp C §1600(c); see §3.9); voting trust agreements filed with the corporation (Corp C §706(b)); accounting books and records (Corp C §1601(a); see §3.13); and minutes of corporate proceedings (Corp C §1601(a); see §3.15). This is sometimes referred to as the "general right" of inspection.

Corporation's Response to Request for Inspection of Corporate Records. The "general right of inspection" (*i.e.,* inspection of the shareholder records by a less-than-5-percent shareholder under Corp C §1600(c) and inspection by any shareholder of the minutes of corporate proceedings and accounting books and records under Corp C §1601) may be exercised only for a "reasonably related" purpose and on written demand. The purposes reasonably related to a shareholder's interests as a shareholder have not been fully defined by court decision, and the statutes do not specify a time within which the demand is to be met. The corporation would presumably be allowed time to evaluate the reasons given by the shareholder as the basis for the request and to receive advice on the validity of those reasons. A delay of some reasonable period beyond the time allowed for delivery of the shareholder list to 5 percent shareholders (*i.e.,* five business days; Corp C §1600(a); see §3.11), would probably be justifiable. The corporation may choose to refuse the demand and allow the courts to determine the validity of the shareholders' reasons for the demand. See 2 MARSH'S CALIFORNIA CORPORATION LAW §14.14 (2d ed).

Miscellaneous Rules. Inspection and copying may be made in person or by agent or attorney. Corp C §§1600(d), 1601(b). The right of inspection includes the right to copy and make extracts. Corp C §1601(b). The statutory rights of shareholders to inspect and copy corporate records cannot be limited by the articles or bylaws. Corp C §§1600(d), 1601(b). Inspection rights apply to all domestic corporations and to foreign corporations that have their principal executive offices in California. Corp C §§1600(d), 1601(a). The right to inspect the record of shareholders also applies to foreign corporations that customarily hold board meetings in California (Corp C §1600(d)), and the right to inspect accounting records and minutes also applies to foreign corporations that keep those records in California (Corp C §1601(a)). The right to inspect accounting records and minutes extends to the records of subsidiaries. Corp C §1601(a).

Sources of Information. If information is not immediately available about where to send a request for information, or the officer on whom it should be served, that information can be obtained from the California Secretary of State's office. All California corporations are required to file annually a Statement of Domestic Corporation. Corp C §1502. A statement similar to that required by Corp C §1502 is required of foreign corporations. Corp C §2117. Additional information on foreign corporations is available from the foreign corporation's initial statement and designation required when filing for its certificate of qualification (Corp C §2105) and from its amended statement and designation filed whenever changes to that information occur (Corp C §2107).

The initial filing for a domestic corporation is made within 90 days of incorporation and annually thereafter. Corp C §1502(a). That statement sets out the names and complete business or residence addresses of its incumbent directors, the number of vacancies on the board (if any), the names and complete residence or business addresses of its chief executive officer, secretary, and chief financial officer, the street address of its principal executive office, the street address of its principal business office in California if its principal executive office is not in California, and a general statement of its principal business activity. Corp C §1502(a). The statement must also designate an agent for service of process. Corp C §1502(b).

If the information changes during the period between filings, the corporation may update its filing but is not required to do so. Corp C §1502(e). The only exception is in the change of an agent for service of process. Whenever the agent for service of process changes, the corporation must file a current statement with all of the information updated. Corp C §1502(e).

While these statements by domestic or foreign corporations do not necessarily provide all the information or the most current information needed in making a demand on the corporation, it is a starting place when other sources fail. As a last resort, serving a demand on the agent for service of process should suffice to constitute a demand made on the corporation.

2. Specific Types of Information

a. Annual Report

§3.3   (1) General Rule

All shareholders must be sent an annual report not later than 120 days after the close of the fiscal year, unless there are fewer than 100 shareholders of record as defined in Corp C §605 and this requirement has been expressly waived in the bylaws. Corp C §§1501(a). This requirement cannot be waived in a close corporation shareholders' agreement. Corp C §300(c). The annual report must include a balance sheet, an income statement, and a statement of changes in financial position for the applicable fiscal year. Corp C §1501(a). For detailed requirements of the annual report to shareholders, see Corp C §1501(a)–(b); see also discussion in §§1.88–1.89.

For corporations with fewer than 100 shareholders, if the requirement for an annual report is expressly waived in the bylaws and no annual report for the last fiscal year has been sent to shareholders, a shareholder, upon written request (preferably addressed to the corporate secretary), is entitled to receive the financial statements required by Corp C §1501(a). Corp C §1501(c).

For further discussion, including legislative history of Corp C §1501, see 2 MARSH'S CALIFORNIA CORPORATION LAW §14.12 (2d ed).

§3.4   (2) Form: Request for Copy of Annual Report

Form 3.4–1

To: [*Name and address of corporation*]
Attn: Corporate Secretary

Dear Secretary:

I am a shareholder of record of the above-named corporation. Please send me a copy of the corporation's latest annual report. If no annual report for the last fiscal year has been sent to shareholders, please send me a balance sheet as of the end of the last fiscal year, an income statement and statement of changes in financial position for that fiscal year, and any other documents, reports, or certificates that may be required by section 1501(a) of the California Corporations Code.

This request is made under section 1501 of the California Corporations Code, and all financial statements are to be prepared as required by that statute. All statements should be accompanied by any report on them by independent accountants, or if there is none, the certificate of an authorized officer of the corporation that they were prepared without audit from the corporation's books and records.

[*Add, if appropriate*]

The requested information should be mailed or delivered to the following person at the following address:

[*Name and address*]

[*Continue*]

Dated: _ _ _ _ _ _

Very truly yours,

[*Signature*]
[*Typed name and address*]

Comment: See discussion at §§3.2–3.3, 3.5. Although the Corporations Code does not so specify, any notice sent to the corporation should be sent registered or certified mail, return receipt requested. This will provide the shareholder with proof of delivery of the notice to the corporation.

b. Annual Financial Statements

§3.5 (1) General Rule

If no annual report for the last fiscal year has been sent to shareholders (see §3.3), any shareholder may make a written request for the financial information required by Corp C §1501(a), which includes a balance sheet, an income statement, and a statement of changes in financial position for the pertinent fiscal year. Corp C §1501(c). The request must be made more than 120 days after the close of the pertinent fiscal year, and the corporation must mail or deliver the requested information to the shareholder within 30 days after receipt of the request. Corp C §1501(c). The requirements for annual financial statements are set forth in Corp C §1501(a)–(b).

For further discussion, see 2 MARSH'S CALIFORNIA CORPORATION LAW §14.12 (2d ed).

§3.6 (2) Form: Request for Annual Financial Statement

Form 3.6–1

To: [*Name and address of corporation*]
Attn: Corporate Secretary

Dear Secretary:

I am a shareholder of record in the above-named corporation.

[*Add, if applicable*]

I understand that this corporation has fewer than 100 shareholders, that the requirement for an annual report to shareholders has been waived in the bylaws of this corporation, and that no annual report for the last fiscal year has been sent to the shareholders.

[*Continue*]

I request that you send me financial statements for the last fiscal year, as required by section 1501(c) of the California Corporations Code, including a balance sheet as of the end of that fiscal year and an income statement and statement of changes in financial position for that fiscal year, accompanied by any other documents that may be required by section 1501(a) of the California Corporations Code.

Dated: _ _ _ _ _ _

Very truly yours,

[*Signature*]
[*Typed name and address*]

Comment: See §§3.2–3.3. The above form can be combined with Form 3.8–1, Request for Existing Quarterly Financial Information. It should be sent registered or certified mail, return receipt requested.

c. Quarterly Financial Information

§3.7 (1) General Rule

In addition to the annual financial information available to all shareholders (see §§3.3–3.6), a shareholder or group of shareholders holding in the aggregate at least 5 percent of the outstanding shares of any class of stock of a corporation is entitled to receive quarterly income statements and balance sheets upon written demand. Corp C §1501(c). Requests may be for the three-month, six-month, or nine-month periods ending more than 30 days prior to the date of the request, and the requested statements must be delivered or mailed to the requesting shareholder(s) within 30 days after receipt of the request. Corp C §1501(c). (For a form of request for quarterly financial information by 5 percent shareholders, see Form §3.8–1.) A copy of these quarterly statements must be kept on file in the principal office of the corporation for 12 months, and must be exhibited at all reasonable times to any shareholder demanding an examination of the statements, or a copy can be mailed to the shareholder. Corp C §1501(c). (For a form of request for existing quarterly financial information, see Form 3.8–2.)

§3.8 (2) Forms: Request for Quarterly Financial Information

Form 3.8–1 Request for Quarterly Financial Statements
(5 Percent Interest Required)

To: [*Name of corporation*]
[*Address*]

1. [*I am/We are*] **the holder(s) of record of at least 5 percent** [*in the aggregate*] **of the outstanding** [*describe class, if any*] **shares of the above-named corporation.**

2. Pursuant to section 1501(c) of the California Corporations Code, you are requested to deliver or mail to [*me/us*]**, within 30 days, an income statement of the corporation for the** [*three-/six-/nine-*] **month period ending**[*date*]**, and a balance sheet of the corporation as of the end of that period.**

Comment: A shareholder or shareholders requesting quarterly income statements *for the current fiscal year* must hold at least 5 percent of the outstanding shares of any class of the corporation. See Corp C 1501(c), second sentence. The date to be inserted (*i.e.,* the date ending the period for which statements are requested) should be more than 30 days prior to the date of the request. Corp C §1501(c).

[*Add, if desired*]

In addition, if no annual report for the last fiscal year has been sent to shareholders, you are requested to include the following: a balance sheet of the corporation as of the end of the last fiscal year, an income statement and statement of changes in financial position for that fiscal year, and any other documents, reports, or certificates required by section 1501(a) of the California Corporations Code.

Comment: See Corp C §1501(c), first sentence. The availability of this information is not limited to 5 percent shareholders. See discussion and form in §§3.5–3.6.

[*Continue*]

3. [*I/We*] also demand copies of all quarterly balance sheets, income statements, statements of changes in financial position, quarterly income statements, and all reports requested by shareholders and required to be kept on file for 12 months under section 1501(c) of the California Corporations Code.

[*Add, if desired*]

[*I/We*] further demand the opportunity to examine those documents at the corporation's principal office, beginning on [*date*] at [*time*].

[*Continue*]

4. This request is made under section 1501 of the California Corporations Code, and all financial statements are to be prepared as required by that statute. All statements should be accompanied by any report on them by independent accountants, or, if there is none, the certificate of an authorized officer of the corporation that they were prepared without audit from the corporation's books and records.

5. The requested information should be mailed or delivered to the following person at the following address:

[*Name and address*]

Dated: _ _ _ _ _ _

[*Signature(s) of shareholder(s)*]
[*Typed name(s)*]

Comment: For discussion, see §§3.2–3.7; see also Comment to Form §3.8–2. This request should be sent registered or certified mail, return receipt requested.

Form 3.8–2 Request for Existing Quarterly Information
(Not Limited to 5 Percent Shareholders)

To: [*Name of corporation*]
[*Address*]

1. I am a shareholder of record of the above-named corporation.

2. I hereby request copies of all existing quarterly balance sheets, income statements, statements of changes in financial position, quarterly income statements, and all reports requested by shareholders and required to be kept on file pursuant to the last sentence of section 1501(c) of the California Corporations Code.

[*Add, if applicable*]

I further demand the opportunity to examine those documents at the corporation's principal office, beginning on [*date*] **at** [*time*].

[*Continue*]

3. This request is made under section 1501 of the California Corporations Code, and all financial statements are to be prepared as required by that statute. All statements should be accompanied by any report on them by independent accountants, or, if there is none, the certificate of an authorized officer of the corporation that they were prepared without audit from the corporation's books and records.

[*If appropriate, add*]

4. The requested information should be mailed or delivered to the following person at the following address:

[*Name and address*]

[*Continue*]

Dated: _ _ _ _ _ _

[*Signature of shareholder*]
[*Typed name*]

Comment: All shareholders (not merely 5 percent shareholders) have the right to demand to examine any quarterly statements prepared for 5 percent shareholders under Corp C §1501(a). See Form 3.8–1. The corporation is required to keep such statements on file for 12 months. The corporation may elect, at its option, to mail a copy of the reports to the shareholder. Corp C §1501(c). See discussion at §§3.2 and 3.7. This request should be sent registered or certified mail, return receipt requested.

d. Shareholder Lists and Records

(1) Available to Any Shareholder for "Reasonably Related" Purpose

§3.9   **(a) General Rule**

Shareholders, unless they have a certain minimum holding (see §3.11), must show "a purpose reasonably related to such holder's interests as a shareholder" to be entitled, as of right, to inspect and copy the corporation's record of shareholders. Corp C §1600(c). The demand on the corporation must be in writing, and the inspection and copying must be performed during usual business hours. Corp C §1600(c). Copies of voting trust agreements filed with the corporation (see §§3.38–3.42) are open to inspection and copying on the same terms as the record of shareholders. Corp C §706(b). This right of inspection applies not only to California corporations but also to foreign corporations having their principal executive offices in California or customarily holding their board meetings here. The right to inspect the corporate records cannot be abridged by provisions in the articles or bylaws. Corp C §1601(b).

Reasonably Related Purpose. The purposes reasonably related to a shareholder's interests as a shareholder under Corp C §1600(c) have not been fully defined by court decision, but should include communications with other shareholders about their vote on matters to be brought before a meeting of shareholders or about matters concerning the sale or purchase of securities. For discussion see 2 MARSH'S CALIFORNIA CORPORATION LAW §§14.13–14.14 (2d ed). The reasons should be stated clearly and concisely. If the relationship between the shareholder requesting access to the record of shareholders and the corporation or its management has reached a point where a formal demand is necessary, it can be assumed that any defect in the demand will be used as a basis for its denial by the corporation.

§3.10   (b) Form: Request To Inspect and Copy Shareholder Records (Purpose Required)

Form 3.10–1

To: [*Name of corporation*]
    [*Address*]

[*First alternative*]

1. I am the owner of [*number*] **shares of** [*class or series, if any*] **stock of this corporation.**

[*Second alternative*]

1. I am the holder of a voting trust certificate representing [*number*] **shares of** [*class or series, if any*] **stock of this corporation.**

Comment: Shares held, to the knowledge of the corporation, subject to a voting trust are considered as held of record by the recordholders of the voting trust certificates. Corp C §605(b)(1). See §§3.38–3.42.

[*Continue*]

2. I, either in person or by my agent or attorney, will inspect [*and copy*] **the record of shareholders, including duplicates of**

any voting trust agreements and extensions thereof on file with the corporation, beginning on [*date*] at [*time*] at the corporation's address set forth above. If the record of shareholders is kept at some other location, please advise me [*or my agent/attorney*] of that location at least 24 hours prior to the time referred to above.

[*Add, if applicable*]

The name, address, and telephone number of my [*agent/attorney*] are as follows: _ _ _ _ _ _ _ _ _ _ _ _.

[*Continue*]

3. This demand is made under section 1600(c) [*and section 706(b)*] of the California Corporations Code. The purpose of the inspection [*and copying*], which is reasonably related to my interests in this corporation, is as follows:

[*State purpose*]

Dated: _ _ _ _ _ _

[*Signature of shareholder*]
[*Typed name and address*]

Comment: The request for inspection and copying of the record of shareholders should give the corporation at least five business days' notice. See Corp C §1600(a). See also §§3.2 and 3.9. If the mails are used, it should be sent registered or certified mail, return receipt requested.

(2) Available to Percentage Shareholders Without Showing Purpose

§3.11   (a) General Rule

Shareholders who in the aggregate hold at least 5 percent of a corporation's outstanding voting shares (or 1 percent if a Schedule 14B relating to the election of directors has been filed with the United States Securities and Exchange Commission) have an absolute right (*i.e.,* no need to show a purpose reasonably related to their interests as shareholders) to do either or both of the following:

(1) Inspect and copy the record of shareholders' names, addresses,

and shareholdings during usual business hours upon five business days' prior written demand on the corporation. Corp C §1600(a)(1). See Form 3.12–1.

(2) Obtain from the corporation's transfer agent, on written demand and on tender of the transfer agent's usual fee, a list of the shareholders entitled to vote for the election of directors, their addresses, and their shareholdings, as of the most recent date for which a list has been compiled or as of a future date specified by the demanding shareholder. Corp C §1600(a)(2). The list should be made available within five business days after the date it is received or the date specified in the request. A corporation has the responsibility for causing its transfer agent to comply with such requests. Corp C §1600(a). See Form 3.12–2.

This right of inspection applies not only to California corporations but also to foreign corporations having their principal executive offices in California or customarily holding their board meetings here. *Valtz v Penta Inv. Corp.* (1983) 139 CA3d 803, 188 CR 922.

§3.12   (b) Forms: Demand by Percentage Shareholders

Form 3.12–1 Request To Inspect and Copy Shareholder Records (Percentage Interest Required)

To: [*Name of corporation*]
[*Address*]

[*First alternative*]

1. [*I am/We are*] **the holder(s) of at least 5 percent** [*in the aggregate*] **of the outstanding voting shares of this corporation.**

[*Second alternative*]

1. [*I am/We are*] **the holder(s) of at least 1 percent** [*in the aggregate*] **of the outstanding voting shares of this corporation and have filed a Schedule 14B with the United States Securities and Exchange Commission relating to the election of directors of the corporation.**

Comment: See Corp C §1600(a). For the Schedule 14B referred to in the form, see 17 CFR §§240.14a–11(c), 240.14a–102.

[Continue]

2. [*I/We*], either in person or by agent or attorney, will inspect [*and copy*] the record of the names, addresses, and holdings of this corporation's shareholders beginning on [*date*] at [*time*] at [*place*]. If the record of shareholders is kept at some other location, please advise me [*or my agent/attorney*] of that location at least 24 hours prior to the time referred to above.

[Add, if applicable]

The [*agent's/attorney's*] name, address, and telephone number are as follows: [*insert information*]

[Continue]

3. This demand is made under section 1600 of the California Corporations Code.

Dated: _ _ _ _ _ _

[Signature(s) of shareholder(s)]
[Typed name(s) and address(es)]

Comment: The request for inspection and copying of the record of shareholders should give the corporation at least five business days' notice. See Corp C 1600(a). See also §§3.2 and 3.11. If the mails are used, it should be sent registered or certified mail, return receipt requested.

Form 3.12–2 Request for Copy of Shareholder List From Transfer Agent (Percentage Interest Required)

To: [*Name of transfer agent*]
[*Address*]

[First alternative]

1. [*I am/We are*] the holder(s) of at least 5 percent [*in the aggregate*] of the outstanding voting shares of this corporation.

[Second alternative]

1. [*I am/We are*] the holder(s) of at least 1 percent [*in the aggregate*] of the outstanding voting shares of this corporation and have filed a Schedule 14B with the United States Securities

and Exchange Commission relating to the election of directors of the corporation.

[*Continue*]

2. [*I/We*] **request a list of the names, addresses, and shareholdings of shareholders who are entitled to vote for the election of directors as of** [*the most recent record date for which it has been compiled/[specify future date*]]. **The list is to be made available on or before the fifth business day after** [*you receive this demand/the date as of which the list is to be compiled*].

3. The list should be mailed or delivered to the following person at the following address:

[*Name and address*]

4. Enclosed is a check for $_ _ _ _ _, which you have stated is your usual charge for such a list.

Dated: _ _ _ _ _ _

[*Signature(s) of shareholder(s)*]
[*Typed name(s)*]

Comment: See discussion at §§3.2, 3.11.

e. Accounting Books and Records
§3.13   (1) General Rule

Any shareholder or holder of a voting trust certificate, on written demand and *for a purpose reasonably related to the holder's interests as a shareholder,* has the right to inspect, copy, and make extracts from the accounting books and records, at the corporation's principal executive office in California, at any reasonable time during usual business hours. Corp C §1601(a). The right may be exercised by the holder in person or by an agent or an attorney. Corp C §1601(b).

§3.14   (2) Form: Request To Inspect and Copy Accounting Books and Records (Purpose Required)

Form 3.14–1

To: [*Name of corporation*]
[*Address*]

[*First alternative*]

1. I am the owner of [*number*] **shares of** [*class or series, if any*] **stock of this corporation.**

[*Second alternative*]

1. I am the holder of a voting trust certificate representing [*number*] **shares of** [*class or series, if any*] **stock of this corporation.**

[*Continue*]

2. I, either in person or by my agent or attorney, will inspect [*and copy*] **the accounting books and records of the corporation, beginning on** [*date*] **at** [*time*] **at the corporation's address set forth above. If the accounting books and records of the corporation are kept at some other location, please advise me** [*or my agent/attorney*] **of that location at least 24 hours prior to the time referred to above.**

[*Add, if applicable*]

The name, address, and telephone number of my [*agent/attorney*] **are as follows:** _ _ _ _ _ _ _ _ _ _ _ _.

[*Continue*]

3. This demand is made under section 1601 of the California Corporations Code. The purpose of the inspection [*and copying*], **which is reasonably related to my interests in this corporation, is as follows:**

[*State purpose*]

Dated: _ _ _ _ _ _

[*Signature of shareholder*]
[*Typed name and address*]

Comment: See discussion at §§3.2 and 3.13. See also 2 MARSH'S CALIFORNIA CORPORATION LAW §§14.13, 14.15 (2d ed).

f. Minute Books

§3.15   (1) General Rule

Any shareholder or holder of a voting trust certificate, on written demand and for a purpose reasonably related to the holder's interests as a shareholder, has the right to inspect, copy, and make extracts from the minutes of proceedings of the shareholders, the board, and committees of the board, at the corporation's principal executive office in California, at any reasonable time during usual business hours. Corp C §1601(a). The right may be exercised by the holder in person or by an agent or an attorney. Corp C §1601(b). See general discussion in §3.2.

§3.16   (2) Form: Request To Inspect and Copy Minutes of Corporate Proceedings (Purpose Required)

Form 3.16–1

To: [*Name of corporation*]
　　[*Address*]

[*First alternative*]

1. I am the owner of [*number*] **shares of** [*class or series, if any*] **stock of this corporation.**

[*Second alternative*]

1. I am the holder of a voting trust certificate representing [*number*] **shares of** [*class or series, if any*] **stock of this corporation.**

[*Continue*]

2. I, either in person or by my agent or attorney, will inspect [*and copy*] **the minutes of proceedings of the shareholders, the board of directors, and committees of the board of the corporation, beginning on** [*date*] **at** [*time*] **at the corporation's address set forth above. If these minutes are kept at some other location, please advise me** [*or my agent /attorney*] **of that location at least 24 hours prior to the time referred to above.**

[*Add, if applicable*]

The name, address, and telephone number of my [*agent/ attorney*] are as follows: _ _ _ _ _ _ _ _ _ _ _ _.

[*Continue*]

3. This demand is made under section 1601 of the California Corporations Code. The purpose of the inspection [*and copying*], which is reasonably related to my interests in this corporation, is as follows:

[*State purpose*]

Dated: _ _ _ _ _ _

[*Signature of shareholder*]
[*Typed name and address*]

Comment: See discussion at §§3.2–3.3, 3.15.

§3.17   g. Bylaws: Right To Inspect

All shareholders are entitled to inspect the bylaws at the corporation's principal executive office in California. Corp C §213. The statute does not state that a written demand or advance notice is necessary, but merely that the bylaws "shall be open to inspection by the shareholders at all reasonable times during office hours." Corp C §213. Foreign corporations operating in California that have no principal executive or business office in California must furnish a copy of the bylaws, as amended to date, to any shareholder upon written request. Corp C §213.

h. Results of Shareholder Vote

§3.18   (1) General Rule

Any shareholder, upon written request to the corporation, is entitled to be informed of the result of any particular vote of shareholders taken at a shareholders' meeting, if the request is made within 60 days following the conclusion of the meeting. Corp C §1509. The information to which the shareholder is entitled includes the number of shares voting for, the number of shares voting against, and the number of shares abstaining or withheld from voting on the particular matter. Corp C §1509. If the matter voted on was the election of directors, the corporation must report the number of shares (or number of votes if voted cumulatively) cast for each nominee for director. If more than one class or series of shares voted, the report must state the appropriate numbers by class and series of shares. Corp C §1509.

The requirements of Corp C §1509 apply to foreign corporations qualified to transact intrastate business in California if the request is made by "a shareholder resident in this state." Corp C §1510(a). The term "a shareholder resident in this state" includes any natural person residing in California, certain banks acting as fiduciaries, and California retirement funds for public employees. Corp C §1510(b). For applicability of Corp C §1509 to foreign corporations not qualified to transact intrastate business in California, see Corp C §1511.

For definition of the term "shareholder" for purposes of Corp C §§1509–1511, see Corp C §1512.

§3.19   (2) Form: Request for Results of Shareholder Vote

Form 3.19–1

To: [*Name of corporation*]
  [*Address*]

   1. I am a shareholder of record of the above-named corporation.

   2. I hereby request the results of the vote of the shareholders of this corporation taken at the shareholders' meeting of [*date*] on the following subject: [*describe*].

   [*First alternative, for matters other than election of directors*]

Please include the number of shares voting for, the number of shares voting against, and the number of shares abstaining or withheld from voting on this particular matter.

   [*Second alternative, for results of election of directors*]

Please include the number of shares, or number of votes if

voted cumulatively, cast for each nominee for director. If more than one class or series voted, please state the appropriate numbers by class or series of shares.

[*Continue*]

3. This request is made under section 1509 of the California Corporations Code.

4. The requested information should be mailed or delivered to the following person at the following address:

[*Name and address*]

Dated: _ _ _ _ _ _

[*Signature of shareholder*]
[*Typed name*]

Comment: The request should be made within 60 days after the conclusion of the meeting at which the vote was taken. Corp C §1509; see §3.18. As with other requests, if the shareholder wants proof of delivery it should be sent by registered or certified mail, return receipt requested.

§3.20   3. Penalties Enforcing Shareholder Rights To Obtain Corporate Information

Failure To Maintain Records. The failure of a corporation to keep or maintain the required record of shareholders or books of account or to prepare and submit the financial statements as required by the Corporation Code will subject the corporation to certain monetary penalties. The penalty is $25 per day for each day that the corporation's failure continues, beginning 30 days after the receipt of a written request that the duty be performed, made by a person entitled to make such a request. The maximum penalty is $1500. Corp C §2200. The penalty is paid to the shareholder or shareholders making the request, but only if a court action is instituted within 90 days after the written request is made. Corp C §2200.

NOTE: The penalty itself seems inadequate and not likely to induce compliance.

This penalty is in addition to any other available remedies for nonperformance of duties by the corporation, its directors, or its officers. Corp C §2202. The court is authorized to reduce these penalties if it finds that the lack of action was inadvertent or excusable. Corp C §2202.

Refusal To Allow Shareholder Inspection of Records. If the corporation refuses a lawful demand under Corp C §1601 to inspect corporate records, the affected person (usually a shareholder or holder of a voting trust certificate) may file suit for enforcement in the appropriate superior court. Corp C §1603. For good cause shown, the court may appoint inspectors or accountants to audit the books and records kept in California and investigate the corporation's property, funds, and affairs. Corp C §1603(a). Corporate officers are required to produce all books and documents in their custody or under their control for review by the appointed inspectors or accountants, and the court has contempt powers if any officer refuses to act. Corp C §1603(b). The expenses of an investigation or audit are paid for by the applicant unless the court orders them to be paid or shared by the corporation. Corp C §1603(c). However, if the court finds that the corporation's failure to comply with a proper demand under Corp C §1600 or §1601 was without justification, it may award damages sufficient to reimburse the applicant for the reasonable expenses incurred, including attorneys' fees. Corp C §1604. See *Valtz v Penta Inv. Corp.* (1983) 139 CA3d 803, 811, 188 CR 922, 927.

False Statements in Reports or Documents. The knowing concurrence by a corporate director, officer, or agent in preparing or publishing a written report or document containing any material false statement or any "untrue or willfully or fraudulently exaggerated" information constitutes a felony. Corp C §2254(a). The same applies if the report or document is intended to or has "a tendency to" give the stock of the corporation a greater or lesser market value than it really has. Corp C §2254(a)(3).

C. Right To Participate in Corporate Affairs

1. Shareholders' Meetings

§3.21   a. General Rules

Shareholders have the right to meet at various times during the corporation's business life in order to act on matters brought before it. These meetings may be held in California or elsewhere as stated in or fixed in accordance with the bylaws. Corp C §600(a). If no other place is so stated or fixed, shareholder meetings are to be held at the corporation's principal executive office. Corp C §600(a).

Annual Meeting. Annual shareholder meetings must be held for the purpose of electing directors on a date and at a time stated in or fixed in accordance with the bylaws. Corp C §600(b). In addition to the election of directors, the shareholders may transact any other proper business at the annual meeting. Corp C §600(b). Normally the annual meeting is held within 120 days following the close of the corporation's fiscal year at a time and place set by the board of directors.

Special Meetings. Special meetings of the shareholders may be called by the board, the chairman of the board, the president, the holders of shares entitled to cast not less than 10 percent of the votes at the meeting, or by such other persons as may be designated in the articles or bylaws. Corp C §600(d). Written notice of a special meeting must designate the general nature of business to be transacted, and no other business may be transacted at that meeting. Corp C §601(a)(1). However, if a shareholder is asked to sign a waiver of notice or consent to the holding of a special meeting, neither the business to be transacted nor the purpose of the meeting needs to be specified (Corp C §601(e)), unless the action to be taken involves one of the following: (1) approval of transactions between the corporation and its directors or between corporations having inter-related directors (Corp C §310); (2) amendments to the articles of incorporation (Corp C §902); (3) approval of the principal terms of a reorganization (Corp C §1201); (4) the election to wind up and dissolve the corporation (Corp C §1900); or (5) approval of a plan of distribution upon dissolution (Corp C §2007). Corp C §601(f).

b. Shareholders' Right To Call or Compel Meetings

(1) Annual Meeting

§3.22   (a) General Rule

If the corporation fails to hold an annual meeting within 60 days after the date designated for it (or, if no date is designated, within

15 months after the date of organization or the last annual meeting), the superior court of the proper county may "summarily" order the meeting to be held, upon the application of any shareholder, after notice to the corporation giving it the opportunity to be heard. Corp C §600(c). The order may specify matters such as the meeting place and time, the record date, and the form of notice. Corp C §600(c). Notwithstanding any provision of the articles or bylaws or of the Corporations Code to the contrary, the shares represented (either in person or by proxy) at a court-ordered meeting and entitled to vote constitute a quorum for purposes of that meeting. Corp C §600(c).

NOTE: This quorum provision of Corp C §600(c) ensures that the majority shareholders will not refuse to attend the meeting in an attempt to prevent the election of new directors or the election of minority representation through cumulative voting. It is a powerful tool in forcing management to call the regular annual meeting. (Note also that in a somewhat similar statute authorizing the court to order *special* shareholder meetings, the quorum provision is absent. See Corp C §601(c) and discussion at §3.24.)

§3.23   (b) Form: Demand for Annual Meeting

Form 3.23–1

DEMAND FOR ANNUAL MEETING OF
[*Name of corporation*]

To: [*Name and title of chairman of the board, president, vice president, or secretary*]

Demand is made that an annual meeting of shareholders be held for the election of directors, for action on any other matters that the board, at the time of the mailing of the notice, intends to present, and for action on any other proper matter that may be submitted to the meeting.

If notice of such a meeting is not given by the corporation within 20 days after receipt of this request, it is the intention of the undersigned to apply to the Superior Court of [*county*] **for an order that the meeting be held, as provided in section 600(c) of the California Corporations Code.**

Dated: _ _ _ _ _ _

> *[Signature of shareholder]*
> *[Typed name]*

Comment: Because Corp C §600(c) is silent with respect to preliminary procedures before seeking a court-ordered annual meeting, the demand and 20-day period are drawn from Corp C §601(c) regarding court-ordered special meetings. See §3.25.

(2) Special Meeting

§3.24   **(a) General Rule**

10 Percent Shareholders. A special meeting of shareholders may be called at any time by holders of at least 10 percent of the shares entitled to vote at the meeting. Corp C §§600(d), 601(c). The 10 percent requirement applies to votes entitled to be cast at the meeting. The number of shares constituting this percentage depends on the subject matter of the meeting, because different numbers of shares may be entitled to vote on different propositions. See 2 MARSH'S CALIFORNIA CORPORATION LAW §14.6 (2d ed).

5 Percent Shareholders. If after the directors have filled a vacancy on the board under Corp C §305(a), less than a majority of the directors have been elected by the shareholders, the holders of 5 percent of the outstanding shares may call a special meeting (or obtain a court order requiring a special meeting) to elect the entire board. Corp C §305(c). For the procedure for obtaining such an order, see Corp C §305(c).

NOTE: Hearings on this matter take precedence over other matters; see Corp C §305(c)). The procedure for calling a meeting is the same as in the case of 10 percent shareholders.

§3.25   **(b) Demand for Call of Special Meeting**

Shareholders seeking the call of a special shareholders' meeting must make a written request to the chairman of the board, president, vice president, or secretary, who must cause notice of the meeting to be given. Corp C §601(c). The date of the shareholders' meeting must be at least 35 days but not more than 60 days after the receipt

of the request by the officer. If notice is not given within 20 days
after the officer receives the request, the shareholders may give notice
themselves or obtain a court order that notice be given. Corp C
§601(c).

Obtaining a court order rather than giving notice directly eliminates
the necessity of obtaining shareholder lists and forces the corporation
to bear the cost of giving notice, both of which may be significant
advantages if there are many shareholders. See 2 MARSH'S CALIFORNIA
CORPORATION LAW §14.6 (2d ed).

NOTE: In many of the larger counties there may be an inherent delay
in seeking judicial relief. An order shortening time may be necessary.

§3.26   (c) Form: Call of Special Shareholders' Meeting

Form 3.26–1

**CALL OF SPECIAL
SHAREHOLDERS' MEETING OF**
[*name of corporation*]

To: [*Name and title of chairman of the board, president,
vice president, or secretary*]

[*I/We*] **call a special meeting of the shareholders of the
above-named corporation, to be held on** [*date*] **at** [*time*] **at**
[*place*], **for the following purpose:** [*state purpose*]. [*I am the
holder/We are the holders*] **of shares entitled to cast at least
10 percent of the votes at that meeting.**

**You are requested to cause notice of that meeting to be given
within 20 days after you receive this call.**

**This call is made under sections 600 and 601 of the California
Corporations Code.**

Dated: _ _ _ _ _ _

[*Signature(s) of shareholder(s)*]
[*Typed name(s) and address(es)*]

§3.27 c. Shareholder Proposals

Meetings of shareholders are generally concerned with shareholder action on a variety of proposals presented by corporate management, such as the election of management's proposed slate of directors. Shareholder proposals may be offered before a shareholders' meeting (which may develop into a proxy contest; see §3.35), or they may be raised at the meeting, commonly in the form of counterproposals from the floor.

Shareholder proposals at meetings must be raised in accordance with the applicable procedures governing the conduct of the meeting. The agenda of the meeting will usually provide for recognition of shareholders for purposes of submitting shareholder proposals. At the time scheduled for the election of directors, shareholders normally may nominate candidates from the floor. The corporate official presiding at the meeting has considerable authority and power to regulate the orderly conduct of the meeting.

Shareholder proposals are subject to the chair's rulings. In the absence of bylaw provisions governing conduct of shareholders' meetings, procedural rules may be established by the chair, subject only to such equitable considerations as may be determined by the court at a later date. 3 Sommer, SECURITIES LAW TECHNIQUES chap 54 (1987). The chair has wide latitude to regulate and limit debate before any vote is taken. See Wetzel, *Conduct of a Stockholders' Meeting,* 22 Bus Lawyer 303, 309 n 14 (Jan. 1967).

Disruptive or disorderly conduct during a meeting is usually ruled out of order and may subject an unruly shareholder to more severe sanctions. See Pen C §403 (misdemeanor to disturb lawful assembly or meeting).

d. Voting

§3.28 (1) General Rules

The right to vote in corporate elections belongs to record owners of shares on the applicable record date. Corp C §701(d). Each record shareholder is entitled to one vote for each outstanding share owned, including fractions of one vote corresponding to fractional shares (Corp C §§700(a), 407), except in the case of cumulative voting for directors (Corp C §708(a); see §3.29) or specific provisions in the articles restricting or eliminating voting rights (Corp C §400). Special statutory rules govern voting jointly held shares (Corp C §704), shares held by fiduciaries, attorneys-in-fact, representatives, receivers, and pledgees (Corp C §702), minors' shares (Corp C §702(d)), and shares held by corporations (Corp C §703). Shareholders may exercise their voting rights through proxies (see §§3.30–3.35) or through voting agreements or voting trusts (see §§3.36–3.42).

§3.29   (2) Cumulative Voting for Directors

Under Corp C §708(a), shareholders have an absolute right, if properly exercised, to vote cumulatively for directors—a rule designed to give minority shareholders a voice in the corporation's management. This right is not granted automatically. At least one shareholder must give notice at the meeting, before the voting for directors begins, of the shareholder's intention to cumulate votes. If any shareholder has given such a notice, all shareholders may cumulate their votes, but only for those candidates whose names have been placed in nomination. Corp C §708(b). But see Corp C §301.5, which allows "listed" corporations to eliminate cumulative voting under certain circumstances.

Under cumulative voting, any shareholder may give one candidate the number of votes equal to the number of directors to be elected multiplied by the number of votes to which the shareholder's shares are normally entitled. Corp C §708(a). For example, if five directors are to be elected, a shareholder holding 20 percent of the total number of voting shares can elect that shareholder's nominee to the board. For a more detailed discussion of cumulative voting and the formulas used, see 1B Ballantine & Sterling, CALIFORNIA CORPORATION LAWS §176.03 (4th ed); 2 MARSH'S CALIFORNIA CORPORATION LAW §11.2 (2d ed).

e. Proxies

§3.30   (1) Granting of Proxies

Every person entitled to vote shares may authorize others to act by proxy. Corp C §705(a). A proxy is a written authorization giving the proxyholder the power to vote the shares. See Corp C §§178,

179. The name of the shareholder may be signed by the shareholder or the shareholder's attorney in fact manually, by typewriter, by telegraphic transmission, or otherwise. Corp C §178. Any proxy purporting to be executed in accordance with these statutes is presumptively valid. Corp C §705(a).

The California Corporations Code provides special rules for proxies distributed to 10 or more shareholders of a corporation with 100 or more shareholders if the corporation has no outstanding class of securities registered or exempted from registration under section 12 of the Securities Exchange Act of 1934. See Corp C §604. Proxies solicited from shareholders of corporations subject to federal proxy rules must meet the much more detailed requirements of Regulation 14A of the Securities Exchange Act of 1934, as amended. See SEC Reg 14A (17 CFR §240.14a–1—240.14a–103). For discussion, see 2 MARSH'S CALIFORNIA CORPORATION LAW §§11.25–11.32 (2d ed).

For termination of proxies, see §3.33.

§3.31   (2) Irrevocable Proxies

Under certain circumstances a proxy, if it so states, may be irrevocable for a specified period. These circumstances are described in detail in Corp C §705(e) and include the granting of proxies in connection with certain pledges, stock purchases or options, extensions of credit, employment contracts, close corporation shareholders' agreements, and trusts. See Corp C §705(e)(1)–(6). Such proxies become revocable, notwithstanding the period of irrevocability specified, when certain events described in the statute occur (*e.g.,* redemption of a pledge). Corp C §705(e).

The fact that shares are subject to an irrevocable proxy must be stated on the face of the share certificate, or on the reverse of the certificate with a reference on the face. Corp C §§174, 418(a)(3), 705(f). If this is not done, the proxy will not be enforceable against a transferee of the shares who does not have actual knowledge of the proxy. Corp C §§418(b), 705(f).

Unless otherwise agreed in writing, a person who holds of record shares that belong to another (*e.g.,* as pledgee) must give the pledgor or owner a proxy to vote the shares, if the pledgor so demands and pays any necessary expenses. Corp C §705(d).

§3.32 (3) Form: Proxy

Form 3.32–1

[*Name of corporation*]
PROXY

[*I/We*], **as record owner(s) of** [*number*] **of the** [*class and series, if any*] **shares of** [*name of corporation*], **revoke any previous proxies and appoint** [*name*] **as** [*my/our*] **proxy to attend** [*all meetings of that corporation's shareholders/the meeting of that corporation's shareholders on* [*date*] *and any adjournment of that meeting*] **and to vote, execute consents, and otherwise represent those shares for** [*me/us*] **in the same manner and with the same effect as if** [*I/we*] **were personally present** [*./,*]

[*If authority is limited, add*]

provided, however, that the authority granted by this proxy is limited

[*First alternative*]

to representing those shares to determine a quorum and voting or otherwise representing those shares with respect to [*, and only in favor of,*] **the** [*election of* [*name of nominee*] *to the corporation's board of directors/* [*state other proposals*]]].

[*Second alternative*]

and the proxyholder shall have no authority to vote for or consent to any proposal for [*e.g., merger, consolidation, sale of corporate assets, dissolution, or winding up of the corporation*].

[*If irrevocable proxy, add*]

This proxy is irrevocable until [*date*], **or until** [*description of event that would make proxy irrevocable under section 705(e) of the California Corporations Code*], **whichever is earlier.**

[*If revocable proxy for specified term, add*]

If not previously revoked, this proxy shall terminate on [*date*].

[*Continue*]

Dated: _ _ _ _ _ _

[*Signature(s) of shareholder(s)*]
[*Typed name(s) and address(es)*]

Comment: This form is for use by corporations with fewer than 100 shareholders.

CAVEAT: If proxies are distributed to 10 or more shareholders of a corporation that has 100 or more shareholders, the form of the proxy (with certain exceptions) must comply with the special requirements of Corp C §604.

§3.33   (4) Termination of Proxies

A proxy expires 11 months after its date unless otherwise provided in the proxy. Corp C §705(b). Therefore, no period of effectiveness need be specified unless a different expiration date is desired.

Attendance and voting at a meeting on the part of the shareholder revokes a proxy, but only for that meeting. An otherwise unexpired proxy will continue in effect for all meetings not attended by the person who executed the proxy. Corp C §705(b).

A proxy may be revoked (1) by written notice delivered to the corporation, or (2) by a subsequent proxy (presumptively determined by the dates stated in the proxies, not by postmarks) executed by the person who executed the prior proxy and presented at the meeting. Corp C §705(b). For form of revocation, see §3.34. The maker's death or incapacity revokes a proxy only if the corporation receives written notice before the vote is counted. Corp C §705(c). An irrevocable proxy is not necessarily revoked by the death or incapacity of the maker, but may be revoked if the purpose for which the proxy was given no longer exists (Corp C §705(e)), or if a transferee of the shares has no knowledge of the existence of an irrevocable proxy (Corp C §705(f)).

§3.34   (5) Form: Revocation of Proxy

Form 3.34–1

[*Name of corporation*]

REVOCATION OF PROXY

[*I/We*], **as record owner(s) of** [*number*] **of the** [*class and series, if any*] **shares of** [*name of corporation*], **revoke all previous proxies, including but not limited to the proxy dated** [*date*] **in which** [*name*] **was named as proxyholder, and revoke all**

authority previously given any person or persons to act on [*my/our*] behalf in any manner with respect to those shares.

Dated: _ _ _ _ _ _

[*Signature(s) of shareholder(s)*]
[*Typed name(s) and address(es)*]

Comment: For a form of substitution of proxyholder, see 3 Ballantine & Sterling, CALIFORNIA CORPORATION LAWS Form 8.21 (4th ed).

§3.35 (6) Proxy Contests

The Corporations Code does not expressly regulate proxy contests, but instead permits a corporation's bylaws to govern the execution, revocation, and use of proxies. Corp C §212(b)(3). Although under Corp C §604, proxies distributed to ten or more shareholders of a corporation with shares held of record by 100 or more persons must allow the shareholder (a) to specify a choice between approval and disapproval of each matter intended to be acted on by the proxyholder, and (b) to withhold the shares from voting in an election of directors (see Corp C §604(a)–(b), the corporation's failure to comply with either of these requirements does not invalidate any corporate action taken but may be the basis for challenging proxies at a meeting, and the superior court may compel compliance at the suit of any shareholder. Corp C §604(c).

Proxy solicitation procedures are also subject to judicial scrutiny. See *Meyberg v Superior Court* (1942) 19 C2d 336, 121 P2d 685; *Ferry v San Diego Museum of Art* (1986) 180 CA3d 35, 225 CR 277; *Braude v Havenner* (1974) 38 CA3d 526, 113 CR 386. Certain proxy solicitations relating to corporate recapitalizations and reorganizations may be subject to provisions of the California Corporate Securities Law. See Corp C §25148, 10 Cal Code of Regs §260.140.60. See also 1 Marsh & Volk, PRACTICE UNDER THE CALIFORNIA SECURITIES LAWS §8.08[2] (rev ed).

Special forms and procedures are required if federal proxy regulations are applicable. See §3.30. Generally speaking, federal rules cover proxy solicitations by corporations whose stock is listed on a national exchange or publicly traded over-the-counter, if the total number of persons solicited is more than ten. See 2 MARSH'S CALIFORNIA CORPORATION LAW §11.25 (2d ed); 17 CFR

§240.14a–2(b)(1). Federal proxy regulation is beyond the scope of this chapter; for discussion see Loss, FUNDAMENTALS OF SECURITIES REGULATION chap 7D (2d ed 1987); 3 Sommer, SECURITIES LAW TECHNIQUES chap 51 (1985).

f. Voting Agreements and Voting Trusts

(1) Voting Agreements

§3.36   (a) General Rules

A group of shareholders may wish to make sure that all their shares are voted in the same way. Common arrangements for this purpose are voting agreements (or pooling agreements), in which the shareholders agree on how shares will be voted, and voting trusts, in which the shares are transferred to a trustee to be voted under a trust agreement. For voting trusts, see §3.38–3.42.

Voting agreements by shareholders of close corporations (and irrevocable proxies to effect such agreements) are provided for in Corp C §§706(a), 706(c), and 705(e)(5). Although it is not uncommon for irrevocable proxies and voting agreements to be included in the "corporate package" of close corporations, practitioners should be cautious about their blanket use.

The enforceability of pooling agreements (and of irrevocable proxies given under such agreements) in corporations other than statutory close corporations has been questioned. This issue is discussed in detail in 3 MARSH'S CALIFORNIA CORPORATION LAW §21.11 (2d ed) (concluding that "[h]ow the California courts will resolve these conflicting arguments is uncertain"); Jordan, *The Close Corporation Provisions of the New California General Corporation Law,* 23 UCLA L Rev 1094, 1130 (1976) (concluding at p 1138 that a "voting trust pursuant to [Corp C] section 706(b) . . . appears to be the only clearly valid pooling arrangement available to corporations other than qualified close corporations"); and Wang, *Pooling Agreements Under the New California General Corporation Law,* 23 UCLA L Rev 1171, 1188 (1976) ("careful examination of sections 705(e) and 706(d) indicates that all pooling agreements can be made self-executing through the use of irrevocable proxies. Therefore, section 706(a) is largely superfluous, and the limitation of its coverage to close corporations is ineffectual, anomalous, and misleading.")

The fact that shares are subject to a voting agreement and to an irrevocable proxy must be stated on the face of the share certificates, or on the reverse with a reference on the face. Corp C §§174, 418(a)(3). If this is not done, the agreement and the proxy will be unenforceable against a transferee of the shares who does not have actual knowledge of them. Corp C §§418(b), 705(f).

A voting agreement under Corp C §706(a) terminates if the corporation ceases to be a close corporation, except to the extent that it is enforceable apart from the statute. Corp C §706(a). An irrevocable proxy given under a voting agreement becomes revocable when the agreement terminates. Corp C §705(e).

§3.37　　　(b) Form: Agreement To Pool Votes

Form 3.37–1

[Name of corporation]
VOTING AGREEMENT

We, as shareholders of [name of corporation], **agree to grant to** [name of proxyholder], **on execution of this agreement, an irrevocable proxy in the form set forth as Exhibit _ _ _ to this agreement.**

[Add, if desired]

This agreement shall terminate when the shares described in that proxy have been voted for the purposes set forth in the proxy.

Dated: _ _ _ _ _ _

[Signatures of shareholders]
[Typed names and addresses]

Comment: This agreement is designed for shareholders of a statutory close corporation. See Corp C §706(a) for statutory authority and restrictions. Unlike the basic close corporation shareholders' agreement, to which all the shareholders must be parties (Corp C §186), a pooling agreement may be between any two or more shareholders. Corp C §706(a).

This simple form of agreement uses proxies as a means of effecting the pool; such proxies are authorized by Corp C §705(e)(5). The proxies will contain the significant substantive provisions. See §3.32 for a form of irrevocable proxy. The statute also provides for specific performance of pooling agreements and permits transfer of the shares to third parties with authority to vote them as provided in the agreement. Corp C §706(a). For possible problems in using such agreements in corporations other than statutory close corporations, see §3.36.

(2) Voting Trusts

§3.38 (a) General Rules

Voting trusts are authorized and regulated primarily by Corp C §706(b). They ordinarily are established by executing a voting trust agreement, transferring the shareholders' shares to the trustee, issuing voting trust certificates, and filing a duplicate of the voting trust agreement with the corporation's secretary. Corp C §706(b). For discussion of the effect of failing to transfer the shares to the trustee or failing to file the agreement with the secretary, see 2 MARSH'S CALIFORNIA CORPORATION LAW §§11.35–11.36 (2d ed).

Beneficial interests in voting trusts and voting trust certificates are securities for purposes of California securities regulation. Corp C §25019. Therefore the issuance of voting trust certificates must be qualified with the Commissioner of Corporations (Corp C §25110), unless the transaction is exempt under Corp C §25102(f) (no more than 35 beneficial owners in the trust), or unless some other exemption applies. See 10 Cal Code Regs §260.102.12; for discussion, see 2 Marsh §11.33. Once the trust certificates have been issued, further issuances resulting from stock splits, reverse stock splits, or stock dividends with respect to the underlying shares are exempt from the qualification requirement. Corp C §25105; 10 Cal Code Regs §260.105.9.

Voting trust certificates are also securities for purposes of federal securities regulation (Securities Act of 1933 §2(1), 15 USC §77b(1); Securities Exchange Act of 1934 §3(a)(10), 15 USC §78c(a)(10)), and therefore are subject to registration requirements and other regulations unless they fall within an exemption. See Securities Act of 1933 §3, 15 USC §77c; Securities Exchange Act of 1934 §3(a)(12), 15 USC §78c(a)(12). See also Loss, FUNDAMENTALS OF SECURITIES

REGULATION chap 3H (2d ed 1987); Gadsby, THE FEDERAL SECURITIES ACT OF 1934 §8.01(c) (rev ed).

If any beneficial owners reside outside California, the applicability of other state securities laws should also be reviewed.

Holders of voting trust certificates have rights similar to those of shareholders to bring derivative actions (Corp C §800(b)); to inspect the record of shareholders (Corp C §1600(c)) and the corporation's accounting books, records, and minutes (Corp C §1601); to bring an action for involuntary dissolution (Corp C §1800(e)); and to purchase other shareholders' shares to avoid dissolution (Corp C §2000(e).

A voting trust is limited to a maximum life of ten years, but this may be extended for additional ten-year periods during the last two years of the term. Duplicates of any extensions must be filed with the corporation's secretary. Corp C §706(b).

§3.39　　　(b) Form: Voting Trust Agreement

Form 3.39–1

[*Name of corporation*]
VOTING TRUST AGREEMENT

1. Introduction and Parties

This voting trust agreement (Agreement) is made as of [*date*] between and among [*names of shareholders*] (Shareholders; also Certificate Holders), who are owners of shares of stock of [*name of corporation*] (Corporation), and [*names of trustees*] (Trustees).

Comment: This is a sample form of agreement for shareholders who wish to pool their votes. For more detailed provisions, see 3 Ballantine & Sterling, CALIFORNIA CORPORATION LAWS Form 8.22 (4th ed); 3 MARSH'S CALIFORNIA CORPORATION LAW Form 87 (2d ed).

2. Exchange of Shares for Voting Trust Certificates

Simultaneously with execution of this Agreement, the Shareholders shall deliver to the Trustees properly endorsed certificates for the number of [*e.g., common*] shares of the Corporation shown opposite their respective names below (the shares). The Trustees shall cause the shares to be transferred

to them on the Corporation's books and [*upon qualification with the California Commissioner of Corporations*] **shall issue and deliver to each of the Shareholders a voting trust certificate, in the form shown in Exhibit A to this Agreement, for the number of shares transferred to the Trustees. The Trustees shall hold the shares transferred to them in trust, subject to the terms of this Agreement.**

Comment: If there are more than 35 beneficial owners of interests in the trust, qualification with the Commissioner of Corporations may be required. Federal securities regulations should also be considered. See §§1.66–1.71. A voting trust certificate may be incorporated in the agreement or attached as an exhibit. For form of voting trust certificate, see §3.41.

3. Trustees' Powers and Duties

(a) Voting of Shares

During the existence of this trust, the Trustees shall have the exclusive right to vote all shares transferred to them in person or by proxy at all shareholder meetings and in all proceedings in which the vote or consent of shareholders may be required or authorized, and shall have all the rights, privileges, and powers of shareholders except as otherwise provided in this Agreement.

Comment: Voting trustees are record holders of the shares held in trust and are entitled to vote the shares on all matters (Corp C §§702(a), 706(b)), unless their voting power is modified to exclude the right to vote on certain matters (*e.g.*, amendments to the articles, reorganizations, mergers, sale of assets) without the prior written consent or instructions of owners of a specified percentage (*e.g.*, majority, two thirds, all) of the shares subject to the trust agreement. The agreement may also provide that the trustees must vote in compliance with the owners' instructions on all matters.

(b) Number and Percentage Vote

The number of Trustees under this Agreement shall be [*e.g., three*]. The Trustees shall act by [*e.g., a majority*] vote in

exercising any powers or taking any action under this Agreement.

(c) Other Trustee Activities

The Trustees may also be parties to this Agreement as share owners holding voting trust certificates. Additionally, they may serve the Corporation as officers or directors or in any other capacity, and may receive compensation from the Corporation for such services.

(d) No Sale of Shares

The Trustees shall have no authority to sell or otherwise dispose of any shares transferred to them under this Agreement.

(e) Replacement or Removal of Trustees

In case of a Trustee's death, resignation, or inability to act, the remaining Trustees shall appoint a successor. If there are no incumbent Trustees, the owners of [*e.g., a majority/two thirds*] of shares subject to this Agreement shall elect successor Trustees to act under this Agreement.

Any Trustee may be removed from office by the affirmative vote of the owners of [*e.g., a majority/two thirds*] of the shares subject to this Agreement.

Comment: The agreement may also provide for appointment of successor trustees by the share owners.

(f) Compensation

The Trustees shall receive [*e.g., no compensation for their services except for reimbursement, by the certificate holders, of expenses incurred in the administration of their duties*].

Comment: Trustees may also be authorized to receive compensation for their services.

(g) Trustees' Liability

The Trustees, and each of them, shall not be liable for any error of judgment or mistake of fact or law, or for any act or omission made in good faith in connection with their powers and duties under this Agreement, except for each Trustee's own willful misconduct or gross negligence. No Trustee shall be liable for the acts or omissions of any other Trustee or Trustees or for the acts or omissions of any employee or agent of any other Trustee or Trustees. The Trustees, and each of them, shall not be liable in acting on any notice, consent, certificate, instruction, or other paper or document or signature believed by them to be genuine and to have been signed by the proper party or parties. The Trustees may consult with legal counsel, and any of their acts or omissions made in good faith in accordance with the opinion of legal counsel shall be binding and conclusive on the parties to this Agreement.

4. Termination

This Agreement shall terminate [*e.g., ten*] years after the date of this Agreement or on any later date to which the term is extended, as provided below, without notice by or to, or action on the part of, the Trustees or the Certificate Holders.

[*Add, if desired*]

This Agreement may be terminated at an earlier date by the vote or written consent of Certificate Holders representing [*e.g., a majority/two thirds*] of the shares subject to this Agreement, upon [*e.g., ten*] days' written notice to the Trustees.

[*Continue*]

As soon as practicable after termination of this Agreement, the Trustees shall re-deliver share certificates representing the appropriate number of shares, properly endorsed for transfer, to the respective Certificate Holders of record, and the Certificate Holders shall surrender to the Trustees their voting trust certificates properly endorsed, together with payment of sums sufficient to cover any taxes and other expenses relating to the transfer or delivery of the share certificates.

If any Certificate Holder refuses to surrender voting trust certificates in exchange for shares, or cannot be located, the Trustees may deliver the share certificates due that Certificate Holder to any bank or trust company in California for the benefit of the person or persons entitled thereto, and thereupon shall be fully discharged with respect to those share certificates.

Comment: The term for a voting trust agreement or an extension may not exceed ten years. See Corp C §706(b). The optional second sentence should not be used if an irrevocable trust is desired. Termination may also be authorized by a vote of the trustees, either by a majority or by some other specified percentage.

5. Extension of Agreement

The term of this Agreement, as prescribed in Paragraph 4, may be extended from the original termination date of this Agreement or from the termination date as last extended in accordance with this paragraph, provided that within two years before the date as originally fixed or as last extended, one or more Certificate Holders, by written agreement, and with the Trustees' written consent, extend the term of this Agreement with respect to their shares for an additional term not to exceed ten years from the expiration date then in effect.

In the event of extension, duplicate copies of this Agreement and of the extension agreement shall be filed with the secretary of the Corporation and shall be open for inspection on the same conditions as the Corporation's record of shareholders.

6. Withdrawal of Shares

Any Certificate Holder may withdraw his or her shares from this Agreement at any time upon giving the Trustees [*e.g., 30*] days' written notice before the effective date of withdrawal and surrendering his or her voting trust certificates to the Trustees. The Trustees shall deliver the withdrawn shares properly endorsed for transfer as in the case of termination under Paragraph 4 above.

7. Notices, Dividends, and Distributions

The Trustees shall promptly forward copies of all notices, reports, statements, and other communications received from the Corporation to the Certificate Holders, indicating the date of receipt.

The Trustees shall promptly distribute all dividends and other distributions received from the Corporation to the Certificate Holders in proportion to their respective interests.

If any dividend or stock split consists of additional shares having voting rights, the Trustees shall hold these shares in trust subject to the terms of this Agreement, and shall issue new voting trust certificates, representing the additional shares, to the Certificate Holders in proportion to their respective interests.

Dated: _ _ _ _ _ _

TRUSTEES

[Signatures of trustees]
[Typed names and addresses]

CERTIFICATE HOLDERS

**Number of Shares
Deposited**

[Signatures of certificate holders]   _ _ _ _
[Typed names and addresses]

§3.40 (c) Additional Provisions

The voting trust agreement set forth in §3.39 may contain additional provisions, including:

- Meetings of certificate holders. See, *e.g.,* 3 Ballantine & Sterling, CALIFORNIA CORPORATION LAWS Form 8.22, Para 5(a) (4th ed).
- Deposit of additional shares. See, *e.g.,* 3 MARSH'S CALIFORNIA CORPORATION LAW Appendix B, Form 87, Para 3 (2d ed).
- Replacement of certificates. See, *e.g.,* 3 Ballantine & Sterling, Form 8.22, Para 1(c).
- Transferability of certificates. See, *e.g.,* 3 Marsh, Form 87 Paras 3 and 4. However, a provision authorizing transfer of certificates may inadvertently raise a public offering problem. See 2 Marsh §§11.33, 11.37.
- Investment representations. Representations by the beneficial owners that interests are acquired for the beneficial owners' own accounts and not with a view to distribution or resale may be included to comply with federal and state securities laws. See, *e.g.,* 1 Marsh & Volk, PRACTICE UNDER THE CALIFORNIA SECURITIES LAWS §5.16 (rev ed).

- Miscellaneous. Arbitration provision; attorneys' fee clause; notices.

§3.41   (d) Form: Voting Trust Certificate

Form 3.41–1

EXHIBIT A

[*Name of corporation*]
VOTING TRUST CERTIFICATE

Certificate No. _ _ _   **_ _ _ Shares**

This certifies that the undersigned Trustees have received certificates for shares [*e.g., of common stock*] **of** [*name of corporation*] **(Corporation) from** [*name of shareholder*] **(Shareholder), and that the Trustees hold these shares subject to the terms and conditions of a voting trust agreement (the Agreement) dated** [*date*], **between** [*names of shareholders*] **(Shareholders; also Certificate Holders), each of whom owns shares of stock in the Corporation, and** [*names of trustees*] **(Trustees). This certificate is Exhibit A to the Agreement. A copy of the Agreement is on file with the secretary of the Corporation.**

1. During the term of the Agreement, the Trustees shall be entitled to vote the shares covered by this certificate and to exercise only those rights, privileges, and powers of shareholders as provided in the Agreement.

2. During the term of the Agreement, the Shareholders shall be entitled to all the benefits of the Agreement, and shall be subject to the terms and conditions arising from the deposit of their shares with the Trustees in accordance with the Agreement.

[*Add, if appropriate*]

3. This certificate is assignable, and a new certificate shall be issued only upon surrender to the Trustees of this certificate properly endorsed.

Comment: See §3.38 and Comment to numbered paragraph 2 in Form 3.39–1.

[Continue]

4. Upon termination of the Agreement, and subject to the terms and conditions of the Agreement, the Trustees shall deliver to the Certificate Holders properly endorsed share certificates representing the number of shares owned by each Certificate Holder, and the Certificate Holders shall surrender their voting trust certificates to the Trustees, properly endorsed, together with payment of a sum sufficient to cover any taxes and other expenses relating to the transfer or delivery of the share certificates.

Dated: _ _ _ _ _ _

TRUSTEES

[Signatures of trustees]
[Typed names and addresses]

§3.42   (e) Form: Extension Agreement

Form 3.42–1

[Name of corporation]
VOTING TRUST EXTENSION AGREEMENT

1. Introduction and Parties

This agreement (Extension Agreement) is made as of *[date]* between and among *[names of voting trust certificate holders]* (Certificate Holders), the holders of voting trust certificates under a voting trust agreement (Voting Trust Agreement) dated *[date]*, and *[names of trustees]* (Trustees), relating to certain shares of stock of *[name of corporation]* (Corporation).

2. Extension of Term of Voting Trust Agreement

The Certificate Holders agree to extend the term of the Voting Trust Agreement for an additional period of *[e.g., ten years]* with respect to the number of shares of the Corporation shown opposite each Certificate Holder's name below.

3. Amendment to Agreement and Certificate

The Voting Trust Agreement and the voting trust certificate

attached to it as Exhibit A are deemed amended to reflect this extension of the term of the Voting Trust Agreement.

4. Delivery of Share Certificates Not Covered by Extension Agreement

The Trustees shall deliver to each Certificate Holder any shares in the Corporation presently on deposit with the Trustees as to which the Voting Trust Agreement is not extended, upon the Certificate Holder's surrender to the Trustees of the voting trust certificate representing those shares, properly endorsed, together with payment of a sum sufficient to cover any taxes and expenses relating to the Trustees' transfer or delivery of the shares.

5. Legend on Voting Trust Certificates

The Certificate Holders to whom this extension is applicable shall make their certificates available to the Trustees for the endorsement thereon of the following legend:

"BY EXTENSION AGREEMENT DATED [date], THE VOTING TRUST AGREEMENT REFERRED TO IN THIS VOTING TRUST CERTIFICATE WAS EXTENDED FOR AN ADDITIONAL TERM OF _ _ _ YEARS, ENDING ON [date]."

6. Filing With Corporation Secretary

The Trustees shall, as soon as practicable, file a duplicate of this Extension Agreement with the secretary of the Corporation.

Dated: _ _ _ _ _ _ _

CERTIFICATE HOLDERS

_____
[Signature]

_____
[Address]

_ _ _ _ _ _ _ _ _ _ _ _ _
[number of shares
covered by extension
agreement]

[*Signature*]

[*Address*]   _ _ _ _ _ _ _ _ _ _ _ _ _
                                   [*number of shares
                                   covered by extension
                                   agreement*]

CONSENT OF TRUSTEES

The undersigned, as the Trustees under the Voting Trust Agreement referred to in this Extension Agreement, consent to this Extension Agreement.

Dated: _ _ _ _ _ _

                        [*Signatures of trustees*]
                        [*Typed names and addresses*]

§3.43   2. Shareholders' Consent to Action Without Meeting

Unless otherwise provided in the articles, any action that could be taken at a shareholders' meeting (annual or special) may be taken without a meeting and without prior notice, if written consent of the shareholders is obtained under rules set forth in Corp C §603. The consent, setting forth the action so taken, must be signed by the holders of outstanding shares having not less than the minimum number of votes that would be necessary to authorize or take that action at a meeting at which all shares entitled to vote on that matter were present and voted. Corp C §603(a).

Written consents may be revoked by a writing received by the corporation before sufficient consents have been received to authorize the action. Corp C §603(c).

Unless the consents of all shareholders entitled to vote have been solicited in writing, notice must be given to the shareholders as follows:

(1) As to matters approved pursuant to Corp C §310 (transactions between the corporation and directors or between corporations having interrelated directors), Corp C §317 (indemnification of corporate agents), Corp C §1201 (corporate reorganization), or Corp C §2007 (approval of a plan of distribution on dissolution of the corporation), notice must be given at least ten days before the consummation

of the action authorized by the approval, if the approval was obtained without a meeting by less than unanimous written consent (Corp C §603(b)(1)); and

(2) Prompt notice must be given of the taking of any other corporate action approved by shareholders without a meeting by less than unanimous written consent, to those shareholders entitled to vote who have not consented in writing (Corp C §603(b)(2)).

The election of directors by written consent requires the unanimous written consent of all shares entitled to vote on this matter (Corp C §603(d)), except that elections by written consent to fill a vacancy (unless the vacancy was created by removal) require only the consent of a majority of the outstanding shares entitled to vote (Corp C §305(b)).

NOTE: As indicated in this section, provisions in the articles, but not the bylaws, may limit the actions that shareholders may take by written consent. Minority shareholders may find little benefit in receiving ten days' notice of the effective date of some major action taken by written consent of the majority shareholders. Any minority shareholder with a substantial equity investment should consider insisting on a provision in the articles of incorporation requiring that certain (or all) actions of the shareholders be taken at a shareholders' meeting or, if such actions are to be taken by written consent, that a sufficiently high percentage of consenting shareholders is required to assure that the minority shareholders will be needed for approval.

D. Property Rights of Shareholders

§3.44   1. Right To Receive Dividends and Other Distributions

One of the most important rights of shareholders is the right to receive dividends and other distributions. For discussion, see chap 4.

§3.45   2. Right To Transfer; Transfer Restrictions

The right to transfer or hypothecate shares is one of the principal property rights of shareholders. However, reasonable restrictions on this right may be stated in the articles or bylaws. Corp C §§204(b),

212(b)(1). Such restrictions are not binding on shares issued before the restriction was adopted, unless the holders of those shares voted in favor of the restriction or agreed to it in writing. Corp C §204(b).

Commonly, a transfer restriction is designed to protect shareholders against the purchase of shares by an outsider, by giving the other shareholders or the corporation a right of first refusal in connection with any proposed sale. See *Yeng Sue Chow v Levi Strauss & Co.* (1975) 49 CA3d 315, 122 CR 816. See also 1 MARSH'S CALIFORNIA CORPORATION LAW §3.40 (2d ed); and BUSINESS BUY-OUT AGREEMENTS chap 1 (Cal CEB 1976). Transfer restrictions may also be used to protect the corporation's special status (as, *e.g.,* a close corporation or an S corporation) or to comply with securities law requirements, by limiting the number or type of shareholders.

Transfer restrictions must be stated on the certificate representing the shares; otherwise they are ineffective against transferees without actual knowledge of the restrictions. Corp C §418(b).

§3.46   3. Shares With Special Rights

If so provided in the articles, or, in certain instances, in the bylaws (see table in ORGANIZING CORPORATIONS IN CALIFORNIA §2.20 (2d ed Cal CEB 1983)) or in a certificate of determination filed with the Secretary of State after filing the articles (Corp C §§202(e), 401; see ORGANIZING CORPS §2.24), a corporation may issue classes or series of shares with special rights. See, *e.g.,* Corp C §§202(e)(3), 400–401 (preferences and privileges); Corp C §402 (redeemable shares); Corp C §403 (convertible shares); Corp C §406 (preemptive rights). For discussion, see ORGANIZING CORPS §§2.24–2.31; FINANCING CALIFORNIA BUSINESSES §§4.4–4.19 (Cal CEB 1976).

§3.47   a. Redeemable Shares

A corporation's articles may provide for one or more classes or series of shares that are redeemable, in whole or in part, (1) at the option of the corporation or (2) on the happening of one or more specified events (Corp C §402(a)); and as to preferred shares, the articles may additionally provide for redemption (3) at the option of the holder or (4) upon the majority vote of the outstanding shares of the class or series to be redeemed. Corp C §402(a). Redemption rights are exercisable in accordance with the enabling provisions of the corporation's articles or certificate of determination, or the director's resolutions establishing the rights of the class of preferred stock. See Corp C §§401–402; FINANCING CALIFORNIA BUSINESSES §4.17 (Cal CEB 1976); 1 MARSH'S CALIFORNIA CORPORATION LAW §5.8 (2d ed).

§3.48   b. Convertible Shares

If so provided in the articles, a corporation may issue convertible shares which, within a specified time or upon the happening of a specified event and upon terms and conditions stated in the articles, may be converted into shares of another class or series (1) at the option of the holder, (2) automatically upon the majority vote of the outstanding shares of the class or series to be converted, or (3) automatically upon the happening of one or more specified events. Corp C §403(a). Unless otherwise provided in the articles, a corporation may issue its debt securities convertible into other debt securities or into shares of the corporation, within a specified time or upon the happening of a specified event and upon such terms and conditions as are fixed by the board. Corp C §403(b); see 1 MARSH'S CALIFORNIA CORPORATION LAW §§5.20, 5.22 (2d ed).

NOTE: Convertible securities are a traditional way of allowing the holders of fixed-income securities (*i.e.,* debentures or preferred stock) to participate in the corporation's capital appreciation by converting their securities to another form of security, such as common stock. For example, holders of convertible preferred stock with preferential rights as to dividends and liquidation but a fixed par value, might be allowed to convert their holdings to common stock, at a ratio based on a fixed price, a formula tied to the market price of the common stock, or some other relevant factor. Holders of debentures or other debt securities could be treated similarly. See 1 MARSH'S CALIFORNIA CORPORATION LAW §5.20 (2d ed); 1 Ballantine & Sterling, CALIFORNIA CORPORATION LAWS §127.03[7] (4th ed). The terms of conversion rights are often heavily negotiated, and a clear understanding of the corporation's value is needed.

§3.49   c. Preemptive Rights

Preemptive rights are a device for permitting the existing

shareholders to maintain their respective equity interests in the corporation by entitling them to purchase a percentage of any subsequent stock issues equal to the shareholder's present holdings. Any provision establishing preemptive rights is effective only if it is contained in the articles of incorporation. Corp C §204(a)(2). Such provisions should be very carefully drafted. The drafter should consider making exceptions for situations in which the corporation might need to issue its securities to others, or situations in which the consideration will be other than cash or debt—*e.g.*, as stock options (to employees or in connection with a merger), stock issued for property or assets, or stock issued upon conversion of convertible securities. See 3 Ballantine & Sterling, CALIFORNIA CORPORATION LAWS Forms 4.33 and 4.44 (4th ed); 3 MARSH'S CALIFORNIA CORPORATION LAW Form 14 (2d ed).

Preemptive rights were more common in the past, when privately held corporations were the norm and additional equity financing commonly came from existing shareholders. These situations no longer predominate. Comparable protection and greater flexibility can probably be achieved through other means, *e.g.*, requiring a supermajority vote on all stock issuances (a provision which must be contained in the articles of incorporation to be effective; see Corp C §204(a)(5)); voting agreements (see §§3.36–3.37); or the establishment of a close corporation (see §§1.91–1.99).

For a more detailed discussion of preemptive rights and procedures, see 1 Ballantine & Sterling §127.03[8]; 1 Marsh §5.24.

§3.50   E. Shareholders' Suits

Recent changes in the Corporations Code permit corporations to limit their directors' liability to the corporation and its shareholders for the breach of their duties as directors, if an appropriate provision is included in the corporation's articles or added by an amendment approved by the shareholders. Corp C §204(a)(10). A corporation may likewise provide for indemnification of its agents (*i.e.*, directors, officers, and employees; see Corp C §317) for monetary damages they might incur from the breach of their duties. Corp C §204(a)(11). Such provisions, if adopted, would limit the rights of shareholders to bring suit against management of the corporation or render such suits less effective because of corporate indemnification of the individual defendants. It should be noted, however, that the statute sets out seven specific categories of acts or omissions from which the directors or agents cannot be protected or indemnified. Corp C §204(a)(10)–(11); see §§2.57–2.61.

In evaluating the rights of shareholders against officers, directors, or other agents of a corporation, the attorney should be familiar with the materials on directors' and officers' liability contained in chap 2. See also §§3.51–3.53.

§3.51   1. Individual Suits by Shareholders

The general rule is that an individual shareholder may not maintain a suit on the shareholder's own behalf alleging that the defendant's wrongful conduct decreased the value of the shareholder's stock and that of other shareholders. See *Sutter v General Petroleum Corp.* (1946) 28 C2d 525, 170 P2d 898. The theory is that when a shareholder invests in a corporation, the shareholder's individual identity is submerged in the corporate entity, and the corporation is entitled to control and manage the investment for the common benefit of all the shareholders. Thus, generally speaking, actions based on the misfeasance or negligence of a corporation's management and resulting in a diminution of the corporate assets are derivative (see §3.52) rather than individual, because the alleged mismanagement injures the corporation directly and only consequentially injures the shareholders. *O'Hare v Marine Elec. Co.* (1964) 229 CA2d 33, 39 CR 799.

For a shareholder to have a personal right of action based on share ownership (and thus avoid the requirements of a derivative suit), the plaintiff must show that the wrongdoer violated some special duty owed to the plaintiff, with a resulting injury peculiar to the plaintiff, not falling alike on all shareholders. See *Truestone, Inc. v Travelers Ins. Co.* (1976) 55 CA3d 165, 127 CR 386.

On the other hand, a shareholder's complaint for vindication of individual rights is not rendered wholly derivative merely because it includes one or more causes of action that could also be maintained by the corporation. However, some individual wrong to the shareholder must appear. *Hagan v Superior Court* (1960) 53 C2d 498, 2 CR 288. That wrong need not be unique to that plaintiff. If the injury is not merely incidental to an injury to the corporation, an individual cause of action exists even though it also affects other shareholders. *Jones v H. F. Ahmanson & Co.* (1969) 1 C3d 93, 107,

81 CR 592, 598. (See discussion of class actions at §3.53; see also discussion of minority rights against the majority at §3.59.)

For examples of cases in which individual shareholders were allowed to sue in their individual capacity as shareholders rather than on behalf of the corporation, see *Smith v Tele-Communication, Inc.* (1982) 134 CA3d 338, 184 CR 571 (sole minority shareholder of subsidiary corporation could sue its directors and the parent corporation in his individual capacity where, after sale of all the assets of the subsidiary, parent and subsidiary filed consolidated tax return allocating all tax benefits from the sale to the parent, thereby depriving plaintiff of a portion of his distributive share); *Crain v Electronic Memories & Magnetics Corp.* (1975) 50 CA3d 509, 123 CR 419 (founding minority shareholders could sue as individuals where it was alleged that acts of the majority shareholder and its agent had deprived plaintiffs of their ownership interests without any compensation whatever); *Low v Wheeler* (1962) 207 CA2d 477, 24 CR 538 (minority shareholder was not told of a higher offer for shares made to gain control of the corporation and thus received substantially less for his shares); *Campbell v Clark* (1958) 159 CA2d 439, 324 P2d 55 (plaintiff was fraudulently induced to sell her interest in a corporation, suffering financial injury); *Sutter v General Petroleum Corp.* (1946) 28 C2d 525, 170 P2d 898 (plaintiff was fraudulently induced to abandon his own oil developments and invest in a corporation whose assets became worthless). See also 2 MARSH'S CALIFORNIA CORPORATIONS LAW §14.21 (2d ed); 1A Ballantine & Sterling, CALIFORNIA CORPORATION LAWS §291.04[1] (4th ed); 12B Fletcher, CYCLOPEDIA OF THE LAW OF PRIVATE CORPORATIONS §§5910–5921 (rev ed 1984).

§3.52 2. Derivative Suits

As stated by the California Supreme Court in *Jones v H. F. Ahmanson & Co.* (1969) 1 C3d 93, 107, 81 CR 592, 598:

> A stockholder's derivative suit is brought to enforce a cause of action which the corporation itself possesses against some third party, a suit to recompense the corporation for injuries which it has suffered as a result of the acts of third parties. The management owes to the stockholders a duty to take proper steps to enforce all claims which the corporation may have. When it fails to perform this duty, the stockholders have a right

to do so. Thus, although the corporation is made a defendant in a derivative suit, the corporation nevertheless is the real plaintiff and it alone benefits from the decree; the stockholders derive no benefit therefrom except the indirect benefit resulting from a realization upon the corporation's assets. The stockholder's individual suit, on the other hand, is a suit to enforce a right against the corporation which the stockholder possesses as an individual.

A shareholder may bring a derivative suit on a corporation's behalf when the directors fail or refuse to act to enforce the corporation's rights. Corp C §800(b)(2). The shareholder is the nominal plaintiff; the corporation is the real party in interest and an indispensable party. See Corp C §800; *Gagnon Co. v Nevada Desert Inn* (1955) 45 C2d 448, 289 P2d 466. As a practical matter, corporate management, directors, and, in certain cases, majority shareholders are frequently named defendants in derivative suits. A shareholder who brings a derivative suit on behalf of the corporation assumes a fiduciary duty towards those on whose behalf the shareholder is suing, and one who assumes such a fiduciary role may not abandon it for personal aggrandizement (*i.e.,* by settling). *Heckmann v Ahmanson* (1985) 168 CA3d 119, 214 CR 177.

In order to bring a derivative suit, two conditions must be met:

"Contemporaneous ownership" requirement. Subject to several exceptions, the plaintiff must allege standing as a record or beneficial shareholder or as the holder of voting trust certificates at the time of the action or transaction alleged to have damaged the plaintiff. Corp C §800(b)(1).

A shareholder who has met the contemporaneous ownership requirement of Corp C §800(b)(1) for shareholder derivative suits has standing to proceed with the suit despite involuntary loss of shareholder status resulting from a merger of the defendant corporation. *Gaillard v Natomas Co.* (1985) 173 CA3d 410, 219 CR 74.

"Demand" requirement. The plaintiff must allege the efforts made to cause the board to bring the suit that plaintiff is bringing, or the reasons for not making that effort ("excuse"), and must allege further that the corporation or the board has been informed in writing of the facts of each cause of action against each defendant or that the plaintiff has delivered to the corporation or the board a true copy of the complaint that has been filed. These allegations must be made "with particularity." Corp C §800(b)(2).

Security Bond. The defendant(s) may move that a security bond be required of the plaintiff, on either of the following grounds: (1) that there is no reasonable possibility that the continuation of the lawsuit will benefit the corporation or its shareholders (Corp C §800(c)(1)), or (2) that the moving party, if other than the corporation, did not participate in the transaction complained of in any capacity (Corp C §800(c)(2)). The filing of a motion for a bond stays the proceedings until ten days after the motion has been disposed of. Corp C §800(f). Because of this stay in proceedings and the expense of the bond to the plaintiff, it can be expected that in most derivative suits, if not all, attorneys for the defense will file a motion for a bond. For further discussion, see 1A Ballantine & Sterling, CALIFORNIA CORPORATION LAWS §§293.01–293.09 (4th ed); 2 MARSH'S CALIFORNIA CORPORATION LAW §24.33 (2d ed).

Business Judgment Rule. In a derivative suit, the plaintiff must at the outset overcome the presumption that a decision of the board of directors (or a duly appointed committee acting on its behalf) to dismiss the suit was made on an informed basis, in good faith, and in the belief that the decision was in the corporation's best interest. See Corp C §§309, 311. The business judgment rule creates a presumption that the directors' decisions are based on sound business judgment, and the plaintiff in a derivative suit must rebut this presumption by showing fraud, bad faith, or gross overreaching on the part of the board. *Eldridge v Tymshare* (1986) 186 CA3d 767, 230 CR 815. Although the California Supreme Court has not ruled directly on this issue, the Ninth Circuit, seeking to apply California law, has followed the "business judgment" approach. See *Gaines v Haughton* (9th Cir 1981) 645 F2d 761; *Greenspun v Del E. Webb Corp.* (9th Cir 1980) 634 F2d 1204; *Lewis v Anderson* (9th Cir 1979) 615 F2d 778; *In re Bankamerica Securities Litigation* (1986) 636 F Supp 419. For an alternative approach (the "structural bias" approach), see *Zapata Corp. v Maldonado* (Del 1981) 430 A2d 779, in which the Delaware Supreme Court held that if disinterested directors decide that a derivate suit is contrary to a corporation's best interests and move to dismiss it, the court will apply its own "independent business judgment," evaluating the director's good faith and examining the result in light of the shareholders' interests and public policy. For discussion, see Yagemann, *The Business Judgment Rule and Shareholders' Suits,*

6 Cal Lawyer No. 4 p 25 (April 1986); 1A Ballantine & Sterling §292.05; 2 Marsh §14.34.

Exculpation of Directors; Indemnification of Agents. Derivative suits for breach of a director's duties to the corporation and its shareholders may be limited by provisions in the corporation's articles. See Corp C §§204(a)(10), 204.5. In addition, a corporation has power to indemnify its "agents," as that term is defined in Corp C §317(a), against liability (Corp C §317), and in certain instances the articles may authorize indemnification in excess of that specified in Corp C §317. Corp C §204(a)(11). See discussion at §3.50. These provisions are complex, and the attorney will need to review the law, the corporation's articles and bylaws, and any indemnity agreements entered into by the corporation and its agents to determine their effect, if any, on the plaintiff's cause of action.

Further References. Derivative suits have many other special aspects and also share many of the problems common to corporate litigation generally. For more detailed discussion, see 1A Ballantine & Sterling §§290–294; 2 Marsh §§14.20–14.37; 9 Witkin, SUMMARY OF CALIFORNIA LAW, *Corporations* §§179–188 (9th ed 1989). See also CALIFORNIA ATTORNEY'S DAMAGES GUIDE chap 5 (Cal CEB 1974).

§3.53   3. Class Actions

Plaintiff's cause of action in a class action derives from the defendant's violation of a duty owed directly to the plaintiff class members, *i.e.,* the shareholders, rather than a duty owed to the corporation as in a derivative suit (see §3.52). Although developed mainly in the federal courts under Rule 23 of the Federal Rules of Civil Procedure, class actions are authorized in California by CCP §382, which provides that "when the question is one of a common or general interest, of many persons, or when the parties are numerous, and it is impracticable to bring them all before the court, one or more may sue or defend for the benefit of all."

A class action on behalf of injured shareholders is not an alternative to a derivative action; ordinarily the two are mutually exclusive. However, if the defendant has also breached a duty to the corporation, a derivative cause of action on the corporation's behalf may be available as well.

A detailed treatment of class actions, either generally or in the corporate context, is beyond the scope of this chapter. For discussion of class actions generally, see 4 Witkin, CALIFORNIA PROCEDURE, *Pleading* §§193–237 (3d ed 1985); for discussion of shareholder class actions, see 2 MARSH'S CALIFORNIA CORPORATION LAW §14.41 (2d ed).

II. SHAREHOLDERS' LIABILITIES AND OBLIGATIONS

A. Liability Under the Alter Ego Doctrine

§3.54 **1. When Is Doctrine Invoked?**

In General. Under normal circumstances, the liability of shareholders is limited to their investment in the corporation. This protection from personal liability may be lost, however, if the courts find a basis for invoking the alter ego doctrine. Under this doctrine, if it would be inequitable not to do so, the courts may disregard the legal fiction of a corporation's separate existence distinct from that of its shareholders, and "pierce the corporate veil," thus exposing the shareholders to personal liability for corporate debts and obligations. See generally 1A Ballantine & Sterling, CALIFORNIA CORPORATION LAWS §§295–300 (4th ed); 2 MARSH'S CALIFORNIA CORPORATION LAW §§15.16–15.26 (2d ed); 9 Witkin, SUMMARY OF CALIFORNIA LAW, *Corporations* §§12–23 (9th ed 1989).

Reasons for Invoking the Doctrine. A common reason for invoking the alter ego doctrine is that failure to do so would work an injustice on the corporation's creditors or other third parties. In other words, the shareholders are attempting to use the corporation as a shield against liabilities that would otherwise inure to them personally. See, *e.g., Minton v Caveney* (1961) 56 C2d 576, 15 CR 641 (tort claims); *Minifie v Rowley* (1921) 187 C 481, 202 P 673) (contractual obligations); *People v Clauson* (1964) 231 CA2d 374, 41 CR 691 (tax liabilities). See also Denvir & Freshman, *Preserving the Corporate Shield Against Individual Liability,* 1 CEB Cal Bus L Practitioner 145 (Fall 1986), and cases cited therein; *Alter-ego liability—Shareholder can be held liable for corporation's tax under alter-ego theory,* 8 CEB Cal Bus L Rep 109 (Dec. 1986).

Two-Pronged Test. As stated by the California Supreme Court, "[T]he two requirements for application of this doctrine are (1) that there be such unity of interest and ownership that the separate personalities of the corporation and the individual no longer exist and (2) that, if the acts are treated as those of the corporation alone, an inequitable result will follow." *Automotriz del Golfo de California v Resnick* (1957) 47 C2d 792, 796, 306 P2d 1, 3. See *Nilsson v Louisiana Hydrolec* (9th Cir 1988) 854 F2d 1538, 1544. Because the alter ego doctrine is equitable, the courts have applied it to many different fact situations in order to arrive at a result that the court believes to be fair, and its application varies according to the circumstances in each case. *Automotriz del Golfo de California v Resnick, supra*. While the doctrine does not depend on the presence of actual fraud, bad faith is an underlying consideration and is found in some form or another whenever the trial court has been justified in disregarding the corporate entity. *Associated Vendors, Inc. v Oakland Meat Co.* (1962) 210 CA2d 825, 838, 26 CR 806, 813.

Typical Fact Patterns. In *Associated Vendors*, the court reviewed and analyzed a number of cases in which the trial court had been upheld in disregarding the corporate entity, and produced the following list of fact patterns, which could serve the attorney as a checklist in determining whether the alter ego doctrine might be applicable (210 CA2d at 838, 26 CR at 813):

> [1] Commingling of funds and other assets, failure to segregate funds of the separate entities, and the unauthorized diversion of corporate funds or assets to other than corporate uses [citations omitted];
>
> [2] [T]he treatment by an individual of the assets of the corporation as his own [citations omitted];
>
> [3] [T]he failure to obtain authority to issue stock or to subscribe to or issue the same [citations omitted];
>
> [4] [T]he holding out by an individual that he is personally liable for the debts of the corporation [citations omitted];
>
> [5] [T]he failure to maintain minutes or adequate corporate records, and the confusion of the records of the separate entities [citations omitted];
>
> [6] [T]he identical equitable ownership in the two entities; the identification of the equitable owners thereof with the domination and control of the two entities; identification of the directors and officers of the two entities in the responsible supervision and management; sole ownership of all of the stock in a corporation by one individual or the members of a family [citations omitted];
>
> [7] [T]he use of the same office or business location; the employment of the same employees and/or attorney [citations omitted];

[8] [T]he failure to adequately capitalize a corporation; the total absence of corporate assets, and undercapitalization [citations omitted];

[9] [T]he use of a corporation as a mere shell, instrumentality or conduit for a single venture or the business of an individual or another corporation [citations omitted];

[10] [T]he concealment and misrepresentation of the identity of the responsible ownership, management and financial interests, or concealment of personal business activities [citations omitted];

[11] [T]he disregard of legal formalities and the failure to maintain arm's length relationships among related entities [citations omitted];

[12] [T]he diversion of assets from a corporation by or to a stockholder or other person or entity, to the detriment of creditors, or the manipulation of assets and liabilities between entities so as to concentrate the assets in one and the liabilities in another [citations omitted];

[13] [T]he contracting with another with intent to avoid performance by use of a corporate entity as a shield against personal liability, or the use of a corporation as a subterfuge of illegal transactions [citations omitted]; and

[14] [T]he formation and use of a corporation to transfer to it the existing liability of another person or entity [citations omitted].

Source and Adequacy of Corporate Funding. If the shareholders have made an equity investment or provided other sources of funding for the corporation's initial operations sufficient to permit it to operate as a viable business entity, the requirement as to adequacy of funding is ordinarily considered to have been met. The initial funding of the corporation need not be solely through equity investments. A key test is whether the corporation had funds available (either as equity or debt) for a sufficient period of time to enable it to begin its business and develop it to the point of economic viability. See 2 Marsh §15.22. Undercapitalization is commonly found in alter ego cases. See, *e.g., Minton v Cavaney, supra; Nillson v Louisiana Hydrolec, supra* (applying California law).

Segregation of Personal and Corporate Affairs. Shareholders should be advised to keep their personal business carefully segregated from the corporation's business. Personal funds or other assets of shareholders should never be commingled with the those of the corporation, and all dealings between shareholders and the corporation should be properly documented and at arm's length. See generally *Associated Vendors, Inc. v Oakland Meat Co., supra*; 2 Marsh §§15.20, 15.23. It is particularly important that corporate assets not be used by the shareholders for their personal benefit. See *Riddle v Leuschner* (1959) 51 C2d 574, 335 P2d 107; see also *Nilsson v Louisiana Hydrolec, supra.*

NOTE: Business creditors, including landlords, often require the principals of small "start-up" corporations to assume liability for or guarantee obligations. Clients should be told to expect these demands as a condition of receiving an extension of credit. This will often render the desired "limited liability" illusory. (Some creditors may also require the corporation to carry sufficient insurance to satisfy prospective tort claimants.)

Observation of Corporate Formalities. A common trap is neglecting corporate formalities. The sole or majority shareholder who runs his corporation "out of his back pocket," fails to hold meetings, and does not keep adequate books and records is especially vulnerable. If such a corporation becomes unable to meet its obligations promptly, creditors may discover and use this disregard of corporate formalities as a significant factor in invoking the alter ego doctrine and obtaining a judgment against the shareholder. See *Temple v Bodega Bay Fisheries* (1960) 180 CA2d 279, 4 CR 300; Denvir & Freshman, *Preserving the Corporate Shield Against Individual Liability,* 1 Cal Bus L Practitioner 145 (Fall 1986); 2 Marsh §15.19. See also §3.55 (sample letter by attorney to client containing checklist for avoiding alter ego liability).

Special Rule for Statutory Close Corporations. California Corporations Code §300(e) provides:

> The failure of a close corporation to observe corporate formalities relating to meetings of directors or shareholders in connection with the management of its affairs, pursuant to a [shareholders'] agreement authorized by [Corp C§300(b)], shall not be considered a factor tending to establish that the shareholders have personal liability for corporate obligations.

See Corp C §158 for definition of the statutory close corporation. For discussion, see Organizing Corporations in California §2.8 (2d ed Cal CEB 1983).

CAVEAT: The provision quoted above, Corp C §300(e), should not be read out of context as indicating that close corporation status can insulate shareholders from liability for corporate obligations. See Corp C §300(d), which provides that as long as the discretion or powers of the board in its management of corporate affairs is controlled by a shareholders' agreement, the liability for managerial acts that would otherwise be imposed on the directors is imposed instead on each shareholder who is a party to the agreement.

§3.55   2. Client's Checklist for Avoiding Alter Ego Liability

Form 3.55–1 (Checklist for New Corporations)

[*Law Firm's Letterhead*]

[*Name and address of client*]

Re: Corporate Do's and Don'ts

Dear Client:

The following list of "do"s and "do not"s is intended to serve as a checklist to help you maintain the limited liability of your shareholders, and to establish other good practices for doing business in the corporate form.

I. DO

A. Hold Meetings.

1. **Your annual shareholders' meeting is set in your bylaws (usually May 1st).**

2. **Your bylaws call for an annual board of directors' meeting to be held immediately afterwards.**

3. **Additional special meetings of the board should be held when matters of importance come up such as:**

This checklist was provided by Harvey W. Stein, Esq., of Oakland, California, who developed it as a form letter to send his "start-up" corporate clients.

    a. Entering into a lease of new premises;

    b. Entering into a substantial funding commitment;

    c. Entering into a substantial leasing commitment;

    d. Entering into any other significant contractual agreement;

    e. Changing an officer's salary;

    f. Filling a vacancy in the board or officer complement;

    g. Entering into a significant new venture;

    h. Considering the sale, in whole or in part, of the assets or the dissolution of the business.

B. Develop a Planning Mechanism.

    1. Review each year's activities during the final month of the fiscal year.

    2. Budget ahead for the longest period reasonably possible and review and analyze results at least semi-annually.

    3. Review the results of 1. and 2. with your CPA to ensure tax planning is properly emphasized.

    4. Begin to develop formal long range planning capacities beyond budgeting if not already in place.

C. Sign all contracts in the name of the corporation in substantially the following form:

[*Name of corporation*]

By _ _ _ _ _ _ _ _ _ _ _ _
       Title

D. Issue all orders in the name of the corporation.

E. Maintain corporate funds in a corporate account or accounts separate and apart from any other account.

II. DO NOT

• Do not fail to hold meetings.

• Do not commingle corporate and personal funds.

• Do not use corporate accounts for personal loans or other personal purposes.

• Do not negotiate loans, leases, etc., between the corporation and a principal other than on an arm's length basis.

• Do not use corporate assets continually for personal use.

• Do not fail to carry reasonable insurance on the corporation having due regard to the risks inherent in the corporation's business.

• Do not fail, in addition, to have a reasonable initial capital base in the corporation.

• Do not fail to set up a review mechanism as to decisions, so that all aspects of a proposed course of action will be considered.

Very truly yours,

[*Attorney's signature*]
[*Typed name*]

Comment: The above checklist is in the form of a letter to be given or mailed to new "start-up" corporate clients shortly after incorporation is complete. It is designed to provide the client with an easy reference to some of the pitfalls of a corporate form of business. While the primary thrust of the list of caveats is toward ensuring that no attempted breach of the corporate veil will be successful, certain of the points raised also entail suggestions which are more particularly aimed at developing good general business procedures.

§3.56 B. Liability of Shareholders for Further Payments or Assessments

Partly Paid Shares. Ordinarily, the shareholder must deliver the full agreed consideration before shares will be issued. See Corp C §§409(a)(1), 410(b). An exception to this rule authorizes issuance of partly paid shares subject to the corporation's call for payment of the balance of the consideration due. Corp C §409(d). Share certificates for partly paid shares must state the total consideration to be paid and the partial amount actually paid, and partly paid shares are entitled to receive dividends only in proportion to the percentage of consideration actually paid. Corp C §409(d). Consideration for shares issued in connection with an employee stock-purchase plan may be made payable in installments. Corp C §408(a); see 1 MARSH'S CALIFORNIA CORPORATION LAW §5.33 (2d ed).

Assessments on Shares. Shares are not assessable except as provided by Corp C §423 or some statute that is not part of the General Corporation Law. Corp C §423(a). However, if the articles expressly authorize the corporation or the board to assess shares, the board may in its discretion levy and collect assessments on any or all classes made subject to assessment by the articles, subject to any limitations contained therein. Corp C §423(a). This authority is in addition to the right of the corporation to recover the unpaid subscription price of shares or the remainder of the consideration to be paid for shares. Corp C §423(a). Any provision granting the corporation the power to levy assessments on the shares or any class of shares must be included in the articles to be effective (Corp C §204(a)(2)), except that statutory close corporations may include such a provision in the shareholders' agreement (see last paragraph of Corp C §204(a)). If shares are assessable, a statement to that effect must appear on the share certificate; otherwise, the liability may not be enforceable against a transferee of the shares without actual knowledge of the liability for assessment. Corp C §§418(a)(2), 418(b). For procedures to levy and enforce an assessment, see Corp C §423(b)–(n); 1 Marsh §§5.39–5.42. For amendments to the articles regarding share assessments, see §§5.14, 5.102, below.

C. Liability for Return of Improper Distributions

§3.57 1. Corporate Distributions Generally

A shareholder with knowledge of facts indicating the impropriety of a corporate distribution who receives such a distribution is liable to the corporation for the benefit of creditors and the other shareholders. Corp C §506; see 1 Ballantine & Sterling, CALIFORNIA CORPORATION LAWS §146.01 (4th ed). See also §4.58. For directors' liability for improper distributions see Corp C §316. See also §§2.32–2.34, 4.57; 1 Ballantine & Sterling §146.02; 2 MARSH'S CALIFORNIA CORPORATION LAW §§13.20–13.22 (2d ed).

Generally speaking, corporate distributions to shareholders must meet statutory retained earnings and asset requirements (Corp C §500); must not cause the corporation to be unable to meet its liabilities as they mature (Corp C §501); if made with respect to junior shares, must not adversely affect the cumulative dividend rights of senior shares (Corp C §503); and, if made upon liquidation with respect to junior shares, must not affect the liquidation preferences of senior shares (Corp C §502). See §§4.8–4.22.

It should be noted that under Corp C §506(a), the requirement is not that the shareholder be aware of the *actual impropriety* of the distribution, only that the shareholder have "knowledge of facts indicating the impropriety" of the distribution. In other words, to trigger shareholder liability for return of an improper distribution, the shareholder need know only the *facts* surrounding the distribution, not the *law* making such a distribution improper.

In making a decision as to the potential liability of shareholders when limitations on distributions have been violated, the practitioner must consider who is entitled to bring suit. Persons entitled to bring suit are limited to (1) creditors whose debts or claims arose prior to the time of the distribution who have not consented to the distribution, and (2) nonconsenting holders of preferred shares. Corp C §506(b).

§3.58 2. Repurchase or Redemption of Shares as Improper Distribution

Repurchase or redemption of its shares by a corporation or its subsidiary is by definition a distribution to shareholders (Corp C §166) and subject to the same restrictions applicable to other distributions. Corp C §§500–511. See §3.57; see also 2 MARSH'S CORPORATION LAW §§13.5–13.16 (2d ed). Restrictions on a corporation's repurchase of its own shares are designed to protect the corporation, its creditors, and innocent shareholders. *Tiedje v Aluminum Taper Milling Co.* (1956) 46 C2d 450, 455, 296 P2d 554, 557. Accordingly, shareholders with knowledge of facts indicating an improper repurchase of their shares may be liable as recipients of an improper distribution. Corp C §506(a).

Exceptions: Deceased or Disabled Shareholders. Redemption of a deceased or disabled shareholder's shares under a repurchase agreement between the corporation and the shareholder, using the proceeds of life insurance or disability insurance applicable to that shareholder in excess of the total amount of all premiums paid by the corporation for the insurance, is specifically exempted from the requirements of Corp C §§500–503. Corp C §§503.1–503.2.

Other Exceptions. The definition of "distribution to its shareholders" (Corp C §166) has been amended to exclude (1) the rescission of the issuance of shares in satisfaction of a final court judgment ordering the recision; (2) the rescission of the issuance of shares made upon a board determination that certain factors exist, and (3) the repurchase of shares issued pursuant to an employee stock purchase plan (Corp C §408), again based on the board's determination that certain factors exist. Corp C §166. See 2 Marsh §13.14B.

NOTE: In evaluating the corporation's ability to repurchase its shares and meet the tests required by Corp C §§500–511 (see §§4.8–4.16), the attorney should consider the time at which payments will be made—particularly if payments are to be made over a period of time, or if payment is made through the issuance of a non-negotiable promissory note. The statutory requirements are applied at the time that the consideration is actually transferred from the corporation to the shareholder, whether or not payment is made pursuant to an earlier contract or a promissory note. See 2 Marsh chap XII; 1A Ballantine & Sterling, CALIFORNIA CORPORATION LAWS chap 8 (4th ed).

§3.59   D. Majority's Duty to Minority Shareholders

Majority shareholders must use their power to control the

corporation for the benefit of all shareholders proportionately and for proper conduct of the corporation's business; they may not use that control to benefit themselves alone or to destroy the minority's interest. See, *e.g., Smith v Tele-Communication, Inc.* (1982) 134 CA3d 338, 184 CR 571 (consolidated group not entitled to all the tax benefits of a member corporation that has a minority shareholder); *Crain v Electronic Memories & Magnetics Corp.* (1975) 50 CA3d 509, 123 CR 419 (freeze-out of minority). In particular, when making any sale or transfer of a controlling block of shares, majority or controlling shareholders have a clear fiduciary obligation to act in good faith and with inherent fairness toward minority shareholders. *Jones v H. F. Ahmanson & Co.* (1969) 1 C3d 93, 81 CR 592; *Fisher v Pennsylvania Life Co.* (1977) 69 CA3d 506, 138 CR 181; *DeBaun v First W. Bank & Trust Co.* (1975) 46 CA3d 686, 120 CR 354; 1 Ballantine & Sterling, CALIFORNIA CORPORATION LAWS §102.03 (4th ed) 9 Witkin, SUMMARY OF CALIFORNIA LAW, *Corporations* §§189–190 (9th ed 1989).

The minority's recovery against majority shareholders who have breached their fiduciary duty depends on the facts of the transaction. See, *e.g., DeBaun v First W. Bank & Trust Co., supra* (46 CA3d at 699, 120 CR at 361); *Brown v Halbert* (1969) 271 CA2d 252, 272, 76 CR 781, 794; *Jones v H. F. Ahmanson & Co., supra* (1 C3d at 118, 81 CR at 606). See also 1 Ballantine & Sterling, CALIFORNIA CORPORATION LAWS §102.03[3] (4th ed). Majority shareholders cannot defend their actions with the assertion that the transaction has been disclosed and approved by the outstanding shares (Corp C §152), even though this may meet the technical requirements for approval of the transaction. *Remillard Brick Co. v Remillard-Dandini Co.* (1952) 109 CA2d 405, 241 P2d 66.

For an extensive discussion of controlling shareholders' obligations, see 1 MARSH'S CALIFORNIA CORPORATION LAW §§10.27–10.33 (2d ed). See also O'Neal & Thompson, O'NEAL'S OPPRESSION OF MINORITY SHAREHOLDERS (2d ed 1981); Dana & Toms, *The New General Corporation Law "Modernizes" a Management Control Fight,* 52 Cal SBJ 120 (1977).

§3.60   E. Disclosure Obligations When Buying or Selling Securities

It is unlawful for any person to offer, sell, or buy a security in

California by means of a written or oral communication that includes an untrue statement of a material fact or omits to state a material fact necessary to make the statements not misleading. Corp C §25401; see Corp C §2254. This rule parallels the federal rule. See Securities Exchange Act of 1934 §10(b) (15 USC §78b); SEC Rule 10b–5 (17 CFR §240.10b–5). See also FINANCING CALIFORNIA BUSINESSES §7.24 (Cal CEB 1976); CALIFORNIA ATTORNEY'S DAMAGES GUIDE §5.14 (Cal CEB 1974). Misrepresentations or nondisclosure of material facts may also give rise to other related claims, *e.g.,* market manipulation (Corp C §§25400, 25500) or "insider" violations (Corp C §§25402, 25502). See DAMAGES GUIDE §§5.16–5.17; 1 Marsh & Volk, PRACTICE UNDER THE CALIFORNIA SECURITIES LAWS §§14.04–14.05 (rev ed).

Litigation concerning the sale or purchase of securities and the obligation to disclose material information is an extensive and continually developing area requiring familiarity with the most current developments in federal and California case law and administrative materials. See, *e.g., Santa Fe Indus. v Green* (1977) 430 US 462. Coverage of this area is beyond the scope of this chapter. For discussion, see 1 Marsh & Volk chap 14; 2 Ballantine & Sterling, CALIFORNIA CORPORATION LAWS §148.02(3)(b) (4th ed); 3 Bromberg & Lowenfels, SECURITIES FRAUD: COMMODITIES FRAUD chap 8 (rev ed 1979).

F. Shareholder Liability After Dissolution of Corporation

§3.61   1. Liability for Known Claims Not Paid or Provided For

Under Corp C §316, directors who approve the distribution of assets to shareholders upon dissolution without paying or adequately providing for all known liabilities of the corporation on which claims were timely filed are liable to the corporation for the benefit of creditors (Corp C §316(a)(2)), and directors who are held liable are entitled to be made whole by the shareholders who received the improper distribution of assets (Corp C §316(f)(2)). Likewise, under Corp C §2009, assets distributed to shareholders without prior payment or adequate provision for payment of corporate debts and liabilities may be recovered by or in the name of the corporation or by its receiver, liquidator, or trustee in bankruptcy. Corp C §2009;

U.S. v Oil Resources, Inc. (9th Cir 1987) 817 F2d 1429. A shareholder's liability is limited to the value of the property distributed, and each shareholder has the right of ratable contribution from other shareholders similarly liable. Corp C §2009(c).

§3.62   2. Liability for Other Claims Asserted After Dissolution of the Corporation

Claims Arising Before Dissolution. After a corporation has been dissolved, its shareholders "may be sued in the corporate name of such corporation upon any cause of action against the corporation arising prior to its dissolution." Corp C §2011(a). See *Allen v Southland Plumbing, Inc.* (1988) 201 CA3d 60, 246 CR 860.

Claims Arising After Dissolution. Claims arising after dissolution are barred by Corp C §2011(a). *Pacific Scene, Inc. v Penasquitos, Inc.* (1988) 46 C3d 407, 250 CR 651 (disallowing recovery against dissolved corporation's former shareholders on an equitable "trust fund" theory.) In *Penasquitos*, the California Supreme Court stated that the legislature has generally occupied the field with respect to the remedies available against the former shareholders of dissolved corporations, thus preempting antecedent common law causes of action, and that, moreover, the trust fund theory conflicts with specific provisions of the Corporations Code. Federal cases applying California law have reached the same result. See, *e.g., U. S. v Oil Resources, Inc.* (9th Cir 1987) 817 F2d 1429; *Levin Metals Corp. v Parr-Richmond Terminal Co.* (ND Cal 1986) 631 F Supp 303. See also Annotation, *Liability of shareholders, directors, and officers where corporate business is continued after its dissolution.* 72 ALR4th (1989).

NOTE: When a California corporation is dissolved, one of the forms sent to the Secretary of State is an Assumption of Liabilities stating what person or entity is liable for the debts of the dissolved corporation. See §§7.35–7.43.

4

Dividends and Other Distributions

Doron M. Tisser

DORON M. TISSER, B.A., 1978, University of California (Los Angeles); J.D. 1981, Southwestern University; LL.M. (Taxation), 1982, New York University. Mr. Tisser practices in Woodland Hills.

I. INTRODUCTION

§4.1   A. Scope of Chapter

Among the responsibilities of a board of directors is deciding whether to make distributions on a class or series of shares. This chapter discusses factors to be considered in making such a decision and the impact of the decision on both the corporation and its shareholders.

After discussing the role of the corporation's attorney (§4.2), this chapter defines and clarifies certain terms (§§4.3–4.7), continuing with a discussion of whether the contemplated distribution is permissible under the applicable statutes and rules (§§4.8–4.22). Once it has been determined that a distribution is permissible, the question arises whether it is desirable. The next part of the chapter (§§4.23–4.53) is devoted to tax considerations in making distributions, including the impact of the distribution on both the corporation and its shareholders. The chapter next discusses certain procedural requirements that apply to declaration and payment of dividends or distributions (§§4.54–4.56). The last part of the chapter (§§4.57–4.58) concerns directors' and shareholders' liabilities if unlawful distributions are made.

We cannot overemphasize the importance of tax planning for corporate clients, or the necessity that counsel advising a corporate client about distributions and dividends have a basic understanding of the tax consequences. This chapter, however, is not intended as a comprehensive discussion of either tax or nontax aspects of distributions. For fuller treatment, see Bittker & Eustice, FEDERAL INCOME TAXATION OF CORPORATIONS AND SHAREHOLDERS chap 7 (Dividends and Other Nonliquidating Distributions) and chap 9 (Stock Redemptions and Partial Liquidations) (5th ed 1987); and 1 Ballantine & Sterling, CALIFORNIA CORPORATIONS LAWS chap 8 (4th ed).

§4.2   B. Attorney's Role

Frequently the attorney representing a corporation will be asked for advice regarding whether a corporation is in a position to make distributions under California law.

Accuracy of Financial Figures. The lawfulness of a corporation's distributions generally is a function of the value of the corporation's assets and its liabilities as well as its retained earnings. See Corp C §500. This type of financial information is usually prepared by a third party, *e.g.,* the corporation's accountant. The attorney should make sure such information is timely and accurate before advising the client as to the legality of the distribution.

Possible Conflict of Interest. If the attorney represents some of the shareholders as well as the corporation, or if the attorney owns any stock in the corporation, there may be an actual or a potential conflict of interest. In this situation, the attorney should take affirmative action to clearly resolve the conflict in a manner satisfactory to all parties, bearing in mind the California Rules of Professional Conduct, effective May 27, 1989. For general discussion of conflicts of interest, see §§2.2–2.15

C. Definition of Terms
§4.3   1. Dividends

The California Corporations Code uses the term "dividend" in various provisions (*e.g.,* Corp C §§166, 507), but does not define the term. Rather, it appears to give the term its generally accepted meaning of a distribution to a shareholder by the corporation without receipt of consideration.

2. Distributions to Shareholders

§4.4　　a. Definition

The first sentence of Corp C §166 contains the following definition:

Distribution to its shareholders" means the transfer of cash or property by a corporation to its shareholders without consideration, whether by way of dividend or otherwise, except a dividend in shares of the corporation, or the purchase or redemption of its shares for cash or property, including the transfer, purchase, or redemption by a subsidiary of the corporation.

CAVEAT: Tax Treatment of Distributions: Merely classifying a transfer by a corporation as a "distribution to its shareholders" will not control the tax treatment of the transfer. Separate rules must be applied to determine the manner in which the distribution will be treated for tax purposes, both with respect to the corporation and the shareholders. See §§4.23–4.53.

§4.5　　b. Exclusions From Definition

Stock Dividends. The term "distribution to its shareholders" does not include stock dividends (see Corp C §166, first sentence) or stock splits (see 10 Cal Code Regs §260.017).

Rescission of Shares. A rescission of the issuance of shares ordered by the final judgment of a court is not a "distribution." Corp C §166. Likewise, a corporation's rescission of the issuance of its shares is not a "distribution" if the board of directors, without counting the vote of any interested director, determines that (1) it is reasonably likely that the holder of the shares in question could legally enforce a claim for rescission, (2) the rescission is in the best interest of the corporation, and (3) the corporation is likely to be able to meet its liabilities (except those for which payment is otherwise adequately provided) as they mature. Corp C §166.

Repurchase of Certain Shares Issued to Employees. Finally, the term "distribution to its shareholders" excludes certain repurchases by a corporation of shares issued pursuant to an employee stock purchase plan or stock option plan. Corp C §§166, 408.

Other Exclusions. Transactions excluded from the definition of "distribution to its shareholders" (Corp C §166) are not subject to the limitations on distributions discussed at §§4.8–4.15.

§4.6   3. Time of Distribution or Dividend

Dividends. The time of any "distribution by way of dividend" is the date that the dividend is declared, rather than the date payment is actually made. See Corp C §166.

CAVEAT: It is imperative that the board of directors, when deciding whether to declare a dividend, base its decision on financial statements that accurately reflect the corporation's financial condition *at the time the dividend is declared.* If, for example, the dividend is declared three months after the date to which the financial statements apply, the corporation's financial position may have changed significantly enough during the three-month period to disqualify the corporation from making the distribution. In such a case, the directors may be subject to personal liability. See §4.57.

Redemption of Shares. The time of a distribution by purchase or redemption of shares (unlike a dividend distribution; see preceding paragraph) is the date on which cash or property is transferred by the corporation, whether or not the transfer is made pursuant to a contract dated earlier than the date of the transfer. Corp C §166; see also Corp C §409. Therefore, in the case of redemptions, the financial statements reviewed by the board of directors should reflect the corporation's financial condition *on the date of the actual transfer of cash or property.*

Exchange of Debt Security for Shares. If a negotiable debt security, as defined in Com C §8102(1) ("uncertificated security") is issued by the corporation in exchange for shares, the time of the distribution (*i.e.,* the time for testing the legality of the distribution) is the date that the corporation acquires the shares in the exchange.

Sinking Fund Payments. A special rule applies with respect to sinking fund payments. In such cases, the transfer of cash or property is deemed to occur "at the time that it is delivered to a trustee for the holders of preferred shares to be used for the redemption of the shares or physically segregated by the corporation in trust for that purpose." Corp C §166.

§4.7   4. Amount of Distribution

Property Distributions. The amount of a distribution payable in property is determined on the basis of the value at which the property is carried on the corporation's financial statements, in accordance with generally accepted accounting principles. Corp C §500.

Note that the corporation's financial statements are used not only in determining whether a distribution lawfully may be made, but also in determining the lawful amount of the distribution. Although the board of directors may rely on the financial statements for these purposes, such reliance is not without limitations. See discussion of Corp C §309(f) in §4.10.

§4.8   II. IS THE CONTEMPLATED DISTRIBUTION PERMISSIBLE?

The Corporations Code provides specific limitations on a corporation's ability to make distributions to its shareholders. For these purposes, distributions include dividends and redemptions. Corp C §166. (The time to which these limitations apply depends on whether the distribution is a dividend or redemption; see §4.6.)

There are three tests with respect to distributions: the insolvency test (see §4.9), the retained earnings test (see §4.10), and the assets test (see §4.11). Although the insolvency test can never be violated, a corporation need only meet *either* the retained earnings test or the assets test, not both of them, to make a lawful distribution.

To the extent a distribution is in violation of the statutory limitations, the board of directors as well as the recipient shareholders may incur personal liability for the distribution. For a discussion of this issue, see §§4.57–4.58.

A. Limitations on Corporation's Right To Make Distributions

§4.9   1. Insolvency Test

A corporation may not make a distribution to its shareholders if the corporation is, or as a result of the distribution would be, likely to be unable to meet its liabilities as they mature (except those whose payment is otherwise adequately provided for). Corp C §501.

This insolvency test must be met, regardless of whether the corporation could meet either the retained earnings test or the assets test (§§4.10–4.11). Therefore, any review of factors in determining the lawfulness of distributions should begin with the insolvency test. If it cannot be met, the other tests are irrelevant.

In addition to the insolvency test, the corporation must meet either the "retained earnings" test (§4.10) or the "assets" test (§4.11).

§4.10   2. Retained Earnings Test

Under the retained earnings test, the amount of the corporation's retained earnings *immediately prior to the distribution* must equal or exceed the amount of the proposed distribution. Corp C §500(a).

If the financial documents being reviewed by the board of directors do not reflect the corporation's retained earnings *immediately prior to the distribution,* the documents should not be relied on; instead, current financial information should be prepared in order to determine whether the corporation has sufficient retained earnings to make the contemplated distribution.

A director may rely on information, opinions, reports, or statements, including financial statements and other financial data, prepared or presented by any of the following (Corp C §309(b)):

(1) One or more officers or employees of the corporation whom the director believes to be reliable and competent in the matters presented;

(2) Counsel, independent accountants or other persons as to matters which the director believes to be within such person's professional or expert competence;

(3) A committee of the board upon which the director does not serve, as to matters within its designated authority, which committee the director believes to merit confidence.

The director, however, must act in good faith, after reasonable inquiry if the need is indicated by the circumstances, and without knowledge that would cause the director's reliance to be unwarranted. Corp C §309(b).

All financial statements, balance sheets, assets, liabilities, and retained earnings (as well as other specified items) must be prepared or determined in conformity with the generally accepted accounting principles ("GAAP") then applicable. Corp C §114.

Special rules apply to a distribution of cash or property in payment of an obligation incurred by a corporation in connection with the purchase of its shares. Corp C §500(b)(2) provides in part:

For the purpose of applying this section to a distribution by a corporation of cash or property in payment in whole or in part of an obligation incurred by the corporation in connection with the purchase of its shares, there shall be added to retained earnings any amount that had been deducted therefrom at the time the obligation was incurred, but not in excess of the principal of the obligation which remains unpaid immediately prior to the distribution and there shall be deducted from liabilities any amount which had been added thereto at the time the obligation was incurred, but not in excess of the principal of the obligation which will remain unpaid after the distribution.

This rule should be reviewed whenever a corporation intends to make a distribution with respect to an obligation previously incurred by the corporation on repurchasing its shares from a shareholder.

§4.11   3. Assets Test

The assets test is met if, *immediately after* giving effect to the distribution, *both* of the following will be true:

(1) The *total corporate assets* (exclusive of goodwill, capitalized research and development expenses, and deferred charges) will be at least 1 1/4 times its liabilities (not including deferred taxes, deferred income, and other deferred credits); and

(2) The corporation's *current assets* will be at least equal to its current liabilities or, in certain specified cases, at least equal to 1 1/4 times its current liabilities. Corp C §500(b).

For purposes of this test, "current assets" may include net amounts which the board of directors has determined in good faith may reasonably be expected to be received from customers. However, in determining the amount of the corporation's assets, unrealized profits derived from an exchange of assets are not included unless the assets received are currently realizable in cash. Corp C §500(b)(2). (The assets test also applies to distributions by a subsidiary corporation to its parent corporation's shareholders.)

NOTE: The "assets test" of Corp C §500(b)(2) cannot be used by corporations that do not classify their assets into current and fixed assets under generally accepted accounting principles. Corp C §502(b).

A corporation that does not meet the assets test may still make a lawful distribution if it meets the retained earnings test, discussed in §4.10.

4. Distributions to Junior Shareholders

§4.12   a. Distributions Affecting Liquidation Preferences of Senior Shareholders

A corporation may not make a distribution to its shareholders on shares of any class or series that is junior with respect to distribution of assets on liquidation to outstanding shares of any other class or series if, after the distribution, the excess of the corporation's assets (with certain exclusions) over the corporation's liabilities (with certain exclusions) would be less than the liquidation preference of all such senior shares. Corp C §502. In addition, the articles of incorporation may impose stricter limitations on such distributions. See §4.15.

Therefore, decisions as to a distribution on the junior shares must take into account the liquidation preferences of any senior classes or series. Since the requirement concerns assets and liabilities after the distribution, it is essential that the financial information reviewed by the board of directors reflect the prospective effect of the proposed distribution.

§4.13   b. Distributions Affecting Cumulative Dividends on Senior Shares

A corporation may not make a distribution to its shareholders on any class or series of shares that is junior to outstanding shares of any other class or series with respect to payment of dividends, unless the amount of the corporation's retained earnings *immediately prior to the distribution* equals or exceeds the amount of the proposed distribution plus the aggregate amount of the cumulative dividends in arrears on all such senior shares. Corp C §503. In addition, the articles of incorporation may impose stricter limitations on such distributions. See §4.15.

The board, before deciding to make a proposed distribution, should therefore take into account the dividend preferences of any senior classes or series of shares and any arrearages in such dividends. For these purposes, the financial information reviewed by the board of directors should reflect the corporation's financial condition immediately preceding the distribution.

§4.14   c. Possible Nonapplicability of Corp C §§502, 503

In California, the rights, preferences, privileges, and restrictions granted to or imposed on any class or series of preferred shares may provide that the limitations of Corp C §502 or §503 regarding distributions to junior shares (see §§4.12–4.13) do not apply. Corp C §402.5. Thus, if the limitations imposed by Corp C §502 or §503 have been made inapplicable to a preferred class or series, distributions to junior shares may be made without regard to the liquidation preferences or dividend arrearages of the preferred class or series. For discussion of Corp C §402.5, see 1 MARSH'S CALIFORNIA CORPORATION LAW §5.4A (2d ed).

NOTE: The rights, preferences, privileges, and restrictions applicable to any class or series of shares must be stated or authorized in the corporation's articles, except that for wholly unissued classes or series they may be set by board resolution. See Corp C §§202(e)(3), 400(a), 401(a)–(b).

§4.15   5. Limitations Set Forth in Charter Documents or Corporate Contracts

In addition to the statutory limitations on distributions, a corporation's articles of incorporation, bylaws, or any other agreement entered into by the corporation may impose additional restrictions on distributions. Corp C §505. For instance, a person or entity lending money to a corporation may require a contractual agreement under which no distributions may be made until the loan is paid in full. If the corporation desires stricter limitations with respect to distributions than are provided by the statutes, consideration should be given to the execution of a document, *e.g.,* a stock repurchase agreement, in which the desired restrictions are set forth in detail.

B. Rules Regarding Redemptions, Stock Dividends, and Stock Splits

§4.16   1. Redemptions

Generally, the same limitations applicable to the making of dividends and distributions apply to making redemptions. Corp C §402(d). Therefore, a corporation may not violate the insolvency test, and it must meet either the retained earnings test or the assets test before making a redemption. See §§4.10–4.11. A violation of these tests can subject the directors or shareholders whose shares are improperly redeemed to personal liability. See §§4.57–4.58.

§4.17   2. Stock Dividends

A stock dividend is generally defined as a pro rata distribution of additional shares of a corporation's stock to its existing shareholders, but does not include a stock split (see §4.17). See 10 Cal Code Regs §260.017.

A stock dividend is excluded from the definition of a "distribution to [a corporation's] shareholders." Corp C §166. Therefore, a corporation making a stock dividend does not have to comply with the limitations on a corporation's ability to make distributions set forth in Corp C §§500–511.

In order for a corporation to issue a stock dividend, the corporation must have sufficient authorized but unissued shares. If this is not the case, the corporation's articles of incorporation must be amended to increase the authorized number of corporate shares. Any such amendment must be approved by the board of directors and by the affirmative vote of the majority of the outstanding shares entitled to vote (Corp C §152). The approval by the outstanding shares may be made either before or after approval by the board of directors. Corp C §902(a). See chap 5 on amendments, generally.

§4.18   3. Stock Splits

A stock split is defined as a pro rata division of all the outstanding shares of a class of stock into a greater number of shares of the same class by an amendment to the articles of incorporation stating the effect of the stock split on the outstanding shares. Corp C §188. Thus, a stock split would result in each shareholder owning additional shares of stock in the corporation. A reverse stock split, on the other hand, is a pro rata combination of all the outstanding shares of a class of stock into a smaller number of shares of the same class by an amendment to the articles of incorporation. Corp C §182.

Stock splits are not subject to the limitations on a corporation's ability to make distributions set forth in Corp C §§500–511.

A stock split requires an amendment to the articles of incorporation stating the effect on outstanding shares. Corp C §188. The amendment to the articles of incorporation is required even if the corporation has sufficient authorized but unissued shares. The amendment must be approved by the board of directors and by the affirmative vote of the majority of the outstanding shares entitled to vote (Corp C §152), except that if the corporation has only one class of shares outstanding, an amendment to the articles of incorporation effecting only a stock split (including an increase in the authorized number of shares in proportion thereto) may be adopted with the approval of the board of directors alone, and no approval of the outstanding shares is required. Corp C §902(a), (c).

C. Nonapplicability of Specific Limitations

§4.19   ### 1. Redemption of Deceased Shareholder's Shares

If the corporation has paid premiums on a policy insuring the life of a deceased shareholder (usually a director, officer, or employee of the corporation), the parties may have entered into a written agreement that certain of the proceeds of the policy may be used by the corporation to fund the corporation's repurchase or redemption of the deceased shareholder's shares.

The provisions of Corp C §§500–503 (*i.e.*, the retained earnings and assets tests, the insolvency test, and the limitations on distributions to junior shareholders; see §§4.9–4.12) do not apply to:

a purchase or redemption of shares of a deceased shareholder from the proceeds of insurance on the life of such shareholder in excess of the total amount of all premiums paid by the corporation for such insurance, in order to carry out the provisions of an agreement between the corporation and such shareholder to purchase or redeem such shares upon the death of the shareholder.

Corp C §503.1.

Therefore, if the corporation has insured the life of any of its shareholders and plans to use its portion of the policy's proceeds to reacquire the shareholder's shares when the shareholder dies, the corporation and the insured shareholder should enter into a written agreement to that effect—either as a separate agreement or as part of a buy-out agreement. See BUSINESS BUY-OUT AGREEMENTS chap 5 (Cal CEB 1976). If the agreement is properly drawn, the limitations on distributions of Corp C §§500–503 will not apply to the redemption transaction.

§4.20 2. Redemption of Disabled Shareholder's Shares

A repurchase or redemption of shares may sometimes be called for if the shareholder (usually a director, officer, or employee) becomes disabled, and the repurchase may be funded by proceeds from a corporation-paid policy of disability insurance. For this purpose, "disability insurance" is statutorily defined as "an agreement of indemnification against the insured's loss of the ability to work due to accident or illness." Corp C §503.2.

Using language parallel to that of Corp C §503.1 for deceased shareholders (see §4.19), Corp C §503.2 allows redemption of a disabled shareholder's shares with proceeds of disability insurance paid for by the corporation, free from the restrictions on distributions of Corp C §§500–503, as long as there is an agreement, entered into between the corporation and the disabled shareholder prior to the disability, allowing this use of the proceeds.

§4.21 3. Distributions Upon Dissolution

The Corporations Code chapter on dividends and reacquisitions of shares (Corp C §§500–511) is expressly made inapplicable to the winding up and dissolution of a corporation, whether the dissolution is voluntary or involuntary. Corp C §508. Thus, the limitations on distributions imposed by Corp C §§500–503 do not apply to distributions made during the winding up and dissolution process. (For dissolution procedures and forms, generally, see chap 7.)

§4.22 D. Limitations on Shareholders' Right To Receive Distributions

A corporation is empowered to issue one or more classes or series of shares, with rights, preferences, privileges, and restrictions as stated or authorized in its articles of incorporation. Corp C §§203, 400(a). All shares of any one class have the same rights, preferences, privileges, and restrictions unless the class is divided into series. Corp C §400(b). A "series" of shares is defined as "those shares within a class which have the same rights, preferences, privileges and restrictions but which differ in one or more rights, preferences, privileges or restrictions from other shares within the same class." Corp C §183. The Corporations Code thus recognizes that a corporation may create a number of classes or series of shares whose shareholder rights, including the right to receive distributions, may vary from class to class or series to series. However, a corporation does not have an unlimited power to limit or deny shareholder's rights, especially with respect to dividends and redemptions.

Dividend or Liquidation Rights. No denial or limitation of shareholders' dividend or liquidation rights by a corporation is effective unless at the time one or more classes or series of outstanding shares, singly or in the aggregate, are entitled to unlimited dividend and liquidation rights. Corp C §400(a).

Redemption and Other Rights. All shares of the same class of stock must have the same redemption rights and other rights, preferences, privileges and restrictions, unless that class of stock is divided into series, in which case all the shares of any one series must have the same redemption rights and other rights, preferences, privileges and restrictions. Corp C §400(b).

III. TAX CONSIDERATIONS

§4.23 A. Distributions Generally

Even though a distribution may be permitted under the Corporations Code, it may result in adverse tax consequences. For instance, a distribution may be treated as a dividend for tax purposes, even though no distribution is made (*e.g.,* interest-free loans from a corporation to its shareholder). It is therefore important for the attorney to have a basic understanding of the tax consequences of distributions.

This chapter does not deal with these matters comprehensively. For a fuller discussion see Bittker & Eustice, FEDERAL INCOME TAXATION OF CORPORATIONS AND SHAREHOLDERS §§7.01–7.44, 9.01–9.35 (5th ed 1987).

§4.24   B. Distributions Treated as Dividends

Under the Internal Revenue Code (IRC), the term "dividend" means, for tax purposes, any distribution of property by a corporation to its shareholders out of the corporation's earnings and profits. IRC §316(a).

NOTE: A payment, to be considered a "distribution," must be made to the shareholder in his capacity as shareholder. Payments made to a shareholder in his capacity as an employee, creditor, or lessor of property, are not distributions for tax purposes, and may be deductible expenses to the corporation. Unless otherwise provided by a specific statute, every distribution is treated as being made from earnings and profits, and thus is subject to classification as a dividend. IRC §316(a). A distribution is treated as being made from accumulated earnings and profits to the extent thereof, or if the distribution exceeds accumulated earnings and profits, from current earnings and profits. IRC §316(a)(1)–(2).

However, distributions are treated as dividends only to the extent of the corporation's current or accumulated earnings and profits. Distributions in excess of current and accumulated earnings and profits are not treated as dividends and may result in no income to the distributee-shareholder. See §§4.32–4.34. Throughout this chapter, however, it is generally assumed that a distribution by a corporation will result in dividend treatment.

§4.25   1. Property

"Property" is defined as money, securities, and any other property, but does not include shares of stock in the corporation making the distribution or the right to acquire such shares. IRC §317(a). Generally, therefore, a corporation's distribution of its own stock and its granting of options to buy stock are not treated as distributions of property; however, these transactions may be classified as distributions of property under IRC §305. See §§4.37–4.43.

§4.26   2. Earnings and Profits

The Internal Revenue Code does not define the term "earnings and profits." Moreover, a corporation's earnings and profits are not necessarily the same as its retained earnings or taxable income. Instead, the computation of earnings and profits generally begins with a corporation's taxable income, to which adjustments are then made. For example, although tax-exempt income will not increase a corporation's taxable income, it will increase the corporation's earnings and profits. Treas Reg §1.312–6(b). Adjustments to earnings and profits are also made for distributions of appreciated property (IRC §312(b)) and depreciation (IRC §312(k)), as well as other items specified in IRC §312. For a more complete discussion of earnings and profits, see Bittker & Eustice, FEDERAL INCOME TAXATION OF CORPORATIONS AND SHAREHOLDERS §7.03 (5th ed 1987).

§4.27   3. Constructive Dividends

Certain other transactions involving the disbursement of money or the transfer of property by the corporation may be treated as dividend distributions for tax purposes. While the transactions discussed below do not constitute a complete list of the types of transactions that will result in "constructive dividend" treatment, they represent several of the more widely applicable transactions that may result in such tax treatment.

§4.28   a. Loans to Shareholders

If a corporation makes a loan to a shareholder and does not charge the shareholder an adequate interest rate for the loan, a dividend distribution is deemed to have been made from the corporation to the shareholder. IRC §7872; see Proposed Treas Reg §1.7872–4(d)(1). In general, the dividend will be based on the difference between the interest rate that should have been charged by the corporation (based on designated interest rates) and the interest rate actually charged by the corporation. However, the entire amount received can be characterized as a constructive dividend if there is no legal obligation to repay the "loan."

De Minimis Exception. If a loan to a shareholder does not have the avoidance of federal tax (with respect to the interest arrangements of the loan) as one of its principal purposes, IRC §7872 will not apply to the loan on any day on which the aggregate outstanding amount of loans between the borrower and the lender does not exceed $10,000. IRC §7872(c)(3).

§4.29   b. Unreasonable Compensation

If a corporation pays a shareholder compensation that is subsequently determined to be in excess of reasonable compensation, the excess may be treated as a dividend, resulting in no deduction to the corporation for the excess. Treas Reg §1.162–8. The excess thus increases the corporation's taxable income and tax liability. (It is generally immaterial to the shareholder whether the payment is classified as compensation or a dividend, since either classification will result in ordinary income to the shareholder.)

§4.30   c. Corporate Payments for Shareholder's Benefit

If a corporation makes a payment on behalf of a shareholder, and the payment is for the personal benefit of the shareholder, the amount of that payment will be treated as a dividend. *Old Colony Trust Co. v Commissioner* (1929) 279 US 716. For example, if a corporation makes a payment on a shareholder's obligation to a third party, the amount of the payment made by the corporation is treated as a constructive dividend to the shareholder, and is not deductible by the corporation.

§4.31   d. Bargain Purchases or Rentals by Shareholders

If a corporation sells property to a shareholder for less than the property's fair market value, or if a corporation rents property to a shareholder for less than the property's fair rental value, the difference between the property's value and the amount that was charged the shareholder is treated as a constructive dividend to the shareholder. Treas Reg §§1.162–8, 1.301–1(j); Rev Rul 58–1, 1958–1 Cum Bull 173.

C. Property Distributions

1. Shareholder Tax Consequences

§4.32 a. Amount of Distribution

The amount of a distribution to a shareholder is the amount of money received by the shareholder, plus the fair market value of all other property received. IRC §301(b)(1). The fair market value of property is determined as of the date of distribution to the shareholder. IRC §301(b)(3). However, the amount of the distribution is reduced by any liabilities that the shareholder assumes or takes subject to, in connection with the distribution. IRC §301(b)(2).

§4.33 b. Amount Taxable

If a distribution of property is made to shareholders with respect to a corporation's stock, the amount of the distribution that does not exceed the corporation's earnings and profits, both accumulated and current, is treated as a dividend and included in the shareholder's gross income. IRC §301(c)(1). The amount of the distribution that is in excess of the corporation's earnings and profits is treated as a tax-free return of capital and reduces the shareholder's adjusted basis in the stock. IRC §301(c)(2). Any amount of the distribution that (1) is not treated as a dividend, and (2) exceeds the shareholder's basis in the stock is treated as gain from the sale or exchange of property. IRC §301(c)(3)(A).

§4.34 c. Basis of Property Distributed

The basis of property received as a dividend distribution is the fair market value of the property, determined as of the date of distribution. IRC §301(d).

2. Corporate Tax Consequences of Property Distributions

§4.35   a. Effect on Corporation's Taxable Income

Generally, a corporation does not recognize gain or loss on a distribution of property. IRC §311(a). (For the definition of "property," see §4.25.) However, if a corporation distributes property (other than an obligation of the corporation) the fair market value of which exceeds the corporation's adjusted basis in the property, the transaction is treated as though the corporation had sold the property to the shareholder, *i.e.,* the corporation will recognize gain in an amount equal to the difference between the property's fair market value and the corporation's adjusted basis in the property. IRC §311(b)(1). Generally, the fair market value of the property is treated as not less than the amount of any liabilities to which the property is subject. IRC §§311(b)(2), 336(b). In addition, a corporation may recognize ordinary income as a result of depreciation recapture. See IRC §§291(a)(1), 1245, 1250.

In order for a corporation to recognize gain on a distribution of property, it is not necessary that the value of the property have appreciated; rather, it is only necessary that the property's fair market value exceed the corporation's adjusted basis in the property. Therefore, if property is being depreciated, for tax purposes, at a faster rate than its economic value is decreasing, gain will be recognized by the corporation if it distributes the property, since the fair market value of the property will exceed its adjusted basis.

§4.36   b. Effect on Earnings and Profits

Internal Revenue Code §312(a) provides in general that on the distribution of property by a corporation with respect to its stock, the corporation's earnings and profits will be decreased by the sum of (1) the amount of money distributed, (2) the principal amount of the corporation's obligations that were distributed, and (3) the adjusted basis of any other distributed property. IRC §312(a). The statute also provides for additional adjustments, including an increase for a distribution of property with a fair market value in excess of its adjusted basis to the corporation. IRC §312(b).

D. Distributions of Stock and Stock Rights

§4.37   1. General Rule: Nontaxability to Shareholder

Generally, a distribution by a corporation of its stock to its shareholders is not taxable to the shareholders. IRC §305(a). The term "stock" includes the right to acquire stock in the corporation, and the term "shareholder" includes persons who hold rights to acquire stock and persons who hold convertible securities. IRC §305(d). Notwithstanding this general rule, the statute contains certain exceptions that will result in tax consequences to the shareholder.

§4.38   2. Exceptions

If any of the following exceptions apply to a distribution by a corporation of its stock, the distribution will be treated as a distribution of property to the shareholders and the tax consequences of the distribution will be governed by the provisions of IRC §301 (potentially resulting in dividend treatment).

§4.39   a. Distributions in Lieu of Money

A distribution is taxable if, at the election of any shareholder, the distribution is payable either in stock of the corporation or in property (*e.g.,* money). IRC §305(b)(1).

§4.40   b. Disproportionate Distributions

A distribution of stock is taxable if it results in (1) the receipt of property by some shareholders, and (2) an increase in the proportionate interest of other shareholders in the assets or earnings and profits of the corporation. IRC §305(b)(2). (For a definition of the term "property," see §4.25.)

§4.41   c. Distributions of Common and Preferred Stock

A distribution of stock is taxable if it (or a series of distributions of which it is one) results in some common shareholders receiving preferred stock and other common shareholders receiving common stock. IRC §305(b)(3).

§4.42   d. Distributions on Preferred Stock

A distribution of stock is taxable if it is made with respect to preferred stock. However, if a change in the conversion ratio of convertible preferred stock is made solely to take account of a stock dividend or stock split with respect to the stock into which the convertible stock is convertible, there will be no tax consequences to the preferred shareholders. IRC §305(b)(4).

§4.43   e. Distributions of Convertible Preferred Stock

A distribution of convertible preferred stock is taxable, unless it is established that the distribution will not result in (1) the receipt of property by some shareholders, and (2) an increase in the proportionate interest of other shareholders in the assets or earnings and profits of the corporation. IRC §305(b)(5); see also IRC §305(b)(2).

§4.44   f. Constructive Distribution Under
Regulations

Under IRC §305(c), subject to treasury regulations, a change in conversion ratio, a change in redemption price, a difference between redemption price and issue price, a redemption subject to IRC §301, or any other transaction having a similar effect on the interest of any shareholder shall be treated as a distribution to any shareholder whose proportionate interest in the corporation's earnings and profits or assets is increased by such transaction. IRC §305(c); Treas Reg §1.305–7.

§4.45   3. Section 306 Stock

Sometimes a corporation, to avoid making dividend distributions, makes a distribution of preferred stock to its common shareholders. Because such a stock distribution comes within the provisions of IRC §305(a) (which states that "gross income does not include the amount of any distribution of the stock of a corporation made by such corporation to its shareholders with respect to its stock"), there are no tax consequences to the shareholder at the time of the distribution.

It might seem that the shareholder recipient could then sell the preferred stock to a third party and recognize the gain from the sale as capital gain, thus converting what otherwise would have been ordinary income from dividend distributions to capital gain on the sale of the preferred stock. To prevent this practice, Congress enacted IRC §306.

Section 306 provides in general that although the distribution of preferred stock is not taxable, if the stock is later sold or otherwise disposed of, some or all of the proceeds of the sale may be taxed to the shareholder as ordinary income. Exceptions apply to certain dispositions of such stock other than redemptions (IRC §306(b)(1)(A)), stock redeemed in a complete liquidation (IRC §306(b)(2)), and stock disposed of at no gain or loss (IRC §306(b)(3)), as well as certain other specified transactions. For a more complete discussion, see Bittker & Eustace, FEDERAL INCOME TAXATION OF CORPORATION AND SHAREHOLDERS chap 10 (5th ed 1987).

CAVEAT: Stock distributions made *to preferred shareholders,* however, are taxable at the time of the distribution. See §4.42.

§4.46   4. Basis of Stock and Stock Rights Acquired in Distributions

If a shareholder receives stock or the right to acquire stock ("new stock") in a nontaxable distribution (see §4.37), then the basis of the new stock and that of the stock with respect to which it is distributed ("old stock"), respectively, are determined by allocating the old stock's adjusted basis between the old stock and the new stock, in proportion to the fair market value of each on the date of distribution. IRC §307(a); Treas Reg §1.307–1(a).

§4.47   E. Redemptions

For tax purposes generally, stock is treated as being redeemed if the corporation acquires its stock from a shareholder in exchange for property, whether the acquired stock is cancelled, retired, or held as treasury stock. IRC §317(b). (For definition of "property," see §4.25).

The distinction between a redemption being treated as a sale or exchange and its being treated as a distribution is significant. If treated as a distribution, the entire amount may be taxable as ordinary income to the shareholder. See §4.24. If, on the other hand, the redemption is treated as a sale, the shareholder will generally recognize gain only to the extent the amount of the redemption exceeds the shareholder's basis in the redeemed stock, and the gain recognized upon redemption generally will be characterized as long-term capital gain. Furthermore, a corporate shareholder may prefer dividend treatment because of the 70 percent or more deduction allowed under IRC §243 of dividends received by corporations.

Generally, if the corporation redeems its stock and the transaction qualifies under the provisions of IRC §302(b)(1), (2), (3), or (4), the redemption will be treated as a distribution in part or full payment in exchange for the stock, rather than as a dividend to the shareholder. IRC §302(a); see §§4.48–4.51. If the distribution fails to meet one of these tests, it will be treated as a dividend. IRC §302(d).

1. Redemptions Treated as Exchanges

§4.48   a. Redemptions Not Equivalent to a Dividend

A distribution is treated as an redemption under IRC §302(a) if it is not essentially equivalent to a dividend. IRC §302(b)(1). The determination of whether a distribution is essentially equivalent to a dividend (*i.e.,* having the same effect as a distribution without any redemption of stock) is made without regard to the corporation's earnings and profits at the time of the distribution. Treas Reg §1.302–2(a). This determination depends on the facts and circumstances of each case. Treas Reg §1.302–2(b).

The 1970 decision in *U.S. v Davis* (1970) 397 US 301, delineates factors considered important in determining what type of redemption is "not essentially equivalent to a dividend." *Davis* states two principles: First, the constructive ownership rules of IRC §318 apply to the dividend equivalence exception. Second, a valid business purpose is irrelevant in determining whether a redemption is equivalent to a dividend.

Under *Davis,* a redemption always has the effect of a dividend if the shareholder's ownership of stock has not been reduced meaningfully.

The following Revenue Rulings set forth the criteria for "meaningful redemption": Rev Rul 75–502, 1975–2 Cum Bull 111; Rev Rul 75–512, 1975–2 Cum Bull 112; Rev Rul 76–364, 1976–2 Cum Bull 91; Rev Rul 76–385, 1976–2 Cum Bull 92; Rev Rul 77–426, 1977–2 Cum Bull 87. Generally, if the corporation has only one class of stock outstanding, distributions in pro rata redemptions of part of a corporation's stock are treated as dividends. Treas Reg §1.302–2(b).

§4.49 b. Substantially Disproportionate Redemptions

A distribution is a "substantially disproportionate" redemption with respect to the shareholder if (1) *immediately after* the redemption the shareholder owns less than 50 percent of the corporation's voting stock, and (2) this is less than 80 percent of the percentage of the corporation's voting stock owned by the shareholder immediately before the distribution. IRC §302(b)(2)(A)–(C). In addition, the redemption cannot be part of a series of redemptions which in the aggregate is not substantially disproportionate. IRC §302(b)(2)(D). See Treas Reg §1.302–3. A substantially disproportionate redemption is an exchange under IRC §302(a) rather than a dividend.

§4.50 c. Complete Termination of Shareholder's Interest

A distribution will qualify as a redemption if it is in complete redemption of all the stock of the corporation owned by the shareholder. IRC §302(b)(3). If, however, close relatives of the shareholder continue to own stock, this ownership will be attributed to the shareholder under the "constructive ownership" rules of IRC §318(a)(1); therefore a complete termination will not have occurred, and the shareholder will not be entitled to redemption treatment on the distribution. Instead, the distribution will be taxed as a dividend.

Under IRC §302(c), the constructive ownership rules of IRC §318(a)(1) do not apply if: (1) immediately after the distribution, the distributee has no interest in the corporation (including an interest as an officer, director or employee), other than an interest as a creditor; (2) the distributee does not acquire any such interest (other than stock acquired by bequest or inheritance) within ten years from the date of the distribution; and (3) the distributee agrees to notify the Internal Revenue Service of any such acquisition within the ten-year period. IRC §302(c)(2); Treas Reg §1.302–4.

§4.51   d. Partial Liquidation

A distribution can be treated as a redemption rather than a dividend if it is (1) in redemption of stock held by a noncorporate shareholder, and (2) in partial liquidation of the corporation. IRC §302(b)(4). A distribution is in partial liquidation of a corporation if (a) the distribution is not essentially equivalent to a dividend (determined at the corporate level rather than at the shareholder level), and (b) the distribution is pursuant to a plan and occurs within the taxable year in which the plan is adopted or within the succeeding taxable year. IRC §302(e)(1). Detailed rules for determining whether the distribution is "not essentially equivalent to a dividend" for purposes of this section are set forth in IRC §302(e)(2)–(3).

NOTE: If a corporation has two or more trades or businesses, the use of the assets of one of those trades or businesses to redeem the stock of a noncorporate shareholder can qualify as a redemption under IRC §302(b)(4).

§4.52   2. Redemptions Treated as Distributions

Generally, the tax consequences to a corporation on a distribution in redemption of stock, with the exception of the effect of such distribution on the corporation's earnings and profits (see IRC §312(n)(7)), are the same as the consequences resulting from other distributions. See §§4.35–4.36.

If a corporation redeems its stock and the transaction does not qualify as a redemption under the provisions of IRC §302(b)(1)–(4), the transaction is treated as a distribution of property to which IRC §301 applies, generally resulting in dividend treatment. IRC §302(d).

§4.53   3. Redemption of Deceased Shareholder's Stock Under IRC §303

Redemption of a deceased shareholder's stock to pay death taxes, even though it does not meet the requirements of IRC §302(b), may nonetheless be eligible for redemption treatment under IRC §303. Four requirements must be met:

(1) The value of the redeemed stock must be included in the decedent's gross estate for federal estate tax purposes. IRC §303(a).

(2) The redemption amount cannot exceed the estate taxes imposed on the estate plus the funeral and estate administrative expenses allowed as estate tax deductions under IRC §2053. IRC §303(a).

(3) The redemption must occur after the decedent's death, and ordinarily within three years and ninety days after the filing of the federal estate tax return. IRC §303(b)(1)(A).

(4) The value of the decedent's stock generally must exceed 35 percent of the excess of the decedent's gross estate (for federal estate tax purposes) over the expenses, indebtedness, taxes, and losses allowable to the estate as deductions. IRC §303(b)(2)(A). The Code also provides rules under which the decedent's stock in two or more corporations which constitutes 20 percent or more of the value of the outstanding stock may be aggregated to meet the 35 percent test. (In determining whether the 20 percent test is satisfied, a surviving spouse's interest held with the decedent in community property, joint tenancy, tenancy in common, or tenancy by the entirety may be aggregated. IRC §303(b)(2)(B).)

IV. PROCEDURE FOR DECLARING AND PAYING DIVIDENDS AND DISTRIBUTIONS

§4.54   A. Authorization by Board of Directors

Generally, only the board of directors may authorize the making of dividends or distributions. An executive committee, although permitted to act on behalf of the board on many matters, is *not* allowed to make a distribution except at a rate, in a periodic amount, or within a price range set forth in the corporation's articles of incorporation or determined by the board. Corp C §311(f).

§4.55   B. Record Date for Distribution Purposes

Once the board of directors has authorized a dividend or other distribution, the right to receive the dividend is determined by the ownership of the shares on the "record date." Corp C §701(d).

The shareholders at the close of business on the record date are entitled to receive the dividend, even though the shares are transferred on the books of the corporation after the record date. However, the corporation's articles of incorporation or an agreement can provide for a different method of determining the persons entitled to the dividends. Corp C §701(d). Thus, if the shares are transferred by a shareholder to a third party after the record date, the transferor is entitled to the dividend (assuming the transferor owned the shares on the record date), unless the parties agree otherwise. On the other hand, if the shares are transferred to a third party before the record date, the transferee would be entitled to the dividend.

If the board of directors desires to do so, it may fix the record date in advance. However, the record date may not be more than sixty days prior to the payment date. Corp C §701(a).

If the board of directors does not fix a record date, the record date is the later of (1) the date the board of directors adopts a resolution declaring the dividend, or (2) sixty days prior to the date the dividend is made payable in the corporate resolution. Corp C §701(b)(3). Therefore, if the payment of the dividend is made within sixty days of the declaration of the dividend, the record date would be the date of adoption by the board of directors. If, on the other hand, the dividend is paid more than sixty days after the adoption of the resolution, the record date would be the 60th day preceding the date provided in the resolution for payment.

§4.56   C. Notice of Source of Dividend

Every dividend distribution by a corporation, other than one chargeable to retained earnings, must be identified in a notice to shareholders as being made from a source other than retained earnings, "stating the accounting treatment thereof." Corp C §507. This enables the shareholder to determine the tax consequences of the dividend, keeping in mind that the notice's classification of the dividend is not controlling for tax purposes. See §4.4. The notice must accompany the dividend or be given within three months after the end of the corporation's fiscal year in which the dividend is paid. Corp C §507.

V. LIABILITY FOR IMPROPER DISTRIBUTIONS

§4.57   A. Directors' Liabilities

Controlling Statute. The liability of directors for improper distributions is controlled by Corp C §316.

Who Is Liable. All directors who approve the making of a distribution that is contrary to the provisions of Corp C §§500–503 (discussed in §§4.8–4.14), including those who are present but abstain, are jointly and severally liable to the corporation for the benefit of all creditors or shareholders entitled to bring a suit against the directors on behalf of the corporation. Corp C §§316(a)(1).

Who May Bring Suit. For distributions that violate the retained earnings, assets, or insolvency tests (Corp C §§500–501), suit may be brought in the name of the corporation by corporate creditors whose debts or claims arose prior to the time of the distribution and who have not consented to the distribution, whether or not they have reduced their claims to judgment. Corp C §§316(c), 506(b). For distributions that violate Corp C §502 or §503 (distributions to junior shares in violation of senior shares' liquidation or cumulative dividend preferences), suit may be brought in the name of the corporation by any holders of preferred shares outstanding at the time of the distribution who have not consented to the distribution. Corp C §§316(c), 506(b).

Damages. The amount of damages recoverable from a director under Corp C §316 is the amount of the illegal distribution, but cannot exceed the amount owed by the corporation to the nonconsenting creditors at the time of the violation or the injury suffered by the nonconsenting shareholders, as the case may be. Corp C §316(d).

Impleading; Contribution; Subrogation; Cross-Complaints. Any director sued under Corp C §316 may implead all other directors liable for the improper distribution and may compel contribution, either in the same action or in an independent action against directors not joined in the original action. Corp C §316(e). Directors liable under Corp C §316 are also entitled to be subrogated to the rights of the corporation against shareholders who received the distribution (Corp C §316(f)(1)), and directors sued under Corp C §316 may file a cross-complaint against persons who are liable to that director as a result of the subrogation and may proceed against them in an independent action (Corp C §316(f)(3)).

Directors' Defenses. Notwithstanding the liability imposed by Corp C §316, directors who perform the duties of a director in good faith, in a manner the director believes to be in the best interests of the corporation and its shareholders, and with the care (including reasonable inquiry) that an ordinarily prudent person in a like position would use under similar circumstances, have no liability based on any alleged failure to discharge their obligations as a director. Corp C §309(a), (c). Furthermore, in making corporate decisions, directors may, without incurring liability, rely on information, opinions, reports, or statements (including financial statements and other financial data) furnished by corporate officers or employees whom the director believes to be reliable and competent as to the matters presented, as well as counsel, independent accountants, or other experts, as long as the director acts in good faith, after reasonable inquiry if the need is indicated by the circumstances, and without knowledge that would cause such reliance to be unwarranted. Corp C §309(b)–(c). Therefore, reasonable reliance on financial information may prevent liability for improper corporate distributions.

NOTE: The liability of a director for monetary damages may be eliminated or limited in a corporation's articles to the extent provided in Corp C §204(a)(10). Corp C §309(c). See §§2.57–2.61; see also §5.134).

Fraudulent Intent. If a director, knowingly and with dishonest or fraudulent purpose, concurs in any vote or act of the directors to make any dividend or distribution except as permitted by law, with the design of defrauding creditors or shareholders, the director is guilty of a misdemeanor punishable by a monetary fine or imprisonment, or both. Corp C §2253.

For fuller discussion of directors' liabilities, see chap 2.

§4.58   B. Shareholders' Liabilities

Controlling Statute. The liability of shareholders for improper distributions is controlled by Corp C §506.

Who Is Liable. Any shareholder who receives a distribution prohibited by Corp C §§500–511 with knowledge of facts indicating the impropriety of the distribution is liable to the corporation for the benefit of all creditors or shareholders entitled to bring an action against the shareholder on behalf of the corporation. Corp C §506(a).

Who May Bring Suit. For distributions that violate Corp C §500 or §501 (retained earnings, assets, or insolvency tests), suit may be brought in the name of the corporation by creditors of the corporation whose debts or claims arose prior to the time of the distribution and who have not consented to the distribution, whether or not they have reduced their claims to judgment. Corp C §506(b). For distributions that violate

Corp C §502 or §503 (distributions to junior shares in violation of senior shares' liquidation or cumulative dividend preferences), suit may be brought in the name of the corporation by any holders of preferred shares outstanding at the time of the distribution who have not consented to the distribution. Corp C §506(b).

Amount of Liability. The shareholder's liability is for the amount of the distribution received by the shareholder with interest at the legal rate on judgments until paid, but not exceeding the corporation's liabilities owed to nonconsenting creditors at the time of the violation or the injury suffered by nonconsenting shareholders, as the case may be. Corp C §506(a).

Impleading; Contribution. Any shareholder sued under Corp C §506 may implead all other shareholders liable under that statute and may compel contribution. Corp C §506(c).

For further discussion of shareholder liabilities, see chap 3.

5

Amending the Articles and Changing the Capital Structure

Hilary Huebsch Cohen

HILARY HUEBSCH COHEN, B.A., 1970, and J.D., 1978, University of California at Los Angeles. Ms. Cohen, of the firm of Hirschtick, Chenen, Lemon & Curtis, practices in Marina del Rey.

This chapter is based on and incorporates portions of Chapter 4 of Operating Problems of California Corporations (Cal CEB 1978) by Michael J. Halloran.

I. INTRODUCTION

§5.1   A. Scope of Chapter

After a corporation has been organized, changing financial or operational needs may require changes in the stock structure, the rights or restrictions on outstanding shares, the corporate powers or purposes, or the corporate name. To effect such changes, amendment of the articles of incorporation may be required.

First, this chapter briefly discusses the general source of a corporation's power to amend its articles and the concomitant limitations on that power, including the "fairness" test. See §§5.3–5.10. Second, it discusses the corporate actions that require amendment of the articles. See §§5.14–5.69. Third, certain actions not requiring amendment of the articles are considered, as are amendments that are prohibited. See §§5.70–5.73. Fourth, the regulation of amendments by the Commissioner of Corporations is discussed in §§5.74–5.89. Finally, the procedures required to put various amendments into effect are presented in §§5.90–5.165.

Attention is given primarily to private California corporations organized for profit and not subject to special regulation of changes in their financial and operational structure. Changes in the capital structure of foreign (*i.e.,* non-California) corporations are not discussed.

§5.2   B. The Attorney's Role

The attorney for the corporation must initially learn from the client the financial or operational problem or need. Then the attorney must consider the equitable and other limitations on possible amendments, and decide which type of amendment will best fill the client's needs. Finally, after verifying the necessary procedural steps, the attorney should prepare a work agenda and a timetable.

This chapter has been written for the guidance of attorneys representing either the corporation, or one or more shareholders. Increasingly, shareholders act in a more sophisticated manner when asked to approve amendments to articles, partly because many institutions have become corporate shareholders. The attorney representing a shareholder may be particularly interested in the possible effects of proposed extensions of provisions protective of directors and officers (see §5.68) as well as equitable, administrative, and other limitations on amendments to articles that the shareholder may raise in an administrative or judicial action to prevent the amendment. See §§5.3–5.10, 5.14–5.69, 5.88–5.89.

II. POWER TO AMEND

§5.3 A. Basic Authority: Corp C §900

Corporations Code §900(a) provides:

> By complying with the provisions of this chapter (*i.e.,* Corp C §§900–911), a corporation may amend its articles from time to time, in any and as many respects as may be desired, so long as its articles as amended contain only such provisions as it would be lawful to insert in original articles filed at the time of the filing of the amendment and, if a change in shares or the rights of shareholders or an exchange, reclassification or cancellation of shares or rights of shareholders is to be made, such provisions as may be necessary to effect such change, exchange, reclassification or cancellation. It is the intent of the Legislature in adopting this section to exercise to the fullest extent the reserve power of the state over corporations and to authorize any amendment of the articles covered by the preceding sentence regardless of whether any provision contained in the amendment was permissible at the time of the original incorporation of the corporation.

Thus, a corporation has blanket statutory authority to amend its articles as long as the amended articles contain only (1) provisions that could be lawfully inserted in original articles at the date of the amendment, and (2) any provisions that may be necessary to effect "a change in shares or the rights of shareholders or an exchange, reclassification or cancellation of shares or rights of shareholders" as a result of the amendment.

At the time the General Corporation Law was adopted (effective January 1, 1977), some authorities questioned whether the courts would accept the blanket provisions of §900(a) as sufficient authority for amendments that take away "vested rights" (see §5.6). In some earlier cases, courts had required specific statutory authority when important rights were being taken away by amendment in order to be sure that the constitutionally reserved power had not been exercised in such a way as to deny the shareholder the constitutional argument of impairment of his contractual obligations or the use of the fundamental change doctrine. See, *e.g., Berger v Amana Soc'y* (Iowa 1959) 95 NW2d 909, 70 ALR2d 830; *Davison v Parke, Austin & Lipscomb, Inc.* (1941) 285 NY 500, 35 NE2d 618; *Consolidated Film Indus., Inc. v Johnson* (Del 1937) 197 A 489, 493. See also Comment, *Corporations—Right of a Majority to Make Fundamental Changes by Amendment,* 45 Iowa L Rev 615, 617 (1960); §§5.5, 5.8. As drafted, Corp C §900(a) attempted to eliminate these problems. The second sentence authorizes any amendment to articles regardless of its effect on shares or shareholders, provided that the substance of the amendment could have appeared in original articles filed at the date of the amendment, and provided further that the amendment obtains the necessary director and shareholder votes and survives the equitable tests imposed by courts and administrative agencies.

The language of the first sentence of Corp C §900(a) was copied from the first sentence of 8 Delaware Code §242(a) and Model Business Corporation Act §58 (superseded by Revised Model Bus Corp Act §10.01). The intent of the provision is illuminated by the following comment on Model Act §58: "One of the major purposes of the Model Act was to sweep aside the complexities of judicial decisions on vested rights which were increasingly handicapping the conduct of business through the corporate form." Model Business Corporation Act §58, Par. 2. In any event, Corp C §900, taken together with Corp C §§902–904, which specify the votes required for certain amendments (see §§5.91–5.109), Corp C §§202–204, which specify required and optional provisions of the original articles (see §§5.14–5.69), and Corp C §§400–404, which specify certain provisions which may be contained in the articles as to shares, probably constitute sufficiently specific statutory authority for most amendments if a court should require such authority. There are few if any reported cases to suggest the continued viability of any argument of insufficient statutory authority for most amendments.

In the years since Corp C §900 was adopted, hostile takeovers have become something of a growth industry, and amendment of the articles to make a takeover less attractive is among the strategies often recommended to a potential target. Regulators have shown some unfriendliness to amendments of this sort. See Securities Exchange Act Release No. 34–15230 (1979). In addition, commentators have questioned the validity of such provisions. For discussion of amendment of articles to prevent a hostile takeover bid, see 1 Fleischer, TENDER OFFERS: DEFENSES, RESPONSES & PLANNING 10 (1983); Cary, *Corporate Devices Used to Insulate Management from Attack*, 25 Bus Lawyer 839 (1970)); 1 Lipton & Steinberger, TAKEOVERS & FREEZEOUTS §1.9.1.1 (1978); Aranow & Einhorn, *Tender Offers for Corporate Control* 259 (1973); Aranow, Einhorn & Berlstein, DEVELOPMENTS IN TENDER OFFERS FOR CORPORATE CONTROL 193 (1977); Mullaney, *Guarding Against Takeovers—Defensive Charter Provisions*, 25 Bus Lawyer 1441 (1970); 2 Winter, Stumpf & Hawkins, SHARK REPELLENTS AND GOLDEN PARACHUTES: A HANDBOOK FOR THE PRACTITIONER §9.10 (1983); 1 MARSH'S CALIFORNIA CORPORATION LAW §10.39 (2d ed). Certain Corporations Code provisions may limit the availability of certain takeover defenses: see Corp C §§301–304 (election and removal of directors); Corp C §305 (filling of vacancies on the Board); Corp C §708 (cumulative voting); and Corp C §900 (amendment of the articles). See also Corp C §2115, which requires foreign corporations doing business in California to comply with California law (discussed at length in ORGANIZING CORPORATIONS IN CALIFORNIA chap 5 (2d ed Cal CEB 1983).

B. Limitations on Power To Amend

§5.4   1. Amendments Inconsistent With the Law

Articles as amended may contain only provisions that could be lawfully inserted in original articles filed at the time the amendment was filed. Corp C §900(a). The original articles in general may contain any lawful provision for the management of the business and the conduct of the corporation's affairs. Corp C §204(d).

Lawfulness is determined under Corp C §§203–204 (see §§5.14–5.69) and also under the common law.

With respect to article provisions that deal with transferability of stock or other rights of the shareholder as an individual, the courts may be willing to overlook inconsistency with the law if it can be shown that the shareholder assented to the restriction or knew of it when acquiring the stock. See §§5.5–5.6. On the other hand, the courts tend to ignore contractual consent and enforce stricter consistency with the law on article provisions that deal with the rights of shareholders as a group or provisions that affect management or the nature of the corporation (*e.g.,* the right to vote for directors, or shareholders' rights that deprive directors of the powers of management or the power to elect officers). See Note, *Articles and By-Laws—Statutory Requirement of Consistency with Law—Contractual Enforcement of Inconsistent Articles and By-Laws,* 31 Notre Dame Law 699 (1956). If a right is guaranteed by statute and consequently cannot be modified by amending the articles, the only alternative may be to attempt to modify the right by private shareholders' agreement. See, *e.g., Sensabaugh v Polson Plywood Co.* (Mont 1959) 342 P2d 1064, in which the court stated that shareholders could validly contract not to vote cumulatively, despite a constitutional guaranty of the right, but the shareholders could not modify or eliminate the right by amendment of the bylaws. See also §5.12.

2. Constitutional Limitations

§5.5 a. Impairment of Contracts

The articles of incorporation are usually regarded as a three-way contract: between the state and the corporation, between the corporation and its shareholders, and among the shareholders themselves. See 7A Fletcher, CYCLOPEDIA OF THE LAW OF PRIVATE CORPORATIONS §3657 (rev ed 1989). A contract cannot be amended without the consent of all the parties unless it otherwise provides. However, California has reserved to itself the power to amend laws concerning corporations. Cal Const art XX, §24. The reserved power includes the power to amend articles of corporations, either by legislative enactment or by action of a specified majority of the shareholders under a legislative enactment permitting them to amend articles. The reserved power provision in the California Constitution is considered part of the three-way contract. See *DeMello v Dairyman's Coop. Creamery* (1946) 73 CA2d 746, 167 P2d 226. Consequently, impairment of contractual obligations is not a ground for limiting the right to amend if the reserved power has been exercised by the legislature. *Tu-Vu Drive-In Corp. v Ashkins* (1964) 61 C2d 283, 38 CR 348; see 1A Ballantine & Sterling, CALIFORNIA CORPORATION LAWS §231.04[2] (4th ed); 2 MARSH'S CALIFORNIA CORPORATION LAW §16.1 (2d ed).

The reserved power is usually exercised by adopting statutes authorizing amendments to articles by action of a specified majority of the shareholders. An example was the enactment in 1987 of enabling legislation (amendments to Corp C §§204, 309) to permit shareholders to amend corporate articles to eliminate or limit directors' personal liability for monetary damages, *e.g.*, for breach of duties to the corporation, and to authorize indemnification of directors, officers, and other corporate agents in excess of that expressly permitted by Corp C §317. See §§5.68. A question often litigated under prior law was whether the statute in fact authorized the amendment to the articles. If not, objecting shareholders could raise impairment of contractual obligations as an objection to the amendment. Some courts required clear statutory authority if important rights were being taken away by the amendment. See *Southern Pac. Co. v Board of R.R. Comm'rs* (CC ND Cal 1896) 78 F 236. It would appear that the California courts should not require statutory specificity under Corp C §900(a) because of the clear expression of legislative intent in the second sentence of Corp C §900(a) to exercise to the fullest extent the state's reserved power over corporations. See §5.3.

If there is adequate statutory authority for the amendment, the shareholder cannot successfully object unless he or she is able to sue in some other capacity. For example, if the shareholder can sue as a creditor, amendments adversely affecting the debt would be an invalid impairment of the shareholder's contract, notwithstanding the reserved power clause. See *Schroeter v Bartlett Syndicate Bldg. Corp.* (1936) 8 C2d 12, 15, 63 P2d 824, 826.

The argument that a subsequently enacted statute cannot apply to previously acquired shares is specifically rejected by Corp C §900(a), which requires only that an amendment be lawful at the time of filing. The argument also had been rejected in earlier cases.

See *Rainey v Michel* (1936) 6 C2d 259, 57 P2d 932; *In re College Hill Land Ass'n* (1910) 157 C 596, 108 P 681.

§5.6   b. Interference With "Vested Rights"

The vested rights doctrine is an aspect of the prohibition against taking property without just compensation. See Lattin, THE LAW OF CORPORATIONS 573 (2d ed 1971). See also §5.7. According to this doctrine, various types of rights provided by articles of incorporation are "vested property rights" that cannot be taken without just compensation. Therefore, any amendment diminishing these rights requires the unanimous consent of the shareholders. However, a majority of the courts that follow this doctrine usually will not find a vested right if the amendment affecting the right is expressly authorized by statute. A specific statute makes it clear that the amendment is authorized by the shareholder's contract (which includes the statute), and, therefore, the right cannot be vested because the shareholder has consented in advance to the amendment. See Note, *The Status of the Doctrine of Vested Rights with Respect to Amendments to the Corporate Charter,* 13 U Pit L Rev 723 (1952).

Although the vested rights doctrine is no longer followed in California (see 2 MARSH'S CALIFORNIA CORPORATION LAW §16.2 (2d ed); see also §5.3), the doctrine does continue to exist in some other states. See, *e.g., Swanson v Shockley* (Iowa 1985) 364 NW2d 252.

§5.7   c. Taking Property Without Just Compensation

The reserved power clause will probably defeat any argument that an amendment constitutes a taking of property without just compensation (due process). *Wilson v Cherokee Drift Mining Co.* (1939) 14 C2d 56, 58, 92 P2d 802, 803; *Heller Inv. Co. v Southern Title & Trust Co.* (1936) 17 CA2d 202, 61 P2d 807. Occasionally, the courts have attempted to avoid confronting this argument directly. See, *e.g., Blumenthal v Di Giorgio Fruit Corp.* (1938) 30 CA2d 11, 85 P2d 580 (no property taken because corporation was in such dire straits that failure to recapitalize might have resulted in liquidation). Note that the reserved power clause operates only on rights derived from the articles. A destruction of rights outside the articles could be a violation of due process. For discussion, see 2 MARSH'S CALIFORNIA CORPORATION LAW §16.3 (2d ed.)

§5.8   3. The Fundamental Change Doctrine

The common law doctrine that requires unanimous consent of the shareholders to effect a fundamental, as distinguished from an auxiliary or incidental, change in the corporation appears to have been rejected by California courts. See *Silva v Coastal Plywood & Timber Co.* (1954) 124 CA2d 276, 268 P2d 510; *DeMello v Dairyman's Coop. Creamery* (1946) 73 CA2d 746, 167 P2d 226. This doctrine antedates the reserved power provisions, and was used primarily to prevent substantial changes in the purposes of a corporation. See also §§5.5–5.6.

4. Equitable Limitations
§5.9   a. The Fairness Test

Beyond the limitations on the power to amend, discussed in §§5.4–5.8, a court of equity has the inherent power to grant injunctive relief when the majority shareholders have acted unfairly toward the minority shareholders. The California test for applying this power is said by one authority to be that stated in *DeMello v Dairyman's Coop. Creamery* (1946) 73 CA2d 746, 751, 167 P2d 226, 228 (quoting from 1A Ballantine & Sterling, CALIFORNIA CORPORATION LAWS §231.04[3][b] (1938)):

> Changes in the rights of outstanding shares may be valid if they can be justified as an exercise of fair business discretion in meeting the needs and exigencies of the corporate enterprise. The more urgent the need or the emergency, the more drastic the amendment or adjustments which fairness will permit.

See also *Bixby v Pierno* (1971) 4 C3d 130, 93 CR 234; *Silva v Coastal Plywood & Timber Co.* (1954) 124 CA2d 276, 268 P2d 510; *Blumenthal v Di Giorgio Fruit Corp.* (1938) 30 CA2d 11, 18, 85 P2d 580, 584.

Thus it appears that, in the event of a challenge, the burden is on the proponents of the amendment (usually the corporate management) to demonstrate (a) the business need or exigency requiring the change, (b) that the amendment would help to meet the need or exigency, and (c) that the adoption of the amendment would appear to be an exercise of fair business discretion in meeting the need, when balanced against the degree of change that would result from the amendment, the available alternatives, and a number of other pertinent factors. See Halloran, *Equitable Limitations On The Power To Amend Articles of Incorporation,* 4 Pac LJ 47 (1973). In summary, the test for granting equitable relief really amounts to balancing various "fairness factors." See §5.10.

§5.10   b. Fairness Factors

Listed below are the principal factors considered by the courts in deciding whether an amendment to the articles should stand or should be enjoined as being inequitable to the objecting shareholders. These factors are also considered by the Commissioner of Corporations in determining whether to issue a permit authorizing an amendment, and by courts in reviewing a decision of the Commissioner. See Orschel, *Administrative Protection for Shareholders in California Recapitalizations,* 4 Stan L Rev 215 (1952). See §§5.74–5.84 for a discussion of when a permit is needed. These factors should be considered both by the attorney advising a corporate client on a proposed amendment and by the attorney for the objecting shareholder. If a permit is required and has been granted, the objecting shareholder will face a particularly difficult task in seeking to convince a court that a proposal is unfair. See 2 MARSH'S CALIFORNIA CORPORATION LAW §16.5 (2d ed).

(1) Corporate necessity. The amendment must be justified by some corporate necessity in terms of business need or exigency. This is basically the test stated in 1A Ballantine & Sterling, CALIFORNIA CORPORATION LAWS §231.04[3] (4th ed), and adopted by the court in *DeMello v Dairyman's Coop. Creamery* (1946) 73 CA2d 746, 751, 167 P2d 226, 228 (membership structure resulted in dissension, hampered operations, caused unnecessary tax payments, and prevented repayment to members of full value of their interests without going into dissolution proceedings). Other examples of such corporate necessity were found in *Tu-Vu Drive-In Corp. v Ashkins* (1964) 61 C2d 283, 38 CR 348 (protection of close corporation and shareholders against unwanted intrusions by outsiders); *Silva v Coastal Plywood & Timber Co.* (1954) 124 CA2d 276, 268 P2d 510 (corporation in financial reorganization proceedings, and amendment required in order to remove restrictions on selling shares, presumably to raise new capital); *Transportation Bldg. Co. v Daugherty* (1946) 74 CA2d 604, 169 P2d 470 (business had never been successful, sole asset was in state of disrepair and decay as a result of payment of dividends out of capital to preferred shareholders, and there was a possibility of sale of the asset to avoid further loss if reorganization was not accomplished); *Blumenthal v Di Giorgio Fruit Corp.* (1938) 30 CA2d 11, 18, 85 P2d 580, 584 (serious financial difficulties, facing probable bankruptcy and dissolution, justified elimination of accrued dividends); and *Heller Inv. Co. v Southern Title & Trust Co.* (1936) 17 CA2d 202, 61 P2d 807 (assets were impaired and new capital was needed in order to continue in business).

(2) Discrimination among or disproportionate treatment of classes or groups of shareholders. The courts have shown considerable interest in whether or not a proposed amendment treats all shareholders alike, or whether there is different treatment of groups or classes of shareholders, particularly if such disparate treatment reflects personal gain to the majority at expense of the minority. See *DeMello v Dairyman's Coop. Creamery, supra* (all members were treated alike); *Lindsay-Strathmore Irr. Dist. v Wutchumna Water Co.* (1931) 111 CA 688, 701, 296 P 933, 939; Note, *Intraclass Discrimination in the Elimination of Accrued Dividends,* 55 Harv L Rev 1196 (1942); see also *Jones v H. F. Ahmanson & Co.* (1969) 1 C3d 93, 108, 81 CR 592, 599 (not an amendment case; however, held broadly that any use to which majority puts the power of control "must benefit all shareholders proportionately").

Lack of a corporate need or business purpose for the amendment, together with discrimination among groups of shareholders, will support the conclusion that its only real purpose is to discriminate against the minority shareholders. *Lindsay-Strathmore Irr. Dist. v Wutchumna Water Co.* (1931) 111 CA 688, 701, 296 P 933, 939; see *DeMello v Dairyman's Coop. Creamery, supra.* When the amendment of the articles increases the authorized number of shares and is followed by issuance of shares, giving each shareholder the right to purchase a pro rata portion of the additional shares (in effect, a preemptive right) will help to eliminate judicial and administrative objections, at least if the price is not grossly unfair. See §§5.15, 5.45.

(3) Size of vote approving amendment and percentage of objecting shares. A favorable shareholder vote approving the amendment, particularly a very large favorable vote, will be given great weight by the courts. There is a presumption of fair dealing by the majority shareholders and by the governing body of the corporation in obtaining their vote, which will control unless it is overcome by contrary evidence. *Transportation Bldg. Co. v Daugherty* (1946) 74 CA2d 604, 614, 169 P2d 470, 476. See also *Western Air Lines, Inc. v Schutzbank* (1968) 258 CA2d 218, 244, 66 CR 293, 310; Dahlquist, *Regulation and Civil Liability Under the California Corporate Securities Act: IV,* 34 Calif L Rev 695, 736 (1946). In addition, if the objecting minority owns a very small number of shares, this factor will weigh in favor of supporting the amendment. Presumably, if the objecting minority shareholders voted for the amendment, they will be estopped from raising a later challenge.

The Commissioner of Corporations also takes careful note of the size of the shareholder vote approving the amendment. The Commissioner usually grants a permit before the shareholders' meeting, and in some circumstances inserts a condition in the permit that a certain percentage of votes be obtained at the meeting. See §5.104.

This factor may be discounted by evidence that the vote has been rigged in favor of the amendment. For example, if the amendment may benefit the common shares at the expense of the preferred shares, and two thirds of the preferred shares are owned by common shareholders, the courts will take this factor into account on a review of the amendment, and the Commissioner may require a higher vote from the preferred shareholders. It is advisable to try to obtain the highest possible independent vote—higher than the majority required by statute—so that this factor will weigh heavily in favor of the proposal.

(4) Available alternatives to the amendment that do less harm to minority shareholders. Courts will sometimes consider whether alternative mechanisms to the amendment adopted might have been available. See, *e.g., Jones v H. F. Ahmanson & Co.* (1969) 1 C3d 93, 115, 81 CR 592, 604; *Keller St. Dev. Co. v Department of Inv.* (1964) 227 CA2d 760, 768, 39 CR 44, 48.

(5) Compensation to minority shareholders. This factor is sometimes called the "compensatory principle." In justifying a recapitalization plan or other amendment to articles, counsel for the majority shareholders and the corporation should usually be able to point to some factor that compensates the adversely affected minority objecting shareholders for the rights they are relinquishing. See *Porges v Vadsco Sales Corp.* (Del Ch 1943) 32 A2d 148 (preferred's accrued dividends were taken away, but voting control passed to preferred); Orschel, *Administrative Protection for Shareholders in California Recapitalizations,* 4 Stan L Rev 215, 224 (1952); Latty, *Fairness—The Focal Point in Preferred Stock Arrearage Elimination,* 29 Va L Rev 1 (1942).

The factor of compensation to minority shareholders requires an appraisal of the right lost by the adversely affected shareholders and what is given to compensate for it. In *McQuillen v National Cash Register Co.* (D Md 1939) 27 F Supp 639, the lost right to accrued dividends was held to be counterbalanced by the gain of an increased equity interest in the company, the permanent right to vote for directors, and the right to participate equally in dividends.

In some situations, *e.g.,* when there is greatly impaired capital, this factor may simply require general financial advantages that accrue to the corporation (*e.g.,* its ability to raise new capital and avoid dissolution), and thus accrue indirectly to the class of shareholders adversely affected by the plan. See §5.36. The attorney for the corporation desiring to recapitalize may wish to consider the standards developed for insolvency reorganizations to ensure fairness to all classes concerned. See Comment, *A Standard of Fairness for Compensating Preferred Shareholders in Corporate Recapitalizations,* 33 U Chi L Rev 97 (1965); Dodd, *Fair and Equitable Recapitalizations,* 55 Harv L Rev 780 (1942).

(6) **Full disclosure to shareholders.** The courts have held that shareholders must be fully and fairly informed of the nature of the plan involving the amendment and of its probable effect on the value of their stock. *Transportation Bldg. Co. v Daugherty* (1946) 74 CA2d 604, 169 P2d 470; see, *e.g., State ex rel Weede v Bechtel* (Iowa 1948) 31 NW2d 853, 857; Comment, *Corporations—Fiduciary Duty of Directors—Amendments to Articles of Incorporation Ineffective Without Adequate Disclosure to Shareholders,* 47 Iowa L Rev 1110 (1962).

(7) **Market prices and financial analysis.** If more than one class of shares will be affected by an article amendment and if all classes of shares are traded on the over-the-counter market or a national securities exchange, their respective prices may be a good indication of what investors consider to be the relative value of the classes of stock. If the exchange ratio is proportionate to the ratio of the

prices, justifying the amendment plan may be easier. In addition, use of financial analysis tests (*e.g.,* capitalizing projected earnings at an appropriate multiplier) may give the court or administrative agency additional insight into whether the recapitalization is justified. See, *e.g., Bailey v Tubize Rayon Corp.* (D Del 1944) 56 F Supp 418, 424.

(8) Hindsight success of business since adoption of amendment. The court or agency may use hindsight in determining the fairness of the plan of amendment, if the review of the plan occurs after a period of its operation. See *Metzger v George Washington Mem. Park, Inc.* (Pa 1955) 110 A2d 425, in which hindsight was used in approving the grant of permanent voting rights to preferred stockholders who had voting control (due to a default in dividends) for many years during which the corporation had been successful. Note, *Protection for Shareholder Interests in Recapitalizations of Publicly Held Corporations,* 58 Colum L Rev 1030 (1958); see Note, *Corporations—Fairness Test Applied to Recapitalization Plan Adopted in Accordance with Statutory Requirements,* 41 Tex L Rev 841 (1963).

§5.11   III. ALTERNATIVE PROCEDURES

Some of the changes in the corporate structure that are listed in §§5.14–5.69 may be accomplished by procedures other than amendment of the articles of incorporation. In addition to changes obtained by a merger, sale of assets, voluntary exchange plans, or repurchase of shares (see §§5.32–5.36, 5.40–5.41, 5.57), or by reorganization under bankruptcy laws (see §5.69), some or all of the following alternatives to amendment may be worth considering in a particular case.

§5.12   A. Agreements Among Shareholders

In some cases, an agreement among the shareholders may be used in lieu of amendment of the articles. The agreement may also sometimes be in the form of bylaws approved by the shareholders, a voting trust (Corp C §706(b)), or an irrevocable proxy (Corp C §705(e)). Certain kinds of amendments may be invalid (*e.g.,* redemption in a one-class share structure, conversion at the option of the corporation), in which case the only alternative may be the use of an agreement among shareholders (see §5.4).

The agreement alternative is of particular use in statutory "close corporations" (Corp C §158). The California corporation statutes (see Corp C §§202–204) appear to have established a norm that the changes in corporate structure discussed in §§5.14–5.69 should be accomplished by amendment of the articles and not by private agreements or by provisions in the bylaws. Statutory close corporations are a specific exception; they may adopt shareholder agreements (Corp C §§300(b), 706(a), (c)) and irrevocable proxies and voting agreements are specifically authorized (Corp C §§705(e)(5), 706(a), (c)).

In addition, agreements may be honored outside the close corporation context. Corporations Code §706(d) and the last sentence of Corp C §204(a) allow the court to enforce an agreement among the shareholders who are parties to the agreement if the court does not feel it is against public policy to do so. For example, suppose that a venture capital investor inserts in the stock purchase agreement with the issuer a right of first refusal to purchase shares sold by the issuer in the future. Such a provision might well be enforceable against shareholders who participated in the agreement. On the other hand, there is some uncertainty whether it would be enforceable against a subsequent shareholder of the issuer who was not a party to the agreement, and counsel should not render an opinion as to the enforceability of such a provision. To the extent the venture capitalist requires a legal opinion or is concerned about the possibility of such a provision not being enforceable, it should insist on a preemptive right in the articles.

Generally, if a shareholder agreement substantially impinges on a statutory norm and is not specifically authorized by statute (*e.g.*, Corp C §158 pertaining to close corporations), the amendment route should be used, at least if the amendment is valid. See Comment, *"Shareholders' Agreements" and the Statutory Norm*, 43 Cornell LQ 68, 76 (1957). See also *Gaskill v Gladys Belle Oil Co.* (Del Ch 1929) 146 A 337; *Nickolopoulos v Sarantis* (NJ 1928) 141 A 792. See §5.105.

§5.13   B. Bylaws

Bylaws or amendments to bylaws should not conflict with the law or the articles of incorporation, but within those basic limits the scope of possible corporate action by bylaw is considerable. See Corp C §212. For example, reasonable restrictions on transfer of shares may be accomplished by amendment of the bylaws. Corp C §212(b)(1). However, no such restriction (whether in articles or bylaws) on shares issued before adoption of the restriction will be binding on nonconsenting shareholders. Corp C §204(b) (which overrules *Tu-Vu Drive-In Corp. v Ashkins* (1964) 61 C2d 283, 38 CR 348 on this point). No filing with the Secretary of State is required; however, a permit from the Commissioner of Corporations may be necessary. Corp C §25103(e)(11); §5.74. See also §5.12 regarding the statutory norm. In the event of any conflict between bylaws and articles, the articles will govern; in the event of any conflict between bylaws and statute (other than variations permitted by statute), the statute will govern. Corp C §212(b). For discussion of statutory rules that may be varied by bylaws, see ORGANIZING CORPORATIONS IN CALIFORNIA §§2.19–2.20, 2.41–2.44 (2d ed Cal CEB 1983).

IV. ACTS THAT REQUIRE AMENDMENT OF ARTICLES

§5.14   A. Stock Assessment

By virtue of the operation of Corp C §900, an amendment to the articles granting the power to levy assessments on shares is authorized by Corp C §204(a)(1). See §5.3. See also Corp C §423 (on assessment of shares), Corp C §904 (requiring consent of all affected shares to amendment authorizing assessment). An amendment making outstanding shares assessable has been upheld despite constitutional objections. *Wilson v Cherokee Drift Mining Co.* (1939) 14 C2d 56, 92 P2d 802.

The average investor will expect that shares are fully paid and nonassessable. Making shares assessable is a major change, not to be anticipated in the ordinary course of business. Thus, shareholder consent is required for such a change. See §5.102. In addition, a permit will typically be required before shareholder approval can be solicited. See §5.75.

Before issuing a permit authorizing an amendment to articles for this purpose, the Commissioner of Corporations will require a showing of corporate necessity for making the shares assessable. See, *e.g., Keller St. Dev. Co. v Department of Inv.* (1964) 227 CA2d

760, 778, 39 CR 44, 48, in which the denial of a permit was upheld when liabilities of the corporation under pending suits had not yet become fixed, the corporation's net worth was not insubstantial, and it had not tried the alternative of borrowing. The Commissioner denied the permit because it appeared that the purpose of the amendment was not to satisfy legitimate needs of the corporation, but rather to freeze out minority shareholders by causing forfeiture of shares for nonpayment of assessment. *Keller* may mark a departure from the previous tendency of California courts to allow amendments authorizing assessment, then to strike down the assessment itself only when it was actually made with such an improper purpose. See, *e.g., Koshaba v Koshaba* (1942) 56 CA2d 302, 312, 132 P2d 854, 860; *Farbstein v Pacific Oil Tool Co.* (1932) 127 CA 157, 15 P2d 766.

The only remedy for the collection of an assessment is sale or forfeiture of the shares, unless remedy by personal action against the shareholders in order to collect the assessment is provided for in the articles. Corp C §423(n). The fact of assessability and the remedy by action against shareholders to collect the assessment, if permitted, must be plainly stated on the face of all share certificates. Corp C §§418(a)(2), 423(n). See also §5.158.

Before consenting to an assessment provision, in most cases, the preferred shareholders should require that the articles provide that assessments on the preferred shares be fully reimbursed before any dividends are paid on the common shares and that, on liquidation, the amount of any assessments plus the liquidation preference be paid to the preferred shareholders before any payment is made to the common shareholders.

A permit from the Commissioner of Corporations is necessary to authorize an amendment to the articles to add, change, or delete assessment provisions, if the change materially and adversely affects any class of shareholders. Corp C §25103(e); see §5.75. For shareholder vote requirements to add or remove an assessment provision, see §5.102.

§5.15 B. Change in Number of Authorized Shares; Capital Reduction; Mandatory Amendment To Provide Shares for Options

A corporation should not amend its articles to decrease the number of its authorized shares of a class or series below the number of issued and outstanding shares of that class or series. To do so would result in an automatic overissue of the outstanding shares of that class or series. To avoid this result, a reverse stock split should ordinarily precede or accompany such an amendment. See §5.16.

An increase or reduction of the authorized number of shares presents few problems as long as each shareholder is left with the same proportionate interest as others of the same and different classes and series. See §§5.92–5.100 as to class and series vote requirements. However, an increase or decrease of one class or series without increase or decrease of another, when followed or accompanied by a subsequent issuance of shares of the increased class or series, or reduction with respect to shares of the decreased class or series, may seriously dilute the holding of one class or series. Such action can raise issues of discrimination among classes or series of shares and violation of equitable limitations on the power of amendment, even though the amendment is approved by the requisite number of outstanding shares. See §§5.9–5.10. See also §5.75 regarding permit requirements.

The most typical situation in which this problem occurs is a capital reduction or reorganization of a corporation in financial difficulty and with a multiple class structure. In such a situation, an amendment may be adopted that decreases the authorized and outstanding shares. The holders of one class of shares are likely to attack the amendment if they feel that the other class of shares is not sufficiently assuming the burden of the reduction. See, *e.g., Kennedy v Carolina Pub. Serv. Co.* (ND Ga 1920) 262 F 803 (reduction of preferred shares by two fifths and common by one fifth held invalid). Such "reduction of capital" cases enunciate a rule that each shareholder must be left with the same proportionate interest as others of the same or different classes or series. However, there is some difference of opinion as to what is a preferred or common shareholder's proportionate interest.

In *Page v Whittenton Mfg. Co.* (Mass 1912) 97 NE 1006, a corporation required new capital or faced the danger of liquidation. It had two classes of outstanding shares: 8000 common, and 2000 6 percent cumulative preferred, with a liquidation preference. It was proposed that an amendment be adopted to reduce the number of authorized outstanding common shares to 1000, leaving the preferred shares intact, then to adopt an amendment increasing the authorized number of common shares and give the shares of both classes the right to subscribe to the new authorized common shares on a prorata basis. The court stated that it would not have allowed the plan, but would have required it to be borne equally by both classes of stock, if the preference of the preferred had been only as to dividends. But because the common could not participate on dissolution until the liquidation preference of the preferred was satisfied, and because failure to adopt the amendment might force the corporation to liquidate (presumably leaving nothing or very little on liquidation for the common), the court concluded that the "contract" between the classes of shareholders was that the common "assumed the burden," and, therefore, "must be first resorted to even to the point of extinction before the preferred stock can be compelled to contribute." 97 NE at 1007. The court in effect adopted the "absolute priority" rule used in solvency reorganizations.

In *Page v American & British Mfg. Co.* (App Div 1908) 113 NYS 734, however, the corporation had two classes of outstanding stock: 80,000 shares of common, and 20,000 shares of preferred, with a dividend and liquidation preference of $100. The common stock was reduced to 20,000 shares, and the number of preferred shares was left intact, although its liquidation preference was also reduced to $50. The court stated that the reduction should have been borne equally by both classes, regardless of the liquidation preference of the preferred, unless there was an express statutory provision authorizing reduction of one class but not another.

The court in *Page v Whittenton Mfg. Co.* (Mass 1912) 97 NE 1006, looked at the problem in terms of proportionate interest in the assets in the event of liquidation. Under this theory, if the preferred has a liquidation preference, the common is the class that must always be reduced, never the preferred. The court in *Page v American & British Mfg. Co., supra,* looked at the problem in terms of voting power. Thus, even though the preferred has a liquidation preference, and even though (in line with the rule adopted in the first case) only the common stock is to be reduced, this reduction is invalid because it reduces the common's proportionate vote. See 11 Fletcher, CYCLOPEDIA OF THE LAW OF PRIVATE CORPORATIONS §§5149, 5150, 5302 (rev ed 1989). A way to satisfy the requirements of both cases is to reduce the number of shares of common, but maintain its proportionate voting strength, if necessary, by giving the common several votes per share or by reducing proportionately the voting power of the preferred. The "absolute priority" rule has been rejected by the commentators for use in the capitalization area, when the company is still a going concern (see articles cited in §5.10(5)). However, when the preferred stock's liquidation preference reduces the common to "a shadow of an equity" in a situation of greatly impaired capital, a capital reduction that includes a reduction of voting rights may be upheld. See 1A Ballantine & Sterling, CALIFORNIA CORPORATION LAWS §231.04 (4th ed).

A capital reduction in either a one- or two-class structure is usually justified when it is necessary to correct the poor financial condition of the corporation, and is not to be for an improper purpose. See Halloran, *Equitable Limitations on the Power To Amend Articles of Incorporation,* 4 Pac LJ 47, 52 (1973); *Hay v Big Bend Land Co.* (Wash 1949) 204 P2d 488 (continual deficits); *Harper v State Bank* (Ill App 1939) 21 NE2d 47 (failing financial condition); Becht, *Changes in the Interests of Classes of Stockholders by Corporate Charter Amendments Reducing Capital, and Altering Redemption, Liquidation and Sinking Fund Provisions,* 36 Cornell LQ 1 (1950). In *Theis v Durr* (Wis 1905) 104 NW 985, an apparently legitimate reduction of the number of authorized and outstanding shares by amendment was enjoined when the purpose of the majority in doing so was "illegitimate," *i.e.,* an attempt to remove the need for paying the balance of the majority shareholders' subscriptions on their shares. The other shareholders had paid for their shares, and the court treated the reduction as intraclass discrimination. Assuming that the requisite corporate need is present and that there is no improper purpose, reduction of the shares of a single outstanding class has not raised equitable objections.

The majority of the shareholders cannot increase the authorized number of shares and issue such shares to themselves with the purpose of increasing their proportionate interest and ousting the minority shareholders from participation in corporate affairs. *Browning v C & C Plywood Corp.* (Ore 1967) 434 P2d 339; *Starr v Engineering Contracting Co.* (Neb 1948) 31 NW2d 213; *Danzig v Lacks* (App Div 1932) 256 NYS 769. See 1 MARSH'S CALIFORNIA CORPORATION LAW §§10.20, 10.41 (2d ed). If minority shareholders will object to issuing additional shares to the majority, judicial and administrative impediments will tend to be reduced if the minority is allowed to purchase its proportion of the shares (a sort of "preemptive right"). See *Bennett v Breuil Petrol. Corp.* (Del Ch 1953)

99 A2d 236, 239; *Gaines v Long Mfg. Co.* (NC 1951) 67 SE2d 350; *Hyman v Velsicol Corp.* (Ill App 1951) 97 NE2d 122; §§5.10(2), 5.45.

An amendment to increase or decrease the authorized number of shares is mandatory in two instances. First, if shares are acquired by the corporation and the articles prohibit reissuing them, the number of authorized shares of the class or series must be amended (without the necessity of shareholder vote) to reflect the reduction. Corp C §510(b); see §5.108. Second, if the corporation is not authorized by its articles to issue enough shares to satisfy option or conversion rights it has granted, the additional number of shares needed when the option or conversion rights are exercised must be authorized by amendment to the articles. Corp C §405(a). It could be argued that such an amendment either requires no shareholder vote, or that an affirmative vote can be compelled by the holders of the rights. A more prudent approach that obviates the issue is to obtain approval of the outstanding shares to issue the option or conversion right. In such a case, it is clear that no further shareholder approval is necessary to increase the number of shares. Corp C §405(b). Any necessity for amendment under Corp C §405 can, and should, be reduced by having the board, by resolution, reserve out of the authorized but unissued shares a sufficient number of shares for issuance on exercise of such rights. Counsel for the holders of the rights should ensure that they are adequately protected in this regard before the rights are issued. Counsel for the corporation should also advise such a reservation to prevent potential problems at the time the rights can be exercised.

C. Change in Number of Outstanding Shares

§5.16   1. Stock Split or Reverse Stock Split

A "stock split" is a pro rata division, other than by a share dividend, of all the outstanding shares of a class into a greater number of shares of the same class, accomplished by an amendment of the articles stating the intended effect on outstanding shares. Corp C §188. The amendment must also increase the authorized number of shares if splitting the shares will otherwise result in the number of outstanding shares exceeding the number of authorized shares.

A stock split may be used to increase the number of outstanding shares while at the same time reducing the market value per share in order to improve share marketability. Another purpose may be to give the shareholders an indication of improved profits of the corporation without distribution of a cash dividend that would be taxable to the shareholders and that might reduce the cash needed for expansion. A stock dividend is another method of accomplishing these purposes.

A "reverse stock split" is a pro rata combination of all the outstanding shares of a class into a smaller number of shares of the same class accomplished by an amendment of the articles stating the effect on outstanding shares. Corp C §182. The purpose may be to increase market value, or sometimes to meet minimum market price requirements of stock exchanges, of underwriters proposing a public offering, or even of the Commissioner of Corporations, none of whom favors "penny stocks." See, *e.g.*, Corp C §25103(f). For qualification requirements for stock splits and reverse stock splits, see §5.76. A reverse stock split can also be used to effect a capital reduction. See §5.15.

§5.17   2. Stock Split versus Stock Dividend

By definition (see §5.16), a stock split or reverse stock split is always accomplished by amending the articles. A stock dividend, on the other hand, is accomplished by a distribution of stock without amending the articles (unless amendment is necessary to authorize sufficient shares). See Mitchell, *Stock Splits and Stock Dividends—The Requirement of a Permit from the Commissioner of Corporations,* 39 LA B Bull 449 (1964). Amendment of the articles to increase the authorized number of shares in order subsequently to declare a large stock dividend is not a stock split under the California Corporations Code; the amendment to the articles must itself effect the split, "stating the effect on outstanding shares." Corp C §188. Amendment of the articles for purposes of a stock split or reverse stock split is authorized by Corp C §900 as "a change in shares."

Three important reasons for distinguishing between a stock split and a stock dividend are (1) the differing requirements of shareholder approval (see §5.101), (2) the differing requirements of administrative approval (see §5.76), and (3) the differing accounting treatment (see

§5.23). Forms for stock splits and reverse stock splits are set forth in §§5.124–5.126.

3. Examples of Stock Split and Stock Dividend

§5.18   a. One-Class Structure

Assume that the corporation has outstanding 500,000 shares of publicly traded common stock with a market price of $40 per share. The board of directors wishes to double the number of outstanding shares, and reduce the market value per share to $20. A two-for-one stock split would accomplish this result. On properly amending the articles of incorporation (see §§5.76, 5.101, 5.124), each outstanding share will be divided into two shares. There is no need to print different share certificates unless the par value of the corporation's stock was also changed. (While the Corporations Code no longer provides for par value, some corporations still retain the concept for their shares; see §5.24.) The outstanding certificates should, however, be replaced with new ones showing the new number of shares. The same results may be obtained by issuing a stock dividend of 500,000 shares, assuming there are at least 1,000,000 authorized common shares. See §5.17.

b. Two-Class Structure

§5.19   (1) Both Classes Affected

Assume that the corporation has a two-class stock structure consisting of 500,000 shares of common stock and 500,000 shares of preferred stock with a dividend rate of $5 per share, a voluntary liquidation preference of $105 per share, and an involuntary liquidation preference of $100 per share. The preferred shares are redeemable at $105 per share. Management desires to double the number of outstanding shares of each class. This may be accomplished by splitting the shares of each class two-for-one, and dividing each preferred share into two shares, each share having half the former dividend rate, voluntary and involuntary liquidation preferences, and a redemption price such that no change in relative preferences will occur.

The drafter should be careful that the amendment does not change the designation of a class; otherwise, the amendment may not be deemed a "stock split." The division must be into a greater number of shares of the same class. Corp C §188. A different shareholder vote may be required if the amendment is not a stock split. See §5.101.

If the doubling of shares had been accomplished by a stock dividend, no amendment to the articles would have been needed (except to the extent required to authorize additional shares). Consequently, there would have been no way to keep the amount of the relative preferences equal by reducing the preference of the doubled number of preferred shares by one half. To avoid an unfair doubling of the preferences of the preferred stock, an acceptable alternative procedure might be to issue, as a stock dividend, 500,000 common shares to the preferred. However, if the preferred had limited voting rights, issuing the new common shares with full voting rights might be objectionable to the old common shareholders. If so, a stock split may be the only acceptable approach. A permit from the California Commissioner of Corporations may be required under Corp C §25103(f). See §5.76.

§5.20   (2) One Class Affected

This situation is the same as that in §5.19, except that only the common shares will be split, two-for-one, after the requisite majority shareholder vote is obtained (see Corp C §§902(a), 903(a)). The common shares will have twice as many votes as the preferred. A reverse stock split of one class will accomplish the opposite result: the class affected will have half as many votes. These results are authorized by Corp C §§182, 188, but if the split were performed for improper purposes, relief would be available under equitable limitations on the exercise of corporate powers. See 1 Ballantine & Sterling, CALIFORNIA CORPORATION LAWS §148.02(3) (4th ed); Comment, *Reverse Stock Splits: The Fiduciary's Obligations Under State Law,* 63 Calif L Rev 1226 (1975). See also §§5.9–5.10. A permit from the Commissioner of Corporations may be required under Corp C §25103(f). See §5.76.

§5.21   (3) One Series Affected

A series of a class of shares may not be split; only the entire class may be split. Corp C §§182, 188. However, a split of a single series of a multiple series class can probably be accomplished by reclassifying the shares into another class or series of shares with an appropriate exchange ratio to reflect the desired split. Because the transaction is not a stock split, none of the exceptions under Corp C §903(a)(1)–(2) apply, and a class vote is required. Corp C §903(a). See §5.76 as to whether a permit from the Commissioner of Corporations will be required.

§5.22   4. Tax Risk of Stock Dividend

Stock issued as a dividend may under certain circumstances be held to be "section 306 stock," with the result that on disposition of the stock by the shareholders the proceeds may be taxable to them at ordinary income rates. IRC §306. This provision was designed primarily to prevent the so-called "preferred stock bail-out," by which a preferred stock dividend distributed to common shareholders was in substance a withdrawal of corporate earnings and profits, taxable at capital gains rates on the subsequent sale of the preferred. See *Chamberlin v Commissioner* (6th Cir 1953) 207 F2d 462. Stock other than common stock received by a shareholder in a tax-free exchange under IRC §351 is section 306 stock if the receipt of money instead of stock would have been taxed as a dividend. IRC §306(c)(3).

Internal Revenue Code §306 poses a hazard which should always be evaluated when considering the distribution of a stock dividend, other than common on common. Ordinary income is realized on various kinds of dispositions of "section 306 stock," including most sales, conversions, and redemptions, but not including transfers on the death of the shareholder to his or her estate or beneficiaries. IRC §306(b). Counsel for a corporation intending to issue a common stock dividend should, if there is more than one class of shares or any convertible securities outstanding, also review IRC §305, which may cause the stock distribution to be taxable at ordinary income rates.

§5.23   5. Accounting Definitions and Treatment

The accounting treatment for stock splits and stock dividends, as well as the applicable definitions used by the accounting profession, are quite different from those used in the California

Corporations Code, whether or not the transaction is accomplished by amendment of the articles; thus a "stock split" for corporation law purposes may or may not be a stock split for accounting purposes. The definitions set forth in the Corporations Code are relevant only for corporate law purposes (*e.g.*, shareholder vote, method of consummation, and Department of Corporations permit requirements).

The basic accounting approach is set forth in Accounting Research Bulletin No. 43, issued by the American Institute of Certified Public Accountants (AICPA). A stock split is an issuance for the purpose of increasing the number of outstanding shares to reduce the unit price, while a stock dividend is an issuance for the purpose of giving shareholders a separate evidence of their prorata interest in accumulated earnings without a property or cash distribution. Distribution of less than 20 or 25 percent of previously outstanding shares would rarely be treated as a stock split, although these percentages are not necessarily the maximum for stock dividend accounting treatment. Accounting Research Bull No. 43, chap 7 §B (1953), CCH AICPA Prof. Stan., AC §5561.02; see 2 MARSH'S CALIFORNIA CORPORATION LAW §16.14 (2d ed); 1 Ballantine & Sterling, CALIFORNIA CORPORATION LAWS §§147.01, 148.01[1][b] (4th ed). Distributions of over 25 percent may "lend themselves to such a [stock dividend] interpretation if they appear to be part of a program of recurring distributions designed to mislead shareholders." Securities and Exchange Commission Financial Reporting Release 1 §214 (Securities Exchange Act Release No. 9618 (June 1, 1972)), CCH Fed Sec L Rep ¶73,055.

The approach set forth in Accounting Research Bull No. 43 is followed generally by the SEC (see Financial Reporting Release 1 §214 (Securities Exchange Act Release No. 9618 (June 1, 1972)), CCH Fed Sec L Rep ¶73,055); the New York Stock Exchange (see NYSE Listed Company Manual §703.02, CCH Accountants SEC Practice Manual ¶3541); and the American Stock Exchange (see American Stock Exchange Company Guide §506, CCH Accountants SEC Practice Manual ¶3606).

If the transaction is characterized as a stock dividend, the AICPA, SEC, NYSE, and ASE require the corporation to transfer from earned surplus "to the category of permanent capitalization (represented by the capital stock and capital surplus accounts) an amount equal to the fair value of the additional shares issued." Accounting Research

Bull No. 43. If it is characterized as a stock split, none of the four bodies requires such a transfer from earned surplus to stated capital except to the extent that the law may require. Accounting Research Bull No. 43, chap 7 §B. The Corporations Code has no such requirement.

The Corporations Code does not specify an account to which the fair value of a stock dividend should be credited. Corporations Code §114, which imposes the concept of generally accepted accounting principles on financial statements prepared under the General Corporation Law, turns the matter back to the accountants. In SEC Financial Reporting Release 1 §214 (Securities Exchange Act Release No. 9618 (June 1, 1972)), CCH Fed Sec L Rep ¶73,055, the SEC stated that if the issuer does not have retained or current earnings against which to charge a stock dividend, the transaction may be part of a scheme giving rise to liability under SEC Rule 10b–5, issued under Securities Exchange Act §10(b) (15 USC §78j(b)), because the shareholders may be misled into thinking that there has been a distribution of earnings equivalent to the value of the shares received. Section 10(b) is applicable to both public and private corporations. Securities Exchange Act §10(b) (15 USC §78j(b)).

§5.24   D. Change In or Deletion of Par Value

Par value is not provided for in the California Corporations Code. Corporations that existed on January 1, 1977, are permitted by the General Corporation Law to amend their articles by board action alone to delete references to par value. Corp C §§2301–2302; see §5.132. Such existing corporations may, if they wish, retain par value in their articles. The articles of corporations formed after January 1, 1977, may (but need not, and often will not) provide for par value under the authority of Corp C §204(d), and the articles of corporations formed before or after that date may be amended to change the par value. Retaining par value is meaningful primarily if it is used to define the shareholders' rights, *e.g.,* outstanding preferred stock preferences are stated as a percentage of par value. Otherwise, statements as to par value in the articles of all corporations are rendered meaningless under the General Corporation Law because it fails to give par value any other substantive effect and has repealed all provisions of the former law relating to par value. Note however that some practitioners continue to set a par value for shares of

California corporations if they anticipate the corporation is likely to do business in a state where the corporation's tax burden can be affected by the par value of its shares.

§5.25 E. Reclassifications

Broad statutory authority exists for every form of amendment to effect changes in preferences, rights, privileges, or restrictions of shares and reclassification of shares, as long as the amended articles could have appeared in the original articles filed at the date of the amendment. Corp C §§204, 900, 903; see §5.3. It has been said that amendments to reclassify shares will be held invalid if discriminatory or confiscatory, unless they can be justified as an emergency or necessary reorganization. 1A Ballantine & Sterling, CALIFORNIA CORPORATION LAWS §§230.03, 231.04 (4th ed). See the fairness test discussed in §§5.9–5.10. Shareholder approval of such an amendment is required. Corp C §§903(a)(4), 903(c); see §§5.98, 5.128.

§5.26 F. Creation of Senior Class or Series

The articles may be amended to create a senior class or series of stock after the requisite shareholder approval is obtained. Corp C §903(a)(5). Procedures for effecting such an amendment are set forth in §§5.97, 5.127. A permit from the Commissioner of Corporations may not be necessary. See §5.75. The board of directors may be authorized under a "blank stock" provision to fix and alter the rights of an unissued class or series of shares, and to alter the number of shares of an unissued series. Corp C §202(e)(3). Doubts have sometimes been expressed that the board of directors, operating under the blank stock provision, can give priority to one series over another series of the same class. However, the language of Corp C §202(e)(3) is broader than that of prior law, giving the board full authority to create and alter rights of an unissued class or series under a blank stock provision approved by the shareholders. Corporations Code §202(e)(3) appears to permit greater freedom to the board than under prior law. For example, it would seem to permit a board to make one series of preferred cumulative as to dividends and another series noncumulative. The operation of a blank stock provision is discussed in §5.72.

The creation of a senior class of stock for the purpose of raising capital is difficult to attack on equitable grounds because the corporation could undoubtedly raise funds by issuing debentures or other forms of indebtedness that would be senior to the common stock and could be given voting rights. Corp C §204(a)(7); see *Heller Inv. Co. v Southern Title & Trust Co.* (1936) 17 CA2d 202, 209, 61 P2d 807, 810 (enough shares were issued to shift voting control from common; strong showing of corporate necessity); see also 1A Ballantine & Sterling, CALIFORNIA CORPORATION LAWS §231.04[2] (4th ed).

If the purpose of creating the senior class is to exchange it for old preferred, there may be unfairness, because the object of the transaction may be to eliminate accrued dividends or to perpetuate a majority in control, rather than to acquire new capital. See Note, *Limitations on Alteration of Shareholders' Rights by Charter Amendment,* 69 Harv L Rev 538, 545 (1956). However, objections to creating a new senior class for such a purpose have not succeeded if there appeared to be adequate corporate need for the new preferred. See, *e.g., Blumenthal v Di Giorgio Fruit Corp.* (1938) 30 CA2d 11, 19, 85 P2d 580, 584; *Bixby v Pierno* (1971) 4 C3d 130, 148, 93 CR 234, 247. See also Curran, *Minority Stockholders and the Amendment of Corporate Charters,* 32 Mich L Rev 743, 768 (1934); 1A Ballantine & Sterling §231.04[3][b]; 2 MARSH'S CALIFORNIA CORPORATION LAW §16.8 (2d ed).

When the articles are amended to provide for two classes of shares, the difference between the classes must be set forth in the articles. See §5.127. The Secretary of State will not accept such an amendment unless it provides substantively different rights for each class established by the amendment, or creates a class or series of blank stock. See §5.72. Further, the distinction between classes must be permanent and cannot disappear at a specified time or event. For example, a provision for one class to have a preferential dividend until a future date, at which time the class will have the same rights as the other class, is not acceptable to the Secretary of State. Also, shares of a single class cannot provide for different rights on the happening of a future event (*e.g.,* a provision that shares held by a shareholder who is not a full-time employee shall have no voting rights). The solution to these problems is to provide for automatic conversion into the other class of shares on the future date or event. See §5.47.

The Secretary of State has taken the position that under Corp C §202(e)(3), the articles cannot provide for any mechanism under the control of the board of directors or shareholders to determine in their discretion the rights or preferences of already issued and outstanding shares. The rights of shares should be certain and not determined by facts ascertainable outside the articles, except to the extent permitted by Corp C §109.5.

§5.27 G. Shareholder Qualifications

Establishing or changing any provisions regarding special qualifications of persons who may be shareholders requires an amendment to the articles of incorporation. Corp C §§204(a)(3), 900. Such provisions are frequently used in professional corporations, and indeed are advisable in these cases. (Statutory restrictions on who can be shareholders in professional corporations apply regardless of the provisions in the articles.) Corp C §§13401–13401.5, 13406–13407; Bus & P C §2408. See also ATTORNEY'S GUIDE TO CALIFORNIA PROFESSIONAL CORPORATIONS §§3.9 (dental), 3.29 (law), 3.50 (medical) (4th ed Cal CEB 1987).

Such provisions may also be used to protect a corporation from outside takeover attempts. The courts will review such a provision closely to see if it was justified by business need and other equitable factors, particularly if the free transferability of shares of nonconsenting shareholders would be affected by the amendment. *Tu-Vu Drive-In Corp. v Ashkins* (1964) 61 C2d 283, 38 CR 348. Such shareholders may be able to block the amendment under Corp C §204(b) if it can be shown that the amendment results in a restriction on the right to transfer shares. Establishing directors' qualifications in the bylaws (Corp C §212(b)(4)) may be an alternative to shareholder qualifications in the articles. See, *e.g., McKee & Co. v First Nat'l Bank* (SD Cal 1967) 265 F Supp 1.

§5.28 H. Supermajority Vote Provisions

Except as discussed below, an amendment to the articles is required to establish or change requirements for a supermajority vote (the vote of all or a larger proportion of shareholders or directors than is otherwise required by the statute for mergers, sales of assets, amendment of articles or bylaws, other corporate transactions), and a change in such provisions must be approved by the required supermajority vote unless the articles provide otherwise. Corp C §§152, 204(a)(5), (a)(9), 902(e); see §5.105. A supermajority vote provision is useful to protect minority shareholders or holders of preferred shares against actions adverse to them, and to make takeover attempts more difficult. Requiring a supermajority vote of directors is useful particularly for a closely held corporation. In general, these supermajority provisions are not effective if they appear only in the bylaws, and not in the articles. One exception is a provision requiring a majority of the authorized number of directors to act. A second, broader, exception obtains in the case of statutory close corporations, which may deal with such matters in a shareholders' agreement. Corp C §204(a).

Corporations existing before January 1, 1977, if they have supermajority provisions in their bylaws, may retain but not amend them. However, pre–1977 corporations that elect or have elected to be governed by Corp C §§202, 204, and 205 (see §§5.132–5.133) must transfer the supermajority vote provisions to the articles. Such a transfer will require a shareholder vote. Corp C §§2302–2302.1. For further discussion, see §5.105.

§5.29   I. Debtholder Voting Rights

An amendment to the articles is required to establish or change provisions for debtholder voting rights (which may be given in the event of, *e.g.,* default), and has been used particularly by corporations in financial difficulties. See Corp C §204(a)(7). Attempts to grant such rights by contract (as in a loan agreement) may not be effective as to anyone who is not a party to the contract. See §5.12.

§5.30   J. Shareholder Rights To Fix Consideration for Shares

An amendment to the articles is required to establish or change a provision that confers on shareholders the right to determine the consideration for which shares shall be issued. See Corp C §§409(c) and 204(a)(8). These provisions are useful primarily for closely held corporations.

K. Change in Certain Dividend Rights

§5.31   1. Change in Accrued Dividend Arrearages

Perhaps the most litigated and controversial aspect of the law of amending articles of incorporation is the elimination of accrued and undeclared dividend arrearages on cumulative preferred shares. An amendment to eliminate accrued dividend arrearages is believed to be authorized by the general terms of Corp C §900, in view of Corp C §903(a)(7), which sets forth the required vote for such an amendment. A form of amendment is set forth in §5.131.

Courts outside California have at times construed statutes strictly to prevent cancellation of accrued dividends. See, *e.g., Schaad v Hotel Easton Co.* (Pa 1952) 87 A2d 227; *Janes v Washburn Co.* (Mass 1950) 94 NE2d 479. See also Buxbaum, *Preferred Stock—Law and Draftsmanship,* 42 Calif L Rev 243, 299 (1954); Meck, *Accrued Dividends on Cumulative Preferred Stocks: The Legal Doctrine,* 55 Harv L Rev 71, 81 (1941); Note, *Amending the Articles of Incorporation,* 15 S Car L Rev 506, 510 (1962). The California courts have generally taken a liberal view of the scope of the power to amend. See Note, *Corporations: Elimination of Dividend Arrearages on Cumulative Preferred Stock by Amendment of the Articles of Incorporation,* 37 Calif L Rev 129 (1949); see also 2 MARSH'S CALIFORNIA CORPORATION LAW §16.7 (2d ed). However, it cannot now be assumed that Corp C §900 makes such an amendment completely safe from attack. If an active dissident group seems ready to take to court the issue regarding an amendment to eliminate dividend arrearages, alternative methods of accomplishing that result should be considered.

§5.32   a. Alternatives to Amendment for Elimination of Dividend Arrearages

There are three principal methods other than amendment of the articles for eliminating dividend arrearages: (1) merger or sale of assets, (2) "voluntary" exchange plan, and (3) repurchase of shares. See 2 MARSH'S CALIFORNIA CORPORATION LAW §§16.7–16.9 (2d ed); see also Comment, *Elimination of Accrued Dividends in Corporate Reorganization,* 28 Tex L Rev 419 (1950). These alternative techniques are usually more complicated and expensive than amendment of the articles of incorporation. Like amendment of the articles, the first two techniques may require a permit from the Department of Corporations.

§5.33   (1) Mergers

A merger may take the following form: Creating a shell corporation or a subsidiary with the desired capitalization, merging the existing corporation into it, and converting the shares with arrearages into shares without arrearages. See 2 MARSH'S CALIFORNIA CORPORATION LAW §16.9 (2d ed). The same result can be accomplished by merger with a going corporation. See, *e.g.*, *Langfelder v Universal Labs., Inc.* (3d Cir 1947) 163 F2d 804. The rationale for this result is that appraisal rights give the shareholder an adequate remedy, and the merger statute is designed to operate retroactively on stock rights. In a merger with a corporation controlled by the existing corporation (see Corp C §160), shareholders may test whether the transaction is "just and reasonable." Corp C §1312(c). In some situations an independent appraiser's opinion on fairness may also be required. Corp C §1203.

§5.34   (2) Exchange Plan

The first step in a voluntary exchange plan is an amendment of the articles to create a new senior preferred stock. The second step is either to offer the new preferred stock in exchange for old preferred and for cancellation of its arrearages, or to effect an amendment to the articles making the old preferred stock convertible into the new preferred at the holder's option. If a holder of the old preferred stock refuses to exchange or convert, that shareholder is relegated to second preference dividends. The new preferred may receive current dividends before payment of dividends to the old preferred and before payment of arrearages on the old preferred shares. The exchange method gives management the flexibility to shorten or extend the period during which old preferred shareholders can obtain the new preferred stock. This technique received judicial approval in *Blumenthal v Di Giorgio Fruit Corp.* (1938) 30 CA2d 11, 85 P2d 580. See 2 MARSH'S CALIFORNIA CORPORATION LAW 16.8 (2d ed).

§5.35 (3) Repurchase of Shares

Use of the technique of share repurchase depends on the voluntary decision of each shareholder. A cash offer for the preferred shares instead of an offer of another security may induce the shareholders to sell. Because in the usual situation the preferred shares will be selling at a depressed price, they can probably be bought for less than the sum of their redemption or liquidation values plus accrued dividends. When using this method, the corporation should consider disclosure of asset values and other material facts to avoid liability under SEC Rule 10b–5 under the Securities Exchange Act of 1934 and the concomitant provisions of California law. See Corp C §25541. For issues of federal law, see *Speed v Transamerica Corp.* (D Del 1951) 99 F Supp 808.

§5.36 b. Evaluation of Alternatives; Equitable Limitations

Of all the alternatives to amendment of the articles to eliminate dividend arrearages, the exchange route is probably the best alternative in California for the following reasons: (1) This method was approved in *Blumenthal v Di Giorgio Fruit Corp.* (1938) 30 CA2d 11, 85 P2d 580; (2) it is probably cheaper and less complicated than the other alternatives, because it takes the form of a simple authorization of a senior class (see §5.26); and (3) an exchange avoids judicial statements that merger, sale of assets, and dissolution statutes meant for one purpose do not apply for any other purpose. See *Mullen v Academy Life Ins. Co.* (1983) 705 F2d 971; *Weckler v Valley City Mill. Co.* (WD Mich 1950) 93 F Supp 444, aff'd (6th Cir 1951) 188 F2d 367; Latty, *Fairness—The Focal Point in Preferred Stock Arrearage Elimination,* 29 Va L Rev 1 (1942).

Even if the statute authorizes elimination of accrued dividends, there are still equitable limitations. See Halloran, *Equitable Limitations On The Power To Amend Articles Of Incorporation,* 4 Pac LJ 47 (1973). When justifying elimination of accrued dividends on equitable grounds, courts have used the argument that the corporation is in financial distress and must free earnings from the claims of the preferred before needed capital can be raised by the sale of additional common or of securities convertible into common. *Blumenthal v Di Giorgio Fruit Corp.* (1938) 30 CA2d 11, 85 P2d 580. Some writers have said that although on its face such an argument has merit, they have found no situations in which such financing has followed the recapitalization plan. See Dodd, *Fair and Equitable Recapitalizations,* 55 Harv L Rev 780, 783 (1942); Comment, *Limitations on Alteration of Shareholders' Rights by Charter Amendment,* 69 Harv L Rev 538, 545 n42 (1959). In addition, an alternative means of obtaining financing (*e.g.,* long term borrowing) may be available that will not be affected by the preferred's claim to accrued dividends. See §§5.9–5.10 for a discussion of this and other fairness factors used in accrued dividend elimination decisions. See also the pros and cons of various fairness arguments in Latty, *Fairness—The Focal Point in Preferred Stock Arrearage Elimination,* 29 Va L Rev 1 (1942).

§5.37   2. Change in Future Dividend Rights or Rates

Amendments that alter future dividend rights or rates should not raise any serious problems if justified by a sufficient corporate need and other fairness factors. See de Funiak, *Reducing Rate of Dividend on Preferred Stock,* 14 Notre Dame Law 23 (1938). In *Transportation Bldg. Co. v Daugherty* (1946) 74 CA2d 604, 610, 169 P2d 470, 474, the right to receive cumulative dividends out of "net cash receipts" was changed to the right to receive cumulative dividends out of surplus or net earnings. Denial of a permit by the Commissioner of Corporations was reversed on the ground that the matter should be decided by the required two-thirds fraction of the preferred shareholders. This conclusion was reinforced by the fact that the corporation had been operating at a deficit, and under the old formula the dividends were being paid out of needed capital.

L. Change in Redemption Provisions
§5.38   1. Compulsory Redemption

Corporations Code §402(a) permits a corporation to provide in its articles for one or more classes or series of shares which are redeemable, in whole or in part, (1) at the option of the corporation, or (2) to the extent and upon the happening of one or more specified events. Articles may not otherwise provide for redeemable shares, except as specifically permitted by §402(a). Consequently, a provision for redemption of common shares at the option of the holder is invalid. See 1 Ballantine & Sterling, CALIFORNIA CORPORATION LAWS

§127.03[5][b] (4th ed); 1 MARSH'S CALIFORNIA CORPORATION LAW §5.8 (2d ed).

Corporations Code §402(a) permits a corporation to provide in its articles for one or more classes or series of preferred shares which are redeemable, in whole or in part, as specified for common shares. Unlike common shares, preferred shares may also be made redeemable at the option of the holder or on the vote of at least a majority of the outstanding shares of the class or series to be redeemed. Corp C §402(a).

An open-end investment company registered under the Investment Company Act of 1940 is permitted, if its articles so provide, to issue shares redeemable at the option of the holder at a price approximately equal to the shares' proportionate interest in the corporation's net assets. See Corp C §§402(a), (c), 504. The statute specifically does not preclude a corporation from creating a sinking fund or similar provision, or entering into an agreement, for the redemption or purchase of its shares to the extent permitted by Corp C §§500–511 (dividends and reacquisitions of shares). Corp C §402(d). A sinking fund, a schedule of mandatory redemption, or an agreement to redeem imposes an obligation on the corporation to redeem at a specified time or on the occurrence of a specified event or condition. Such an obligation is enforceable only to the extent that the corporation meets the tests for making the distribution under Corp C §§500–511. Corp C §402(d). See Corp C §2308 regarding application of these tests to purchase or redemption provisions entered into before January 1, 1977.

Any redemption permitted under Corp C §402 must be effected at the price or prices, within the time, and on the terms and conditions stated in the articles. Corp C §402(b). When the articles permit partial redemption, the articles must prescribe the method of selecting the shares to be redeemed. Corp C §402(b). Among the permitted methods are pro rata, by lot, or at the discretion of or in a manner approved by the board. The articles may specify other methods. Corp C §402(b).

§5.39   2. Redemption of Single Class or Series

Redemption rights cannot be provided with respect to one class or series of outstanding shares unless there is another class of outstanding shares not subject to redemption. Corp C §402(c). See

1 Ballantine & Sterling, CALIFORNIA CORPORATION LAWS §§127.03, 144.02 (4th ed); see also 1 MARSH'S CALIFORNIA CORPORATION LAW §5.8 (2d ed). One class or series of common shares may be redeemable, if a second class or series of outstanding common shares is not redeemable. Redeemable common stock is sometimes issued to employees. On termination of employment, the stock can be redeemed. Exceptions to these restrictions on redemption exist for open-end investment companies, professional corporations, and corporations that hold a government license or franchise that is conditioned on shareholders having certain qualifications. Corp C §§402(c), 403(a)(2).

§5.40   3. Making Outstanding Nonredeemable Shares Redeemable

A question exists whether nonredeemable shares may be made redeemable by amendment of the articles. The Commissioner of Corporations may object to such a change, particularly in publicly held corporations. See 1A Ballantine & Sterling, CALIFORNIA CORPORATION LAWS §231.05 (4th ed). In a closely held corporation, making nonredeemable shares redeemable and then exercising the power to redeem may in some circumstances be used to squeeze out one or more undesired minority shareholders. The only California statutory authority for such an amendment is Corp C §900 (the general amendment provision). Such an amendment would have to be approved by a majority class vote (Corp C §903(a)(4)) and by a majority vote of all of the outstanding voting shares (Corp C §903(c)). In *Cowan v Salt Lake Hardware Co.* (Utah 1950) 221 P2d 625, such an amendment was permitted under a general statutory provision comparable to Corp C §900 (but the corporation's charter was to expire shortly in any event). However, several cases in other jurisdictions have held that such amendments are invalid under a generally worded statute. See *Breslav v New York & Queens Elec. Light & Power Co.* (App Div 1936) 291 NYS 932, affd (1937) 7 NE2d 708; *Yukon Mill & Grain Co. v Vose* (Okla 1949) 206 P2d 206.

The California courts have often taken a liberal view of the scope of the amendment power. Consequently, if the corporation is not likely to be faced with objecting shareholders, the risks of the amendment procedure should be acceptable, because it is the easiest method of making nonredeemable shares redeemable. If there may be objecting shareholders, counsel and the corporation should consider the alternative routes that have met with less judicial opposition: (1) The voluntary exchange plan (see *Johnson v Lamprecht* (Ohio 1938) 15 NE2d 127; *Kreicker v Naylor Pipe Co.* (Ill 1940) 29 NE2d 502); (2) the merger or sale of assets (see *Clarke v Gold Dust Corp.* (3d Cir 1939) 106 F2d 598; *Dratz v Occidental Hotel Co.* (Mich 1949) 39 NW2d 341); or (3) repurchase of shares. See §§5.32–5.35.

§5.41   4. Change in Redemption Price

An amendment changing the redemption price of stock on some reasonable basis is probably valid. In *Transporation Bldg. Co. v Daugherty* (1946) 74 CA2d 604, 169 P2d 470, the court indicated that it would sustain an amendment reducing the redemption price from $50 to $30 per share on the ground that the present market value of the corporation's assets did not support more than the lower figure. See *Morris v American Pub. Util. Co.* (Del 1923) 122 A 696; *Sander v Janssen Dairy Corp.* (D NJ 1940) 36 F Supp 512. Voluntary plans and sale-of-assets reorganizations changing the redemption price have also been upheld. See *Shanik v White Sewing Mach. Corp.* (Del 1941) 19 A2d 831.

A question exists whether an amendment can change the nature of the consideration to be received on redemption, *e.g.,* from money to stock or debentures. In *Bowman v Armour & Co.* (Ill 1959) 160 NE2d 753, an amendment by which the right to receive cash on redemption was changed to the right to receive debentures was held invalid on the ground that a generally worded statute similar to Corp C §§900 and 903 did not authorize the amendment. See also *Berger v Amana Soc'y* (Iowa 1959) 95 NW2d 909, 70 ALR2d 830 (right to receive cash held to be right to receive shares; held invalid). Corporations Code §180 now makes it clear that "redemption price" includes "cash, property or securities, or any combination thereof"; an express provision is required if the redemption price is payable other than in cash. Corp C §180.

§5.42   5. Change in Date for Redemption

An amendment changing the date for redemption at the holder's option has been held invalid. See *Weckler v Valley City Mill. Co.* (WD Mich 1950) 93 F Supp 444, aff'd (6th Cir 1951) 188 F2d 367; *Hay v Big Bend Land Co.* (Wash 1949) 204 P2d 488. But see *King v Ligon* (SC 1936) 185 SE 305, which allowed the removal of a provision for compulsory redemption on a specified date.

§5.43   6. Removal of Redemption Provision

Amendments removing a provision for redemption at the option of the corporation have had a mixed reception by the courts. In *Davis v Louisville Gas & Elec. Co.* (Del 1928) 142 A 654, such an amendment was approved, the court resorting to the presumption that the majority of the shareholders acted in good faith in concluding that the change would facilitate additional capitalization. See §5.10. But see *Koeppler v Crocker Chair Co.* (Wis 1929) 228 NW 130.

§5.44   7. Removal of Sinking Fund Provision

Several decisions outside California have refused to permit removal of sinking fund provisions. See, *e.g., Yoakam v Providence Biltmore Hotel Co.* (D RI 1929) 34 F2d 533, 543; *Davison v Parke, Austin & Lipscomb, Inc.* (1941) 285 NY 500, 35 NE2d 618. An amendment authorizing a reduction in the amount required to be paid into the sinking fund has been permitted in some cases, *e.g., Johnson v Bradley Knitting Co.* (Wis 1938) 280 NW 688, 117 ALR 1276. The "voluntary" plan has been used to avoid sinking fund payments. See *Longson v Beaux-Arts Apts., Inc.* (App Div 1942) 38 NYS2d 605.

M. Change in Preemptive Rights
§5.45   1. Grant or Enlargement

Preemptive rights entitle shareholders to subscribe to new issues of stock in proportion to their interests in the corporation, thus offering a certain protection against dilution of their interests. Although at common law shareholders were entitled to preemptive rights, since 1931 California law has accorded such rights only when the articles specifically grant them. Corp C §406; 1 MARSH'S CALIFORNIA CORPORATION LAW §§3.28, 5.24 (2d ed). Amendments of the articles to grant or enlarge preemptive rights are authorized by Corp C §§204(a)(2), 406, 900, 903(a). See §5.3.

Preemptive rights may entail the following disadvantages:

(1) Legitimate financing may be delayed by a requirement of a prior offer to shareholders, to the detriment of the corporation.

(2) In complex stock structures, it may be difficult to find any fair basis for apportioning a new issue between the different classes of shares.

(3) The preemptive right may be subject to so many exceptions (*e.g.*, stock issued for property) that its value to shareholders as a protection against dilution may be doubtful.

(4) Depending on the circumstances and identity of the shareholders at the time the right is exercised, exemptions from federal and California securities law requirements may not be available.

(4) At least in large publicly held corporations, a new issue does not necessarily result in substantial dilution of the interest of each individual shareholder.

(5) Equitable limitations, sometimes called quasi-preemptive rights, exist to prevent issuance of shares at substantially less than a fair price and consequent dilution in the interests of the shareholders, and to prevent stock issuance from being used as a device to obtain or retain control of a corporation. See 1 Ballantine & Sterling, CALIFORNIA CORPORATION LAWS §127.03[8] (4th ed); 1 Marsh §5.25; Comment, *Pre-emptive Rights Restricted,* 4 Stan L Rev 449 (1952); *Shaw v Empire Sav. & Loan Ass'n* (1960) 186 CA2d 401, 9 CR 204 (discussed at 49 Calif L Rev 561 (1961)); *Schwab v Schwab-Wilson Mach. Corp.* (1936) 13 CA2d 1, 55 P2d 1268).

In view of these possible objections, counsel for the corporation should consider carefully whether granting preemptive rights by amendment or otherwise may adversely affect the corporation's flexibility to a degree that outweighs the possible protection of shareholders against dilution.

The drafter of an effective preemptive rights provision should first consider the judicial exceptions to the preemptive right and decide if it is in the best interests of the client to draft against them. See 1 Ballantine & Sterling §127.03[8]; 1 Marsh §5.24; Comment, *Corporations: Preemptive Rights: Importance of Drafting in Protecting Shareholder Against Dilution of Interest and Compulsory Reinvestment,* 40 Calif L Rev 132 (1952). The drafter should define the respective preemptive rights of each class if the corporation has a multiple class structure. Finally, the drafter should consider inserting in the provision appropriate language to protect against an amendment of the article that revokes or restricts the right. See §5.46.

For forms of preemptive rights provisions for articles, see ORGANIZING CORPORATIONS IN CALIFORNIA §2.28 (2d ed Cal CEB 1983); 3 Ballantine & Sterling, CALIFORNIA CORPORATION LAWS App A, Forms 4.33–4.44 (4th ed); 3 MARSH'S CALIFORNIA CORPORATION LAW App C, Form 14 (2d ed).

§5.46   2. Restriction or Revocation

Amendments to articles that restrict or revoke previously existing preemptive rights are likely to be objectionable to minority shareholders. However, any effort by them to block the amendment by litigation is unlikely to be successful in California in view of the general amendment authority provided in Corp C §§900 and 903(a). See also *Silva v Coastal Plywood & Timber Co.* (1954) 124 CA2d 276, 278, 268 P2d 510, 512; but see *Casady v Modern Metal Spinning & Mfg. Co.* (1961) 188 CA2d 728, 10 CR 790 (applying vested rights approach to limit effect of amendment to later-issued shares). Some commentators consider *Casady* to have been implicitly overruled by *Tu-Vu Drive-In Corp. v Ashkins* (1964) 61 C2d 283, 38 CR 348. See Halloran, *Equitable Limitations On The Power To Amend Articles Of Incorporation,* 4 Pac LJ 47, 50 n14 (1973). For further discussion, see McNulty, *Corporations and the Intertemporal Conflict of Laws,* 55 Calif L R 12, 46 (1967).

The minority shareholder who thinks that a preemptive rights provision is beneficial should bargain for protection of this provision against later restriction or revocation. The minority shareholder should request that the articles of incorporation require an affirmative vote of a sufficiently high percentage of the outstanding shares to amend or repeal the preemptive rights provision. A majority class vote is required by statute to remove the provision. Corp C §903(a)(4).

Under Corp C §§900 and 903(a)(4), preemptive rights may be restricted without being eliminated. A corporation expecting opposition to a complete elimination of rights should consider asking for shareholder approval of article amendment that merely excepts certain stock from the preemptive rights. Such a limited waiver of rights is not uncommon with respect to shares to be issued for foreign financing, on conversion of debt securities, or under employee stock plans.

N. Creation of or Change in Conversion Rights

§5.47   1. Creation of Conversion Right

An amendment to the articles may make a class of shares convertible on the happening of one or more specified events or the vote of at least the majority of the outstanding shares of the series or class to be converted. Corp C §403(a). To be effective, such an amendment requires the approval of a majority of the outstanding shares of the class to be convertible, of the class into which the shares are convertible, and of the outstanding voting shares. Corp C §§900, 903(a)(3)–(5), (c). However, the conversion price or ratio must not be so grossly unfair as to indicate that the directors are engaged primarily in a maneuver to obtain or retain control. See Hills, *Convertible Securities—Legal Aspects and Draftsmanship*, 19 Calif L Rev 1, 8 (1930); *Schwab v Schwab-Wilson Mach. Corp.* (1936) 13 CA2d 1, 55 P2d 1268; *Shaw v Empire Sav. & Loan Ass'n* (1960) 186 CA2d 401, 9 CR 204, discussed at 49 Calif L Rev 561 (1961), as to duty to sell shares for the largest possible return and not at a low price for purposes of obtaining or retaining control.

Making outstanding nonconvertible shares convertible, at the holder's option, into another class of shares is authorized by Corp C §§403(a)(1), 900. See §5.3.

An appropriate antidilution provision in the conversion amendment may be needed. See 1 Ballantine & Sterling, CALIFORNIA CORPORATION LAWS §127.03[7][c] (4th ed); 1 MARSH'S CALIFORNIA CORPORATION LAW §5.22 (2d ed). The California Commissioner of Corporations requires antidilution provisions for convertible senior securities in the case of stock splits, stock dividends, and other recapitalizations. The Commissioner authorizes, but does not require, antidilution provisions covering issuance of additional shares below the conversion price or the then-current market price. 10 Cal Code Regs §260.140.6. For discussion of necessity for permit from Commissioner of Corporations, see §§5.74–5.84.

The articles may provide for automatic conversion at the happening of one or more events, conversion at the holder's option, conversion on the vote of at least a majority of the outstanding shares of the class or series to be converted, or, in certain instances, conversion at the corporation's option when necessary to prevent the loss of a governmental license or franchise or national securities exchange membership. Conversion provisions can be drafted to become exercisable on almost any specified set of events, terms, or conditions (Corp C §403(a)), *e.g.,* on the shareholder's reaching the age of majority (*Larsen v Lilly Estate* (Wash 1949) 208 P2d 150). A provision for automatic conversion on a specified event is authorized by Corp C §403(a)(1). Such a provision might be used in a series of common stock sold to employees, which is automatically convertible into a smaller number of shares of the common series sold to nonemployees if the employee leaves before completing a specified period of employment.

A provision for conversion at the option of the corporation is not valid except when it is necessary to protect a license or franchise. Corp C §403(a)(2). See §5.39. When it is decided to allow the corporation to force conversion to another class, but not to protect a license or a franchise, a redemption-in-kind provision (*i.e.,* a redemption for another class of security) can be used. See §5.41. A conversion amendment providing that a junior security is convertible into a senior security (an upstream conversion), or vice versa, is authorized by Corp C §403(a)(1), but only "into shares of any class or series," not into debt.

§5.48   2. Alteration of Conversion Rights

An amendment that changes conversion rights is authorized by the Corporations Code if it is approved by a majority vote of the class changed (see Corp C §§900, 903(a)(3)–(5)), and if the amendment is also approved by the outstanding voting shares (see Corp C §903(c)). If the rights, preferences, or privileges of another class could be affected by the amendment, approval by a majority vote of that class is also needed. Corp C §903(a)(5). See discussion in §5.96.

§5.49   O. Change in Liquidation Preferences

Use of article amendments to change or eliminate liquidation preferences is authorized by Corp C §§900 and 903(a)(4), and such amendments should not be disturbed by the courts when adequate corporate necessity, compensating advantages for rights lost, a sufficiently high vote, and other fairness factors can be shown. See §§5.9–5.10. See *Transportation Bldg. Co. v Daugherty* (1946) 74 CA2d 604, 169 P2d 470, in which the reduction of a liquidation preference from $50 to $30 by amendment was held to be fair (contrary to decision by the Commissioner of Corporations) when the value of all the corporation's assets did not support a figure of more than $30. See also *Bailey v Tubize Rayon Corp.* (D Del 1944) 56 F Supp 418 (elimination of liquidation preference that was impaired on assets basis, when voting control given by exchange for common, market prices held to justify the exchange ratio); *Sander v Janssen Dairy Corp.* (D NJ 1940) 36 F Supp 512 (reduction of preference by 60 percent plus elimination of accrued dividend upheld when capital was impaired, 82 percent voted in favor, and compensating advantages given). These and other cases in the amendment of articles area tend not to require the common stock to bear the full weight of the capital reduction (*i.e.*, these cases do not impose the "absolute priority" principle applicable in insolvency proceedings) when the business is a going concern and liquidation is not reasonable. See §5.15. See also Becht, *Changes in the Interests of Classes of Stockholders by Corporate Charter Amendments Reducing Capital, and Altering Redemption, Liquidation and Sinking Fund Provisions,* 36 Cornell LQ 1, 20 (1950).

P. Change in Term of Corporate Existence

§5.50   1. Shortening Term

All corporations formed under or electing to be governed by the General Corporation Law exist perpetually unless the law or the articles of incorporation expressly provide otherwise. Corp C §200(c). Since the articles may contain a provision ending the corporation's life at a specified date (Corp C §204(a)(4)), they may be amended to limit the corporation's term. Corp C §900. See §5.3.

§5.51   2. Extending Term or Reviving Corporation

Corporations exist perpetually unless the law or the articles expressly provide for a shorter term. Corp C §200(c). The articles of a corporation organized for a shorter term may be amended to delete the provision for a limited term and provide for perpetual existence. Corp C §§900, 909.

For an amendment to be effective in reviving a corporation with a limited term that has already lapsed (perhaps for the purpose of trading on its former name), the corporation must have continuously acted as a corporation and done business as such after expiration of the term and up to the date of the amendment effecting the revival, and must so state in the certificate of amendment. Corp C §909. Corporations Code §909 requires that the amendment extending the term of a corporation whose term has already expired must actually provide for perpetual existence; it is not sufficient merely to delete the limited term provision from the articles. See also 45 Ops Cal Atty Gen 3 (1965). This opinion indicates that the question is whether the corporation has been conducting transactions for financial gain and also indicates that proof that the corporation is a "de facto" corporation is sufficient. A mere nameholder probably could not qualify. 8 Fletcher, CYCLOPEDIA OF THE LAW OF PRIVATE CORPORATIONS §3838 (rev ed 1989). However, a certified copy of the certificate of amendment extending a term that has expired is itself prima facie evidence of performance of the conditions necessary to adoption of the amendment. Corp C §908. Thus, the burden of proof is on the objector to the filed amendment.

The general rule appears to be that a shareholder does not have a contractual right to prevent extension or revival. See Lynch, *The Majority's Power to Effect Fundamental Changes in Shareholder Rights,* 2 Corp Prac Comment Nos. 4, 1, 16 (1961); Note, *Corporations—Extension or Revival of Corporate Existence—Rights of Minority Stockholders,* 36 Minn L Rev 267, 268 (1952); *Garzo v Maid of the Mist Steamboat Co.* (NY App Div 1951) 106 NYS2d 4. However, a shareholder may sue for involuntary dissolution on the ground that the period for which the corporation was formed has terminated without extension. Corp C §1800(a)(3), (b)(6). See also *Rossi v Caire* (1921) 186 C 544, 199 P 1042, which indicates that the shareholder of a corporation with a term already expired has a better array of arguments for blocking an extension than does a shareholder of a corporation with an unexpired term.

§5.52   Q. Alteration of Voting Rights

Because corporations may provide in their original articles for one or more classes or series of shares with full, limited, or no voting rights, they may amend the articles to provide for such voting rights. Corp C §§202(e)(3), 400, 900; see §5.3. In *Heller Inv. Co. v Southern Title & Trust Co.* (1936) 17 CA2d 202, 61 P2d 807, the court held that under a predecessor of Corp C §400 a corporation could deny any voting privileges to a class of stock. However, complete elimination of voting rights is impossible because the Corporations Code grants voting rights even to nonvoting shares with respect to certain matters, *e.g.,* reorganizations (Corp C §§117, 1201), certain amendments of the articles (Corp C §§117, 903–904), and a plan of distribution of assets in a dissolution (Corp C §§117, 2007). A voting trust agreement among shareholders or an irrevocable proxy may be the only ways to affect votes on such matters. See §5.12. The major categories of limitations on changing voting power by article amendment are considered in §§5.53–5.56.

§5.53   1. Statutory Limitations

First, at least one class of outstanding shares (which need not be the same class with respect to each matter) must be able to vote on all matters on which shareholders may vote. Corp C §400(a). For example, an amendment making common shares nonvoting and authorizing a new voting preferred appears to be unacceptable because at the time the amendment becomes effective, none of the voting preferred shares are outstanding. This problem probably could be solved by reclassifying a small ratio of common shares to preferred in connection with the amendment, so that there will be a class of outstanding shares with complete voting rights after the amendment.

Second, except in certain listed corporations (Corp C §301.5; see §5.70), cumulative voting is required as to shares entitled to vote for the election of directors, and may not be limited by a provision in the articles. Corp C §708(a). In addition, the board of directors may not be classified to give the directors staggered terms of more than a year. See Corp C §301(a). However, one class of shares may be given the right to vote for some directors and another class may vote for the others. Corp C §301(a).

Third, it appears that each share is entitled by statute to one full vote per share on the matters on which all shares (including nonvoting shares) are given voting rights (*e.g.,* reorganizations; see the discussion of these matters above), regardless of whether on other matters the shares are given more or less than one vote each. See Corp C §700(a); 1A Ballantine & Sterling, CALIFORNIA CORPORATION LAWS §171.02 (4th ed).

§5.54   2. Limitations by Commissioner of Corporations

The Commissioner of Corporations will not allow voting power arrangements that he or she deems unfair. For example, the Commissioner typically will require that the articles of a corporation that has nonparticipating, nonconvertible, nonvoting, preferred shares, provide for a "voting switch." The switch comes in the event of cumulative default of eight quarterly dividends, and gives the preferred shares "reasonable representation" on the board of directors until all arrearages in dividends are paid in full. The right to elect a majority of the board is stated to be presumptively reasonable. 10 Cal Code Regs §260.140.2. Common shares and similar equity securities should normally carry equal voting rights on all matters. 10 Cal Code Regs §260.140.1. These regulations of the Commissioner merely set forth guidelines, and, when justified, a variation from them will be granted, particularly in the case of limited offerings (10 Cal Code Regs §260.140) or when adversely affected shareholders consent. For example, nonvoting common stock is often used for investment company management companies to prevent shifts in control that necessitate frequent investment company shareholder votes; it is also used for retiring family members or employees who will have no further participation in the management of the business.

The basis for restrictions imposed on nonvoting common stock is that such a security allows control of the corporation to shift at a considerably reduced investment and risk. Reclassifications that break up outstanding voting stock into two classes, one voting and one nonvoting, have been criticized as a device used by the majority to perpetuate itself in voting control with less capital, with the result that the minority shareholders are partially disenfranchised. See Comment, *Manipulation of Voting Control—The Stock Split,* 4 Stan L Rev 575 (1952).

This complaint was made by the minority shareholders in *Bixby v Pierno* (1971) 4 C3d 130, 93 CR 234. Despite the objection, the

Commissioner granted the permit, partly because the applicant complied literally with the Commissioner's regulations. Instead of creating two classes of common, one nonvoting, in violation of 10 Cal Code Regs §260.140.1, the issuer created nonvoting, nonconvertible, nonparticipating preferred with the right to elect a majority of the board in the event of default of dividends for eight quarters. The hearing officer in the Department of Corporations found that development of the real estate holdings of this closely held corporation required stability and continuity of management, and the proposed recapitalization would make passage of control less likely in the event of a shareholder's death, because the nonvoting preferred stock (which had a high liquidation preference, making it valuable) could be sold by the estate of each deceased shareholder to provide cash to meet costs of death, taxes, and administration, while the voting common stock could be distributed to heirs. The California Supreme Court held that the Department of Corporations was entitled to conclude that the advantages of the plan out weighed its adverse effects. The application and use of the equitable "fairness factor" analysis to this case (see §5.10) is discussed in detail in Halloran, *Equitable Limitations On The Power To Amend Articles Of Incorporation,* 4 Pac LJ 47, 61 (1973).

§5.55   3. Limitations by Stock Exchanges

The Securities and Exchange Commission requires that registered national securities exchanges and associations have rules prohibiting the listing, continuation of listing, or quotation or transaction reporting through an automated inter-dealer quotation system,

> of any common stock or other equity security of a domestic issuer, if the issuer of such security issues any class of security, or takes other corporate action, with the effect of nullifying, restricting, or disparately reducing the per share voting rights of holders of an outstanding class or classes of common stock of such issuer registered pursuant to section 12 of the [Securities Exchange Act of 1934]. . . .

Rule 19c–4(a), (b) (17 CFR 140.19c–4(a), (b)). For examples of actions that are presumed to have or not to have the prohibited effect, see Rule 19c–4(c) (17 CFR 140.19c–4(c)). See New York Stock Exchange Listed Company Manual §§313.00, 801.00–802.00; American Stock Exchange Company Guide §§122–124.

§5.56   4. Judicial Limitations

The indirect impairment of voting rights as a result of creating a senior class should not be upset by the courts if the purpose is to raise new capital or make new acquisitions. See §5.10. However, the courts may strike down an indirect impairment of voting rights in connection with a capital reduction that discriminates against one outstanding class or group of shareholders with respect to voting rights. See §5.15.

Limitations on amendments changing voting rights have appeared primarily in cases in which there is a direct shrinkage in voting rights of outstanding shares in favor of a direct expansion of voting rights of another group or class of outstanding shares. See *Faunce v Boost Co.* (NJ Sup 1951) 83 A2d 649, in which the reclassification of outstanding shares into nonvoting shares, and the authorization and issuance of a new voting class of shares in exchange for cancellation of the recipient's contractual preemptive rights, were held invalid on grounds of lack of statutory authority, unfairness, and removal of the "vested" right to vote. The court in *Asarco Inc. v Court* (D NJ 1985) 611 F Supp 468, citing *Faunce v Boost Co.*, upheld the rule that a corporation may not issue classes of shares that would give different voting rights to shareholders within the same class.

Other courts, however, have refused to overturn voting rights amendments either without some evidence that indicates fraud (see *Topkis v Delaware Hardware Co.* (Del 1938) 2 A2d 114 (preferred shares given exclusive right to vote)), or when various fairness factors weighed in favor of the amendment. See §§5.9–5.10. See also *Metzger v George Washington Mem. Park, Inc.* (Pa 1955) 110 A2d 425, discussed in §5.10(8); *Berger v Amana Soc'y* (Iowa 1959) 95 NW2d 909, 914, 70 ALR2d 830 (although following "fundamental change" doctrine, court allowed creation of another class that, in its view, took away sole voting rights and control from common shares). See also *Honigman v Green Giant Co.* (8th Cir 1962) 309 F2d 667, in which the corporation had two classes of shares, one publicly held nonvoting and one privately held voting. Amendments to the articles were adopted under which both classes were exchanged for a voting common, but because the privately held shares were surrendering their voting rights, they were given a much more favorable exchange ratio than the publicly held shares. The court stated that, although a sufficient vote under the statute had been obtained, it preferred to base its decision on the fact that "no fraud or inequitable conduct was resorted to in consummating the amendment, and the proposed plan was fair, equitable and beneficial both to the non-voting . . . stockholders and to the corporation." 309 F2d at 671. In its review of fairness, the court noted that the corporation had prospered through the years under the management of the holders of the privately held shares, the plan was adopted by 92.3 percent of the outstanding, nonvoting, publicly held stock (of which the majority owner of the privately held shares and his family owned only 20 per cent), and the premium received by the privately held shares seemed commensurate with the benefit received by the corporation in having publicly held voting shares.

The drafter of an amendment affecting voting rights should evaluate the amendment in terms of fairness, and weigh financial advantages that a disenfranchised shareholder will receive against the loss of voting power. See Note, *Corporations: Alteration of Voting Right by Amendment,* 37 Cornell LQ 768, 777 (1952). An amendment providing for transfer of voting rights from common to preferred in exchange for preferred dividend arrearages should not necessarily be considered unfair to the common stock, because the transfer of control would be to a class with a financial interest in running the corporation more profitably. See Comment, *Limitations on Alterations of Shareholders' Rights by Charter Amendment,* 69 Harv L Rev 538, 550 (1956). The opposite situation occurred in *Transportation Bldg. Co. v Daugherty* (1946) 74 CA2d 604, 169 P2d 470, in which the preferred shareholders had the right before the amendment to elect all but one of the directors. The amendment gave the common stock the exclusive right to vote, except that in the event of failure to pay dividends on the preferred stock for 18 months, the preferred shares would have the right to elect a majority of the directors as long as the default existed. The court reversed the Commissioner's finding of unfairness. The court was convinced that the plan was fair because (a) the company's operations had never been successful, (b) failure to adopt the recapitalization plan might have encouraged a sale of the corporate property in order to avoid further loss, and (c) there was lack of management of the property that could be corrected by giving common stock with voting rights to the new manager under a seven-year management contract.

§5.57   5. Alternatives to Amendment on Voting Rights

If voting rights cannot be altered directly by amendment of the articles, it may be possible to modify them by merger or another form of corporate reorganization. Impairment of voting rights by such methods has been upheld. See *Clarke v Gold Dust Corp.* (3d Cir 1939) 106 F2d 598, 603; but see *Outwater v Public Serv. Corp.* (NJ 1928) 143 A 729, aff'd (NJ 1929) 146 A 916. See also §5.12.

§5.58   R. Change in Corporate Powers or Purposes; Election To Be Governed by Corp C §202(b)(1)

An amendment to articles of incorporation to change a corporation's powers or purposes is seldom required for a corporation formed on or after January 1, 1977, because such a corporation may provide in its articles that its purpose is to "engage in any lawful act or activity for which a corporation may be organized" under the Corporations Code, other than the banking or trust company business or the practice of a profession. Corp C §§202(b)(1), 206. The articles may, however, contain limitations or restrictions on the corporation's business or powers (Corp C §204(a)(6)), although such limitations are relatively uncommon in current practice.

Corporations in existence before January 1, 1977, may amend their articles by board action alone to elect to be governed by Corp C §§202, 204, and 205, and conform the statement of powers and purposes to Corp C §202(b). Corp C §2302. This appears to be so even though such corporations may presently have a provision limiting their business, because the policy of the present Corporations Code provision is to eliminate disputes and litigation over powers and purposes. Moreover, Corp C §2303 provides that any statement in the articles of a pre–1977 corporation relating to the purposes or powers of the corporation is not to be construed as a limitation unless expressly stated as such. In addition, Corp C §2303 provides that Corp C §§206 and 207 automatically apply to corporations existing on January 1, 1977. In view of the broad language of Corp C §206 (permitting business corporations to "engage in any business activity"), an election under Corp C §2302 is not necessary for most corporations as far as powers or purposes are concerned. See §§5.132–5.133.

A business corporation may convert into a nonprofit corporation by amendment of its articles. Unanimous consent or approval of all shares is required.

§5.59   S. Change of Corporate Name

An article amendment that adopts a new corporate name is subject to the rules governing selection and reservation of a name on initial incorporation. Corp C §§201(b), 202(a); see ORGANIZING CORPORATIONS IN CALIFORNIA §§2.5–2.6 (2d ed Cal CEB 1983).

§5.60   1. Choice of New Name

As a general rule, a corporation may choose any corporate name as long as the new corporate name is (a) not likely to mislead the public; and (b) not the same as, and does not resemble so closely as to tend to deceive, the name of another domestic corporation or of a foreign corporation that is authorized to transact intrastate business, or of a corporation that has registered or reserved its name with the Secretary of State. Corp C §201(b). Restrictions are placed on the use of certain words, however. See, *e.g.,* Corp C §201(a) ("bank," "trust," "trustee," and related words); Corp C §12311 ("cooperative" or its abbreviation); 36 USC §380 ("Olympic" or "olympiad"). The name of a close corporation (see Corp C §158) must contain the word "corporation," "incorporated," or "limited," or an abbreviation of one of those words. Corp C §202(a).

For additional requirements applicable to certain types of corporations, see Corp C §201.5 (insurers); Bus & P C §§1804 (dental corporation), 2275, 2415 (medical corporation); 5536 (architectural corporation); 6738(a)(3) (engineering corporation); 8729 (land surveying and civil engineering corporations); 12302 (consumer cooperatives). For law corporation requirements, see Bus & P C §6171 and Law Corporation Rules of the State Bar of California (West's Annotated California Codes, vol 23, part 2, p 695; Deering's California Codes Annotated, Law Corporation Rules of the State Bar of California, p 247). Copies of the State Bar Law Corporation Rules may be obtained from the State Bar of California, 555 Franklin

St., San Francisco, CA 94102). See also Corp C §13409 (names of professional corporations generally).

For discussion of possible trademark and trade name problems, see ADVISING CALIFORNIA PARTNERSHIPS §§3.12–3.18 (Cal CEB 1988). See also ATTORNEY'S GUIDE TO THE LAW OF COMPETITIVE BUSINESS PRACTICES chap 6 (Cal CEB 1981), and ATTORNEY'S GUIDE TO TRADE SECRETS (Cal CEB 1971).

The filing of articles or an amendment containing a name that violates Corp C §201(b) does not preclude a court from enjoining the use of that name: Objections to the new name may be raised by a corporation having a similar name. However, if the objector is no longer actively engaged in the business conducted by the corporation desiring the new name, a court will usually allow the use of the new name, at least if there is a distinguishing word in the name that to some extent will serve to prevent injury to the objector in the event it resumes its business. See *Petition of Los Angeles Trust Co.* (1910) 158 C 603, 112 P 56.

If the objector is a new nameholder not yet fully organized, instead of a corporation that went out of business after its organization, the use of a similar name by another corporation can probably be prevented. See 6 Fletcher, CYCLOPEDIA OF THE LAW OF PRIVATE CORPORATIONS §2452 (rev ed 1989).

Formation of a nameholder corporation by an adversary is a real danger to a corporation intending to change its name. If the change of name cannot be effected by filing an amendment within the 60-day period for reservation of the name (see §5.62), *e.g.,* because of the time required to obtain the necessary shareholder vote, it is advisable to incorporate a nameholder corporation. After adoption of the amendment, the principal corporation may file the amendment, accompanied by a consent of the nameholder corporation under Corp C §201(b); the nameholder corporation can then have its name changed, in turn, or be dissolved if there is no further need for its existence. In the alternative, the nameholder corporation, if formed as a wholly owned subsidiary, may be merged into the parent, with the parent taking on the name of the disappearing subsidiary. See §5.67.

A change of name has no effect on the identity of a corporation, and in no way affects its rights, privileges, or obligations. *Mutual Bldg. & Loan Ass'n v Corum* (1934) 220 C 282, 30 P2d 509; *American Trust Co. v Jones* (1933) 130 CA 651, 20 P2d 346.

2. Procedural Considerations in Changing Corporate Name

a. Name Check and Reservation

§5.61 (1) Name Check

A name check by telephone call to the Secretary of State's office ((916) 322–2387) will indicate whether a desired corporate name is available before the final selection and approval, but provides no assurance that it will continue to be available. It therefore ordinarily is followed by reservation of the name (see §5.62). Only two names may be checked per call. A separate written request for a name check is not necessary—if a telephone check is not feasible, the written request for a name check can be combined with a request for name reservation. In any event, a telephone check should be followed by a letter reserving the desired name(s). See Form 5.62–1. Name reservations may also be made in person over the counter at the Secretary of State's Sacramento, San Francisco, Los Angeles, or San Diego offices. A $6.00 special handling fee is charged for over-the-counter reservations. 2 Cal Code Regs §21904(f).

§5.62 (2) Form: Request for Reservation of Name

Form 5.62–1

Secretary of State
1230 J Street
Sacramento, California 95814

Re: Reservation of Corporate Name

Dear Secretary:

Request is hereby made for the reservation of a corporate name. Please issue a name reservation certificate for the first available corporate name according to the order of preference. The names to be considered in order of preference are as follows:

[*First choice corporate name*]

[*Second choice corporate name*]

[*Third choice corporate name*]

[*Fourth choice corporate name*]

A check for $10 is enclosed to cover the name reservation fee. Please send the certificate of reservation to us. Thank you.

Sincerely,

[*Signature of attorney*]
[*Typed name*]

Comment: When an available name has been selected, particularly if there may be a delay in board of directors and shareholder action to amend the articles of incorporation changing the name (see §5.63), the proposed name may be reserved for 60 days on payment of a $10 fee (see Govt C §12199). Corp C §201(c). The Secretary of State will issue a certificate of reservation for 60 days. The Secretary cannot reserve the same name for, or for the benefit of, the same applicant for consecutive 60-day periods. Corp C §201(c); see §5.61. However, a reservation may be reapplied for after a one-day lapse, if the name has not been reserved by another in the interim. Note that while only two names may be cleared by telephone (see §5.61) up to four names may be checked on written request.

§5.63   b. Amendment of Articles of Incorporation

When the new corporate name has been selected, a resolution amending the articles of incorporation must be prepared. See §§5.110–5.114, 5.117. The amendment must then be approved by the board of directors and the outstanding shares. Corp C §§902–903; see §5.91. (If no shares have been issued, only approval of the incorporators or directors is needed. Corp C §901.) Any special requirements in the articles, bylaws, or shareholders' agreement should also be complied with. A certificate of amendment is then filed with the Secretary of State. The form of the certificate and filing procedures are discussed in §§5.140–5.143. The amendment becomes effective when the certificate is filed. Corp C §908.

§5.64   c. Notification of Third Parties

Consideration should be given to the notices and revisions that may be necessary or advisable because of the name change. These include product label changes required by consumer protection regulations (see, *e.g.,* 21 USC §343(e)(1)); notices to licensing agencies; changes to outstanding powers of attorney, *e.g.,* powers of attorney to represent the corporation before the IRS; and amendments to qualifications to do business in other states. It is good practice to give notice to customers, suppliers, lenders, and others with whom the corporation transacts business under its corporate name, and in some instances, such notification may be required by contract, or other instrument. Such notice may not be necessary if business is to be conducted (1) under the prior name, or (2) under a fictitious business name following the name change. However, consideration should be given to filing and publishing appropriate fictitious business name statements. See ADVISING CALIFORNIA PARTNERSHIPS §§3.20–3.27 (2d ed Cal CEB 1988).

Although a corporate seal is no longer required by California law, if one is used, a new one should be adopted, reflecting the corporation's new name but retaining the original date of incorporation. See Corp C §207(a). For form of minutes that can be adapted for this purpose, see §1.59. Any bylaw provisions relating to the corporate name or seal should also be conformed.

§5.65   d. Change of Share Certificates

Stock exchanges require that the new name appear on all share certificates issued after the amendment. A proposed overprint or new form of certificate bearing the new name and revised corporate seal to be placed on the issuer's supply of unissued stock certificates should be submitted to the stock exchange for approval in advance of the amendment. The Corporations Code does not contain a requirement that the certificates bear the new name. Even if not required to do so, the board may choose to obtain new certificates for use after the name change. See also Corp C §422 (board's authority to cancel and replace outstanding certificates).

§5.66   e. Use of New Name When Transferring Property

There is no need to change title to real and personal property. When existing property is sold or transferred in the future, the transferor should be referred to in its new name, followed by "(formerly named [former corporate name])" so that persons searching the record will have no difficulty in determining its chain of title. Certified copies of the name-changing amendment may be helpful or necessary adjuncts to such later transfers.

§5.67   3. Change of Name on Merger

A change of name of a corporation may be accomplished in connection with a merger without separate shareholder approval for the name change. The agreement of merger may provide that the acquiring company's name, subject to Corp C §201(b), be changed to a name that is the same as that of the disappearing corporation. Corp C §1101(b). This feature of the merger provisions of the Code also apply to a short-form merger, *i.e.,* a merger of a 90 percent or more owned subsidiary into its parent company. Thus, a board wishing to change a corporation's name without the need for a vote of the shareholders may create a wholly owned subsidiary with the desired name, then effect a short-form merger of the subsidiary into the parent under Corp C §1110, providing in the agreement of merger for the surviving corporation to take the name of the disappearing subsidiary. Because no shareholder approval is required for this procedure (Corp C §1101), no dissenters' rights attach under Corp C §1300. See Corp C §181.

§5.68   T. Indemnification and Exculpation

Corporations Code §309 sets forth a director's duty of care in discharging his or her obligations, and provides that a person who complies with its standards "shall have no liability based upon any alleged failure to discharge the person's obligations as a director." Corp C §309(c). The articles may further limit a director's liability in a derivative action for breach of his or her duties. Corp C §204(a)(10). A corporation's power to indemnify its agents (including directors, officers, and employees) is established by Corp C §317. Again, the articles may authorize indemnification (by bylaw, agreement, or otherwise) in excess of the express limits set by Corp C §317 for breach of duty to the corporation or its shareholders. Corp C §204(a)(11). Exculpation of directors under Corp C §204(a)(10) and indemnification under Corp C §204(a)(11) are permitted only to the extent an appropriate provision is included in the articles. Corp C §204(a). See §§5.134–5.135 for forms.

In addition to the limitations discussed above, liability for breach of duty to the corporation or its shareholders cannot be limited or eliminated for any of the following:

(1) Acts or omissions involving intentional misconduct or knowing and culpable violations of the law (Corp C §204(a)(10)(A)(i));

(2) Acts or omissions that a director believes to be contrary to the best interests of the corporation or its shareholders (Corp C §204(a)(10)(A)(ii));

(3) Acts done without good faith on the part of a director (Corp C §204(a)(10)(A)(ii));

(4) Acts from which a director derives an improper personal benefit (Corp C §204(a)(10)(A)(iii));

(5) Acts or omissions that show a reckless disregard for a director's duty to the corporation or its shareholders when the director was or should have been aware, in the ordinary course of performing a director's duties, of a risk of serious injury to the corporation or its shareholders (Corp C §204(a)(10)(A)(iv));

(6) Acts or omissions that make up an unexcused pattern of inattention that amounts to abdication of a director's duty to the corporation or its shareholders (Corp C §204(a)(10)(A)(v));

(7) Violations of Corp C §310, which requires the disclosure of material facts in transactions between a corporation and its director or a corporation and an entity in which one or more of its directors has a material financial interest (Corp C §204(a)(10)(A)(vi)); or

(8) Violations of Corp C §316, which subjects a director to liability for improper distributions, loans, or guaranties (Corp C §204(a)(10)(A)(vii)).

One of the goals of the 1987 amendments to Corp C §309 and the addition of Corp C §204(a)(10)–(11) was to harmonize current decisional law (particularly in Delaware) with the Model Business Corporation Act and California General Corporation Law approach of defining directors' duties by statute. See Stats 1987, ch 1203 §4. Delaware does not define directors' duties by statute, although a definition continues to be developed by case law. See, *e.g., Smith v Van Gorkom* (Del 1985) 488 A2d 858. A further distinction between California and Delaware law is that Corp C §309's exculpation provision applies only to derivative suits and not to shareholder class actions against the directors. This may be a distinction without a difference (except when the corporation is insolvent) because, given an appropriate provision in the articles, a corporation may authorize indemnity in shareholder class actions, subject to the limits of Corp C §204(a)(11), without being subject to attack on the ground of violation of public policy. See §§5.134–5.135 for forms of articles and §5.136 for a form of bylaw limiting such liability.

One of the most significant effects of Corp C §204(a)(11) is to authorize corporations to enter into indemnity agreements. These agreements had become popular in other states, but before this provision was added in 1987 the enforceability of such agreements had been questionable in California. Corporations may find indemnity agreements useful in recruiting outside directors or other special talent. Current management may also feel more confident relying on indemnity based on such an agreement, rather than merely on bylaw provisions. There may be a concern, particularly in corporations that may be takeover candidates, that bylaws could be amended to alter indemnification provisions. Although it could be argued that the director, officer, or agent has a vested right to indemnification for matters arising before amendment of the bylaws, an agreement offers protection for matters arising even after any bylaw amendment. In addition, indemnification agreements can be tailored for special needs. For example, an agreement could provide for mandatory indemnification, or it could provide for discretionary indemnification and yet protect the director, officer, or agent against the potential negative effects of having such discretion exercised by new management following a takeover by appointing an outside party to make the discretionary decision in such circumstances. See §5.137 for a form of indemnification agreement incorporating such provisions.

§5.69   U. Amendment in Connection With Plan of Reorganization Under Bankruptcy Law

A corporation may amend its articles and make any change in its capital or shares, or effect any other amendment, change, alteration, or provision authorized by Division 1 of the California Corporations Code, in connection with any plan of reorganization or arrangement under federal law. Corp C §1400. The corporation has full power and authority to carry out the plan of reorganization and the orders of the court relating to the plan, without director or shareholder action. It may exercise authority by the court-appointed trustee or, if there is no trustee, by its officers or other court-appointed official with the same effect as if done by unanimous action of the directors and shareholders. Corp C §1400(a).

The certificate of amendment made by the trustee or other authorized person must certify that provision for making the certificate is contained in the order of a court having jurisdiction of the reorganization or other proceeding under federal law. Corp C §1401(b). The certificate is filed according to the usual procedures. See Corp C §§1401(a), 1403. See also §§5.140–5.143.

Bankruptcy reorganizations are governed by Chapter 11 of the Bankruptcy Code (11 USC §§1101–1174). (That code now refers only to "reorganizations"; the term "arrangements" is no longer used). Plans of reorganization under chapter 11 are subject to acceptance by a class vote of shareholders and creditors, but if the prescribed vote is not obtained the court may still confirm a plan if it finds it fair and equitable after a hearing and other requirements are met. 11 USC §§1126–1129; see 5 COLLIER ON BANKRUPTCY chap 1126–1129 (15th ed 1988).

No permit from the California Department of Corporations is required to solicit shareholder approval for or to effect a change in the rights, preferences, privileges, or restrictions of outstanding shares if the soliciting is done under a plan of reorganization under the Bankruptcy Code. Corp C §25102(k); 10 Cal Code Regs §260.103.

After the final decree in the reorganization proceeding is entered, closing the case and discharging any trustee, the normal procedures for adoption of amendments apply (see §§5.110–5.131). Corp C §1402.

V. ACTS THAT DO NOT REQUIRE AMENDMENT

§5.70   A. Change in Authorized Number or Classification of Directors (When Not Specified in Articles)

The articles need not specify the authorized number of directors. Corp C §202. This matter is frequently covered in the bylaws so that changes in the number of directors will not require amendment of articles. See Corp C §212(a). Bylaw amendments of the number of directors authorized may require shareholder action but do not require a filing with the Secretary of State. See Corp C §212(a). Adjustments in the number of directors (if not specified in the articles) may be effected by the board without shareholder action if the bylaws provide for an indefinite number of directors, within the range of a minimum (but not less than three) and maximum (which may not be greater than two times the minimum minus one) stated in the bylaws. Corp C §212(a).

The articles of corporations existing on January 1, 1977, that have not since amended their articles to delete such a provision will specify the number of directors. Corporations Code §2304 provides that Corp C §212(a) does not apply to such corporations, which will continue to be governed by prior law until a Corp C §2302 amendment is adopted (see §5.133). Because prior law (see former Corp C §500) permits the authorized number of directors to be changed by amendment of bylaws (even though there is a provision in the articles, and the bylaw amendment creates an inconsistency with the number of directors provided in the articles), there was and is no need to amend the articles to change the number of directors of existing corporations unless the articles provide otherwise. Nonetheless, on making the Corp C §2302 amendment, the articles should be amended to delete the statement as to the number of directors to eliminate possible confusion, and to preserve the flexibility of being able to amend the bylaws to change the number of directors. See §5.103.

"Listed corporations" (those whose shares are listed on the New York or American Stock Exchange, and some whose shares are traded on the National Association of Securities Dealers Automatic Quotation System) similarly may, within limits, amend their articles or bylaws to provide for two or three classes of directors or eliminate cumulative voting, or both. A corporation which has issued shares but is not yet listed may adopt such an amendment to become effective when it becomes listed. Any such amendment requires approval of the board and the outstanding shares voting as a single class. If articles are amended for this purpose, the certificate of amendment must include a statement of facts showing that the corporation is a listed corporation. Corp C §301.5.

§5.71   B. Change of Office Location (When Not Specified in Articles)

Corporations formed on or after January 1, 1977, are not required to set forth the location of their principal office in the articles of incorporation. See Corp C §202 (required provisions of the articles). Corporations formed before that date may elect to be governed by Corp C §202 and delete their principal office statement by filing an amendment to the articles. See Corp C §2302. See also §§5.132–5.133. Every corporation must inform the Secretary of State of the street address of its principal executive or business office in California, in the annual statement required by Corp C §1502. The location of the principal executive or business office may also be set forth in the bylaws; see Corp C §212(b).

A corporation formed before January 1, 1977, that has not elected under Corp C §2302 to be governed by Corp C §202 must amend its articles if it wishes to change the location of its principal office to any other county within the state, but no amendment is required if the principal office is changed from one location to another in the same county. See former Corp C §3600. If such an amendment becomes necessary, the corporation may want to elect to be governed by Corp C §202 and delete the principal office statement to avoid the future need for such filings. A pre–1977 corporation that does not make such an election may not change its principal office to a place outside California. See former Corp C §301(c).

The principal office specified in the articles or the principal executive or business office set forth in the Corp C §1502 statement (see §5.133) probably will be the place of residence of the corporation for purposes of residual venue of an action against it. See 3 Witkin, CALIFORNIA PROCEDURE, *Actions* §§610 (3d ed 1985); *Hardin v San Jose City Lines* (1951) 103 CA2d 688, 230 P2d 31.

§5.72 C. Blank Stock; Filing the Certificate of Determination

No amendment of the articles is required or deemed to have been made as a result of filing a certificate of determination of preferences under Corp C §401, even though that filing may indirectly revise the relative rights and priorities of an outstanding class or series of shares by creating a senior class or series. The corporation's shareholders authorize this action by previously approving an article provision giving the board of directors authority to fix the rights, preferences, privileges, and restrictions of a wholly unissued class or series of shares, *i.e.,* a blank stock provision. See Corp C §202(e)(3). See also §5.26. The filing of the certificate of determination is the method by which the directors exercise their authority in this matter.

Amended certificates of determination may be filed by the board before shares covered by the certificate are issued. Corp C §401(b). Once shares of any class or series have been issued, no right, preference, privilege, restriction, or other matter pertaining to those shares may be altered or revoked by a certificate of determination that purports to specifically affect such shares. This may be done only by amendment to the articles with any required shareholder vote (see §5.96). Corp C §401(d). The one exception permitted, if the articles so provide, is that the number of shares of a series of a class can be increased or decreased. Corp C §202(e)(3)). Such an increase or decrease must be within the limits originally stated in the articles or in board resolutions (reflected in a prior certificate of determination) that originally fixed the number of shares in the series, and no decrease may reduce the number of shares below the number of shares of the series then outstanding. Corp C §202(e)(3). Care should be taken as well not to eliminate shares that will be needed upon the exercise of options, warrants, or similar rights. Such an increase or decrease requires board action and the filing of an amended certificate of determination. Corp C §401(c).

If it is desired to provide maximum board flexibility, an amendment to give the board of directors authority to fix, by resolution, the rights and preferences of a senior class should provide that the class may be issued in one or more series, and that the directors may fix the rights, preferences, and designations of the various series by resolution. See Corp C §202(e)(2). The board can then create several series with different terms as financial needs require, *e.g.,* different yields required by underwriters or institutional purchasers, or different preferences required by acquisition candidates. When exercising its blank stock power (see §5.26), the board should designate the first issued class as a series (*e.g.,* "Preferred Stock, Series 1"), or it will have eliminated the possibility of issuing more preferred stock under its blank stock power with different rights. This is because any later attempt to file a certificate of determination redesignating an outstanding preferred stock as "Preferred Stock,

Series 1" would specifically affect that stock. This cannot be done without amendment of the articles. See Corp C §401(d).

§5.73 D. Change in Bylaw Restrictions on Transfer of Shares

Reasonable restrictions on the right to transfer shares may be inserted in the articles, but no such restrictions are binding with respect to shares issued before adoption of the restriction unless the holders of the shares vote in favor of the restriction. Corp C §204(b) (which effectively overrules *Tu-Vu Drive-In Corp. v Ashkins* (1964) 61 C2d 283, 38 CR 348, on this point). In view of the ease of adoption of transfer restrictions in bylaw form (no filing with the Secretary of State is required; however, a permit from the Commissioner of Corporations may be required under Corp C §25103(e)(11); see §5.74(1)), or in the form of agreements among shareholders, which do not require a permit at present (except in a close corporation; see §§5.12, 5.74), there appears to be no reason for placing such provisions in the articles. See also §5.96.

VI. AMENDMENTS THAT REQUIRE QUALIFICATION WITH COMMISSIONER OF CORPORATIONS

§5.74 A. Requirement of Qualification by Permit

Any amendment of the articles that would result in "any change in the rights, preferences, privileges, or restrictions of or on outstanding securities," requires a qualification by permit from the Commissioner of Corporations unless the securities or the transaction is exempt. Corp C §§25017(a), 25120–25121. (For discussion of the application for a permit, see §§5.85–5.87; for form, see §5.87.)

Exemptions from this qualification requirement are available for the following:

(1) All changes in rights, preferences, privileges, or restrictions (other than certain stock splits or reverse stock splits), except for the changes enumerated in Corp C §25103(e) if such enumerated changes "materially and adversely affect any class of shareholders" (see §5.75);

(2) All stock splits and reverse stock splits, except for certain types enumerated in Corp C §25103(f) (see §5.76);

(3) Changes in which the holders of less than 25 percent of any class of substantially and adversely affected shares are California residents, under Corp C §25103(b) (see §5.78);

(4) All transactions involving securities of certain organizations exempted under Corp C §25100 (see §5.79); and

(5) Certain securities transactions exempted by rules of the Commissioner of Corporations (see §§5.80–5.84).

It should be noted that under prior law, the Commissioner of Corporations took the position that changes effected by agreements among shareholders, even when the corporation was a party to the agreement, were not subject to these qualification provisions as long as the articles and bylaws (or other charter documents) are not changed, because such agreements gave rise to purely personal obligations and did not change the corporate structure. See 5 Ops Cal Comm'r Corps 73/72C, 73/73C, 73/74C (1973); 4 Ops Cal Comm'r Corps 72/29C, 72/63C (1972); 3 Ops Cal Comm'r Corps 71/105C (1971). See also §5.12. However, the Commissioner's position appears to have changed in this regard as to shareholder agreements of close corporations. See Commissioner of Corporations Release Nos. 50-C (Feb. 9, 1977), 52-C (Sept. 14, 1977).

The Department of Corporations has indicated informally that amendments eliminating or limiting personal liability under Corp C §204(a)(10) or providing for indemnity under Corp C §204(a)(11) (see §5.68) will not be viewed as changes in the rights, preferences, privileges, or restrictions of shares and therefore a permit will not be required for such changes. Both the Department of Corporations and the Secretary of State's office have indicated, however, that they would have serious problems with any of these provisions that contained language such as "to the full extent of the law *as it now exists or may hereafter be amended.*" See §5.68, 5.134–5.135. Thus, although a permit is not required for an amendment simply changing the exculpation or indemnification provisions of the articles, the Department of Corporations has indicated that if articles with the offending language are submitted in connection with a permit application at any time, it will require deletion of the language before granting a permit. Corporations subject to the Department's permit jurisdiction therefore may want to avoid such language in order to avoid delays in later permit applications.

B. Exempted Amendments

§5.75 1. Changes in Rights Set Forth in Corp C §25103(e)

Before the adoption of the Corporate Securities Law of 1968, the securities law contained only the broad definition of "sale" that included any change in rights, preferences, privileges, or restrictions of outstanding securities, with very few exemptions. Virtually any amendment to the articles affecting rights of shares was potentially subject to the permit requirements, and there was great uncertainty as to which amendments required a permit.

The Corporate Securities Law of 1968 (Corp C §§25000–25706) attempts to solve this problem by exempting from the permit requirements *all* changes in rights, preferences, privileges, or restrictions of outstanding shares except those specifically enumerated in Corp C §25103(e) and (f). Corporations Code §25103(e) identifies thirteen categories of changes *not* exempt from the permit requirement if they "materially and adversely affect any class of shareholders," as follows:

(1) Addition, change, or deletion of assessment provisions;

(2) Change in dividend rights;

(3) Change in redemption provisions;

(4) Change to make the securities redeemable;

(5) Change in amounts payable on liquidation;

(6) Change, addition, or deletion of conversion rights;

(7) Change, addition, or deletion of voting rights;

(8) Change, addition, or deletion of preemptive rights;

(9) Change, addition, or deletion of sinking fund provisions;

(10) Rearrangement of relative priorities of outstanding shares;

(11) Imposition of, change in, or deletion of transfer restrictions in articles or bylaws;

(12) Change in shareholder rights with respect to calling special meetings of shareholders;

(13) Change, addition, or deletion of rights, preferences, privileges, or restrictions of, or on, outstanding shares or memberships of a mutual water company or other corporation organized primarily to provide services or facilities to its shareholders or members. Corp C §25103(e). For the changes enumerated by Corp C §25103(f), see §5.76.

Section 25103(e) still embodies the pre–1968 principle that an amendment affecting one class of outstanding shares (favorably, so as not to require a permit) may also affect another class of outstanding shares materially and adversely, so as to require a permit. See Commissioner's Policy Letter No. 131, and 5 Ops Cal Comm'r Corps 73/68C (1973) (acceleration of conversion rights of preferred shares adversely affects common and requires a permit); Commissioner's Policy Letter No. 25 (grant of voting rights to shares that did not have them adversely affects class that already has voting rights); 4 Ops Cal Comm'r Corps 72/2C (1972) (amendment to change from two classes to one not exempt under Corp C §25103(e) when relative voting rights of the two shareholders would change, especially because one shareholder's voting power would be reduced from 72 percent to 64 percent, less than the two thirds needed to approve mergers and other fundamental changes); 4 Ops Cal Comm'r Corps 72/16C (1972) (increase in interest rate on debentures substantially and adversely affects common shareholders by reducing common equity (even though by only $27,000 per year), thus requiring a permit under the provisions of Corp C §25103(g), which is similar to §25103(e)).

Although the authorization of a new class of shares or the issuance and sale of additional shares of an outstanding or a senior class may well have the indirect effect of diluting or modifying the economic position of outstanding shares, such an action does not constitute a change "in the rights, preferences, privileges, or restrictions of or on previously outstanding shares" under Corp C §25103(e). 10 Cal Code Regs §260.103.1. See 1 Marsh & Volk, PRACTICE UNDER THE CALIFORNIA SECURITIES LAWS §7.03[2][b] (rev ed). However, a permit will be required under Corp C §25110 or §25120 to offer or sell shares of any new class, unless another exemption is available. Moreover, if the new senior class is not issued under a blank stock provision (see §§5.26, 5.72), it may be wise to file an application for permit to issue the shares even before the amendment is adopted, so that any changes required by the Commissioner in the rights of the new class can be made before the amendment is adopted.

Corporations Code §25103(e) does include the clarification that changes in rights, preferences, privileges, or restrictions of or on outstanding shares do not "materially and adversely" affect any class of shareholders if they arise from (1) amendment of the articles of incorporation to adopt or terminate close corporation status, (2) involuntary cessation of close corporation status, or (3) termination of a shareholders' agreement under Corp C §300(b). Such changes therefore do not require a permit. But see Wang, *The California Statutory Close Corporation: Gateway to Flexibility or Trap for the Unwary?* 15 San Diego L Rev 687 (1978) for a discussion of rules of the California Commissioner of Corporations relating to close corporations.

At a minimum, favorable changes should not require a permit unless they are favorable to one class and unfavorable in a material and adverse way to another. It would appear that the "material and adverse" standard should be applied by reference to whether the change would have materially affected the investment decision of the shareholder had it been in effect before the securities were purchased. See 1 Marsh & Volk §7.03[3]. In applying the standard, however, the Commissioner bases the determination "primarily on an analysis of its issuer's stock structure and not on such facts as its present financial condition, shareholder relationships and unanimity of the board of directors at the time of the proposed change." 9 Ops Cal Comm'r Corps 78/2C (1978) (elimination of assessibility of common shares was material with respect to senior securities despite factual unlikelihood that common shares ever would be assessed to pay senior securities' dividend and liquidation preferences). Potential purchasers of preferred stock usually demand, and drafters of protective provisions usually include, protective provisions that neither expects will ever have operative effect (*e.g.,* supermajority vote provisions; see §5.28). If, however, an event occurs that would trigger a protective provision, the provision becomes important. A change in such a protective provision is usually considered "material" by the Commissioner of Corporations, however remote the occurrence of the triggering event may seem at the time of the change. It was held under prior law that changes in the articles affecting substantial voting rights required a permit. See *Western Air Lines, Inc. v Sobieski* (1961) 191 CA2d 399, 414, 12 CR 719, 728.

Cases defining materiality under various securities statutes, both state and federal, may be useful. A request for an interpretive opinion under Corp C §25618 and Comm'r Corps Rel No. 61-C (June 25, 1980), may be sought to protect against liability if no permit is obtained, although the Commissioner is rather conservative in issuing such opinions, and it may be more practical to simply seek a permit.

But see 9 Ops Cal Comm'r Corps 78/2C (1978), *supra*; 4 Ops Cal Comm'r Corps 72/126C (1972) (amendment to delete preemptive rights in one-class structure substantially and adversely affects outstanding shares, because it abrogates the right to maintain proportionate interests), 5 Ops Cal Comm'r Corps 73/44C (1973) (adding to the articles restrictions identical to those in shareholder agreement substantially and adversely affects outstanding shares, because the agreement gave rise merely to personal obligations).

A change in or deletion of transfer restrictions in articles or bylaws may be material and adverse even though it may grant greater freedom to transfer shares without compliance with the restriction, on the ground that it also limits the ability of other shareholders to exercise their rights of first refusal (5 Ops Cal Comm'r Corps 73/36C, 73/159C (1973), 2 Ops Cal Comm'r Corps 70/29 (1970); Commissioner's Policy Letter No. 120). The insertion or deletion of supermajority provisions in the articles will require a permit under Corp C §25103(e)(7) (see 6 Ops Cal Comm'r Corps 74/101C (1974)). See also §5.28.

§5.76   2. Stock Splits, Reverse Stock Splits; Stock Dividends

Corporations Code §25103(f) exempts from the permit requirement any stock split or reverse stock split, except the following: (1) any stock split or reverse stock split if the corporation has more than one class of shares outstanding and the split would have a material effect on the proportionate interests of the respective classes as to voting, dividends, or distributions; (2) any stock split of a stock which is traded in the market and its market price as of the date of directors' approval of the stock split, adjusted to give effect to the split, was less than two dollars per share; and (3) any reverse stock split, if the corporation has the option of paying cash for any fractional shares created by such reverse split and as a result of such action the proportionate interests of the shareholders would be substantially altered.

The first clause is designed to prevent, or to permit the Commissioner to review, any possible material adverse discrimination against one class for the benefit of the other by splitting or reverse-splitting one class but not the other, or at least to ensure that this is not done on a materially disproportionate basis. 7 Ops

Cal Comm'r Corps 75/14C (1975), 4 Ops Cal Comm'r Corps 72/6C (1972); see §5.16.

The second clause is designed to allow the Commissioner to exercise his or her discretion in light of the traditional view (see 10 Cal Code Regs §260.140.70) that stock should not be traded on the market at low prices, which permits speculation and fraud in trading transactions involving "penny stocks." The term "traded in the market" is defined in 10 Cal Code Regs §260.103.4.

The third clause is designed primarily to prevent substantial elimination of shareholders by use of a reverse stock split, followed by payment for fractional shares in cash. Such a reverse stock split "will not normally be approved." 10 Cal Code Regs §260.140.70. See also Corp C §407, which prohibits cash payment for fractional shares if that action would result in cancellation of more than 10 percent of the outstanding shares of any class. There is little authority on what is "substantial alteration" for Corp C §25103(f) purposes. See 9 Ops Cal Comm'r Corps 78/4C (1978) (reduction of number of shareholders must be considered as well as number of shares to be eliminated; reduction of number of shareholders from 633 to 234 is substantial alteration); 10 Ops Cal Comm'r Corps 79/5C (1979) (reduction of number of shareholders from 42 to 3 is substantial alteration); 2 Ops Cal Comm'r Corps 70/98 (1970) (.0009594 percent change in proportionate interests is not substantial); 3 Ops Cal Comm'r Corps 71/23C (1971) (reverse split to cash out 496 public shareholders holding less than 2 percent of the outstanding shares requires permit, unless a market exists at the time the public shareholders are advised of the reverse split so that they may choose between selling on the market or awaiting the cashout); 4 Ops Cal Comm'r Corps 72/19C (1972).

The definitions of "stock split" and "reverse stock split" used in Corp C §25103(f) appear in 10 Cal Code Regs §260.103.2 and are essentially the same as in the General Corporation Law. See §5.16. A "stock dividend" is distinguished from a "stock split." A "stock dividend," as used in Corp C §25017, is defined in 10 Cal Code Regs §260.017 also in accordance with its legal meaning and not according to its accounting definition. See §§5.17, 5.23. (The reference in the California Code of Regulations to par value is obsolete for California corporations, and one should focus on "stated value," which is probably the number of outstanding shares of the class, divided into the capital attributable to those shares.) See §5.24.

A stock dividend is excluded from the definitions of "offer" and "sale" (which has the effect of exempting it from all qualification and permit requirements of the Corporate Securities Law) if (a) it is made with respect to common stock solely (except for cash or scrip paid for fractions) in shares of such common stock (but if the shareholders are given an option to take cash, the "solely" requirement is not met; see 10 Cal Code Regs §260.017(b), second sentence); and (b) the corporation has no other class of voting stock outstanding. Corp C §25017(f)(2); see 3 Ops Cal Comm'r Corps 71/40C (1971).

"Voting stock" is defined in 10 Cal Code Regs §260.017.1 to mean stock presently entitling the owner or holder to vote in the election of directors. The term excludes shares that have a right to vote only on a contingency, *e.g.*, a default in dividends. A transaction can be exempt if it is done in the form of a stock dividend and not as a stock split. See, *e.g.*, 3 Ops Cal Comm'r Corps 71/91C (1971) (a stock dividend on one class of voting shares but not the other class of nonvoting shares was exempt, but might not be exempt as a stock split if it could have an effect on dividends and distributions, because the voting shares would receive more shares). See also 10 Cal Code Regs §260.103.1; 3 Ops Cal Comm'r Corps 71/38C (1971).

Any stock dividend (other than a cash-option stock dividend) that is not exempt from qualification under Corp C §25017(f) and 10 Cal Code Regs §260.017 is a change in rights, preferences, and privileges requiring qualification under Corp C §25110 or §25120, unless otherwise exempted by Corp C §25100, §25102, §25103, or §25105. This means that the exemption in Corp C §25103(e) should be considered for such a stock dividend. See 2 Ops Cal Comm'r Corps 70/45 (1970) (nonvoting stock dividend on two classes of voting stock is a sale under Corp C §25017, but exempt under Corp C §25103(e), because no change in voting or other rights was affected by that dividend; but 9 Ops Cal Comm'r Corps 77/11C (1977) may have overruled this opinion); 4 Ops Cal Comm'r Corps 72/23C (1972) (Corp C §25103(e) exemption unavailable for stock dividend on common, because the reduction of the preferred's voting power from 6.8 percent to 4.7 percent is a substantial and adverse effect on preferred when viewed as a class, because it would be a one-third reduction). Other exemptions in connection with Corp C §§25100 and 25103 should also be considered (see §§5.78–5.84).

§5.77   3. Changes in Debt Securities

Corporations Code §25103(g) exempts any change in the rights of outstanding debt securities. Again, as in the case of changes to rights of outstanding stock (see §5.75), the statute contains a lengthy list of exceptions. They include:

(1) Change in the right to interest;

(2) Change in redemption provisions;

(3) Change to make the securities redeemable;

(4) Change to extend the maturity of the securities or to change the amount payable at maturity;

(5) Change in voting rights;

(6) Change in conversion rights;

(7) Change in sinking fund provisions; and

(8) Change to subordinate the securities to other debt.

§5.78   4. Fewer Than 25 Percent California Residents

Corporations Code §25103(b) exempts any change in rights, preferences, privileges, or restrictions, unless the holders of at least 25 percent of the outstanding shares of any class of securities that will be directly or indirectly affected substantially and adversely by such change have addresses in California according to the issuer's records. See §5.75 for a discussion of which class is adversely affected by a change in one class. Only the residency of holders of each class adversely affected need be ascertained for purposes of Corp C §25103(b). Securities held by broker-dealers or their nominees, and securities controlled by any one person who controls more than 50 percent of the class, are excluded in making the determination of whether the 25 percent test is met. Corp C §25103(d). Under this test, a change in rights affecting a sole (100 percent) shareholder or two 50 percent shareholders is exempt from the permit requirements (5 Ops Cal Comm'r Corps 73/150C (1973); 4 Ops Cal Comm'r Corps 72/9C (1972); 3 Ops Cal Comm'r Corps 71/97C (1971), 3 Ops Cal Comm'r Corps 71/38C (1971); Commissioner's Policy Letter No. 170C). For example, if a 60 percent shareholder resides in Nevada, his or her shares will be excluded, and the test will be whether 25 percent of the remaining 40 percent, *i.e.*, 10 percent, have addresses in California. See 5 Ops Cal Comm'r Corps 73/77C (1977).

A study of outstanding shares and shareholder residency before an amendment may reveal that, with proper planning, the exemption can be claimed to exist at the time it is to be tested—the record date for the determination of shareholders entitled to vote or consent on the action (or, if no shareholder vote is required, the date of the directors' approval of the action). Corp C §25103(d). For example, transfer of shares out of the name of a California bank trustee into the name of a New York bank trustee or into the name of a broker nominee may be helpful. It is advisable that such a transfer be made on a permanent basis and not with the intent of switching back after the test date. When it is not certain whether the test will be met on the record date, it may be advisable to file a permit application and pay the nonrefundable filing fee (see 10 Cal Code Regs §250.16), then withdraw if the test is met, so that there is no delay in mailing the proxy material while a permit is obtained. (For discussion of proxy materials, see §5.86.)

§5.79   5. Securities of Certain Organizations

No permit is required for amendment of the articles of various U.S. and foreign governmental entities; national and California state banks; California trust companies; certain savings and loan and similar associations; corporations whose securities require authorization from the California Insurance Commissioner, Public Utilities Commissioner, or Real Estate Commissioner; certain real property subdivisions; certain credit unions; federally and state-regulated railroads, common carriers, utilities, and utility holding companies; certain nonprofit corporations; and agricultural cooperative corporations organized under Food & Ag C §§54001–54294. Corp C §25100(a)–(m). As to nonprofit corporations, see also 10 Cal Code Regs §260.105.20. Amendments to articles of corporations relating to securities listed or approved for listing on the New York Stock Exchange or American Stock Exchange, or designated or approved for designation as a National Market System security on an interdealer quotation system of the National Association of Securities Dealers, Inc., are also exempt. See Corp C §§25100(*o*), 25100.1; 10 Cal Code Regs 260.105.17; Commissioner of Corporations Release Nos. 27-C (Mar. 4, 1972), 87-C (Sept. 22, 1989). Also exempt are amendments to articles of certain consumer cooperatives. See Corp C §25100(r). Corporations Code §25100 does not exempt an amendment changing the rights of securities other than those covered by the exemption. Thus, a proposed increase in dividend rate of an unlisted preferred stock would not be exempt under Corp C §25100(*o*), even though the corporation's common stock is listed. If the preferred were listed and the common were not listed, the dividend increase might not be exempt, because it might be regarded under prior Attorney General Opinions (see §5.75) as a change in rights of the common stock.

An amendment that creates a new security or changes an outstanding security will be exempt even before the exchange approves the amended listing application (which might not occur until after the proxy material has been sent out), thus eliminating the need for a permit before mailing the proxy material. See 10 Cal Code Regs §260.105, which exempts the offer of a security if at the time of actual issuance it is an exempt security under Corp C §25100 (*i.e.*, the amended listing application must have been approved before or concurrently with filing the amendment). See §5.85. The amendment should be conditioned on exchange approval being obtained (either by board resolution or by a statement in the proxy material), unless such approval can be obtained before the proxy statement is mailed out or unless a permit is obtained.

The application of the "new security" concept is difficult in connection with other exemptions that are based on authorization by another public agency, *e.g.*, a public utilities commission. If the agency does not require such authorization for the changed security, does the exemption exist on the basis that authorization was originally given by the agency for the unchanged security? In the absence of a rule similar to that of 10 Cal Code Regs §260.105, it is possible to argue that an authorization is required for the new changed security. In that situation, it is better practice to find another exemption or obtain a permit.

§5.80   6. Certain Securities Transactions Exempted by Commissioner's Rule

The Commissioner is authorized to exempt transactions by rules. See Corp C §25105. Thus, amendments to the articles of corporations organized under the Moscone-Knox Professional Corporation Act (Corp C §§13400–13410) are exempt from the permit requirements of Corp C §§25110 and 25120. 10 Cal Code Regs §260.105.6(a).

The Commissioner's rule in 10 Cal Code Regs §260.103(a) exempts from the permit requirements any amendment that, if it had involved issuance of a new security containing the changed rights, would have been exempt from the issuer qualification requirements under Corp C §25102 or 10 Cal Code Regs §260.105.14. By virtue of this rule, the additional exemptions set forth in §§5.81–5.84 are available.

§5.81   a. Nonpublic Offerings

Nonpublic Offerings of Debt Securities. An amendment of the articles affecting the terms of an outstanding debt security is exempt from qualification if it does not involve any public offering. Corp C §25102(e); 10 Cal Code Regs §260.102.2; ORGANIZING CORPORATIONS IN CALIFORNIA §4.73 (2d ed Cal CEB 1983). This exemption does not apply to debt securities that are convertible into equity securities, unless the security into which they are convertible is also exempt. 10 Cal Code Regs §260.102.3.

Nonpublic Offerings of Equity Securities. An amendment of the articles affecting the terms of an outstanding equity security is likewise exempt from qualification if it involves only a limited offering. Corp C §25102(f); see 10 Cal Code Regs §§260.102.12–260.102.14, 260.103 (allows unlimited number of "excluded purchasers" under 10 Cal Code Regs §260.102.13, plus up to 35 other investors). See also Corp C §25102(h); ORGANIZING CORPORATIONS §§4.49–4.56.

For a discussion of Corp C §25102, which lists issuer transactions that are exempt from the sale qualification requirements of Corp C §25110, see *People v Graham* (1985) 163 CA3d 1159, 210 CR 318.

§5.82   b. Institutional Investors

An exemption from qualification applies to an amendment of the articles of any corporation that has no investors other than institutional investors, *e.g.,* banks, savings and loan associations, trust companies, insurance companies, investment companies registered under the Investment Company Act of 1940, pension or profit-sharing trusts (other than such a trust of the issuer, a self-employed individual retirement plan or IRA), and such other institutional investors as may be defined by rule. Corp C §25102(i). Also included in the definition of institutional investor are certain corporations with outstanding securities registered under §12 of the Securities Exchange Act of 1934 (15 USC §78*l*) and their wholly owned subsidiaries (see also §5.84). By rule, the Commissioner has added a range of tax-exempt charities to the institutional investor category, specifically those organizations exempt from federal income taxes under IRC §501(c)(3) that have total assets of $5,000,000 or more. 10 Cal Code Regs §260.102.10(a). The definition also includes certain corporations with a net worth of $14,000,000 if, among other things, less than 25 percent of the issuer's outstanding common shares are owned by California residents, or the institutional investor does not own more than 5 percent of the issuer's outstanding common shares. 10 Cal Code Regs §260.102.10(b). Finally, any wholly owned subsidiary of an institutional investor as defined in Corp C §25102(i) or 10 Cal Code Regs §260.102.10 is defined as an institutional investor. 10 Cal Code Regs §260.102.10(c). See Corp C §25102(i); ORGANIZING CORPORATIONS IN CALIFORNIA §§4.71–4.72 (2d ed Cal CEB 1983). See §5.83 for a discussion of shares owned by pension and profit-sharing plans.

Because Corp C §25102(i) requires that the purchaser make a written investment representation in connection with any amendment to articles for which no permit is being obtained in reliance on this exemption, each shareholder should be required to reaffirm in writing its investment intent. Note that this requirement that each purchaser express an investment intent appears to grant any objecting shareholder a veto to prevent an amendment from being effected without a permit under this exemption merely by refusing to reaffirm a previously expressed intent not to distribute the securities. As a result, there may be circumstances in which it is advisable to apply for a permit for an amendment otherwise exempt under Corp C §25102(i), particularly where timing is a factor. The cost of obtaining a permit may also be less than the cost of soliciting shareholder representations in some cases.

§5.83   c. Bankruptcies; Pension and Profit-Sharing Plans

Bankruptcy reorganizations or arrangements. An amendment of articles is exempt if effected under a reorganization or arrangement subject to court confirmation under the federal bankruptcy law. Corp C §25102(k); see §5.69.

Pension and profit-sharing plans. Corporations Code §25102(m) exempts from qualification an amendment to the articles of a corporation, the shares of which are owned by one or more pension, profit-sharing, stock bonus, or employee stock ownership plans meeting the requirements for qualification under IRC §401, provided that no individual employee contributions are required or permitted. The exemption applies regardless of whether the stock is contributed to the plan, purchased from the issuer with contributions by the issuer or an affiliate, or purchased from the issuer with funds borrowed from any source.

§5.84   7. Common Stock of Quality Corporations

Changes involving the offer or sale of certain publicly traded, nonassessable, voting common stocks of corporations meeting certain net worth, capitalization, audit, and income requirements are exempt under 10 Cal Code Regs §260.105.17, provided there is only one class of common stock outstanding. An amendment to the articles of a large corporation not exempt under Corp C §25102(i) (see §5.82), or a stock split, reverse stock split, or stock dividend of voting common stock not exempt under Corp C §25103(f) (see §5.76), could be exempt under this rule.

C. Application for Permit To Issue Securities in Connection With Amendment

§5.85   1. When To Apply

The issuer of securities must obtain a permit from the Commissioner of Corporations either to offer or to sell a security in connection with a change in rights, preferences, privileges, or restrictions, unless the transaction is exempt (see §§5.75–5.84). Corp C §25120. Even though the transaction may necessitate registration of the new security under the Securities Act of 1933 (see §5.155), qualification by coordination is not available for a transaction subject to Corp C §25120—qualification must be by permit. Corp C §§25110, 25120, 25121. A permit must be obtained before the "offer" of the changed or new security is made by means of a general solicitation of shareholder approval of the amendment. Negotiations and agreements before that time are exempt (*e.g.*, discussions of, and agreements on, the terms of the amendment by the board or with a few selected shareholders). See Corp C §25103(a).

The policy of the Commissioner is to require that a definitive permit be applied for before general solicitation of shareholder approval, that the Commissioner act on the application before distribution of the proxy soliciting material, and that the definitive permit be conditioned on shareholder approval (the condition may require a separate vote of those who do not have a "conflict of interest in connection with the adoption" of the amendment; see §5.104). 10 Cal Code Regs §260.140.63. This procedure usually eliminates the need for two permits: One to make the "offer" to the shareholders (a so-called "negotiating permit"), and a definitive permit to permit the "sale" (filing the amendment with the Secretary of State)—unless the proxy materials need to be distributed before the Commissioner is expected to issue the definitive permit, in which case a negotiating permit must be obtained. 10 Cal Code Regs §260.140.63. See Corp C §25102(c).

§5.86 2. Proxy Material

Proxy material must be filed as an exhibit to the application for permit. 10 Cal Code Regs §§260.121(b), item (15)(D), 260.140.60–260.140.63.

What information should be furnished to shareholders in connection with solicitation of approval of an amendment to articles? Although all proxy material must be filed as an exhibit to the application (10 Cal Code Regs §260.121(b), item (15)(D)), no formal requirement of the Commissioner of Corporations exists that a proxy statement be used. See §5.155 as to SEC proxy statement requirements for publicly held companies, and Corp C §604 as to minimum California proxy solicitation requirements. When the shareholders are not all sophisticated or closely affiliated persons, and the effect of the amendment is not apparent on its face, some explanatory proxy material is generally desirable and may be required by the Commissioner as a condition to issuance of a permit, whether the shareholders are acting at a meeting or by written consent. In these situations, information required to be included in the application for a permit that is material to shareholders voting on the amendment should generally be included in the material furnished to shareholders.

§5.87   3. Official Form: Application for Permit

(Department of Corporations Use Only)	
Fee Paid _____	

Receipt No. _____

Initial Review _____

Deficiency Letters_____

Effective Date _____

Orders Issued _____

DEPARTMENT OF CORPORATIONS
FILE NO.

(Insert file number of previous filings of Applicant
before the Department, if any)

FEE: _____
(To be completed by Applicant)

Date of Application: _____

DEPARTMENT OF CORPORATIONS
STATE OF CALIFORNIA
FACING PAGE
APPLICATION FOR QUALIFICATION OF SECURITIES, UNDER THE CORPORATE SECURITIES LAW OF 1968,
BY *(Check Only One)*

☐ COORDINATION,   SECTION 25111   ☐ POST-EFFECTIVE   AMENDMENT
☐ NOTIFICATION,   SECTION 25112   NUMBER_____
☐ PERMIT,   SECTION 25113   TO APPLICAT'ON
☐ PERMIT,   SECTION 25121   FILED UNDER
                                                                    SECTION_____
☐ NEGOTIATING PERMIT, SECTION 25102(c)   ☐ PRE-EFFECTIVE   DATED _____

This application is for an ☐ open or ☐ limited offering qualification as defined in Section 260.001 of the rules (check as applicable)

1. Name of applicant

2. (a) Is applicant a corporation, partnership, trust or other entity? _____
   (b) State of incorporation or jurisdiction under which organized? _____
   (c) If a corporation, is applicant in good standing in the State of its incorporation? (Indicate "yes" or "no") ___
   (d) Is applicant a registered investment company? (Indicate "yes" or "no") _____

3a. Address of principal executive office of applicant.
    Number and Street   City   State   Zip Code

  b. Is the principal location of applicant's books and records at the address of the principal executive office, above? (Indicate
     "yes" or "no"). If "no", provide address:
     Number and Street   City   State   Zip Code

4. Name and address of person to whom correspondence regarding this application should be addressed.

5.	(a)	(b)	(c)	(d)	(e)
	Description of Securities (See instructions on reverse side)	Total number of shares or units of each class of securities being qualified in California (e.g., "20,000")	Proposed maximum offering price per unit (e.g., "$10")	Proposed maximum aggregate offering price for securities being qualified in California (e.g., "200,000") Note: Fee calculated on total of this column	Does a public market exist for this class of securities? (Indicate "yes" or "no." If "yes," insert CUSIP number.)

6. Consideration to be paid for securities: if cash, state "cash", or if other than cash and the aggregate value is ascribed thereto by the Board of Directors of the issuer so state (e.g., "Real Property, $100,000," or "Assets of a going business, $50,000.").

7. There is no adverse order, judgment or decree entered in connection with the offering by any State regulatory authority,
   any court or the Securities and Exchange Commission, except as follows: *(If none, so state)*

260 110 (12 84)

INSTRUCTIONS

The following instructions must be adhered to with respect to all applications for qualification by permit under Sections 25102(c), 25113 and 25121; by coordination under Section 25111, and notification by Section 25112:

Completion of Application. The facing page on the reverse side hereof, must be completed in full and in addition to the facing page, applications must continue by completion of each item of the applicable following forms:

Application for qualification by coordination,	Form No. 260.111
Application for qualification by notification,	Form No. 260.112
Application for permit pursuant to Section 25113,	Form No. 260.113
Application for permit pursuant to Section 25121,	Form No. 260.121
Application for Negotiating Permit pursuant to Section 25102(c),	Form No. 260.113

The numbering sequence in the forms must be adhered to. Any item which is inapplicable should be listed by the number on the form, followed simply by the word "inapplicable."

Form of Application. The application should be typewritten or printed in the English language, on one side only of either legal or letter-size paper.

Signing of Applications. Applications should be signed by an officer or general partner of the applicant; however, it may be signed by another person holding a power of attorney for such purposes from the applicant, and if signed on behalf of the applicant pursuant to such power of attorney, should include as an additional exhibit a copy of said power of attorney or a copy of the corporate resolution authorizing the attorney to act.

Item 5 — "Public Market." A "public market" exists for this class of securities if it (1) is listed on a national securities exchange, (2) is traded in the over-the-counter market and quoted in the *Wall Street Journal* or other newspaper of general circulation, or (3) is held of record or beneficially by 500 or more persons.

Incorporation by Reference. In lieu of answering any specific item in this form, an applicant may incorporate the information called for by reference to any attached document, or to any document currently on file with the Department. Such reference should indicate the pages or portion of the document where the information is located.

Amendments to Applications. An amendment to any application for qualification should contain only the information being amended *by item number* and should be verified in the form prescribed for the application. Each amendment should be accompanied by a facing page in the form prescribed by Section 260.110 of the rules on which the applicant shall insert the fact that the filing is an amendment and the number of the amendment if more than one amendment.

Filing Fee Calculation. The filing fee fixed by Section 25608 must accompany each application and the amount of filing fee paid is to be set forth on the facing page in the upper right hand corner. By way of illustration, the filing fee for qualification of securities by coordination, notification, or permit under Sections 25113 or 25121 is computed by taking 1/10th of 1% of the maximum aggregate offering price of securities being qualified in California, see appropriate column on facing page, and adding $100. Thus, a qualification, for $275,250 would be computed by moving the decimal point three places to the left, $275.25, and adding $100 for a total of $375.25. However, the maximum filing fee, including the $100, is $1,750 for applications filed under Sections 25112, 25113, and 25121 and is $1,550 for applications filed under Section 25111.

Description of Securities Being Qualified. State title of each class of securities (e.g. $10 par value common stock) and include rights, warrants, options and convertible securities and the securities to be issued upon exercise or conversion thereof.

A Customer Authorization of Disclosure of Financial Records Form (Form No. QR 500.259) must also be filed as an exhibit to the application.

DEPARTMENT OF CORPORATIONS
STATE OF CALIFORNIA

INSTRUCTIONS FOR APPLICATION FOR QUALIFICATION OF RECAPITALIZATIONS AND REORGANIZATIONS (SECTION 260.121)

An application pursuant to Section 25121 of the Code for the qualification of the offer and sale of securities in connection with any change in the rights, preferences, privileges, or restrictions of or on outstanding securities or in any exchange of securities by the issuer with its existing security holders exclusively or in any exchange in connection with any merger or consolidation or purchase of corporate assets in consideration wholly or in part of the issuance of securities shall, in addition to the facing page required by Section 260.110 of these rules, continue on the following form:

NOTE: Any item which is inapplicable should be listed by number on the form followed simply by the word "inapplicable."

(a) IF THE TRANSACTION INVOLVES a merger, consolidation or purchase of corporate assets:

ITEM 8. DESCRIPTION OF PLAN.

Describe the material features of the plan, the reasons therefor, the general effect thereof upon the rights of existing security holders, the approximate number of shareholders of each corporation involved, the vote needed for its approval, the proposed date for the mailing of proxies and the proposed date of the shareholders' meeting.

ITEM 9. EXECUTION OF PLAN.

Describe the method by which the plan described in Item 8 will be carried out, including the names of any broker-dealers or agents to be employed by each corporation in effecting purchases or sales of securities pursuant to the plan and the compensation to be paid such persons, or other consideration to be received by such persons, or any other persons, in connection with the sale or purchase of securities.

If agents (other than licensed broker-dealers) are to be employed by the applicant in connection with the distribution of securities in California pursuant to the plan, the applicant is required to comply with Sections 260.141.30 and 260.141.31, Title 10, California Administrative Code, and the following information is to be furnished:

a. The name and business address of each person who will represent the applicant as an agent in this state.

b. The name and business address of the officer or other official who will supervise such agents on behalf of the applicant.

c. A statement that all such agents are employees of the applicant.

d. A statement of the compensation to be paid to such agents. A statement of the compensation to be paid to such supervisory personnel, other than their regular salaries if they are regular employees of the applicant.

e. Describe any order, judgment or decree of any governmental agency or administrator, or of any court of competent jurisdiction revoking or suspending for cause any license, permit or other authority of such agent or supervisory person or of any corporation of which he is an officer or director, to engage in the securities business or in the sale of a particular security or temporarily or permanently restraining or enjoining any such person or any corporation of which he is an officer or director from engaging in or continuing any conduct, practice, or employment in connection with the purchase or sale of securities, or convicting such person of any felony or misdemeanor involving a security or any aspect of the securities business, or of theft or of any felony.

f. A surety bond complying with Section 260.216.15, Title 10, California Administrative Code.

ITEM 10. DESCRIPTION OF BUSINESS.

Describe the business of the issuer and each other corporation involved in the transaction.

ITEM 11. DIVIDENDS IN ARREARS OR DEFAULTS.

A statement concerning any dividends in arrears or defaults in principal or interest in respect of any securities of the issuer and any other corporation involved in the transaction, and concerning the effect of the plan thereon.

ITEM 12. HIGH AND LOW SALES PRICES WITHIN 2 YEARS.

As to each class of securities of the issuer and of each other corporation involved in the transaction which is admitted to trading on a securities exchange or with respect to which a market otherwise exists, and which will be materially affected by the plan, state the high and low sale prices (or, in the absence of such information, the range of the bid prices) for each quarterly period within two years.

ITEM 13. DIRECTORS AND EXECUTIVE OFFICERS.

(a) List the names of all directors and officers of the issuer and of each other corporation involved in the transaction, indicating all positions and offices held by each person named.

(b) Describe any order, judgment, or decree of any governmental agency or administrator, or of any court of competent jurisdiction revoking or suspending for cause any license, permit or other authority of such person or of any corporation of which he is an officer or director, to engage in the securities business or in the sale of a particular security or temporarily or permanently restraining or enjoining any such person or any corporation of which he is an officer or director from engaging in or continuing any conduct, practice, or employment in connection with the purchase or sale of securities, or convicting such person of any felony or misdemeanor involving a security or any aspect of the securities business, or of theft or of any felony.

260 121 (12 84)

ITEM 14. PRINCIPAL HOLDERS OF SECURITIES.

State any material interest in the transaction, of each person who, with respect to the issuer or any other corporation involved in the transaction, is a director or officer or person occupying a similar status or performing similar functions, or owns of record or beneficially (if known to the issuer) 10% or more of the outstanding shares of any class of equity securities, or is a promoter if the issuer or such other corporation was organized within the past three years.

(Instruction: An interest of one of the specified persons which arises solely from the ownership of securities of only one of the corporations involved in the transaction is not a material interest where the specified person receives no extra or special benefit not shared on a pro rata basis by all holders of securities of that class.)

ITEM 15. EXCHANGE RATIO.

State the basis of the ratio for the exchange of the securities of the issuer corporation for the securities of the constituent corporation(s).

ITEM 16. EXHIBITS.

Attach and incorporate by reference the following exhibits.

NOTE: Any exhibit which is inapplicable should be listed by letter on the form followed simply by the word "inapplicable."

A. With respect to the issuer and each other corporation involved in the transaction, the financial statements required by Section 260.d613 of Title 10 of the California Administrative Code, and pro forma financial statements giving effect to the proposed transaction.

B. A copy of the plan of reorganization if it is set forth in a written document, including any request for delayed effectiveness of the filing of such document with the Secretary of State or similar authority.

C. Copies (which may be in a restated or composite form) of the current charter documents (as defined in Section 260.001, Title 10, California Administrative Code) of the issuer and of each constituent corporation involved in a merger or consolidation.

D. A copy of any contract made or to be made by the issuer affecting any of the rights, preferences, privileges, or transferability of the securities.

E. Subject to the following instruction, a copy of any agreement made or to be made by or among shareholders of the issuer which materially affects, or will materially affect, any of the rights, preferences, privileges, or restrictions of or on securities of the issuer or the management of the issuer (including any voting agreement, irrevocable proxy or shareholders' agreement).

Instruction: If a copy of an agreement is not available to the issuer, so state and furnish a brief description of the agreement including therein such information regarding the parties and terms as is known to the issuer. Nothing contained herein shall be construed as requiring the issuer to disclose information concerning agreements of which it has no knowledge.

F. A preliminary copy of the proxy material to be used to solicit the vote or consents of security holders (amended copies of such proxy material and final copies should be submitted as supplemental information to this application), and the consent of any attorney, accountant or other expert named in such proxy material, if such expert's consent is required pursuant to Section 260.504.2.2, Title 10, California Administrative Code, in the form required by that section.

G. The Consent to Service of Process if required by Section 25165 of the California Corporations Code.

H. A Customer Authorization of Disclosure of Financial Records Form (Form No. QR 500.259).

ITEM 17. REPORTS OF FINANCIAL CONDITION.

Pursuant to Section 25146 of the California Corporations Code and Section 260.146 of Title 10 of the California Administrative Code, applicant hereby undertakes, as long as required under the foregoing sections and subject to the exceptions therein contained, to file with the Commissioner: (a) within 120 days after the end of each fiscal year a report of financial condition and a related statement of income and expenses covering such fiscal year; and (b) within 90 days after the first six months of each fiscal year, a like report and statement covering such six months period.

(b) IF THE TRANSACTION INVOLVES a change in rights, preferences, privileges or restrictions of or on outstanding securities or an exchange by an issuer with its existing security holders exclusively:

ITEM 8. OUTSTANDING SECURITIES TO BE MODIFIED.

State the title and amount of outstanding securities to be modified.

ITEM 9. DESCRIPTION OF OUTSTANDING SECURITIES AND MODIFIED SECURITIES.

Describe any material differences between the outstanding securities and the modified or new securities.

ITEM 10. DESCRIPTION OF PROPOSED MODIFICATION.

State the reasons for the proposed modification, the general effect thereof upon the rights of existing security holders, the basis of the ratio for the exchange of securities by an issuer with its existing security holders, the vote needed for approval, the proposed date for the mailing of proxies and the proposed date of the shareholders' meeting.

ITEM 11. DIVIDENDS IN ARREARS OR DEFAULTS.

A statement as to arrears in dividends or as to defaults in principal or interest with respect to outstanding securities which are to be modified, and such other information as may be appropriate in the particular case to disclose adequately the nature and effect of the proposed action.

ITEM 12. METHOD OF SELLING THE SECURITIES.

If the applicant will employ broker-dealers or agents in connection with the recapitalization described in Items 9 and 10, describe the functions such persons will perform, furnish their names, and state the compensation to be paid such persons, or other consideration to be received by such persons, or any other persons, in connection with the sale or purchase of securities under the plan of recapitalization.

If agents are to be employed by the applicant in connection with the distribution of securities pursuant to the plan, the applicant is required to comply with Sections 260.141.30 and 260.141.31, Title 10, California Administrative Code, and the following information is to be furnished:

a. The name and business address of each person who will represent the applicant as an agent in this state.

b. The name and business address of the officer or other official who will supervise such agents on behalf of the applicant.

c. A statement that all such agents are employees of the applicant.

d. A statement of the compensation to be paid to such agents. A statement of the compensation to be paid to such supervisory personnel, other than their regular salaries if they are regular employees of the applicant.

e. Describe any order, judgment or decree of any governmental agency or administrator, or of any court of competent jurisdiction revoking or suspending for cause any license, permit or other authority of such agent or supervisory person or of any corporation of which he is an officer or director, to engage in the securities business or in the sale of a particular security or temporarily or permanently restraining or enjoining any such person or any corporation of which he is an officer or director from engaging in or continuing any conduct, practice, or employment in connection with the purchase or sale of securities, or convicting such person of any felony or misdemeanor involving a security or any aspect of the securities business, or of theft or of any felony.

f. A surety bond complying with Section 260.216.15, Title 10, California Administrative Code.

ITEM 13. DIRECTORS AND EXECUTIVE OFFICERS.

(a) List the names of all directors and officers of the issuer indicating all positions and offices held by each person named.

(b) Describe any order, judgment, or decree of any governmental agency or administrator, or of any court of competent jurisdiction revoking or suspending for cause any license, permit or other authority of such person or of any corporation of which he is an officer or director, to engage in the securities business or in the sale of a particular security or temporarily or permanently restraining or enjoining any such person or any corporation of which he is an officer or director from engaging in or continuing any conduct, practice, or employment in connection with the purchase or sale of securities, or convicting such person of any felony or misdemeanor involving a security or any aspect of the securities business, or of theft or of any felony.

ITEM 14. PRINCIPAL HOLDERS OF SECURITIES.

State any material interest in the transaction of each officer or director of the issuer, or any person occupying a similar status or performing similar functions, any person owning of record or beneficially (if known to the issuer) 10% or more of the outstanding shares of any class of equity security of the issuer, and any promoter of the issuer if the issuer was organized within the past three years.

ITEM 15. EXHIBITS.

Attach and incorporate by reference the following exhibits.

NOTE: Any exhibit which is inapplicable should be listed by letter on the form followed simply by the word "inapplicable."

A. With respect to the issuer, the financial statements required by Section 260.613 of Title 10 of the California Administrative Code.

B. A copy of the plan of recapitalization if it is set forth in a written document, including any request for delayed effectiveness of the filing of such document with the Secretary of State or similar authority.

C. Copies (which may be in a restated or composite form) of the current charter documents (as defined in Section 260.001, Title 10, California Administrative Code) of the issuer and of each constituent corporation involved in a merger or consolidation.

D. A preliminary copy of the proxy material to be used to solicit the vote or consents of security holders (amended copies of such proxy material and final copies should be submitted as supplemental information to this application), and the consent of any attorney, accountant or other expert named in such proxy material, if such expert's consent is required pursuant to Section 260.504.2.2, Title 10, California Administrative code, in the form required by that section.

E. A copy of any contract made or to be made by the issuer affecting any of the rights, preferences, privileges, or transferability of the securities.

F. The Consent to Service of Process if required by Section 25165 of the California Corporations Code.

G. Subject to the following instruction, a copy of any agreement made or to be made by or among shareholders of the issuer which materially affects, or will materially affect, any of the rights, preferences, privileges, or restrictions of or on securities of the issuer or the management of the issuer (including any voting agreement, irrevocable proxy or shareholders' agreement).

H. A Customer Authorization of Disclosure of Financial Records Form (Form No. QR 500.259).

Instruction: If a copy of an agreement is not available to the issuer, so state and furnish a brief description of the agreement including therein such information regarding the parties and terms as is known to the issuer. Nothing contained herein shall be construed as requiring the issuer to disclose information concerning agreements of which it has no knowledge.

ITEM 16. REPORTS OF FINANCIAL CONDITION.

Pursuant to Section 2514 of the California Corporations Code and Section 260.146 of Title 10 of the California Administrative Code, applicant hereby undertakes, as long as required under the foregoing sections and subject to the exceptions therein contained, to file with the Commissioner: (a) within 120 days after the end of each fiscal year, and; (b) within 90 days after the first six months of each fiscal year, a like report and statement covering such six months period.

(c) SIGNATURES: The application must be signed and verified in the following form:

The applicant has duly caused this application to be signed on its behalf by the undersigned, thereunto duly authorized.

_____
(Applicant)

By _____

_____
(Title)

I certify (or declare) under penalty of perjury under the laws of the State of California that I have read this application and the exhibits thereto and know the contents thereof, and that the statements therein are true and correct.

Executed at_____, on_____ , 19 ____.
(Place)   (Date)

_____
(Signature)

Comment: The form of application for permit is set forth in 10 Cal Code Regs §260.110, which provides the form of facing page, and §260.121, which provides the balance of the form. One or two copies of the forms may be obtained without charge at any office of the Department of Corporations. Only the original application need be filed. The filing fee is $100, plus one tenth of 1 percent of the aggregate value of securities to be sold in California, up to a maximum aggregate fee of $1750. Corp C §25608(e), (h). If a negotiating permit is sought, the fee is $50. Corp C §25608(b). To the extent the corporation does have shareholders whose rights are affected and who are exempt institutional investors under Corp C §25102(i), the issuer may save filing fees by excluding from the permit application the securities sold to such investors. Fees should be submitted with the application, and checks should be made payable to "Department of Corporations." For extensive discussion of permit applications, see ORGANIZING CORPORATIONS IN CALIFORNIA §§4.82–4.118 (2d ed Cal CEB 1983).

The requirement that financial statements submitted with the application be audited (see 10 Cal Code Regs §260.613) usually will be waived by the Commissioner in the case of a closely held corporation if the unaudited financial statements that are submitted appear to have been carefully prepared.

The permit application must cover the securities of all shareholders (whether residents of California or not) if the offer will be made to them "in this state" (Corp C §25008). An offer that "originates from" California, even though it is directed to nonresident shareholders, is defined in Corp C §25008(b) as having been made "in this state." Thus, mailing proxy material from this state will necessitate qualification of all the securities affected. If the shareholders direct their acceptance back into this state, an offer is deemed made in this state (Corp C §25008(b)). Most foreign-based issuers can limit the qualification to securities offered to California residents. See §5.114 as to permit authority to cover the sale of fractional shares.

§5.88   D. Department Hearings on Proposed Amendments

A hearing may be held before the Department of Corporations on applications for permits relating to proposed amendments to articles. Two Corporations Code sections provide for a hearing on request: §§25142 and 25143(b).

Under Corp C §25142, the Commissioner is authorized to hold a hearing on the fairness of the terms and conditions of the issuance and exchange of securities for outstanding securities, claims, or property. Such a hearing will be ordered by the Commissioner at the request of the applicant for the permit. 10 Cal Code Regs §260.142. The applicant must bear the expense of the hearing. 10 Cal Code Regs §250.25.

Hearings are often requested and obtained by applicants under Corp C §25142 to exempt the transaction from registration under the Securities Act of 1933, by virtue of §3(a)(10) of that Act. See Glickman, *The State Administrative Fairness Hearing and Section 3(a)(10) of the Securities Act—Some Questions,* 45 St John's L Rev 644 (1971), for discussion of the use of this procedure. See also §5.155. Hearings are also requested when opposition is anticipated, and it is desired to preempt the opposition's move for a hearing by having management make the first request.

Although both Corp C §§25142 and 24143(b) provide only for a hearing at the request of the applicant for the permit (or on the Commissioner's own motion), an objecting shareholder who requests a hearing will probably be granted one, even though there is no provision for granting a hearing on request of a nonapplicant. See §5.10 as to the factors on which the Commissioner will base a decision.

§5.89   E. Judicial Review

Every final order or other official act of the Commissioner of Corporations is subject to judicial review. Corp C §25609. Review is obtained by filing a petition for a writ of mandate in accordance with CCP §1094.5. This appears to be the exclusive avenue to judicial review of the Commissioner's adjudicatory actions. See CALIFORNIA ADMINISTRATIVE MANDAMUS §1.4 (2d ed Cal CEB 1989). Any person beneficially interested may seek a writ of mandate. CCP §1086. Thus, a shareholder who is objecting to a permit authorizing an amendment to the articles of the corporation may petition for judicial review. An applicant aggrieved by the Commissioner's failure to grant a permit may also seek judicial review. The court will not overturn the Commissioner's decision unless it finds a "prejudicial abuse of discretion" on the ground that the findings are not supported by the evidence (CCP §1094.5(b), (c)), and the review will ordinarily be based on the administrative record with no rehearing of evidence by the court (see CCP §1094.5(d)). Some question exists whether a presumption of correctness attaches to the Commissioner's decision, but the courts will in any case be reluctant to overrule it. See *Bixby v Pierno* (1971) 4 C3d 130, 150, 93 CR 234, 248; CAL ADMIN MANDAMUS, chap 4.

VII. DIRECTOR AND SHAREHOLDER ACTION TO AMEND

§5.90   A. Before Shares Issued

The client may decide, after incorporation but before shares have been issued, that a different name or capital structure would better suit the proposed business. At that point the appropriate amendments may be adopted by a writing signed by a majority of the incorporators, if directors were not named in the articles and have not been elected, or if directors were named in the articles or have been elected by a resolution adopted by the majority of the directors then in office. Corp C §§164, 901. The required "writing" may be the certificate of amendment signed and filed under Corp C §906. See §5.139. If directors have been named, they may also act by resolution at a meeting or by unanimous written consent, then file a certificate of amendment under Corp C §§905, 906.

This procedure is available only if no shares have been "issued" within the meaning of Corp C §901. If shares have been issued, meetings of both the shareholders and the board of directors must be called, noticed, and held, or the written consent of each group must be obtained, after which a certificate of amendment must be filed. Corp C §§902–905; see §5.141.

"Issuance" is not merely the execution and delivery of a share certificate after payment for the shares. Although the term is difficult to interpret, "issuance" probably occurs, for purposes of Corp C §901, when the corporation receives payment for its shares. See *Garretson v Pacific Crude Oil Co.* (1905) 146 C 184, 188, 79 P 838, 840. But see 1 Ballantine & Sterling, CALIFORNIA CORPORATION LAWS §123.03 (4th ed). See also Corp C §25017, defining "sale" under the Corporate Securities Law of 1968. In *People v Beber* (1951)

104 CA2d 359, 367, 231 P2d 516, 522, the court held that the issuance of shares "means the act or contract of the corporation by which shares become vested in a person as a member or stockholder." It would appear that the simplified amendment procedure provided in Corp C §901 may be used whether or not there is a subscription agreement as long as the shares have not been paid for in part. See former Corp C §3630 (requiring vote of subscribers); Dahlquist, *Regulation and Civil Liability Under the California Corporate Securities Act II,* 34 Calif L Rev 344, 346 (1946) (no "issuance" under Corporate Securities Act until valuable consideration given); and Comment, *Legal Effect of Preincorporation Subscription Agreements in California,* 19 Hastings LJ 1418 (1968) (because incorporation is acceptance of preincorporation subscription agreement, former Corp C §3630 is of no use when such an agreement existed). Of course, it would be prudent to obtain subscriber approval in these circumstances, if that is feasible.

B. After Shares Issued

§5.91 1. General Requirement of Shareholder and Director Approval

After shares have been issued, the director and shareholder action required to adopt an amendment is governed by Corp C §§902–905. Generally, amendments may be adopted only if approved both by the board of directors and by the outstanding voting shares before or after board approval. Corp C §902(a). However, board approval alone is sufficient if the amendment comes within one of the specific provisions set forth in §5.109.

When board approval is necessary, that approval must be by the board as a whole, and not by a committee of the board, unless shareholder approval is not required. Corp C §311(a). (Curiously enough, while in certain circumstances authority to amend the articles may thus be delegated to a committee, authority to amend the bylaws may not be. Corp C §311(d).) Shareholder approval under Corp C §902(a) must be by the vote (or written consent; see Corp C §194) of a majority of outstanding shares entitled to vote. Corp C §152. Nonvoting shares, or shares not permitted by the articles to vote on certain amendments, would not be entitled to vote on an amendment governed only by Corp C §902(a).

A group of shareholders with sufficient votes to adopt an amendment is sometimes unable to persuade the board of directors (who may be elected by the remainder of the shareholders) to adopt the amendment. There appears to be no other way for counsel for those shareholders to obtain adoption of the amendment than to advise them to call a special meeting of shareholders to remove the present directors and to elect new ones, for Corp C §902(a) requires both board and shareholder approval. Where a statute contemplates corporate action by the board, an amendment that is approved merely by the requisite majority of the shareholders is not binding on the other shareholders (see 7A Fletcher, CYCLOPEDIA OF THE LAW OF PRIVATE CORPORATIONS §3719 (rev ed 1989)). A suggestion made by the Department of Corporations during the drafting of the General Corporation Law to reverse this result was not approved by the State Bar Committee on Corporations and did not become a part of the General Corporation Law.

If the corporation has 100 or more shareholders, special requirements apply to amendments of the articles that include supermajority vote requirements (requirements that particular corporate acts be approved by a greater than majority vote). These supermajority provisions cannot require a vote greater than 66 2/3 percent of the outstanding shares or of a class or series of outstanding shares. In addition, such a requirement must be adopted by a vote at least as great as the supermajority specified in the provision, and the provision is effective for only two years, subject to renewal. Corp C §710.

§5.92   2. Additional Approval of Class or Series Affected

Separate votes by class or series and supermajority votes are not necessary unless required by the articles (see Corp C §152), by Corp C §903 or §904, (see §§5.93–5.100), or by an agreement among the shareholders (see §5.12).

§5.93   a. Requirements of Corp C §903

The most generally applicable requirement that a proposed amendment must also be approved by the outstanding shares of a class affected in certain ways is set forth in Corp C §903. See

§§5.95–5.100. Generally, in addition to approval by the outstanding shares entitled to vote (Corp C §903(c), which in effect repeats the Corp C §902(a) vote requirement), a separate vote of approval is needed from any class, whether or not it is otherwise entitled to vote, affected in any of the ways enumerated in Corp C §903(a). Under Corp C §903(a) it is irrelevant whether the effect on a particular class is adverse, beneficial, or neutral (except as discussed in §5.97 with respect to an increase in rights of a senior class under Corp C §903(a)(5)). Whether or not the change is adverse is a question that need be addressed only under Corp C §903(b).

§5.94   b. Separate Approval by a Series of a Class

If a series (defined in Corp C §183) of a class of outstanding shares would be adversely affected by the amendment in a different manner than other outstanding shares of the same class, the approval of the series voting as if it were a separate class is required. Corp C §903(b). A single amendment could affect a class in such a manner as to trigger the Corp C §903(a) approval requirement by the entire class, and the approval of a particular series of the same class, voting as if it were a separate class, could also be required. If two series of cumulative preferred stock with different dividend rates were outstanding, an amendment to make both series noncumulative requires a vote of the entire class, but probably not the approval of either series voting separately as a class, because both series would be affected *in the same manner* (even though it may be argued that the series with the higher dividend rate might be more adversely affected by loss of the cumulative feature).

§5.95   c. Amendment Changing Authorized Number of Shares of a Class

One type of amendment requiring class approval under Corp C §903 is an amendment to increase or decrease the number of authorized shares of the class, other than an increase incident to a stock split (see §5.101) or required to satisfy option or conversion rights under Corp C §405(b). Corp C §903(a)(1). Also, a class vote of a junior class is required when the preferences or number of authorized shares of a senior class is increased. Corp C §903(a)(5); see §5.97.

§5.96   d. Amendment Changing Share Rights or Restrictions

Any change in the rights, preferences, privileges, or restrictions of a class of shares requires a vote of the class (Corp C §903(a)(4)), as well as a majority vote of all the outstanding voting shares. Corp C §903(a)(4). Similar language appeared in the former Corporate Securities Law and led to some problems because of the breadth of the language (see §5.75). The intention of the drafters of Corp C §903(a)(4) was that the word "change" be read to require the amendment to actually reach out and directly modify the rights, preferences, privileges, or restrictions of the outstanding shares whose vote is required. For example, an authorization of additional shares of preferred stock or increase in the preferred's dividend rate does not directly change the rights or preferences of the common shares, even though there may be an indirect impact on the common, *e.g.*, with respect to dividends. *Hartford Acc. & Indem. Co. v W. S. Dickey Clay Mfg. Co.* (Del 1942) 24 A2d 315; *In re Kinney* (NY 1939) 279 NY 423, 18 NE2d 645. It was further intended that such amendments require a class vote of another class indirectly affected only to the extent specifically required by Corp C §903(a)(5).

If the opposite position were taken, class votes could be required to effect amendments in situations in which the General Corporation Law drafting committee had no intention to extend the law (*e.g.*, an amendment increasing or decreasing the number of directors when no class is entitled to elect any particular number of directors at that time; or eliminating a series of preferred shares, all the outstanding shares of which had been previously redeemed). See also Small, *Changes in Rights, Preferences, Privileges and Restrictions on Outstanding Securities Under the California Corporate Securities Law,* 14 Hastings LJ 94, 98 (1962), for these and other examples of the length to which this position might be carried, if accepted. Thus, an increase in the authorized number of shares of common (in connection with a stock split of common or otherwise (see §5.101)) does not require a class vote of preferred under either Corp C §903(a)(4) or (5), even though it may be argued that the preferred is indirectly affected by the potential dilution created by the increase in the authorized number of common shares.

A change that affects rights of all classes on a uniform basis will still require a class vote under Corp C §903(a)(4) if the rights of each class are being *directly* affected, *e.g.*, elimination of preemptive rights or right-of-first-refusal provision that applies to all of the outstanding shares of the corporation. (This is unlike Corp C §903(b), which requires the change to affect each series in a "different manner" to trigger a series vote.) Thus, it may be preferable to include a right-of-first-refusal provision in the bylaws or an agreement rather than in the articles.

§5.97 e. Amendment Creating Senior Class or Increasing Its Rights

A class vote of junior shares is required whenever a senior class is created or the rights or number of shares of the senior class is increased. Corp C §903(a)(5). It would appear that an amendment adding a "blank stock" provision to the articles requires a class vote of each then-outstanding class if it gives the directors the right to create and issue a senior class. See §§5.26, 5.72. The necessity of a class vote every time a new class is to be created with senior preferences might be avoided if the board of directors obtains authority for a blank stock provision with authorization of a large number of shares and any number of series. The board can then issue series senior to the prior series of the same class without having to obtain any further vote, because Corp C §903(a)(5) refers only to a junior "class," and Corp C §903(b) requires that different series within the same class be treated in a different manner before they can be given a vote as a "class." See §5.94.

§5.98 f. Reclassification of Shares

The typical method of changing the rights of an outstanding class of shares is to "reclassify" the shares within the meaning of Corp C §903(a)(2). For example, 6 percent preferred stock may be reclassified into 5 percent preferred stock either by a direct change by amendment in its rights and class name, or by creating a new class of stock into which the 5 percent preferred stock is automatically exchanged or reclassified on filing the amendment. Corporations Code §903(a)(2) and (4) would each require a class vote in a situation where shares of the class are exchanged, reclassified, or cancelled (the subparagraphs of Corp C §903 overlap to a great extent in actual operation). Corporations Code §903(a)(3) requires a similar vote where shares of another class are given a right of exchange into shares of the subject class. Because it is usually necessary to offer compensation for rights lost (see §5.10(5)), the preferred might also receive some shares of common stock. This could also be accomplished under Corp C §903(a)(2) and (3) by effecting an automatic exchange of the old 6 percent preferred stock into shares of 5 percent preferred stock plus some shares of common. The express wording of the amendment should be drafted to accomplish this result automatically on filing the amendment (for a form such an amendment, see §5.128). Corporations Code §903(a)(3) requires a class vote of the common in such a situation. As in other cases, the approval of a majority of the outstanding shares (Corp C §152) is also required. Corp C §§902(a), 903(c).

§5.99　　g. Change To Add One or More Series of Preferred When Preferred Class Already Outstanding

If preferred shares have been issued as a class but not as a series, a senior series cannot be created by the board alone, even under a blank stock provision. Such a change would require an amendment to divide the preferred class into series or to designate the existing preferred class as a specific series of the new preferred class, and this amendment requires a class vote. Corp C §903(a)(6).

§5.100　　h. Other Amendments Affecting Outstanding Shares

A class vote is required to cancel or otherwise affect accrued dividends. Corp C §903(a)(7). See discussion in §5.31. No reference is made in Corp C §903(a) to an amendment making nonredeemable shares redeemable, but it probably requires a class vote under Corp C §903(a)(4). Some constitutional and other objections may exist to such an amendment. See §5.40.

§5.101　　3. Stock Splits; Reverse Stock Splits

If the corporation has only one class of shares outstanding (whether or not more than one class is authorized in the articles), an amendment effecting only a stock split may be adopted by the board of directors alone. Corp C §902(c). Any increase in the authorized number of shares in proportion to the stock split may also be adopted by the board alone, without shareholder vote. Corp C §§902(c), 903(a)(1)–(2). Thus, a corporation with 100,000 authorized common shares and 50,000 outstanding may, in connection with a two-for-one split, increase the authorized number of shares to 200,000 (while it increases the outstanding to 100,000) without a shareholder vote.

An amendment effecting a stock split must be approved by a majority of all outstanding shares if the corporation has more than one class of shares outstanding. Corp C §902(a), (c). No class vote of the class of shares being split is required. Corp C §903(a)(1)–(2). If it is necessary to increase the number of preferred shares to effect the split, a class vote of the common shares is required under Corp C §903(a)(5) (see §5.97). Even if there are enough authorized preferred shares to effect the split without increasing the number of preferred shares, the split must maintain the relative rights, preferences, or privileges by reducing them per share, proportionate to the amount of the split; otherwise, if the rights of the preferred are decreased, Corp C §903(a)(4) will require a class vote of the preferred.

If it is desired to split only the common shares, the preferred shares will not be entitled to a class vote on the amendment but will vote with the common in a Corp C §902(a) vote if the preferred shares have voting rights under the articles provisions. In such a case, if the preferred shares are outvoted by the common in the Corp C §902(a) vote, equitable limitations may protect the preferred from any unfair dilution resulting from a split of common only. See §§5.10, 5.20.

Amendment of the articles effecting a reverse stock split almost always requires approval of the outstanding shares under Corp C §902(a). A class vote of the shares being combined appears to be necessary, because the reverse split ordinarily results in an exchange or cancellation of shares. Corp C §903(a)(2). A reverse split is usually accompanied by payment of cash in lieu of fractional shares, and there are statutory and perhaps equitable limitations on that procedure (see §§5.10, 5.161–5.162).

A stock dividend as such does not require a shareholder vote, and may be a simple alternative to a stock split when there is more than one class of outstanding shares and if there are sufficient authorized shares for the stock dividend. In a one-class structure, however, a stock split is just as easy as a stock dividend and also allows retention of the same proportionate number of authorized shares, all conducted by board action alone. See §§5.17–5.18.

§5.102   4. Amendments Regarding Share Assessments

A unanimous vote of all outstanding shares affected (as well as a Corp C §902(a) vote of the outstanding shares), regardless of limitations or restrictions on their voting rights, is required to authorize the corporation to levy assessments on any fully paid shares or to authorize action against a shareholder for collection of an assessment on fully paid shares. Corp C §904. The vote or written consent of a majority of outstanding shares of the corporation is required to remove an assessment provision from the articles or to alter an assessment provision. Corp C §902(a). A class vote of an assessable class may be required if there is more than one class, because removal or alteration of an assessment provision is probably a change in rights and restrictions under Corp C §903(a)(4).

§5.103   5. Amendment Changing Number of Directors or Classifying Board

After the issuance of shares, any amendment of the articles (or bylaws) that would reduce the authorized number of directors below five cannot be adopted if the votes cast against it (or in an action by written consent, the shares not consenting) are equal to more than one sixth (16 2/3 percent) of the outstanding shares entitled to vote. Corp C §212. (The purpose of this requirement is to protect minority shareholders who have the right under cumulative voting to elect one out of five directors.)

If this impediment is overcome, an amendment of the articles reducing or changing the number of directors must be approved by a majority of all outstanding shares under Corp C §902(a). A similar vote is required if the provision is in the bylaws, unless there is a "flexible" board. See Corp C §212(a). There appears to be no utility in placing a "flexible" (minimum-maximum) board provision in the articles, because there is no exception from the requirement of a shareholder vote to adjust the number of directors in the articles within the range. Corp C §212(a). See also §5.70. If a class is entitled to vote on its own for a particular number of directors, a proposal to reduce the number of directors electable by the class may be a change in "rights," requiring a class vote under Corp C §903(a)(4). See §5.96.

Certain "listed corporations" may amend their articules or bylaws to provide for two or three classes of directors or eliminate cumulative voting, or both. Corp C §301.5; see §5.70. Such amendments require the approval of the board and the outstanding shares (Corp C §152) voting as a single class, notwithstanding the provisions of Corp C §903. Corp C §301.5(a).

6. Requirement of Greater Than Statutory Vote

§5.104   a. By Commissioner of Corporations

Regardless of the statutory percentage of shareholder approval required for adoption of an amendment, in all transactions involving a permit, the California Commissioner of Corporations has the power to evaluate whether a proposed plan of recapitalization, reorganization, or other change in the rights, preferences, privileges, or restrictions of outstanding shares is fair, just, and equitable to all security holders affected. Corp C §25140(c). The Commissioner may impose conditions to ensure fairness, which may require a greater than statutory vote. Corp C §25141; see Dahlquist, *Regulation and Civil Liability Under the California Corporate Securities Act II,* 34 Calif L Rev 344, 351 (1946).

The Commissioner's permit may condition the approval of a recapitalization or reorganization on the obtaining of an affirmative vote of a specified percentage of the shares held by persons other than those who have a "conflict of interest" in connection with the transaction. 10 Cal Code Regs §260.140.63. For example, a simple majority class vote of preferred shareholders approving an amendment that adversely affects their rights might not be acceptable to the Commissioner if a substantial number of common shareholders also hold preferred shares.

The Commissioner may question whether adequate disclosure of the terms of the plan was made to shareholders if a substantial number of the independent shareholders do not vote on the plan, and if the plan had potentially unfair aspects for them. See Orschel,

Administrative Protection for Shareholders in California Recapitalizations, 4 Stan L Rev 215, 223 (1952).

§5.105   b. In Articles of Incorporation or Agreements Among Shareholders

Provisions in the articles requiring approval of certain actions by some specified percentage of shareholders greater than the statutory minimum, or agreements among shareholders to that effect, must be observed. See §§5.12, 5.28.

Although a requirement for unanimity can be so unwieldy as to paralyze a corporation, on occasion such a provision may be appropriate. In any event, a provision requiring a unanimous vote of shareholders in most circumstances is expressly authorized by Corp C §204(a)(5). The statute does create exceptions for the removal of directors (Corp C §303(a)(2)), cumulative voting for directors (Corp C §708(c)), and dissolution (Corp C §§402.5(b), 1900). Thus, when by the provisions of the articles, the holders of the shares of any class or series, voting as such, are entitled to elect one or more directors, such director(s) may be removed only by a vote of the electing class or series. Corp C §303(a)(2). Cumulative voting may not be defeated by supermajority voting provisions. Corp C §708(c). And while a supermajority requirement may be imposed for voluntary dissolution under Corp C §1900, such a provision is permissible only for certain preferred stock, and then not in excess of 66 2/3 percent. See Corp C §§204(a)(5), 402.5(b), 1900(a). See also Corp C §§152 and 153, which respectively define "[a]pproval by the outstanding shares" and "approval by the shareholders," and both of which specifically authorize unanimous vote requirements. Unanimity provisions have been upheld in several cases. See O'Neal, *Giving Shareholders Power to Veto Corporate Decisions: Use of Special Charter and By-Law Provisions,* 18 Law & Contemp Prob 451, 468 (1953); *Benintendi v Kenton Hotel* (NY 1945) 60 NE2d 829, 249 NY 112, 159 ALR 280.

A corporation may attempt to circumvent a supermajority vote requirement by issuing additional preferred shares to friendly shareholders in sufficient number to reduce the holdings of the present preferred shareholders to less than the fraction that could veto the amendment, then holding a meeting to adopt the amendment. Although equitable relief might be obtained (see §§5.9–5.10), the problem may be avoided if a protective provision is inserted in the articles stating that additional shares of preferred stock may be issued, or additional shares of preferred stock may be authorized, but only with approval by the supermajority vote of the preferred shares. Such a provision may be coupled with a preemptive right to purchase new shares. See §5.45.

Another technique for circumventing a supermajority requirement is to merge the corporation into another corporation, which requires only a majority class vote (Corp C §1201), then to exchange the surviving corporation's preferred shares with, *e.g.*, a lower dividend rate, for the preferred shares of the disappearing corporation. Such an action was upheld in *Langfelder v Universal Labs., Inc.* (3d Cir 1947) 163 F2d 804. Alternatively, the corporation may sell all of its assets to a new corporation in exchange for shares, including preferred stock with a lower dividend rate, then dissolve and distribute the preferred with the lower dividend rate to the preferred shareholders. Sale of the assets requires only a majority class vote (Corp C §1201), and dissolution requires a class vote of only 50 percent of all shares entitled to vote (Corp C §1900) or a majority class vote (Corp C §2007). Either of these maneuvers may be prevented by inserting a protective provision in the articles requiring that any merger or sale of assets be approved by a supermajority vote of the preferred shares.

A voluntary dissolution of an active corporation that has not been adjudicated bankrupt requires a shareholder vote of at least 50 percent of the voting power. Corp C §1900. See also *Kavanaugh v Kavanaugh Knitting Co.* (NY 1919) 226 NY 185, 123 NE 148. This requirement apparently may not be changed in the articles of incorporation, because unlike Corp C §§902–903 and 1201, Corp C §1900 does not refer to Corp C §152. See Corp C §204(a)(5). The 50 percent vote required for dissolution may not be increased except for certain preferred stock, and then not in excess of 66 2/3 percent. See Corp C §§204(a)(5), 402.5(b), 1900(a).

The Secretary of State will not accept for filing any articles of incorporation that provide for a higher or lower percentage vote for voluntary dissolution than the 50 percent vote required by Corp C §1900 (except for other percentages established for preferred shares under §402(b)). See Comment, *Rights of the Minority Shareholders to Dissolve the Closely Held Corporation,* 43 Calif L Rev 514, 518 (1955). Statutory close corporations (Corp C §158) may be able to achieve the same result, however, by use of a shareholder agreement. See Corp C §300(b), (c). For discussion of whether other closely held corporations may do so, see 43 Calif L Rev 514; 2 O'Neal, CLOSE CORPORATIONS §9.06 (3d ed 1983). See also Corp C §§204(a), 706(d).

§5.106   7. Amendments in Connection With Merger

The articles of a surviving California corporation in a merger may be amended in the merger agreement on filing with the Secretary of State the officers' certificate and the merger agreement under Corp C §1103, or a certificate of ownership under Corp C §1110(d). See Corp C §§905(d), 1101(b), 1103. See also Corp C §1110(f) with respect to a short-form merger. The vote required for the merger, including amendment of the articles, is specified in Corp C §1201, unless the merger is a short-form merger under Corp C §1110 (where no vote is required). Although there are a number of exemptions from the vote requirement in Corp C §1201(b), Corp C §1201(d) requires a majority vote of a class of shareholders whenever they would receive shares of the surviving or acquiring corporation in the merger having different rights, privileges, preferences, or restrictions than those shares they held before the merger. In addition, Corp C §1201(c) requires the vote normally required for amendments of articles if any amendment is made to the articles of the surviving corporation. In effect, Corp C §1201(c)–(d) ensure that the same majority class vote required by Corp C §903(a)(2), (4), will always pertain.

It appears that certain amendments may be accomplished by merger that would otherwise require a greater or unanimous vote, *e.g.*, authorization to levy assessments (see Corp C §904) and reduction of the number of directors (see Corp C §212). An objecting shareholder could exercise dissenter's rights under Corp C §1300 when shares of the class held by that shareholder are entitled to vote on the merger as a result of the operation of Corp C §1201(a), (b), or (e), or when the merger is a short-form merger. Corp C §1300(a). Note that a vote that is required only because of Corp C §1201(c) or (d) does not trigger dissenters' rights under Corp C §1300(a). Thus, if Corp C §1201(b) is applicable, the Corp C §1201(a) vote requirement will be eliminated. This would occur when the merger was into a new shell corporation. In that situation, the vote of the preferred on its changed rights will derive only from Corp C §1201(d), which means there are no dissenters' rights. This is so that there will be no difference in rights of shareholders merely because such a merger is used to effect the change in rights. The amendment may be subject to equitable limitations when dissenters' rights do not exist, or in the case of a short-form merger. See Corp C §1312. See also §5.10.

§5.107   8. Amendments To Extend Corporate Existence

An amendment to extend the existence of a corporation with a limited period of existence in its articles requires the approval of a majority of the outstanding voting shares. Corp C §§902(a), 909; see §5.51. One limited exception to this requirement is for an extension of the existence of a corporation organized before adoption of the perpetual existence statute on August 14, 1929. Corp C §902(b); see Stats 1929, ch 711.

9. When Shareholder Vote Not Required

§5.108   a. Mandatory Reduction of Authorized Shares

No shareholder vote is required to authorize the mandatory amendment to reflect reduction in the authorized number of shares or elimination of a class or series of shares due to reacquisition by the corporation of such shares, which, according to the articles, cannot be reissued. Corp C §510(b); see §5.15. Action by the board of directors is still required because a certificate of amendment must be made and filed in accordance with the other requirements of Corporations Code ch 9. Corp C §510(b).

§5.109   b. Miscellaneous Amendments That Do Not Require Shareholder Vote

Amendments that do not require a shareholder vote include:

(1) An amendment to delete close corporation status on acquiring more than the maximum specified number of shareholders (Corp C §158(e));

(2) An amendment to increase the authorized number of shares to cover options or convertible securities that have been issued after shareholder approval (Corp C §405(b); see §5.15);

(3) An amendment effecting a stock split when only one class of shares is outstanding (Corp C §902(c); see §§5.18, 5.101);

(4) An amendment deleting names and addresses of the first directors, if any, or of the initial agent (Corp C §902(d); the Corp C §1502 statement must first have been filed; Corp C §900(b));

(5) An amendment to change the name of a parent corporation in connection with a short-form merger (Corp C §1110(c); see §5.67);

(6) An amendment effecting certain other reorganizations (Corp C §1201(b); see §5.91);

(7) Certain amendments adopted in a reorganization under the federal bankruptcy laws (Corp C §1400; see §5.69); and

(8) Certain amendments by which corporations organized before January 1, 1977, elect to be governed by the provisions of the new General Corporation Law (Corp C §2302; see §§5.132–5.133).

In addition, there is no need for shareholder approval of certificates filed with the Secretary of State that do not amend the articles (*e.g.,* a certificate restating but not amending the articles of incorporation (Corp C §910), a certificate of determination of rights and preferences (Corp C §401), or a certificate of correction (Corp C §109)) do not require shareholder action) but do require director action before filing.

C. Amendment Procedure

1. Shareholder Action: By Written Consent or at Meeting

§5.110   a. Form: Adoption at Meeting

Form 5.110–1 (Resolution Adopting Amendment)

RESOLVED, that the following amendment to the articles of incorporation of this corporation is adopted and approved:

[Insert amendment]

Comment: Shareholders may act at a meeting or by written consent. Corp C §§601–605. This form of resolution is appropriate for use when action is taken at a meeting. For a form to use when action is taken by written consent, see §5.111. The "adopted and approved" wording in the resolution is intended to comply with Corp C §902. See §5.142. If shareholder rights are adversely affected by the amendment, the Department of Corporations may require changes in the amendment before it is submitted to shareholders (see §5.85). The forms of amendment to be inserted are set forth in §§5.117–5.135.

§5.111   b. Forms: Adoption by Written Consent

Form 5.111–1 (Shareholder Consent to Amendment—Corporation With Fewer Than 100 Shareholders)

WRITTEN CONSENT OF SHAREHOLDERS OF
[*name of corporation*]

The undersigned shareholders of [*name of corporation*], a California corporation, holding of record the number of outstanding shares of capital stock of the corporation entitled to vote as set forth opposite their respective signatures below, adopt, approve, and consent to the following amendment to the articles of incorporation of the corporation:

[*Insert amendment*]

This consent is granted under section 603 of the California Corporations Code with respect to the number of shares held by the undersigned set forth below.

Shareholders	Number of outstanding shares held by shareholders	Date
[*Signatures of shareholders*]	_____	_____
[*Typed names*]	_____	_____

Comment: See Comment to Form 5.111–2.

Form 5.111–2 (Corporation With 100 or More Shareholders If Consent Distributed to Ten or More Shareholders)

WRITTEN CONSENT OF SHAREHOLDERS OF
[name of corporation]

The undersigned shareholders of *[name of corporation]*, **a California corporation, holding of record the number of outstanding shares of capital stock of the corporation entitled to vote as set forth opposite their respective signatures below, take the following action:**

[ ] Adopt, approve, and consent to

[ ] Disapprove

[ ] Abstain from voting on

the following amendment to the articles of incorporation of the corporation:

[Insert amendment]

This action is taken under section 603 of the California Corporations Code with respect to the number of shares held by the undersigned set forth below.

Shareholders	Number of outstanding shares held by shareholders	Date
[Signatures of shareholders]	_____	_____
[Typed names]	_____	_____

Comment: Shareholders may act on a proposed amendment by written consent if the holders of the minimum number of shares required to authorize the amendment sign the consent. Corp C §603; see §5.91. This form is appropriate for use in that situation. If the corporation has over 100 shareholders and the written consent is being distributed to ten or more shareholders, the written consent must provide the options regarding disapproval or abstention from voting. Corp C

§604. Apparently, this requirement applies regardless of whether proxies or written consents are being solicited by management or by dissidents. See Corp C §701 as to the record date if a transfer of shares takes place in the middle of soliciting consents. Unless the consents of all shareholders entitled to vote have been solicited in writing, prompt notice of filing the amendment with the Secretary of State must be given to all shareholders who did not consent in writing to the amendment. Corp C §603(b)(2). If the consent is in connection with a merger or reorganization under Corp C §1201, notice of shareholder approval without a meeting must be given at least ten days before consummation. Corp C §603(b)(1).

2. Directors' Action: By Written Consent or at Meeting

§5.112   a. Form: By Consent

Directors may act at a board meeting or by written consent. Corp C §307(b). Whereas shareholders may act by majority approval (Corp C §603(a); see §5.111), the written consent of directors must be unanimous to be effective. Corp C §307(b). Directors may attend a meeting by conference telephone or similar communications equipment so long as all directors participating can hear one another; participation in this manner constitutes presence in person at the meeting. Corp C §307(a)(6). Directors may not act by proxy.

Form 5.112–1 (Directors' Written Consent)

**UNANIMOUS WRITTEN CONSENT
OF BOARD OF DIRECTORS OF**
[name of corporation]

The undersigned, being all of the directors of *[name of corporation]*, **a California corporation, unanimously adopt, approve, and consent to the following resolution:**

RESOLVED, that the following amendment to the articles of incorporation of this corporation is adopted and approved:

[Insert amendment]

This action is taken under section 307(b) of the California Corporations Code.

Directors	**Date**
[*Signatures of directors*]	_ _ _ _ _ _ _ _
[*Typed names*]	_ _ _ _ _ _ _ _

Comment: The written consent of the directors must be unanimous. Corp C §307(b). The same rule applies to action by a committee of directors. Corp C §307(c); see §5.91. The forms of amendment to be inserted are set forth in §§5.117–5.133.

§5.113   b. Form: Adoption at Meeting

Form 5.113–1 (Sample Form: Directors' Resolution With Preamble)

The name of this corporation no longer accurately reflects the business in which this corporation is engaged, and this corporation requires additional authorized shares so that the corporation may issue additional shares from time to time for corporate purposes.

The board of directors of this corporation deems it to be in the best interests of this corporation and its shareholders that the articles of incorporation be amended to change the corporate name to [*new name*] **and to increase the authorized number of shares of capital stock from** _ _ _ _ _ _ **to** _ _ _ _ _ _ **shares of capital stock.**

In view of the above, it is

RESOLVED that the following amendments to the articles of incorporation of this corporation are adopted and approved:

[*Insert amendments*]

Comment: A preamble may be useful in some situations as an expression of considerations that led to adoption of the amendment, *e.g.,* when a sensitive issue is involved or when the board wishes to reflect its business judgment. Some practitioners prefer to introduce each clause of a preamble with "WHEREAS,". Procedures for changing the corporation's name are discussed in §§5.59–5.67. The "adopted and approved" wording is intended to comply with Corp C §902.

§5.114   c. Forms: Additional Director Resolutions in Connection With Amendment

Form 5.114–1 (Directors' Resolution To Authorize Seeking Permit)

RESOLVED, that the officers, or any of them, are authorized and directed on behalf of this corporation to make any necessary or proper application or applications, or any amendments or supplements to them, to the California Commissioner of Corporations for the purpose of procuring any necessary or proper permit or permits and any amendment or amendments to them in connection with the proposed amendment to Article [*e.g., FOUR*] of this corporation's articles of incorporation.

Comment: In addition to authorizing the amendment itself, authority may be needed to have the permit cover sale of fractional shares on the market if that is the method chosen to eliminate fractional shares. See Corp C §407. See also §5.162.

Form 5.114–2 (Directors' Resolution To Authorize Submission to Shareholders)

RESOLVED, that [*on obtaining such permit or permits as may be required,*] the amendment of Article [*e.g., FOUR*] of the articles of incorporation of this corporation shall be submitted to the shareholders of this corporation for adoption and approval by them by their vote or written consent.

RESOLVED FURTHER, that under the provisions of Section ____ of Article ____ of the bylaws of this corporation, a special meeting of shareholders is hereby called by this board of directors to be held on [*date*], at ___.m., at [*address and city*], California, for the purpose of considering and acting on the amendment, and the secretary or any assistant secretary of this corporation is authorized and directed to give written notice of this special meeting as provided by law and the bylaws of this corporation.

RESOLVED FURTHER, that the close of business on [*date*]**, is fixed as the record date of the determination of the shareholders entitled to notice of and to vote at this special meeting of shareholders.**

Comment: The first portion in brackets in the first line of the resolution would be inserted only if a permit is required. Even if the shareholders' vote is to be obtained by written consent without a meeting, the board may wish to adopt a resolution setting the record date for determining shareholders who are entitled to vote or consent. See Corp C §701(a). If no record date is fixed, it will be determined under Corp C §§194, 701(b). If a shareholders' meeting is to be held, the board may adopt additional resolutions appointing proxies and inspectors of election, approving proxy material, and recommending to shareholders that they vote affirmatively. If there is time pressure to act on the proposed amendment and there is a possibility a necessary permit may not be obtained in time, the board may delegate to a committee or certain officers the right to adjourn or reschedule the meeting. Note, however, that only the board or a committee of the board may set the record date. Corp C §§701, 311.

Form 5.114–3 (Omnibus Resolution)

RESOLVED, that [, *if the holders of a majority of all outstanding shares of this corporation and the holders of a majority of the outstanding shares of preferred stock of this corporation shall adopt and approve the foregoing amendment,*] **the officers of this corporation, and each of them, is authorized and directed to execute, verify, and file a certificate of amendment in the form and manner required by the laws of California, and to execute and deliver any and all certificates, authorizations, and other written instruments and papers and in general to do all acts and things necessary to effect this amendment.**

Comment: This resolution is ordinarily adopted by the board for all amendments in order to give the officers adequate authority to carry out all amendment proceedings and filings. The portion in brackets is inserted only if a shareholders' vote is required. The form assumes that a class vote is required under Corp C §903.

Form 5.114–4 (Resolutions To Eliminate Fractional Shares)

RESOLVED, that no fractional shares of capital stock shall be issued in connection with the adjustments in outstanding shares required by the foregoing amendment, but in lieu thereof cash will be paid to each shareholder of record as of the date of filing the certificate of amendment reflecting the foregoing amendment with the California Secretary of State, [*in an aggregate amount not to exceed the net proceeds received from the sale of the next highest whole number of shares resulting from cumulating all fractional shares, as set forth in the immediately following resolution*], **and under section 407 of the California Corporations Code it is hereby determined by this board of directors that the fair value of the fractional shares shall be** [*$_ _ _ _ _ _/the mean between the bid and the asked prices as quoted on National Association of Securities Dealers Automated Quotation (NASDAQ) System on the date of filing the certificate of amendment/the amount of the net proceeds received on the issuance and sale of the shares*].

Comment: See §§5.161–5.165. Corporations Code §407 allows three methods of disposing of fractional shares, one of which is provided in this resolution: Payment in cash of the fair value as of the time when those entitled to receive such fractions are determined (usually the date of filing the certificate; see §5.162). The fair value may be determined by the board or by reference to the market or other means, and then the cash may be paid directly and the fractions eliminated, or the decision may be made to cumulate the fractions and sell them on the market to raise the cash to pay off fractions. In the latter case, the fair value is, in effect, set by the net proceeds obtained from sale on the market, and the following additional resolution may be adopted:

[*Add, if appropriate*]

RESOLVED, that to provide funds to be distributed to each shareholder of record who would otherwise be entitled to receive a fraction of a share in connection with the amendment, the president or secretary of this corporation is authorized and directed to cause to be issued and sold shares of capital stock of this corporation in an amount not to exceed the next highest whole number of shares resulting from the cumulation of all

fractional shares that would otherwise be distributable in connection with the amendment, such sale to be consummated in a regular transaction [*e.g., on the New York Stock Exchange/in the over-the-counter market*], such issuance and sale to be consummated in such manner that they will be exempt from registration under the Securities Act of 1933 [*insert provision for compliance with any stock exchange or over-the-counter market requirement, e.g., and comply with the rules of the New York and Pacific Stock Exchanges*].

Form 5.114–5 (Resolution Authorizing Corp C §507 Notice)

RESOLVED, that concurrently with the distribution of the shares pursuant to this amendment, the president or secretary of this corporation is hereby authorized and directed to send a notice to all shareholders, complying with section 507 of the California Corporations Code [*and (citation to stock exchange requirement, if any)*].

Comment: If the distribution to shareholders resulting from the amendment causes a charge to some account other than retained earnings, then it is best to give a Corp C §507 notice, even though Corp C §507 refers to "dividends." The notice should be given either at the time of the distribution or within three months after the end of the fiscal year in which the distribution is made. A resolution picking one method or the other and reminding the directors and officers of it is often desirable. The "notice" is often included in a president's letter to shareholders accompanying the distribution, or in the annual report if it is sent out within three months after the end of the year.

Form 5.114–6 (Resolution Ordering Surrender and Exchange of Share Certificates)

RESOLVED, that the board of directors hereby orders, effective on filing the certificate of amendment with respect to the above amendment with the Secretary of State, all holders of outstanding certificates for shares of capital stock to surrender all such certificates to the corporation [*or the transfer agent for the corporation*] and exchange such certificates for new certificates for this company's common stock reflecting the above amendment to the articles, on or before a date [*e.g., 45*]

days after such filing, which this board of directors hereby determines to be a reasonable time, and in the event any holder of outstanding shares does not so surrender such certificates for outstanding shares on or before such date, the board orders that any such holder shall not be entitled thereafter to vote or to receive dividends or to exercise any of the other rights of a shareholder of shares represented by such certificates for outstanding shares, until such holder has so surrendered such share certificates.

Comment: Reclassifications, changes of name, and other amendments affect the statements contained in the certificates for outstanding shares. Corporations Code §422 authorizes the board of directors to order holders of outstanding certificates for shares to surrender and exchange them within a reasonable time to be fixed by the board. The board may provide that a holder of any certificate who does not surrender it cannot receive dividends or exercise any of the other rights of a shareholder until the holder has complied with the order. This resolution is designed to permit the board to take advantage of Corp C §422.

§5.115 d. Other Board Resolutions

The board may wish to adopt other resolutions as appropriate, such as resolutions:

(a) Authorizing the filing of a registration statement under the Securities Act of 1933, or proxy statement under the Securities Exchange Act of 1934, if required for the amendment (see §5.155);

(b) Reserving additional shares under so-called antidilution provisions of outstanding stock option agreements, convertible securities, and other instruments that require adjustments on a stock split or other capital adjustment (see §5.15);

(c) Authorizing the filing of an application for listing on whatever stock exchange on which the company's securities are listed of additional or changed shares issued in connection with a stock split or other capital adjustment;

(d) Amending bylaws to conform with any amendments to articles;

(e) Adopting a new form of share certificate, if required as a result of the amendment (see §5.156), and overprinting any existing supply of old certificates if the client wishes to use them;

(f) Authorizing appropriate filings under securities laws other than those of California if the amendment affects the right of outstanding shares whose holders reside in other jurisdictions and if it appears that the securities laws of such other jurisdictions may apply (see §5.148); and

(g) When there is a large number of shareholders, appointing an exchange agent to exchange new share certificates for old (see §5.156).

§5.116   3. Drafting Amendments

The language of an amendment to the articles of incorporation must comply with Corp C §907. Section 907(a) provides:

> (a) The certificate of amendment shall establish the wording of the amendment or amended articles by one or more of the following means:
>
> (1) By stating that the articles shall be amended to read as set forth in full in the certificate.
>
> (2) By stating that any provision of the articles, which shall be identified by the numerical or other designation given it in the articles or by stating the wording thereof, shall be stricken from the articles or shall be amended to read as set forth in the certificate.
>
> (3) By stating that the provisions set forth in the certificate shall be added to the articles.

The Secretary of State interprets the word "provision" in Corp C §907(a)(2) and (3) to mean a complete paragraph, sentence, or clause that has a subject and a predicate. A phrase, word, or line is not considered to be a "provision."

The statute requires that, if an existing provision of the articles is to be stricken or amended, the provision must be identified in the amendment either by referring to it by the numerical or letter designation given to the existing provision in the articles or by quoting the wording of the existing provision in full. In addition, the amendment must state either that the provision shall be stricken from the articles or that the provision shall be amended to read as it is quoted in full in the amendment. Corp C §907(b).

The amendment should not select a particular word, phrase, or line out of a provision, refer to it, and strike that portion of the provision. The provision must be referred to by its numerical or other designation or quoted in full, and then amended by quoting the amended provision in full but omitting the stricken word, phrase, or line. It is also improper to try to add one word, phrase, or line to the articles by an amendment that merely states that the word, phrase, or line is inserted at a certain place in a provision; instead, the entire provision must be quoted with the word, phrase, or line added to it.

If a new provision is to be added to the articles, the amendment should state that the new provision, which is quoted in full, is added to the articles. Corp C §907(a)(3).

The attorney drafting the amendment must be careful to do so accurately, because the Secretary of State is likely to reject for filing any amendment that does not comply. Moreover, the power of a court to reform the articles of incorporation has been held to be much more limited than its power to reform private contracts, on the ground that the articles constitute "legislative acts" (acts authorized by the legislature through its statutes) and consequently are not subject to reformation any more than are statutes. *Casper v Kalt-Zimmers Mfg. Co.* (Wis 1914) 149 NW 754.

The statute continues by providing:

> (b) If the purpose of the amendment is to effect a stock split or reverse stock split or to reclassify, cancel, exchange, or otherwise change outstanding shares, the amended articles shall state the effect thereof on outstanding shares.

Thus, if the amendment will have some effect on outstanding shares, the effect or change must actually be set forth in the amendment itself. For example, if the amendment will effect a five-for-one stock split, the amendment must actually state that each outstanding share is split up and converted into five shares. If the amendment reclassifies Class B shares into Class C shares, the amendment must state that each outstanding Class B share is reclassified and changed into one Class C share.

If a second class of shares is added, and no statement of effect on outstanding shares or certificate of determination is filed, Corp C §907(c) determines the status of the outstanding shares and states:

> (c) In the event of an amendment to change the statement of authorized shares from a single class of shares to two classes, the shares outstanding immediately prior to the amendment are automatically considered to be the same number of shares of the common stock class. If the designation of only one of the two classes includes "common," that class is the common stock class. If the designation of both classes or of neither class includes "common" but one of the two classes has limited or

no voting rights, the class whose voting rights are not limited is the common stock class for the purpose of this subdivision. This subdivision has no application if the amendment of articles includes a statement of the effect of the amendment on outstanding shares pursuant to subdivision (b).

Finally, Corp C §907(d) provides that an amendment changing the stated par value is not necessarily subject to Corp C §907(b):

An amendment which adds or eliminates a stated par value or changes the stated par value and which does not also state the effect of the amendment on outstanding shares is not thereby subject to subdivision (b).

Drafting amendments that comply with Corp C §907 will be easier if the original articles have been divided into numbered articles and lettered paragraphs as appropriate. For example, a provision granting preemptive rights to shareholders should be set forth in a separate article, or a separate paragraph of the article, describing rights of shareholders so that it can later be amended out by simple reference to the article number, or the paragraph letter and article number, without having to quote the entire provision. See Organizing Corporations in California §2.28 (2d ed Cal CEB 1983).

The following amendments are examples of the application of the rules set forth above. These forms would be used with the forms of consents or resolutions in §§5.110–5.115. Cross-references are made to discussion of such amendments elsewhere in the chapter.

For a discussion of statements of effect of amendment on outstanding shares, see §5.129.

§5.117 a. Form: Amendment Changing Article Provision

Form 5.117–1

Article ONE of the articles of Incorporation Is amended to read In Its entirety as follows:

"ONE. The name of the corporation is [*new name of corporation*]**."**

Comment: The wording of the superseded article with the old name provision need not be quoted because the provision has a separate identifying number, *i.e.,* "ONE." See Corp C §907(a)(2). When identifying a provision in the articles by referring to its numerical or letter designation, the reference must be exact. For example, an article designated *"FIRST"* should not be referred to as Article "1st," "first," "First," "FIRST" (without underscoring), ONE, or some other designation in any way different from that in the original articles. When amending an entire numbered article or a lettered paragraph of an article, state that it is amended "to read in its entirety" as set forth in the amendment. See Corp C §907(a); §5.116.

§5.118 b. Form: Amendment Striking Out Article Provision

Form 5.118–1

Paragraph [*e.g., (b)*] of Article [*e.g., FOUR*] of the articles of incorporation is stricken from the articles of incorporation.

Comment: If a provision in the paragraph is to be retained, the amendment should quote the entire provision to be stricken, then strike it out using the form below. See Corp C §907(a); §5.116.

Form 5.118–2

The provision of Article [*e.g., FOUR*] of the articles of incorporation that now reads "[*provision to be stricken, quoted in full*]" is stricken from Article [*e.g., FOUR*] of the articles of incorporation.

Comment: See Corp C §907(a); §5.116. In the alternative, the amendment may set out only the language to be retained, using the form in §5.119.

§5.119 c. Form: Changing Paragraph of Article

If a provision is in a separate article, or a lettered or numbered paragraph of an article, and it is desired to change the provision in some way, but not strike it completely, the following form should be used.

Form 5.119–1

Paragraph [*e.g., (a)*] **of Article** [*e.g., FOUR*] **of the articles of incorporation is amended to read in its entirety as follows:**

[*Insert revised paragraph*]

Comment: The revised paragraph as set forth in the amendment does not say "FOUR (a)," because the article designation "FOUR" is not considered by the Secretary of State to be part of paragraph (a).

§5.120   d. Form: Changing Portion of Combined Paragraph

Although it is recommended that articles not be drafted to contain combined paragraphs (see §5.116), at times, counsel will be confronted with existing articles with such unartful drafting. In such a case, the following form may be used:

Form 5.120–1

The provision of paragraph [*e.g., (a)*] **of Article** [*e.g., FOUR*] **of the articles of incorporation that now reads:**

[*Insert provision in paragraph to be revised*]

is amended to read as follows:

[*Insert revised provision of paragraph*]

Comment: This form of amendment may be used if the provision to be amended is not set forth as a separate article or paragraph of an article, but is combined in a paragraph that also contains provisions not to be amended. If the articles are inartfully drafted, counsel may recommend restating the articles in a more appropriate form at the time they are amended. See §5.123 for form.

§5.121   e. Form: Adding New Article

An Article designated [*e.g., FIVE*] **is added to the articles of incorporation to read as follows:**

[*Insert new article*]

f. Restating Articles

§5.122 (1) Restating Entire Articles of Incorporation

Articles of incorporation may be restated at any time. Restatement is particularly appropriate if the articles are poorly drafted. If there have been numerous amendments, restatement may be indicated in order to simplify future reference to the document. For form, see §5.123. See also 1A Ballantine & Sterling, CALIFORNIA CORPORATION LAWS §235 (4th ed); 2 MARSH'S CALIFORNIA CORPORATION LAW §16.33 (2d ed). Note that certificates of determination are considered part of the articles, so the restated articles should include the provisions of any such certificates, designated as articles. Corp C §§154, 910(c).

§5.123 (2) Form: Amending and Restating Entire Articles of Incorporation

Form 5.123–1

The articles of incorporation are amended and restated to read in their entirety as follows:

[*Insert restated articles, including any amended provision*]

Comment: An amendment of the entire articles of incorporation should state that the articles are amended to read as set forth in full in the amendment. See Corp C §907(a). The articles as amended may be restated in a single certificate by complying with Corp C §910(a). Any certificates of determination that are still operative are to be included in the body of the articles as restated and given an article designation (*e.g.,* "Article FOUR (a)"). In restating the articles, the statements of effects on outstanding shares that were included in prior amendments should be omitted. Such statements, once included in a filing, have served their purpose, and need not be repeated in a subsequent amendment. Corp C §910(a), (c).

g. Amendments Affecting Outstanding Shares

§5.124 (1) Form: Stock Split; Increase in Authorized Shares

Form 5.124–1

Article [*e.g., FOUR*] of the articles of incorporation is amended to read in its entirety as follows:

[If no additional shares are to be authorized]

"[*E.g., FOUR*]. **This corporation is authorized to issue** [*existing number, e.g., 500,000*] **shares of capital stock. On the amendment of this article, each outstanding share of capital stock is split up and converted into** [*e.g., five*] **shares of capital stock.**"

[If additional shares are to be authorized]

"[*E.g., FOUR*]: **This corporation is authorized to issue** [*e.g., 500,000*] **shares of capital stock. On the amendment of this article to read as set forth above, each outstanding share of capital stock is split up and converted into** [*e.g., five*] **shares of capital stock:**"

Comment: The first alternative presumes that there are sufficient authorized shares to effect the split, and there is no desire to increase the authorized number of shares. (This could also be accomplished simply by amending the article to add the last sentence to it, effecting the split.) The second alternative presumes there are not sufficient authorized shares to effect the split. Thus, if the articles formerly authorized the corporation to issue 100,000 shares of capital stock, and it has 50,000 outstanding shares and desires to effect a five-for-one split, the amendment would have to increase the authorized number of shares to at least 250,000. To keep the same relationship of authorized shares to outstanding shares, the directors could decide to increase the authorized shares to 500,000. Although the increase in number of authorized shares may change the information to that effect on the stock certificates, resulting in the need for ordering in and cancelling presently outstanding certificates, it has no effect on the outstanding "shares" (see Corp C §907), *i.e.,* the units into which the proprietary interests in the corporation are divided (see Corp C §184). Consequently, no statement of the effect of an increase in the authorized number of shares is required. See §§5.16–5.23, 5.76, 5.101, as to stock splits.

§5.125   (2) Effective Date of Amendment

An amendment to the articles of incorporation is effective on the date of filing the certificate of amendment with the Secretary of State. See Corp C §908; 1A Ballantine & Sterling, CALIFORNIA CORPORATION LAWS §234.04[4] (4th ed); 2 MARSH'S CALIFORNIA CORPORATION LAW §16.32 (2d ed). Consequently, the date on which the amendment is to take effect, *e.g.,* the date the stock split and increase in authorized shares is to occur, is not placed in the amendment. Filing the certificate automatically splits the outstanding shares and increases the number of shares at the time of filing. See §5.124. However, the Secretary of State will delay the filing at the request of the party submitting the certificate for up to 90 days after the receipt of the certificate. Corp C §110(a). A later date may be specified as the date a filed amendment is to become effective, provided it is within 90 days of the date of filing (*i.e.,* the date the certificate of amendment is received by the Secretary of State). See §5.142.

§5.126 (3) Form: Reverse Stock Split

Form 5.126–1

Article [*e.g., FOUR*] of the articles of incorporation is amended by adding the following provision to it:

"On the amendment of this article, each outstanding [*e.g., five*] shares of capital stock are converted into [*e.g., one*] share of capital stock."

Comment: This amendment would add the provision above to the original article provision authorizing issuance of the shares. If the corporation does not wish to issue fractional shares, the board of directors should adopt appropriate resolutions. See §5.162. The amendment need not include any statement about disposing of fractional shares, but this is sometimes done to enhance the prospect of obtaining a favorable shareholder vote on the method of disposing of fractions, particularly if a number of shareholders will be eliminated from the enterprise as a result of the adjustment. See the discussion of stock splits and reverse stock splits in §§5.16–5.23, 5.76, 5.101.

§5.127 (4) Form: Creation of Senior Class

Form 5.127–1

Article [*e.g. FOUR*] of the articles of incorporation is amended to read in its entirety as follows:

"[*E.g., FOUR*]: (a) This corporation is authorized to issue two classes of shares to be designated respectively "Common" shares and "Preferred" shares. The number of authorized Preferred shares is [*e.g., 100,000*], and the number of authorized Common shares is [*e.g., 100,000*]. On amendment of this Article [*e. g., FOUR*] to read as set forth above, each outstanding share of capital stock is reclassified and changed into one Common share."

(b) A statement of the rights, preferences, privileges, and restrictions granted to or imposed on the respective classes or series of shares or on the holders of them is as follows:

[*Insert statement of dividend rights, redemption provisions, liquidation rights, voting rights, and the like, of respective classes; and protective provisions for rights of preferred shares. A blank stock provision may be inserted here. See §§5.26, 5.72.*]

Comment: Corporations Code §907 requires that, if an amendment to change the statement of authorized shares from a single class to two classes is made, the shares outstanding are considered to be the number of shares of the common stock class unless there is a statement of the effect of the amendment on outstanding shares, as specified. Corp C §907(c). In addition, Corp C §907(d) provides that an amendment affecting stated par value is not subject to the requirement of a statement of the effect on outstanding shares. See §5.116. If no statement of effect on outstanding shares is included in the amendment (see §5.129) or, alternatively, if no certificate of determination is filed, Corp C §907(c) provides the method of determining the status of the outstanding shares. For filing a certificate of determination, see Corp C §910. See also 1 Ballantine & Sterling, CALIFORNIA CORPORATION LAWS §127.04 (4th ed); 2 MARSH'S CALIFORNIA CORPORATION LAW §16.23 (2d ed).

The board of directors should order the shareholders to surrender old capital stock certificates, exchanging them for new common stock certificates. The new common stock certificates must contain the statements regarding the preferred stock required by Corp C §417. See §§5.156–5.160.

§5.128 (5) Form: Reclassification of Shares

Form 5.128–1

On amendment of this paragraph [*e.g., (b)*] of Article [*e.g., FOUR*] to read as set forth herein, each outstanding share of preferred stock, series [*e.g., A*], shall be reclassified and changed into one share of preferred stock, series [*e.g., M*], and one tenth (1/10th) of one share of common stock:

Comment: The substantive effect on outstanding shares need not be stated, only the capital adjustment of the outstanding shares, *e.g.,* that each share is split up and converted into more shares, converted into or reconstituted as fewer shares, or reclassified into a differently named class or classes or series. Even though the reclassification may change the dividend rate, make the shares redeemable or convertible, or change liquidation preferences or voting rights, such effects need not be stated, because that is accomplished by the statement that the shares are reclassified into another series, the rights of which will be set forth in the articles. See §§5.25, 5.98.

§5.129 (6) Statement of Effect on Outstanding Shares

A statement of the effect of the amendment on outstanding shares should not be included in the amendment unless outstanding shares (*i.e.,* the units into which the proprietary interests are divided in the articles (see Corp C §184)) are to be changed. Many amendments may have great substantive effect on the rights of shareholders but do not require any statement as to their effect on outstanding shares. For example, a change in dividend rate may often be accomplished by direct amendment of the rate without any reclassification or change in the outstanding shares as such. However, if the dividend rate is part of the designated name of the class or series (*e.g.,* "$8.50 preferred shares, series A"), a statement of effect on outstanding shares would be required as part of the amendment to reclassify the shares to, *e.g.,* "$10.00 preferred shares, series A."

The effect of the following amendments on outstanding shares ordinarily need not be stated if the shares are not reclassified as part of the change: (1) Change in voting rights (*e.g.,* from one vote to two votes per share); (2) grant of conversion or preemptive rights; (3) change or elimination of liquidation preferences or redemption rights; and (4) insertion of supervote provisions or qualifications of shareholders. All such amendments ordinarily leave the outstanding units intact; the units are the same in number and kind, they merely have greater or lesser rights or preferences. The statement of effect on outstanding shares is inserted only when necessary as an operative clause to convert the outstanding units from one number and kind to another. Nevertheless, the drafter may want to state the effect for clarity.

§5.130   (7) Equality of Effect of Amendment Within Class or Series

An amendment must provide for equal treatment of each outstanding share of the same class or series. See Corp C §§202(e), 400(b), 900(a). For example, an amendment providing that half the outstanding shares of capital stock are converted into common stock, and the other half into preferred, will not be accepted by the Secretary of State. This problem may sometimes be solved by going outside the amendment process—perhaps by having the corporation repurchase half of the capital stock in exchange for an equal number of shares of newly authorized preferred stock. See §5.47.

§5.131   (8) Form: Eliminating Accrued Dividends

Form 5.131–1

Paragraph [*e.g., (b)*] of Article [*e.g., FOUR*] of the articles of incorporation is amended by adding the following provision:

"Dividends accrued and unpaid to and including [_ _ _ _ _ _, *19_ _/the date this amendment is filed with the Secretary of State*] on outstanding shares of [*e.g. $8.50 Preferred Stock*] are cancelled and eliminated."

Comment: Accrued dividends are often eliminated by reclassifying the shares into a new class or series of shares (see §5.32). If this method is used, the reclassification amendment should include the statement in the above form so that the intended effect of the reclassification is made completely clear. No such statement is needed for a change in dividend rate because a comparison of the new rate with the old rate shows the effect. With respect to accrued dividends, nothing in the articles states that such accruals exist, so the statement in the above form is needed in the amendment. See §§5.31–5.36 with respect to limitations and alternative procedures in the area of eliminating accrued dividend arrearages.

h. Amendments Electing To Be Governed by New General Corporation Law

§5.132 (1) Considerations In Making Election

Counsel may encounter corporations organized before the January 1, 1977, effective date of the General Corporation Law that have not considered whether to elect under Corp C §2302 to be governed by that law. Unless and until it so elects, such a corporation is not governed by Corp C §202 (relating to required provisions of the articles, Corp C §204(b), (c), and (d), or Corp C §205 (relating to par value of shares). A corporation that does not so elect continues to be governed by prior law on matters covered by those code sections. (There is nothing left of the prior law on par value. See §5.24 as to par value.) See 2, 3 MARSH'S CALIFORNIA CORPORATION LAW §§16.18, 24.1–24.16 (2d ed).

One advantage of making the Corp C §2302 election is that the articles may be amended (with approval of the outstanding shares) to take advantage of the wider limits on the flexible number of directors permitted by Corp C §212. See Corp C §2304. The only disadvantages to making the election are that (a) Corp C §204(b) might make unenforceable any transfer restrictions previously imposed in the articles and bylaws that had not been consented to by all shareholders (see §§5.13, 5.73) and (b) supermajority provisions appearing in the bylaws must be transferred to the articles, which will require a shareholder vote (see §5.28).

§5.133 (2) Form: Election Under Corp C §2302

Form 5.133–1

Article [*e.g., TWO*] of the articles of incorporation is amended to read in its entirety as follows:

"[*E.g., TWO*]. The purpose of the corporation is to engage in any lawful act or activity for which a corporation may be organized under the General Corporation Law of California other than the banking business, the trust company business, or the practice of a profession permitted to be incorporated by the California Corporations Code."

Articles [*e.g., THREE and FOUR*] of the articles of incorporation are stricken from the articles of incorporation.

Article [*e.g., SIX*] is added to the articles of incorporation to read in its entirety as follows:

"[*E.g., SIX*]. The corporation elects to be governed by all of the provisions of the new law (as defined in section 2300 of the California Corporations Code) not otherwise applicable to the corporation under chapter 23 of the new law."

Comment: The article being amended is the purposes and powers article, which is required by Corp C §202(b) to be in the language quoted in that section. See §5.58. The articles being stricken are the principal office article (see §5.71) and the name, address, and number of directors article or articles, because none of these is required by Corp C §202. (These may be left in the articles if desired, but see §5.70 as to the disadvantage of leaving the number of directors provision in the articles on a Corp C §2302 amendment.) However, the names and addresses of directors cannot be deleted until after the corporation has filed the Corp C §1502 statement with the Secretary of State (see Corp C §900(b)), so it is advisable to file such statement before a Corp C §2302 amendment is made. There is another reason to file the §1502 statement: Corp C §202(c) and the last sentence of Corp C §2302 require a statement in the articles of the name and address of the initial agent, unless a §1502 statement has been filed. The above form assumes that the statement has been filed, and does not add a new article regarding the initial agent.

The corporation may also delete all references to par value from the article dealing with the stock structure. This is permitted, but not required, by Corp C §§202(e) and 205, which carry out the statutory intent to render par value statements meaningless in California. See §5.24. Where revisions are extensive, counsel may prefer to amend and restate the articles to facilitate future consultation of the document. See §5.122.

The Secretary of State takes the position that the actual Corp C §2302 election must be a separate article. Because of the extensive changes resulting from the Corp C §2302 election, many practitioners make the election as part of an amendment and restatement of the entire articles. See §5.123.

§5.134　　i. Form: Limitation on Directors' Liability

Form 5.134–1

An Article designated [*e.g., FIVE*] is added to the articles of incorporation to read as follows:

"[*E.g., FIVE*]: The liability of the directors of the corporation for monetary damages shall be eliminated to the fullest extent permissible under California law."

Comment: This form contains the statutory language of Corp C §204.5(a). Although the statutory language is not the exclusive form of article provision that may be adopted to limit the personal liability of directors (Corp C §204.5(b)), the Secretary of State's office has indicated that it will accept only language that exactly tracks the statute for amendments under Corp C §204(a)(10).

Note also that both the Department of Corporations and the Secretary of State's office have indicated that they would have serious problems with language such as "to the full extent of the law *as it now exists or may hereafter be amended.*" See §5.74.

The language in this form insulates the directors to the fullest extent permissible from personal liability for monetary damages for breach of a director's duties to the corporation or its shareholders and for other acts, omissions, and transactions not involving a breach of duty to the corporation or shareholders. Corp C §204(a)(10). The provision does not operate to change the otherwise applicable standards or duties of disclosure to shareholders in connection with approval of such a provision in the articles. Corp C §204.5(c). See Corp C §309 on duties of directors; see §5.68 for further discussion.

The new article does not limit liability for acts done before the article's adoption and limits the director's liability in his or her capacity as a director only; liability as an officer or other agent is not affected. See §§5.68, 5.135–5.137 on indemnification of officers and other agents.

j. Forms: Indemnification of Agents

§5.135   (1) Form: Indemnification of Officers and Directors (Articles of Incorporation)

Form 5.135–1 (Indemnification of Officers and Directors)

An Article designated [*e.g., SIX*] is added to the articles of incorporation to read as follows:

"[*Article number*]: The corporation is authorized to indemnify the directors and officers of the corporation to the fullest extent permissible under California Law."

Comment: The articles may authorize the corporation, by bylaw, agreement, or other means, to permit indemnification of corporate agents in excess of the express limits of Corp C §317 for breach of duty to the corporation or its shareholders. Corp C §204(a)(11). See §5.68 for discussion. "Agent" as used in the statute means (Corp C §317(a)):

> any person who is or was a director, officer, employee or other agent of the corporation, or is or was serving at the request of the corporation as a director, officer, employee or agent of another foreign or domestic corporation, partnership, joint venture, trust or other enterprise or was a director, officer, employee or agent of a foreign or domestic corporation which was a predecessor corporation of the corporation or of another enterprise at the request of the predecessor corporation . . . .

The language of Form 5.135–1 is drawn from Corp C §317(g) and has been suggested by the Secretary of State's office. That office states that this language is "limited to indemnification of directors and officers because Section 317 has always specifically permitted the corporation to indemnify other persons as the corporation's board of directors determines and without the necessity of an article provision for 'excess' indemnification." Note that agents may not be indemnified for acts for which a director may not be relieved of liability (see §5.68) nor in circumstances in which indemnity is expressly prohibited by Corp C §317.

See §5.136 for form of bylaws permitting indemnification to the fullest extent possible, and §5.137 for a form of indemnification agreement.

§5.136 (2) Sample Forms: Indemnification of Agents (Bylaws)

Form 5.136–1 (Indemnification of Directors, Officers, Employees, and Other Agents—Short Form)

ARTICLE [*Number*]

INDEMNIFICATION OF DIRECTORS, OFFICERS, EMPLOYEES, AND OTHER AGENTS

The corporation shall, to the maximum extent permitted by the California General Corporation Law, have power to indemnify each of its agents against expenses, judgments, fines, settlements, and other amounts actually and reasonably incurred in connection with any proceeding arising by reason of the fact that any such person is or was an agent of the corporation, and shall have power to advance to each such agent expenses incurred in defending any such proceeding to the maximum extent permitted by that law. For purposes of this Article, an "agent" of the corporation includes any person who is or was a director, officer, employee, or other agent of the corporation, or is or was serving at the request of the corporation as a director, officer, employee, or agent of another corporation, partnership, joint venture, trust, or other enterprise, or was a director, officer, employee, or agent of a corporation which was a predecessor corporation of the corporation or of another enterprise serving at the request of such predecessor corporation.

Comment: See Comments to Form 5.136–2.

Form 5.136–2 (Indemnification of Directors, Officers, Employees, and Other Agents—Long Form)

ARTICLE [*Number*]

INDEMNIFICATION OF DIRECTORS, OFFICERS, EMPLOYEES, AND OTHER AGENTS

Section 1. AGENTS, PROCEEDINGS, AND EXPENSES. For the

purposes of this Article, "agent" means any person who is or was a director, officer, employee, or other agent of this corporation, or is or was serving at the request of this corporation as a director, officer, employee, or agent of another foreign or domestic corporation, partnership, joint venture, trust, or other enterprise, or was a director, officer, employee, or agent of a foreign or domestic corporation which was a predecessor corporation of this corporation or of another enterprise at the request of such predecessor corporation; "proceeding" means any threatened, pending, or completed action or proceeding, whether civil, criminal, administrative, or investigative; and "expenses" includes, without limitation, attorneys' fees and any expenses of establishing a right to indemnification under Section 4 or Section 5(c) of this Article [*Number*].

Section 2. ACTIONS OTHER THAN BY THE CORPORATION. This corporation shall have the power to indemnify any person who was or is a party, or is threatened to be made a party, to any proceeding (other than an action by or in the right of this corporation to procure a judgment in its favor) by reason of the fact that such person is or was an agent of this corporation, against expenses, judgments, fines, settlements, and other amounts actually and reasonably incurred in connection with such proceeding if that person acted in good faith and in a manner that the person reasonably believed to be in the best interests of this corporation, and, in the case of a criminal proceeding, had no reasonable cause to believe the conduct of that person was unlawful. The termination of any proceeding by judgment, order, settlement, conviction, or on a plea of nolo contendere or its equivalent shall not, of itself, create a presumption that the person did not act in good faith and in a manner that the person reasonably believed to be in the best interests of this corporation or that the person had reasonable cause to believe that the person's conduct was not unlawful.

Comment: Section 2 of this form tracks the provisions of Corp C §317(b), acknowledging the corporation's power to indemnify, but leaving that indemnification to the decision of the board, independent counsel, or shareholders. See Section 5 of form. In the past, some corporations have modified the introductory language to read, "This corporation shall indemnify . . . ," making indemnification mandatory. The intent was to give corporate agents, and particularly directors, the comfort of knowing they would be indemnified to the full extent permitted by law. In troubled corporations, such comfort could be an essential prerequisite to recruiting qualified directors, particularly outside directors.

Indemnification agreements are now recognized by statute in California. See §§5.68, 5.137. In most cases they are likely to be preferable to bylaw provisions because they provide more flexibility, and avoid problems that might result from future bylaw amendments. For example, a corporation might want to enter into agreements for mandatory indemnity for directors (and perhaps officers), yet reserve the right to decide indemnity claims on a case-by-case basis for other agents. While comparable provisions may be included in the bylaws, the employees may prefer to have direct contractual obligations.

Note, however, that in certain circumstances a corporation may be obligated to indemnify a California employee regardless of the provisions of Corp C §317. See, *e.g.*, Lab C §2802, which provides:

> An employer shall indemnify his employee for all that the employee necessarily expends or loses in direct consequence of the discharge of his duties as such, or of his obedience to the directions of the employer, even though unlawful, unless the employee, at the time of obeying such directions, believed them to be unlawful.

Because both the Corporations Code and Form 5.136–2 make their respective indemnification rights nonexclusive, the potential conflict between the bylaw indemnification provisions and Lab C §2802 should not pose a problem unless indemnification required in a specific instance by Lab C §2802 would violate California public policy or the express prohibitions against indemnification found in Corp C §317. The interaction between Corp C §317 and Lab C §2802 apparently has not been settled judicially. The Labor Code provision is important to remember if a corporation wishes to adopt an exclusive indemnification policy more restrictive than Lab C §2802. Also, if the board has been given discretion to indemnify employees and agents, it should be aware of the limits on its discretion found in Lab C §2802.

Section 3. ACTIONS BY OR IN THE RIGHT OF THE CORPORATION. This corporation shall have the power to indemnify any person who was or is a party, or is threatened

to be made a party, to any threatened, pending, or completed action by or in the right of this corporation to procure a judgment in its favor by reason of the fact that such person is or was an agent of this corporation, against expenses actually and reasonably incurred by such person in connection with the defense or settlement of that action, if such person acted in good faith, in a manner such person believed to be in the best interests of this corporation and its shareholders. No indemnification shall be made under this Section 3 for the following:

(a) With respect to any claim, issue, or matter as to which such person has been adjudged to be liable to this corporation in the performance of such person's duty to the corporation and its shareholders, unless and only to the extent that the court in which that proceeding is or was pending shall determine upon application that, in view of all the circumstances of the case, such person is fairly and reasonably entitled to indemnity for expenses and then only to the extent that the court shall determine;

(b) Of amounts paid in settling or otherwise disposing of a pending action without court approval;

(c) Of expenses incurred in defending a pending action that is settled or otherwise disposed of without court approval.

Section 4. SUCCESSFUL DEFENSE BY AGENT. To the extent that an agent of this corporation has been successful on the merits in defense of any proceeding referred to in Section 2 or 3 of this Article [Number], or in defense of any claim, issue, or matter therein, the agent shall be indemnified against expenses actually and reasonably incurred by the agent in connection therewith.

Section 5. REQUIRED APPROVAL. Except as provided in Section 4 of this Article [number], any indemnification under this section shall be made by the corporation only if authorized in the specific case, on a determination that indemnification of the agent is proper in the circumstances because the agent has met the applicable standard of conduct set forth in Section 2 or 3 by one of the following:

(a) A majority vote of a quorum consisting of directors who are not parties to such proceeding;

(b) Independent legal counsel in a written opinion if a quorum of directors who are not parties to such a proceeding is not available;

(c) (i) The affirmative vote of a majority of shares of this corporation entitled to vote represented at a duly held meeting at which a quorum is present; or

(ii) the written consent of holders of a majority of the outstanding shares entitled to vote (for purposes of this subsection 5(c), the shares owned by the person to be indemnified shall not be considered outstanding or entitled to vote thereon); or

(d) The court in which the proceeding is or was pending, on application made by this corporation or the agent or the attorney or other person rendering services in connection with the defense, whether or not such application by the agent, attorney, or other person is opposed by this corporation.

Comment: A corporation that elects to provide in its bylaws for mandatory indemnification could also elect to eliminate the case-by-case determination required by this Section 5. In that event, the corporation should first adopt an article authorizing indemnification in excess of Corp C §317. See Comment to Section 2 of this form. See also §5.135 for forms of articles.

Section 6. ADVANCE OF EXPENSES. Expenses incurred in defending any proceeding may be advanced by the corporation before the final disposition of that proceeding on receipt of an undertaking by or on behalf of the agent to repay those amounts if it shall be determined ultimately that the agent is not entitled to be indemnified as authorized in this Article [*number*].

Comment: As with indemnification, advance of expenses may be made mandatory in the bylaws, by agreement, or otherwise, if there is appropriate authorization in the articles. See §§5.68, 5.135.

Section 7. OTHER CONTRACTUAL RIGHTS. The indemnification

provided by this Article [*number*] shall not be deemed exclusive of any other rights to which those seeking indemnification may be entitled under any bylaw, agreement, vote of shareholders or disinterested directors, or otherwise, both as to action in an official capacity and as to action in another capacity while holding office, to the extent such additional rights to indemnification are authorized in the articles of the corporation. The rights of indemnity under this Article [*number*] shall continue as to a person who has ceased to be a director, officer, employee, or agent and shall inure to the benefit of the heirs, executors, and administrators of the person. Nothing contained in this section shall affect any right to indemnification to which persons other than such directors and officers may be entitled by contract or otherwise.

Comment: See §§5.68 and 5.135 regarding authorization in the articles.

Section 8. LIMITATIONS. No indemnification or advance shall be made under this Article [*number*], except as provided in Section 4 or Section 5(c), in any circumstance if it appears:

(a) That it would be inconsistent with a provision of the articles or bylaws, a resolution of the shareholders, or an agreement in effect at the time of the accrual of the alleged cause of action asserted in the proceeding in which expenses were incurred or other amounts were paid, which prohibits or otherwise limits indemnification; or

(b) That it would be inconsistent with any condition expressly imposed by a court in approving settlement.

Section 9. INSURANCE. This corporation may purchase and maintain insurance on behalf of any agent of the corporation insuring against any liability asserted against or incurred by the agent in that capacity or arising out of the agent's status as such, whether or not this corporation would have the power to indemnify the agent against that liability under the provisions of this Article [*number*]. Notwithstanding the foregoing, if this corporation owns all or a portion of the shares of the company issuing the policy of insurance, the insuring company or the policy, or both, shall meet the conditions set forth in section 317(i) of the Corporations Code.

Comment: Corporations Code §317(i) imposes certain restrictions on directors' and officers' liability insurance purchased through companies in which they have an ownership interest (so-called captive insurers).

Section 10. FIDUCIARIES OF CORPORATE EMPLOYEE BENEFIT PLAN. This Article [*number*] does not apply to any proceeding against any trustee, investment manager, or other fiduciary of an employee benefit plan in that person's capacity as such, even though that person may also be an agent of the corporation. The corporation shall have the power to indemnify, and to purchase and maintain insurance on behalf of any such trustee, investment manager, or other fiduciary of any benefit plan for any or all of the directors, officers, and employees of the corporation or any of its subsidiary or affiliated corporations.

Section 11. EFFECT OF AMENDMENT. Any amendment, repeal, or modification of this Article [*number*] shall not adversely affect an agent's right or protection existing at the time of such amendment, repeal, or modification.

Section 12. SETTLEMENT OF CLAIMS. The corporation shall not be liable to indemnify any agent under this Article [*number*] for (a) any amounts paid in settlement of any action or claim effected without the corporation's written consent, [*which consent shall not be unreasonably withheld,*] or (b) any judicial award, if the corporation was not given a reasonable and timely opportunity to participate, at its expense, in the defense of such action.

Section 13. SUBROGATION. In the event of payment under this Article [*number*], the corporation shall be subrogated to the extent of that payment to all of the rights of recovery of the agent, who shall execute all papers required and shall do everything that may be necessary to secure such rights, including the execution of such documents as may be necessary to enable the corporation effectively to bring suit to enforce those rights.

Section 14. NO DUPLICATION OF PAYMENTS. The corporation shall not be liable under this Article [*number*] to make any payment in connection with any claim made against the agent

to the extent the agent has otherwise actually received payment, whether under a policy of insurance, agreement, vote, or otherwise, of the amounts otherwise indemnifiable under this Article.

Comment: Before any of these optional provisions will be effective, the corporation must adopt an article authorizing indemnification in excess of that provided by Corp C §317. See §§5.68, 5.135.

Because Corp C §317 does not set forth the exclusive provisions for indemnification of directors, officers, and agents, some counsel advise including one or more of the optional provisions above. Section 11, imported from indemnification agreements (see §5.137), underlines the contractual nature of the agent's right to indemnification. Section 12, on the other hand, protects the corporation by obligating it to indemnify for settlements and judgments only when it is consulted or has an opportunity to participate. Section 13, giving the corporation rights of subrogation, and 14, eliminating any liability for duplicate payments, are also for the corporation's benefit.

Section 11 does not address the extent to which any amendment of the bylaws (including an amendment implementing this version of expanded indemnification rights) can be applied to acts or omissions occurring before the amendment. The interaction between Corp C §204 and §317 is unclear on this point. When bylaws or an indemnification agreement provide for indemnification to the fullest extent of the law, if retroactive application is possible, there is an argument that the language of Section 11 encompasses it.

Some corporations may wish to take the opposite approach from that in these forms and limit indemnification as much as possible. If so, the bylaw should prohibit indemnification except where required by law. See Corp C §317(h)(1) which, by inference, permits the articles or bylaws to limit indemnification.

§5.137 (3) Sample Form: Indemnification of Agents (Indemnification Agreement)

Form 5.137–1 (Indemnification Agreement)

INDEMNIFICATION AGREEMENT

THIS AGREEMENT is entered into as of [*date*]**, between** [*name* of corporation], a California corporation ("the Company"), and [name of indemnitee] ("Indemnitee").

RECITALS

A. The Company believes that it is essential to its best interests to attract and retain highly capable persons to serve as directors, officers, and agents of the Company.

B. Indemnitee is or has been selected to be a director, officer, and/or agent of the Company.

C. The Company and Indemnitee recognize the increased risk of litigation and other claims being asserted against directors, officers, and other agents of corporations.

D. In recognition of Indemnitee's need for substantial protection against personal liability, in order to enhance Indemnitee's [continued] service to the Company, and in order to induce Indemnitee to [continue to] provide services to the Company as a director, officer, and/or agent, the Company wishes to provide in this Agreement for the indemnification of and the advancement of expenses to Indemnitee to the fullest extent permitted by law and as set forth in this Agreement, and, to the extent applicable insurance is maintained, for the coverage of Indemnitee under the Company's policies of directors' and officers' liability insurance.

IN CONSIDERATION of the foregoing and of Indemnitee's [providing/continuing to provide] services to the Company directly or, at its request, with another enterprise, the parties agree as follows:

Section 1. DEFINITIONS.

a. Board: the board of directors of the Company.

b. Change in Control: a state of affairs that shall be deemed to have occurred if:

(i) any person is or becomes the "beneficial owner" (as that term is defined in Rule 13d–3 under the Securities Exchange Act of 1934, as amended (the "Exchange Act")), directly or indirectly, of securities representing 20 percent or more of the total voting power of the Company's then-outstanding voting securities; or

(ii) during any period of two consecutive years, individuals who, at the beginning of such period, constitute the board, together with any new director whose election by the board or nomination for election by the Company's shareholders was approved by a vote of at least two thirds of the directors then in office who either were directors at the beginning of the two-year period, or whose election or nomination was previously so approved, cease for any reason to constitute a majority of the board; or

(iii) the shareholders of the Company approve a merger or consolidation of the Company with any other corporation, other than a merger or consolidation that would result in the voting securities of the Company outstanding immediately prior to such merger or consolidation continuing to represent (either by remaining outstanding or by being converted into voting securities of the surviving entity) at least 80 percent of the total voting power represented by the voting securities of the Company or such surviving entity outstanding immediately after such merger or consolidation; or

(iv) the shareholders of the Company approve a plan of complete liquidation of the Company, or an agreement for the sale or disposition by the Company (whether in one transaction or a series of transactions) of all or substantially all of the Company's assets.

c. Expenses:

(i) Any expense, liability, or loss, including attorneys' fees, judgments, fines, ERISA excise taxes and penalties, amounts paid or to be paid in settlement;

(ii) any interest, assessments, or other charges imposed on any of the items in part (i) of this subsection (c); and

(iii) any federal, state, local, or foreign taxes imposed as a result of the actual or deemed receipt of any payments under this Agreement paid or incurred in connection with investigating, defending, being a witness in, or participating in (including on appeal), or preparing for any of the foregoing in, any proceeding relating to any indemnifiable event.

d. Indemnifiable Event: any event or occurrence that takes place either before or after the execution of this Agreement and that is related to

(i) the fact that Indemnitee is or was a director or an officer of the Company, or while a director or officer is or was serving at the request of the Company as a director, officer, employee, trustee, agent, or fiduciary of another foreign or domestic corporation, partnership, joint venture, employee benefit plan, trust or other enterprise, or was a director, officer, employee, or agent of a foreign or domestic corporation that was a predecessor corporation of the Company or another enterprise at the request of such predecessor corporation, or

(ii) anything done or not done by Indemnitee in any such capacity, whether or not the basis of the proceeding is an alleged action in an official capacity as a director, officer, employee, or agent, or in any other capacity while serving as a director, officer, employee, or agent of the Company, as described in this subsection d.

e. Independent Counsel: the person or body appointed in connection with Section 3.

f. Person: "person" (as that term is used in sections 13(d) and 14(d) of the Exchange Act), other than a trustee or other fiduciary holding securities under an employee benefit plan of the Company acting in such capacity, or a corporation owned directly or indirectly by the shareholders of the Company in substantially the same proportions as their ownership of shares of the Company at the date of this Agreement.

g. Participant: a person who is a party to, or witness or participant (including on appeal) in, a proceeding.

h. Potential Change in Control: a state of affairs that shall be deemed to exist if:

(i) the Company enters into an agreement or arrangement,

the consummation of which would result in the occurrence of a change in control; or

(ii) any person (including the Company) announces publicly an intention to take or to consider taking actions that, if consummated, would constitute a change in control; or

(iii) any person who is or becomes the beneficial owner, directly or indirectly, of securities of the Company representing 10 percent or more of the combined voting power of the Company's then-outstanding voting securities, increases his or her beneficial ownership of such securities by 5 percent or more over the percentage owned by such person on the date of this Agreement; or,

(iv) the board adopts a resolution to the effect that, for purposes of this Agreement, a potential change in control has occurred.

i. Proceeding: any threatened, pending, or completed action, suit, or proceeding, or any inquiry, hearing, or investigation, whether conducted by the Company or any other party, that Indemnitee in good faith believes might lead to the institution of any such action, suit, or proceeding, whether civil, criminal, administrative, investigative, or other.

j. Reviewing Party: the person or body appointed in accordance with Section 3.

k. Voting Securities: any securities of the Company that have the right to vote generally in the election of directors.

Section 2. AGREEMENT TO INDEMNIFY.

a. General Agreement. In the event Indemnitee was, is, or becomes a participant in, or is threatened to be made a participant in, a proceeding by reason of (or arising in part out of) an indemnifiable event, the Company shall indemnify Indemnitee from and against any and all expenses to the fullest extent permitted by law, as the same exists or may hereafter be amended or interpreted (but in the case of any such amendment or interpretation, only to the extent that such amendment or interpretation permits the Company to provide broader indemnification rights than were permitted prior to that amendment or interpretation). The parties to this Agreement intend that this Agreement shall provide for indemnification in excess of that expressly permitted by statute, including, without limitation, any indemnification provided by the Company's articles of incorporation, its bylaws, a vote of its shareholders or disinterested directors, or applicable law.

b. Initiation of Proceeding. Notwithstanding anything in this Agreement to the contrary, Indemnitee shall not be entitled to indemnification under this Agreement in connection with any proceeding initiated by Indemnitee against the Company or any director or officer of the Company unless:

(i) the Company has joined in or the Board has consented to the initiation of such proceeding;

(ii) the proceeding is one to enforce indemnification rights under Section 5; or

(iii) the proceeding is instituted after a change in control and independent counsel has approved its initiation.

c. Expense Advances. If so requested by Indemnitee, the Company shall, within ten business days of such request, advance all expenses to Indemnitee (an "expense advance"). Notwithstanding the foregoing, to the extent that the reviewing party determines that Indemnitee would not be permitted to be so indemnified under applicable law, the Company shall be entitled to be reimbursed by Indemnitee for all such amounts, and Indemnitee hereby agrees to reimburse the Company promptly for the same. If Indemnitee has commenced legal proceedings in a court of competent jurisdiction to secure a determination that Indemnitee should be indemnified under applicable law, as provided in Section 4, any determination made by the reviewing party that Indemnitee would not be permitted to be indemnified under applicable law shall not be binding, and Indemnitee shall not be required to reimburse the Company for any expense advance until a final judicial determination is made with respect thereto and all rights of appeal therefrom have been exhausted or have lapsed. Indemnitee's obligation to reimburse the Company for expense advances shall be unsecured and no interest shall be charged thereon.

d. **Mandatory Indemnification.** Notwithstanding any other provision of this Agreement, to the extent that Indemnitee has been successful on the merits in defense of any proceeding relating in whole or in part to an indemnifiable event or in defense of any issue or matter in such proceeding, Indemnitee shall be indemnified against all expenses incurred in connection with that proceeding.

e. **Partial Indemnification.** If Indemnitee is entitled under any provision of this Agreement to indemnification by the Company for a portion of expenses, but not for the total amount of expenses, the Company shall indemnify Indemnitee for the portion to which Indemnitee is entitled.

f. **Prohibited Indemnification.** No indemnification under this Agreement shall be paid by the Company on account of any proceeding in which judgment is rendered against Indemnitee for an accounting of profits made from the purchase or sale by Indemnitee of securities of the Company under the provisions of Section 16(b) of the Exchange Act, or similar provisions of any federal, state, or local laws.

Section 3. REVIEWING PARTY. Before any change in control, the reviewing party shall be any appropriate person or body consisting of a member or members of the board or any other person or body appointed by the board who is not a party to the proceeding for which Indemnitee is seeking indemnification; after a change in control, the reviewing party shall be the independent counsel. On all matters arising after a change in control (other than a change in control approved by a majority of the directors of the board who were directors immediately before such change in control) concerning the rights of Indemnitee to indemnity payments and expense advances under this Agreement, any other agreement, applicable law, or the Company's articles of incorporation or bylaws now or hereafter in effect relating to indemnification for indemnifiable events, the Company shall seek legal advice only from independent counsel selected by Indemnitee and approved by the Company (which approval shall not be unreasonably withheld), and who has not otherwise performed services for the Company or the Indemnitee (other than in connection with indemnification matters) within the previous five years. The independent counsel shall not include any person who, under the applicable standards of professional conduct then prevailing, would have a conflict of interest in representing either the Company or Indemnitee in an action to determine Indemnitee's rights under this Agreement. Such counsel, among other things, shall render a written opinion to the Company and Indemnitee on whether and to what extent the Indemnitee should be permitted to be indemnified under applicable law. The Company agrees to pay the reasonable fees of the independent counsel and to indemnify fully such counsel against any and all expenses, including attorneys' fees, claims, liabilities, loss, and damages arising out of or relating to this Agreement or the engagement of independent counsel under this Agreement.

Section 4. INDEMNIFICATION PROCESS AND APPEAL.

a. Indemnification Payment. Indemnitee shall receive indemnification of expenses from the Company in accordance with this Agreement as soon as practicable after Indemnitee has made written demand on the Company for indemnification, unless the reviewing party has given a written opinion to the Company that Indemnitee is not entitled to indemnification under this Agreement or applicable law.

b. Suit To Enforce Rights. Regardless of any action by the reviewing party, if Indemnitee has not received full indemnification within 30 days after making a demand in accordance with Section 4a, Indemnitee shall have the right to enforce its indemnification rights under this Agreement by commencing litigation in any court in the State of California seeking an initial determination by the court or challenging any determination by the reviewing party or any aspect thereof. The Company hereby consents to service of process and to appear in any such proceeding. Any determination by the reviewing party not challenged by the Indemnitee shall be binding on the Company and Indemnitee. The remedy provided for in this Section 4 shall be in addition to any other remedies available to Indemnitee in law or equity.

c. Defense to Indemnification, Burden of Proof, and Presumptions. It shall be a defense to any action brought by Indemnitee against the Company to enforce this Agreement (other than an action brought to enforce a claim for expenses incurred in defending a proceeding in advance of its final disposition when the required undertaking has been tendered to the Company) that it is not permissible, under this Agreement or applicable law, for the Company to indemnify Indemnitee for the amount claimed. In connection with any such action or any determination by the reviewing party or otherwise on whether Indemnitee is entitled to be indemnified under this Agreement, the burden of proving such a defense or determination shall be on the Company. Neither the failure of the reviewing party or the Company (including its board, independent legal counsel, or its shareholders) to have made a determination before the commencement of such action by Indemnitee that indemnification is proper under the circumstances because the Indemnitee has met the standard of conduct set forth in applicable law, nor an actual determination by the reviewing party or Company (including its board, independent legal counsel, or its shareholders) that the Indemnitee had not met such applicable standard of conduct, shall be a defense to the action or create a presumption that the Indemnitee has not met the applicable standard of conduct. For purposes of this Agreement, the termination of any claim, action, suit, or proceeding, by judgment, order, settlement (whether with or without court approval), conviction, or on a plea of nolo contendere, or its equivalent, shall not create a presumption that Indemnitee did not meet any particular standard of conduct or have any particular belief or that a court has determined that indemnification is not permitted by applicable law.

Section 5. INDEMNIFICATION FOR EXPENSES INCURRED IN ENFORCING RIGHTS. The Company shall indemnify Indemnitee against any and all expenses. If requested by Indemnitee, the Company shall, within ten business days of such request, advance to Indemnitee such expenses as are incurred by Indemnitee in connection with any claim asserted against or action brought by Indemnitee for

(a) indemnification of expenses or advances of expenses by the Company under this Agreement, or any other agreement, or under applicable law, or the Company's articles of incorporation or bylaws now or hereafter in effect relating to indemnification for indemnifiable events, and/or

(b) recovery under directors' and officers' liability insurance policies maintained by the Company, for amounts paid in settlement if the independent counsel has approved the settlement.

The Company shall not settle any proceeding in any manner that would impose any penalty or limitation on Indemnitee without Indemnitee's written consent. Neither the Company nor the Indemnitee will unreasonably withhold its consent to any proposed settlement. The Company shall not be liable to indemnify the Indemnitee under this Agreement with regard to any judicial award if the Company was not given a reasonable and timely opportunity, at its expense, to participate in the defense of such action; however, the Company's liability under this Agreement shall not be excused if participation in the proceeding by the Company was barred by this Agreement.

Section 6. ESTABLISHMENT OF TRUST. In the event of a change in control or a potential change in control, the Company shall, on written request by Indemnitee, create a trust for the benefit of the Indemnitee ("the Trust") and from time to time on written request of Indemnitee shall fund the Trust in an amount sufficient to satisfy any and all expenses reasonably anticipated at the time of each such request to be incurred in connection with investigating, preparing for, participating in, and/or defending any proceeding relating to an indemnifiable event. The amount or amounts to be deposited in the Trust under the foregoing funding obligation shall be determined by the reviewing party. The terms of the Trust shall provide that on a change in control:

(a) The Trust shall not be revoked or the principal invaded without the written consent of the Indemnitee.

(b) The Trustee shall advance, within ten business days of a request by the Indemnitee, all expenses to the Indemnitee (provided that the Indemnitee hereby agrees to reimburse the Trust under the same circumstances for which the Indemnitee would be required to reimburse the Company under Section 2c of this Agreement).

(c) The Trust shall continue to be funded by the Company in accordance with the funding obligation set forth in this Section 6.

(d) The Trustee shall promptly pay to the Indemnitee all amounts for which the Indemnitee shall be entitled to indemnification under this Agreement or otherwise.

(e) All unexpended funds in the Trust shall revert to the Company on a final determination by the reviewing party or a court of competent jurisdiction that the Indemnitee has been fully indemnified under the terms of this Agreement.

The Trustee shall be chosen by the Indemnitee subject to the approval of the [reviewing party/company]. Nothing in this Section 6 shall relieve the Company of any of its obligations under this Agreement. All income earned on the assets held in the Trust shall be reported as income by the Company for federal, state, local, and foreign tax purposes. The Company shall pay all costs of establishing and maintaining the Trust and shall indemnify the Trustee against any and all expenses, including attorneys' fees, claims, liabilities, loss, and damages arising out of or relating to this Agreement or the establishment and maintenance of the Trust.

Section 7. NONEXCLUSIVITY. The rights of Indemnitee under this Agreement shall be in addition to any other rights Indemnitee may have under the Company's articles of incorporation, bylaws, applicable law, or otherwise. To the extent that a change in applicable law (whether by statute or judicial decision) permits greater indemnification by agreement than would be afforded currently under the Company's articles of incorporation, bylaws, applicable law, or this Agreement, it is the intent of the parties that Indemnitee enjoy by this Agreement the greater benefits afforded by such change.

Section 8. LIABILITY INSURANCE. To the extent the Company maintains an insurance policy or policies providing directors' and officers' liability insurance, Indemnitee shall be covered by such policy or policies, in accordance with its or their terms, to the maximum extent of the coverage available for any Company director or officer.

Section 9. PERIOD OF LIMITATIONS. No legal action shall be brought, and no cause of action shall be asserted, by or on behalf of the Company or any affiliate of the Company against Indemnitee, Indemnitee's spouse, heirs, executors, or personal or legal representatives, after the expiration of two years from the date of accrual of such cause of action, or such longer period as may be required by state law under the circumstances. Any claim or cause of action of the Company or its affiliate shall be extinguished and deemed released unless asserted by the timely filing of a legal action within such period; provided, however, that if any shorter period of limitations is otherwise applicable to any such cause of action, the shorter period shall govern.

Section 10. AMENDMENT OF THIS AGREEMENT. No supplement, modification, or amendment of this Agreement shall be binding unless executed in writing by both of the parties to it. No waiver of any of the provisions of this Agreement shall operate as a waiver of any other provisions of this Agreement (whether or not similar), nor shall such waiver constitute a continuing waiver. Except as specifically provided in this Agreement, no failure to exercise or delay in exercising any right or remedy under it shall constitute a waiver of the right or remedy.

Section 11. SUBROGATION. In the event of payment under this Agreement, the Company shall be subrogated to the extent of that payment to all of the rights of recovery of Indemnitee, who shall execute all papers required and shall do everything that may be necessary to secure such rights, including the execution of any documents necessary to enable the Company effectively to bring suit to enforce such rights.

Section 12. NO DUPLICATION OF PAYMENTS. The Company shall not be liable under this Agreement to make any payment in connection with any claim made against Indemnitee to the extent Indemnitee has otherwise received payment (under any insurance policy, bylaw, or otherwise) of the amounts otherwise indemnifiable under this Agreement.

Section 13. BINDING EFFECT. This Agreement shall be binding on and inure to the benefit of and be enforceable by the parties to it and their respective successors (including any direct or indirect successor by purchase, merger, consolidation, or otherwise to all or substantially all of the Company's business or assets or both), assigns, spouses, heirs, and personal and legal representatives. The Company shall require and cause any successor (whether direct or indirect, by purchase, merger, consolidation, or otherwise) to all, substantially all, or a substantial part, of the Company's business or assets or both, by written agreement in form and substance satisfactory to Indemnitee, expressly to assume and agree to perform this Agreement in the same manner and to the same extent that the Company would be required to perform if no such succession had taken place. The indemnification provided under this Agreement shall continue for Indemnitee for any action taken or not taken while serving in an indemnified capacity pertaining to an indemnifiable event even though Indemnitee may have ceased to serve in such capacity at the time of any proceeding.

Section 14. SEVERABILITY. If any portion of this Agreement shall be held by a court of competent jurisdiction to be invalid, void, or otherwise unenforceable, the remaining provisions shall remain enforceable to the fullest extent permitted by law. Furthermore, to the fullest extent possible, the provisions of this Agreement (including, without limitation, each portion of this Agreement containing any provision held to be invalid, void, or otherwise unenforceable, that is not itself invalid, void, or unenforceable) shall be construed so as to give effect to the intent manifested by the provision held invalid, void, or unenforceable.

Section 15. GOVERNING LAW. This Agreement shall be governed by and construed and enforced in accordance with the laws of the State of California applicable to contracts made and to be performed in such State without giving effect to the principles of conflicts of laws.

Section 16. NOTICES. All notices, demands, and other communications required or permitted under this Agreement shall be made in writing and shall be deemed to have been duly given if delivered by hand, against receipt, or mailed, first class postage prepaid, [*certified or registered mail, return receipt requested,*] and addressed to the Company at:

[*Address*]

Attn: _ _ _ _ _

and to Indemnitee at:

[Address]

Notice of change of address shall be effective only when given in accordance with this Section. All notices complying with this Section shall be deemed to have been received on the date of delivery or on the third business day after mailing.

Comment: If desired, the notices section may be modified to also provide for notices to counsel.

IN WITNESS WHEREOF, the parties hereto have duly executed and delivered this Agreement as of the day specified above.

COMPANY:	*[Name of company]*
	by *[Signature; typed name and title below]*
INDEMNITEE:	*[Signature; typed name below]*

Comment: Before this agreement is used, the corporation should adopt an article authorizing agreements for indemnification in excess of that provided for by Corp C §317. See §§5.68, 5.135. The agreement will be valid only on or after the date of that amendment. Although indemnity is typically covered in the bylaws, many corporations are now considering entering into indemnification agreements with certain officers and directors. This may be particularly useful when new management is recruited, if the company is a takeover target, if officers and directors seem particularly exposed to claims of liability, or when outside directors are recruited.

4. Certificate of Amendment

a. Before Shares Issued

§5.138   (1) Contents of Certificate

The certificate of amendment sets forth the amendment (see §§5.117–5.135) and any facts necessary to show that it has been duly adopted. Corp C §§905–907. If the amendment is adopted before any shares have been issued by the corporation (see §5.90), the contents are prescribed by Corp C §906. If no directors have been elected, the certificate must be executed by the incorporator(s), and must state that the signers constitute at least a majority of the incorporators and that directors were not named in the original articles and have not been elected. Corp C §906. If directors were named in the original articles or were elected by the incorporators, the certificate must state that the signers constitute at least a majority of the corporation's directors. A certificate of either incorporators or directors made before shares have been issued must also (a) state that they adopt the amendment or amendments set forth in the certificate (if the amendment is made before issuance of shares, the certificate can serve as the "writing" by which the amendment is adopted under Corp C §901); (b) state that the corporation has issued no shares; and (c) be signed and verified by the signers.

If a "listed corporation" amends its articles to classify its board of directors or eliminate cumulative voting, the certificate must include a statement of facts showing the corporation is a listed corporation. Corp C §301.5; see §5.70.

§5.139   (2) Form: Certificate of Amendment, Before Any Shares Issued

Form 5.139–1

CERTIFICATE OF AMENDMENT OF ARTICLES OF INCORPORATION OF
[name of corporation]

[Names of incorporators or directors] certify that:

1. They constitute at least a majority of the [incorporators/directors] **of** [name of corporation], **a California corporation:**

2. They adopt the following amendment(s) to the articles of incorporation of the corporation:

[Insert amendment(s)]

3. The corporation has issued no shares.

[Insert 4 if the amendment is by the incorporators]

4. Directors were not named in the articles of incorporation and have not been elected.

[*Continue*]

[*Signatures of incorporators or directors*]
[*Typed names*]
[*Incorporator/Director*]

Each of the undersigned declares under penalty of perjury that the statements contained in the foregoing certificate are true and correct of his or her own knowledge, and that this declaration was executed on _ _ _ _ _ _, 19_ _, at _ _ _ _ _ _, California.

[*Signatures of incorporators or directors*]
[*Typed names*]

Comment: See §5.138. The forms of amendment to be inserted are set forth in §§5.117–5.135. This form uses a verification by declaration under penalty of perjury as permitted by Corp C §193(b). Verification by affidavit is also permitted (see Corp C §193(a)), but is more cumbersome because notarization is required, and would rarely be used. A certificate of amendment may be verified by declaration under penalty of perjury within or outside California. Corp C §193(b).

b. After Shares Issued

§5.140 (1) Contents of Certificate

When the certificate of amendment is adopted after any shares have been issued by the corporation, the certificate of amendment must meet the following requirements:

(a) It must be an "officers' certificate" signed and verified by the chairman of the board, the president or any vice president, and by the secretary, the chief financial officer, the treasurer, any assistant secretary, or any assistant treasurer. Corp C §173.

(b) It must state that the board of directors has approved the amendment. The date and manner of adoption (*e.g.,* written consent) need not be stated. Corp C §905(b).

(c) It must state the wording of the amendment. The exact wording of the amendment (see §§5.117–5.135) should be copied into the certificate, and no more. The resolution of the board of directors need not be copied into the certificate. Corp C §905(a).

(d) If the amendment required shareholder approval (see §§5.91–5.107), the certificate of amendment must state: (1) That the amendment was approved by the required vote (which also means written consent; see Corp C §194) in accordance with Corp C §902, §903, or §904 (if both Corp C §§902(a) and 903(a) apply, only Corp C §903 usually need be mentioned, because Corp C §903(c) duplicates Corp C §902(a) as far as the shareholder vote is concerned); (2) the total number of outstanding shares entitled to vote on the amendment, broken down by class if there is more than one class and by series if a series is given a separate vote (see §5.94); (3) the percentage vote (usually a majority; see §§5.91–5.93) required of the outstanding shares to approve the amendment (broken down by class if there is more than one class and by series if a series is given a separate vote); and (4) that the number of outstanding shares entitled to vote (of each class) and voting in favor of the amendment either equalled or exceeded the vote required. The amendment need not contain the shareholders' resolution, the time and place of meeting, the number of shares voting in favor, or the method of adoption. Corp C §905(c).

(e) If the amendment does not require shareholder approval, but is one that can be adopted with approval by the board alone (see §§5.108–5.109), the certificate of amendment must state the facts entitling the board alone to adopt the amendment. Corp C §905(d).

(f) If a "listed corporation" amends its articles to classify its board of directors or eliminate cumulative voting, the certificate must include a statement of facts showing the corporation is a listed corporation. Corp C §301.5; see §5.70.

§5.141   (2) Form: Certificate of Amendment, After Shares Issued

Form 5.141–1

CERTIFICATE OF AMENDMENT OF ARTICLES OF INCORPORATION OF
[*name of corporation*]

[*Names of officers*] **certify that:**

1. They are the [*e.g., president and secretary*], **respectively, of** [*name of corporation*], **a California corporation.**

2. The following amendment to the articles of incorporation of the corporation has been duly approved by the board of directors of the corporation:

[*Insert amendment*]

[*Insert appropriate paragraph 3 below*]

[*First alternative: majority vote required*]

3. The amendment was duly approved by the required vote of shareholders in accordance with section 902 of the California Corporations Code. The total number of outstanding shares entitled to vote with respect to the amendment was [*number*], the favorable vote of a majority of such shares is required to approve the amendment, and the number of such shares voting in favor of the amendment equaled or exceeded the required vote.

[*Second alternative: more than one class; supermajority vote of preferred*]

3. The amendment was duly approved by the required vote of shareholders in accordance with section 903 of the California Corporations Code. The total number of outstanding shares of each class entitled to vote on the amendment was [*number*] shares of common stock and [*number*] shares of preferred stock; the favorable vote of [*e.g., a majority*] of such shares of common stock and [*e.g. 80 percent*] of such shares of preferred stock is required to approve the amendment; and the number of such shares of each such class voting in favor of the amendment equalled or exceeded the required vote for that class.

[*Third alternative: board action alone; Corp C §2302 election*]

3. The amendment makes no change in the articles of incorporation other than conforming the statement of purposes and powers to subdivision (b) of section 202 of the California Corporations Code, and deleting references to par value and location of principal office, in accordance with the corporation's election under section 2302 of the California Corporations Code. The above amendment makes no change that would require approval of the outstanding shares under section 2304 of the California Corporations Code. Accordingly, the amendment is one that may be adopted with approval by the board alone.

[*Add, if desired*]

4. The amendment shall become effective on _ _ _ _ _**, 19**_ _
[*, which date is not more than 90 days after the date of filing the certificate of amendment*].

[*Continue*]

[*Signatures of officers*]
[*Typed names and titles*]

[*Verification*]

Comment: See §5.140. The verification may be by affidavit or by declaration under penalty of perjury in the same form as provided in §5.139. See Corp C §193. Optional paragraph 4, delaying the effective date, is discussed in §§5.125, 5.142.

§5.142   c. Filing Requirements

The original, signed certificate of amendment must be filed in the office of the Secretary of State. See Corp C §§169, 905–906, 908. The filing must be made in Sacramento. If a difference of opinion arises as to the appropriateness of the certificate for filing, the opinion of counsel procedure described below can be used.

Either letter-size or legal-size paper may be used, one side only. A space at least three inches square should be left in the upper right-hand corner for the filing stamp of the Secretary of State. Backing sheets should not be used. The sheets should be stapled once in the upper left-hand corner. Typewriter ribbon originals or documents made by multilith are acceptable. The Secretary of State will also accept photocopies if the printing appears to be permanent and cannot be easily smudged or erased. All signatures must be manual, and the names of the signers should always be typed or printed below signature lines. The Secretary of State microfilms the documents.

The Secretary of State must file the certificate of amendment as of the date it is received, if it conforms to law. Corp C §110. This does not mean the document is actually reviewed and filed on the date received. It means that, after it is reviewed by the Secretary of State and found acceptable for filing, it is filed as of the date of receipt. If the filing or the effectiveness of the amendment is to be delayed (see §5.125), counsel should request in the transmittal letter that the certificate of amendment be withheld from filing until the specified date, or delaying language can be included in the certificate of amendment (see optional paragraph 4 in Form 4.135–1). The filing can be delayed no more than 90 days after receipt of the certificate by the Secretary of State, and effectiveness can be delayed no more than 90 days after filing. The date of effectiveness or the requested future filing date can be a Saturday, Sunday, or holiday (*e.g.*, it may be desirable to have an amendment filed or become effective on the last day of the tax or accounting year). See Corp C §110.

If the attorney does not wish to rely on the mails, or wishes to have the document actually filed on the date of receipt, the certificate may be hand-delivered to the Office of the Secretary of State. A special handling fee for expediting the filing of corporate documents in the amount of $15 will be charged. See Govt C §12208, 2 Cal Code Regs §21904.

The Secretary of State must determine that the certificate of amendment conforms to law. Corp C §110. If it is determined that it does not, the Secretary of State's office will return the certificate to the attorney.

If the attorney and the Secretary of State cannot agree on whether the certificate conforms to the law, Corp C §110(b) provides a procedure to resolve the dispute. An attorney who is a member of the California State Bar may submit the certificate, accompanied by a written opinion that the specific provision of the certificate objected to by the Secretary of State does conform to law, and state the points and authorities on which the opinion is based. The Secretary of State is required to rely on such a written opinion in most cases. Corp C §110(b).

For filing procedures generally, see the "Corporations Check List" published by and available from the Secretary of State's office. This pamphlet is updated periodically.

§5.143   d. Fees of Secretary of State

The filing fee for certificates of amendment is $30. Govt C §12205. One certified copy of the filed certificate of amendment should be requested for the corporation's minute book. Additional certified copies may be needed for filing in other states and for special purposes (see §§5.147–5.155), but no copies need be filed with California county clerks or recorders. The Secretary of State will compare and certify up to two copies of the filed certificate without charge, provided that the attorney submits the copies to the Secretary of State with the original certificate to be filed. Govt C §12209. Copies not submitted by the attorney with the original certificate, and more than two copies submitted with the original filing, will require a fee of $8 each for comparing and certification. Govt C §12186.

5. Certificate of Correction

§5.144   a. When Used

Defective filings of certificates of amendment may be corrected under Corp C §109 by a certificate of correction filed and verified in the same manner as a certificate of amendment. See §§5.139, 5.141. Certificates of correction may be filed at any time after the original defective filing. Corp C §109.

A certificate of correction may not be filed if the amendment was defective when submitted to the board of directors or shareholders. Corp C §109. The only way to correct such an error is to hold a new board or shareholders' meeting, adopt a new amendment, and file a new certificate of amendment. As a practical matter, a certificate of correction may be used only when the amendment language in the certificate differs from the wording adopted by the board or the shareholders or when the error is in the certificate of amendment outside the amendment language. A certificate of correction may not be used to effect a corrected amendment of articles if the amendment as corrected would not in all respects have complied with Corporations Code requirements in existence when the certificate of amendment being corrected was filed.

§5.145   b. Form: Certificate of Correction

Form 5.145–1

CERTIFICATE OF CORRECTION OF CERTIFICATE OF AMENDMENT OF ARTICLES OF INCORPORATION OF
[*name of corporation*]

[*Names of officers*] **certify that:**

1. They are the [*e.g., president*] **and the** [*e.g., secretary*], **respectively, of** [*name of corporation*].

2. The name of the corporation is [*name of corporation*], **a California corporation.**

3. The instrument being corrected is titled "CERTIFICATE OF AMENDMENT OF ARTICLES OF INCORPORATION OF [*name of corporation*]**," and the instrument was filed with the California Secretary of State on** _ _ _ _ _ _, **19_ _.**

4. Paragraph [*e.g., 2*] **of the Certificate of Amendment is corrected to read as follows:**

[*Insert corrected paragraph*]

5. Paragraph [*e.g., 2*], **as corrected, conforms the wording of the amendment set forth therein to the wording of the amendment as approved by the board of directors and shareholders.**

[*Signatures of officers*]
[*Typed names and titles*]

Each of the undersigned declares under penalty of perjury that the statements contained in the foregoing certificate are true and correct of his or her own knowledge and that this declaration was executed on _ _ _ _ _ _, **19_ , at** _ _ _ _ _, **California.**

[*Signatures of officers*]
[*Typed names*]

Comment: The fees for filing and certifying a certificate of correction and the clerical requirements of the Secretary of State are the same as those for a certificate of amendment. See §5.143. The requirements for a verification are also the same. See §§5.139–5.141.

§5.146 VIII. FILING REQUIREMENTS IN SPECIAL CASES

A certificate, notice, or other document describing the amendment may be required to be filed with or submitted to governmental agencies other than the Department of Corporations, or creditors, stock exchanges, or other entities. Some form of license or consent may be required from one or more of them. Such requirements depend on the nature and business of the corporation and the laws to which it may be subject. Corporate counsel should develop a checklist of requirements for a particular corporate client after becoming familiar with the client's business and operations, reviewing all of the client's significant contracts and checking the laws and regulations of the jurisdictions where the client does business and any governmental agencies that regulate the client. The following summary (see §§5.147–5.155) indicates some of the matters that should be examined in planning the transaction and in developing a checklist for the particular corporation before any official action by the corporation, its board of directors, or its shareholders.

§5.147 A. Filings in Other States Where Corporation Is Qualified

Amendments to the articles of incorporation may need to be filed with, or notice given to, the Secretary of State, the Corporations Commissioner, or other officials of states in which the corporation is qualified to do business as a foreign corporation, and notice of amendments may be required to be published in such states. The laws of each state in which the corporation is qualified to do business as a foreign corporation should be reviewed to determine any such filing requirements. In addition, counsel should consider contacting the relevant official or agency in each of these states to ask whether any other state or local laws or regulations would be applicable, and whether the official or agency interprets or applies the laws and regulations in any manner that might not be apparent from a fair reading of the laws and regulations. Local counsel or one of the reputable corporate agents may be employed to assist in making these determinations.

§5.148 B. Securities Law Filing Where Shareholders Reside

Amendment of the articles may require a permit under the California Corporate Securities Law (see §§5.74–5.89). Similarly, the securities or "blue sky" laws of each state where any of the corporation's shareholders reside, and the regulations under such laws, should be surveyed to determine if the amendment could be construed to constitute an exchange or distribution of securities, or a change in the rights, preferences, privileges, or restrictions of outstanding shares that would require a permit, registration, or qualification before shareholder approval is solicited. The matter might be discussed with the state securities administrator if a question of interpretation arises. For example, if only one or two shareholders reside in the state, a statutory "isolated transaction" exemption may be available.

§5.149   C. Filing for Particular Business

Laws and regulations applicable to the corporation by virtue of the business in which it is engaged must also be reviewed, both those of California and of any other state in which the corporation may do business. For example, a change in rights, preferences, privileges, or restrictions of outstanding securities of an insurance company would be governed by Ins C §822 (which, by virtue of Ins C §1140, preempts the Corporations Code, including the Corporate Securities Law). Such a change would most likely require a permit from the Insurance Commissioner, because there are almost no exemptions in the Insurance Code provisions. See §5.75 for a discussion of the "change in rights, preferences, privileges, or restrictions" language.

For a public utility, the governing authority would be Pub Util C §816, and the permit would have to be obtained from the Public Utilities Commission. Many codes regulate specialized corporations in California and elsewhere, and those corporations may be required to obtain the consent of, or at least to notify, the cognizant administrative officers. See, *e.g.,* Ins C §§707, 713–714 (insurance companies); Fin C §§600 (banks or trust companies), 5650–5651 (savings and loan associations).

§5.150   D. Professional Corporations

Special requirements are applicable to professional corporations. The statutory provisions are set forth in Corp C §§13400–13410, but the regulatory agency governing each profession issues its own regulations. See ATTORNEY'S GUIDE TO CALIFORNIA PROFESSIONAL CORPORATIONS (4th ed Cal CEB 1987).

§5.151   E. Tax-Exempt Corporations

Corporations exempt from federal or state taxes, or both, are typically required to provide copies of amendments of articles to the relevant federal and state taxing agencies. Copies may also need to be filed with other regulatory agencies. See, *e.g*, ADVISING CALIFORNIA NONPROFIT CORPORATIONS §8.32 (Cal CEB 1984) (requirement that public benefit corporation file copy with Attorney General).

§5.152   F. Fictitious Business Name

If the corporation does business under a fictitious business name and the amendment would result in a change of the corporation's name, the California requirements (see Bus & P C §17913) and those of any other states in which the corporation does business must be observed. See §§5.59–5.67. In California, a corporation's prior fictitious business name statement expires 40 days after the amendment changing its name becomes effective. See Bus & P C §17920(b).

§5.153   G. Securities Exchange and NASD Requirements

If any of the corporation's outstanding securities are listed on a securities exchange, advance notice of the amendment may need to be given to the exchange. Specified action may be required by the exchange in the event of any proposed change in outstanding listed securities or setting a record date for shareholders' meetings, and copies of material to be mailed to shareholders with respect to an amendment typically must be filed with and reviewed by the exchange. See, *e.g.*, New York Stock Exchange Listed Company Manual §§204.03–204.31.

The Securities and Exchange Commission requires disclosure to the securities markets of certain amendments to articles. See, *e.g.*, 17 CFR §240.10b–17, making it a manipulative or deceptive device or contrivance to fail to notify the securities exchange, or, if the security is traded in the over-the-counter market, the National Association of Securities Dealers (NASD), before the record date of various proposed actions, *e.g.*, stock splits and other amendments to articles that may result in distributions to holders of outstanding shares.

§5.154   H. Advance Tax Ruling

An advance ruling from the Internal Revenue Service as to tax effects of an amendment (*e.g.,* recapitalizations or changes in the rights, preferences, privileges, or restrictions of outstanding securities) will occasionally be desirable. This matter is within the purview of tax counsel.

§5.155   I. SEC Registration, Proxy, and Other Requirements

Amendments to articles may sometimes be subject to the registration provisions of the Securities Act of 1933, which require filing a registration statement with the SEC and delivering a prospectus to security holders. The exemption in Securities Act §3(a)(9) (15 USC §77c(a)(9)) will usually be available ("exchange" of security by issuer with existing securities holders exclusively, provided there is no renumeration paid for soliciting approval of the exchange). See Hicks, *Recapitalizations under Section 3(a)(9) of the Securities Act of 1933,* 61 Va L Rev 1057 (1975). If all shareholders reside in California, the intrastate offering exemption of Securities Act §3(a)(11) (15 USC §77c(a)(11)) and Securities Act Rule 147 issued under that provision will often be available for a California corporation doing most of its business in California. Finally, the exemption provided in Securities Act §3(a)(10) (15 USC §77c(a)(10)) may be available when a hearing is requested under Corp C §25142 (see §5.88).

Stock dividends have historically been considered to be exempt from the Securities Act of 1933, even if the shareholder is given an option to take cash or stock. Securities Act Release No. 929 (July 29, 1936). If no exemption applies, Securities Act Rules 145 (17 CFR §230.145) and 153a (17 CFR §230.153a) should be reviewed ("reclassifications" other than stock splits or reverse stock splits require registration). See §5.25. Purchases and sales of fractional shares will be exempt from the registration provisions of the Securities Act of 1933 by virtue of Securities Act Rule 152a(17 CFR §230.152a) (buy-sell order form technique; see §§5.163–5.165) or Securities Act Rule 236 (17 CFR §230.236) (sale of shares to provide funds to pay off fractional interests; see §5.162); Rule 236 requires advance notice to the SEC. If the corporation has securities registered under the Securities Exchange Act of 1934, counsel must have the client comply with the applicable proxy or information statement rules under Exchange Act Regs 14A (17 CFR §§240.14a–1—240.14a–102) or 14C (17 CFR §§240.14c–1—240.14c–101) and the reporting requirements of SEC Forms 8–K, 10–K, and 10–Q. Other statutes, *e.g.,* the Public Utility Holding Company Act of 1935, the Trust Indenture Act of 1939, the Investment Company Act of 1940, and the Investment Advisers Act of 1940, may also apply to amendments of the articles of particular corporations.

IX. POSTAMENDMENT PROCEDURES

§5.156   A. Exchange of Certificates

When the articles are amended in a manner that changes the share distribution (*e.g.,* a two-for-one stock split; see §5.18), to the extent possible, the old share certificates should not be exchanged for new certificates. Instead, certificates representing additional shares should be distributed, leaving the old certificates outstanding. The old certificates generally may be replaced by any new form of stock certificate when they are submitted for transfer in the normal course. See, *e.g.,* New York Stock Exchange Listed Company Manual §501.07. The board of directors does have the power to call in the certificates for exchange. Corp C §422; see *Heller Inv. Co. v Southern Title & Trust Co.* (1936) 17 CA2d 202, 61 P2d 807. Such an exchange would be necessary in any event if the number of shares represented by each certificate is reduced, as in the case of a reverse stock split, or if the amendment requires changing any statement or legend on the certificates. See §5.114.

If an exchange of certificates does not occur, the board of directors may provide by resolution that each outstanding share certificate continues to represent the number of shares it represented before the amendment, and distribute additional share certificates. An alternative procedure is for the board to resolve that each outstanding share certificate shall be deemed to represent the changed shares, and that new certificates will be issued and exchanged as the old certificates are submitted for transfer in the normal course. The first alternative procedure is simpler, because under it, the paperwork is completed sooner after consummation of the transaction and avoids the confusion that can result if some shareholders do not receive notice of the amendment. Counsel should coordinate these procedures with the corporation's transfer agent, if any.

§5.157 B. Statements on New Certificates

New certificates issued in exchange for or in addition to existing certificates should bear any legend or statement that was necessary or advisable on the old certificates, unless the amendment necessitates altering the legends or statements on the old certificate, as well as any additional legends or statements made necessary or advisable by the amendment. A variety of such legends or statements may be necessary or desirable under provisions of federal law or the California Corporations Code. See, *e.g.,* Corp C §25103(f) (second sentence), Corp C §25017(f)(2), and 10 Cal Code Regs §260.103.5, which require the same legends with respect to promotional and other restrictions of the Commissioner of Corporations on presplit shares or prestock dividend shares to be placed on postsplit shares or poststock dividend shares. See also FINANCING CALIFORNIA BUSINESSES §§4.4–4.12 (Cal CEB 1976). Several examples of such statements that are required under Corp C §417 on occasion of an amendment that creates a two-class or series stock structure are set forth in §§5.158–5.159. Legends imposed under Corp C §25102(h) may not be removed by an exchange that would be exempt under Corp C §25102(f) and 10 Cal Code Regs §260.103. 11 Ops Cal Comm'r Corps 85/1C (1985).

§5.158 1. Sample Form: Summary Statement of Rights, Preferences, Privileges, and Restrictions

Form 5.158–1 (Statement Under Corp C §417(b))

As more fully described in the Certificate of Determination of Preferences and the Articles of Incorporation, shares of series [*e.g., A*] preferred stock are redeemable at [*e.g., ten cents*] per share plus accrued dividends, under certain specified

circumstances. **Holders of shares of preferred stock are entitled to elect** [*e.g., a majority*] **of the members of the board of directors. Each share of preferred stock is convertible into** [*e.g., one*] **share(s) of common stock until the** [*e.g., fifth*] **day before the redemption date declared by the corporation, and will be automatically converted (unless redeemed) into** [*e.g., one*] **share(s) of common stock on the effectiveness of a registration statement filed under the Securities Act of 1933 covering any securities of the corporation of an aggregate offering price of** [*e.g., $1,000,000*].

Comment: Any such statement would be derived from the terms of the instrument governing the rights, preferences, privileges, and restrictions of the stock represented by the certificate. An entire statement of rights under Corp C §417(a) is seldom feasible because of limited space on the stock certificate. The following additional sentence should be added when a blank stock provision exists in the articles (see §§5.26, 5.72), because Corp C §417(a) refers to classes "authorized to be issued."

[*Add, if appropriate*]

The articles of incorporation of the corporation authorize the board of directors to fix the dividend rights and rates, conversion, voting, and redemption rights, redemption prices, liquidation preferences, and number of shares constituting any unissued series of preferred stock.

§5.159   2. Form: Alternative Statement of Place Where Statement Can Be Obtained

Form 5.159–1 (Statement Under Corp C §417(c))

A statement of the rights, preferences, privileges, and restrictions granted to or imposed on each class or series authorized to be issued and on the holders of such class or series will be furnished without charge to any shareholder on request addressed to the secretary of the corporation at the corporation's principal office], [*or to the office of the transfer agent of the corporation*].

§5.160 3. Form: Statement on Face of Certificate When Statements on Reverse

If any of the statements in Forms 5.151–1 or 5.152–1 appear on the reverse of the certificate, Corp C §417 (by use of the term "on the certificate" (see Corp C §174)) requires that a statement appear on the face of the certificate referring to the statement on the reverse side. The statement on the face of the certificate may read as follows:

Form 5.160–1

See the reverse of this certificate for a [*statement/summary*] **of the rights, preferences, privileges, and restrictions of each** [*class/series*] **of shares.**

C. Fractional Shares

§5.161 1. Issuance of Fractional Shares

The corporation may issue fractional shares to shareholders entitled to them under the terms of the amendment. See discussion in §5.114. Fractional shares create bookkeeping difficulties when dividends are declared, the shareholders vote, or action is taken that requires determining the proportionate interests of shareholders. The corporation may avoid these difficulties by not issuing fractional shares, either on original issuance of whole shares or on transfer of shares. Corp C §407. See also California Legislature, *Report of the Assembly Select Committee on the Revision of the Corporations Code* p 65 (1975) (reprinted in Appendix A in 3 MARSH'S CALIFORNIA CORPORATION LAW 324 (2d ed)), which recites that the policy of former Corp C §1113 "permitting, but not requiring, a corporation to issue fractions of a share either originally or upon transfer is continued."

§5.162 2. Alternatives to Fractional Shares

If a corporation does not issue fractional shares, it must take one of three alternative courses of action: (1) Arrange for disposition of fractional interests by those entitled to them, (2) pay the fair value of the fractions as of the time when their holders' entitlement is determined, or (3) issue scrip or warrants (which may be in registered or bearer form) entitling the holder to receive a certificate for a full share on the surrender of the scrip or warrants aggregating a fall share. The scrip may be made subject to conditions, *e.g.,* a cutoff date by which the scrip must be exchanged for full shares or become void. Corp C §407.

These alternatives are subject to three provisos. First, in a merger or reorganization, fractions of a share may be disregarded or shares issuable in a merger may be rounded off to the nearest whole share when the fraction of a share that any person would otherwise be entitled to receive is less than half of 1 percent of the total shares that person is entitled to receive, if the merger or reorganization agreement so provides. The second proviso is that the second alternative (cash payments by the corporation) is not available if it would result in the cancellation of more than 10 percent of the outstanding shares in any class. Corp C §407. Third, there are equitable limitations. See §5.10.

Cash payment for the fractions is the simplest way to dispose of fractional shares, and is ordinarily the preferable alternative if the corporation has the necessary funds and meets the statutory requirements to effect what amounts to a purchase of the shares. See Corp C §§166, 500. If funds are not available, the statutory tests are not met, or the corporation does not wish to make the expenditure, the simpler of the remaining alternatives would ordinarily be to arrange for disposition of the fractional interests. All fractional interests ordinarily can be disposed of at one time with little difficulty. See §5.114 for forms of resolutions.

§5.163   3. Buy-Sell Order Form

One common method of disposing of fractional interests is the so called "buy-sell order form" technique that permits the shareholder to elect either (a) to purchase an additional fraction of a share sufficient to give the shareholder a whole share or (b) to sell the fraction to another shareholder or on the market. See Corp C §407. For form, see §5.165. Shareholders should receive adequate instructions with the buy-sell order form, including the advice that failure to make the election before a specified date will be construed as an election either to purchase or to sell. For form, see §5.164.

§5.164   4. Form: Instructions to Shareholders When Buy-Sell Form Used

This form of instructions assumes that the buy-sell order form is used to dispose of fractional shares arising from a three-for-one reverse stock split. These instructions assume an exchange of certificates, but if there is no exchange, the instructions can be modified appropriately.

Form 5.164–1 (Sample Instructions)

If the number of old shares surrendered by you is not evenly divisible by three, the number of new shares to which you would otherwise be entitled will result in a fraction. No fractional shares will be issued. However, if you would otherwise be entitled to a fraction of a share, you may elect on or before [*date*], either to (a) purchase the additional fractional share interest needed to make one whole share, or (b) sell the fractional share interest to which you are entitled. Such election must be indicated on the attached Letter of Transmittal at the time the certificates are surrendered for exchange. Each shareholder electing to purchase a fractional share interest will receive from the corporation's transfer agent, [*name of transfer agent*], a bill for the purchase and the brokerage commission. Each shareholder electing to sell a fractional share interest will receive a check for the proceeds less the brokerage commission.

Promptly after [*date*], [*name of transfer agent*] will sell, for the account of the holders of the shares, the number of full new shares equivalent to the sum of the aggregate of existing fractional share interests for which instructions have not been received. Thereafter, [*name of transfer agent*] will hold and will pay to such holders on surrender of their old shares the prorata proceeds of such sale.

Purchases and sales of fractional share interests for the accounts of shareholders will be effected as promptly as practicable after [*date*], on the basis of market prices on the [*e.g., New York Stock Exchange*] on the dates when the transactions are made. [*Name of transfer agent*] will offset buying and selling orders to the extent possible. Service charges and brokerage commissions in connection with such purchases or sales will be paid by the shareholders.

Comment: Purchases and sales of fractional shares will ordinarily be exempt from the registration provisions of the Securities Act of 1933 if the fractional shares result from a stock split, reverse stock split, conversion, merger, or similar transaction, and the appropriate notice is filed. See §5.155.

§5.165   5. Sample Form: Letter of Transmittal

Like the form of Instructions to Shareholders in §5.164, the following form assumes a three-for-one reverse stock split. It may be modified for use in other situations.

Form 5.165–1 (Sample Letter of Transmittal)

[*Address of corporation or transfer agent*]

Dear Sir or Madam:

Enclosed please find my stock certificate(s) numbered as follows:

representing _ _ _ _ _ _ shares of the [*e.g., common*] stock of [*name of corporation*]. I deliver these certificates to you for exchange in connection with the three-for-one reverse stock split.

**(Shareholder—strike the following paragraph
if the number of old shares surrendered
by you is evenly divisible by three)**

The number of old shares I am surrendering is not evenly divisible by three. As a result, I would ordinarily be entitled to receive fractional shares. Since no fractional shares are to be issued, I hereby elect to:

_____ (a) purchase the additional fractional share needed to make one whole share

OR

_____ (b) sell the fractional share interest to which I am entitled.

I understand that if I have elected to purchase, I will receive from the corporation's transfer agent a bill for the purchase

price and the brokerage commission, and that if I have elected to sell, I will receive a check for the proceeds less the brokerage commission.

_____

Signature

_____

Typed or printed name

_____

Date

6

Mergers and Acquisitions

Jerry W. Monroe

JERRY W. MONROE, A.B., 1959, Columbia University; J.D., 1966, University of Utah. Mr. Monroe, of the firm of Luce, Forward, Hamilton & Scripps, practices in San Diego.

The author wishes to express his appreciation for the invaluable assistance provided by his colleagues at Luce, Forward, Hamilton & Scripps who reviewed and edited those portions of this chapter which were outside his area of expertise.

§6.1   I. INTRODUCTION; SCOPE OF CHAPTER

The three basic methods of corporate acquisition or combination in California are through sales of stock, sales of assets, and mergers. These three methods are not interchangeable; each requires different procedures and has different effects.

This chapter begins with a brief summary of the fundamentals of mergers and acquisitions (§§6.2–6.57), including a review of the statutory framework and the use of terms (§6.2); a discussion of the three types of acquisitions and their variations (§§6.3–6.22); a discussion of "reorganizations" under the California Corporations Code (§§6.23–6.32); and an analysis of the stages of a merger or acquisition from the viewpoint of the lawyer advising a corporate client (§§6.29–6.57).

Next follows a treatment of the tax aspects of mergers and acquisitions, including a discussion of the three types of "reorganizations" as that term is used in the Internal Revenue Code (§§6.58–6); California income tax aspects (§6.75); and California real property taxes (§6.76).

Non-tax considerations when planning a merger or acquisition are discussed in §§6.77–6.113. Particular topics include compliance with state and federal securities law requirements (§§6.78–6.85); problems concerning transferability of assets (§§6.86–6.88); effect of the acquisition on third parties (§§6.89–6.94); antitrust considerations (§§6.95–6.104); employment problems (§§6.105–6.109); and environmental considerations (§§6.110–6.113).

The formalities of accomplishing a merger are discussed in §§6.114–6.147, including the merger agreement (§§6.114–6.118); required action by directors (§§6.119–6.123); required action by shareholders (§§6.124–6.129); dissenters' rights and procedures (§§6.130–6.142); and consummation of the merger (§§6.143–6.147).

The chapter concludes with discussions of foreign corporations (§6.148), and the "short-form" merger between a parent corporation and a subsidiary (§§6.149–6.153).

This chapter is not intended as an in-depth treatment of the various matters discussed herein, nor does it contain detailed forms of the agreement and auxiliary documents for complex mergers and acquisitions. For this type of coverage, references are made to more specialized treatments, in particular to DRAFTING AGREEMENTS FOR THE SALE OF BUSINESSES (2d ed Cal CEB 1988) short-cited as SALE

OF BUSINESSES, which contains detailed forms with comments and practice tips. See also Table of References at the end of this volume.

II. FUNDAMENTALS OF MERGERS AND ACQUISITIONS

§6.2   A. Statutory Framework

This chapter assumes that a California business lawyer has a basic understanding of the California General Corporation Law (Corp C §§100–2319). In dealing with mergers and acquisitions, the lawyer needs to be familiar with the Code chapters on mergers (Corp C §§1100–1112); reorganizations (Corp C §§1200–1203); and dissenters' rights (Corp C §§1300–1312), as well as pertinent definitions in Corp C §§100–195, particularly Corp C §181 ("reorganizations"). The attorney should also have a basic understanding of certain aspects of federal taxation of corporate organizations and reorganizations, as set forth in §§351–385 of the Internal Revenue Code of 1986, particularly sections 358, 362, 368, and 381–382.

A table of statutes is provided at the end of this volume.

§6.3   B. Types of Acquisitions; Reorganizations

There are three principal forms of business acquisitions: sales of stock, sales of assets, and mergers. The acquiring corporation is frequently referred to as the buyer or the surviving corporation. The acquired corporation may be referred to as the disappearing corporation, the "target," or the seller. Either of these parties may be either a parent or a subsidiary of another corporation.

Sales of Stock. In a sale of stock acquisition, the buyer does not deal at all with the "selling" corporation. Instead, the corporation itself is sold, and the consideration goes directly to its shareholders. The corporation continues to exist; the only change is that ownership of its stock passes from one shareholder or group of shareholders to another. See §§6.4–6.9.

Sales of Assets. In a sale of assets acquisition, the selling corporation may sell either all or a portion of its assets to the buyer. Similarly, all or a portion or even none of its liabilities may be assumed by the buyer. The consideration passes to the selling corporation, which continues to exist; its shareholders remain the same. See §§6.10–6.14.

Mergers. A merger can take place only if both the buyer and the seller are corporations. A merger combines the two entities in accordance with a statutory scheme. One corporation is said to merge into the other, with the former "disappearing" and the latter "surviving." The surviving corporation takes on both the assets and the liabilities of the disappearing corporation and continues to exist as a combination of the previously existing entities. See §§6.15–6.22.

Reorganizations. A "reorganization," under the California Corporations Code, is not actually a form of business acquisition. Rather, it is the term used to characterize an overlay of statutory requirements brought into play when shareholder rights are affected in certain ways. As defined in Corp C §181, the category includes mergers, "exchange reorganizations," and "sale-of-assets reorganizations." Under former law, there were differences in voting requirements, dissenters' rights, and other statutory requirements, depending on the form of acquisition selected (although the general effect on shareholders may have been essentially the same). The present law covering reorganizations (Corp C §§1200–1203) seeks to resolve inconsistencies and introduce greater protection for shareholders.

CAVEAT: The word "reorganization" is used both in the Corporations Code (see §§6.23–6.27) and in the Internal Revenue Code (see §§6.58–6.73). Although both refer to the same general type of transaction, one is not necessarily the same as the other. In any given case, the attorney should understand clearly which type of reorganization is under consideration.

§6.4   1. Sale of Stock

A sale of stock is the most straightforward of the three methods of acquisition, although its ease of execution will depend largely on the number of shareholders. Conceptually, it is essentially the same transaction as the purchase of shares in the open market. An individual or corporation negotiates for the purchase of shares directly with the shareholders. The board of directors does not become involved, and the corporation itself is not a party to the transaction. Consideration for the purchase is paid to the shareholders.

§6.5 a. Advantages and Disadvantages

The salient characteristic of a sale of stock is that the target corporation continues to exist and its assets remain intact. Nothing changes other than the ownership of the stock, and, unlike a merger, either a total or a partial ownership interest can be acquired. Since the target's corporate structure is not affected by the transaction, the business being acquired can be contained in a neat package that can easily operate, be accounted for, and stand on its own. This is a particularly desirable feature if limited liability is an important consideration, as when the business has a greater than usual likelihood of failure or the nature of the business involves high risks.

Occasionally, a business becomes available at a bargain basement price because of existing financial difficulties. Sometimes a seller will even give it away in return for the buyer's relieving the seller of certain guaranties or other personal liabilities. If the business is shaky enough to be sold on this basis, the buyer will probably not want to become individually liable for existing obligations other than those being assumed to protect the seller. The business being acquired may also involve significant risks in areas such as product liability or protection of the environment. Maintaining the corporate integrity of the business may help to cordon off such risks.

The principal strength of the stock acquisition is also one of its principal weaknesses. A partial interest in a business can be acquired by purchasing a single share, but it takes purchases from 100 percent of the shareholders to purchase 100 percent of the business. This should be contrasted with the other two acquisition methods, which ordinarily require only a majority shareholder approval in order to purchase the entire business. When the stock method is used, the buyer deals with the shareholders of the target corporation; in a merger or a purchase of assets the buyer negotiates with the target corporation itself, through its officers and directors. If there is only one shareholder, obviously this is not a problem at all. However, the more shareholders there are, the greater the problem becomes. Often a purchase of a majority of the stock is followed by a merger to buy out the minority who did not participate in the original purchase.

If the target is a publicly traded corporation, a general solicitation is required in compliance with the tender offer rules of the Securities and Exchange Commission.

b. Variations

§6.6   (1) Straight Sale of Stock

The seller transfers stock of the target to the buyer in return for money or other property. The buyer, becomes a shareholder of the target. The extent to which the ownership of the target changes depends on the number of shares purchased as compared with the total outstanding shares of the target.

Diagram 1: **STRAIGHT SALE OF STOCK**

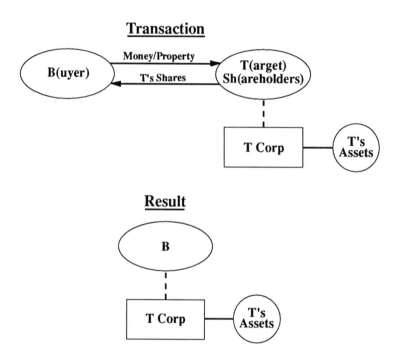

*In this group of diagrams (§§6.6–6.20), "B" refers to the buyer, "T" refers to the target corporation (seller), and "Sh" refers to shareholders (*e.g.,* B Sh means buyer's shareholders).

§6.7 (2) Corporate Buyer

If the buyer is a corporation, the target becomes the partially or wholly owned subsidiary of the buyer, depending on whether all or a portion of the outstanding shares of the target are sold.

Diagram 2: **STRAIGHT SALE OF STOCK - CORPORATE BUYER**

Transaction

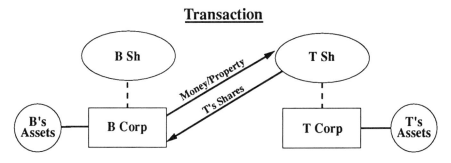

Result

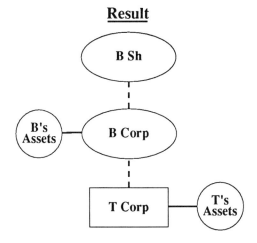

§6.8   (3) Shares for Shares

If the consideration for the shares of the target corporation consists of shares of the buyer, the target becomes the subsidiary of a corporate buyer and the shareholders of the target become shareholders of the buyer.

Diagram 3: **SALE OF STOCK, SHARES FOR SHARES**

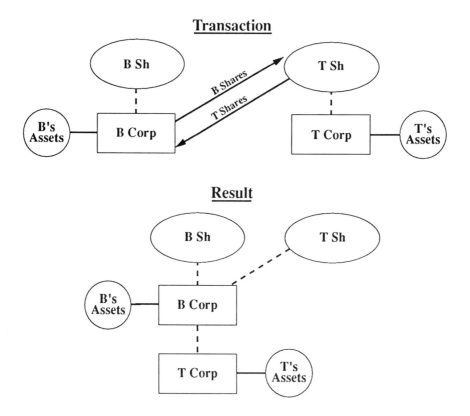

§6.9   c. Corporate Formalities in Sales of Stock

Not surprisingly, there are no corporate formalities on the part of the target in connection with an acquisition of a corporation by purchasing its stock. The reason is quite simple: The target corporation is not ordinarily involved in the transaction, which is merely a sale between the buyer corporation and the shareholders of the target. This remains true even if the transaction is a "reorganization" under Corp C §181 (see §§6.23–6.27), but in that event, board approval as well as shareholder approval may be necessary.

2. Sale of Assets

§6.10   a. Advantages and Disadvantages

The salient feature of a sale of assets is that it allows the buyer to acquire only a portion of the assets of a corporation and to assume a portion of its liabilities. In fact, when a corporation proposes to sell an unincorporated division of its business, a sale of assets is ordinarily the only method by which this can be accomplished.

This method is also very useful when a buyer is acquiring a troubled business that has a high risk of failure or has contingent liabilities. It allows the buyer to acquire only certain assets and to assume only certain liabilities. However, in California the purchaser of assets may incur liabilities if (1) there is an express or implied agreement to that effect, (2) the transaction really amounts to a merger or consolidation of the two corporations, (3) the purchasing corporation is a mere continuation of the seller, or (4) the transfer of assets is merely a fraudulent attempt to escape liability. *Ray v Alad Corp.* (1977) 19 C3d 22, 28, 136 CR 574, 578; *Lodestar Co. v County of Mono* (ED Cal 1986) 639 F Supp 1439, 1447. For an example of such successor liability, see *RRX Indus. v Lab-Con, Inc.* (9th Cir 1985) 772 F2d 543, 546.

NOTE: The acquisition agreement should state as precisely as possible which liabilities are actually being transferred—whether all, or none, or something in between. Whatever the understanding between the parties, it should be clearly stated in the acquisition agreement. Particular care must be given to describing the allocation of post-closing liabilities, *e.g.*, liabilities arising after the closing but related to the operation of the business before the closing.

Transfer of Assets Problems. In a merger, assets are transferred by operation of law, and in a sale of stock, the corporation itself (via the stock) is transferred rather than its assets. In a sale of assets, however, particular assets must be transferred by deed or bill of sale and in accordance with special regulations, *e.g.*, those pertaining to transfer of title to automobiles, airplanes, and boats. See §§6.86–6.87. If the Bulk Transfer law applies, there may be further requirements for filings, publication, and escrow, which, unless waived by the buyer, can cause additional expense and delay. For discussion of the Bulk Transfer law, see §6.91.

Effect on Existing Contracts. Perhaps the greatest problem with a sale of assets is the potential that the transfer will cause existing contractual rights to be lost or fall into default. Leases, vendor and purchaser contracts, loan agreements, and many other common business agreements frequently contain prohibitions against or conditions relating to assignment. Although problems in this regard may sometimes arise in other types of acquisitions, prohibitions against assignment do not ordinarily apply to a merger, which is a transfer by operation of law (see Corp C §1107), nor do they apply to a sale of stock, which does not make any assignments of contracts but merely changes the ownership of the corporate entity. In a sale of assets, however, contractual prohibitions against assignment can pose a real problem. Of course, consents to assignment can be sought, but even if the other parties to the contract are willing to consent to its assignment, there is still the process of obtaining the consents. This process can be troublesome, causing delays and inviting the person from whom a consent is solicited to seek terms that are more favorable than those in the existing contract.

b. Variations

§6.11 (1) Straight Sale of Assets

A sale of assets works basically the same way whether the seller is a corporation, a partnership, or an individual. The owner of the assets sells them to someone else.

Diagram 4: **STRAIGHT SALE OF ASSETS**

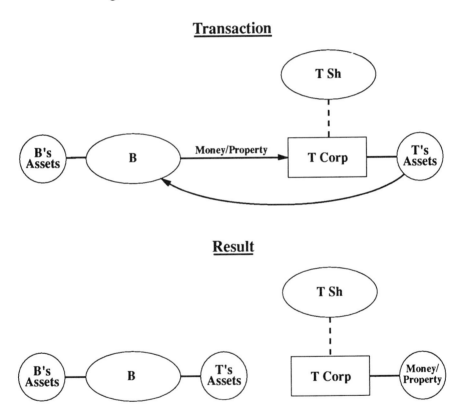

§6.12   (2) Corporate Buyer

The fact that the buyer is a corporation does not make any difference unless the transaction meets one of the tests of a reorganization under Corp C §181 (see §§6.23–6.28).

Diagram 5: **SALE OF ASSETS TO CORPORATE BUYER**

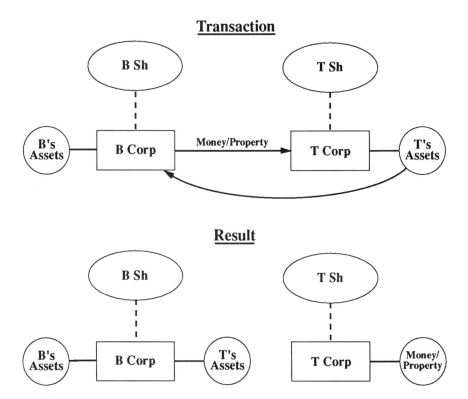

§6.13   (3) Shares for Assets

If shares of the buyer are issued, the target corporation becomes a shareholder of the buyer unless it distributes the stock to its shareholders or resells the stock (*i.e.,* if the buyer is publicly traded).

Diagram 6: **SALE OF ASSETS, SHARES FOR ASSETS**

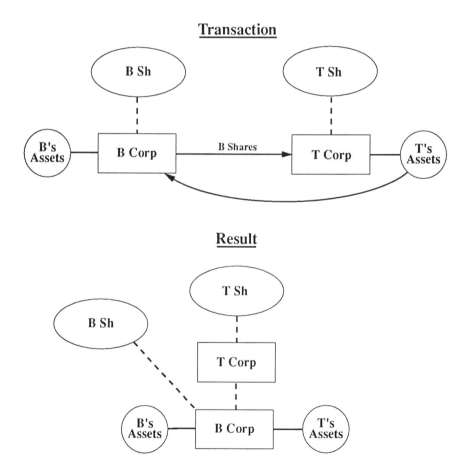

§6.14   c. Corporate Formalities in Sales of Assets

The consideration for purchase of the assets of a corporation can be money, property, or the securities of any other corporation, either domestic or foreign. Corp C §1001(c). If the transaction involves all or substantially all of the assets of the corporation, the principal terms must be approved by the board of directors of the selling corporation (Corp C §1001(a)(1)), and (unless the transaction is in the usual and regular course of business) by shareholders owning a majority of the outstanding shares of the selling corporation (Corp C §1001(a)(2)). However, if the buyer of the assets is in control of or under common control with the seller, approval is required by 90 percent of the voting power of the shareholders of the seller (unless the consideration for the sale is the unredeemable common shares of a corporate buyer or of its parent). Corp C §1001(d).

§6.15   3. Merger

A statutory merger can take place only between corporations, of which there may be two or more. Corp C §1100. A merger extinguishes the separate existence of the disappearing corporation, and the surviving corporation succeeds, without other transfer, to all the rights, property, debts, and liabilities of the disappearing corporation. Corp C §1107(a).

§6.16   a. Advantages and Disadvantages

A merger, which combines corporate entities merely by filing a document with the Secretary of State, has the advantage of simplicity as compared with other methods of acquisition. The transfer of assets and liabilities occurs by operation of law, as does the transfer of contractual rights and obligations. This reduces transfer documentation to a minimum. (It may be desirable, however, to make certain record changes just in order to avoid future name confusion. Examples of record changes are interests in real property (see Corp C §1109) and titles to automobiles, boats, and airplanes.)

A merger may avoid problems that could arise in other types of acquisitions if there are important contractual relationships to be preserved or if a transfer might accelerate some of the target's obligations. Although California law favors the assignability of contracts, it is clear that a contractual provision precluding assignment can create a default or trigger other undesirable results. A merger frequently circumvents such provisions (although a particular contract may have been drafted to include merger as an event of default; see §6.87).

However, a merger is an all-or-nothing proposition. Unlike a sale of assets or stock, a merger *necessarily* results in the purchase of a 100 percent interest in the entire business, including all its assets and all its liabilities. There is no way to buy only a partial interest or to take only certain assets or certain liabilities. As a result of this simplicity, in a merger, the buyer automatically becomes subject to the liabilities of the target. Although a decision to assume *known* liabilities is ordinarily a matter of business judgment and risk evaluation, in a merger, the *unknown* liabilities are assumed along with the known.

NOTE: This problem is often addressed by using a triangular merger (see §§6.19–6.20). Rather than merging directly with the target, the buyer corporation forms a subsidiary and the target is merged into it. Thus, the target's liabilities are maintained in a separate corporation, and the buyer enjoys the same insulation from unknown liabilities that might have been accomplished by a stock purchase.

b. Variations

§6.17   (1) Straight Merger

In a straight merger, the target is merged into the buyer, and target's shareholders receive the agreed consideration, which may be cash, property, or shares of the buyer. If the consideration is shares of the buyer, the target's shareholders become shareholders of the buyer along with its existing shareholders.

Diagram 7: **STRAIGHT MERGER**

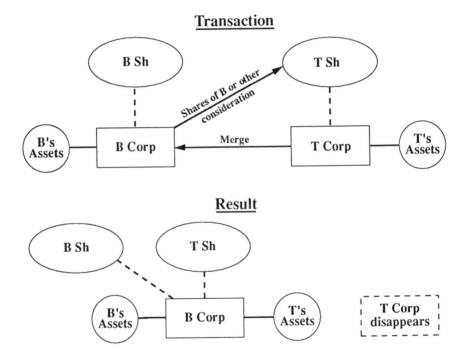

§6.18   (2) Reverse Merger

A reverse merger is like a straight merger (see §6.17), except that the buyer is merged into the target. The buyer shareholders exchange their shares for shares of the target (or their shares are deemed to be automatically converted into shares of the target). Usually, the shareholders of the target exchange their shares for other consideration, leaving the buyer shareholders as the sole owners of the target.

Diagram 8: **REVERSE MERGER**

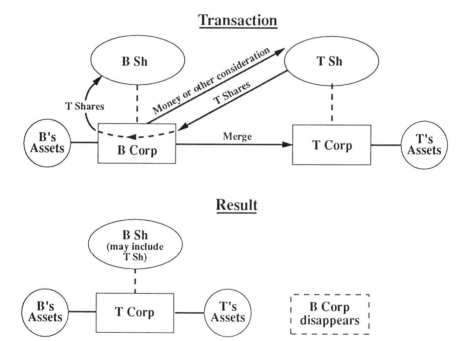

§6.19   (3) Triangular Merger

As the name suggests, a triangular merger involves three corporations. They are usually the target, the buyer ("parent"), and the buyer's subsidiary (often created expressly for this transaction). The target is merged into the buyer's subsidiary, and the target's shareholders exchange their shares for shares or other securities of the parent. Thus, the parent corporation becomes the sole shareholder of the merged subsidiary and target corporations, and the target's former shareholders become shareholders of the parent.

Diagram 9: **TRIANGULAR MERGER**

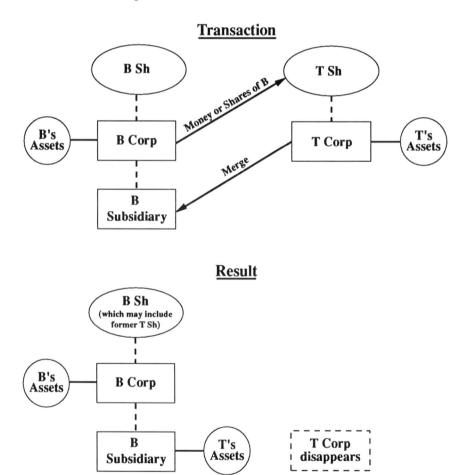

Transaction

Result

§6.20 (4) Reverse Triangular Merger

A reverse triangular merger is like a triangular merger (see §6.19), except that the buyer's subsidiary is merged into the target rather than vice versa. Target's shareholders are issued shares or other securities of the parent, and the parent becomes the sole shareholder of the target corporation. The end result is the same as in a straight triangular merger, except that the name and structure of the target survive, rather than those of the buyer's subsidiary.

Diagram 10: **REVERSE TRIANGULAR MERGER**

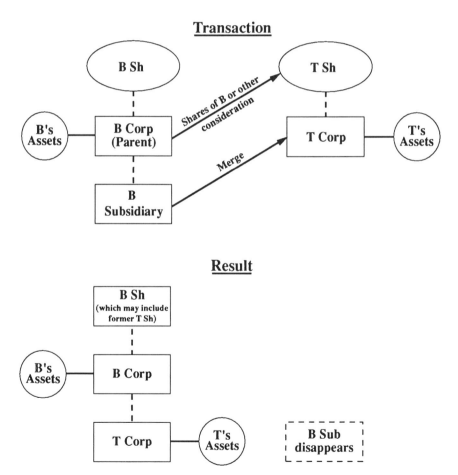

§6.21   (5) Upstream and Downstream Mergers

"Upstream" and "downstream" mergers involve only a parent corporation and its subsidiary. If the subsidiary is merged into the parent it is an upstream merger; if the parent is merged into a subsidiary it is a downstream merger.

If the parent owns 90 percent or more of each class of the subsidiary's shares, upstream mergers can be handled as "short form" mergers under Corp C §1110, thus dispensing with many of the standard merger formalities. See §§6.149–6.153. Upstream and downstream mergers are normally used as a means of restructuring within a corporate hierarchy rather than as a means of acquisition. However, they are sometimes used as one of the steps of an acquisition, or they may be used to freeze out minority shareholders. In an upstream merger, the shares of the subsidiary are simply extinguished. In a downstream merger, the parent's shares are exchanged for shares of the target/subsidiary.

§6.22   c. Corporate Formalities in Mergers

Effectuating a Merger. Two or more corporations can be combined into a single entity by filing an agreement of merger with the Secretary of State, accompanied by officers' certificates of each of the constituent corporations, attesting to the appropriate approval of the merger by the corporation's by board and shareholders. Corp C §1103. See §§6.143, 6.146. Tax clearance is required before a Certificate of Merger will be issued, and this often takes some time. See §§6.144–6.145. Since a merger is by definition a reorganization (see Corp C §181(a)), the agreement of merger must be approved by the board of each constituent corporation, and the principal terms of the agreement must ordinarily be approved by the shareholders. Corp C §§1101, 1103, 1200–1201. Unless its principal terms are altered, the agreement of merger can be amended by action of the board without further shareholder action. Corp C §1104. Similarly, the merger can be abandoned by action of the board alone. Corp C §1105. Consideration to be paid to the shareholders of the disappearing corporation can be cash, property, rights, or securities. Corp C §1101 (last paragraph).

Protection of Minority Shareholders. Certain protections are built into the Corporations Code in order to preclude the majority shareholders from freezing out a minority. See §§6.130–6.142.

NOTE: In a short-form merger (see §§6.149–6.153), if the minority of the disappearing corporation holds no more than 10 percent of its outstanding shares, then, subject to dissenters' rights of appraisal, they can be required to exchange their shares for other consideration. Corp C §1110(b). However, if any constituent corporation owns more than 50 percent of the voting power of any other constituent corporation, holders of common shares of the disappearing corporation can receive only common shares of the surviving corporation, unless there is unanimous approval of a contrary plan. See Corp C §1101 (last paragraph).

4. Reorganizations (Corp C §181)

§6.23   a. Definition; Types of Reorganizations

Chapter 12 of the Corporations Code (Corp C §§1200–1203), entitled "Reorganizations," applies to some but not all acquisitions. All California mergers except short-form mergers (Corp C §1110; see §§6.149–6.153) are reorganizations ("merger reorganizations"). Corp C §181(a). For non-merger acquisitions, the principal factor is whether the target's shareholders will receive securities of the buyer. If a corporation exchanges its equity securities (shares) for shares of another corporation, the transaction is an "exchange reorganization." Corp C §181(b). A sale of all or substantially all of a corporation's assets is a "sale-of-assets reorganization" if the consideration, in whole or in part, is either (a) equity securities of the buyer or its parent, or (b) debt securities of the buyer or its parent which are not adequately secured and have a maturity date more than five years after the acquisition. Corp C §181(c).

§6.24   b. Special Requirements for Reorganizations

If an acquisition is deemed a reorganization under Corp C §181, an overlying network of statutory requirements must be dealt with. These requirements are described in §§6.25–6.28.

§6.25   (1) Board Approval of the Transaction

Corporations Code §1200 requires that the transaction be approved by the boards of the following:

(1) Each constituent corporation in a merger reorganization;

(2) The acquiring corporation in an exchange reorganization;

(3) The acquiring corporation and the corporation whose property and assets are acquired in a sale of assets reorganization; and

(4) The corporation in control of any constituent or acquiring corporation referred to above if its securities are issued or transferred in the reorganization.

See discussion and forms in §§6.119–6.120.

§6.26   (2) Shareholder Approval

General Rule. If board approval of the acquisition is required, the principal terms of the acquisition generally must be approved by a majority of the outstanding shares entitled to vote. See Corp C §§1201(a), 152.

Exception to General Rule. There is an exception for any corporation if it or its shareholders, immediately before the reorganization, will own (immediately after the reorganization) equity securities with more than five sixths of the voting power of the surviving or acquiring corporation or parent party. Corp C §1201(b). Thus, an acquiring corporation or its parent need not obtain shareholder approval if it parts with no more that one sixth of its voting shares in the course of the reorganization. Arithmetically, the buyer can issue additional shares equal to 20 percent of its outstanding shares before it drops below the five-sixths test.

Exceptions to the Exception. There are two exceptions to the exception. First, a reorganization must be approved by the outstanding shares of the surviving corporation if any amendment is made to its articles which would otherwise require such approval. Corp C §1201(c). Second, a merger or sale of assets reorganization must be approved by the outstanding shares of any class of any party corporation if holders of that class receive shares of the surviving or acquiring corporation or parent party having different rights, preferences, privileges, or restrictions than the shares surrendered. Corp C §1201(d). Shares of foreign corporations received in exchange for shares of a domestic corporation have different rights, preferences, privileges, and restrictions within the meaning of this provision. Corp C §1201(d).

See discussion and forms in §§6.124–6.129.

§6.27 (3) Dissenters' Rights of Appraisal

Shareholders whose vote is required for approval of a reorganization have the right to dissent and call for cash payment of the fair market value of their shares. Corp C §1300. This is their sole remedy; they are specifically precluded from attacking the validity of the reorganization or seeking to have it set aside or rescinded. Corp C §1312. See *Steinberg v Amplica, Inc.* (1986) 42 C3d 1198, 233 CR 249.

See discussion and forms in §§6.130–6.142.

§6.28 c. Reorganizations Involving Management Buy-Outs

Corporations Code §1203 was enacted in 1987 and amended in 1988 to provide protection to the shareholders in "management buyout" (MBO) situation. If the purchaser in a corporate reorganization is actively involved in the corporation's management, the potential for abuse is clear. Management has superior knowledge concerning the intrinsic value of the corporation and controls the mechanisms of communication with the shareholders. Because of these and other factors, MBOs have sometimes resulted in short term profits for management at the expense of shareholders.

If a party either directly or indirectly controls a corporation or is involved in its management and proposes to acquire the corporation by a reorganization, Corp C §1203 has several requirements: There must be a report by an independent appraiser that the offer is just and reasonable as to the shareholders. Corp C §1203(a). If, while the management proposal is pending, any competing proposal is made by other persons, that proposal must be transmitted by the corporation to its shareholders along with any documents provided by the offeror. Corp C §1203(b)(1). If the later competing offer requires a vote of shareholders, the shareholders must be given at least ten days to consider the later offer and withdraw any vote, consent, or proxy given on the initial proposal, or at least ten days to withdraw any tendered shares. Corp C §1203(b)(2). Although management is not prohibited from amending its offer in light of any later offer, if it does so, the requirements of Corp C §1203 would apparently apply anew.

Section 1203 is too new to have been interpreted by the courts. The 1988 amendment cleared up many ambiguities in the 1987 version, but, inevitably, more will be discovered as the section is applied and interpreted in the courts.

C. Stages of a Merger or Acquisition

§6.29 1. Role of Counsel in the Various Stages

It is important for counsel advising a party to an acquisition to understand that the client's perspective will be much different from an attorney's. As a business person, the client's perspective focuses on such things as purchase price, labor considerations, key employees, and the financing of the transaction. A business person may initially consider few of the matters with which counsel is particularly concerned, sometimes even postponing the "due diligence" investigation until negotiations are in full swing. The business person tends to look beyond the acquisition to the future operation, but in so doing may overlook details that could be of major consequence to the future success of the business.

Counsel's ultimate goal may be the successful closing of the acquisition, but the client may view the acquisition as merely a bothersome obstacle that needs to be cleared as quickly as possible so that the business operation can get started. The lawyer must understand and respect the client's motivation to complete the acquisition as soon as possible and to get on with running the business.

For further discussion, see SALE OF BUSINESSES §§1.1–1.8 (2d ed CEB 1988).

§6.30 2. The Decision To Combine

Frequently, the attorney is not actively involved in arriving at the initial decision to buy, sell, or combine with another corporation. It is to be hoped, however, that counsel will be consulted in the early stages of the transaction, because numerous factors that are not readily apparent to the average business person could cause delay or even business disaster.

Whether consulted early or late in the process, and whether representing the buyer or the seller in the transaction, counsel should understand from the outset the client's principal motives for entering into the transaction. A buyer may be seeking, *e.g.,* to expand or diversify an existing business, or to make better use of liquid funds, or perhaps merely to take advantage of a good opportunity. Some buyers may also be looking for a business through which to earn a living or supply a job for a family member. A seller may be motivated by a desire to decrease the size of an existing business or to spin off an unprofitable or unrelated division. Some sellers may be in need of cash or may even be forced to sell. The point to recognize is that the motivation for buying or selling a business comes in all shapes and sizes, and that overt, covert, or ulterior motives can play an important role in determining questions like purchase price, timing, and terms. Counsel must understand the client's motives in order to guide the client into the most favorable negotiating position.

Counsel must also differentiate as clearly as possible between legal advice, business advice, and specialized knowledge (*e.g.,* labor, toxic waste matters), and must know *and communicate* the limits of his or her expertise. See SALE OF BUSINESSES §1.8 (2d ed CEB 1988).

3. The Initial Evaluation

§6.31   a. A New Area: Does It "Fit"?

The annals of financial disaster are replete with examples of ambitious executives who have ventured into new areas of business without fully understanding the importance of asking whether the new business "fits." Successful businesses can suddenly become unsuccessful when they branch into a new location, market, technical field, or area in which they have little or no experience. Counsel will obviously not be much help in this aspect of the evaluation, except to anticipate and ferret out regulatory roadblocks and areas with significant potential for liability. For instance, ladies' ready-to-wear may sound like a safe and uncomplicated business, but if the business is located on real property formerly occupied by a gas station, or if it imports its clothes from the far east and sells them by mail-order catalogue, there may be more regulatory surprises than the client's pocketbook can tolerate. Counsel should be alert to point out the pitfalls of heavy regulation, the consequences of being unable to obtain insurance in a business with product liability exposure, and the myriad of other legal ramifications of entering into new business areas.

§6.32 b. Purchase Price

Counsel should have a basic grasp of the process by which a business is valued. Although the client and advisors (*e.g.,* accountants, appraisers, investment bankers) are likely to have far more to do with the valuation process than counsel, counsel should understand the valuation dialogue and be able to recognize a clearly incorrect appraisal.

"Fair market value" is usually defined as the price at which a given thing will change hands in an open market where neither buyer nor seller is under any compulsion to trade. In the practical world, however, motivation of the parties and particular circumstances and market conditions will influence the price. A buyer who has ready cash and is merely following up an opportunity obviously has a distinct advantage over a seller whose lines of credit have run out and who is near the point of going out of business.

Apart from the motivation and particular circumstances of the parties, there are accepted standards for arriving at the valuation of a business entity. The valuation methods described in §§6.33–6.37 are commonly used in the purchase and sale of businesses. They are presented here in a rudimentary form that may be sufficient for attorneys who will have no more than a passing involvement in the process. For fuller discussion, see Desmond & Kelly, Business Valuation Handbook (rev ed 1988); Pratt, Valuing Small Businesses and Professional Practices (1986); Schnepper, The Professional Handbook of Business Valuation (1982).

§6.33 (1) Earnings

Anticipated Income. In the long run, the real value of a going business is its ability to generate income. This is true whether a business is to be operated, sold, or held for future sale. However, the present income of a business must always be weighed against both the potential that anticipated future income may not be realized and the risk that all or a portion of the investment might be lost.

Price/Earnings Ratio. In evaluating a business, there are often intangible factors that must be taken into consideration. An example is the innate appeal of the type of business in the minds of potential investors or buyers. Regardless of income, a biotechnology company is more likely to bring a good price than a company that manufactures broom handles. (The same concept seems to apply to shiny red cars as contrasted with dull brown cars.) The volatility of a business and its stage of maturity are other examples. For whatever reason, different types of businesses seem to bring different prices relative to their respective profitability. This is an important concept and is commonly expressed as a price/earnings or "PE" ratio for a particular type of business. We can establish a ratio between the earnings of a company and the price its stock sells for or, more commonly, brings on the open market. From this data we can obtain a "multiplier" to use when comparing this company with similar businesses.

Return on Investment. We can also calculate "return on investment," which is the percentage of a given investment returned to the investor in the form of income. For instance, if a business with annual earnings of $500,000 sells for $2 million, it has a return on investment of 25 percent ($500,000 ÷ $2,000,000), or a multiplier of four ($2,000,000 ÷ $500,000). Using this multiplier to evaluate a similar business whose earnings are $600,000, we arrive at an anticipated price of $2.4 million (4 x $600,000). This is sometimes called "capitalizing" earnings. Similarly, a buyer who is looking for an investment that will return at least 25 percent cannot pay more than $2.4 million for a business with anticipated earnings of only $600,000 ($600,000 ÷ 0.25).

NOTE: The above description does not take into account the effect of debt in a purchase but assumes that the purchase price is all cash from the buyer's pocket.

§6.34 (2) Liquidation Value

If a business has relatively little income compared with the value of its assets, an assets appraisal is likely to be the more accurate test of value. The value of assets, of course, can be what they would bring if sold item by item in the ordinary course of business. It can also be the price they would bring if sold all at the same time. The liquidation value, however, is what they would bring if they were sold under circumstances that called for their immediate disposal, *e.g.,* if the business failed and all its assets had to be sold in bankruptcy. This, presumably, is the buyer's ultimate risk and the lowest price at which a seller could be expected to sell.

§6.35   (3) Book Value

Many businesses are sold strictly by book value according to the target company's latest balance sheet. This approach, whether using audited or unaudited financial statements, does not necessarily generate a value that is consistent with either an earnings evaluation or an assets evaluation. This is because of a general conservative attitude in the application of "generally accepted accounting principles," and also because of a relatively great margin for accounting errors in certain types of businesses. Accountants record assets at either depreciated purchase price or market value, whichever is lower. Consequently, balance sheet value is quite likely to be undervalued if the company's assets include property or heavy machinery that may be obsolescent. On the other hand, assets that include high-tech inventory or high-fashion garments are likely to be overvalued.

Accountants have wide latitude in determining whether or not a company is required to reduce the value of goods to market value. One can easily imagine the rapidity with which certain types of inventory could become obsolescent and the difficulty of determining when that takes place. Nevertheless, book value is a popular method of price determination. This may be because it is simple, obvious, and unlikely to produce a hard-fought negotiation.

§6.36   (4) Comparables

Valuation experts frequently attempt to compare the target company with the established value of other companies. This approach is an interesting and sometimes valuable check but can rarely stand on its own. It is better for valuing real estate than businesses, because it is much easier to find similar pieces of real property than it is to find truly comparable businesses. Although there may be businesses similar to that of the target company, it is unlikely that they will be the same size, operate in the same locality, or have the same executive staff and other similarities essential for making a close comparison. It is even more unlikely that there will have been a recent sale of a comparable company and that the price and terms of sale will be available.

Nevertheless, it is important to make a comparison, and an appraiser's report will almost invariably include a list of comparable companies. Usually these will be companies whose per-share stock price is readily available because it is listed on a national exchange or traded in the over-the-counter market. The stock price can then be multiplied by the number of shares outstanding to arrive at the theoretical value of the company. The appraiser will then make numerous adjustments that will attempt to correct for differences. Even more importantly, the profit/earnings ratio (see §6.33) of comparable companies can be used to establish a comparative multiplier for application of the earnings test.

§6.37 (5) Other Methods

There are numerous other methods of valuation, some of which are variations and refinements of the foregoing. For the most part, however, a basic understanding of the approaches described above will be sufficient for dealing with valuation questions with which counsel might be expected to become involved.

§6.38 c. Financing the Transaction

Many acquisitions do not require that the full purchase price be paid in cash at the closing; frequently some other arrangement better suits the buyer, the seller, or both.

Buyer's Point of View. Buyers generally seek to leverage their cash, often by borrowing from third parties, *e.g.,* banks or other financial institutions or private sources of cash. (For large amounts, a buyer might try insurance companies, pension funds, or foreign capital.) Sometimes the buyer can borrow part or all of the purchase price from the seller. This can be done in as simple a manner as giving the seller a promissory note for all or a portion of the purchase price, or it can take a more complex form, *e.g.,* an issuance of securities from the purchasing company or even the target company. The securities might be common stock, preferred stock, or debentures, and the deal might even call for options or warrants.

Seller's Point of View. Although the seller may prefer cash because it is the most secure form of consideration, an all-cash payment has drawbacks. Generally, the tax on cash consideration is difficult for the seller to defer. Furthermore, a seller who offers terms can usually negotiate a better price, and may also obtain a higher interest rate on the capital investment than would be available from other sources. Securities in the buyer's company may also represent a potential for future growth, and the seller may even be able to negotiate some down-side protection. For instance, an issuance of preferred stock could be tied to the value of common stock but would be redeemable at a given price; or the company could issue a debt security that would be convertible into common stock at the instance of the seller.

The "Earn-Out." A variation that is popular with both buyers and sellers is an "earn-out," under which the seller may become entitled to additional cash or shares if the target company meets certain earnings goals. This can seem like a bonus to a seller, and it can be a hedge for a buyer. If the target performs well, the buyer may not mind sharing the wealth. If it does not, then perhaps enough consideration was paid on the front end. The difficulty in the earn-out is developing an earnings formula that will be satisfactory to both buyer and seller. Another problem is describing the extent to which the seller will be involved with the target in producing the earnings. Earn-outs are always difficult to define well, and often lead to disputes later.

§6.39   d. Key Employees

The importance of the target company's management team as a factor in negotiating an acquisition depends on the extent to which the buyer intends to become involved in operations after the closing. Management may not be a factor at all in a small company that is being purchased for the buyer or buyer's family to operate. On the other hand, it may be extremely important to a buyer who intends to stay out of management or has relatively little knowledge about the particular business.

In almost any case, however, there will be key employees who must be retained, at least during the start-up period. Key employees may be in management, or they may be technical people, artists, professionals, salespersons, scientists, or even the CEO's secretary, who knows where all the skeletons are closeted. Counsel will probably be asked to prepare employment contracts ensuring, to the extent possible, that these important employees will remain with the company.

Counsel should explain to the client in the clearest terms that no contract will ensure these employees' continued value to the company or even their continued retention. Keeping key employees on the job means keeping them happy, and this is a task that will transcend even the most tightly drafted contract. The buyer will not be able to ensure that key employees stay with the company, no matter what the contracts say. This is important to keep in mind, particularly if the value of the target consists largely of its key employees. Probably most buyers already understand this, but it bears repeating nevertheless. Furthermore, when a key employee falls out of grace, buyers tend to look to the contract for a way to cure the problem, but the contract rarely contains the ideal solution. Even the least sophisticated of key employees will rarely sign a contract that allows termination at will or even a contract containing language sufficient to allow termination when performance is not at the level desired by the buyer.

For problems related to employee contracts, see §§6.105–6.109.

4. Accounting Decisions

§6.40   a. Determining the Accounting Method

In the planning process, it is always important and sometimes critical to gain an early understanding of how an acquisition will be presented in the financial statements of the buyer or continuing entity.

The method of accounting may be a key factor in the buyer's ultimate decision to proceed, since financial presentation is an important element in any corporate financing, either debt or equity. This subject should be discussed at an early stage with the buyer's independent public accountants, because the accounting treatment will have to meet with their approval. If the Securities and Exchange Commission has jurisdiction over the accounting treatment, or if there is a reasonable possibility of such jurisdiction in the future (*e.g.*, if there may be a public sale of securities), the buyer should obtain an opinion from its certified public accountants as to whether the desired accounting treatment will be accepted by the SEC.

The method used to account for an acquisition can make a great deal of difference in the financial statements of the combined corporation. In fact, accounting treatment can be determinative of the acquisition method and it can even dictate whether or not the target is an appropriate acquisition candidate.

§6.41   (1) Types of Accounting Methods

Business acquisitions are accounted for either by the "purchase" method or the pooling of interests ("pooling") method. (Note that accounting treatment does not necessarily correspond to tax treatment, and must be analyzed separately.) The method used is extremely important because of the differences in treatment of significant matters, including the amounts used to record assets, the impact on the buyer's net income, and the carryover of surpluses or deficits.

Under current accounting guidelines, business combinations may be accounted for as poolings of interest only if certain specified criteria are met. See §6.43. These criteria can often be quite difficult to meet given the varied interests and complexity of many business deals. Business combinations that do not meet all of the specified criteria for poolings are accounted for as purchases.

Purchase Method. The purchase method of accounting treats a business combination as the buyer's acquisition of the target's assets and assumption of its liabilities. The buyer records the total assets and liabilities of the acquired corporation at cost and allocates cost to individual assets and liabilities on the basis of fair value; the buyer's income will include income from the target's operations earned after the acquisition. All identifiable assets acquired, either individually or by type, and liabilities assumed, whether or not shown in the financial statements of the acquired enterprise, are assigned a portion of the cost of the acquired enterprise, normally equal to their fair values at date of acquisition. Independent appraisals are often used as an aid in determining the fair values of some assets and liabilities. The excess of the cost of the acquired enterprise over the sum of the amounts assigned to identifiable assets acquired less liabilities assumed is recorded as goodwill.

Goodwill is not depreciable for tax purposes, but for accounting purposes is written off against future earnings over a period of years. Neither historical earnings nor retained earnings of the target are presented in the financial statements of the acquiror in a purchase transaction, and the same is true of losses and deficits.

Pooling Method. If an acquisition meets pooling of interests criteria (see §6.43), the respective financial statements of the combined companies are blended, somewhat as though their operations had been combined from their inception. The recorded assets and liabilities of the separate enterprises become the recorded assets and liabilities of the combined enterprise. The earnings (or loss) of the target for the year of the acquisition are taken into the earnings of the buyer, and retained earnings and surpluses are added to the buyer's corresponding accounts. Financial statements and financial information of the separate enterprises presented for years prior to the combination are restated on a combined basis. Most importantly (and perhaps best of all), no goodwill is created.

Under the pooling method, the buyer records the target's assets at the amounts previously carried by the acquired company (instead of at fair value, as would be done in a purchase); and income of the combined corporation includes income of the target for all fiscal periods presented, even those predating the acquisition.

§6.42 (2) Chart: Purchase and Pooling Compared

The following chart summarizes the principal differences between the two methods of accounting:

Purchase	*Pooling*
(a) Goodwill created if price exceeds values that can be assigned to assets. Goodwill must be written off against earnings over a period not exceeding 40 years (Accounting Principles Board Opinion No. 17 (1970)), but is not deductible for tax purposes. Special rules are applicable when the purchase price is less than the fair value of the assets acquired.	No goodwill created.
(b) New basis acquired for all assets (even if old tax basis carried forward).	Continue to use old basis for all assets (even if new tax basis created).

(c) Undervalued assets must be written up to fair values.	No writeups.
(d) Overvalued assets must be written down to fair values (particularly useful for slow-moving or obsolete inventories).	No writedowns as part of transaction unless otherwise done under good accounting practice. Concurrent writedowns are possible, but with the same effect on earnings as if the assets were in the acquiring company.
(e) Retained earnings not carried over.	Retained earnings and paid-in surplus are added to corresponding accounts of acquired company.
(f) Deficit in retained earnings not carried over.	Deficit in retained earnings must be carried over to reduce total retained earnings of the combined companies.
(g) Earnings or losses of the acquired company for periods before acquisition date are not combined with those of the acquiring company.	Earnings or losses of the acquired company must be reported as part of acquiring company's earnings; preacquisition earnings or losses must be "pooled back" and reported for the preacquisition periods.
(h) Retained earnings available for dividends under state law and under indentures and loan agreements are not increased.	Retained earnings available for dividends under state law and under indentures and loan agreements usually (but not always) are increased by retained earnings of acquired company.

§6.43   (3) Criteria for Pooling Treatment

The Corporations Code requires that accounting statements of corporations must be prepared in conformity with generally accepted accounting principles. Corp C §114. The accounting treatment to be used in a particular transaction is determined primarily by pronouncements of the Financial Accounting Standards Board, the Accounting Principles Board of the American Institute of Certified Public Accountants (AICPA), and, with respect to public companies, by the Securities and Exchange Commission. (The requirements set forth in SEC accounting releases and interpretations should be considered not only for corporations that are already publicly traded but also for those that are likely to become subject to SEC requirements in the future.) The corporation's accountants should be satisfied that the transaction as structured will meet the parties' accounting objectives. It is usually desirable to obtain a written opinion from the corporation's certified public accountants concerning the accounting treatment of a business combination.

Accounting Principles Board Opinion No. 16 (1970) sets forth and discusses in detail the tests for determining whether a transaction should be accounted for as a purchase or as a pooling of interests. In effect, this opinion provides that all of the 12 criteria listed below must be met in order to treat a transaction as a pooling of interests; if any of them is not met, the transaction should be treated as a purchase. These criteria are subject to numerous interpretations by the AICPA and the SEC, and should be treated as general guidelines only.

(1) Each combining corporation must be autonomous and cannot have been a subsidiary or division of another corporation within two years before the plan of combination is initiated.

(2) Each of the combining corporations must be independent of the other combining corporations.

(3) The combination must be effected in a single transaction or completed in accordance with a specific plan within one year after the plan is initiated.

(4) The buyer can issue only common stock with rights identical to those of the majority of its outstanding voting common stock, in exchange for substantially all (at least 90 percent) of the voting stock interest of the target.

(5) Each individual common shareholder who exchanges shares must receive a voting common stock interest exactly in proportion to the shareholder's relative voting interest before the combination.

(6) The voting rights of shareholders in the combined corporation cannot be restricted.

(7) Each of the combining corporations must maintain substantially the same voting common stock interest with no exchanges, retirements, or distributions in contemplation of the combination.

(8) Each of the combining corporations may reacquire shares

of voting common stock only for purposes other than business combinations, and may reacquire no more than a normal number of shares between the date the plan of combination is initiated and the date of consummation.

(9) The combined corporation cannot agree to issue contingent or escrowed shares or to distribute other considerations at a later date to the former shareholders of a combining corporation. (This requirement virtually eliminates pooling of interest accounting treatment for "earn-outs," in which shares are to be issued later on the basis of the company's earnings over a specified period.)

(10) The combined corporation cannot agree to retire or reacquire any part of the common stock issued to effect the combination.

(11) The combined corporation cannot make special financial arrangements for the benefit of the former shareholders of a combining corporation.

(12) The combined corporation should not intend or plan to dispose of a significant part of its assets within two years after the combination, except in the ordinary course of business or to eliminate duplicate facilities or excess capacity.

NOTE: In the Financial Accounting Standards Board Technical Bulletin issued January 3, 1986, 18 SEC Reg & L Rep 55 (BNA), the board stated that an exchange of stock between two subsidiaries of a common parent, one or both of which are partially owned, that involves stock of minority shareholders, should be accounted for by the purchase method based on fair value. However, if the exchange "lacks substance," it is not a purchase and should be accounted for based on existing carrying amounts. The board further stated that a "downstream merger" (wherein a partially owned subsidiary exchanges its common stock for outstanding voting stock of the parent; see §6.21) cannot be accounted for as a pooling of interests.

§6.44   b. Audit of Target Corporation

When contemplating an acquisition, the buyer should determine whether the target's audited financial statements are available, and if not, what the cost and time required to obtain them will be.

Buyers frequently require an audit of the target's books and records as a condition of the closing. This is an excellent supplement to the buyer's due diligence process, and it may be essential in the financing package to be used by the buyer in making the acquisition. (Lenders are invariably more comfortable with an audit.) The audit can be undertaken either by the buyer's accountants or by those of the target.

CAVEAT: If target's accountants are used, it is important that the buyer's accountants agree beforehand that they will accept the audit in future auditing processes without conducting a re-audit. Such acceptance is common practice between the major accounting firms, but may be out of the question if target's accountant is a small local firm with whose work the buyer's accountants are unfamiliar. A possible consequence of not obtaining advance acceptance is substantially higher auditing expenses connected with the merger or acquisition.

Finally, a significant acquisition by a public corporation will require audited financial statements of the target for Securities and Exchange Commission reporting purposes. The SEC requires that it be notified of any acquisition of a "business" of a certain size within 15 days after the closing, and, no later than 60 days after the notification, the acquiror must furnish to the SEC audited financial statements of the acquired entity for the past one to three years. See Securities & Exchange Form 8–K, General Instructions, Bulletin No. 126 (3–3–89).

§6.45   5. Early Negotiations

Negotiations start when the parties first begin to discuss the possibility of an acquisition. They end when the transaction is completed and the parties no longer have any continuing rights or obligations to each other.

The cardinal rule for the attorney is to coordinate the efforts of the negotiation team. If each member of the team is free to contact the opposing parties and their advisers, the final result will be less favorable than it should have been for one party or the other. Unfortunately, there is a tendency for clients to consider themselves to be above this rule. The ancient military principle of "divide and conquer" is especially applicable to negotiations. A party who realizes that counsel can be circumvented when the going gets tough may be inclined to do so each time the opportunity presents itself.

There are two levels of negotiation: deal points and details. Deal points are the principal bailiwick of the client, and details are the province of the client's advisers, including legal counsel. However, counsel's most significant contribution may be in analyzing and setting priorities for deal points.

§6.46   a. Deal Points

Deal points usually include price, terms, assets to be purchased, major liabilities and risks to be assumed, tax treatment, and executive perquisites. In actuality, a deal point can be anything that either of the parties chooses to call a deal point, but for the most part they are the major financial aspects of the transaction. Some elements of the transaction can fall into either category, depending on the circumstances. Thus, for example, the form of the acquisition (sale of stock, sale of assets, or merger) may be a deal point or a detail, depending on its importance in accommodating the needs of the parties.

Although deal points are often primarily business considerations and therefore out of the usual sphere of counsel, it is usually unwise for the buyer to either negotiate them or attempt to reduce them to writing without the assistance of counsel. Although the client must ultimately decide deal points, counsel can be of great value at this stage. Frequently, clients do not even know what all the deal points should be, *e.g.,* the structure of the deal may be dictated by tax factors that the client may be unaware of. In many situations, counsel needs to be actively involved in negotiating deal points and advising the client about them. Of course, every deal is different, and some will require less legal expertise than others, but every deal contains risks unless a legal review is undertaken before the handshake. Many of the details (see §6.48) will have a distinct bearing on the structuring and negotiation of deal points. Unless this is recognized, negotiators are likely to find themselves renegotiating when the effect of the details becomes apparent.

§6.47   b. The Letter of Intent: Checklist

Deal points and the framework of the details are often summarized in a relatively short document usually referred to as a letter of intent.

It can be binding or not binding as the draftsman provides. A letter that is properly drafted to accomplish its purposes of setting out the basic terms of the agreement and assuring the parties that they have a general understanding, if it does not specify whether it is binding or not, will generally be considered a "contract to contract" and will thus obligate the parties to negotiate in good faith the terms of the final agreement. See, *e.g., Heritage Broadcasting Co. v Wilson Communications, Inc.* (Mich Ct App 1988) 428 NW2d 784, 787 (letter of intent that includes all essential terms to be included in final contract is a contract to contract); *Foley v Interactive Data Corp.* (1988) 47 C3d 654, 683, 257 CR 211, 227 (all contracts impose on each party a duty of good faith and fair dealing in their performance).

The purpose of the letter of intent is twofold. The first is to assure the parties that they do in fact have a general understanding, before significant time and energy is expended in further efforts. The second is to set out the nature of that understanding in definitive form so that there will be less likelihood of future disagreement about the basic terms. A true letter of intent is not designed to be binding, and it may be sufficiently brief that its lack of specificity would render it unenforceable even in the absence of language in the document stating the intention not to be bound. In such a document, only the most salient features of the transaction are dealt with. The parties intend that they will not be bound until a certain amount of due diligence has been undertaken and more of the details have been agreed on.

The following elements should be considered for inclusion in the letter of intent:

- The precise names of the parties;
- A description of the thing to be sold, the purchase price, and the form of the consideration to be paid;
- The payment terms;
- Assumption of liabilities and risks;
- Contingencies such as the agreement of certain key employees to remain with the company, the satisfactory completion of an audit verifying certain results, and certain reviews and investigations of the target;
- Special tax considerations and tax requirements of the parties;
- Requirements for the concurrence of certain third parties, *e.g.,* labor unions, important suppliers, customers;

- Compliance with securities and trade laws and regulations and other applicable regulatory measures;
- Procedures to be followed in carrying out the due diligence investigation;
- The method of handling any brokers' commissions and finders' fees, or a statement that the parties have not become obligated for any commissions or finders' fees;
- A statement that the acquisition agreement, when prepared, will contain the terms, conditions, warranties, and representations usual (or not unusual) for transactions of a similar nature;
- A statement concerning whether or not the parties intend to be bound by the letter of intent; and
- A covenant that each party will negotiate in good faith and will not negotiate with or consider offers made by third parties.

For sample form and further discussion of letters of intent, see SALE OF BUSINESSES §§3.1–3.18 (2d ed Cal CEB 1988).

A word should be said about "binding" letters of intent. Not infrequently, the parties may wish to be bound at an early stage of the negotiation. The document used to memorialize such an understanding should state specifically that the parties intend to be bound by the terms contained in the letter notwithstanding a failure at a later date to reach an agreement on details yet to be negotiated. Such a document is substantially more difficult to draft than a letter of intent. It must bind, but in the briefest of terms. It must indicate that definitive terms are contemplated, but it is necessarily too brief to specify them. A binding letter of intent should be drafted with the same or even greater care than the final agreement, because it is quite possible that it will be the final agreement.

§6.48   c. Negotiation of Details

After the letter of intent is drawn up, the parties embark on the somewhat more lengthy process of negotiating the definitive terms of the acquisition. This painstaking task is conducted primarily by counsel for the various parties. The onus of preparing a first draft is usually on buyer's counsel, because the buyer usually bears the greatest investigatory burden and requires more in the way of warranties and representations than the seller. However, practice varies greatly with respect to who prepares which document. Many attorneys feel that there is an advantage of momentum if they prepare the first comprehensive draft.

The burden for the related documentation is spread among counsel for all of the parties.

The acquisition agreement and related documents form the basis for the detailed negotiation. The buyer's first draft is handed to seller's counsel, who will review it in detail and make appropriate changes, additions, and comments. This joins the issue, and the negotiation proceeds from there, sometimes face to face and sometimes by telephone or correspondence. Each successive draft brings the parties closer to their goal, and eventually the document is carved into something on which both sides can agree.

For detailed forms for a sale of stock agreement, a sale of assets agreement, and a "reverse triangular" merger agreement, see chaps 4, 5, and 6 respectively, of SALE OF BUSINESSES (2d ed Cal CEB 1988).

§6.49 6. Coordinating the Acquisition

In many transactions, the responsibility for coordinating the acquisition—making sure that each participant knows what is expected and when it must be done, and following up to ensure compliance—falls on the attorney, because other participants lack the necessary training, professional focus, or overall point of view.

In such situations, the attorney may find it helpful to

- Maintain a list of all persons involved in the transaction, with phone numbers and addresses;
- Prepare a critical path chart (time and responsibility chart) outlining the steps needed to complete the transaction, the anticipated date of each step, and the persons primarily responsible for completing each step; and
- Prepare a closing chart (closing memorandum), detailing each step to be taken at closing.

For further discussion and sample forms, see SALE OF BUSINESSES §§1.9–1.13 (2d ed Cal CEB 1988).

§6.50 a. Reviewing Data: Checklist

Appropriate representatives of each corporation should review, as early as possible, not only its own corporate affairs, to detect obstacles or conditions to its right to combine, but also the corporate affairs of the other parties, to ascertain as far as possible, *e.g.,* that the other parties' assets and liabilities are as believed or represented, and that contracts assumed will not be too burdensome.

The scope of review of the other parties' affairs (see discussion of "due diligence," in §6.54) will vary widely, depending on the parties' prior dealings with each other, the complexity of their corporate affairs, and other factors. The following list illustrates subjects that typically would be reviewed by both corporations:

(1) Corporate name, place of incorporation, and good standing.

(2) Articles of incorporation, bylaws, and minute books from the date of incorporation. Particular attention should be paid to validity of organization, authorization of stock issues, and authorization of merger.

(3) Outstanding shares; number and geographical distribution of shareholders; identity of principal shareholders; and other outstanding securities and rights to purchase securities, including stock options and option plans. The share records should be examined or an independent transfer agent's certificate obtained.

(4) Names, addresses, salaries, and brief biographical information about principal officers and directors.

(5) States in which corporation is qualified to do or is doing business.

(6) Method and location of operations, markets and principal customers, and national security clearances.

(7) Names of corporation's banks, attorneys, and accountants.

(8) Most recent audited balance sheet and five-year audited operating statements, and most recent unaudited financial statements (if more recent than audited financial statements).

(9) State and federal tax returns, other tax data, *e.g.,* record of tax basis of assets and tax accounting methods, and status of tax examinations.

(10) Pending or threatened litigation.

(11) Title to corporate property and any liens, encumbrances, or exceptions.

(12) Contracts and commitments. Particular attention should be paid to contracts or commitments that restrict or require consent to mergers, that must be amended or replaced, or that might be unintentionally extended in scope if taken over unchanged by the enlarged business (*e.g.,* "requirements" or "output" contracts, or those

whose terms are tied to corporate income). Matters to be considered include bonds or debenture indentures, credit and loan agreements, and stock exchange listing agreements; leases, patents, licenses, franchises, distributorship agreements, and insurance policies; and employment agreements, collective bargaining contracts, pension, retirement, profit-sharing, and similar plans.

(13) Annual reports to shareholders, proxy statements, reports filed with the Securities and Exchange Commission, and similar documents likely to contain important information.

§6.51   b. Related Activities

A number of actions that may need to be taken in connection with a merger or acquisition are likely to be time consuming, and should be started as far in advance of closing as possible. Such actions include:

- Satisfying conditions or obtaining necessary consents;
- Obtaining a Franchise Tax Board tax clearance certificate (see §§6.144–6.145);
- Making a "blue sky" survey and filing necessary documents with state securities regulatory agencies;
- Filing notice of the proposed transaction with the Federal Trade Commission or Justice Department, if required by antitrust legislation (see §§6.98–6.101);
- Transferring property in other jurisdictions;
- Qualifying to do business as a foreign corporation, and withdrawing disappearing corporations;
- Protecting corporate names;
- Meeting requirements of stock transfer agents or registrars;
- Obtaining new share certificates;
- Selecting and engaging any new auditors; and
- Obtaining auditors' approval of the proposed accounting treatment (see §§6.40–6.44).

§6.52   c. Time Schedule; Allocation of Responsibility

As soon as possible, counsel should circulate a preliminary time schedule showing the expected date by which each principal action is to be taken. This should be followed by a more detailed time schedule. If the complexity of the proceeding or the number of working parties requires it, the more detailed schedule should indicate when and by whom drafts or proofs are to be prepared and circulated, and a conference should be held to ensure complete understanding of the problems and of the allocation of responsibility.

§6.53   7. Documentation

The acquisition agreement (sometimes called a reorganization agreement or a merger agreement) is the core document. It sets forth the terms and conditions of the understanding, and it usually forms the framework for a thorough investigation of the target company. It contains numerous representations and warranties, many of which refer to exhibits and schedules. The parties become bound by a combination of the language of the agreement itself and the documents to which it refers.

Most acquisition agreements follow the same general format. First there are recitations that establish the purpose, intent, and form of the transaction. These are followed by agreements concerning price, terms, and a description of the thing being sold. The great bulk of the agreement contains covenants concerning the conduct of the business pending the closing, warranties and representations of the parties, procedures at the closing, indemnification, and the ever present miscellaneous provisions, *e.g.*, waiver, notices, attorneys' fees, severability. The length of an acquisition agreement can range from as few as eight or ten pages to well over one hundred pages, depending on the complexity of the transaction.

In addition to the acquisition agreement and its many exhibits and schedules, there will probably be opinions of counsel, merger documents, escrow agreements, corporate action, employment contracts, regulatory applications and approvals, and other documents especially suited to the particular transaction.

Documentation is perhaps counsel's most crucial task. This is where the details reside and where liability can be created or avoided. Formbooks are replete with examples of ways that others have done their acquisitions, and corporate counsel may have office files showing the results of past negotiations. See §§6.114–6.118 for discussion and sample forms that could be adapted to an uncomplicated merger transaction. For more detailed forms and comments, see SALE OF BUSINESSES chap 4 (sale of stock agreement);

chap 5 (sale of assets agreement); chap 6 (merger agreement) (2d ed Cal CEB 1988).

A form can be a great place to begin the drafting process. Be advised, however, that each acquisition is different. Nothing replaces the analysis and imagination of counsel in anticipating, providing for, and heading off the problems of the particular transaction.

8. Due Diligence
§6.54   a. The Investigative Process

In General. "Due diligence" refers generally to the investigative process that ensures that a given state of affairs is as it appears to be or as the other party represents it to be. In the acquisition context, although it may include an investigation not only of the seller but also the buyer of the target company, the heart of the investigation is the examination of the business itself.

Role of Counsel. Due diligence is primarily the client's responsibility. The attorney's area of expertise ordinarily does not include non-legal matters, *e.g.,* operations, finances, management, product suitability, and counsel should not accept responsibility for more than the legal aspects of the due diligence process. It is the client, not counsel, who has the laboring oar in this aspect of the acquisition, and the client should be made fully aware of this. Counsel, however, may often be involved in coordinating the effort. See §§6.49–6.52. For further discussion and a sample checklist, see SALE OF BUSINESSES §§1.14–1.32 (2d ed Cal CEB 1988).

Investigation of the Buyer. Obviously, the target company must always be investigated. The buyer should also be investigated, particularly if the purchase price is comprised in part of the securities of the buyer or if the purchase price will be paid over a period of time. Even if the terms are cash at the closing, the buyer should still be investigated, because the seller needs assurance that the buyer has the capacity to raise the money. It will be a red-faced seller (or worse) who goes through the throes of the acquisition process only to find that the buyer does not and never did have the wherewithal to finance the purchase.

Stages of the Process. The due diligence process will probably be carried out in stages roughly approximating the progress of the negotiations. Thus, when talks are just beginning, the investigation may be limited to publicly available information. At the letter of intent stage, both the buyer and the seller may be more generous in providing confidential information. Finally, when the transaction is fully documented and executed, the due diligence review can be undertaken to the fullest extent. The buyer or the buyer's financial advisors will visit the premises of the target company and talk to key employees. There may be appraisals of critical assets, and major vendors and customers may be contacted. Contractual obligations will be evaluated, and banking relationships and credit may be reviewed. If the target company does not have audited financial statements, or if target's auditors are not acceptable to the buyer, a certified audit may be called for.

Confidentiality Agreement. The due diligence process involves review of information that includes the most highly confidential aspects of the respective businesses and the financial affairs of the parties. If the acquisition should fall through, some kinds of confidential information could be used by the other party in connection with anti-competitive practices or for insider trading or market manipulation; other kinds of information could be used to defeat proprietary rights in technological trade secrets. It is therefore a good idea for the parties to enter into a confidentiality agreement (see §6.55) governing their use of information gained during the investigation in the event that the transaction is not completed as planned. At a minimum, neither party would want the other to have unbridled use of information gained in the course of the due diligence investigation.

§6.55   b. Form: Confidentiality Agreement

Form 6.55–1

Dear Sir or Madam:

This will confirm that we have agreed to provide you with certain confidential information concerning the business of this corporation and allow you access to our facilities and such books and records as you may reasonably require to complete your evaluation.

In the course of your investigation, you may encounter information on such matters as marketing plans and procedures,

data, strategies, forecasts, customer lists, or other confidential information that constitutes proprietary or trade secret information of this corporation. Consequently, we must ask that you hold all such information in the strictest confidence and agree not to use or disclose it unless such information is commonly known in the industry or is otherwise in the public domain.

We also request, in the event that you do not acquire substantially all of the assets of this corporation, that you refrain from using any non-public information obtained in the course of your investigation to your own business advantage, and that you promptly return any documents or other materials obtained in the course of visits or investigation.

Please indicate your agreement by signing a copy of this letter and returning it to me. We look forward to your visit and to the consummation of a mutually beneficial sale.

Very truly yours,

[*Signature*]
[*Typed name*]

AGREED AND ACCEPTED:
[*Name of corporation*]
By_____

Comment: This form of agreement contains the essential elements of a confidentiality understanding, namely, an acknowledgment that the proposed buyer will be exposed to confidential information, a description of the information, the buyer's agreement to maintain confidentiality and not use if for the buyer's own purposes if the transaction is not consummated. This form is very brief, and is set up like a letter to avoid any controversy at the early stages of the negotiations. It is quite adequate for the usual business transaction. However, there are circumstances where a due diligence investigation will disclose information that is highly sensitive, *e.g.,* if the target's business is dependent on trade secrets or if marketing information is critical. In such instances, the confidentiality agreement should be more thorough, especially in the description of the information, and it should provide for remedies in the event of breach by the buyer.

For an alternative form that could be adapted to this purpose, see SALE OF BUSINESSES §4.74 (2d ed Cal CEB 1988).

§6.56   9. Closing

Timing. Acquisitions are usually structured to provide a hiatus between the date on which the parties are bound by executing the agreement and the closing date. This period of time is used to complete the due diligence review (see §6.54) and to prepare for the actual transfer of the target company. It is during this period that regulatory matters are attended to, shareholder votes are taken, and waiting periods (*e.g.,* those required by bulk transfer and trade regulation laws) expire. See generally SALE OF BUSINESSES §§2.54–2.74, 2.80, 2.82 (2d ed Cal CEB 1988).

General Nature of the Closing. The closing takes place at a prearranged time and place. The parties meet and execute the documentation needed to complete the transaction. The closing may involve nothing more than payment of cash for an endorsed stock certificate, or it may be so complicated that it requires several hours to sign and exchange all the documents and complete the other necessary procedures. The parties may exchange cashier's checks, stock certificates, certified resolutions authorizing the transfer, bills of sale, deeds to real property and opinions of counsel. Supplementary escrows may be entered into, representations updated, boards of directors reorganized, regulatory compliances attested to, and documents of merger filed. It is a time when things rarely go right, and counsel must be prepared for inevitable last-minute negotiations and amendments to documentation. It is usually a good idea to schedule a "pre-closing" on the day prior to the closing date for the purpose of coordinating these last-minute details. This can help assure that the actual closing will occur as planned.

Closing Memorandum. For sample "closing memorandum" to assist the attorney in keeping track of all the steps that need to be taken before, at, and after the closing, see SALE OF BUSINESSES §1.10.

§6.57   10. Post-Closing

Once the deal is completed, the buyer can finally run the business, the seller can begin spending his money, and counsel can start the examination to be certain that all the loose ends have been tied. The process that has gone on before may have involved time pressure, a myriad of documents, and complexities that defy on-the-spot analysis. Immediately after the closing is the time to organize the files, contemplate the entire situation, document oral understandings, cure defects, and calendar any potential future problems. However onerous it may be for counsel to retrace all the steps preceding the culmination, it is a necessary last step to a successful acquisition.

As a part of this process, counsel should prepare a "closing book" containing copies of all documents used anywhere in the transaction. They should be carefully indexed and should contain notes that can be used later to refresh faded memories. The closing book is an invaluable source of information when later questions arise.

III. TAX ASPECTS OF MERGERS AND ACQUISITIONS

§6.58   A. Federal Tax Law: Types of Tax-Deferred Reorganizations

The federal tax law relating to mergers and acquisitions is highly complex and difficult in many respects. It is a field for the tax specialist, not for the general practitioner who brushes with the tax law from time to time. An adequate treatment of the tax elements and consequences involved in corporate acquisition is beyond the scope of this chapter. Therefore, the material that follows is not designed to impart the tax knowledge necessary to plan or consummate a corporate acquisition. Rather, it is intended to summarize basic tax principals that are likely to appear in an acquisition situation, and to serve as a basis from which a lawyer who is not a tax specialist can anticipate basic issues and communicate with a specialist concerning them.

Corporate acquisitions having the characteristics described in IRC §368 generally incur neither gain nor loss at the time of the acquisition, and are sometimes referred to as "tax free" reorganizations. However, the basis of the assets and shares involved generally carry over to serve as the measure of tax to be incurred at some letter date; therefore, it may be more accurate to refer to them instead as "tax-deferred" transactions.

The principal tax-deferred acquisitions are:

- **Merger ("A" Reorganization).** An "A" reorganization is a merger or consolidation under applicable state law. IRC §368(a)(1)(A). See §§6.60–6.64.
- **Stock-for-Stock Reorganization ("B" Reorganization).** A "B" reorganization is an acquisition by one corporation of substantially all of the stock of another corporation solely in exchange for voting stock of the acquiring corporation or of a corporation that is in control of the acquiring corporation. IRC §368(a)(1)(B). See §§6.65–6.68.
- **Stock-for-Assets Reorganization ("C" Reorganization).** A "C" reorganization is an acquisition by one corporation of substantially all of the assets of another corporation solely (subject to certain exceptions) in exchange for voting stock of the acquiring corporation or of a corporation that is in control of the acquiring corporation. IRC §368(a)(1)(C). See §§6.69–6.73.

NOTE: The use of the word "reorganization" in both the Corporations Code and the Internal Revenue Code may be confusing. Both refer to the same general type of transaction. However, one is not necessarily the same as the other. The Corporations Code refers generally to any type of statutory corporate reorganization whether or not qualified under the Internal Revenue Code; to qualify as a "reorganization" under the Internal Revenue Code, the transaction must satisfy distinct statutory and case law criteria, discussed in §§6.60–6.73.

§6.59   B. Requirements and Pitfalls Common to All Reorganizations

Although each type of reorganization has its own unique requirements, as outlined below, there are also a series of requirements common to all three. Failure to satisfy any one of the criteria could endanger the tax-deferred status of the "A," "B," or "C" type. The first of the following tests is applied in the acquisition situation, and the last four are applied after the acquisition.

(1) **Business Purpose Test.** It is well established that a reorganization without a bona fide business purpose independent of tax considerations will be denied tax-deferred treatment. *Gregory v Helvering* (1935) 293 US 465; Treas Reg §§1.368–1(b), 1.368–2(g). The taxpayer is not required to select the approach that will produce

the least desirable tax result, but must be able to show that tax considerations are of secondary importance to the business reasons for the transaction.

(2) **Continuity of Interest.** The rationale behind deferring the tax on a corporate reorganization is that shareholders should not be taxed currently if their investment vehicle is merely changing shape or size. If there is good reason to reorganize, that reorganization should not be inhibited by a substantial taxable event. However, if the shareholders take back little or no equity interest in the new entity or if they promptly dispose of that interest, the transaction falls outside this rationale. The Internal Revenue Service takes the position for ruling purposes that to come within the rationale, an equity interest in the acquiring corporation must be acquired by target shareholders, and this interest must have a value that is at least 50 percent of the value of the target corporation. Rev Rul 66–234, 1966–2 Cum Bull 436; Rev Proc 77–37, 1977–2 Cum Bull 568. The interest in the acquiring corporation must be held by target's shareholders for a substantial period of time, and they must have no intention of disposing of it at a particular date in the future. *McDonald's Restaurants v Commissioner* (7th Cir 1982) 688 F2d 520.

(3) **Continuity of Business.** On a theory related to the continuity of interest test, the Internal Revenue Service imposes the requirement that the surviving entity must either continue the acquired corporation's "historic business" or that it must continue to use a significant portion of the acquired corporation's "historic business assets." Treas Reg §1.368–1(d). It should be noted that the test does not refer to the acquired corporation's assets or business immediately before the acquisition. Rather, it looks to the historic business assets to determine if the requirement has been satisfied. Rev Rul 81–25, 1981–1 Cum Bull 132.

(4) **Contingent Payments.** Contingent or "earn out" shares are frequently used in a reorganization if the parties are unable to negotiate a fixed price. They are also used if it is desirable to give additional equity incentive to shareholders who will be key employees of the surviving entity, or if the buyer wants security for potential liabilities. In an "earn-out" the buyer agrees to issue shares in addition to those paid at the closing based on the performance of the target during a specified period in the future. Usually the number of shares to be issued is based on a formula, and it is agreed that they will be issued only after the deduction of certain future liabilities.

While the Internal Revenue Service initially took the position that shares issued subsequent to the reorganization were "other property," in violation of the "solely for voting stock" requirement, it has since taken a more lenient position. If the six guidelines set out in Rev Proc 77–37, 1977–2 Cum Bull 568, amplified and increased to nine by Rev Proc 84–42, 1984–1 Cum Bull 521, are followed, the Internal Revenue Service will rule that the contingent shares are not "other property." Among other things, the guidelines provide that there must be a valid business reason for not issuing all the stock, that the maximum number of contingent shares is specific, and that the shareholders cannot control the triggering mechanism for the issuance.

(5) Step Transaction Doctrine. Sometimes a reorganization is one of a series of steps intended by the parties to be interdependent and to achieve an integrated result. In that event the Internal Revenue Service can be expected to take the position that all of the steps must be considered together in determining whether the reorganization qualifies under IRC §368. The danger is that although one of the steps taken alone may satisfy all the appropriate criteria, if the entire transactional series is perceived as one, then it may not qualify as a tax-deferred reorganization. Factors considered are (1) the timing of the transactions, (2) the intention of the parties, (3) the interdependence of the steps, and (4) the ultimate result. *Hirotoshi Yamamoto* (1980) 73 TC 946. Because of its flexibility and relative lack of technical requirements, the doctrine is usually less dangerous to the "A" reorganization (merger) than to the others. In analyzing the potential for disqualification, consideration must be given to planned activities both before and after a reorganization.

C. "A," "B," and "C" Reorganizations

§6.60 1. "A" Reorganizations (Mergers)

The only express requirement for an "A" reorganization imposed by IRC §368(a)(1)(A) is that the merger must qualify as a merger under the appropriate state statute. However, additional requirements and restrictions have been imposed by regulation and by case law.

§6.61 a. Boot

If the shareholders receive nothing other than stock, the transaction is completely tax-deferred. If, however, they receive "boot" (money or other property), gain is recognized if the total value of the boot and the shares received exceeds the shareholder's cost basis in the shares surrendered. The amount of gain is limited to the amount of boot, and any such gain will be characterized as ordinary income to the extent it is treated as a dividend; any remaining gain is generally treated as capital. Treas Reg §1.356–1(b). Unfortunately for the shareholder with a high cost basis, although gain can be recognized, loss cannot. IRC §356(c).

A distribution of boot to shareholders in proportion to their shareholdings may result in dividend treatment. If dividend treatment occurs, the shareholders are taxed at ordinary income rates rather than at capital gain rates, and cannot offset their basis in the shares, while the corporation receives no offsetting deduction. Dividend treatment can be avoided if the distribution to shareholders is substantially disproportionate to the number of shares they hold. IRC §302(b)(1).

§6.62   b. Basis

Exchanging Shareholders' Basis. If the merger qualifies as a reorganization, the basis of the shares exchanged generally carries over to the shares received. IRC §358. Any potential gain or loss is preserved for realization at the time of some later disposition. If for some reason the transaction is not completely tax-deferred (*e.g.,* boot is received), the basis of the non-recognition property decreased by the fair market value of the boot received and the amount of any loss recognized, and increased by the amount of any dividend and any capital gain taxed to the recipient. IRC §358. Any basis adjustment for property received as boot is made according to its fair market value.

Acquiring Corporation's Basis. In general, the acquiring corporation's basis in the acquired property is the same as the transferor's, though it may be increased to the extent any gain is recognized by the transferor. IRC §1.362–1; Treas Reg §1.362–1.

§6.63   c. Taxable Mergers

A business combination that is properly consummated as a merger under state law can nevertheless fail to qualify as a tax-deferred reorganization for various reasons. A taxable merger will have the general tax consequences described below.

Taxable Regular Mergers. The acquiring corporation does not incur any tax obligation when it issues its stock in a two-party taxable merger. Assuming, as is probably the case, that a taxable merger will be treated as a taxable sale of assets by the acquired corporation followed by a liquidation of the acquired corporation, the acquired corporation will recognize gain on the sale of assets, and in addition, the subsequent liquidation distribution to the shareholders of the acquired corporation will also be taxable to the shareholders as capital gain.

Taxable Triangular Mergers. A special additional tax problem may be present in triangular mergers if the shares of the parent corporation are considered to be transferred by the parent to its subsidiary and in turn by the subsidiary to the acquired corporation. The subsidiary, if not protected by IRC §1032, would realize taxable gain on the full value of the parent's stock exchanged, because it would have a zero basis in that stock. Although there is some indication that the separate entity of the subsidiary will be ignored if the subsidiary is a dummy corporation created for the purpose of the triangular merger, counsel should further protect against this problem by having the acquired corporation issue the stock directly to the acquired corporation's shareholders. See Rev Rul 73–427, 1973–2 Cum Bull 301.

Impact of Tax Liability. If a merger is treated as a taxable sale of assets, the incidence of tax liability is on the acquired corporation, and the liability for the tax on the liquidation distribution is borne by the acquired corporation's shareholders. However, because the surviving corporation (either the acquiring corporation or its subsidiary) by operation of law assumes all of the acquired corporation's obligations and liabilities, the acquiring corporation in fact bears the impact of any income tax liability for a taxable sale of assets, unless the merger agreement provides otherwise.

Carryover of Basis and Attributes. As described above, in a typical tax-deferred merger, various attributes (*e.g.,* net operating loss carryovers and accounting methods) of the acquired corporation may be carried over to the surviving corporation under IRC §381. In addition, the acquiring corporation carries over the acquired corporation's basis in the assets. IRC §362. In a taxable merger, however, there is generally no carryover of any of the "tax history" of the acquired corporation, because IRC §381 does not apply. See IRC §382(a). The acquiring corporation obtains a cost basis in the acquired corporation's assets. IRC §1012.

§6.64 d. Advantages and Disadvantages

A "B" reorganization and some "C" reorganizations require that an acquisition be solely for the voting stock of the acquiring corporation. In an "A" reorganization, however, an extra payment by the acquiring corporation (in addition to the stock) will not result in the disqualification of the reorganization as a tax-deferred transaction as long as there is sufficient continuity of interest.

If an "A" reorganization is selected, a short taxable year may result, which could affect the carryforward of net operating losses unless the merger takes place on the last day of the fiscal year of that corporation. Other than that, the problems lie only in the area of corporate law in such things as satisfying the formalities for approval, and the automatic assumption of liabilities.

§6.65 2. "B" Reorganizations (Stock for Stock Exchanges)

A "B" reorganization is an exchange of stock for stock. Its principal requirements are that (1) the consideration received by the shareholder of the target be "solely . . . the voting stock" of the buyer or its parent and that (2) immediately after the acquisition the "acquiring corporation have control" of the target. IRC §368(a)(1)(B).

§6.66 a. Solely for Voting Stock

This test is strictly construed by the courts. *Heverly v Commissioner* (3d Cir 1980) 621 F2d 1227. If the buyer gives any consideration other than voting stock to the target shareholders, the transaction will not qualify as a "B" reorganization. The stock must, in fact, be stock, not rights or warrants to purchase additional stock. *Helvering v Southwest Consolidated Corp.* (1942) 315 US 194. The stock must vote, not merely have the right to vote under certain circumstances. For example, if preferred stock has voting rights in arrearage situations and an arrearage exists at the time of the reorganization (and thus the stock has at least temporary voting rights), such stock would appear to be voting stock. However, if no arrearage existed, it would not be voting stock. The acquirer may pay certain legitimate expenses of the reorganization that would otherwise fall to the target and its shareholders. Rev Rul 73–54, 1973–1 Cum Bull 187; Rev Rul 76–365, 1976–2 Cum Bull 110. The acquirer may also pay cash to target's shareholders in lieu of issuing fractional shares. *Mills v Commissioner* (5th Cir 1964) 331 F2d 321. However, payments for fractional shares that freeze out minority shareholders may disqualify a "B" reorganization. Rev Rul 78–351, 1978–2 Cum Bull 148. The buyer can agree to undertake an SEC registration of the stock of target shareholders without violating the "solely for voting stock" requirement. Rev Rul 67–275, 1967–2 Cum Bull 142. Employee-shareholders of the target can receive employment contracts that provide for reasonable compensation. Contracts that pay excessive compensation may be deemed additional consideration, and violate the "solely for voting stock" requirement.

§6.67   b. Control of the Target

"Control" means ownership of at least 80 percent of the voting stock and at least 80 percent of the shares of each other class of stock of the corporation. IRC §368(c). Even though 100 percent of all other stock has been acquired, the failure to obtain at least 80 percent of a single small class will disqualify the reorganization. The entire 80 percent need not be obtained all at the same time, but the reorganization will be placed in jeopardy if 80 percent is not acquired within 12 months as part of a clearly pre-existing plan of acquisition. Treas Reg §1.368–2(c). *American Potash & Chem. Corp. v U.S.* (Ct Cl 1968) 399 F2d 194.

§6.68   c. Basis

The voting stock issued by the acquirer in consideration of the stock of the target takes on the same basis as the target stock. The stock of the target received by the acquirer retains the same basis as it had in the hands of the target shareholders. If the target shareholders surrender blocks of stock in which they have different bases, the bases in the new stock is not averaged. Instead, the new stock is divided into blocks, each of which has a basis corresponding to the shares previously owned. Rev Rul 68–23, 1968–1 Cum Bull 144. Theoretically, the acquiring corporation must learn the basis of each of the target shareholders, a nearly impossible task if the target was widely held. Practically speaking, however, the acquiring corporation does not usually attempt to gather such information, and if the acquiring corporation is later sold it may be done in such a way as to make the prior basis immaterial. However, in certain cases the Internal Revenue Service does allow an acquiring corporation to determine its basis by statistical sampling. Rev Proc 81–70, 1981–2 Cum Bul 729.

§6.69   3. "C" Reorganizations (Stock for Assets Exchanges)

A "C" reorganization is an exchange of voting stock for assets. Its principal requirements are that (1) the consideration received by the shareholder of the target be "solely . . . the voting stock" of the buyer or its parent and that (2) the buyer acquires "substantially all of the properties of" the target. IRC §368(a)(1)(C).

§6.70   a. Solely for Voting Stock

This test is similar to the corresponding test in a "B" reorganization (see §6.67). However, IRC §368(a)(2)(B) provides that money or other property in addition to voting stock can be paid to the target shareholders if the property for which voting stock is issued has a fair market value that is at least 80 percent of the fair market value of all of the property of the target corporation. In other words, the target shareholders can receive money or other property for 20 percent of the value of the assets conveyed by the target corporation. (See discussion of tax consequences of receiving "boot" in §6.61.) At first glance, this provision appears to allow significantly greater flexibility than the "B" reorganization, which has no similar flexibility to its "solely voting stock" requirement; however, the percentage test is applied to gross assets rather than net assets. In computing the 20 percent limitation, the existing liabilities of the target corporation that are assumed by the acquirer must be taken into consideration if any boot is received. Treas Reg §1.368–2(d)(3). For example, if the target's liabilities are $150,000 and the value of its property (assets) is $1,000,000, the target has a net worth of $850,000.

If the purchase price is the same as the net worth (of course, in normal circumstances it could be either more or less), then the purchase price would be 85 percent of the value of the property. Since a "C" reorganization requires that voting stock be issued for not less than 80 percent of the fair market value of the property if boot is received, 5 percent of the purchase price could be paid in cash or other property. The problem is that most operating businesses are unable to function without borrowings in excess of 20 percent of the value of assets. The result is that the 20 percent cash or property flexibility is mostly illusory: It is available in theory but not in practice.

Fortunately, the liabilities of the target corporation are not taken into consideration for any purpose other than computing the 20 percent money or property exception. By the express terms of IRC §368(a)(1)(C), the assumption of liabilities of the target is not a factor in determining whether the exchange is solely for stock. Otherwise, a "C" reorganization would rarely be available.

§6.71   b. Substantially All of the Properties

There is no statutory definition of "substantially all," but the Internal Revenue Service will rule that the test is satisfied if the target conveys 90 percent of the fair market value of its net assets and 70 percent of the fair market value of its gross assets. Rev Proc 77–37, 1977–2 Cum Bull 568. The courts have defined assets in this sense to mean operating assets and, to that extent, have excluded non-operating assets from those to be considered in determining what is "substantially all." Therefore, it may be proper for a target to withhold from acquisition the investment portfolio of a manufacturing company, even though it constitutes more than 25 percent of gross assets. *Commissioner v First Nat'l Bank* (3d Cir 1939) 104 F2d 865. Similarly, the courts have looked favorably on situations in which the target corporation has withheld funds for the purpose of paying retained liabilities. *Western Indus. Co. v Helvering* (DC Cir 1936) 82 F2d 461. Presumably, these funds were not considered necessary for or an essential part of the functional business of the target.

Regular dividends paid prior to the reorganization are not considered in determining whether substantially all of the assets are transferred. Rev Rul 74–457, 1974–2 Cum Bull 122. However, a spin off of assets prior to the reorganization could very well be fatal to the "substantially all" test since such assets might be considered part of the total assets of the acquired corporation.

§6.72   c. Required Distribution

In order to qualify as a "C" reorganization, the corporation whose assets have been acquired must distribute, pursuant to the reorganization, all of the stock, securities, and other property received in the transaction, as well as its other properties.

§6.73   d. Basis of Acquired Assets and Exchanged Stock or Securities

"C" reorganizations, like "A" and "B" reorganizations, utilize the general "substitution of basis" rule. The acquiring corporation takes the acquired corporation's basis for the assets transferred. IRC §362(b). Shareholders who receive stock keep the basis they had in the surrendered stock. IRC §358(a)(1). If the acquired corporation does not liquidate and continues to hold the stock, then its basis is equal to its basis in the assets transferred. IRC §358(a).

§6.74   D. Net Operating Loss Carryovers

The tax characteristics of a target corporation may make it attractive to a prospective buyer. A corporation with a loss carryforward on its books (a "loss corporation") has a potential asset equal to the tax that would be paid on an equivalent amount of income. The asset cannot be realized, however, unless there is a profit. If the loss corporation merges into another corporation that is profitable and whose profitability is certain, the loss may possibly be treated as that of the fused entities so that the tax asset may be realized as profits are generated. The acquired corporation's net operating losses can be used as allowed in IRC §§381–382.

There are at least five limitations on the use of losses following a corporate acquisition. First, a merger that does not have an independent business purpose will be denied tax-deferred status altogether. *Gregory v Helvering* (1935) 293 US 465; Treas Reg §§1.368–1(b)–(c), 1.368–2(g).

Second, even though the merger or acquisition may have an

independent business purpose so that it qualifies under IRC §368, loss carryovers are denied if the principal purpose of the transaction is to obtain the benefit of the tax deduction and (1) one corporation gains control of another corporation, or (2) assets are obtained from an unrelated corporation in a tax-free transaction. IRC §269(a).

A third limitation on loss carryovers is imposed by the separate return limitation year (SRLY) rules of the consolidated return regulations. Under the SRLY rules, if one or more members of an affiliated group acquires another corporation, the acquired corporation's preacquisition losses can only be used to offset future income of the acquired corporation. Those losses may not be used to offset future income of the acquiring corporation or other members of the affiliated group.

A fourth limitation on loss carryovers applies if there is an ownership change involving an aggregate increase in ownership of a loss corporation of more than 50 percent, by one or more 5 percent shareholders during a three year period. (Detailed rules define a "5% shareholder," the definition embracing four separate categories of shareholders.) If IRC §382 applies, the loss corporation and its successor are limited in the use of the preacquisition losses in any postacquisition period, to an amount determined by multiplying the value of the loss corporation by the applicable long-term tax-exempt rate. Special rules allow additional net operating loss to be utilized to the extent of certain built-in gains.

A fifth limitation is imposed by IRC §384, which applies if a loss corporation acquires the assets of or acquires control of the stock of a corporation with built-in gain pursuant to a tax-free reorganization. If §384 applies, the loss corporation's preacquisition loss cannot be used to offset any recognized built-in gain that is attributable to the disposition of an asset with built-in gain or economically accrued income during a five-year period beginning on the acquisition date.

For purposes of IRC §§382 and 384, the term "loss corporation" generally includes any corporation that has a current year's net operating loss, a net operating loss carryover, or a net unrealized built-in loss. A built-in loss means that the bases of the corporation's assets exceed their fair market value by more than 25 percent. A corporation is considered to have a built-in gain if the fair market value of the corporation's assets exceeds their tax bases by more than 25 percent.

§6.75　E. California Income Tax Aspects

The California income tax consequences of a business acquisition are substantially the same as under federal law with respect to nonrecognition of gain or loss and the basis of the stock, securities, or property exchanged. The California Revenue and Taxation Code either incorporates provisions of the Internal Revenue Code by reference, as in Rev & T C §§17321, 23251, 23253, 24551, 24561, and 24591–24594, or uses language almost identical to that of the Internal Revenue Code. However, California does modify federal law somewhat, so state law must still be reviewed to check for such modifications. See Petersen, Plant & Eager, CALIFORNIA TAXATION §42.01[1] (1989). For example, California treats net operating losses significantly differently from the federal government. See Rev & T C §24416.

§6.76　F. Real Property Tax

In 1976, the California Constitution was amended through the initiative process by passage of Proposition 13. This law proscribes the reassessment of real property for taxation purposes except when a change in ownership occurs. Cal Const art 13A §2. Under Rev & T C §64 (transfers of the stock of a corporation), either an issuance of shares by a corporation or a transfer of shares by shareholders that results in a change in the majority ownership interest of the corporation constitutes a change in ownership within the meaning of Proposition 13. This is true whether it takes place in a single event or cumulatively over a period of time. A change in ownership of a parent corporation triggers reassessment of the real property owned by wholly-owned subsidiaries of the parent. *Sav-On Drugs v County of Orange* (1987) 190 CA3d 1611, 236 CR 100. Similarly, it would not matter whether the change took place through a transfer of stock or a merger. There is an exception to the general rule that a reorganization results in a change of ownership, but only if the reorganization is among members of an affiliated group. For this purpose, a group is affiliated if each member is either wholly owned by the parent corporation or is 100 percent owned by one or more other members of the group. Rev & T C §64.

In *Pueblos Del Rio South v City of San Diego* (1989) 209 CA3d 893, 257 CR 578, the court held that to qualify for the exemption under Rev & T C §64(b) for transfers of corporate property between members of an "affiliated group" in a reorganization, the group members must be affiliated *after* the reorganization as well as before and during the transaction. The exemption of Rev & T C §64(b) did not apply to a two-step process that ultimately transferred land from a corporation to one of its shareholders in exchange for the shareholder's shares in a "divisive" reorganization; instead, the transaction constituted a true change of ownership under Rev & T C §64(c), and a Proposition 13 reassessment was proper.

IV. NON-TAX PLANNING CONSIDERATIONS
§6.77   A. In General

The following sections summarize factors which, if not anticipated and planned for in the early stages of an acquisition, may result in delays, difficulties, and even substantial liabilities for one or more of the parties. An exhaustive analysis of any of these factors is not intended—each subheading could, in itself, be the subject of a treatise. And as is the case in any complex legal situation, no two corporate acquisitions are alike and no checklist can cover every possible consideration. However, there are certain factors that appear frequently, with which counsel should become acquainted.

B. Compliance With Securities Law Requirements
§6.78   1. In General

Although the securities law becomes an issue only if the transaction involves the issuance or transfer of a security, securities are involved in the vast majority of corporate acquisitions. Obviously, stock is a security and a sale of stock requires securities compliance whether the consideration is cash, property, or other securities.

The applicability of securities law to mergers is somewhat less obvious. In essence, a merger is nothing more than a transfer of the ownership of the capital stock of a corporation from one owner or group of owners to another. The transfer is effected by operation of law when the certificate of merger is filed with the Secretary of State. Since ownership of stock is changing, securities law compliance is an issue and is required.

A sale of assets is the only type of acquisition in which securities compliance may not be required. However, even a sale of assets frequently involves securities of one sort or another as consideration.

CAVEAT: Do not forget that a promissory note may be a security.

§6.79 2. State Securities Laws

California is well known for having one of the toughest and most comprehensive blue sky laws in the country, and California's Department of Corporations is as tough as the law it enforces. The present law, Corp C §§25000–31516, was adopted in 1968 and has been amended annually since that time. The amendments to the Code and the Regulations have introduced refinements that have not only kept the law workable, but, to the extent possible, have coordinated it with federal securities law developments.

§6.80 a. Qualification

In California, the offer or sale of a security must be qualified by the Department of Corporations unless an exemption from qualification is available. Qualification involves the preparation of an application detailing the proposed transaction and the submission of comprehensive information concerning the parties. The Department then passes on whether the transaction is "fair, just and equitable" to all concerned.

In the acquisition context, the statutes most likely to be encountered by corporations that are not publicly traded are Corp C §§25110 and 25120. Unless an exemption applies (see §6.81), Corp C §25110 requires qualification of any offer or sale of securities in an issuer transaction, and Corp C §25120 requires qualification of an offer, sale, or exchange of securities in connection with a "merger or . . . purchase of corporate assets." The two statutes cover all three of the means by which corporations are sold.

The qualification process can be time-consuming at best. In addition, the Department may disagree with the applicants concerning the question of whether the transaction is fair, just, and equitable to all parties. For these reasons, it is important to search for an exemption from qualification.

§6.81   b. Exemptions

A stock for stock exchange is governed by Corp C §25110, the principal exemption from which is provided by Corp C §25102(f). This exemption is available if no more than 35 persons are to receive securities and if each of them either has a preexisting business or personal relationship with the issuer or its executives or meets certain standards of financial sophistication. The offer cannot be advertised, and all offerees must represent that they are purchasing for their own account "and not with a view to or for sale in connection with any distribution of the security." Corp C §25102(f). A notice must be filed with the Department of Corporations within 15 days after the issuance. 10 Cal Code Regs §260.102.14. The notice is not a condition of the exemption, but failure to file it can result in the assessment of a penalty equal to the fee for filing an application for qualification. See Corp C §25102(f)(4).

Unfortunately, the §25102(f) exemption is not available for mergers and sales of assets, which are subject to Corp C §25120. This is evident from Corp Sec Rule 260.103, 10 Cal Code Regs §260.103, which makes §25102(f) applicable to two of the types of transactions covered by §25120, but omits mergers and sales of assets. Conceptually, there seems to be no compelling reason why this distinction should be made. Consequently, it may be a trap for the unwary.

There are numerous exemptions for special situations set forth not only in the Corporations Code but also in the regulations. The potential for an exemption should always be reviewed carefully before efforts are made to qualify the transaction.

3. Federal Securities Laws

§6.82   a. Registration

The Securities Act of 1933 (the "Securities Act"), section 5 (15 USC §77e) requires that every sale of a security in interstate commerce must be registered unless it comes within an exemption. See also Rule 145 (17 CFR §230.145).

Federal registration is such an expensive and time-consuming process that many smaller transactions would not be feasible if there were no alternative. Registration should be considered only if the acquisition is large and cannot qualify for any available exemption.

b. Exemptions

§6.83   (1) Intrastate Transactions

An acquisition that is wholly within a single state can probably escape federal registration. Section 3(a)(11) of the Securities Act (15 USC §77c(a)(11)) reserves to the states the regulation of sales of securities that are part of an issue offered and sold to persons resident within a single state, if the issuer is incorporated and doing business within that same state.

The intrastate exemption is further defined by Rule 147, 17 CFR 230.247. Rule 147 defines "part of an issue," "person resident," and "doing business within." It also requires from each issuer a written representation concerning residency, prohibits resales within nine months of the issuance, requires the imposition of a legend on the security certificates and a stop transfer notice to the transfer agent, and requires that the transfer restrictions be disclosed to the offerees.

§6.84   (2) Exemption Under Regulation D

The Securities Act as originally enacted contained two very important exemptions from registration: Section §4(2), 15 USC §77d(2), which exempts issuer transactions not involving a public offering, and section 3(b), 15 USC §77c(b), which enables the SEC to adopt regulations providing for the exemption of small issues. For many years section 4(2) was thought to exempt all issuances that were not made to the public at large. Then, in *SEC v Ralston Purina Co.* (1953) 346 US 119, the United States Supreme Court severely limited the exemption. For several decades thereafter, securities lawyers were left to seek case-by-case interpretive opinions issued by the SEC (called "no-action letters"). Finally in 1982 the SEC promulgated Regulation D, 17 CFR 230.147, which provides a safe harbor for issuers under section 4(2) and revises and coordinates the regulations authorizing exemptions under section 3(b). It applies to "business combinations" described in Rule 145, and to certain stock-for-stock transactions.

The use of Regulation D can be simple or complex, depending on the characteristics of the issuees and the monetary size of the offering. For instance, if the issuees are all "accredited investors," as defined by Regulation D, the requirements are few. The issuer must (1) make reasonable inquiry to ensure that the purchaser is acquiring the securities for himself and not others; (2) make written disclosure to each purchaser that the securities are not registered under the Securities Act and cannot be sold except upon registration or pursuant to an available exemption; (3) place a legend on the share certificate indicating lack of registration and the restriction on transferability; and (4) file a notice of the transaction with the SEC within 15 days after the first sale. Failure to file the Regulation D notice, like failing to file notice of exemption under California Corp C §25102(f), does not necessarily result in losing the exemption. See Securities Act Release 6825 (3–14–89).

Where the issuees are not "accredited," however, there are more stringent requirements. For instance, there can be sales to no more than 35 unaccredited investors, and each such offeree may have to be delivered offering materials which, in a sizable offering, may be comparable to a prospectus prepared in connection with a registration statement. "Accredited investors" under Rule 501(d) are those categories of entities and persons whom the SEC considers do not need the protection afforded the general public in a registered securities offering.

The "offering" under Regulation D may be considered to include purchasers and securities involved in transactions six months before and six months after the issuance in question. Consequently, one must look at the recent history of securities issuances and count not only the number of issuees within six months but also the dollar amount of consideration received for the securities. Similarly, securities issuances during the following six months may be restricted. Furthermore, the securities received cannot be resold unless it is either registered or exempt from registration.

For a detailed analysis of Regulation D, see Hicks, 1989 LIMITED OFFERING EXEMPTIONS: REGULATION D (new edition issued annually).

Failure to qualify under Regulation D does *not* necessarily mean that issuer cannot qualify for the section 4(2) exemption. However, the issuer is then subject to the ambiguous and often strict case-law interpretation (see above) of the section 4(2) exemption.

§6.85   (3) Restricted Securities and Rule 144

Restricted securities are those that are owned by affiliates of the issuer or are issued in an unregistered transaction not involving a public offering. Restricted securities cannot be offered or sold without registration except pursuant to an exemption. All transactions under Regulation D are considered to create restricted securities.

Rule 144, 17 CFR §230.144, is not actually an exemption. Rather, it is a "safe harbor" that defines the availability of the exemption provided by section 4(1) of the Securities Act, 15 USC §77d(1). The essence of Rule 144 is that, under specified circumstances, restricted securities may be sold on the open market after a two-year holding period, and may be sold without restriction after three years. When using Rule 144, study it carefully. It is far more complex than it initially appears.

The concept of restricted securities is a very important planning consideration. It is crucial to recognize that restricted securities not only cannot be readily sold but, for that reason, they are almost invariably less valuable than unrestricted securities. This is true whether their owner wants to sell them, pledge them as security for a loan, or merely show them as assets on a balance sheet. They are an asset whose full value cannot normally be realized until holding requirements have been fulfilled.

NOTE: Registration under the Securities Act is actually far more the exception than the rule. The exemptions outlined above and many others that are equally viable but more specialized make registration an alternative which, with the imagination and planning of counsel, is limited primarily to significant offerings to the general public. However, it should be remembered that there is no exemption to either the federal or the state anti-fraud provisions. The stringent securities fraud test will still apply to every securities issuance, whatever the exemption. Therefore, adequate and accurate factual disclosure is necessary in every instance.

§6.86 C. Problems Concerning Transferability of Assets

Sometimes problems involving the transferability of assets can be cured by changing the form of the acquisition. See §6.87. Occasionally, however, the problem may be incurable, either because of the nature of the restriction or because of the character of the acquiring party. For instance, the asset may be real property that is subject to a common law condition subsequent. If the condition would be breached by the transfer, the asset may be lost unless an understanding can be reached with the person or entity possessing the possibility of reverter.

More frequently, the untransferable asset is a contract right that requires the prior consent of a third party before a transfer can be effectuated.

§6.87 1. Lease and Contract Rights

Almost every lease contains a provision precluding assignment without the consent of the landlord. Similar restrictions can also be found in other contracts. Although presumably intended to protect parties from being involuntarily thrust into new and unsatisfactory relationships, such provisions are often used by the protected party as a way of extracting additional consideration or concessions from the other party. Fortunately, the California Supreme Court has acted to hold this practice to a minimum. In *Kendall v Ernest Pestana, Inc*. (1985) 40 C3d 488, 220 CR 818, the court held that if an assignment requires the prior consent of the lessor, the lessor may not withhold consent unless a commercially reasonable objection exists. Some of the factors a court will consider in determining whether consent is reasonably withheld are the financial responsibility of the proposed assignee, the suitability of the use for the particular property, the legality of the proposed use, the need for alteration of the premises, and the nature of the occupancy. Denying consent solely on the basis of personal taste, convenience, or sensibility is not commercially reasonable. 40 C3d at 501, 220 CR at 826. In other types of contracts, as well as leases, there is an implied covenant of good faith and fair dealing, and thus any discretionary powers of one party must be exercised with this in mind. See also *California Lettuce Growers, Inc. v Union Sugar Co.* (1955) 45 C2d 474, 484, 289 P2d 785, 791.

If it is necessary to obtain the consent of third parties before contract rights can be transferred, the logistics can be a formidable obstacle to a timely closing. For example, the other party to the contract or lease may be a large corporate organization located in a different part of the country whose leasing department has no particular reason to expedite the consent.

Acquisition agreements commonly require that the seller obtain the necessary written consents, and make the obtaining of such consents a condition precedent to the closing. If the necessary consents are not available when the closing date arrives, the buyer will have to decide whether to close, await the consent, or cancel the acquisition. The decision will usually depend on the importance of the asset to which the consent relates and on whether the seller is able to provide adequate assurances to protect the buyer. If the lease or contract right is important but not crucial to the transaction, the buyer may be willing to proceed based on the seller's agreement to indemnify for any harm caused by an eventual failure to obtain the consent.

Form of the Acquisition as Solution. There is no substitute for a careful reading of the contract or other document that requires consent to transfers. These provisions vary widely, depending on the draftsman and the situation. In some instances, a careful reading may indicate that a solution can be found in the form of the acquisition. The attorney should realize that it is comparatively easy to draft a contractual provision requiring the protected party's consent before the contract may be directly transferred, as in a sale of assets acquisition. It is somewhat more difficult to draft a contractual provision requiring the protected party's consent to a sale of stock by the other party, as in a sale of stock acquisition. It is even more difficult to draft a provision requiring the protected party's consent to a merger of the other party with another corporation—particularly if the transaction is a reverse merger in which the buyer merges into the target. All other things being equal, the solution may lie in the form of the transaction.

For restrictions on transfer contained in loan documents, see §6.89.

§6.88   2. Liquor Licenses

In a surprisingly large number of business transactions, the transfer of a liquor license from seller to buyer may be involved. For many proposed deals, particularly those involving restaurants and bars, the license may be an integral part of the transaction. Without it, the buyer may well decline to go through with the purchase.

In California, the sale of alcoholic beverages is strictly regulated. The license cannot simply be transferred to the buyer along with the other assets of the business. Rather, the statutory scheme set forth in Bus & P C §§24070–24082 must be complied with. The transfer requirements apply not only to outright sales but also to changes in ownership, *e.g.*, those occurring in stock sales or mergers. Bus & P C §24071.1.

Compliance can be complicated and may involve filing notice with the appropriate county recorders, application to the Department of Alcoholic Beverage Control for approval, and satisfaction of the Department's qualification standards. Any transfer is subject to an investigation of the transferee by the Department. Bus & P C §23958.

Because of the complexity of the license transferring process and the probable importance of the license, care must be taken to comply with all statutory and administrative requirements, or a valuable asset could be lost.

D. Effect of the Acquisition on Third Parties

§6.89   1. Creditors

The transfer of a corporation's assets is almost always proscribed in loan documents negotiated with a commercial lender. The loan document may call for repayment of the loan in the event of a sale of stock, sale of assets, or merger.

"Due on Sale" Clauses. Under 17 USC §1701j–3, which preempts state law, a "due on sale" clause in a promissory note secured by a deed of trust on real property is enforceable. If no real property security is involved, the California Commercial Code controls, and the clause is likewise enforceable. See *Guild Wineries & Distilleries v Land Dynamics* (1980) 103 CA3d 966, 166 CR 348. There is no solution to the problem of a due on sale clause except to deal with the lender. If the contract is important in the overall transaction, the buying corporation should be sure that satisfactory terms with the lender have been arrived at before making a final commitment to the acquisition.

§6.90   2. Encumbrances

The acquisition agreement should contain warranties and representations against liens on the target's real and personal property. However, the wary buyer will want to make its own investigation, and to that end will obtain a search by a title company covering each parcel of real property. In most situations, title companies are able to provide information on real property liens on fairly short notice.

As to encumbrances on personal property, the buyer should have a search service check with the Secretary of State for any UCC–1 Financing Statement filings (which are required to perfect a security interest in personal property located within the state). The seller may also want such a search, to support its representation that its assets are "free and clear of all encumbrances." This information may take somewhat longer to obtain than information from a title company.

§6.91   3. Bulk Transfers

The Bulk Transfer law, Division 6 of the Commercial Code (Com C §§6101–6111), was designed to protect a seller's creditors by allowing them to reach assets sold unless certain notice and payment requirements have been met. It governs only sales of assets transactions and applies only if the seller's "principal business is the sale of merchandise, including those who manufacture what they sell, or that of a baker, cafe or restaurant owner, garage owner, or cleaner and dyer" (Com C §6102(3)), and if the sale is of "a substantial part of the materials, supplies, merchandise or other inventory" (Com C §6102(1)). If such assets of any of the enumerated businesses are sold, the buyer must make certain that a specified form of notice is filed with the county recorder, published in a newspaper of general circulation, and mailed to the county tax collector. Com C §6107. Otherwise the transfer will be deemed "fraudulent and void against any creditor of the transferor" (Com C §6105), and action can be brought to levy against the goods for a period of one year after the transfer (Com C §6111). If the consideration for the sale is less than $1,000,000, and is substantially all cash or an obligation to pay cash in the future, the transferee or an escrow holder must follow a complex payment framework in order to pay creditors from the consideration resulting from the transfer. Com C §§6106, 6106.1.

Compliance with the Bulk Transfer law is frequently "waived" by the buyer, particularly if the seller is substantial. (Strictly speaking, compliance is not waived; rather, the parties merely elect not to comply. Since such a transaction is by definition a "fraudulent transfer," a question arises whether counsel can recommend or even participate in such a transaction.) The buyer in such circumstances often prefers to rely on the seller's warranty and indemnification covenants rather than to endure the tribulations of the notice and escrow provisions of the Commercial Code.

Oddly enough, however, the Bulk Transfer law is sometimes used for businesses to which it does not technically apply. The buyer may be concerned that the seller's trade creditors will not appreciate the fact that there is a new proprietor and will insist on payment by the buyer. The stringent procedures of the Bulk Transfer law increase the likelihood that the majority of the seller's creditors will be paid and also provide an easily understandable reason why those who do not assert their rights in a timely fashion are not entitled to payment.

The Bulk Transfer law, by its terms, protects only those creditors of the seller who hold claims based on transactions or events occurring before the bulk transfer. Com C §6109. However, if the seller files for bankruptcy, the trustee in bankruptcy (or the seller as debtor in possession) has the power to set aside a sale for the benefit of all creditors whose claims arose either before or after the bulk transfer, if there is any creditor of the seller who could claim the protection of the Bulk Transfer law. Bankr C §544(b), 11 USC §544(b). Thus, after a bulk sale a seller could incur substantial debt that has no relationship to that sale or to the business assets sold, and the bulk sale could be set aside for the benefit of all the seller's creditors as of the time of the bankruptcy filing. This possibility should be significant incentive for advising compliance with the Bulk Transfer law in every applicable instance, unless the seller's financial strength is unmistakable.

§6.92   4. The Insolvent Target

A buyer seeking to acquire a troubled business for a fire-sale price should consider the situation carefully before committing funds. If "reasonably equivalent value" is not paid for the assets, the transfer from the seller may be set aside if the seller (1) was insolvent at the time of or as a result of the transaction, (2) had unreasonably small capital remaining for its business, or (3) intended to incur, or believed that it would incur, debts beyond its ability to pay such debts as they mature. CC §3439.05 (Fraudulent Transfer Act); Bankr C §548, 11 USC §548. Under the Bankruptcy Code, the buyer retains a lien for the consideration paid but is not entitled to post-sale appreciation, which under some circumstances could be substantial. See Bankr C §548(c), 11 USC §548(c).

CAVEAT: An even more difficult situation is presented under the doctrine of *Dean v Davis* (1917) 242 US 438. If a purchaser is aware that the seller intends to use the proceeds of sale to prefer a creditor, a trustee in bankruptcy arguably can set the sale aside. Furthermore, even though the purchaser was unaware of any intention of the part of the seller to make a preference, it is arguable that the effect of Bankr C §§547(b) and 550(a) is to allow a trustee to set such a transaction aside.

NOTE: Perhaps the most troubling aspect of the foregoing is that there may be no defenses for the buyer, except to be certain that the seller is solvent and be able to prove it if the transaction is attacked (often an impossible burden). Any purchaser out of bankruptcy or from an insolvent seller should retain qualified bankruptcy counsel. This area is too specialized and too risky unless counsel is very familiar with the relevant law.

§6.93   5. The Leveraged Buy-Out

A common financing strategy of the buyer is to use the assets of an incorporated business to secure the purchase price for the stock of that corporation. Alternatively, the corporation may guarantee the buyer's purchase price obligation. In many such transactions, the corporation itself receives no benefit from having pledged its assets or guaranteed the buyer's debt. Thus, the transaction may be vulnerable to attack as a fraudulent transfer if either (1) the corporation was insolvent at the time of the transaction or as a result of the transaction (often true because the new liability is unaccompanied by any new asset); (2) the corporation had an unreasonably small amount of capital left for its business; or (3) the corporation intended to incur, or believed that it would incur, debts beyond its ability to pay them as they mature. See 11 USC §548(a)(2)(B) (the federal Bankruptcy Code); CC §§3439.04(b), 3409.05.

NOTE: The corporation's board of directors should be attuned to these issues. Directors have a high level of fiduciary duty here. See chap 2.

§6.94   6. Tort Liability

Nearly every business of significant size has pending or potential tort liability. Sometimes this tort liability can be insured against and sometimes it cannot. An important point in the negotiations is the allocation of the responsibility for unknown or contingent tort liabilities.

Merger and Sale of Stock. In a merger or a sale of stock, tort liability ordinarily goes along with the corporation, and if the seller is to retain any part of it, such retention must be clearly spelled out in the acquisition agreement.

Sale of Assets: Buyer's Liability. In a sale of assets (unlike a merger or sale of stock), the buyer ordinarily takes only those assets and those liabilities agreed upon. However, the California Supreme Court has carved out an important exception to this rule. In *Ray v Alad Corp.* (1977) 19 C3d 22, 136 CR 574, a corporation bought all the assets of a ladder manufacturer and began doing business under the seller's trade name, and the seller promptly wound up and dissolved. The court held the buyer liable for personal injuries caused by a ladder manufactured before the acquisition. Using the rationale of strict product liability, the court indicated that the buyer enjoyed its predecessor's goodwill and was in the best position to bear the burden of damage caused by the predecessor's faulty ladder. Later decisions have tended to narrow the holding of *Ray* rather than broaden it. See *Lundell v Sidney Mach. Tool Co.* (1987) 190 CA3d 1546, 236 CR 70 (purchaser not liable where business purchased was reduced in size and goodwill was not enjoyed); *Kline v Johns-Manville* (9th Cir 1984) 745 F2d 1217 (only part of business and assets were purchased); *Potlatch Corp. v Superior Court* (1984) 154 CA3d 1144, 201 CR 750 (if stock is acquired, rather than assets, liability does not extend beyond the acquired corporation). Nevertheless, the law in California continues to put a purchaser of assets in jeopardy for product liability claims.

Sale of Assets: Seller's Continuing Primary Liability. It is important to realize that whether or not the *Ray* doctrine applies, and no matter what the agreement of the parties, in a sale of assets transaction the seller continues to be primarily liable to third persons, even for liabilities assumed by the buyer. Since there is no way for the seller to get rid of this liability to third persons short of a novation and release, the seller must rely on the buyer's obligation to indemnify, as provided in the acquisition agreement.

Environmental Concerns. In any type of acquisition, counsel for both parties should be alert for any possible environmental liabilities. Because of the difficulty of proving when pollutants were introduced, the buyer should consider including environmental testing as part of its due diligence investigation (see §§6.54 and 6.110).

§6.95 E. Antitrust Considerations

Since a violation of the antitrust laws can involve both civil damages and criminal penalties, it is important to review every acquisition in light of applicable federal and state laws relating to restraint of trade and unfair competition. The problem is that these laws are so complex in their interpretation by the courts that in a close case only a lawyer who is truly an expert can make an accurate evaluation. Nevertheless, there are certain basic principles that can be applied to the clear cases.

The antitrust laws are numerous and very broad in their coverage. A complete discussion of their impact on mergers and acquisitions is beyond the scope of this chapter. For a basic treatment of the antitrust laws generally, see Hills, ANTITRUST ADVISER (3d ed 1985), particularly chapter 8, Compliance.

Section 7 of the Clayton Antitrust Act, 15 USC §18, deals specifically with corporate acquisitions in its first paragraph, as follows:

> No person engaged in commerce or in any activity affecting commerce shall acquire, directly or indirectly, the whole or any part of the stock or other share capital and no person subject to the jurisdiction of the Federal Trade Commission shall acquire the whole or any part of the assets of another person engaged also in commerce or in any activity affecting commerce, where in any line of commerce or in any activity affecting commerce in any section of the country, the effect of such acquisition may be substantially to lessen competition, or to tend to create a monopoly.

In applying this statute to a particular acquisition, the main question is how great a reduction in competition in the particular geographic and product market will result from the acquisition. In a large market with many small competitors, the competitive effect of combining any of them will probably be very slight. In a narrow market with few competitors, however, a merger can result in a substantial shift in market power and overall reduction in competition.

§6.96   1. Horizontal, Vertical, and Conglomerate Mergers

Horizontal Merger. A conflict with the antitrust laws is most likely to be encountered in a "horizontal" merger, in which the participants do business at the same level of the production/distribution chain. The merger of retailer with retailer or of manufacturer with manufacturer lessens competition by reducing the number of competitors in the market place. As a rule, the fewer the competitors, the greater the potential for one or two of them to control production and prices. See, *e.g., U.S. v Topco Assoc., Inc.* (1972) 405 US 596.

Vertical Merger. An acquisition is "vertical" if the combination is between entities doing business at different levels in the production/distribution chain, *e.g.,* manufacturer with wholesaler, wholesaler with retailer. A vertical merger may have anti-competitive effects, at least in the theoretical sense, but it is far less likely to be construed as a violation of the antitrust laws than a horizontal merger would be. In fact, the economic effect of a vertical combination is often beneficial, in that it increases the efficiency of the production/distribution chain without unduly affecting competition. See, *e.g., Continental T.V., Inc. v GTE Sylvania, Inc.* (1977) 433 US 36.

Conglomerate Merger. The antitrust laws are rarely a problem in acquisitions that involve entities in different industries and different markets. See, *e.g., U.S. v Connecticut Nat'l Bank* (1974) 418 US 656. Trouble will be encountered only if the parties are so large that the combination of their economic strength in itself is sufficient to affect the marketplace.

§6.97   2. The Relevant Market

Competition is defined in relation to the market in which the participants are doing business. Definition of the "relevant market" is invariably a central issue. There are two aspects to the determination of a relevant market: the product market and the geographic market. *Indiana Farmer's Guide Publishing Co. v Prairie Farmer Publishing Co.* (1934) 293 US 268. Definition involves complex economic considerations of product or source alternatives. In an acquisition, each participant's share in the relevant market and the relative shares of other competitors in that same market are measured, to determine the degree of concentration in the market and the degree to which competition may be reduced by an acquisition.

§6.98   3. Hart-Scott-Rodino Act: Premerger Notification

Under section 7A of the Clayton Act, 15 USC §18a, popularly referred to as the Hart-Scott-Rodino Act, the parties to acquisitions meeting certain size criteria must give 30 days' notice to the Federal Trade Commission and to the Department of Justice before the acquisition may be consummated. See §§6.99–6.100. The notification must include a comprehensive description of the characteristics of both participants, their relevant markets, their competitive positions, and their business plans. The fine for failing to file is $10,000 per day.

The time needed for the preparation of the application plus the 30-day waiting period can result in substantial delay to an acquisition unless compliance is begun at the earliest stage of the acquisition process.

§6.99   a. Size Requirements

The premerger notification requirements of the Hart-Scott-Rodino Act, 15 USC §18a, come into play only if either the buyer or seller is doing business in interstate commerce and each meets certain size criteria. Size is considered in two aspects, size of the participants and size of the transaction.

The first test, a measure of the size of the companies themselves, is met if either (a) a manufacturing company with total assets or annual net sales of $10 million or more is being acquired by a company with total assets or annual net sales of $100 million or more; (b) a company not engaged in manufacturing with total assets of $10 million or more is being acquired by a company with total assets or annual net sales of $100 million or more; or (c) any company with total assets or annual net sales of $100 million or more is being acquired by a company with total assets or annual net sales of $10 million or more. 15 USC §18a(a)(2). In assessing the size of the participating parties, all affiliated entities up to the ultimate parent entity or owner must be included.

Size of the Transaction. In addition to the foregoing, the acquiring party, as a result of the proposed acquisition, must hold either (a) 15 percent or more of the acquired party's voting securities or (b) an aggregate total of $15 million or more of the acquired party's voting securities or assets. 15 USC §18a(a)(3).

§6.100   b. Waiting Period

If a proposed merger or acquisition is subject to the Hart-Scott-Rodino Act, 15 USC §18a, it cannot be consummated until after the expiration of 30 days following receipt by the Justice Department and the Federal Trade Commission of the notice and required informational material. The waiting period can be shortened by joint action of the two agencies, or it can be extended. An extension may be imposed if additional documentary materials or information relevant to the proposed acquisition are requested. Requests for additional materials are often extensive and may take time to comply with. The extension may continue for not more than 20 days after receipt of such materials and information. Thereafter, no further delay may be imposed except by order of a United States District Court. 15 USC §18a(b), (e)(2). However, the agencies may, and often do, ask for voluntary extensions.

§6.101   c. Exemptions

The Hart-Scott-Rodino Act is intended to apply to industrial business combinations subject to the antitrust laws. It does not apply to (1) goods or realty transferred in the ordinary course of business, (2) acquisitions of non-voting securities, (3) acquisitions of voting securities that do not result in the increase in the acquiring party's percentage ownership of the issuer, (4) specified acquisitions of voting securities solely for investment purposes, (5) transactions to which the antitrust laws do not apply, (6) transfers to or from government agencies, or (7) specified transactions requiring government agency approval. 15 USC §18a(c).

§6.102   4. Challenges Based on Antitrust Violations

A proposed combination may be challenged by either public or private plaintiffs. The filing of a suit by a public agency depends on whether the agency considers the combination to be significantly anti-competitive. Filing of a suit by a private interest depends largely on whether that private interest is being sufficiently harmed by the combination, considers that it has a significant chance to win the suit, and has the funds to pursue protracted litigation.

§6.103   a. Public Plaintiffs

The most likely public plaintiffs are the Department of Justice, the Federal Trade Commission, and the Attorney General of the appropriate state. In addition, local enforcement agencies, such as district attorneys, may be empowered to enforce federal and state statutes aimed at anti-competitive practices.

Each of the various agencies with power to enforce the antitrust laws has its own set of published guidelines. If a particular merger transaction requires a premerger notice under Hart-Scott-Rodino (see §§6.98–6.101), the guidelines of all these agencies should certainly be consulted. Even if the acquisition is too small to fall within the purview of Hart-Scott-Rodino, the potential competitive impact of the transaction should be reviewed in light of these guidelines and state and federal court interpretation of the statutes involved.

§6.104   b. Private Plaintiffs

There are no published guidelines on when a private plaintiff may file suit to enjoin a combination. Counsel therefore should seek to discover what (if any) business interest may be harmed by it. Because of the complex economic issues involved, antitrust suits are invariably protracted and expensive. This in itself is a significant deterrent to litigation. Nevertheless, an injunction against the creation of a too powerful competitor may be less expensive and less risky than a fight in the marketplace. The possibility that a competitor may exercise its private right of action should never be ignored.

§6.105   F. Employee Matters

Poor labor relations, bad union contracts, or unfunded pension plans can be a serious drain on business profits. These are problems that may contribute to business failure following an acquisition.

§6.106   1. Union Contracts

Unions should be regarded with respect and handled with expertise. An attorney who is not experienced in the labor relations field should not hesitate to obtain assistance from a specialist. Most importantly, wherever there is a collective bargaining agreement, the buyer and seller must each make sure that someone with labor expertise reads it and advises concerning its present and future ramifications.

In a sale of stock transaction, the corporation remains intact and the buyer normally inherits the union contract along with the corporation. In a merger, the obligations of the disappearing corporation, including union contracts, normally become those of the surviving corporation. See Corp C §1107.

Although the assets of a business can usually be sold in a sale of assets transaction without binding the buyer to the seller's existing contracts, this rule does not necessarily apply to labor contracts. The Supreme Court has refused to adopt the normal corporate law distinctions between mergers, reorganizations, and sales of assets in the labor area. *Golden State Bottling Co. v NLRB* (1973) 414 US 168, 182 n5. Instead, the court has developed a concept of "successor" liability for union contracts, so that in appropriate circumstances, the successor employer may have to bargain with the previous union representative, regardless of whether the change in the employing entity occurred by merger, reorganization, or sale of assets. *NLRB v Burns Int'l Sec. Servs., Inc.* (1972) 406 US 272. In determining whether a corporation qualifies as a "successor" in this context, judicial and NLRB inquiries focus on continuity of the work force, continuity in the employing industry, continuity in the bargaining unit's appropriateness, and the impact of any suspension in operations. See Morris, THE DEVELOPING LABOR LAW 713 (2d ed 1983).

It is important to note that the court in *Burns* drew a distinction between successor liability for *bargaining* obligations versus *contractual* obligations. Successor liability does not automatically include an obligation to assume the predecessor's union contract terms. In several situations, however, the predecessor's contract obligations may be imposed on the successor. First, a successor that has expressly or constructively adopted the contract will be bound by the contract's terms. Constructive adoption can arise if the successor continues to follow the substantive terms of the union contract after the change in ownership. *Audit Servs., Inc. v Rolfson* (9th Cir 1981) 641 P2d 757; *Eklund's Sweden House Inn, Inc.* (1973) 203 NLRB 413. A similar result applies if it is held that the successor is the alter ego of the predecessor because of common ownership and control of the enterprise, among other things. See, *e.g., J. M. Tanaka Constr., Inc. v NLRB* (9th Cir 1982) 675 F2d 1029. Contract obligations also normally survive ownership changes via stock transfer transactions, if the corporate entity continues. *TKB Int'l Corp.* (1979) 240 NLRB 1082; *Western Boot & Shoe, Inc.* (1973) 205 NLRB 999.

NOTE: A corporation that is deemed a "successor" corporation may be liable for its predecessor's unfair labor practices if the successor was aware of the practices. *Golden State Bottling Col. v NLRB, supra; NLRB v Winco Petroleum Co.* (8th Cir 1982) 668 F2d 973.

Some collective bargaining agreements may contain a provision that, in the event of a sale of assets, the seller must require the purchaser to assume the union agreement. Failure of the seller to do so, and of the purchaser to assume the agreement, could lead to a breach of contract action against the seller and a tortious interference with contract action against the buyer. The union might even attempt to enjoin or set aside the sale if such a provision is ignored.

§6.107   2. Non-Union Employment Contracts

Contracts with individual employees can generally be dealt with on the same basis and following the same legal principles as other contracts. In an acquisition, however, it is important for the buyer to become informed as to which of the seller's employees have contracts, and what the terms of such contracts are. The problem lies in obtaining that information.

Although the selling corporation may believe it has contracts with only a few specific employees, it may actually have more (see below).

It is necessary to ferret out all of the seller's written agreements, consulting agreements, oral agreements, independent contractor agreements, sales representative agreements, and the like, to determine which of them should be considered employment contracts. To obtain this type of information, the buyer may have to engage in extensive discussions with all of the seller's officers and managers.

Employment contracts can be not only written or oral but also implied. See *Foley v Interactive Data Corp.* (1988) 47 C3d 654, 254 CR 211. The buyer should try to obtain all of the seller's personnel manuals and employee handbooks, and should treat such documents as if they were binding contracts with all the employees.

Of course, if the contract is implied, not even the seller may be aware of its terms. This area of uncertainty can be an important point of negotiation in a sale of stock or merger, and should not be neglected by a buyer even in a sale of assets. The buyer should demand protection in the form of appropriate representations, warranties, indemnities, and agreements to defend. If a buyer hires the seller's employees without clear understandings with them concerning their terms of employment, and without an express declaration that the buyer is not assuming any of the seller's obligations with respect to past employment terms, the seller's implied contracts of employment (if any) could carry forward to the new owner.

In a sale of assets, if it is the buyer's intention to hire some of the seller's employees but not to take on past employment-derived obligations, it is common practice for the seller to terminate all employees at or just before the closing. The seller may then have obligations relating to past employment, but the buyer is free to negotiate new terms of employment with each employee. Caution should be taken to avoid employment or hiring practices that could indicate a pattern of racial, sexual, or other forbidden types of discrimination.

§6.108   3. Employee Benefit Plans

It is not extraordinary for a company's retirement plan to be either its largest asset or its largest liability. The plan can involve a single employer, or it can be a multiemployer plan, typically sponsored and maintained by a union, over which a single employer may have little control. A multiemployer plan can have obligations in the millions or even billions. If assets have been accumulated to meet a company's obligations under a retirement plan, it is said to be fully funded. If excess assets have been accumulated, the plan is overfunded, and if the assets are deficient, the plan is underfunded.

Obviously, the extent of a company's obligations under a retirement plan cannot be finally determined until all of the retirements occur (and, under some plans, until all of the retirees die). There is a similar problem in making a present determination of the amount of funds that will be available in the future to make retirement payments. An actuary can make a statistical calculation of funding, and such a calculation may be sufficient for many purposes. It does not, however, determine ultimate liability. Considered thought should be given to the extent of assets and liabilities associated with retirement plans, as well as the responsibilities of each of the parties to such plans.

Unfunded Liability. Perhaps the most significant concern in the merger and acquisition context is the potential for unfunded liability in employee retirement plans. In a merger or sale of stock, unfunded liability follows the company's assets by operation of law. Corp C §1107. Only the actuarial calculations and the seller's warranties and representations determine the theoretical extent of that liability.

In a sale of assets, the situation is somewhat different. The Employee Retirement Income Security Act of 1974 (ERISA), 29 USC §§1001–1461, a complex piece of federal legislation governing employee benefit plans, was drafted with major corporations and unions in mind but applies equally to smaller entities. Under ERISA, a "withdrawal" from a multiemployer plan may be deemed to have occurred when a sale of the assets takes place, resulting in the buyer's immediate liability for the seller's proportionate portion of unfunded liability of the entire multiemployer plan. See 29 USC §§1381–1461. This liability could be immense. Withdrawal liability can be avoided if the buyer assumes the seller's obligations under the plan and a bond is posted to ensure continued contributions. See 29 USC §1384.

ERISA also creates potential liability for past violations. A transaction prohibited by ERISA can result in personal liability on the part of plan fiduciaries. 29 USC §1109. It is important for the buyer to investigate this possibility during the due diligence process and require the seller to make strong warranties against it.

Group Health Plans. Under the health care continuation provisions of the Comprehensive Omnibus Budget Reconciliation

Act of 1986 ("COBRA"), 29 USC §§1161–1168, any employee health plan provided by an employer must give certain health plan beneficiaries, including terminated employees, the option of continuing expiring health coverage for a period of time after regular coverage terminates on account of certain specified causes. If the parties, particularly in a sale of assets, are not vigilant on this issue, one or the other could incur the statutory COBRA liability for the coverage, with no right of indemnification from the other party and without the support of an insurance carrier. To find out after the fact that a party is self-insured for such coverage could be an absolute disaster, particularly if a large number of employees are not retained by the buyer.

Furthermore, COBRA provides *severe penalties* for violations, with only oblique guidance as to who is responsible for such coverage in a sale of assets. See 26 USC §4980 (IRC §4980), 29 USC §§1451–1453. The parties should carefully carve up COBRA responsibility in the acquisition or merger agreement.

The intricacies of ERISA are the bailiwick of specialists, and if problems are encountered, the general business practitioner should not attempt to deal with them unassisted.

§6.109   4. Accrued Wages and Benefits

In a sale of assets, the buyer and seller can pick and choose which of the assets and which of the liabilities will be included in the sale. Therefore, the decision as to which employees will remain on the payroll and which of their benefits will be assumed by the buyer becomes a subject of negotiation. Accrued vacations, unpaid wages, and benefit packages can add up to substantial sums, and therefore call for the close attention of both buyer and seller. If the dollar amount of such obligations could be significant relative to the size of the acquisition, specific numbers rather than mere generalities should be negotiated and set forth in the acquisition agreement.

§6.110   G. Environmental Considerations

The Comprehensive Environmental Response, Compensation, and Liability Act of 1980 (CERCLA), 42 USC §§9601–9675, has given rise to a body of law that cuts through many common law protections for corporations, their shareholders, officers and directors. CERCLA created a $1.6 billion fund to enable federal and state agencies to begin immediately cleaning up dangerous hazardous waste disposal sites. It also authorized federal and state governmental agencies to recover "response costs," which include clean-up costs and damages for injuries to natural resources, from the private sector. The principal effect of CERCLA on corporate acquisitions is the liability that it imposes not only on polluters but also on current owners of polluted real property.

§6.111   1. The Sweep of Liability

The owner of real property is responsible for disposing of hazardous waste contamination. Furthermore, the courts have uniformly held that corporate officers may be individually liable for hazardous waste cleanup under CERCLA. See, *e.g., State of New York v Shore Realty Corp.* (2d Cir 1985) 759 F2d 1032; *U.S. v Northeastern Pharmaceutical & Chem. Co.* (8th Cir 1986) 810 F2d 726. Individual liability may be imposed against corporate shareholders, officers, and directors, irrespective of actual wrongful conduct, provided only that the individuals had the power to control the disposal of waste. 42 USC §9607(a). CERCLA requires only a minimal showing of causation, tacitly imposes strict liability and joint and several liability, and allows the corporation to avoid liability only if the violations were occasioned by an act of God, an act of war, or, in extremely limited circumstances, the acts of a third party. 42 USC §9607(b).

§6.112   2. Successor Liability

From the perspective of the successor corporation, the threat of liability under CERCLA for the environmental violations of the prior owner and operator is significant. Liability will be imposed on the current owner or operator without reference to whether that corporation caused or contributed to the release of hazardous waste. The court in *State of New York v Shore Realty Corp.* (2d Cir 1985) 759 F2d 1032, discussed the rationale behind the rule imposing strict liability against a successor corporation: "It is quite clear that if the current owner of a site could avoid liability merely by having purchased the site after chemical dumping had ceased, waste sites certainly would be sold, following the cessation of dumping, to new owners who could avoid the liability otherwise required by CERCLA." 759 F2d at 1045. Obviously, a thorough investigation of all premises of a potential target is essential in the early planning stages. The fact is that the potential cost of a cleanup can approach and even exceed the value of the property itself.

§6.113 3. Dealing With the Problem

Appropriate warranties and representations are obviously a necessity in any transaction in which real property will be involved or in which the target corporation is involved in manufacturing or other processes which may produce pollutants. It is important to note, however, that the protection of the seller's indemnity obligations to the buyer is limited to the seller's financial ability to respond in damages. While this is true in any circumstances, it is even more important to consider in the toxic-waste context because of the potentially disproportionate liability and because insurance coverage may be extremely expensive or unavailable. Enforceable warranties of the seller should be considered generally insufficient where the potential risks are significant. The developments in this area of the law have caused the dramatic expansion of the industry involved in the discovery, analysis, and disposal of toxic waste. An expert in this field should be retained to assess the site and thoroughly examine the land use history of the target's real property. In fact, if bank financing is involved, the lender can be expected to require such an investigation.

There are circumstances under which the buyer may wish to proceed without sufficient contractual protections from the seller or without thorough investigation. In such instances, it will be important to utilize a corporation to shield the principal assets of the seller. The target business should remain in a corporation separate from the buyer until hazardous waste questions have been laid to rest. This can be done using either the stock purchase method or by forming a separate corporation to receive the assets of or to merge with the target. However, the principles enunciated in cases such as *State of New York v Shore Realty Corp.* (2d Cir 1985) 759 F2d 1032 (see §6.112) must be scrupulously observed. In the current state of the law, it would appear that directors and officers of a corporation can be held personally liable for continued pollution and that an individual shareholder may be similarly liable if that shareholder was in a position to control the handling of pollutants. Thus far, the courts have not gone beyond this. However, it is a relatively short jump from this holding to a holding that a parent corporation is liable for the activities of its wholly owned and controlled subsidiary.

V. THE MERGER: REQUIRED FORMALITIES

A. The Merger Agreement

§6.114   1. Required Contents

To effectuate a merger, a merger agreement must be filed with the California Secretary of State, along with officer's certificates for each of the constituent corporations. Corp C §1103. The statutory requirements for contents of the merger agreement (Corp C §1101) are as follows:

(1) The terms and conditions of the merger (Corp C §1101(a));

(2) Any amendments to the surviving corporation's articles to be effected by the merger (Corp C §1101(b));

(3) The names and places of incorporation of the constituent corporations, and identification of the surviving corporation (Corp C §1101(c)); and

(4) A specific description of the method of converting shares and of any other consideration that shareholders are to receive (Corp C §1101(d)).

When drafting the merger agreement, counsel should also refer to Corp C §§1100–1112, 1200–1203 ("reorganizations"), and 1300–1312 (dissenters' rights), for other matters that may be applicable.

The Secretary of State reviews merger documents submitted for filing to determine whether they meet statutory requirements. However, except for certain questions regarding corporate names, the Secretary of State must ultimately rely on an appropriate written legal opinion of California counsel with respect to whether an instrument conforms to law. Corp C §110(b).

NOTE: Filing by the Secretary of State does not prevent others from attacking the merger agreement on the ground that it does not meet the statutory requirements.

In a merger of affiliated corporations (*e.g.*, parent and subsidiary), an agreement that includes little more than the statutory requirements may be sufficient. An acquisition merger, however, involves the purchase and sale of a corporate business, so most of the matters ordinarily included in an agreement for the sale of stock or the sale of assets must be either included or covered in a separate agreement (see §6.115). Among the general provisions common to all types of business acquisitions are:

- A statement of the consideration (*e.g.,* shares) to be exchanged;
- Representations and warranties of the parties;
- Conditions precedent to the obligation of the parties to consummate or close the transaction;
- Covenants regarding conduct of business and other matters during the period preceding the closing;
- The time, place, and procedure for closing;
- Postclosing covenants and obligations, including covenants for registering securities;
- Miscellaneous provisions, *e.g.,* notices, attorney fees, governing law. For examples of such provisions, see SALE OF BUSINESSES chap 6 (2d ed Cal CEB 1988).

§6.115   2. Use of Separate Reorganization Agreement

Many of the subjects not required by statute to be included in the merger agreement (see §6.114) may be covered in a separate agreement, often called a reorganization agreement or an acquisition agreement. Unlike the formal merger agreement, the reorganization agreement is not filed with the Secretary of State. The substantive scope and effect of the provisions are generally the same whether they are contained in one agreement or two. Therefore, the decision to use a separate reorganization agreement is dictated by practical considerations, *e.g.,* the desire to facilitate amendments before closing, or to limit the matters disclosed in the public records. If a separate reorganization agreement is used, its provisions must be consistent with those of the formal merger agreement.

For a detailed form of merger acquisition agreement, see SALE OF BUSINESSES chap 6 (2d ed Cal CEB 1988).

§6.116   3. Merger Agreement Forms

The following sample forms of merger agreement include primarily the basic provisions required by statute, and are for filing with the

Secretary of State. The first (Form 6.117–1) is for a simple two-party merger. The second (Forms 6.118–1 through 6.118–7) is for a triangular merger between affiliated corporations, but may be adapted for a merger of unrelated corporations if the factual situation is not complicated. For a more detailed form of agreement for use in an acquisition, see SALE OF BUSINESSES chap 6 (2d ed Cal CEB 1988).

§6.117 a. Form: Merger Agreement, Two Party (For Filing With Secretary of State)

Form 6.117–1

AGREEMENT OF MERGER

This Agreement of Merger is entered into between [*name*], a California corporation (herein "Surviving Corporation") and [*name*], a California corporation (herein "Disappearing Corporation").

1. Disappearing Corporation shall be merged into Surviving Corporation.

[*First alternative*]

2. The outstanding shares of Disappearing Corporation shall be cancelled and no shares of Surviving Corporation shall be issued in exchange therefor.

[*Second alternative*]

2. Each outstanding share of Disappearing Corporation shall be converted to _____ share(s) of Surviving Corporation.

[*Continue*]

3. The outstanding shares of Surviving Corporation shall remain outstanding and are not affected by the merger.

4. Disappearing Corporation shall, from time to time, as and when requested by Surviving Corporation, execute and deliver all documents and instruments and take all actions necessary or desirable to evidence or carry out this merger.

5. The effect of the merger and the effective date of the merger are as prescribed by law.

IN WITNESS WHEREOF the parties have executed this Agreement.

[*Name of surviving corporation*]

By [*Signature*]
[*Typed name*]
President

By [*Signature*]
[*Typed name*]
Secretary

[*Name of disappearing corporation*]

By [*Signature*]
[*Typed name*]
President

By [*Signature*]
[*Typed name*]
Secretary

§6.118   b. Form: Merger Agreement (Triangular Merger, Affiliated Corporations)

Form 6.118–1 (Introduction and Parties)

AGREEMENT OF MERGER

This agreement of merger (Agreement) is entered into between [*name of surviving corporation*] **(Survivor), a California Corporation, and** [*name of disappearing corporation*] **(Disappearing), a California Corporation, the constituent corporations in this merger.**

Comment: The name and place of incorporation of each constituent corporation must be included. Corp C §1101(c).

Form 6.118–2 (Recitals)

A. The issued and outstanding stock of Disappearing consists of _ _ _ _ common shares.

B. The issued and outstanding stock of Survivor consists of ____ common shares.

[Add, if applicable]

C. [*Name of parent corporation*] (Parent) is a California corporation that owns 100 percent of the issued and outstanding shares of both Disappearing and Survivor.

Form 6.118–3 (Statement of Merger)

Survivor and Disappearing agree that Survivor and Disappearing shall, on the effective date of the merger stated in this Agreement, be merged into a single corporation, Survivor, and that the terms and conditions of the merger are as stated in this Agreement. On the effective date of the merger, the separate existence of Disappearing shall cease, and Survivor, as the surviving corporation, shall succeed, without other transfer, to all the rights and property of Disappearing, and shall be subject to all the debts and liabilities of Disappearing, in the same manner as if Survivor itself had incurred them.

Comment: This provision designates the surviving corporation, as required by Corp C §1101(c). The statement of the basic effect of the merger (Corp C §1107(a)) is advisable, although not required by statute.

Form 6.118–4 (Articles, Bylaws, Officers, and Directors)

The articles of incorporation of Survivor in effect on the effective date of the merger shall continue in effect until altered or amended as provided by this Agreement or by law. The bylaws of Survivor shall not be altered by this Agreement. The officers and board of directors of Survivor shall not be altered by this Agreement.

Comment: Although not required by statute, it may be desirable to document these aspects of the transaction. If the articles of the survivor are to be amended, see Corp C §1101(b). There is no provision for amending bylaws in a merger agreement.

Form 6.118–5 (Manner of Converting Shares)

[First Alternative: No Shares Issued or Consideration Given]

The shares of Survivor outstanding on the effective date shall not be changed or converted as a result of the merger, but shall remain outstanding as shares of Survivor. The outstanding shares of Disappearing shall be cancelled, and no shares of Survivor shall be issued in exchange for them.

Comment: This provision is advisable if no additional shares are issued and no other consideration is given, and shares of both corporations are held in the same proportion by the same shareholders. A statement of what happens to the outstanding shares of each constituent should be included even if these is no change. See Corp C §1101(d); 1 MARSH'S CALIFORNIA CORPORATION LAW §18.27 (2d ed).

[Second Alternative: Shares Converted]

The shares of Survivor outstanding on the effective date shall not be changed or converted as a result of the merger, but shall remain outstanding as shares of Survivor. On the effective date, each issued and outstanding common share of Disappearing shall be converted into _ _ _ _ common share(s) of Survivor. No fractional shares shall be issued[./,]

[Add, if appropriate]

but each shareholder of Disappearing who would otherwise be entitled to receive a fraction of a share of Survivor shall receive, in lieu of a fractional share, an amount in cash equal to the value of that fraction, based on the fair value of the shares of Survivor as determined by the board of directors of Survivor in office immediately after the effective date.

Comment: The manner of converting the shares must be stated. Corp C §1101(d).

Form 6.118–6 (Effective Date)

An executed counterpart of this Agreement of merger and officers' certificates of each of the constituent corporations shall be filed in the office of the California Secretary of State.

[First alternative]

The merger shall become effective on the date of that filing.

[*Second alternative*]

The merger shall become effective on [*date*], **which date is not more than 90 days after the date of that filing.**

Comment: It is advisable, although not required, to recite the filing procedure. Unless otherwise specified, the merger is effective on the date of filing. Corp C §1103. The second alternative is designed to take advantage of Corp C §110(c), which permits a delayed effective date not more than 90 days after the date of filing. Use of a delayed effective date, however, is often impractical for mergers of unrelated corporations.

Form 6.118–7 (Signatures)

IN WITNESS WHEREOF, Survivor and Disappearing, as duly authorized by their respective boards of directors, have caused this Agreement of merger to be executed as of [*date*].

[*Name of surviving corporation*]

By _____
[*Title*]

By _____
[*Title*]

[*Name of disappearing corporation*]

By _____
[*Title*]
By _____
[*Title*]

Comment: Each corporation must sign the agreement by its chairman of the board, president, or a vice president, and by its secretary or assistant secretary. Corp C §1102. No corporate seal, verification, or notarial acknowledgment of the signatures is required by the Corporations Code. They may, however, be desired by the parties or required by governmental agencies or private institutions involved in the particular merger.

B. Action by Directors

§6.119   1. Authorization and Related Actions

The board of directors of each corporation ordinarily must approve the agreement of merger (including the separate acquisition or reorganization agreement, if used). See Corp C §§1101, 1200. For form of resolution, see §6.120. The agreement may also be approved by a committee of the board (to the extent permitted by the bylaws or board resolution), unless the merger requires approval by the outstanding shares or the merger agreement contains other matters not within the statutory competence of a committee. See Corp C §311. If the merger is to be approved at a special meeting of the board, it is good practice (although not required by statute; see Corp C §307(a)(2)) to indicate the purpose of the meeting in the notice.

A complete copy of the proposed form of merger agreement should be submitted to each director, and one copy should be permanently retained in the corporate minute books or files. The approval can be given at a board meeting or by written consent of all directors without a meeting. Corp C §307(b); see §§1.5–1.30. For a checklist of various other actions that must be taken by the boards of directors, see §6.121.

§6.120   a. Form: Resolution of Acquired Corporation Approving Merger (Triangular Merger)

Form 6.120–1

There has been submitted to and discussed at this meeting an agreement of merger [*and related reorganization agreement*] **between and among this corporation,** [*name of parent acquiring corporation*] **(Parent), and** [*name of parent's subsidiary corporation*] **(Subsidiary), providing for the merger of this corporation with and into Subsidiary. The board of directors of this corporation deems it in the best interests of this corporation and its shareholders that this corporation enter into that merger with Subsidiary.**

In view of the above, it is

RESOLVED that the merger of this corporation with and into Subsidiary, and the terms and conditions of the merger as set

forth in the agreement of merger [*and related reorganization agreement*] dated [*date*] are approved.

RESOLVED FURTHER that the chairman of the board, president or any vice president, and the secretary or any assistant secretary of this corporation are authorized and directed by and on behalf of this corporation and in its name to execute and deliver to Subsidiary the agreement of merger [*and related reorganization agreement*] between the parties named above and this corporation [*substantially*] in the form in which [*that agreement was/those agreements were*] presented and discussed at this meeting [*./,*]

[*Add, if appropriate*]

but with such changes as the officers executing [*it/them*] shall deem appropriate, as conclusively evidenced by their execution of [*it/them*].

[*Continue*]

RESOLVED FURTHER that the secretary of this corporation is directed to place [*a copy/copies*] of the agreement of merger [*and reorganization agreement*], in the form presented and discussed at this meeting, in the minute book following the minutes of this meeting.

Comment: These resolutions are for the acquired corporation in a triangular merger, but, with minor changes, would be appropriate for the subsidiary. The resolutions adopted by the parent's board would be similar, but would reflect that the actual merger would be between the subsidiary and the acquired corporation. These resolutions can be adapted for use in a regular two-party merger. The officers who may sign the agreement are specified by Corp C §1102.

If the optional language permitting corporate officers to make changes in the form of agreement is used, note that the agreements must remain substantially in the form presented to and approved by the board. See Corp C §§1101, 1103; 2 Ballantine & Sterling, CALIFORNIA CORPORATION LAWS §258.03 (4th ed). Although the law is unclear, counsel should consider the advisability of having the board ratify any changes made by the officers, before the officers' certificate is filed. Any amendment to the executed agreement must be approved in the same manner as the original agreement. Corp C §1104.

§6.121   b. Table: Other Actions

In addition to approval of the merger, the following other actions ordinarily would be taken by the directors of one or more of the parties to the merger, as indicated. This table assumes a triangular merger in which the subsidiary is the surviving corporation and is wholly owned by the parent corporation.

	Parent	*Subsidiary*	*Acquired Corporation*
(a) Call a shareholder's meeting to consider approving the agreement, unless the time of the regular annual meeting renders it unnecessary, or unless the shareholder's approval will be obtained by written consent. See §§6.124–6.129. Approval by the parent as the subsidiary's sole shareholder ordinarily would be by written consent.	X	X	X
(b) Fix a record date for voting at the shareholders' meeting. Corp C §701.	X		X
(c) Appointment inspectors of election (if desired) for shareholders' meeting. Corp C §707.	X		X
(d) Designate the persons to be named as proxies in any proxy form distributed by management to shareholders. See §§6.127–6.128.	X		X
(e) Approve any amendment to the articles of incorporation. See §5.106.	X	X	
(f) Authorize preparation, or approve the form, of any material to be sent to shareholders, and direct that it be timely sent.	X		X
(g) Authorize preparation and filing of the application for permit with the California Department of Corporations. See §§5.74–5.89.	X		

	Parent	Subsidiary	Acquired Corporation
(h) Authorize any necessary filing with blue sky authorities of other states, stock exchanges, banks, trustees, or other authorities or institutions.	X	X	X
(i) Authorize filing with the Securities and Exchange Commission (1) the proxy material, or information statement, if required; and (2) any necessary registration statements or SEC Regulation A materials.	X		X
(j) Authorize all necessary or proper filings and recording of the merger agreement after all approvals are obtained from shareholders or others.		X	X
(k) State by resolution the fair value of nonmonetary consideration (shares of acquired corporation) for which shares are to be issued. Corp C §409(e).	X		
(l) Authorize officers to sell and issue stock pursuant to the merger, the Commissioner of Corporations permit, any other blue sky qualifications, and an effective registration statement with the Securities and Exchange Commission, if applicable.	X		
(m) Authorize execution of written assumption of liabilities of the acquired corporation to be filed with the Franchise Tax Board. See §§6.144–6.145.		X	
(n) Authorize any necessary amendment of any contracts, licenses, pension plans, or similar documents.	X	X	X
(o) Approve form of any new stock certificates.	X		
(p) Authorize any assumption of stock options of acquired corporation.	X		

	Parent	Subsidiary	Acquired Corporation
(q) Authorize execution of supplemental indentures if acquired corporation has outstanding bonds or debentures.		X	
(r) Authorize any filings to qualify to do business in states where acquired corporation does business.			
(s) Authorize application for business permits and licenses held by acquiring corporation.		X	
(t) Authorize execution of all documents and all other action the officers consider necessary or proper to carry out the purposes of the other resolutions.	X	X	X

§6.122   2. Amendment of Merger Agreement

The merger agreement may be amended, before consummation of the merger, by approvals of the same kind, given in the same manner, as required for the original agreement. The amended agreement must be signed in the same way as an original agreement. Corp C §1104.

§6.123   3. Abandonment of Merger

The directors of any corporation may abandon a merger, subject to the rights of third parties (including other constituent corporations) under any related contracts, without further shareholder action or approval, any time before the merger becomes effective. Corp C §1105. If a merger agreement providing for a delayed effective date has been filed with the Secretary of State, the merger can be abandoned by a certificate to that effect by any of the constituent corporations (Corp C §161) filed before the specified effective date. Corp C §110(c). For form of certificate, see 3 MARSH'S CALIFORNIA CORPORATION LAW App B, Form No. 103 (2d ed). However, the merger agreement itself may restrict abandonment *e.g.,* by requiring the consent of all parties or permitting unilateral abandonment only in specified situations.

C. Shareholder Approval

§6.124   1. Requirements

A merger reorganization (Corp C §181(a)) ordinarily must be approved by the outstanding shares of each class of each corporation whose directors are required to approve the merger agreement. This includes the constituent corporations and any parent corporation whose shares are used in the merger (a "parent party"; see Corp C §1200(d)). Corp C §§117, 1201(a). This requirement does not apply to short-form mergers (discussed in §§6.149–6.153). Corp C §181(a). "Approved by the outstanding shares" means approved by the affirmative vote of a majority (unless the articles require a higher percentage) of the outstanding shares of each class or series, regardless of restrictions on the voting rights of the class or series. If a corporation's articles require a higher percentage vote of any class or series, the merger reorganization must be approved by that higher percentage. Corp C §152. Shareholder approval may be given before or after that of directors (Corp C §1201(f)), but ordinarily would be sought afterwards. Approval may be either by written consent or by vote at a shareholder meeting. Any amendment to the merger agreement is subject to the same shareholder approval requirements as the original agreement. Corp C §1104.

There are two major exceptions to the requirement of shareholder approval:

(1) No approval by preferred shareholders, as a class, of the surviving corporation or parent party is required if the rights, preferences, privileges, and restrictions of those shares remain unchanged by the merger, unless an amendment is made to the articles that would otherwise require this approval (Corp C §1201(a), (c)), or unless the articles require a class vote by those shares (Corp C §1201(a)). This exception prevents a small class of the preferred shareholders of the surviving or parent corporation from blocking the merger.

(2) Shareholder approval is generally not required of the acquiring corporation or its parent if those who were the corporation's shareholders immediately before the merger own, immediately after the merger, equity securities possessing more than five sixths of the voting power of the surviving corporation or parent party. The theory behind this exception is that, in such a situation, the dilution will

not be substantial. In calculating voting power for this purpose, special rules are provided to remove the effects of cross-ownership and to exclude securities whose potential for dilution is relatively remote. Corp C §1201(b).

Qualification of the Voting Power Dilution Exception. The voting power dilution exception is, however, subject to three qualifications:

(1) Shareholder approval is required if any amendment that would require shareholder approval is made to articles of the surviving corporation (*e.g.,* an amendment to increase the authorized shares, or create a new class or series). Corp C §1201(c).

(2) Approval by class vote is required if the class will receive shares of the surviving corporation or shares of a corporation whose shareholder rights, preferences, privileges, or restrictions are different from those of the shares surrendered. Identical shares issued by a foreign corporation are considered different for this purpose. Corp C §1201(d).

(3) If, in the merger, shareholders of a statutory close corporation (Corp C §158) receive shares of a corporation that is not a statutory close corporation, an affirmative vote of at least two thirds of each class of the outstanding shares of the close corporation is necessary, unless the articles provide for a lesser vote (but in no event less than a majority vote). Corp C §1201(e).

If the number of shares to be issued by the acquiring corporation is indefinite (*e.g.,* if the number is tied to fluctuating factors such as earnings of the acquired company or the market price of the shares at the closing of the merger), a merger agreement that meets the tests of the voting power dilution exception when the agreement is signed might possibly not qualify at the time the transaction is closed. In that situation, either the maximum number of shares to be issued in the transaction should be limited to ensure that the exception will apply, or shareholder approval should be obtained.

2. Meeting To Consider Proposed Merger

§6.125   a. Timing of Meeting

Shareholder approval of a merger reorganization may be given by written consent or at an annual or special meeting. See §§1.31–1.63 for general requirements for shareholder meetings.

Factors in fixing the date of the meeting include (a) the time needed to obtain a permit, if required, from the Commissioner of Corporations, and approval by the Securities and Exchange Commission of proxy material, if required; (b) the time required after that to give notice of the meeting and to solicit proxies for, or to ensure sufficient personal attendance at, the meeting; (c) the proposed date for consummating the transaction; and (d) the time schedule for matters to be attended to after the meeting and before consummation (*e.g.,* the time for sending notice of approval of merger, and the date by which the necessary papers must be dispatched for filing.

§6.126   b. Form: Notice of Meeting

Form 6.126–1

NOTICE OF SPECIAL MEETING OF SHAREHOLDERS OF
[*Name of corporation*]
ON [*date*]

To the shareholders of [*name of corporation*]**:**

A special meeting of the shareholders of [*name of corporation*] **will be held at** [*address and city*]**, California, on** [*date*] **at** [*time*]**, solely for the purpose of considering and voting on the approval of the agreement of merger** [*and related reorganization agreement*] **dated** [*date of agreement*]**, providing for the merger of** [*name*]**, a California corporation, into** [*name*]**, a California corporation** [*, which is a wholly owned subsidiary of [name*]**, a California corporation**].

Enclosed with this notice are a form of proxy for the meeting and a proxy statement describing the general terms of the merger and containing a copy of the agreement of merger [*and related reorganization agreement*]**.**

[*Insert notice of dissenters' rights, if required*]

[*Continue*]

Shareholders of record on the books of the corporation at the close of business on [*date*] **will be entitled to vote at the meeting. All shareholders are cordially invited to attend the**

meeting in person, BUT THOSE WHO ARE UNABLE TO DO SO ARE URGED TO SIGN, DATE, AND RETURN THE ENCLOSED PROXY AT THEIR EARLIEST CONVENIENCE.

Dated: _ _ _ _ _ _

> **By order of the board of directors**
> [*Signature*]
> **Secretary**

Comment: For a general discussion of notice requirements and general forms of notice and declaration of mailing, see §§1.35–1.47.

This notice is for shareholders of the parent corporation in a triangular merger or for shareholders of the acquired corporation. Normally, the approval of the parent as sole shareholder of the subsidiary in a triangular merger is by written consent. Notice to holders of certain publicly traded stock must include appropriate notice of dissenters' rights. Corp C §1300(b)(1); see §§6.130–6.142.

The general nature of the proposal (unless approval is unanimous) must be stated in the notice or in any written waiver of notice. Corp C §601(f). It is not necessary to send shareholders a copy of the complete merger or reorganization agreement. However, such copies are usually a helpful supplement to the disclosure in the proxy statement, and it is desirable to qualify any description of those agreements by reference to the agreements themselves. Publicly held companies subject to the reporting requirements of the Securities Exchange Act of 1934 (15 USC §§78a–78kk) must provide a proxy statement that includes substantial information about the constituent corporations and the effect of the merger. SEC Reg 14A (17 CFR §§240.14a–1 through 240.14a–103). Corporations subject to the proxy rules must comply with them in connection with soliciting consents and with any meeting of the shareholders even if proxies are not solicited. Even corporations not subject to the federal proxy rules may nevertheless be required to make similar disclosure by Securities Exchange Act of 1934 §10(b) (15 USC §78j(b)) and Exchange Act Rule 10b–5 (17 CFR §240.10b–5), which require full and fair disclosure to shareholders. Moreover, the California Commissioner of Corporations may require that a proxy statement similar to that required under the proxy rules be sent to each person to whom an offer is made in connection with a merger. Corp C §25148.

c. Proxy

§6.127 (1) Use of Proxy

Every person entitled to vote shares may authorize others to act by proxy with respect to those shares. Corp C §705(a). A proxy is a written authorization signed by a shareholder or his or her attorney in fact giving another person power to vote shares. Corp C §178. No proxy is valid after the expiration of 11 months from its date, unless it provides otherwise. Corp C §705(b). A proxy may be made irrevocable under certain conditions. See Corp C §705(e). Any revocable proxy may be revoked, before it is voted, by a writing delivered to the corporation, by a subsequent proxy presented to the meeting, or by the maker's attendance at the meeting and voting in person. Corp C §705(b).

§6.128 (2) Form: Proxy

Form 6.128–1

**PROXY SOLICITED ON BEHALF OF
THE BOARD OF DIRECTORS FOR
THE MEETING OF SHAREHOLDERS**

The undersigned, as record owner of the shares of [*name of corporation*] **(the "Corporation"), a California corporation, described below, hereby appoints the following person:**

[ ] [*Name of proxy*]

as his or her agent and proxy, with full power of substitution, to vote all shares of the Corporation that the undersigned would be entitled to vote at the Meeting of Shareholders of the Corporation to be held at [*time and date*] **or at any adjournment thereof, at** [*place of meeting*]**.**

The undersigned instructs that the shares of the undersigned be voted as follows:

[ ] IN FAVOR of the proposed merger of the Corporation with _ _ _ _ _ _ _ _ _.

[ ] AGAINST the proposed merger.

The undersigned confers upon the proxy hereby appointed discretion to act on all other matters that may properly be brought before the Meeting or any adjournment or adjournments thereof, including any changes in the terms, conditions, requirements or other aspects of the proposed merger.

THIS PROXY WHEN PROPERLY EXECUTED WILL BE VOTED IN THE MANNER DIRECTED HEREIN, BUT IF NO CONTRARY DIRECTION IS MADE, IT WILL BE VOTED FOR THE PROPOSED MERGER AND IN THE PROXY HOLDER'S SOLE DISCRETION, FOR OR AGAINST ALL OTHER MATTERS WHICH MAY PROPERLY BE BROUGHT BEFORE THE MEETING OR ANY ADJOURNMENT OR POSTPONEMENT THEREOF.

The undersigned hereby executes this Proxy as of _ _ _ _ _ _, 19_ _.

Number of shares owned: _ _ _ _ _ _

_____
Signature of Shareholder

_____
Signature of Shareholder

SHAREHOLDER: Please sign, date, and return in the enclosed business reply envelope. Signature(s) must correspond with the name(s) shown on your share certificate. Each joint owner should sign; executors, administrators, trustees, and other persons signing in representative capacity should give full titles.

§6.129   d. Form: Shareholder Resolution Approving Merger

Form 6.129–1

There has been presented to this meeting a form of agreement of merger [*and a related reorganization agreement*] between this corporation and [*name of other corporation*]. [*This agreement has/These agreements have*] been approved by the boards of directors of this corporation and [*name of other corporation*], and executed by the officers of both corporations in the manner required by section 1102 of the California Corporations Code.

It is in the best interests of the shareholders of this corporation that the terms and conditions of [*that agreement/those agreements*] **be approved and performed.**

In view of the above, it is

RESOLVED that the form, terms, and provisions of the agreement of merger [*and related reorganization agreement*] **between this corporation and** [*name of other corporation*] **submitted to this meeting are approved as submitted.**

Comment: This resolution is for shareholders of a constituent party to the merger rather than those of a parent, and assumes that shareholder approval follows approval by the directors. Shareholder approval may be given either before or after approval by the directors. Corp C §1201(f).

When read together, Corp C §§1201 and 1103 require that the shareholders approve both the principal terms of the reorganization and the principal terms of the merger agreement. These requirements will be met if both the merger agreement and any reorganization agreement are attached to the proxy statement and the resolution is adopted. Amendments to the merger agreement must be approved in the same manner as the original agreement. Corp C §1104.

D. Dissenters' Rights

§6.130   1. Qualification of Dissenting Shares

The statutory provisions concerning dissenting shares are complex. The complexity, however, is primarily due to the many exceptions and provisos added to the general rule.

The general rule is that, subject to the requirements discussed below, shareholders who do not vote in favor of a reorganization have the right to demand and receive payment from the corporation for their shares at fair market value.

Requirement That Shares Be Outstanding on Record Date. "Dissenting shares" as defined in Corp C §1300(b) must be outstanding on the date for the determination of shareholders entitled to vote on the reorganization. Corp C §1300(b)(2).

Requirement That Stocks Not Be "Listed." Subject to exceptions discussed below, the stocks, immediately before the reorganization or short-form merger, must not have been listed either on a national securities exchange or on the Federal Reserve's list of OTC margin stocks. Corp C §1300(b)(1). This exclusion does not apply:

- If the notice of meeting of shareholders to act on the reorganization fails to summarize the provisions of Corp C §§1300–1304 regarding dissenters' rights;
- If transfer of the shares is restricted by the corporation or by any law or regulation; or
- As to any class of stock, if demands for payment are filed with respect to 5 percent or more of the outstanding shares of that class. Corp C §1300(b)(1).

Requirements as to Voting on the Reorganization. The general rule is that, in order to qualify as dissenting shares, the shares must not have been voted in favor of the reorganization. Corp C §1300(b)(2). However, as to any "listed" stock (see above), the shares must actually be voted *against* the reorganization, unless approval of the reorganization is sought by written consent rather than at a meeting, in which case the general rule (not voted in favor) applies. Corp C §1300(b)(2).

Procedural Requirements. In addition to the above requirements, the dissenting shareholders must perfect their rights by complying with statutory procedures; see §§6.132–6.137.

For more detailed discussion of dissenters' rights, see 1A Ballantine & Sterling, CALIFORNIA CORPORATION LAWS §262.05 (4th ed); 2 MARSH'S CALIFORNIA CORPORATION LAW §§19.1–19.14 (2d ed).

2. Perfection of Dissenters' Rights

§6.131 a. Corporation's Notice to Dissenting Shareholders

If a reorganization has been approved by the outstanding shares and any of the shareholders have a right to demand cash payment (*i.e.,* voted against or did not vote in favor of the reorganization; see §6.130), the corporation must, within ten days after the approval, mail each such dissenting shareholder a notice of the approval. Corp C §1301(a). See also Corp C §603(b). The notice must contain (1) a statement of the price determined by the corporation to be the fair market value of the dissenting shares, (2) a brief description of the procedure to be followed if the shareholder desires to exercise appraisal rights, and (3) a copy of Corp C §§1300–1304. The corporation's statement of price constitutes its offer to purchase the dissenting shares at that price.

§6.132 b. Form: Notice to Shareholders of Approval of Reorganization

Form 6.132–1

NOTICE OF SHAREHOLDERS' APPROVAL OF REORGANIZATION

TO THE SHAREHOLDERS OF [*name of corporation*]:

NOTICE IS HEREBY GIVEN that at a meeting of shareholders of this corporation held on [*date*], at [*address*], California, the outstanding shares of each class of this corporation approved the principal terms of reorganization whereby this corporation will

[*First alternative; sale of stock*]

acquire _ _ _ percent of the outstanding shares of [*name of selling corporation*] in return for the issuance to the shareholders thereof of _ _ _ shares of [*class*] stock of this corporation.

[*Second alternative; exchange of shares*]

acquire all or substantially all of the assets of [*name of selling corporation*] in exchange for _ _ _ shares of this corporation's [*name of class*] stock.

[*Third alternative, merger*]

merge with [*name of corporation*], in accordance with the terms of a Merger Agreement executed on [*date*].

If the shares of the corporation held by you were outstanding on the date for the determination of shareholders entitled to vote on the reorganization and were not voted in favor of the reorganization, you are entitled to demand that the corporation acquire them for cash at their fair market value.

The following is a brief description of the procedure to be followed if you desire to exercise your rights to require a purchase of your shares pursuant to California Corporations

Code sections 1300–1306. This description does not purport to be a complete statement of the law relating to dissenters' rights and is qualified in its entirety by reference to the foregoing Code sections, a copy of which is attached to this Notice.

1. Within 30 days of the date of this Notice you must make a written demand upon the corporation for the purchase of your shares and the payment to you in cash of their fair market value. Your demand must state (a) the number and class of shares held of record by you in respect of which you are demanding purchase, and (b) the dollar amount which you claim to be the fair market value of those shares as of the day before the announcement of the proposed reorganization. After a demand has been made, it cannot be retracted without the consent of the corporation. Your statement of fair market value will constitute an offer by you to sell the shares to the corporation at the price stated.

2. Within 30 days of the date of this Notice you must submit to the corporation at its principal office the certificate or certificates representing any shares which you demand that the corporation purchase, to be stamped or endorsed with a statement that the shares are dissenting shares or to be exchanged for certificates of appropriate denomination so stamped or endorsed.

3. If you and the corporation fail to agree on a price for which your shares are to be purchased, you may file a lawsuit within six months of the date shown on this Notice in the Superior Court of the County of [appropriate California county], praying the court to determine whether the shares are dissenting shares or to determine the fair market value of the dissenting shares or both.

You are hereby notified that the corporation has determined that the price of $_ _ _ _ _ _ per share is the fair market value of the dissenting shares of this corporation as of the day before the first announcement of the terms of the reorganization, excluding any appreciation or depreciation in consequence thereof and adjusted for any stock split, reverse stock split or share dividend accruing in the meantime. This constitutes an offer to purchase your dissenting shares at the price indicated above.

Dated: _ _ _ _ _ _

[Name of corporation]

By_____
Secretary

§6.133   c. Dissenting Shareholder's Demand for Purchase

The holder of shares that qualify as dissenting shares can perfect dissenters' rights by making written demand on the corporation that the shares be purchased for cash at their fair market value. Corp C §§1300(b)(3), 1301. The demand must be received by the corporation or its transfer agent either: (1) for "listed" stocks (see §6.130), not later than the date of the shareholders' meeting at which the reorganization will be voted on, or (2) for unlisted stocks (see §6.131), within 30 days after the date on which the notice of the approval of the reorganization by its outstanding shares was mailed to the shareholder. Corp C §1301(b).

The demand must state the number and class of the dissenting shares and the price that the shareholder claims to be their fair market value as of the day before the announcement of the proposed reorganization. The shareholder's statement of fair market value constitutes an offer by the shareholder to sell the shares at that price. Corp C §1301(c).

A dissenting shareholder may not withdraw a demand for payment unless the corporation consents. Corp C §1308.

NOTE: Only the record holder of shares may perfect appraisal rights. Corp C §1300(c). The record transfer of shares is frequently within the sole control of the corporation, and even if there is a transfer agent, can involve significant delay. Therefore, shareholders who are not holders of record should make arrangements for the transfer of record well in advance of the shareholders' meeting. The Code is very explicit that a late demand has no effect. See Corp C §1301(b).

§6.134   d. Form: Shareholder's Demand for Purchase

Form 6.134–1

DEMAND FOR PURCHASE OF SHARES

TO: [*Name of corporation*], **a California Corporation**

I am the holder of record of [*number of shares*] **shares of the** [*class*] **stock of this corporation, evidenced by stock certificate No.** [*stock certificate number*].

I hereby demand that the corporation purchase the foregoing shares for cash at their fair market value as of the day before the first announcement of the terms of the reorganization, [*describe reorganization*], **excluding any appreciation or depreciation in consequence of the reorganization and adjusted for any stock split, reverse stock split, or share dividend which became effective thereafter.**

I hereby submit to you the share certificate referred to above so that the certificate may either (a) be endorsed with a statement indicating that these are dissenting shares, or (b) exchanged for a certificate of appropriate denomination so stamped or endorsed.

Please return the endorsed certificate to me promptly at the address indicated below.

Dated: _ _ _ _ _ _

[*Signature*]
[*Shareholder's name and address*]

Comment: See discussion at §6.133.

§6.135   e. Endorsement of Shares

One of the conditions of perfection of the appraisal right is that the shares be submitted to the corporation or its transfer agent for endorsement within 30 days after the date on which the corporation mails notice of the approval of the reorganization. A legend must be placed on the share certificate indicating that the shares are dissenting, or the certificate may be replaced with one bearing such a legend. Corp C §1302.

Dissenters continue to have all rights and privileges incident to their shares until their fair market value is agreed upon or determined by the court. Corp C §1308. Dissenting shares are transferrable, and the transfer includes the dissenter's right of appraisal. However, the transfer of dissenting shares prior to endorsement terminates their status as dissenting shares. Corp C §1309(b).

§6.136   f. Agreed Value

The Code places significant emphasis on avoiding a contest on the question of fair market value. Both the corporation and the dissenter are obliged to commit themselves to a price at the outset. Presumably, both of these offers remain outstanding until the court renders its judgment. During this period, either party may bring the matter to a close merely by accepting the offer of the other.

Both parties are well advised to make their offers reasonable, inasmuch as the court has discretion to assess or apportion the costs of the action. This is particularly important for the corporation, because if the appraisal exceeds the price offered by the corporation, the corporation *shall* pay the costs, and if the appraisal exceeds 125 percent of the price offered by the corporation, the court has discretion to include attorneys' fees, expert witness' fees, and interest, as part of the costs. Corp C §1305(e). See §6.140.

§6.137   g. Court Determination of Value

If the dissenter and the corporation are unable to agree or the corporation denies that the shares are dissenting shares, then either of them may file an action for a determination in Superior Court. Corp C §1304(a). Two or more dissenters may be joined as plaintiffs or as defendants and two or more such actions may be consolidated. Corp C §1304(b). Suit must be filed not later than six months after the corporation mails notice of the approval of the reorganization. If the status of dissenting shares is at issue, the court will determine that question first. If the fair market value of dissenting shares is at issue the court may either make the determination or appoint one or more appraisers for that purpose. Corp C §1304(c). The appraisers must make and file a report within ten days of their appointment or at such other time fixed by the court. If the court finds the report to be reasonable, the court may confirm it. Corp C §1305(a). If the appraisers fail to file the report at the appointed time, or if the report is not confirmed by the court, then the court shall determine the fair market value. Corp C §1305(b). The judgment rendered by the court is payable upon delivery and endorsement of the shares. Corp C §1305(d).

§6.138   h. Costs of Proceedings

The cost of court proceedings, including reasonable compensation to the appraisers, may be apportioned equitably by the court, but if the appraisal exceeds the price offered by the corporation, the corporation must pay the costs. Corp C §1305(e). If the court awards a value for the shares that exceeds 125 percent of the price offered by the corporation in the notice mailed to the shareholder, the court in its discretion may also require the corporation to pay attorneys' fees, fees of expert witnesses, and interest at the legal rate on judgments from the date of compliance with Corp C §§1300–1302. Corp C §1305(e).

§6.139   i. Interim Rights of Dissenting Shares

Cash dividends declared and paid on dissenting shares after the date of shareholders' approval of the merger, and before the corporation purchases the shares, are credited against the purchase price. Corp C §1307. With this exception, dissenting shares have all rights of other shares of their class until fair market value is determined. Corp C §1308.

§6.140   j. Payment for Dissenting Shares

If the corporation and a dissenting shareholder agree on the price for the shares (see §6.136), the shareholder, upon surrender of the share certificates, is entitled to payment within 30 days after the agreement, together with interest at the legal rate on judgments from the date of the agreement. Corp C §1303. Shareholders who receive a court judgment that their shares are dissenting and a determination of their value are entitled to payment, with interest from the date of the judgment, upon endorsement and delivery of the certificates. Corp C §1305(c)–(d). The dissenting shareholder's right to payment is, however, subject to the statutory limitations on a corporation's ability to reacquire shares (Corp C §§500–510). To the extent that these provisions prohibit payment, the dissenting shareholders become creditors of the corporation, subordinate to all other creditors in a liquidation proceeding. Corp C §1306.

§6.141 k. Loss of Dissenting Status

A dissenting shareholder may withdraw a demand for payment, but only with the corporation's consent. Corp C §§1308, 1309(d). Dissenting shares also lose their status as dissenting shares (and the shareholder loses the right to require purchase) if:

- The corporation abandons the transaction (in this situation, shareholders who instituted proceedings in good faith may recover their expenses, including reasonable attorney fees);
- There is no agreement as to dissenting status or value and there is no complaint filed for, or intervention in, an appropriate court action within the specified period; or
- The shares are transferred or surrendered for conversion into shares of another class before endorsement as dissenting shares. Corp C §1309.

§6.142 3. Attacking Validity of a Reorganization

Subject to minor exceptions, shareholders who would be entitled to dissenters' rights cannot attack the validity of an approved merger or have it set aside or rescinded, except in an action to test whether the required number of shares voted in favor of the transaction. Corp C §1312(a).

The rule is not applicable in the following situations:

(1) Holders of shares that specify the amount to be paid on a merger are not bound by the dissenters' rights provisions but are entitled to payment in accordance with those terms. Corp C §1312(a).

(2) If one of the parties to a merger is controlled by, or under common control with, another party, minority shareholders of the controlled corporation who have not demanded payment for their shares may bring an action to attack the validity of the merger. Corp C §1312(b). A shareholder who institutes such an action may not later claim dissenters' rights. Corp C §1312(b). The court in any such action cannot restrain or enjoin consummation of the merger except on ten days' notice to the corporation and on the court's determination that no other remedy will protect the complaining shareholder or the class of shareholders of which the complainant

is a member. Corp C §1312(b). In such an action, the corporation in control has the burden of proving that the transaction is just and reasonable to such shareholders. Corp C §1312(c).

For the corporation, the quid pro quo for dissenters' rights of appraisal is the dissenter's inability to attack the validity of the reorganization except as noted above. *Sturgeon Petroleums, Ltd. v Merchants Petroleum Co.* (1983) 174 CA3d 134, 195 CR 29. This protection can be an extremely important right, which the corporation may wish to take particular pains to preserve.

E. Consummation of Merger

§6.143   1. Filing Requirements Generally

After director and shareholder approval, the merger is consummated by filing with the Secretary of State an executed copy of the merger agreement (see §§6.114–6.118), with an officers' certificate for each constituent corporation attached (see §6.146). The agreement and officers' certificates will not be filed until a Franchise Tax Board tax clearance certificate (see §§6.144–6.145) for the disappearing corporation has been filed. A merger between California corporations becomes effective when the agreement with attached officers' certificates is filed, unless the merger agreement provides otherwise. These documents are "filed" as of the date the Secretary of State receives them, in the absence of contrary instructions. Corp C §§110, 1103. A filing date not more than 90 days after the Secretary of State receives the documents may be requested, and an effective date not more than 90 days after the filing date may be specified in the merger agreement. Corp C §110(a),(c). If a delayed effective date is specified, either constituent corporation may prevent the merger agreement from becoming effective by filing a revocation certificate before the effective date. Corp C §110(c).

Effect on Property Rights. When the merger becomes effective, the separate existence of the disappearing corporation ceases. The surviving corporation succeeds, without other transfer, to all rights and property of each constituent corporation. Corp C §1107. Copies of the agreement certified by the Secretary of State, or a certificate prescribed by the Secretary of State, should, however, be recorded in any California counties in which any real property of the disappearing corporation is located, to evidence the new record ownership of the property in the surviving corporation. See Corp C §1109. Any other filings or documentation required by jurisdictions other than California should also be made. Documents evidencing title to property (*e.g.,* motor vehicles or securities) that are standing in a discontinued name should be tendered for reissuance in the new name.

Effect on Liabilities. When the merger becomes effective, the surviving corporation becomes subject to all the debts and liabilities of the constituent corporations. This liability is not limited to the value of the assets received in the merger transaction, but attaches as if the surviving corporation itself had incurred the liability. Corp C §1107(a). All creditors' rights and all liens on property of each constituent corporation are preserved unimpaired, but the liens on property of the disappearing corporation are limited to property affected by the liens immediately before the effective date of merger. Corp C §1107(b). Any pending action or proceeding by or against a constituent corporation may be prosecuted to a judgment that binds the surviving corporation, or the surviving corporation may be proceeded against or substituted for the constituent corporation. Corp C §1107(c).

2. Franchise Tax Board Clearance

§6.144   a. Obtaining Tax Clearance Certificate

A tax clearance certificate, certifying that the disappearing corporation's franchise taxes have been paid or are secured, must be obtained from the Franchise Tax Board before the Secretary of State will file the merger agreement. Corp C §1103. This should be arranged for well in advance; Rev & T C §23334 provides for action by the FTB within 30 days after it receives a request for such a certificate.

CAVEAT: This can be an important timing issue in the transaction. In particular, year-end transactions sometimes encounter delays in obtaining FTB clearance certificates, due to the rush of transactions at the end of the calendar year.

The certificate ordinarily can be obtained by filing with the board an assumption by the surviving corporation of all franchise tax liabilities of the disappearing corporation. See §6.145. The Franchise

Tax Board will send its original certificate to the taxpayer and a copy to the Secretary of State.

§6.145   b. Form: Assumption of Tax Liability

Form 6.145–1

BEFORE THE FRANCHISE TAX BOARD
STATE OF CALIFORNIA

In the matter of the assumption of tax liability of [*name of disappearing corporation*], a corporation (Corporation No. _ _ _) By [*name of surviving corporation*], a corporation (Corporation No. _ _ _	))))))) CORPORATION ASSUMPTION OF TAX LIABILITY

[*Name of surviving corporation*], **a corporation incorporated or qualified to do business in California, unconditionally agrees that it will assume and agree to pay in full, without reservation or restriction, all accrued or accruing franchise taxes, and delinquent charges on those taxes, of** [*or assumed by*] [*name of disappearing corporation*] **to the Franchise Tax Board under the provisions of the California Bank and Corporation Tax Law, and that it will file or cause to be filed with the Franchise Tax Board such returns and data as may be required of** [*name of disappearing corporation*]**, such assumption and agreement to be effective on the effective date of the merger of** [*name of disappearing corporation*] **into** [*name of surviving corporation*] **under section 1103 of the California Corporations Code.**

[*Name of assuming corporation*]

By_____

[*Typed name and title of officer*]

STATE OF _____)
) SS.
COUNTY OF _____)

[*Name of officer*]**, being first duly sworn, on oath deposes** and says that [*he/she*] is the [*title of officer*] of[*name of assuming corporation*], the corporation that executed the above and foregoing instrument, and is the officer of that corporation who signed the name of the corporation to the above instrument in [*his/her*] official capacity; that at the time of executing the above instrument, affiant had full power and authority to execute that instrument on behalf of the corporation and to bind the corporation to carry out each, every, and all of the terms, conditions, obligations, and undertakings recited and set forth therein.

_____[*Signature of officer*]_____
[*Typed name and title*]

Subscribed and sworn to
before me on [*date*]

[*Signature*]
Notary Public

Comment: The Franchise Tax Board provides copies of a form, FTB 2568, similar to this. That form, however, does not condition the assumption of liability on the effectiveness of the merger, a provision which should be included. In addition, the assumption should not limit the surviving corporation's right to contest taxes or charges it does not consider proper.

In a triangular merger, the Franchise Tax Board will accept the assumption of franchise tax obligations by the surviving subsidiary corporation without requiring an assumption by the parent corporation.

The assumption of tax liability should be sent to the Franchise Tax Board, Corporation Audit Section, P.O. Box 1468, Sacramento 95807; Attn: Tax Clearance Unit.

§6.146   3. Form: Officers' Certificate

Form 6.146-1

OFFICERS' CERTIFICATE OF APPROVAL
OF
AGREEMENT OF MERGER

[*Name of officer*] and [*name of officer*] certify that:

1. They are the [*chairman of the board/president/vice president*] **and the** [*secretary/assistant secretary/chief financial officer/treasurer/ assistant treasurer*], **respectively, of** [*name of corporation*], **a California corporation.**

[*First alternative: approval by shareholders*]

2. The principal terms of the agrement of merger in the form attached to this certificate were approved by the shareholders of this corporation.

[*Second alternative: approval by board alone*]

2. The agreement of merger in the form attached to this certificate was approved on behalf of the corporation by its board of directors. The merger was entitled to be approved by the board of directors alone under the provisions of section 1201 of the California Corporations Code.

[*Continue*]

3. The total number of outstanding shares of each class of the corporation entitled to vote on the agreement of merger is, and was at the time of that approval, as follows: [*number*] [*e.g., common*] **shares.**

[*If approved by shareholders, insert*]

[4.] Under the corporation's articles of incorporation and applicable law the percentage vote required of each class of shares of the corporation for agreement is as follows: [*e.g., a majority of the common shares*]. **The agreement of merger was approved by the vote of** [*number*] [*e.g., common*] **shares,** [*which is a percentage greater than 50 percent of the outstanding common shares*].

[*Insert in certificate of subsidiary, if applicable*]

[5.] [*Name of parent corporation*], **a California corporation, is the parent corporation of** [*name of subsidiary*]. **Equity securities of that parent corporation are to be issued in the merger, and** [*no vote of the shareholders of that parent corporation is required/the required vote of the shareholders of that parent corporation was obtained*].

[*Continue*]

IN WITNESS WHEREOF, the undersigned have executed this certificate on [*date*].

> [*Signature*]
> [*Typed name and title*]
>
> [*Signature*]
> [*Typed name and title*]

Each of the undersigned declares under penalty of perjury that the statements in the above certificate are true of his or her own knowledge, and that this declaration was executed on [*date*] **at** [*city and state*].

> [*Signature*]
>
> [*Signature*]

Comment: Officers' certificates of each constituent corporation are required, and their contents are prescribed by Corp C §§173 and 1103. in a triangular merger, the constituent corporations are the acquiring corporation's subsidiary and the acquired corporation. However, if equity securities of the parent corporation are issued in a triangular merger, the officers' certificate of the subsidiary must state either that no vote of the parent's shareholders is required or that the required vote was obtained. Corp C §1103.

The officers who may sign the certificate are specified by Corp C §173. Verification is required. Corp C §§173, 193.

§6.147   4. Exchanging Share Certificates

The surviving corporation (or the parent corporation in a triangular merger) issues new certificates to shareholders of the disappearing constituent corporation upon surrender of their certificates for shares in the disappearing corporation. See Corp C §1101. The acquiring corporation ordinarily does not issue new certificates to its own shareholders unless they receive stock of a different class, or a different number of shares. If major changes in authorized capital are made, or if the corporate name is changed, however, it may be desirable to request the shareholders to exchange their certificates, even if the provisions of their shares are not changed.

Shareholders who exchange more than one certificate for the same class of shares, representing shares with different tax bases, should obtain a separate certificate for each certificate turned in.

§6.148   VI. FOREIGN CORPORATIONS

The merger of domestic (California) corporations with foreign corporations may be effected if the foreign corporation is authorized by the laws under which it is formed to effect such a merger. The surviving corporation may be any one of the constituent corporations, and continues to exist under the laws of the state or place of its incorporation. Corp C §1108(a).

If the surviving corporation is a California corporation, the agreement and officer's certificate of each California or foreign constituent corporation must be filed in California. Corp C §1108(c). If the surviving corporation is a foreign corporation, the merger proceedings may be in accordance with the laws of the state or place of incorporation of the surviving corporation (Corp C §1108(b)), and shall become effective in accordance with the law of the jurisdiction under which the surviving corporation is organized, but shall be effective as to any California disappearing corporation as of the time of effectiveness in the foreign jurisdiction upon the filing in California of specified merger documents (Corp C §1108(d)). Each foreign disappearing corporation that is qualified to transact intrastate business automatically, by such a filing, surrenders its right to transact intrastate business. Corp C §1108(c)–(d).

"Pseudo-Foreign" Corporations. Under Corp C §2115, many foreign corporations are subject to California law (to the exclusion of the law of their states of incorporation) with respect to certain matters, including shareholder approval and dissenters' rights. Corporations whose stock is listed on a national securities exchange or qualified for trading on the NASDAQ national market system are exempt from Corp C §2115, as are those whose stock is wholly owned by an exempt corporation. Corp C §2115(e). A foreign corporation is subject to Corp C §2115 if (a) the average of its property factor, payroll factor, and sales factor (as defined in Rev & T C §§25129, 25132, and 25134) is more than 50 percent allocable to California during its latest full income year, and (b) more than one half of its outstanding voting securities are held of record by persons having addresses in California. Corp C §2115(a). For discussion see 2 MARSH'S CALIFORNIA CORPORATION LAW §§24.17–24.20 (2d ed).

§6.149   VII. "SHORT-FORM" MERGERS

A California corporation may merge one or more California subsidiary corporations into itself by a summary "short-form merger" (Corp C §187) if the parent owns at least 90 percent of each class of outstanding shares of each such subsidiary. Corp C §1110. This procedure may also be used if either the parent or the subsidiary is a foreign corporation, if permitted by the laws of its jurisdiction of incorporation. Corp C §1110(g)–(h); see §6.157.

§6.150   A. Procedure

A short-form merger is accomplished by (1) adoption of a resolution by the board of directors of the parent corporation, and, if there are minority shareholders, of the subsidiary; (2) giving notice to any minority shareholders of a domestic subsidiary at least 20 days before the merger (see §6.158); (3) obtaining and filing Franchise Tax Board certificates of satisfaction for any disappearing subsidiaries (Corp C §1110(e); see §6.149) with the Secretary of State; and (4) filing an officer's certificate of the parent corporation (certificate of ownership) with the Secretary of State, together with a copy of the certificate for each domestic and qualified foreign subsidiary being merged. Corp C §1110(d)-(f) (see §6.159). The certificate of ownership contains a resolution of the parent's board of directors providing for the merger and assumption of the liabilities of the merged subsidiary. Corp C §1110(a), (d). The merger, and any amendment of the articles of incorporation of the surviving corporation set forth in the certificate of ownership, are effective on filing the certificate (unless a delayed effective date is provided as permitted by Corp C §110).

§6.151   B. Foreign Corporations

Short-form mergers are permitted if the parent is a foreign corporation and at least one subsidiary is a California corporation (Corp C §1110(g)), or if the parent is a California corporation and one or more subsidiaries are foreign corporations (Corp C §1110(a), provided that this procedure is permitted by the laws of the foreign corporation's jurisdiction of incorporation (Corp C §1110(h)). If the parent is a foreign corporation, a copy of the certificate of ownership is filed as to each domestic and each qualified foreign subsidiary, but not as to the foreign parent. Corp C §1110(g).

§6.152   C. Rights of Minority Shareholders

In a short-form merger no approval of the shareholders of the parent corporation or of the minority shareholders of the subsidiary is required. Short-form mergers are expressly exempted from the requirement of Corp C §1110 that there be a shareholder vote if (a) one constituent corporation owns 50 percent or more of another, and (b) nonredeemable common shares are not exchanged for nonredeemable common shares of the surviving corporation.

However, minority shareholders of the subsidiary are entitled to dissenters' rights similar to those provided in other mergers. Corp C §1110(i). The parent corporation must give such shareholders notice at least 20 days before the merger. The notice must advise shareholders of the date on or after which the merger will become effective, must advise shareholders of their dissenters' rights (Corp C §1301), and must contain a copy of the resolutions of the boards of parent and subsidiary. Corp C §1110(i). The form of notice of approval of merger in §6.137 may, with those required additions, be adapted for this purpose.

Some other protections are afforded the minority shareholders. The subsidiary's board of directors must approve the fairness of the consideration to be given to minority shareholders. Corp C §1110(b). In addition, in a short-form merger, as in any other merger reorganization in which one of the constituent corporations is under the control of or under common control with the other, the minority is not limited to dissenters' rights, but may attack the validity of the reorganization. If such an action is brought, the parent corporation has the burden of proving that the transaction is just and reasonable as to the minority shareholders of the subsidiary. Corp C §1312(c).

§6.153   D. Form: Certificate of Ownership

Form 6.153–1

CERTIFICATE OF OWNERSHIP

[Name of officer] **and** [name of officer] **certify that:**

1. They are the [chairman of the board/president/vice president] **and the** [secretary/chief financial officer/treasurer/assistant secretary/assistant treasurer], **respectively, of** [name of parent corporation], **a California corporation.**

2. [Name of parent] **owns** [100 percent of the outstanding shares/at least 90 percent of the outstanding shares of each class] **of** [name of subsidiary], **a California corporation.**

3. At a duly held meeting of the board of directors of [name of parent], **the following resolutions were adopted:**

RESOLVED that under section 1110 of the California Corporations Code this corporation merge [name of subsidiary] **into itself and assume all the obligations of** [name of subsidiary].

[If subsidiary is not 100 percent owned by parent, insert]

RESOLVED FURTHER that this corporation shall [issue/pay/deliver/grant] [describe securities, cash, property, or rights] **on surrender of each share of** [name of subsidiary] **not owned by** [name of parent].

[If parent's name is to be changed, insert]

RESOLVED FURTHER that Article [e.g., One] **of the articles of incorporation of** [name of parent] **is amended in its entirety to read as follows:**

"[E.g., ONE]. **The name of the corporation is** [new name of parent].

[Continue]

RESOLVED FURTHER that the chairman of the board, president, or a vice president, and the secretary or assistant secretary of this corporation are authorized to execute, verify (by their declaration under penalty of perjury or otherwise), and file a certificate of ownership under section 1110 of the California Corporations Code, and to take all other action they consider necessary and proper to consummate the merger.

[*If subsidiary is not 100 percent owned by parent, insert*]

4. At a duly held meeting of the board of directors of [*name of subsidiary*], **the following resolution was adopted:**

RESOLVED that this board of directors approves the fairness of the consideration [*describe*] **to be received for each share of this corporation not owned by** [*name of parent*].

[*Insert, if desired*]

5. The effective date of the merger described above shall be [*date*].

[*Continue*]

[*Officer's signature*]

[*Typed name and title*]

[*Officer's signature*]

[*Typed name and title*]

Each of the undersigned declares under penalty of perjury that the statements in the above certificate are true of his or her own knowledge, and that this declaration was executed on [*date*] **at** [*city and state*].

[*Officer's signature*]

[*Officer's signature*]

Comment: The contents of the certificate are prescribed by Corp C §1110(d). The required corporate resolutions are specified in Corp C §§1110(a)–(b).

After the required Franchise Tax Board clearances have been obtained (see §6.149), one executed copy of the certificate must be filed with the Secretary of State on behalf of the parent corporation (unless it is a foreign parent), and a copy filed for each merged California or qualified foreign subsidiary. Corp C §1110(d).

In a short-form merger, the parent corporation may change its name, regardless of whether the new name is the same as or similar to that of any of its subsidiaries. Inexplicably, the parent corporation's name can be changed in this situation without the approval of its shareholders, contrary to the general rules applicable to articles. Compare Corp C §1110(c) with Corp C §902(a). Any amendment to change the parent's name must provide and establish the wording of the amendment of its articles to change the name. Corp C §1110(c).

The short-form merger provisions (Corp C §1110), unlike those for other mergers (Corp C §1103), do not expressly refer to Corp C §110(c), which permits use of a delayed effective date. However, the provisions of Corp C §110(c) are absolute, and appear to control.

The officers who may sign and verify the certificate are listed in Corp C §173; verification requirements are set forth in Corp C §193.

7

Dissolving the Corporation

William T. Manierre

WILLIAM T. MANIERRE, B.A., 1970, Yale University; J.D., 1975, Hastings College of the Law, University of California. Mr. Manierre, of the firm of Bronson, Bronson & McKinnon, practices in San Francisco.

This chapter is based on and incorporates portions of Chapter 6 of Operating Problems of California Corporations (Cal CEB 1978) by Miles A. Cobb and Richard L. Greene.

I. INTRODUCTION

§7.1 A. General Principles of Dissolution

The dissolution of a corporation is the termination of its existence as a legal person. Dissolution generally involves the liquidation of the corporation, but liquidation as a legal concept is different from dissolution. The liquidation of a corporation is the settling or winding up of its affairs: assets are collected, debts are identified and paid or provided for, and any remaining assets are distributed to shareholders. Liquidation is a part of the process of dissolving a corporation.

The statutes governing the dissolution of a California corporation establish procedures requiring that shareholders and creditors receive notice of the event and that the priority of their interests in the assets of the corporation be respected. Corp C §§1800–2011, 2314–2315. The considerations involved and the safeguards established by law are similar to those associated with probating an estate after the death of a natural person, with the shareholders in the role of the heirs.

Professional corporations are generally subject to the dissolution provisions of the General Corporation Law, but special rules may apply to particular professions, such as those governing the work in progress of law corporations. Corp C §13403. See *Fox v Abrams* (1985) 163 CA3d 610, 210 CR 260.

§7.2   B. Decision To Dissolve

The decision to dissolve a corporation, particularly one with an ongoing business, has serious consequences for its shareholders and all others involved. The corporation's liquidation value may be far less than its value as a going concern. Shareholders should be alerted to considerations that will affect the amounts they may receive from the corporation in a dissolution, as well as any income tax liability that may result, and the possible need to set aside corporate assets to secure contingent liabilities. An attorney asked to handle a dissolution should make sure that alternatives to dissolution have been properly considered.

Another preliminary consideration in exploring the dissolution of a corporation is the role of the attorney and any conflicts of interest that may be involved. A lawyer retained by a corporation owes allegiance to the entity. See Cal Rules of Prof Cond 3–600(A). The interests of particular shareholders may differ from those of the corporation and of other shareholders. An attorney retained to represent more than one party must consider whether such representation is appropriate and whether the informed written consent of the parties is required. Cal Rules of Prof Cond 3–600(D)–(E), 3–310.

§7.3   C. Methods

Assuming that a decision to dissolve has been made (see §§7.2–7.9), the existence of a California corporation may be terminated under the California Corporations Code by (1) voluntary dissolution without court supervision, (2) court-supervised voluntary proceedings, (3) involuntary proceedings instituted by the directors or shareholders of the corporation, subject to court supervision, or (4) involuntary proceedings instituted by the State. The existence of a California corporation may also be terminated by merger or consolidation into another corporation (see chap 6), expiration of its term of existence (if it does not have unlimited life), or forfeiture of its corporate existence. De facto dissolution, or abandonment or liquidation of a corporation without formal dissolution, is generally inadvisable. See 1A Ballantine & Sterling, CALIFORNIA CORPORATION LAWS §313.03 (4th ed).

This chapter addresses voluntary dissolution proceedings without court supervision (§§7.15–7.58), court-supervised voluntary proceedings (§§7.53–7.69), and involuntary proceedings (§§7.70–7.83).

§7.4   D. Checklist for Predissolution Planning

The following actions should be considered in planning for dissolution:

(1) Evaluate other methods of accomplishing shareholders' objectives, such as a merger or a sale of assets or stock.

(2) Determine the federal and state income tax consequences of the dissolution to the corporation and the shareholders, and ascertain any procedural requirements of the Internal Revenue Service and the Franchise Tax Board.

(3) Consider the requirements of other federal and state agencies, such as the FCC, PUC, ABC, State Board of Equalization, and the California Employment Development Department.

(4) Identify necessary actions by the board of directors, including (a) determination of the necessity or desirability of dissolution, and (b) adoption of the appropriate resolutions, including granting of authority to act to the appropriate corporate officers.

(5) Review necessary actions by shareholders, including approval of appropriate resolutions, consents, and elections.

(6) Review the corporation's assets and liabilities, including contingent assets and liabilities.

(7) Review list of corporate creditors, and check financing agreements for restrictions against dissolution or liquidation; also check for any acceleration provisions of secured obligations.

(8) Determine methods for satisfying claims against the corporation and providing reserves for payment of contingent liabilities. Consider insurance to protect against unknown claims (*e.g.,* product liability claims).

(9) Review corporation's leases and contracts for right of assignment and potential liabilities for breach or early termination.

(10) Identify any provisions in articles, bylaws, and shareholders' agreements relating to liquidation preferences, and review all instruments creating conversion rights with respect to the corporation's stock.

(11) Prepare a plan of liquidation that provides for sale as a going concern or sale of individual assets by negotiation, auction, or other means. Review bulk sales notice requirements. Consider provisions for distributing assets to shareholders and retention of assets to satisfy liabilities. In appropriate cases consider use of a liquidating trust. Investigate possibility of selling or licensing use of corporate name.

(12) Identify pending litigation affecting the corporation. Arrange for continued participation by corporate successor and for payment of litigation costs.

(13) Consider methods for preserving corporate rights under licenses and other executory contracts that may produce future income.

(14) Review plans for making distributions to shareholders. Examine list of shareholders. Arrange for receipt and cancellation of share certificates. Determine procedure for shareholders who do not surrender certificates.

(15) Consider the desirability of court supervision of dissolution in cases in which the shareholders disagree, claims of certain corporate creditors are disputed, or any unusual steps during liquidation are foreseen by the corporation.

§7.5   II. TAX CONSIDERATIONS

The dissolution of a corporation will often generate significant income tax liability for both the corporation and its shareholders. See §§7.7, 7.9. The combined effect of these two levels of taxation must be considered in estimating the net amounts that the shareholders will realize. The Internal Revenue Code of 1986 addresses the subject of corporate liquidations at IRC §§331–346. The California law, which directly incorporates many of the provisions of the federal law, is set forth in Rev & T C §§24501–24520.

Double Taxation on Dissolution. Prior to the enactment of the Tax Reform Act of 1986 (Pub L 99–514, 100 Stat 2085 (1986); hereinafter "1986 Act"), double taxation on dissolution could usually be avoided. The 1986 Act and related California legislation, however, repealed the *General Utilities* doctrine (see former IRC §§336, 337; former Rev & T C §§24511–24514; *General Utilities Operating Co. v Helvering* (1935) 296 US 200), which had provided for nonrecognition of gain at the corporate level on liquidation sales and distributions. By repealing the *General Utilities* doctrine, the 1986 Act substantially increased the tax cost of most corporate liquidations. The prior law remains in partial effect with respect to liquidations completed before 1989 by qualified closely held corporations valued at $10 million or less. See Tax Reform Act of 1986 §633(d), 100 Stat 2278 (set forth following 26 USC §336). See also Wheeler & Thompson, *General Utilities—R.I.P.,* Bus Lawyer Update (July/August 1987); Schmehl, *How Liquidations and S Elections May Avoid the Impact of TRA '86,* 67 J Tax 30 (1987).

Effect on S Corporations. The repeal of the *General Utilities* doctrine is less significant for S corporations than for C (regular) corporations. In general, gain recognized at the corporate level of an S corporation flows through, to be taxed to the shareholders and increase their basis in the stock of the corporation. See generally IRC §§1361–1379. The increased basis of the stock reduces by like amount any gain that would otherwise be recognized at the shareholder level by reason of the receipt of distributed property, generally resulting in less aggregate tax liability than would result from the liquidation of an otherwise comparable C corporation. To prevent C corporations from escaping the effects of the repeal of the *General Utilities* doctrine by electing S corporation status shortly before liquidation, the Internal Revenue Code as amended by the 1986 Act imposes a tax at the corporate level on an S corporation that liquidates or sells its assets within 10 years after converting from a C corporation to an S corporation. IRC §1374. The prior law, still in effect for C corporations electing S corporation status before 1987 and partially in effect for qualified closely held C corporations filing an S election before 1989, imposed a corporate-level tax if liquidation or sale of assets occurred within *three* years after the conversion. Tax Reform Act of 1986 §633, 100 Stat 2277 (set forth following 26 USC §336); former IRC §1374.

"Liquidation-Reincorporation" Doctrine. If liquidation is preceded or followed by the transfer of a substantial portion of the corporation's operating assets to another corporation owned by most of the same shareholders, the "liquidation-reincorporation" doctrine (although less significant since the passage of the 1986 Act) may still apply. Under this doctrine, the liquidation may be deemed incomplete and the transaction recharacterized for tax purposes in a manner disadvantageous to the shareholders. See Treas Reg §1.331–1(c); *Atlas Tool Co.* (1978) 70 TC 86, aff'd (3d Cir 1980) 614 F2d 860. For discussion see Bittker & Eustice, FEDERAL INCOME TAXATION OF CORPORATIONS AND SHAREHOLDERS §11.05 (5th ed 1987); Nuzum, *Recast by IRS of 337 Liquidation as a Reorganization Creates a Dividend to Distributee,* 50 J Tax 214 (1979).

Use of a Liquidating Trust. In certain cases, it may be necessary or convenient to distribute the assets of a liquidating corporation to a liquidating trust, either (1) for the benefit of creditors or missing shareholders, or (2) as a title-holding device to allow an orderly disposition of the corporation's property to all of its shareholders. See §§7.46–7.47. If the trustee is not permitted to engage in business, the liquidation of the corporation is considered complete for tax purposes, and the assets are considered received by the shareholders for purposes of determining the gain or loss on the liquidation, when the assets are distributed to the trust. Treas Reg §301.7701–4(d). The trust's future income is taxed to the shareholders under the grantor trust rules of IRC §671. Rev Rul 80–150, 1980–1 Cum Bull 316; Rev Rul 75–379, 1975–2 Cum Bull 505; Rev Rul 72–137, 1972–1 Cum Bull 101; Rev Rul 57–140, 1957–1 Cum Bull 118; Treas Reg §301.7701–4(d).

A. Taxation at the Shareholder Level

§7.6   1. General Rules

The liquidation of a corporation is treated as an exchange of a shareholder's stock for the amounts received in liquidation, thus resulting in full recognition of gain or loss at the shareholder level.

IRC §331; Rev & T C §24501. (Certain "parent-subsidiary" liquidations are exempt from this rule; see §7.7.) The amount received by a shareholder is the sum of the cash and the fair market value of the other assets distributed, less the liabilities assumed, or to which distributed assets are subject. IRC §1001(b); Rev & T C §18031. Gain or loss will be recognized to the extent that the amount received exceeds or is less than the basis for the shareholder's stock. IRC §1001; Rev & T C §18031. The gain or loss generally will be a capital gain or loss, unless the stock is not considered a capital asset in the shareholder's hands (see IRC §1221) or the corporation is collapsible (see IRC §341).

Shareholder's Use of Installment Reporting. If gain is recognized, the full amount of gain is reported in the year in which the distributions are received. Thus, the installment method of reporting income (IRC §453(a)–(b)) cannot be used in most liquidations. But if (1) a shareholder receives an installment obligation acquired by the corporation in respect of a sale or exchange made by the corporation during the 12-month period beginning on the date a plan of complete liquidation is adopted, and (2) the liquidation is completed within that 12-month period, the shareholder may recognize gain with respect to that obligation on the installment method. IRC §453(h). (In this situation, however, the distribution of the installment obligation will result in gain recognition at the corporate level without the receipt of funds to pay the resulting tax. See IRC §453B.) It may also be possible for a shareholder to achieve installment sale reporting by selling the stock before the liquidation occurs, with payment for the stock to be in installments over a number of years. Installment sale reporting is not allowed if the intermediate purchaser-seller is a person whose ownership of the stock would be attributed to the first seller under the stock attribution rules of IRC §318(a). See IRC §453(e).

§7.7   2. Parent-Subsidiary Exception

An exception to the general rule on recognition of gain by the corporation or a shareholder applies to the liquidation of a solvent 80-percent-or-more owned subsidiary. Although a written election is not required, the parent and subsidiary corporations must formally adopt a plan of liquidation. IRC §332; Treas Reg §1.332–6(a); *George L. Riggs, Inc.* (1975) 64 TC 474, acq 1976–2 Cum Bull 2. The parent will not recognize gain if the dissolution is in complete cancellation or redemption of all the subsidiary's stock and is completed either (a) within one taxable year, or (b) in accordance with a plan of liquidation adopted within three years after the taxable year in which the first of a series of distributions is made. IRC §332; Rev & T C §24502. The basis of property received by the parent in such a dissolution is the same as the subsidiary's basis. IRC §334(b)(1); Rev & T C §24504. (The parent-subsidiary exception cannot be used by minority shareholders of a liquidating corporation or by the corporation with respect to such minority shareholders. IRC §§332, 337.)

To satisfy the stock ownership requirement of the parent-subsidiary exception, the parent corporation must own at least 80 percent of the total value of the stock in the corporation being liquidated, in addition to at least 80 percent of the corporation's voting power. IRC §§332(b)(1), 1504(a)(2). Under IRC §1504(a)(5)(A)–(B), regulations will be promulgated to define stock for the purposes of the ownership tests of §1504(a)(2). The Internal Revenue Service announced that for the purposes of IRC §332(b)(1) such regulations will not apply to plans of liquidation adopted on or before the date the proposed regulations are published in the Federal Register. IRS Notice 87–63, 1987–39 Int Rev Bull 17.

Prior to the Tax Equity and Fiscal Responsibility Act of 1982 (TEFRA, Pub L 97–248, 96 Stat 324), it was often advantageous for a corporation that had purchased 80 percent or more of the stock of a target corporation to liquidate the target to achieve a step-up in basis of the target's assets, under former IRC §334(b)(2) and *Kimbell-Diamond Milling Co.* (1950) 14 TC 74. TEFRA repealed IRC §334(b)(2) and added IRC §338, which allows an acquiring corporation meeting certain requirements to achieve a step-up in basis simply by making an election to treat the transaction as if it had been a purchase of assets. The 1986 Act, however, amends IRC §338 so that gain must be recognized at the subsidiary level when the acquiring corporation makes a section 338 election. See 1986 Act §631(b)(1), 100 Stat 2269, IRC §338(a)(1).

§7.8 B. Taxation at the Corporate Level

With certain exceptions, some of which are noted below, gain or loss is recognized by a corporation upon distribution of its property in complete liquidation as if the corporation had sold its property to the distributee at its fair market value. IRC §336(a); Rev & T C §24511. If the property so distributed is subject to a liability or if the distributee assumes a liability of the corporation in connection with the distribution, the fair market value of the property is deemed to equal the greater of its fair market value or the amount of the liability. IRC §336(b); Rev & T C §24511.

Exceptions. No gain or loss is recognized by a liquidating subsidiary corporation with respect to distributions made to a parent corporation owning 80 percent or more of the stock of the subsidiary, provided the parent distributee takes a carry-over basis in the distributed property. IRC §§332, 337(a); Rev & T C §24512. Similarly, no gain or loss is recognized in connection with tax-free reorganizations if the distributee does not recognize gain or loss on the receipt of the property. IRC §336(c); Rev & T C §24511.

A liquidating corporation cannot recognize loss on a distribution of property to a "related person" (as defined in IRC §267) if the distribution is not made on a prorata basis or if the property is "disqualified property." IRC §336(d); Rev & T C §24511. "Disqualified property" is property acquired by the liquidating corporation in a transaction to which IRC §351 applied, or as a contribution to capital, during the five-year period ending on the date of the distribution, including any other property whose adjusted basis is determined by reference to the adjusted basis of such disqualified property. IRC §336(d)(1)(B). In addition, a liquidating corporation cannot recognize loss on the sale, exchange, or distribution of "built-in loss" property contributed to the corporation for the purpose of creating a loss. IRC §336(d)(2).

§7.9   C. S Corporations: Tax on Built-In Gains

In general, the provisions of the tax law governing the liquidation of C (regular) corporations apply to S corporations as well (see IRC §1371(a)(1); Bittker & Eustace, FEDERAL INCOME TAXATION OF CORPORATIONS AND SHAREHOLDERS §6.09 (5th ed 1987), but because the income of an S corporation is ordinarily taxed only to its shareholders, less aggregate tax liability is usually incurred upon liquidation of S corporations than C corporations. To discourage C corporations from electing S corporation status shortly before liquidation, IRC §1374 imposes a special tax on the "recognized built-in gain" of any S corporation that (1) was formerly a C corporation, (2) elected S corporation status on or after January 1, 1987, and (3) disposed of its assets in liquidation or sale of assets within ten years after the effective date of its election of S corporation status. "Recognized built-in gain" means any gain recognized during that ten-year period on the disposition of any asset owned by the corporation at the beginning of its first year as an S corporation, that does not exceed the excess (if any) of the asset's fair market value over its adjusted basis at that time. See IRC §1374(d). Partial relief is afforded qualifying closely held corporations that elected S corporation status during 1987 and 1988. See 1986 Act §633(b)–(c), 100 Stat 2277, set forth following 26 USC §336. Corporations that elected S corporation status prior to 1987 are subject to the provisions of IRC §1374 as it existed before amendment by the 1986 Act. 1986 Act §633(d), 100 Stat 2278, set forth following 26 USC §336; see Rev Ruling 86–141, 1986–2 Cum Bull 151. See also §7.5.

§7.10 D. Filing of Federal Tax Forms

Within 30 days after a corporation adopts a plan of liquidation, it must file a notice on Form 966 with the Internal Revenue Service. Every corporation making a distribution of $600 or more to any shareholder in liquidation of its capital stock must file a Form 1099-DIV for each shareholder along with the related transmittal form, Form 1096. In certain cases, shareholders may wish to request a prompt determination by the IRS of any tax liability owed by the corporation beyond that shown on its final return. See IRC §6501(d) for procedure; see §7.14 for sample letter.

§7.11   1. Official Form: IRS Form 966—Corporate Dissolution or Liquidation

Form 7.11–1

Form **966** (Rev. June 1987) Department of the Treasury Internal Revenue Service	**Corporate Dissolution or Liquidation** (Required under Section 6043(a) of the Internal Revenue Code)	OMB No. 1545-0041 Expires 6-30-90

Please type or print

Name of corporation			Employer identification number
Address (Number and street)			Check type of return
City or town, state, and ZIP code			☐ 1120 ☐ 1120L ☐ 1120-IC-DISC ☐ 1120S ☐ Other ▶

1 Date incorporated	2 Place incorporated	3 Type of liquidation ☐ Complete ☐ Partial

4 Internal Revenue Service Center where last income tax return was filed and tax year covered	Service Center	Tax year ending Month Year

5 Date of adoption of resolution or plan of dissolution, or complete or partial liquidation	6 Tax year of final return . . . . Was final return filed with a parent corporation (consolidated return)? . . ☐ Yes ☐ No If "Yes," enter: Name of parent corporation ▶ _____ Employer identification number ▶ _____ IRS Center where consolidated return was filed ▶

		Common	Preferred
7 Total number of shares outstanding at time of adoption of plan or liquidation			

8 Dates of any amendments to plan of dissolution. . . . .

9 Section of the Code under which the corporation is to be dissolved or liquidated. . . . .

10 If this return concerns an amendment or supplement to a resolution or plan for which a return was filed, give the date filed. . . . .

Attach a certified copy of the resolution or plan, together with all amendments or supplements not previously filed.

Under penalties of perjury, I declare that I have examined this return, including accompanying schedules and statements, and to the best of my knowledge and belief it is true, correct, and complete.

▶ _____   _____   ▶ _____
Signature of officer   Date   Title

Instructions

Paperwork Reduction Act Notice.—We ask for this information to carry out the Internal Revenue laws of the United States. We need it to ensure that taxpayers are complying with these laws and to allow us to figure and collect the right amount of tax. You are required to give us this information.

Who Must File.—A corporation files Form 966 if it is to be dissolved or if any of its stock is to be liquidated. Exempt organizations are not required to file Form 966. These organizations should see the instructions for Form 990 or 990-PF.

When To File.—File Form 966 within 30 days after the resolution or plan is adopted to dissolve the corporation or liquidate any of its stock. If the resolution or plan is amended or supplemented after Form 966 is filed, file an additional Form 966 within 30 days after the amendment or supplement is adopted. The additional form will be sufficient if you show the date the earlier form was filed and attach a certified copy of the amendment or supplement and all other information required by Form 966 and not given in the earlier form.

Where To File.—File Form 966 with the Internal Revenue Service Center where the corporation is required to file its income tax return.

Section 333 Repealed

Section 333 has been repealed by the Tax Reform Act of 1986. Transitional rules, however, allow small businesses to liquidate under section 333. In addition, corporations will have to include a portion of the gain from the liquidation in income. For more information, see sections 631(e) and 633 of the Tax Reform Act of 1986, and **Form 964-A,** Computation of Gain or Loss Recognized by Corporations on Section 333 Liquidations.

Signature.—The return must be signed and dated by the president, vice president, treasurer, assistant treasurer, chief accounting officer, or any other corporate officer (such as tax officer) authorized to sign. A receiver, trustee, or assignee must sign and date any return required to be filed on behalf of a corporation.

§7.12 2. Official Form: IRS Form 1099-DIV—Dividends and Distributions

Form 7.12–1

☐ CORRECTED (if checked)

PAYER'S name, street address, city, state, and ZIP code	1a Gross dividends and other distributions on stock (Total of 1b, 1c, 1d, and 1e) $	OMB No. 1545-0110	
	1b Ordinary dividends $	**19 89** Statement for Recipients of	**Dividends and Distributions**
PAYER'S Federal identification number | RECIPIENT'S identification number	1c Capital gain distributions $	1d Nontaxable distributions $	**Copy B For Recipient**
RECIPIENT'S name (first, middle, last)	1e Investment expenses $	2 Federal income tax withheld $	This is important tax information and is being furnished to the Internal Revenue
Street address	3 Foreign tax paid $	4 Foreign country or U.S. possession	Service. If you are required to file a return, a negligence penalty or
City, state, and ZIP code	**Liquidation Distributions**		other sanction will be imposed on you if this dividend income is
Account number (optional)	5 Cash $	6 Noncash (Fair market value) $	taxable and the IRS determines that it has not been reported.

Form **1099-DIV**   Department of the Treasury · Internal Revenue Service

☐ CORRECTED (if checked)

PAYER'S name, street address, city, state, and ZIP code	1a Gross dividends and other distributions on stock (Total of 1b, 1c, 1d, and 1e) $	OMB No. 1545-0110	
	1b Ordinary dividends $	**19 89** Statement for Recipients of	**Dividends and Distributions**
PAYER'S Federal identification number | RECIPIENT'S identification number	1c Capital gain distributions $	1d Nontaxable distributions $	**Copy B For Recipient**
RECIPIENT'S name (first, middle, last)	1e Investment expenses $	2 Federal income tax withheld $	This is important tax information and is being furnished to the Internal Revenue
Street address	3 Foreign tax paid $	4 Foreign country or U.S. possession	Service. If you are required to file a return, a negligence penalty or
City, state, and ZIP code	**Liquidation Distributions**		other sanction will be imposed on you if this dividend income is
Account number (optional)	5 Cash $	6 Noncash (Fair market value) $	taxable and the IRS determines that it has not been reported.

Form **1099-DIV**   Department of the Treasury · Internal Revenue Service

☐ CORRECTED (if checked)

PAYER'S name, street address, city, state, and ZIP code	1a Gross dividends and other distributions on stock (Total of 1b, 1c, 1d, and 1e) $	OMB No. 1545-0110	
	1b Ordinary dividends $	**19 89** Statement for Recipients of	**Dividends and Distributions**
PAYER'S Federal identification number | RECIPIENT'S identification number	1c Capital gain distributions $	1d Nontaxable distributions $	**Copy B For Recipient**
RECIPIENT'S name (first, middle, last)	1e Investment expenses $	2 Federal income tax withheld $	This is important tax information and is being furnished to the Internal Revenue
Street address	3 Foreign tax paid $	4 Foreign country or U.S. possession	Service. If you are required to file a return, a negligence penalty or
City, state, and ZIP code	**Liquidation Distributions**		other sanction will be imposed on you if this dividend income is
Account number (optional)	5 Cash $	6 Noncash (Fair market value) $	taxable and the IRS determines that it has not been reported.

Form **1099-DIV**   Department of the Treasury · Internal Revenue Service

Instructions for Recipient

Box 1a.—Gross dividends include any amounts shown in Boxes 1b, 1c, 1d, and 1e. If you file **Form 1040A**, report the sum of Boxes 1b and 1e. If you file **Schedule B (Form 1040)**, report Box 1a on Schedule B. If you file Form 1040 without Schedule B, report the sum of Boxes 1b and 1e on the "Dividend income" line and Box 1c on **Schedule D (Form 1040)** or the "Capital gain distributions" line.

The amount shown may be a distribution from an employee stock ownership plan (ESOP). Although you should report the ESOP distribution as a dividend on your income tax return, treat it as a plan distribution, not as investment income, for any other purpose.

Box 1b.—Ordinary dividends are fully taxable and are included in Box 1a.

Box 1c.—Capital gain distributions are included in Box 1a.

Box 1d.—Amounts shown are usually a return of capital that reduce your basis in the stock. Once you have received an amount equal to your cost or other basis, these distributions are taxable to you as a capital gain even if the payer lists them as nontaxable. This amount is included in Box 1a. For more information, see **Pub. 550**, Investment Income and Expenses.

Box 1e.—Any amount shown is your share of the expenses of a nonpublicly offered regulated investment company, generally a nonpublicly offered mutual fund, which is included as a dividend in Box 1a. The full amount shown in Box 1a must be reported as income on your tax return. The expenses shown in Box 1e are deductible as a "Miscellaneous Deduction" on **Schedule A (Form 1040)** subject to the 2% limit. Generally, the actual amount you should have received or had credited to you is the amount in Box 1a less the amount in Box 1e.

Box 2.—Any amount shown represents backup withholding. For example, persons not furnishing their taxpayer identification number to the payer become subject to backup withholding at a 20% rate on certain payments. See **Form W-9,** Request for Taxpayer Identification Number and Certification, for information on backup withholding. Include this amount on your income tax return as tax withheld.

Nominees.—If your Federal identification number is shown on this form and two or more recipients are shown or the form includes amounts belonging to another person, you are considered a nominee recipient. You must file Form 1099-DIV for each of the other owners showing the income allocable to each. File Form(s) 1099-DIV with **Form 1096,** Annual Summary and Transmittal of U.S. Information Returns, at the Internal Revenue Service Center for your area. On Forms 1099-DIV and 1096, you should be listed as the "payer." On Form 1099-DIV, the other owner(s) should be listed as the "recipient." A husband or wife is not required to file a nominee return to show payments for the other.

Comment: A separate Form 1099-DIV is required for each shareholder who receives a distribution of $600 or more. These are to be attached to IRS Form 1096; see Comment to Form 7.13–1.

§7.13   3. Official Form: IRS Form 1096—Annual Summary and Transmittal of Information Returns

DO NOT STAPLE   6969   ☐ CORRECTED

Form **1096** Department of the Treasury Internal Revenue Service	**Annual Summary and Transmittal of U.S. Information Returns**	OMB No. 1545-0108 19**89**

⌐ Type or machine print FILER'S name (or attach label) ⌐

Street address

City, state, and ZIP code

If you are not using a preprinted label, enter in Box 1 or 2 below the identification number you used as the filer on the information returns being transmitted. Do not fill in both Boxes 1 and 2.	Name of person to contact if IRS needs more information Telephone number ( )	**For Official Use Only** ☐☐☐☐☐☐☐☐ ☐☐

1 Employer identification number	2 Social security number	3 Total number of documents	4 Federal income tax withheld $	5 Total amount reported with this Form 1096 $

Check only one box below to indicate the type of forms being transmitted.   If this is your FINAL return, check here . . . . . . ☐

W-2G 32	1098 81	1099-A 80	1099-B 79	1099-DIV 91	1099-G 86	1099-INT 92	1099-MISC 95	1099-OID 96	1099-PATR 97	1099-R 98	1099-S 75	5498 28
☐	☐	☐	☐	☐	☐	☐	☐	☐	☐	☐	☐	☐

Under penalties of perjury, I declare that I have examined this return and accompanying documents and, to the best of my knowledge and belief, they are true, correct, and complete.

Signature ▶ ....   Title ▶ ....   Date ▶ ....

Please return this entire page to the Internal Revenue Service. Photocopies are NOT acceptable.

Instructions

Purpose of Form.—Use this form to transmit Forms W-2G, 1098, 1099, and 5498 to the Internal Revenue Service.

Completing Form 1096.—If you received a preprinted label from IRS with Package 1099, place the label in the name and address area of this form inside the brackets. Make any necessary corrections to your name and address on the label. However, do not use the label if the taxpayer identification number (TIN) shown is incorrect. If you are not using a preprinted label, enter the filer's name, address, and TIN in the spaces provided on the form. **The name, address, and TIN you enter on this form must be the same as those you enter in the upper left area of Form 1099, 1098, 5498, or W-2G.** A filer includes a payer, a recipient of mortgage interest payments, a broker, a barter exchange, a person reporting real estate transactions, a trustee or issuer of an individual retirement arrangement (including an IRA or SEP), and a lender who acquires an interest in secured property or who has reason to know that the property has been abandoned. Individuals not in a trade or business should enter their social security number in Box 2; sole proprietors and all others should enter their employer identification number in Box 1. However, sole proprietors who are not required to have an employer identification number should enter their social security number in Box 2.

Group the forms by form number and submit each group with a separate Form 1096. For example, if you must file both Forms 1098 and Forms 1099-A, complete one Form 1096 to transmit your Forms 1098 and another Form 1096 to transmit your Forms 1099-A.

In Box 3, enter the number of forms you are transmitting with this Form 1096. Do not include blank or voided forms in your total. Enter the number of correctly completed forms, not the number of pages, being transmitted. For example, if you send one page of three-to-a-page Forms 5498 with a Form 1096 and you have correctly completed two Forms 5498 on that page, enter 2 in Box 3 of Form 1096. Check the appropriate box to indicate the type of form you are transmitting.

No entry is required in Box 5 if you are filing Form 1099-A or 1099-G. For all other forms, enter in Box 5 of Form 1096 the total of the amounts from the specific boxes of the forms listed below:

Form W-2G	Box 1
Form 1098	Box 1
Form 1099-B	Boxes 2, 3, and 6
Form 1099-DIV	Boxes 1a, 5, and 6
Form 1099-INT	Boxes 1 and 3
Form 1099-MISC	Boxes 1, 2, 3, 5, 6, 7, 8, and 10
Form 1099-OID	Boxes 1 and 2
Form 1099-PATR	Boxes 1, 2, 3, and 5
Form 1099-R	Boxes 1 and 8
Form 1099-S	Box 2
Form 5498	Boxes 1 and 2

If you will not be filing Forms 1099, 1098, 5498, or W-2G in the future, either on paper or on magnetic media, please check the "FINAL return" box.

If you are filing a Form 1096 for corrected information returns, enter an "X" in the CORRECTED box at the top of this form.

For more information about filing, see the separate Instructions for Forms 1099, 1098, 5498, 1096, and W-2G.

For Paperwork Reduction Act Notice, see separate Instructions for Forms 1099, 1098, 5498, 1096, and W-2G.   Form **1096** (1989)

Form 1096 (1989)   Page **2**

When To File.—File Form 1096 with Forms 1098, 1099, or W-2G by February 28, 1990. File Form 1096 with Forms 5498 by May 31, 1990.

Where To File.— Send all information returns filed on paper to the following:

If your principal business, office or agency, or legal residence in the case of an individual, is located in ▼	Use the following Internal Revenue Service Center address ▼
Florida, Georgia, South Carolina	Atlanta, GA 39901
New Jersey, New York (New York City and counties of Nassau, Rockland, Suffolk, and Westchester)	Holtsville, NY 00501
New York (all other counties), Connecticut, Maine, Massachusetts, New Hampshire, Rhode Island, Vermont	Andover, MA 05501
Illinois, Iowa, Minnesota, Missouri, Wisconsin	Kansas City, MO 64999
Delaware, District of Columbia, Maryland, Pennsylvania, Virginia	Philadelphia, PA 19255
Indiana, Kentucky, Michigan, Ohio, West Virginia	Cincinnati, OH 45999
Kansas, New Mexico, Oklahoma, Texas	Austin, TX 73301
Alaska, Arizona, California (counties of Alpine, Amador, Butte, Calaveras, Colusa, Contra Costa, Del Norte, El Dorado, Glenn, Humboldt, Lake, Lassen, Marin, Mendocino, Modoc, Napa, Nevada, Placer, Plumas, Sacramento, San Joaquin, Shasta, Sierra, Siskiyou, Solano, Sonoma, Sutter, Tehama, Trinity, Yolo, and Yuba), Colorado, Idaho, Montana, Nebraska, Nevada, North Dakota, Oregon, South Dakota, Utah, Washington, Wyoming	Ogden, UT 84201
California (all other counties), Hawaii	Fresno, CA 93888
Alabama, Arkansas, Louisiana, Mississippi, North Carolina, Tennessee	Memphis, TN 37501

If you have no legal residence or principal place of business in any Internal Revenue district, file with the Internal Revenue Service Center, Philadelphia, PA 19255.

★ U S GPO 1989-0-246-262

Comment: Form 1096 must be filed on or before February 28 of the year following the calendar year in which the liquidating dividend or dividends were distributed to the shareholders. Form 1096 must show the name and address of the corporation and the number of Forms 1099-DIV attached.

§7.14   4. Form: Letter Requesting Prompt Assessment

Form 7.14–1 (Letter to District Director of Internal Revenue)

Dear Sir or Madam:

Pursuant to Internal Revenue Code section 6501(d), it is hereby requested that prompt assessment of federal taxes against [*name of corporation*] **be made. The following information is furnished:**

1. The corporation was a California corporation until _ _ _ _ _ _, 19_ _, on which date it was formally dissolved under California law.

2. On _ _ _ _ _ _, 19_ _, a plan of complete liquidation was adopted by the shareholders, under which all assets of the corporation were distributed to the shareholders in complete redemption and cancellation of all the capital stock of the corporation.

3. The liquidation and dissolution were made in good faith, there being no intent on the part of the shareholders to reactivate the corporation.

4. The corporation as such ceased all corporate activities on _ _ _ _ _ _, 19_ _, and it has had no income since that time.

5. The corporation's income tax return for the taxable year ending _ _ _ _ _ _, 19_ _, was filed with the [*IRS branch and location*] **on _ _ _ _ _ _, 19_ _. All required forms** [*including Forms 966, 1099-DIV and 1096*] **have been filed.**

Dated: _ _ _ _ _ _

[*Name of corporation*]

By _____
[*Typed name and title*]

Comment: In certain situations a prompt federal tax assessment can be requested if a taxpayer wants a quick determination of the tax consequences of the dissolution. If the Internal Revenue Service fails to assess any additional taxes arising out of the dissolution within 18 months from the date of the request, it is barred from such an assessment except in the case of a false or fraudulent return, substantial omissions from gross income on the return, or personal holding company tax liability. IRC §6501(d). The request may not be made until after the corporation's final tax return has been filed.

III. VOLUNTARY PROCEEDINGS WITHOUT COURT SUPERVISION

A. Commencement of Proceedings

§7.15   **1. Procedure; Effect of Commencement**

Voluntary proceedings for dissolution begin with the adoption of authorizing resolutions. These resolutions are generally adopted by the shareholders, but in certain limited cases may be adopted by the directors. Corp C §1900; see §§7.16–7.17. Once voluntary proceedings have been commenced, a certificate of election to wind up and dissolve must be filed with the Secretary of State, and written notice must be sent promptly by mail to all shareholders except those who voted in favor of the dissolution and to all known creditors and claimants whose addresses appear on the corporation's records. Corp C §§1901, 1903(c).

The corporation is not dissolved by these acts. Dissolution and winding up are merely authorized, and shareholders and creditors are given notice that actual dissolution may follow. Even though voluntary proceedings have been commenced, the board of directors continues to act as a board and has full powers to wind up and settle the corporation's affairs. Corp C §1903(b). After the commencement of voluntary proceedings, however, the corporation must cease to carry on business except to the extent necessary to wind up its affairs or preserve its goodwill or going-concern value pending a sale of the business or assets. Corp C §1903(c). If normal business operations are continued, the directors may be exposed to the risk of personal liability. See *Matawan Bank v Matawan Title Co.* (NJ 1949) 65 A2d 729.

During the winding-up period, the directors are required to settle the rights and claims of creditors, sell or otherwise dispose of the assets of the corporation, and make final distribution of the remaining assets to the parties entitled to them. Corp C §2001. For treatment of the winding up and liquidation process, see §§7.28–7.58.

2. Authorization by Board of Directors Alone

§7.16 a. General Rule

An election to wind up and dissolve voluntarily may be authorized by resolutions of the board of directors alone if one of the following is applicable: (1) the corporation has issued no shares, (2) a relief order under chapter 7 of the federal bankruptcy law has been entered for the corporation, or (3) it has disposed of all of its assets and has not conducted any business during the five-year period immediately preceding the date of adoption of the resolutions electing to dissolve. Corp C §1900(b). In addition, if the corporation's term of existence as fixed by its articles of incorporation has expired without renewal or extension, the board is required to terminate the corporation's business and wind up its affairs. Corp C §1906.

§7.17 b. Form: Directors' Resolutions Authorizing Dissolution Before Issuance of Shares

Form 7.17–1

This corporation was duly formed on _ _ _ _ _ _, 19_ _, by filing its articles of incorporation on that date in the office of the California Secretary of State. This corporation has issued no shares whatsoever. It is deemed advisable by the board of directors that this corporation be wound up and dissolved.

In view of the above, it is

RESOLVED that the board of directors elects to wind up and dissolve this corporation.

RESOLVED FURTHER that the officers or directors of this corporation are authorized and directed to file the certificate and to give the written notice required under sections 1901 and 1903(c) of the California Corporations Code.

RESOLVED FURTHER that the officers of this corporation are authorized and directed to take such further action as may

be necessary or proper to wind up the affairs of this corporation and to dissolve it.

§7.18   c. Form: Directors' Resolution Appointing Representative To Act After Dissolution

Form 7.18–1

The Chairman then stated that the occasion may arise when someone should act on behalf of the corporation after it has been dissolved. After discussion, the following resolution was adopted:

RESOLVED that [*name of person authorized to act*] is nominated and authorized to act on behalf of the corporation in any and all matters that may arise after the corporation has been finally dissolved and liquidated.

Comment: The foregoing resolution may be adopted when it appears that it may be useful to identify a specific individual to handle any corporate matter arising after dissolution.

3. Authorization by Shareholders

§7.19   a. General Rule

Voluntary proceedings to wind up and dissolve are normally commenced by the shareholders. The general rule is that dissolution is commenced if shareholders holding 50 percent or more of the voting power of the corporation adopt a resolution electing to wind up or file with the corporation a written consent to that effect. Corp C §1900(a).

CAVEAT: If the corporation has preferred shares, its articles of incorporation may provide that dissolution requires the vote of a supermajority, not exceeding 66 2/3 percent, of a class or series of preferred shares. Corp C §402.5(b). The articles of incorporation should be examined to determine if they include provisions requiring such a supermajority shareholder vote for dissolution.

The date of adoption of the shareholders' resolution or written consent is the date when voluntary proceedings are considered to commence. Corp C 1903(a). A sample written election of shareholders to voluntarily wind up and dissolve is set forth in §7.20.

The power of the holders of 50 percent or more of the voting power to dissolve the corporation is not absolute; it must be exercised in good faith and not to injure other shareholders. See *In re Security Fin. Co.* (1957) 49 C2d 370, 317 P2d 1. For example, if dissolution were voted for the purpose of taking from minority shareholders the fair value of their investment in the ongoing business, the minority would be entitled to damages. *Jones v H. F. Ahmanson & Co.* (1969) 1 C3d 93, 81 CR 592. See 1 MARSH'S CALIFORNIA CORPORATION LAW §10.44 (2d ed).

Board action is not ordinarily required to commence proceedings for voluntary dissolution. Nevertheless, it is good practice for the board, before submitting the matter to shareholders, to adopt resolutions determining that, in its judgment, it is in the best interest of the corporation and its shareholders that the corporation wind up its affairs and dissolve.

§7.20   b. Form: Shareholders' Election and Consent

Form 7.20–1

WRITTEN ELECTION OF SHAREHOLDERS
TO VOLUNTARILY WIND UP AND DISSOLVE
[*Name of corporation*]
AND CONSENT TO WIND UP AND DISSOLVE

Each of the undersigned shareholders of [*name of corporation*]**, a California corporation, holding of record the number of shares of capital stock of the corporation opposite such shareholder's signature at the end of this certificate:**

(1) States that it is in the best interests of the corporation and its shareholders that the corporation be dissolved and its affairs wound up;

(2) Elects that the corporation be wound up and dissolved and consents to such winding up and dissolution;

(3) Authorizes and directs the officers and directors of the

corporation to take such action as may be necessary or proper to wind up the affairs of the corporation and to dissolve it; and

(4) Waives notice of the commencement of proceedings to wind up and dissolve the corporation.

IN WITNESS WHEREOF, the undersigned have signed their names and the date of signing and the number of shares of the corporation entitled to vote held by them of record on such date, all of which shares in the aggregate constitute 50 percent or more of the voting power of the corporation.

Shareholder	Date	No. of shares held
_____	_____	_____
_____	_____	_____
_____	_____	_____

§7.21   c. Form: Certificate of Election To Wind Up and Dissolve

Form 7.21–1

**CERTIFICATE OF ELECTION
OF
[*Name of corporation*]
TO WIND UP AND DISSOLVE**

[*Name of corporation's president*] **and** [*name of secretary*], **certify that:**

1. They are the president and secretary, respectively, of [*name of corporation*], **a California corporation.**

2. The corporation has elected to wind up and dissolve.

3. The election was made by the vote of [*number*] **shares of the corporation voting for the election and representing at least 50 percent of the voting power of the corporation.**

[*Or*]

3. The corporation has not issued any shares, and the election was made by the board of directors of the corporation.

We further declare under penalty of perjury under the laws of the State of California that the matters set forth in the certificate are true and correct of our own knowledge.

Dated: _ _ _ _ _ _

_____

President

_____

Secretary

Comment: If a corporation has elected to wind up and dissolve, a certificate evidencing the election must be filed in the office of the Secretary of State. The certificate must be signed and verified by either (1) the president, vice president, or chairman of the board, and the secretary, assistant secretary, treasurer, or assistant treasurer; (2) a majority of the directors then in office; or (3) one or more shareholders authorized to do so by shareholders holding 50 percent or more of the voting power of the corporation. Corp C §1901. The above form contemplates signature by the president and the secretary of the corporation.

4. Notice to Creditors

§7.22   a. General Rule

Promptly after commencement of proceedings for voluntary dissolution, written notice is required to be sent to all known creditors and claimants whose addresses appear on the records of the corporation, as well as all shareholders except those who voted in favor of the dissolution. Corp C §1903(c). In cases in which voluntary proceedings are commenced by written consent of shareholders, the consent form may contain a waiver of notice as to the signing shareholders.

§7.23   b. Form: Notice of Commencement of Proceedings To Wind Up and Dissolve

Form 7.23–1

NOTICE OF COMMENCEMENT OF PROCEEDINGS
OF
[Name of corporation]
TO WIND UP AND DISSOLVE

TO ALL SHAREHOLDERS, CREDITORS, AND CLAIMANTS OF *[name of corporation]*:

YOU ARE HEREBY NOTIFIED that *[name of corporation]*, **a California corporation, has voluntarily elected to wind up its affairs and dissolve the corporation.**

YOU ARE FURTHER NOTIFIED that the winding up of the corporation commenced on _ _ _ _ _ _, 19_ _, by the signing on that date, by the shareholders of the corporation representing 50 percent or more of the voting power, of a written consent to the voluntary winding up and dissolution of the corporation.

Dated: _ _ _ _ _ _

_____
President

_____
Secretary

§7.24   5. Avoiding Dissolution by Buy-Out of Shares

In a proceeding for voluntary dissolution initiated by the vote of shareholders representing only 50 percent of the corporation's voting power, dissolution can by avoided by the purchase for cash of the initiating shareholders' shares at their fair value, by either the corporation or the other shareholders. The corporation's election to purchase requires "approval of the outstanding shares" under Corp C §152; that is, the affirmative vote of a majority of the outstanding shares entitled to vote, excluding shares held by the initiating shareholders. Corp C §2000(a). If the corporation does not elect to purchase, the holders of 50 percent or more of the corporation's voting power may do so. Corp C §2000(a). (The rules of Corp C §2000 also apply to involuntary dissolutions; see §7.76.)

The fair value of the shares is determined on the basis of their liquidation value but taking into account the possibility, if any, of sale of the entire business as a going concern in a liquidation. If the initiation of the dissolution is a breach by any initiating shareholder of an agreement with the purchasing party or parties, the amount of any damages resulting from the breach may be deducted from the amount payable to the initiating shareholder (except where involuntary dissolution is sought on the ground of fraud or mismanagement under Corp C §1800(b)(4); see §§7.70, 7.76). Corp C §2000(a). If the parties are unable to agree on the fair value of the shares to be purchased, the value may be determined by a court on proper application by the purchasing parties. Corp C §2000(b).

6. Revocation of Election To Dissolve
§7.25   a. General Rule

A voluntary election to wind up and dissolve may be revoked before distribution of any corporate assets. Revocation requires the vote or written consent of shareholders representing a majority of the voting power of the corporation (or a resolution of the board of directors if the election to wind up and dissolve was made by the directors alone; see §7.17).

NOTE: Although the vote or written consent of only 50 percent of the corporation's voting power is necessary for a voluntary election to wind up and dissolve, revocation of such an election to dissolve requires the vote or written consent of a *majority* of the corporation's voting power. See Corp C §§1900(a), 1902.

Revocation is effective when a duly signed and verified certificate of revocation (see §7.27) is filed in the Secretary of State's office in the same manner as the certificate of election to wind up and dissolve. Corp C §1902.

§7.26   b. Form: Revocation of Election To Wind Up and Dissolve

Form 7.26–1

REVOCATION OF ELECTION TO WIND UP AND DISSOLVE CORPORATION

The undersigned shareholders of [*name of corporation*], a California corporation, each holding of record the number of shares of capital stock of the corporation set down opposite such shareholder's signature at the end of this document, state as follows:

1. We revoke the election to wind up and dissolve the corporation effected by the written consent of shareholders holding 50 percent or more of the voting power of the corporation, dated _ _ _ _ _ _, 19_ _, a Certificate of Election to Wind Up and Dissolve having been filed in the office of the Secretary of State of the State of California on _ _ _ _ _ _, 19_ _.

2. No assets of the corporation have been distributed under the previous election to wind up and dissolve.

IN WITNESS WHEREOF, the undersigned have executed this revocation and, following the signature, have inserted the date of signing and the number of shares of the corporation held of record on the date of signing, all of which shares are entitled to vote, and all of which shares in the aggregate constitute a majority of the voting power of the corporation.

Shareholder	Date	No. of shares held
_____	_____	_____
_____	_____	_____
_____	_____	_____

§7.27   c. Form: Certificate of Revocation of Election To Wind Up and Dissolve

Form 7.27–1

CERTIFICATE OF REVOCATION
OF ELECTION OF
[Name of corporation]
TO WIND UP AND DISSOLVE

The undersigned, [names of corporate officers] certify that they are and have been at all times herein mentioned respectively, the duly elected and acting [e.g., vice president and secretary] of [name of corporation] a California corporation, and they further certify that:

1. A certificate, signed and acknowledged in accordance with section 1901 of the California Corporations Code, was filed with the California Secretary of State stating that the corporation had elected to wind up and dissolve;

2. The corporation has revoked its election to wind up and dissolve;

3. No assets of the corporation have been distributed under this election;

4. By written consent of the shareholders of the corporation, duly executed on _ _ _ _ _ _, 19_ _, shareholders holding _ _ _ _ shares entitled to vote consented to revoke voluntary election to wind up and dissolve; and

5. The total number of outstanding shares entitled to vote on or consent to such revocation was _ _ _ _.

We further declare under penalty of perjury under the laws of the State of California that the matters set forth in this certificate are true and correct of our own knowledge.

_____
President

_____
Secretary

B. The Winding Up Process Generally

§7.28   1. Powers and Authority of the Board

Whether dissolution proceedings are voluntary or involuntary, the board of directors continues to function as a board during the process of winding up. The Corporations Code gives the board adequate authority to act in the name and on behalf of the corporation. See Corp C §§1903(b), 2001. A court having jurisdiction over the dissolution can impose restrictions on the board's authority, but such restrictions are unlikely except on application of an interested party.

The powers and duties of the board in dissolution proceedings include the power "to make contracts and to do any and all things in the name of the corporation which may be proper or convenient for the purposes of winding up, settling and liquidating the affairs of the corporation." Corp C §2001(h). Specific powers also include the powers to elect officers, carry out existing contracts, collect accounts, pay debts, defend actions brought against the corporation, prosecute actions by the corporation, and sell the property of the corporation without court order. Corp C §2001(a)–(g).

Under Corp C §2001(g), the directors of a corporation in dissolution may sell all or part of the corporate assets *for cash* without the shareholder approval otherwise required by Corp C §1001, unless the sale is made to a controlling party of the corporation, in which case approval by at least 90 percent of the voting power is required. Corp C §§1001(d), 2001(g). However, any transfer of assets in a transaction that constitutes a reorganization under Corp C §181 requires shareholder approval. Corp C §§1200, 1201, 2001(g)]. Even where shareholder approval is required, there are no dissenters' rights (Corp C §§1300–1312) in dissolution proceedings. Corp C §2001(g). See 2 MARSH'S CALIFORNIA CORPORATIONS LAW §20.24 (2d ed).

Following commencement of voluntary proceedings, a corporation is authorized to continue to conduct business for "such period as the board may deem necessary to preserve the corporation's goodwill or going-concern value pending a sale of its business or assets, or both, in whole or in part." Corp C §1903(c).

§7.29   2. Vacancies on Board

A vacancy on the board may be filled during a winding up proceeding in the same manner as if the corporation had not elected to dissolve. Corp C §§305, 2002. If vacancies exist on the board, it may be necessary for at least some of the vacancies to be filled in order to enable the acting directors to satisfy the quorum requirements of Corp C §307(a)(7) for board action.

When the identity of the directors or their right to hold office is in doubt, or if they are dead or unable to act, or they fail or refuse to act or their whereabouts cannot be ascertained, any interested person may petition the superior court of the proper county (the county in which the principal executive office of the corporation is located, or Sacramento County if the office is outside California or there is no such office; see Corp C §177) to determine the identity of the directors, or, if there are no directors, to appoint directors to wind up the affairs of the corporation, after hearing upon such notice to such persons as the court may direct. Corp C §2003. The petition should set forth the facts of dissolution or commencement of dissolution or winding up, and the names and addresses, to the extent known, of the persons who were directors or the fact that they are dead, unknown, or unable to act in the winding up. Presumably, any person named in the petition or any person claiming to be a director or trustee or receiver for the corporation is entitled to be heard on the petition.

§7.30   3. Adoption of Plan of Distribution

Once voluntary proceedings to wind up and dissolve have commenced, it is good practice for the board of directors to adopt resolutions outlining the steps to be taken in the dissolution and authorizing the officers of the corporation to proceed. See §7.32 for sample form. There is no general requirement that a plan of distribution be formally adopted by the board or shareholders, unless the plan contemplates a change in the normal liquidation rights of the shareholders (see §7.31).

§7.31   a. Varying the Liquidation Rights and Preferences

In general, preferred shareholders are entitled to receive the amount of their liquidation preference in cash before any assets are distributed to nonpreferred shareholders. Nevertheless, a plan of distribution of the corporation's non-money assets which is not in accordance with the liquidation rights of the preferred shares as specified in the articles may be adopted by approval of (1) the board, and (2) the outstanding shares of each class (Corp C §152). Corp C §2007(a). Such a plan might be useful if, for example, the dissolving corporation has sold its assets for the securities of the another corporation and it is more advantageous to distribute the securities to the preferred shareholders than to make special arrangements to distribute cash.

The board must cause notice of the adoption of such a plan to be given by mail, within 20 days after its adoption, to all holders of shares having a liquidation preference. Corp C §2007(b). The plan of distribution is binding on all shareholders except those who have a liquidation preference and dissent from the plan. For procedure necessary to preserve dissenters' rights, see §7.34.

§7.32   b. Form: Directors' Resolution Adopting Plan of Distribution

Form 7.32–1

Shareholders representing at least 50 percent of the voting power of the corporation have elected [*by written consent*] **to wind up and dissolve the corporation.**

The certificate of election to wind up and dissolve has been filed with the California Secretary of State.

The corporation must proceed to wind up its affairs.

In view of the above, it is

RESOLVED that the officers of the corporation are authorized and directed to sell any or all of those assets on the terms and conditions, and for such consideration, as the officers deem reasonable and expedient, and to execute all deeds and other documents necessary to transfer title to such assets.

RESOLVED FURTHER that the officers of the corporation are authorized and directed to pay or to make adequate provisions for all of the debts and liabilities of the corporation.

RESOLVED FURTHER that after the debts and liabilities of

the corporation have been paid or adequately provided for, the officers are authorized and directed to distribute the remaining assets to the shareholders, on receipt from the shareholders of the duly executed share certificates representing their shares, as follows: [*Set forth method of distribution, e.g., undivided interests according to their respective shareholdings*].

RESOLVED FURTHER that the officers of this corporation are authorized and directed to obtain the vote or written consent approving this plan of distribution of shareholders holding at least a majority of the shares of each class of issued and outstanding stock of the corporation [*or all the shares if there is only one class outstanding*].

RESOLVED FURTHER that upon distribution of all the assets of the corporation under this plan of distribution, the directors of this corporation are authorized and directed to execute and file a certificate of dissolution.

§7.33   c. Forms: Written Consent of Shareholders to Plan of Distribution

Form 7.33–1 (Shareholders' Consent)

WRITTEN CONSENT OF SHAREHOLDERS TO PLAN OF DISTRIBUTION

The undersigned shareholders of record of [*name of corporation*] (the corporation), a California corporation, whose shares constitute at least a majority of the shares of each class of the corporation's issued and outstanding stock, approve and consent to the plan of distribution of the assets of the corporation adopted by the board of directors at a meeting duly held on _ _ _ _ _ _, 19_ _, a copy of which plan is attached as Exhibit A and incorporated into this consent.

Each of the undersigned shareholders has signed the shareholder's name below and entered the date of signing and the number and class of the corporation's voting shares held by such shareholder of record on that date, and by so doing consents to the adoption of the plan of distribution set forth in Exhibit A.

Shareholder	Date	No. of Voting Shares Held	Class of Shares
_____	_____	_____	_____
_____	_____	_____	_____
_____	_____	_____	_____

Comment: A copy of Form 7.32–1 or of 7.33–2 should be attached as Exhibit A.

Form 7.33–2 (The Plan of Distribution)

PLAN OF DISTRIBUTION OF
[Name of corporation]

As part of this corporation's plan of liquidation, it is deemed by the board of directors of this corporation to be in the best interests of this corporation and its shareholders to adopt a plan of distribution of this corporation's assets among its shareholders in accordance with section 2007 of the California Corporations Code.

In view of the above, it is

RESOLVED that subject to approval by a majority of each class of this corporation's shareholders, the following plan of distribution of this corporation's assets among its shareholders is adopted.

1. *[Specify how assets are to be distributed]*;

2. The officers and directors of this corporation are authorized, empowered, and directed to execute and deliver all documents and to do all other things that are necessary or advisable to carry out the purposes and intentions of this plan of distribution;

3. All distributions before final distribution under the foregoing plan of distribution shall be in partial satisfaction of, and the final distribution under the foregoing plan of distribution shall be in complete satisfaction of, the rights of

any of this corporation's shareholders on distribution and liquidation of assets; and

4. This corporation's stock transfer books shall be closed as of the close of business on _ _ _ _ _ _, 19_ _.

§7.34   d. Dissenters' Rights

Unless the plan of distribution is abandoned, a dissenting shareholder is entitled to be paid the amount of the liquidation preference in cash if, within 30 days after the date of mailing of the notice of the adoption of the plan of distribution, the shareholder files a written demand for payment with the corporation, stating the number and class of shares held of record by the dissenting shareholder. Corp C §2007(c).

Abandonment of Plan of Distribution. If a demand for cash payment is filed, the board, in its discretion, may abandon the plan without further approval of the outstanding shares, and all shareholders are then entitled to distributions according to their rights and liquidation preferences. Corp C §2007(d).

C. The Distribution Phase

1. Paying or Providing for Debts and Liabilities

§7.35   a. General Rule

Debts and liabilities, including taxes (see §§7.39–7.43) must be paid or adequately provided for before distributions may be made to shareholders. See Corp C §§2004–2005.

Provision for the payment of corporate debts and liabilities is deemed adequate (1) if payment has been assumed or guaranteed in good faith by one or more financially responsible corporations or other persons (usually some or all of the shareholders) or by the United States Government or any agency of the government, and the corporation's board of directors has determined in good faith and with reasonable care that such provision for payment of debts and liabilities is adequate at the time of the distribution of assets to shareholders; or (2) if the amount of the debt or liability has been deposited with the State Treasurer or with a bank or trust company in California, in the manner specified in Corp C §2008.

See Corp C §2005. The foregoing are not the exclusive means of making adequate provision for debts and liabilities. In dissolutions that are not under court supervision, however, directors should be cautioned against adopting methods other than those specified in the Corporations Code and thereby risking personal liability. See §7.37.

§7.36   b. Form: Shareholders' Assumption of Debts and Liabilities

Form 7.36–1

**ASSUMPTION BY SHAREHOLDERS OF DEBTS
AND LIABILITIES OF**
[*Name of corporation*]

The undersigned, being the owners of all of the issued and outstanding shares of [*name of corporation*] **(the corporation), a California corporation, jointly assume and agree to pay all debts, obligations, and liabilities of the corporation; provided, however, that this assumption and agreement is limited, as to each of the undersigned, to the value of the property and assets of the corporation distributed to that shareholder.**

This assumption is made in consideration of the distribution upon dissolution of the corporation of all of its property and assets to the undersigned, who are all of the shareholders of the corporation, and is to be effective as of the time of distribution of those assets to the undersigned. This assumption includes all further expenses of liquidation of the corporation to the extent that they are unpaid at the date of dissolution.

Dated: _ _ _ _ _ _

> [*Signature(s) of shareholder(s)*]
> [*Typed name(s)*]

Comment: It may be necessary to provide for the assumption of other corporate debts and liabilities by financially responsible persons, or to deposit the amount of the debt or liability with the State Treasurer. Corp C §§2005, 2008; see §7.39.

c. Liability for Debts Not Paid or Provided For

§7.37   (1) Known Debts and Liabilities

Directors' Liability. Directors are liable to the corporation if they approve the distribution of assets to shareholders upon dissolution without paying or adequately providing for all *known* liabilities of the corporation on which claims were timely filed. Corp C §316(a)(2). Any one or more creditors of the corporation whose debts or claims arose prior to the initiation of dissolution proceedings and who have not consented to the improper distribution, whether or not they have reduced their claims to judgment, may bring suit in the name of the corporation to enforce this liability. Corp C §316(c). Directors who are sued may implead and compel contribution from other liable directors (Corp C §316(e)), and directors who are held liable are entitled to be subrogated to the rights of the corporation against the shareholders who received the distribution of assets. Corp C §316(f)(2).

CAVEAT: Although some other rules regarding directors' liability were liberalized in 1987, Corp C §204(a)(10)(A)(vii) was added at that time, specifically prohibiting any provision in the articles that would eliminate or limit directors' liability for monetary damages under Corp C §316.

Recovery From Recipient Shareholder. Assets distributed to shareholders without prior payment or adequate provision for payment of corporate debts and liabilities may be recovered by or in the name of the corporation or by its receiver, liquidator, or trustee in bankruptcy. Corp C §2009; *U.S. v Oil Resources, Inc.* (9th Cir 1987) 817 F2d 1429. A shareholder's liability is limited to the value of the property distributed, and each shareholder has the right of ratable contribution from other shareholders similarly liable. Corp C §2009(c).

§7.38   (2) Unknown Debts and Claims

Claims Arising Before Dissolution. After a corporation has been dissolved, its shareholders may be sued in the corporate name upon any cause of action against the corporation arising *prior to* the dissolution. Corp C §2011(a); *Allen v Southland Plumbing, Inc.* (1988) 201 CA3d 60, 246 CR 860.

Claims Arising After Dissolution. The California Supreme Court has ruled that claims arising after dissolution, barred by Corp C §౽౿.1(a), cannot be asserted on an equitable "trust fund" theory. *Pacific Scene, Inc. v Penasquitos, Inc.* (1988) 46 C3d 407, 417, 250 CR 651, 657. The court held that the legislature, in enacting Corp C §2011(a) and related sections addressing virtually all claims that formerly could have been asserted in equity against the shareholders of dissolved corporations, has occupied the field; moreover, said the court, the trust fund theory conflicts with specific provisions of the Corporations Code. 46 C3d at 409, 250 CR at 652.

The same result has been arrived at by the Ninth Circuit applying California law. In *U.S. v Oil Resources, Inc.* (9th Cir 1987) 817 F2d 1429, the Internal Revenue Service sued former shareholders of a dissolved corporation for satisfaction of its tax liabilities. The district court held the shareholders liable under the trust fund doctrine, but the Ninth Circuit reversed, reasoning that the statutory remedies of Corp C §§2009–2011 superseded the common law cause of action, and that the court "must therefore apply the statutory scheme in resolving this dispute." 817 F2d at 1433. See also *Levin Metals Corp. v Parr-Richmond Terminal Co.* (ND Cal 1986) 631 F Supp 303, aff'd (9th Cir 1987) 817 F2d 1448, holding that Corp C §§2010 and 2011(a) "do not authorize suits against dissolved corporations based on causes of action arising subsequent to dissolution." 631 F Supp at 304.

In appropriate situations, however, claimants may be entitled to sue under the Uniform Fraudulent Transfer Act, CC §§3439–3439.12. See §7.84.

§7.39   d. Provision for Payment of State Taxes

California franchise taxes will normally have to be assumed by financially responsible persons (*e.g.*, a majority or all of the shareholders) unless a final return is prepared and filed on the date the dissolution is to be completed. The Franchise Tax Board must issue a tax-clearance certificate before the Secretary of State will file the certificate of dissolution. Corp C §1905(d); Rev & T C §23334. To obtain the tax-clearance certificate a form of assumption of tax liability is usually filed with the Franchise Tax Board.

CAVEAT: The official forms of assumption required by the Franchise Tax Board (Forms 7.41–1 and 7.42–1) do not condition the assumption on the filing of a certificate of dissolution, and the Franchise Tax Board will not accept amendments to these forms. Consequently, a person should not file an assumption of tax liability with the Franchise Tax Board unless he or she is willing to assume the corporation's tax liability even if the dissolution is abandoned.

NOTE: If the corporation has not done any business in California during the taxable year and complies with statutory procedures, the minimum franchise tax for taxable year can be waived. Rev & T C §23332.

§7.40   (1) Official Form: Request for Tax Clearance
                  Certificate (FTB 3555)

Form 7.40–1

STATE OF CALIFORNIA

FRANCHISE TAX BOARD

***REQUEST FOR
TAX CLEARANCE CERTIFICATE
SUPPLEMENTAL INFORMATION**

MAIL TO: CORPORATION AUDIT SECTION
             ATTN: TAX CLEARANCE UNIT
             P.O. Box 1468
             Sacramento, CA 95807-1468

             Phone Sacramento
             (916) 369-4144

CORPORATE NAME	CALIFORNIA CORPORATION NUMBER
Date taxpayer ceased or will cease to do business in California:	Latest income period for which a California return has been filed:

The Franchise Tax Board will issue a Tax Clearance Certificate when all taxes have been paid or secured.

> ***ATTACH CORPORATE ASSUMPTION OF TAX LIABILITY, FORM FTB 2568, OR INDIVIDUAL ASSUMPTION OF TAX LIABILITY, FORM FTB 2569, TO THIS REQUEST.**

Supplemental Information. Please furnish the following information if the business carried on in California will be continued by another corporation after the taxpayer's dissolution or withdrawal.

NAME OF TRANSFEREE	CALIFORNIA CORPORATION NUMBER OF TRANSFEREE
ACCOUNTING PERIOD OF TRANSFEREE	Section of the Internal Revenue Code applicable to the Transfer of Taxpayer's Business or assets: _____

If the Tax Clearance Certificate is to be mailed to someone other than the Corporation listed above, please complete the following: *(A copy of the Tax Clearance Certificate will be sent to the Secretary of State)*

NAME
ADDRESS

FTB 3555 (REV 6-86)

Comment: To obtain a tax-clearance certificate, the corporation should file the above form with the Franchise Tax Board, along with either a corporate assumption of tax liability (Form 7.41–1) or an individual assumption of tax liability (Form 7.42–1).

§7.41 (2) Official Form: Corporate Assumption of Tax Liability (FTB 2568)

Form 7.41–1

FRANCHISE TAX BOARD

CORPORATION ASSUMPTION
OF TAX LIABILITY

MAIL TO: CORPORATION AUDIT SECTION
ATTN: TAX CLEARANCE UNIT
P.O. Box 1468
Sacramento, CA 95807-1468

Phone Sacramento
(916) 369-4144

The Assumption of Tax Liability

of (1) _____)
)
_____ A corporation) _____
)   Corporate No.
by (2) _____)
)
_____ A corporation) _____
                                                                    Corporate No.

incorporated or qualified to do business within the State of California, unconditionally agrees to file with the Franchise Tax Board all returns and data that is required and unconditionally agrees to pay in full all tax liabilities, penalties and interest of (1) _____

_____ ;

(2) _____
                          Exact Corporate Name

_____
Signature and Title of Officer

STATE OF _____)
) ss.
COUNTY OF _____)

_____ , Being first duly sworn, state

that I am the, _____
of the corporation referred to in (2) above and that in such official capacity; I signed the name of that corporation to the assumption agreement; and that at the time of executing the agreement, I had full power and authority to execute the agreement on behalf of the corporation, and to bind the corporation to carry out each, every, and all the terms, conditions, obligations and undertakings set forth therein.

Subscribed and sworn to before me this _____ *day of* _____ *, 19* _____ .

_____   _____
Signature and Title of Officer   Notary Public

FTB 2568 (REV 7-86)

§7.42   (3) Official Form: Individual Assumption of Tax Liability (FTB 2569)

Form 7.42–1

STATE OF CALIFORNIA

FRANCHISE TAX BOARD

**INDIVIDUAL ASSUMPTION
OF TAX LIABILITY**

MAIL TO: CORPORATION AUDIT SECTION
                  ATTN: TAX CLEARANCE UNIT
                  P.O. Box 1468
                  Sacramento, CA 95812-1468

                  Phone Sacramento
                  (916) 369-4144

CORPORATE NAME	CALIFORNIA CORPORATION NUMBER

I unconditionally agree to file or cause to be filed with the Franchise Tax Board, under the provisions of the Bank and Corporation Tax Law, such returns and data that may be required and to pay in full all accrued or accruing liabilities for tax, penalty and/or interest due from the above corporation.

My net worth (assets minus liabilities) is not less than: $ _____ .

(A detailed financial statement, form FTB 3565, is required).

NAME OF INDIVIDUAL ASSUMER. (Must be resident of California)	SOCIAL SECURITY NO.

ADDRESS

DATE	SIGNATURE

FOR PRIVACY ACT NOTICE, SEE FORM FTB 1131.

FTB 2569 (REV 3-89)

Comment: This form must be accompanied by a detailed financial statement of the assumer (Form 7.43–1).

Note that an assumption of tax liability is not conditioned on the corporation's filing of a Certificate of Dissolution; see *Caveat* in §7.39.

§7.43 (4) Official Form: Financial Statement for Assumers (FTB 3565)

Form 7.43–1

STATE OF CALIFORNIA
FRANCHISE TAX BOARD

FINANCIAL STATEMENT FOR INDIVIDUAL ASSUMER

STATEMENT OF ASSETS AND LIABILITIES

ITEM	PRESENT VALUE	LIABILITIES BALANCE DUE	EQUITY IN ASSET
CASH			
BANK ACCOUNTS			
STOCKS AND BONDS			
CASH OR LOAN VALUE OF INSURANCE			
HOUSEHOLD FURNITURE			
REAL PROPERTY			
VEHICLES			
OTHER ASSETS (Describe)			
FEDERAL TAXES OUTSTANDING			
LOANS			
OTHER (Include judgements)			
TOTAL			$

GENERAL INFORMATION

Net Annual Income

Source (Name of Business or Employer)

Banks and Savings and Loan Accounts (Names and Addresses)

Description and license number of each vehicle

Stocks and Bonds (Name of company, number of shares, etc.)

Real Property (Brief descriptions and locations)

I certify that the above data is correct to the best of my knowledge.

Assumer's Name

Assumer's Address

Signature _____ Date _____

FTB 3565 (REV 9-86)

88 50546

2. Distributions to Shareholders

§7.44   **a. General Rule: Prorata Distribution**

Distributions to shareholders may be made at one time or in installments, and may be in cash or in kind.

Prorata Distribution. In general, after a corporation's debts have been paid or adequately provided for, the remaining corporate assets must be distributed among the shareholders "according to their respective rights and preferences." Corp C §2004. Not only must liquidation preferences of preferred shares be respected, but the holders of shares of the same class must be treated equally in the distribution of assets. Therefore assets must be distributed pro rata among shareholders of the same class. The board may not distribute assets in kind to certain of the shareholders while distributing cash to others, even though an effort is made to ensure that each shareholder receives the same value. *In re San Joaquin Light & Power Corp.* (1942) 52 CA2d 814, 127 P2d 29; *Zimmerman v Tidewater Associated Oil Co.* (1943) 61 CA2d 585, 143 P2d 409. Presumably, however, if 100 percent of the shareholders of a specific class were to agree on a non-prorata distribution of assets amongst themselves, the board could make such a distribution based on the shareholders' authorization.

§7.45   **b. Distribution According to Plan**

For distributions according to a plan of distribution (which may or may not vary the shareholders' liquidation rights and preferences), see §§7.31–7.34.

c. Trust Agreement

§7.46   **(1) When To Use**

It may be advisable to establish a liquidating trust to complete the winding up, particularly if there are (1) missing shareholders, (2) unliquidated debts, (3) too many shareholders to administer the estate practically as tenants in common, or (4) difficulties in disposing of the corporation's assets in an orderly manner. The trust agreement should be drafted to accomplish the purposes for which it is created, but for purposes of avoiding income tax problems it should have a definite term (preferably no longer than five years), and the trustee should not be authorized to engage in a business. The sample form in §7.47 addresses problems raised by situations (3) and (4), and should be adapted to the particular case.

§7.47   (2) Form: Trust Agreement

Form 7.47–1

TRUST AGREEMENT

This agreement is made on _ _ _ _ _ _, 19_ _, between [name of corporation] (the corporation), a California corporation in the process of dissolution, and [name of bank or trust company] (Trustee).

RECITALS

The corporation has shares of outstanding stock owned by the persons in the amounts and percentages set forth on the list of shareholders attached as Exhibit A and incorporated into this agreement. In this agreement, persons on the shareholder list are referred to as "beneficiary" or "beneficiaries."

On _ _ _ _ _ _, 19_ _, persons owning 50 percent or more of the corporation's outstanding voting stock elected in writing to wind up and dissolve the corporation, authorized its directors to adopt a plan of liquidation, and authorized and directed its officers to take such action as may be necessary or proper to wind up the affairs of the corporation and dissolve it. Under this authority, on _ _ _ _ _ _, 19_ _ the corporation's directors adopted a plan of complete liquidation and distribution. A certified copy of the directors' resolution adopting this plan is attached as Exhibit B and incorporated into this agreement.

[Insert, if applicable]

On _ _ _ _ _ _, 19_ _, the corporation's directors requested and obtained court supervision, by the [name of superior court] (the Court), of the corporation's winding up and dissolution under the provisions of section 1904 of the California Corporations Code.

[Continue]

In accordance with the plan, the corporation has to date sold several parcels of real property, and contemplates selling additional parcels. The proceeds from these sales have been, and are expected to be, in the form of cash, promissory notes, accounts receivable, or a combination thereof.

[*Describe actions taken, e.g., the corporation has sold one parcel of real property to _ [name of buyer]*] for cash and a promissory note in the face amount of $_ _ _ _ _ _, bearing annual installments commencing on _ _ _ _ _ _, 19_ _. The corporation has requested [*name of maker of note*] to break this note down into small denominations so that it can be divided among the beneficiaries in accordance with the percentages shown on the shareholder's list, but [*maker*] has refused to comply with the request. The corporation's officers feel that the same problem may arise in connection with other promissory notes.

In view of the above, the corporation's directors and persons owning _ _ _ _ percent of the corporation's outstanding voting stock approved the following plan of distribution of the corporation's assets among the corporation's shareholders in complete liquidation:

1. All cash and unsold assets which, in the opinion of the corporation's board of directors, are reasonably susceptible of division in kind shall be distributed to the corporation's shareholders on a prorata basis.

2. All other assets, including without limitation unsold real property, promissory notes, accounts receivable, and other assets which, in the opinion of the corporation's board of directors, are not reasonably susceptible of division in kind shall be distributed, subject to any remaining corporate obligations, to a trustee appointed by the Court (Trustee) under the terms of a trust approved by the Court for the following purposes: (a) receiving the assets for and on behalf of the beneficiaries in complete liquidation of the corporation (b) converting the assets to cash, (c) paying any and all debts to which those assets are subject, (d) distributing the remaining cash forthwith, and (e) distributing any other assets remaining on termination of the trust to the beneficiaries.

A certified copy of the directors' and shareholders'

resolutions adopting the foregoing plan of distribution is attached as Exhibit C and incorporated into this agreement.

On _ _ _ _ _ _, 19_ _, [*name of trustee*] was appointed Trustee by the [*Court/(specify other)*], to receive certain of the corporation's assets for the benefit of the corporation's shareholders under the plan of distribution, and was directed to hold those assets in accordance with the terms of and for the purposes set forth in this agreement.

[*Add, if applicable*]

A copy of the Court's order is attached as Exhibit D and incorporated into this agreement.

[*Continue*]

IT IS AGREED:

1. CREATION OF TRUST ESTATE. Contemporaneously with the execution of this agreement, the corporation has executed and delivered to Trustee assignments of the assets set forth on the list attached to and incorporated into this agreement as Exhibit E. From time to time, the corporation may transfer to Trustee additional assets, which may be subject to the corporation's obligations or liabilities; the corporation will execute and deliver to Trustee all documents necessary to transfer these assets to Trustee. These future additions, any obligations to which they are subject, the assets listed on Exhibit E, and any income earned on any assets transferred to Trustee, shall be the trust estate.

2. POWERS OF TRUSTEE. Trustee is empowered and authorized to act as follows:

(a) Promissory Notes and Accounts Receivable. Trustee shall collect the installments of principal and interest on any notes and accounts receivable which are part of the trust estate. After deducting from such collections Trustee's estimate of a reasonable reserve for trust expenses and any obligations to which any of the trust estate is subject, Trustee shall distribute to each beneficiary, at the address set forth on the shareholders' list, such beneficiary's prorata portion, in accordance with the shareholder list (Exhibit A), of these collections. Distributions under this paragraph shall be made to the beneficiaries [*specify frequency or time of distribution; e.g., monthly/quarterly/at appropriate intervals within Trustee's reasonable discretion/as soon as practical after receipt by Trustee].*

If there is a default in payment of any installment of principal or interest on any note or account receivable, Trustee shall take all necessary action to collect the defaulted installment, or, if Trustee deems it to be in the best interests of the beneficiaries, Trustee shall accelerate the entire balance due and shall institute suit to recover such balance. If Trustee institutes suit, Trustee shall be entitled to all its reasonable and necessary costs and expenses, including attorney fees, if any, in connection with the suit.

(b) All Other Assets. Trustee shall hold the trust estate, other than cash, notes, and accounts receivable, for disposition, upon the terms and for the consideration determined by Trustee in its absolute discretion to be in the best interests of the beneficiaries. Trustee shall have full power to do everything necessary to consummate any disposition of the trust estate, including the power of sale [*add other powers, if any.*]

(c) General. Under no circumstances shall Trustee conduct any business of any nature on behalf of the trust estate. Trustee's activities shall be limited to the collection, disposition, and distribution of the trust estate as set forth in this agreement. If all the trust estate cannot be disposed of within the time period provided in this agreement, at the termination of the trust Trustee shall distribute the remaining trust estate among the beneficiaries in accordance with the percentages set forth on the shareholder's list (Exhibit A).

3. ADDITIONAL DUTIES OF TRUSTEE. Trustee shall have the following duties as trustee in addition to those set forth in Paragraph 2:

(a) Preparing and filing all federal and state tax returns required to be filed by the trust;

(b) Preparing, filing with the proper governmental authorities, and mailing to the beneficiaries at the addresses shown on the shareholder list, annual information returns showing each beneficiary's share of the trust's net income and the nature of the income;

(c) From the cash proceeds of the trust estate, paying any obligations to which the trust estate is subject;

(d) Keeping and maintaining adequate books and records of all Trustee's transactions as trustee, and annually furnishing to each beneficiary a statement showing the trust's remaining assets, gross receipts, and gross disbursements other than distributions to beneficiaries; and

(e) On termination of the trust, preparing and making available for inspection at Trustee's office at _ _ _ _ _ _ _, California, a complete account of all Trustee's transactions as trustee under this agreement.

4. TERM OF TRUST. This trust shall be irrevocable and shall terminate on _ _ _ _ _ _, 19_ _, or an earlier date on which the trust estate has been distributed to the beneficiaries.

5. SUCCESSOR TRUSTEE. If Trustee resigns, or refuses or is unable to act as trustee, a new trustee shall be appointed by the [Court/(specify other)] who, upon execution of a written acceptance of the appointment, shall succeed to all the rights and duties of Trustee.

6. LIABILITY OF TRUSTEE. Trustee shall not be liable for (1) any distribution made by it in accordance with the percentages set forth on the shareholder list (Exhibit A), (2) any disposition of the trust estate as set forth in Paragraph 2(b) of this agreement, or (3) any other act, omission, or conduct specifically authorized by the terms of this agreement [or by the Court], except to the extent of Trustee's own willful misconduct.

[Add Trustee's requested exculpatory clause, if appropriate]

7. TRUSTEE'S EXPENSES. All expenses of Trustee in carrying out the purposes of this trust shall be paid from the trust estate. Such expenses shall include, without limitation, Trustee's fee for acting as trustee, real or personal property taxes on the trust estate, attorneys' or accountants' fees, or both, and costs of collecting or selling any assets in the trust estate.

8. COMPENSATION OF TRUSTEE. Trustee shall be paid a reasonable fee for its services in administering this trust. [*Insert, if appropriate, an agreed fee or a percentage of assets in the trust estate.*]

9. INSTRUCTIONS TO TRUSTEE. Trustee is granted broad powers to carry out the specified purposes of this agreement and shall not be required to obtain consent of the beneficiaries in matters within the powers described.

[*Add, if appropriate*]

If questions arise concerning interpretation of this agreement, Trustee shall request instructions from the Court.

[*Continue*]

IN WITNESS WHEREOF, the parties have executed this trust agreement on _ _ _ _ _ _, 19_ _.

[*Name of corporation*]

By _____
[*Typed name and title*]

_____
Trustee

Comment: This is a sample form of trust agreement, and should be adapted to the facts and circumstances of the particular corporation.

§7.48   3. Final Distribution

After determining that all the known debts and liabilities of the corporation have been paid or adequately provided for, the board must distribute all the remaining corporate assets among the shareholders according to their respective rights and preferences, or, if there are no shareholders, to the persons entitled to the remaining assets. Corp C §2004.

Distribution should be made as soon as reasonably possible after adequate provision for corporate debts and liabilities. Corp C §2006. Distribution may be either in money or in kind, as long as distribution is fair and reasonable and there is compliance with provisions of the articles of incorporation concerning shareholders' rights. Corp C §2006. Preferred shareholders may have a right to demand payment of the amount of their liquidation preference in cash, if the articles of incorporation so provide. See §7.31. Common shareholders have no right to demand a cash distribution, and they may be required to accept prorata distribution in kind. Corp C §2006. See 1A Ballantine & Sterling, CALIFORNIA CORPORATION LAWS §317.02 (4th ed).

Following are sample forms of a conveyance and assignment to complete the liquidation of assets (§7.49), and the corporation's receipt for shareholders' stock certificates (§7.50).

§7.49   a. Form: Corporation's Conveyance and Assignment to Shareholders or to Liquidating Trust

Form 7.49–1

CONVEYANCE AND ASSIGNMENT

Under the plan of complete liquidation adopted _ _ _ _ _ _, 19_ _, [*name of corporation*] (the corporation), a California corporation, hereby grants, conveys, sells, assigns, and transfers over to [*e.g., names of shareholders*], equal undivided interests in the following properties of the corporation:

1. All of the corporation's bank accounts, cash, and currency;

2. All of the corporation's accounts receivable, promissory notes, mortgages, pledges, other encumbrances, other evidences of indebtedness, and other obligations of others owing to the corporation;

3. All of the corporation's causes of action and choses in action;

4. All of the corporation's stock, bonds, and other securities;

5. All of the corporation's miscellaneous property of any and all kinds; and

6. Any and all other property of whatever kind or nature and

wherever located, and all the corporation's right, title, and interest in that property.

The specific enumeration or description of properties in this conveyance and assignment is not intended to limit the assets and properties that it covers; it is the intent of the corporation by this instrument to convey all of the corporation's assets and properties of any and all kinds or character to the shareholders listed above.

This conveyance and assignment is made under the plan of liquidation and distribution adopted and approved by written consent of the above-named shareholders of the corporation on _ _ _ _ _ _, 19_ _, in complete liquidation of the corporation and in complete cancellation of all outstanding shares of capital stock of the corporation.

Title to all properties specified as being conveyed and transferred shall become fully and completely conveyed and transferred to the above-named shareholders by the making of this instrument and delivery of it to the shareholders, but the corporation agrees, at the shareholders' request, to make, execute, and deliver to the shareholders such other and further deeds, bills of sale, checks, conveyances, and assignments as may be desirable or convenient to further evidence the conveyance, assignment, and transfer effected by this conveyance and assignment.

IN WITNESS WHEREOF, the corporation has caused this conveyance and assignment to be executed and its corporate seal to be affixed by its duly authorized officers on _ _ _ _ _ _, 19_ _.

[*Name of corporation*]

_____
President

_____
Secretary

[*Corporate Seal*]

[*Acknowledgment*]

State of California, County of _ _ _ _ _ _:

On _ _ _ _ _ _, 19_ _, before me, the undersigned, a notary public for the State of California, personally appeared _ _ _ _ _ _ _ _, known to me or proved to me on the basis of satisfactory evidence to be the person(s) who executed this instrument as officer(s) or on behalf of the corporation named therein, and acknowledged to me that the corporation executed it.

[*Seal*]

_____
Notary Public

§7.50   b. Form: Corporation's Receipt for Shareholders' Stock Certificates

Form 7.50–1

TO: [*name of shareholder*]

RECEIPT IS ACKNOWLEDGED of share certificate No(s). _ _ _ _ issued by this corporation to you, evidencing a total of _ _ _ _ shares of the capital stock of this corporation. Each such share certificate has been duly endorsed by you, and is received by the corporation for complete cancellation, in exchange for the transfer to you of your [*prorata/agreed*] share, as a shareholder of this corporation, of all the corporation's property and assets in the course of the corporation's winding up and dissolution.

Dated: _ _ _ _ _ _

[*Name of corporation*]

By _____
[*Corporate seal*]   **Secretary**

D. Procedure for Completing Unsupervised Dissolution

§7.51   1. Certificate of Dissolution, Generally

When a corporation has been completely wound up without court supervision, a majority of directors then in office must sign and verify a certificate of dissolution stating:

(1) That the corporation has been completely wound up.

(2) That its known debts and liabilities have been actually paid, adequately provided for, or paid or provided for as far as its assets permitted, or that it has incurred no known debts or liabilities, as the case may be. (If provision for payment of known debts or liabilities has been made, the certificate must specify the provisions and furnish detailed information to allow creditors to claim payment; see Corp C §1905(a)(2).)

(3) That its known assets have been distributed to the persons entitled thereto or that it acquired no known assets, as the case may be.

(4) That the corporation is dissolved. Corp C §1905(a).

The corporate existence ceases (except for the purpose of further winding up, if needed) when the certificate of dissolution is filed in the office of the Secretary of State. However, before the corporation may file a certificate of dissolution, it must file or cause to be filed a certificate of satisfaction of the Franchise Tax Board that all taxes imposed under the Bank and Corporation Tax Law have been paid or secured. Corp C §1905(b).

§7.52   2. Form: Certificate of Dissolution

Form 7.52–1

CERTIFICATE OF DISSOLUTION OF
[*name of corporation*]

[*Names of a majority of corporation's directors*] **certify that:**

1. They constitute a majority of the directors now in office of [*name of corporation*], **a California corporation.**

2. The corporation has been completely wound up.

3. The corporation's known debts and liabilities have been actually paid.

[*Or*]

3. The corporation's known debts and liabilities have been adequately provided for by their assumption by the following named persons:

Name	Address
_____	_____
_____	_____
_____	_____

[*Continue*]

4. The corporation's known assets have been distributed to the persons entitled thereto.

[*Or*]

4. The corporation has acquired no known assets.

[*Continue*]

5. The corporation is dissolved.

Dated: _ _ _ _ _ _

_____
Director

_____
Director

Each of the undersigned declares under penalty of perjury that the matters set forth in the foregoing certificate are true and correct. Executed on _ _ _ _ _ _, 19_ _, at_ _ _ _ _ _ _ _, California.

_____

_____

Comment: For general information on dissolution filings, see California Secretary of State, *Corporations Check List* (1986) p 48. Filing of the certificate of dissolution is only informative in nature and is not determinative of dissolution for federal income tax purposes; in that context, dissolution depends on whether the corporation has ceased doing business for all practical purposes. See *A B C Brewing Corp. v Commissioner* (9th Cir 1955) 224 F2d 483; *Bank of Alameda County v McColgan* (1945) 69 CA2d 464, 159 P2d 31. If there are disputes with shareholders or creditors, winding up may have to continue after the filing of the certificate. See Corp C §2010.

IV. COURT-SUPERVISED VOLUNTARY PROCEEDINGS

§7.53   A. In General

In voluntary dissolution proceedings, court supervision of winding up the affairs of a corporation is available if it appears necessary for the protection of any parties in interest. Corp C §1904. The court's jurisdiction may be invoked at any stage during the winding up process.

The power to invoke the court's jurisdiction in all cases is not entirely clear. See *In re San Joaquin Light & Power Co.* (1942) 52 CA2d 814, 127 P2d 29. See also *In re Security Fin. Co.* (1957) 49 C2d 370, 317 P2d 1. The party petitioning for court supervision (see §7.56) must persuade the court that the application is meritorious and in good faith and that supervision is necessary.

Court supervision can be valuable if disputes occur or are anticipated in settling claims against the corporation, determining the terms and conditions of a sale of the corporation's assets, or arriving at a plan of distribution on completion of liquidation.

Even if winding up has been accomplished without court proceedings, the board, in lieu of filing the certificate of dissolution, may petition the court for an order declaring the corporation duly wound up and dissolved. Corp C §1907(a). See §§7.65–7.69. This may be desirable if the corporation has a large number of shareholders or if the propriety of the directors' conduct during the winding up of the corporation's affairs is questioned by shareholders or creditors. A copy of the court order will be filed in the office of the Secretary of State in the same manner as a certificate of dissolution (see §§7.51–7.52). Corp C §§1907(d), 1808–1809. This procedure has the advantage of barring claims of persons with notice who fail to appear (see Corp C §1907(c)), as well as providing the directors with a court determination that the winding up has been satisfactorily completed.

After dissolution is completed, the corporation continues to exist for an indefinite period to wind up its affairs, prosecute and defend actions, collect and discharge obligations, dispose of and convey property, and collect and divide its assets. Corp C §2010(a). See §7.84.

§7.54   B. Superior Court Jurisdiction and Powers

The superior court of the county in which the principal office of the corporation is located, or of Sacramento County if the office is located outside California or if there is no such office, has jurisdiction to make orders and to adjudge all matters concerning the winding up of the corporation. Corp C §§177, 1800(a), 1806, 1904. The court's broad powers include:

(1) Requiring timely proof of all claims and demands against the corporation, whether due or not yet due, contingent, unliquidated, or sounding only in damages, and barring from participation in any distribution of general assets all creditors and claimants failing to make and present claims and proofs within such time as the court may direct, generally within four to six months after the first publication of notice to creditors (Corp C §§1806(a), 1807(a));

(2) Determining or compromising all claims against the corporation, and determining the amount of money or assets to be retained by the corporation to pay or provide for the payment of claims (Corp C §1806(b));

(3) Determining the rights of shareholders to assets of the corporation (Corp C §1806(c));

(4) Requiring and ruling on intermediate and final accounts by the corporation's directors or other persons appointed to conduct

the winding up, and discharging such persons from their duties and liabilities (Corp C §1806(d));

(5) Appointing a commissioner to hear and determine any or all matters, with such power or authority as the court may deem proper (Corp C §1806(e));

(6) Filling any vacancies on the board which the directors or shareholders are unable to fill (Corp C §1806(f));

(7) Removing any director who appears to be guilty of dishonesty, misconduct, neglect, or abuse of trust in conducting the winding up, or who is unable to act, and providing for the filling of vacancies caused by such removals (Corp C §1806(g));

(8) Staying prosecution of any action against the corporation and requiring the parties seeking relief against the corporation in such an action to present and prove their claims in the same manner as required of other claimants (Corp C §1806(h));

(9) Determining whether adequate provision has been made for payment or satisfaction of all debts and liabilities not actually paid (Corp C §1806(i));

(10) Making orders for the withdrawal or termination of proceedings to wind up and dissolve, subject to conditions for the protection of shareholders and creditors (Corp C §1806(j));

(11) Making an order, upon the allowance or settlement of the final accounts, that the corporation has been duly wound up and is dissolved (Corp C §1806(k));

(12) Making orders to bring in new parties as the court deems proper for the determination of all questions and matters (Corp C §1806(*l*)). Although set forth in the chapter on involuntary dissolutions (Corp C §§1800–1809), these powers also apply in court proceedings for voluntary winding up and dissolution. Corp C §1904.

C. Petition and Orders for Court Supervision

§7.55   1. Who May Petition

Court supervision of voluntary winding up and dissolution may be initiated by a verified petition filed by any of the following: (1) the corporation, (2) the holders of 5 percent or more of the outstanding shares of any class of the corporation's stock (without regard to voting rights), (3) any shareholder of a close corporation, or (4) three or more creditors. Corp C §1904.

§7.56 2. Form: Shareholder Petition for Court Supervision of Voluntary Winding Up

Form 7.56–1

IN THE MATTER OF	) No. _ _ _ _ _ _
[name of corporation], A	)
CALIFORNIA CORPOR-	) PETITION FOR JUDICIAL
ATION IN THE PROCESS	) SUPERVISION OF WINDING UP
OF VOLUNTARY	) AFFAIRS OF CORPORATION
WINDING UP	) (Corp C §1904)

Petitioner(s) allege(s):

1. [Name of corporation] (the corporation), a California corporation, is, and at all times mentioned was, a corporation duly organized and existing under and by virtue of the laws of California, with its principal office in _ _ _ _ _ _ _ _ County, California.

2. Petitioner(s) [is/are] [e.g., the holder(s) of record of [number] shares of stock of the corporation constituting 5 percent or more of the total number of the corporation's outstanding shares]

3. The corporation is in the process of winding up by virtue of the adoption, on _ _ _ _ _ _, 19_ _, of an election by the [e.g., shareholder(s)] of the corporation to wind up and dissolve.

4. Supervision by the Court over all matters concerning the winding up of the affairs of the corporation is in the best interest of all parties in that [e.g., supervision will facilitate the settlement of claims against the corporation].

WHEREFORE, petitioner(s) pray(s) that:

1. The Court direct notice to the corporation and to all shareholders, creditors, and claimants of the corporation requiring them to appear before the Court at the time and place appointed, then and there to show cause why the Court should not take jurisdiction over, make orders, and adjudge as to any and all matters concerning the winding up of the affairs of the corporation, including all matters set forth and permitted in sections 1802–1808 of the California Corporations Code;

2. The court enter an order prescribing the notice to be given to the corporation and other persons interested in the corporation as shareholders, creditors, or claimants;

3. After the hearing on the order to show cause, this Court enter its order and decree assuming jurisdiction over the winding up of the affairs of the corporation, including all matters contained in sections 1802–1808 of the California Corporations Code;

4. For such other and further relief as the Court considers proper.

Dated: _ _ _ _ _ _

_____

Petitioner

_____

Attorney for Petitioner

VERIFICATION

I am [*a/the*] petitioner in this action; the foregoing petition is true of my own knowledge, except as to the matters stated in it on my information or belief, and as to those matters I believe it to be true.

I declare under penalty of perjury that the foregoing is true and correct, and that this declaration was executed on _ _ _ _ _ _, 19_ _, at _ _ _ _ _ _ _ _, California.

_____

Petitioner

_____

Attorney for Petitioner

Comment: See §7.54 for discussion of reasons for requesting court supervision. The above form should be modified appropriately for petitioners other than shareholders; see §7.65 for discussion of who may petition for court supervision of voluntary proceedings.

§7.57 3. Form: Order Approving Petition for Court Supervision of Winding Up of Corporation

Form 7.57–1

[*Caption; see*
Form 7.56–1]

No. _ _ _ _ _ _

ORDER APPROVING
PETITION FOR COURT
SUPERVISION OF WINDING
UP OF CORPORATION

The Court having read and filed the verified petition of [*name of petitioner*], and good cause appearing,

IT IS ORDERED that the petition be granted, and this Court takes jurisdiction of and supervision of the winding up of [*name of corporation*], and shall make orders and adjudge as to any and all matters concerning the winding up of the affairs of the corporation and determining the rights of shareholders, creditors, and claimants in and to the assets of such corporation.

Dated: _ _ _ _ _ _

_____
Judge

§7.58 4. Form: Order for Notice to Creditors

Form 7.58–1

[*Caption; see*
Form 7.56–1]

No. _ _ _ _ _ _

ORDER FOR NOTICE
TO CREDITORS

GOOD CAUSE APPEARING, IT IS ORDERED that:

1. The time within which claims are to be presented to the corporation shall be [*e.g., six months*] after the first publication of notice to creditors.

2. Publication of this notice shall be made in [*name of*

newspaper], **a newspaper of general circulation in _ _ _ _ _ _ _ _
County, California, once a week for three consecutive weeks.**

**3. A copy of this published notice shall be mailed to each
person shown as a creditor or claimant on the books of the
corporation, and also to all shareholders of record** [*e.g., and
to all former shareholders who tendered their stock to the corporation
for purchase under the corporation's tender offer made on _ _ _ _ _ _,
19_ _*]**.**

**4. Any claims against the corporation shall be filed in the
office of the Clerk of the Superior Court of _ _ _ _ _ _ _ County,
California, or such claims shall be presented at the office of**
[*name and address of attorney*], **attorney for** [*name of corporation*]**.**

IT IS FURTHER ORDERED that any creditor or claimant [*e.g.,
and former shareholders above described*] **shall be barred from
participation in any distribution of the general assets of the
corporation if such person fails to make and present a claim,
and proof of such claim, whether due or not yet due, within
the period of** [*e.g., six months*] **from the date of first publication
of this notice.**

Dated: _ _ _ _ _ _

_____
Judge

Comment: See Corp C §§1907(b), 1807(b). For claims procedure,
see §7.59.

D. Claims Procedure

§7.59   1. General Rules

A significant aspect of court supervision of voluntary proceedings is
the court's power to require presentation and proof of all claims and
demands against the corporation, and to bar creditors and claimants
who fail to comply from participating. See Corp C §1806(a). Creditors
and claimants may be barred from participation in the distribution of
general assets if they fail to make and present claims and proofs within
the time set by the court, which must be not less than four nor more than
six months after the first publication of notice of creditors, unless it

appears by affidavit that there are no claims, in which case the time limit may be three months. Corp C §1807(a). The court may allow a claim to be filed or presented at any time before distribution is completed if it is shown that the claimant did not receive notice. Corp C §1807(a). For requirements for publication of notice and the persons to whom personal notice should be sent, see Corp C §1807(b). Secured creditors who fail to present their claims are barred only as to the right to claim against the corporation's general assets for any deficiency in the amount realized on their security. Corp C §1807(c).

Before any distribution to the shareholders may be made, the undisputed claims must be paid, and the amount of any unmatured, contingent, or disputed claim that has been presented and has not been disallowed must be paid into court, subject to appropriate adjustments or other provisions deemed adequate by the court. See Corp C §1807(d).

Suits against a corporation on rejected claims must be commenced within 30 days after written notice of rejection. Corp C §1807(e). Under Corp C §1806(h), the court may stay prosecution of any suit, proceeding, or action against the corporation, and require the parties to present and prove their claims in the manner specified by the court, which is normally the same procedure followed in probate proceedings.

§7.60   2. Form: Notice for Presentation of Claims Against Corporation

Form 7.60–1

[*Caption; see Form 7.56–1*]

No. _ _ _ _ _ _

NOTICE FOR PRESENTATION OF CLAIMS AGAINST CORPORATION

To creditors and claimants of [*name of corporation*] **a California corporation:**

NOTICE IS HEREBY GIVEN that voluntary proceedings have been commenced for the winding up and dissolution of [*name of corporation*] **(the corporation), and that this Court has assumed jurisdiction over these proceedings under section 1904 of the California Corporations Code.**

In accordance with an order of this Court dated _ _ _ _ _ _ , 19_ _, all claims and demands against the corporation, whether due or not yet due, contingent, unliquidated, or for damages only, must be filed, together with proof thereof, with [*name of designated officer*] at the principal office of the corporation at [*address*] within [*e.g., 60/90 days*] after the date of first publication of this notice, which is _ _ _ _ _ _ , 19_ _.

Any creditor or claimant who fails to make and present claims and proofs within the time directed by the Court may be barred from participation in any distribution of the general assets of the corporation.

Dated: _ _ _ _ _ _

[*Name of corporation*]

By _____
[*Typed name and title*]

Comment: The notice may be adapted to the circumstances of a particular case or to a court order prescribing the form of notice.

E. Forms for Court Approval of Plan of Distribution

§7.61 **1. Form: Petition for Order Approving Plan of Distribution**

Form 7.61–1

[*Caption; see Form 7.56–1*]

No. _ _ _ _ _ _

PETITION FOR ORDER APPROVING PLAN OF DISTRIBUTION, FIRST LIQUIDATING DISTRIBUTION [*Add, if appropriate*] , **LIQUIDATING TRUST AGREEMENT, AND APPOINTMENT OF TRUSTEE**

The petitioner, [*name of corporation*], a California corporation, respectfully shows:

On _ _ _ _ _ _, 19_ _, persons owning more than 50 percent of the outstanding voting stock of [*name of corporation*] elected in writing to wind up and dissolve the corporation, authorized its directors to adopt a plan of liquidation; and authorized and directed its officers and directors to take necessary and proper action to wind up the affairs of the corporation and dissolve it. Under this authority, on _ _ _ _ _ _, 19_ _, the directors of [*name of corporation*] adopted a plan of complete liquidation.

On _ _ _ _ _ _, 19_ _, the directors of [*name of corporation*] applied for and obtained Court supervision of the above-entitled Court under the provisions of section 1904 of the California Corporations Code.

[*State facts concerning adopting a plan of distribution of corporate assets*].

For the foregoing reasons, a plan of distribution was adopted by the board of directors of [*name of corporation*] on _ _ _ _ _ _, 19_ _, providing in effect that [*state assets*] be distributed to the shareholders in trust. A copy of the plan of distribution is attached as Exhibit A and incorporated by reference in this petition.

Thereafter, the directors of [*name of corporation*] declared its first liquidating distribution to its shareholders, in the form of Exhibit B, attached and incorporated by reference in this petition, which distribution consisted of [*describe distribution*].

Under the provisions of section 2007 of the California Corporations Code, this distribution requires, in addition to the resolution of the board of directors, the vote or written consent of holders of a majority of each class of the outstanding shares of [*name of corporation*]. A meeting of the shareholders has been called and noticed for _ _ _ _ _ _, 19_ _, to consider, among other things, approval of the resolution of the board of directors as shown in Exhibit B. As of the date of this petition it is anticipated that the necessary approval of more than a majority of each class of shares of [*name of corporation*] will be obtained for the resolution. By the date of hearing on this petition the shareholders' meeting will have been held, and the results of the vote of the shareholders on the first liquidating distribution will be known.

[*Add, if appropriate*]

In conformity with the plan of distribution (Exhibit A), and the directors' resolution declaring the first liquidating distribution, a liquidating trust agreement has been prepared with [*name of bank or trust company*]. A copy of the trust agreement is attached as Exhibit C and is incorporated by reference in this petition.

[*Continue*]

WHEREFORE, petitioner respectfully prays:

1. That a date be set for the hearing of this petition, and notice of the time and place of the hearing be sent at least ten days before the hearing to all shareholders at the addresses shown on the books of the corporation, and that the notices be deposited in the United States mail in a sealed envelope with postage prepaid;

2. For an order approving the plan of distribution (Exhibit A) [*,/and*] the declaration of a first liquidating distribution (Exhibit B) [*;/,*]

[*Add, if appropriate*]

and the execution by the officers of the corporation of the trust agreement (Exhibit C);

[*Continue*]

3. For an order appointing [*name of bank or trust company*] as trustee;

4. For an order approving all distributions to shareholders [*under the trust agreement*] and reciting that these distributions are considered to be a fair and ratable distribution and a distribution in accordance with the respective rights of the shareholders of [*name of corporation*], and that all these distributions are in partial satisfaction of the rights of the shareholders [*;*]

[*Add, if appropriate*]

upon distribution and liquidation of the assets assigned and transferred to the trustee under this trust agreement;

[*Continue*]

5. For such further orders as the Court may deem reasonable under the circumstances.

Dated: _ _ _ _ _ _

> [*Name of corporation*]
>
> **By** _____
> [*Typed name and title*]

VERIFICATION

I am the [*title of officer*] **of** [*name of corporation*], **a petitioner in this action; I have read the foregoing petition; I am informed and believe that the matters in it are true and on that ground allege that the matters stated in the petition are true.**

I declare under penalty of perjury that the foregoing is true and correct and that this declaration was executed on _ _ _ _ _ _, 19_ _, at _ _ _ _ _ _ _ _, California.

> [*Signature*]
>
> _____
> [*Name and title*]

§7.62   2. Form: Order Fixing Time and Place of Hearing

Form 7.62–1

[*Caption; see Form 7.56–1*]

No. _ _ _ _ _ _

ORDER FIXING TIME AND PLACE OF HEARING ON PETITION FOR ORDER APPROVING PLAN OF DISTRIBUTION, FIRST LIQUIDATING DISTRIBUTION [*Add, if appropriate*] , **LIQUIDATING TRUST AGREEMENT, AND APPOINTMENT OF TRUSTEE**

On reading and filing the verified petition of [*name of petitioner*], **in dissolution:**

IT IS ORDERED that the petition for an order approving a

plan of distribution [*and/,*] resolution declaring a first liquidating distribution,

[*Add, if appropriate*]

liquidating trust agreement, and appointment of trustee,

[*Continue*]

will be heard before the above-entitled Court, Department No. _ _ _ _, located at _ _ _ _ _ _ _ _, California, on_ _ _ _ _ _, 19_ _, at _ _ _.m., and that notice of the time and place for the hearing of the petition shall be given to all shareholders of [*name of corporation*] by its secretary, in the form attached, by depositing this notice in the United States mail, in a sealed envelope with postage prepaid, addressed to the shareholders at their respective addresses as shown on the books of the corporation, at least ten days before the date of the hearing.

Dated: _ _ _ _ _ _

_____

Judge

§7.63   3. Form: Notice of Hearing on Petition for Order Approving Plan of Distribution

Form 7.63–1

[*Caption; see*   **No.** _ _ _ _ _ _
Form 7.56–1]

NOTICE OF HEARING ON PETITION FOR ORDER APPROVING PLAN OF DISTRIBUTION, FIRST LIQUIDATING DISTRIBUTION [*Add, if appropriate*] , **LIQUIDATING TRUST AGREEMENT, AND APPOINTMENT OF TRUSTEE**

NOTICE IS HEREBY GIVEN that [*name of corporation*] has petitioned the Superior Court of _ _ _ _ _ _ _ _ County, California, in the above-entitled proceeding, for an order approving a plan of distribution [and/,] resolution declaring a first liquidating distribution,

[Add, if appropriate]

liquidating trust agreement, and appointment of trustee,

[Continue]

and that the petition will be heard before the above-entitled Court, Department No. _ _ _ _, located at _ _ _ _ _ _ _ _, California, on _ _ _ _ _ _, 19_ _, at _ _ _.m.

Dated: _ _ _ _ _ _

[Name of corporation]

By _____
[Typed name and title]

Comment: A copy of the petition should be attached to the notice.

§7.64   4. Form: Order Approving Plan of Distribution

Form 7.64–1

[Caption; see   No. _ _ _ _ _ _
Form 7.56–1]
                        ORDER APPROVING PLAN
                        OF DISTRIBUTION, FIRST
                        LIQUIDATING DISTRIBUTION
                            [Add, if appropriate],
                        LIQUIDATING TRUST
                        AGREEMENT, AND
                        APPOINTMENT OF TRUSTEE

The petition of [name of corporation] (the corporation), a California corporation, in dissolution, for an order approving its plan of distribution [,/and] resolution declaring a first liquidating distribution,

[Add, if appropriate]

liquidating trust agreement, and appointment of trustee,

[Continue]

having come on regularly for hearing on _ _ _ _ _ _, 19_ _, [name *of attorney*] **appearing on behalf of petitioner, and no appearance having been made by any of the shareholders of petitioner, and proof of service of notice of this hearing as required in the order of this Court on _ _ _ _ _ _, 19_ _, having been made, and the Court having received evidence both oral and documentary, and being fully advised in the premises:**

IT IS ORDERED that the plan of distribution, Exhibit A to the petition, adopted by the board of directors on _ _ _ _ _ _, 19_ _, and approved by the vote of more than a majority of each class of the shareholders of the corporation on _ _ _ _ _ _, 19_ _, at a meeting duly called and held for that purpose, is approved.

IT IS FURTHER ORDERED that the resolution of the board of directors adopted on _ _ _ _ _ _, 19_ _, declaring its first liquidating distribution to its shareholders, in the form set forth in Exhibit B to the petition and approved by the vote of more than a majority of each class of the shareholders of the corporation on _ _ _ _ _ _, 19_ _, which distribution consisted of [describe distribution], is approved.

[Add, if appropriate]

IT IS FURTHER ORDERED that [name of bank or trust company] is appointed trustee under the trust agreement set forth as Exhibit C to the petition, which trust agreement is approved, and the officers of the corporation are authorized to execute the same on behalf of the corporation.

[Continue]

IT IS FURTHER ORDERED that all distributions made to shareholders

[Add, if appropriate]

under the trust agreement

[Continue]

shall be deemed to be a fair and ratable distribution in accordance with the respective rights of petitioner's share holders [,/.]

[Add, if appropriate]

and that these distributions are and will be in partial satisfaction of the rights of the shareholders on distribution and liquidation of the assets assigned and transferred to the trustee under the trust agreement.

[Continue]

Dated: _ _ _ _ _ _

_____

Judge

§7.65 F. Court Approval of Accounting and Order of Dissolution

Dissolution proceedings under court supervision are concluded by the directors' filing of an accounting and a petition for an order settling the accounting and declaring the corporation duly wound up and dissolved. Corp C §1808; see §7.66 for form. Notice of hearing is by mail and publication of an order to show cause why the corporation should not be declared duly wound up and dissolved. Corp C §1907; see §§7.67–7.68 for forms.

Upon issuance of the court's order declaring the corporation dissolved (see §7.69), the corporation's existence ceases, except for any necessary further winding up, and the directors and trustees are discharged from their duties and liabilities, except for completion of the winding up. Corp C §1808(b). A copy of the court order declaring the corporation dissolved, certified by the clerk of the court, must be filed with the Secretary of State. Corp C §1809.

§7.66 1. Form: Directors' Account and Petition

Form 7.66–1

[*Caption; see*   **No.** _ _ _ _ _ _
Form 7.56–1]
                                 **FIRST AND FINAL ACCOUNT
                                 OF DIRECTORS [*AND
                                 TRUSTEE*]; PETITION FOR
                                 ORDER APPROVING
                                 ACCOUNT, DECLARING
                                 CORPORATION DULY
                                 WOUND UP AND
                                 DISSOLVED, AND
                                 DISCHARGING DIRECTORS
                                 [*AND TRUSTEE*] FROM
                                 LIABILITY**

The petition of [*name of corporation*] (the corporation), a California corporation, in voluntary proceedings for winding up and dissolution, and the first and final account of its directors [*and trustee*] respectfully show that:

1. On _ _ _ _ _ _, 19_ _, persons owning more than [*e.g., 50 percent*] of the corporation's outstanding voting stock elected in writing to wind up and dissolve the corporation, authorized its directors to adopt a plan of liquidation, and authorized and directed its officers and directors to take such action as might be necessary and proper to wind up the corporation's affairs and dissolve it. Under this authority, on _ _ _ _ _ _, 19_ _, the directors adopted a plan of complete liquidation.

2. On _ _ _ _ _ _, 19_ _, the corporation's directors applied for and obtained court supervision by the above-entitled court ("the Court") under the provisions of section 1904 of the California Corporations Code.

3. On _ _ _ _ _ _, 19_ _, the Court made its order providing that notice be given to creditors, and fixing a period of [*e.g., six months*] within which claims were to be presented; that notice should be effected by publication in [*name of newspaper*], a newspaper of general circulation in _ _ _ _ _ _ _ County, once a week for three consecutive weeks; that a copy of this published notice should be mailed to each person shown as a creditor or claimant on the corporation's books, and also to all shareholders of record; that all claims should be either filed in the office of the Clerk of the Superior Court of _ _ _ _ _ _ _ County, California, or

presented at the office of [name and address of attorney], California, the corporation's attorney; and that any creditors, claimants, or former shareholders who failed, within the period of _ _ [e.g., six months] from the date of first publication of the notice, to make and present their claims and proof of amounts due or not yet due would be barred from participation in any distribution of the corporation's general assets.

4. Notice was duly mailed to all persons as provided in the Court's order and published in the [name of newspaper] for three consecutive weeks, the first publication having been made on _ _ _ _ _ _, 19_ _. Affidavits of mailing and of publication are on file in the records of this Court. The period for the filing of claims expired on _ _ _ _ _ _, 19_ _.

5. Attached to and incorporated in this account and petition as Exhibit A is a first and final account of the directors of the corporation from the commencement of liquidation to and including [cutoff date], showing all of the corporation's known assets as of the date of commencement of the dissolution, all known liabilities, all payments made during this period, and all disbursements to shareholders made during this period. Also shown are the remaining assets and liabilities of the corporation as of [cutoff date].

6. On the hearing of this petition, petitioners will file a supplement to this first and final account, covering the period from [cutoff date] to the date of hearing, at which time all remaining liabilities will have been paid or adequately provided for, and a final liquidating dividend will have been made to shareholders.

7. On _ _ _ _ _ _, 19_ _, a petition was filed by the corporation for an order approving a plan of distribution [,/and] a resolution declaring a first liquidating distribution [,/.]

[Add, if appropriate]

a liquidating trust agreement, and for appointment of a trustee under the trust agreement,

[Continue]

and that an order fixing time and place for hearing of the petition was duly made by this Court on _ _ _ _ _ _, 19_ _. Notice of time and place of hearing was given to all shareholders, and on _ _ _ _ _ _, 19_ _, by an order duly given and made, this Court approved: (1) the plan of distribution [,/and] (2) the resolution declaring a first liquidating distribution [;/,]

[*Add, if appropriate*]

(3) the liquidating trust agreement; and (4) the appointment of the trustee.

[*Continue*]

All of these documents are incorporated by reference in this account and petition.

[*Add, if appropriate*]

[8.] On _ _ _ _ _ _, 19_ _, [*name of bank or trust company*], the trustee named by the Court, and the corporation entered into the trust agreement approved by the Court. The trust agreement provided for the distribution in trust by the corporation to the trustee, for the equal prorata benefit of the shareholders, of all of its assets not capable of distribution in kind. The assets remaining in the corporation which were not sold, its promissory notes, and its other assets not capable of distribution in kind, with the exceptions of those referred to in the next following paragraph, have been or will be, at the time of hearing, transferred to the trustee under the terms of the trust agreement, as well as sufficient funds to cover subsequently arising expenses and any obligations and expenses of the trustee in connection with administering the trust.

[*Add, if appropriate*]

[9.] Certain real estate owned by the corporation known as _ _ _ _ _ _ _ _, situated in or near _ _ _ _ _ _ _ _, consisting of approximately _ _ _ _ acres, has not been disposed of, and the trustee cannot accept this asset under the trust agreement because it is situated outside the State of California. A separate trust agreement was entered into between the corporation and [*name of out-of-state trustee*] (the out-of-state trustee), by virtue of which the corporation assigned to the out-of-state trustee the above-described real estate, with power of sale or other disposition, for the purpose of liquidating the property and making a prorata distribution of the proceeds to the corporation's shareholders. Authority for the entry into the trust agreement was granted by resolution of the board of directors and approved by the written consent of more than [*e.g., a majority of each class*] of the shareholders of the corporation, and by an order duly made by the Court dated _____, 19__. That petition and order are incorporated by reference in this account and petition.

[Add, if appropriate]

[10.] The corporation has been party to certain leases previously entered into on a number of properties that had been owned and then sold during the course of liquidation. In each instance, the properties have been sold to a financially responsible person and the obligations of the lessor under these leases have been assumed by the purchasers of the properties, and the purchasers have agreed to indemnify and hold [*name of corporation*] harmless from any liability under the leases. All of the purchasers are fully able to perform the assumed obligations under the leases. The names of the parties who have assumed such obligations, and their addresses, are as follows:

Name	Address
_____	_____
_____	_____
_____	_____

[Continue]

[11.] The following claims, and only the following claims, have been filed: [*List and describe claims filed*].

[12.] With the filing of the supplemental account on the date of hearing of this petition, all of the corporation's assets will have been distributed [*pro rata to/in accordance with the rights and preferences of*] its shareholders, and all of its debts and obligations will have been paid or will have been adequately provided for. Therefore the Court may on the hearing make its order (1) approving and settling the first and final account of the directors and the supplemental account, and (2) declaring that the corporation's affairs have been duly wound up, its known assets have been distributed, all taxes or penalties due under the Bank and Corporation Tax Law have been paid, its other known debts, obligations, and liabilities have been actually paid or adequately provided for, the accounts of its directors have been settled, the directors [*and trustee*] are discharged from their duties and liabilities to creditors or shareholders, and the corporation is dissolved; for which order petitioner respectfully prays.

Dated: _ _ _ _ _ _

> [*Typed name of corporation*]
> [*Signature of officer*]
>
> [*Typed name*]

VERIFICATION

I am the [*title of officer*] of [*name of corporation*]. I have read the foregoing account and petition; I am informed and believe that the matters in it are true and on that ground allege that the matters stated in the account and petition are true.

I declare under penalty of perjury that the foregoing is true and correct and that this declaration was executed on _ _ _ _ _ _, 19_ _, at _ _ _ _ _ _ _ _,California.

> [*Signature*]
> _____
> [*Typed name and title*]

§7.67   2. Form: Order Fixing Time and Place of Hearing

Form 7.67–1

*[Caption; see
Form 7.56–1]*

No. _ _ _ _ _ _

**ORDER FIXING TIME AND
PLACE FOR HEARING ON
PETITION FOR ORDER
APPROVING ACCOUNT,
DECLARING CORPORATION
DULY WOUND UP AND
DISSOLVED, AND
DISCHARGING DIRECTORS
[*AND TRUSTEE*] FROM
LIABILITY**

The Court having filed and read the verified petition of [*name
of corporation*], a California corporation, in dissolution,

IT IS ORDERED that the time and place for the hearing of
the petition for an order settling and approving the first and
final account of the directors [*and trustee*], and for an order
declaring the corporation duly wound up and dissolved and
the directors [*and trustee*] discharged from their duties and
liabilities to creditors and shareholders, shall be _ _ _ _ _ _,
19_ _, at _ _ _.m.

IT IS FURTHER ORDERED that notice of the time and place
for the hearing of the petition be given to all shareholders of
[*name of corporation*] by its secretary, in the form attached, by
depositing this notice in the United States mail, in a sealed
envelope with postage prepaid, addressed to the shareholders
at their respective addresses as shown on the books of the
corporation.

Dated: _ _ _ _ _ _

_____
Judge

§7.68   3. Form: Notice of Hearing

Form 7.68–1

[*Caption; see*
Form 7.56–1]

No. _ _ _ _ _ _

**NOTICE OF HEARING ON
PETITION FOR ORDER
APPROVING ACCOUNT,
DECLARING CORPORATION
WOUND UP AND DISSOLVED,
AND DISCHARGING DIRECTORS
[*AND TRUSTEE*] FROM LIABILITY**

NOTICE IS HEREBY GIVEN THAT [*name of corporation*] **has petitioned the Court for an order approving the first and final account of directors** [*and trustee*], **and for an order declaring the corporation duly wound up and dissolved and the directors** [*and trustee*] **discharged from their duties and liabilities to creditors and shareholders. Reference is made to the petition for further particulars. This petition will be heard before the above-entitled Court, Department No. _ _ _, located at _ _ _ _ _ _ _, California, on _ _ _ _ _ _ _,19_ _, at _ _ _ _m.**

Dated: _ _ _ _ _ _

[*Name of corporation*]

By _____
[*Typed name and title*]

Comment: A copy of the petition should be attached to the notice.

§7.69 4. Form: Order Approving Accounts and Declaring Corporation Dissolved

Form 7.69–1

[*Caption; see*
Form 7.56–1]

No. _ _ _ _ _ _

**ORDER APPROVING FIRST
AND FINAL ACCOUNT,
DECLARING CORPORATION
DULY WOUND UP AND
DISSOLVED, AND DISCHARGING
DIRECTORS [*AND TRUSTEE*]
FROM LIABILITY**

The first and final account of directors [*and trustee*], **the**

supplemental account, and the petition for an order approving the same and declaring [*name of corporation*] duly wound up and dissolved and its directors [*and trustee*] discharged from their duties and liabilities to creditors and shareholders, was heard on _ _ _ _ _ _, 19_ _, and oral and documentary evidence was submitted to the Court.

On proof being made to the satisfaction of the Court, the Court finds that:

1. The first and final account and the supplemental account should be approved and settled.

2. The corporation's affairs are in a condition for the corporation to be wound up and dissolved.

3. Any tax or penalty due under the Bank and Corporation Tax Law has been paid or secured, and a certificate of the Franchise Tax Board to that effect has been filed with the California Secretary of State.

4. All of the corporation's known debts and liabilities have been paid or adequately provided for.

[*Add, if appropriate*]

In connection with those liabilities that have been adequately provided for, the only known contingent liabilities of the corporation arise out of certain leases made by it as lessor to tenants of properties previously owned by the corporation and which have been sold during the course of liquidation. In each instance, the properties have been sold to a financially responsible person and the obligations of the lessor under the leases (principally the obligation to grant tenant the quiet and peaceable possession of the properties during the term of such leases) have been assumed by the purchasers, and the purchasers have agreed to indemnify and hold the corporation harmless from any liability. A designation of the properties and the names and addresses of the parties who have assumed such obligations are set forth in Exhibit A attached to and incorporated in this order.

[*Continue*]

5. All known assets of the corporation have been distributed to its shareholders.

IT IS ORDERED that:

1. The first and final account and the supplemental account of the directors [*and trustee*] are approved and settled as filed.

2. The corporation is duly wound up and dissolved.

3. The accounts of the directors [*and trustee*] having been settled, the directors [*and trustee*] are discharged from their duties and liabilities to creditors and shareholders.

Dated: _ _ _ _ _ _

_____

Judge

V. INVOLUNTARY PROCEEDINGS

§7.70   A. Grounds

Involuntary dissolution proceedings may be instituted under Corp C §1800 on any one or more of the following grounds:

(1) The corporation has abandoned its business for more than one year (Corp C §1800(b)(1));

(2) The corporation has an even number of directors who are equally divided and cannot agree as to the management of its affairs, so that the corporate business can no longer be conducted to advantage or so that there is danger that its property and business will be impaired or lost, and the holders of the voting shares are so divided into factions that they cannot elect a board consisting of an uneven number (Corp C §1800(b)(2));

(3) There is internal dissension, and two or more factions of shareholders are so deadlocked that the corporate business can no longer be conducted to advantage, or the shareholders have failed at two consecutive annual meetings, at which all voting power was exercised, to elect successors to directors (Corp C §1800(b)(3));

(4) Those in control of the corporation have been guilty of or knowingly countenanced persistent and pervasive fraud, mismanagement or abuse of authority, or persistent unfairness toward any shareholders, or the corporation's property is being misapplied or wasted by its directors or officers (Corp C §1800(b)(4));

(5) There are no more than 35 shareholders, and liquidation is

reasonably necessary for the protection of the rights of the complaining shareholders (Corp C §1800(b)(5)); or

(6) The period for which the corporation was formed has terminated and has not been extended (Corp C §1800(b)(6)).

In addition, the Attorney General may file suit in certain specified situations, under Corp C §1801. See §7.72.

Proceedings for involuntary winding up and dissolution are initiated by filing a verified complaint (see §7.77) in the Superior Court of the county in which the principal executive office of the corporation is located (or in Sacramento County if the office is outside California or there is no such office). Corp C §§1800(a), 177.

§7.71 B. Who May File

Involuntary proceedings may be initiated by (1) one half or more of the directors; (2) shareholders who hold not less than 33–1/3 percent of either the outstanding shares (assuming conversion of any convertible preferred shares), the outstanding common stock, or the equity of the corporation, exclusive in each case of shares owned by persons who have personally participated in any of the transactions enumerated in Corp C §1800(b)(4) (see §7.70), or any shareholder of a close corporation as defined in Corp C §158; (3) any shareholder if the ground for dissolution is that the term of corporate existence has expired; or (4) any other person expressly authorized to do so in the articles. Corp C §1800(a). In addition, the Attorney General may initiate proceedings (see §7.72). Any shareholder or creditor may intervene before trial. Corp C §1800(c).

§7.72 C. Attorney General Action

The Attorney General may bring an action in the name of the people of California to dissolve any domestic corporation, based on the Attorney General's own information or on the complaint of a private party, on any of the following grounds (Corp C §1801(a)):

(1) Serious violation of any statutory provision regulating corporations;

(2) Fraudulent abuse or usurpation of corporate privileges or powers;

(3) Violation of any provision of law by any act or default which is a ground for forfeiture of corporate existence; or

(4) Failure to pay any tax imposed by the Bank and Corporation Tax Law for a period of five years.

If the Attorney General's action is based on a matter or act that can be corrected by amendment of the corporation's articles or other corporate action, the Attorney General may not commence the action unless, at least 30 days before the institution of the action, the corporation has been given written notice of the matter or act done or omitted to be done and the corporation fails to institute proceedings to correct the matter or act within the 30-day period, or later fails to complete the proceedings. Corp C §1801(b).

In any action brought by the Attorney General, the court, as in other dissolution proceedings, may order dissolution or such other or partial relief as it deems just and expedient. A receiver may also be appointed, or the court may order that the corporation be wound up by its board subject to court supervision. Corp C §1801(c); see §§7.73, 7.75.

Service of process on the corporation is made in accordance with the requirements of Corp C §§1700–1702 or by written notice to the president or the secretary of the corporation at the address indicated in the corporation's last tax return. In addition, the Attorney General must also publish a notice to the shareholders of the corporation concerning commencement of the action once in a newspaper of general circulation in the county of the principal executive office of the corporation (or Sacramento County if the office is outside California or there is no such office). Corp C §1801(d).

§7.73   D. Appointment of Provisional Director

If the ground for the complaint for involuntary dissolution is that the board of directors is deadlocked (Corp C §1800(b)(2)), the court may appoint a provisional director, even though a vacancy does not exist on the board. Corp C §1802. The provisional director, who must be an impartial person who is neither a shareholder or creditor of the corporation nor a relative of any of the other directors, has all the rights and powers of a director until the deadlock is broken or until the provisional director is removed by order of the court or by approval of a majority of the voting shares of the corporation. Corp C §308(c).

§7.74 E. Appointment of Receiver

If the court determines that the interests of the corporation and its shareholders will suffer pending determination of the complaint for involuntary dissolution unless a receiver is appointed, the court, after a hearing on notice to the corporation and on the giving of security under CCP §567 by the persons seeking involuntary dissolution, may appoint a receiver to take over and manage the corporation's business and affairs and preserve its property pending the hearing and determination of the complaint for dissolution. Corp C §1803.

§7.75 F. Effect of Commencement of Involuntary Proceeding

After a hearing on the complaint for involuntary dissolution, the court, if cause is shown, may decree a winding up and dissolution of the corporation and, with or without winding up and dissolution, may issue orders, decrees, and injunctions as justice and equity require. Corp C §1804; see §7.78.

Involuntary proceedings for winding up a corporation commence when the order for winding up is entered. Corp C §1805(a). Once an involuntary proceeding for winding up has commenced, the winding up of the corporation's affairs must be conducted by the board, subject to the supervision of the court, unless the court, on good cause shown, appoints other persons to conduct the winding up. Subject to any restrictions imposed by the court, the directors or other persons conducting the winding up may exercise all their powers through the executive officers without order of court. Corp C §1805(b). See §7.28 for a discussion of the powers and authority of the board during the winding up process.

After an involuntary proceeding for winding up has commenced, the corporation must cease to carry on business except to the extent necessary for the beneficial winding up of the corporation and except during the period the board deems necessary to preserve the corporation's goodwill or going-concern value pending a sale of its business or assets. The directors must cause written notice of commencement of the proceeding for involuntary winding up to be mailed to all shareholders and to all known creditors and claimants whose addresses appear on the corporation's records (see §7.79), unless the order for winding up has been stayed (see §§7.80–7.82) or the proceeding or the execution of the order has been enjoined. Corp C §1805(c).

The jurisdiction and powers of the court, which are the same for involuntary and voluntary proceedings, are set forth at length in Corp C §1806. Corp C §§1804, 1904. See *Howard v Data Storage Assocs.* (1981) 125 CA3d 689, 178 CR 269 (in corporate dissolution proceedings, court has power under Corp C §1806(l) to being in such new parties as it deems proper). See also §§7.28.

After dissolution is completed, the corporation continues to exist for an indefinite period to wind up its affairs, prosecute and defend actions, collect and discharge obligations, dispose of and convey property, and collect and divide its assets. Corp C §2010(a). See §7.84.

§7.76   G. Buy-Out of Plaintiff Shareholder To Avoid Dissolution

To avoid involuntary dissolution or the appointment of a receiver, the corporation or the holders of 50 percent or more of the outstanding shares may purchase the plaintiff's shares at their fair value for cash in the same manner as in a voluntary dissolution (see §7.24), and a stay of the proceedings may be obtained from the court pending determination of the fair value of the plaintiff's shares. Corp C §2000; see §§7.80–7.83 for forms.

H. Court Forms

§7.77   1. Form: Complaint for Involuntary Winding Up and Dissolution

Form 7.77–1

[*Name of Plaintiff*]	) No. _ _ _ _ _ _
v	)
[*Name of Defendant*],	) **COMPLAINT FOR**
A California Corporation	) **INVOLUNTARY DISSOLUTION**
	) **OF A CORPORATION**
	) **(Corp C §1800)**

Plaintiff(s) allege(s) that:

1. Defendant is a corporation duly organized and existing under the laws of the State of California. Defendant's principal office is located in _ _ _ _ _ _ _ _ County, California.

2. Defendant is not subject to the Banking Law, Public Utilities Act, Savings and Loan Association Law, or sections 1010–1062 of the California Insurance Code.

[If complaint is by directors under Corp C §1800(a)(1), insert]

3. At a shareholders' meeting of defendant corporation held on _ _ _ _ _ _, 19_ _, each of the plaintiffs was elected a director of defendant corporation, and thereafter has acted as a director of defendant corporation. The total number of directors of the corporation is _ _ _ _, and the *[number]* plaintiffs constitute *[one half/more than one half]* of the total number of acting directors of the corporation.

[If complaint is by shareholders under Corp C §1800(a)(2), insert]

3. Plaintiffs are the holders of record of an aggregate of *[number]* shares of stock of defendant corporation. The number of shares of defendant corporation issued and outstanding is _ _ _ _ shares. There are no outstanding preferred shares of this corporation convertible into common shares *[e.g., except for _ _ _ _ shares which, assuming conversion, increase the number of issued and outstanding shares to _ _ _ _]*. The shares held by plaintiffs constitute at least 33–1/3 percent of the number of outstanding shares of defendant corporation *[e.g., exclusive of the [number] shares owned by [name] who, as alleged, personally participated in the transactions complained of]*.

[If complaint is by shareholder on expiration of term of corporate existence under Corp C §1800(a)(3), insert]

3. Plaintiff is the holder of record of *[number]* shares of defendant corporation. Defendant corporation was duly formed on _ _ _ _ _ _, 19_ _, and its articles of incorporation provide that the term for which it was to exist was *[number]* years from and after the date of its incorporation. This term of existence has expired without renewal or extension.

[Continue]

[Allege one or more of the following grounds]

4. Defendant corporation has abandoned its business for more than one year.

[Or]

4. The board of directors of defendant corporation consists of an even number of directors, namely, *[number]* **directors. At a meeting of the shareholders on _ _ _ _ _ _, 19_ _, the following persons were elected as directors:** *[names of directors]*. **Each of these persons was qualified and accepted the office, and thereafter has acted as a director of defendant corporation. At a meeting of the board of directors at which all these directors were present, held on _ _ _ _ _ _, 19_ _, the following matters concerning management of the affairs of the corporation were submitted for resolution and vote:** *[specify matters]*. **The directors were evenly divided on all of these matters, in that** *[number]* **directors voted in favor of, and** *[same number]* **directors voted against each matter. At that meeting and at all subsequent meetings of the board of directors, the directors have been and continue to be equally divided as to the management of the affairs of defendant corporation so that** *[e.g., the business of the corporation can no longer be conducted to advantage/there is danger that its property and business will be impaired and lost]* **in the following respects:** *[allege facts supporting conclusion]*. **The holders of the voting shares of defendant corporation are so divided into factions that they cannot agree on or elect a board of directors consisting of an uneven number.**

[Or]

4. There is internal dissension and two or more factions of shareholders in defendant corporation are so deadlocked that *[e.g., its business can no longer be conducted with advantage to its shareholders/the shareholders have failed at two consecutive annual meetings, at which all voting power was exercised, to elect successors to directors [name]* **and** *[name]*, **whose terms have expired or would have expired on election of their successors]*.

[Or]

4. *[The directors/names of persons in control]* **of defendant corporation have been guilty of or have knowingly countenanced persistent and pervasive** *[fraud/mismanagement/ abuse of authority/unfairness toward any shareholder]* **in the following respects:** *[allege facts supporting conclusion]*.

[Or]

4. Defendant corporation's property is being *[misapplied/ wasted/lost]* **by its** *[directors/officers]* **in the following respects:** *[specify]*.

[Or]

4. Defendant corporation has *[35 or fewer shareholders]* **and its liquidation is reasonably necessary for the protection of the rights and interests of** *[the complaining shareholder(s)]*, **specifically,** *[number]* **shareholder(s) holding a total of** *[number]* **shares of record of defendant corporation, in that** *[allege facts supporting conclusion]*.

[Continue]

WHEREFORE, plaintiff(s) pray(s) judgment as follows:

1. That the Court decree a winding up and dissolution of defendant corporation;

2. That the Court entertain those proceedings as may be necessary or proper for the involuntary winding up or dissolution of defendant corporation, and make those orders for winding up and dissolution of defendant corporation as justice and equity require;

3. For costs of suit herein incurred; and

4. For such other and further relief as the court may deem proper.

[Signature]

_____

[Typed name]
Attorney

VERIFICATION

I am *[a/the]* **plaintiff in this action; the foregoing complaint is true of my own knowledge, except as to the matters stated in it on my information or belief, and as to each of those matters I believe it to be true.**

I declare under penalty of perjury that the foregoing is true and correct, and that this declaration was executed on _ _ _ _ _ _, 19_ _, at _ _ _ _ _ _ _ _, California.

[*Signature*]

_____

[*Typed name*]
Plaintiff

Comment: The complaint should be adapted to the facts of the particular case. The term "caption" used in the court forms in this chapter represents the names of the court and county in which the action is brought and the title of the action. For examples of general format and caption of court papers, see 1 California Civil Procedure Before Trial §7.17, chap 22 (Cal CEB 1977).

§7.78   2. Form: Court Order Directing That Corporation Be Wound Up and Dissolved

Form 7.78–1

[*Caption; see*   **No. _ _ _ _ _ _**
Form 7.77–1]
                                   **ORDER THAT CORPORATION
                                   BE WOUND UP AND
                                   DISSOLVED**

The verified complaint of [*name(s) of plaintiff(s)*] **for the involuntary winding up and dissolution of** [*name of corporation*], **a California corporation, came on regularly for hearing before this Court on this date. Plaintiff(s) appeared by** [*name of counsel*]; **and** [*specify any other appearances*].

On proof to the satisfaction of the Court that an order should be made directing that defendant corporation be wound up and dissolved,

IT IS ORDERED that:

1. [*Name of corporation*], **a California corporation, be wound up and dissolved.**

2. The present directors of the corporation, [*name of each* *director*], **are directed to conduct the winding up of the affairs of the corporation.**

3. In winding up the affairs of the corporation, the directors shall have the powers and duties conferred on directors in voluntary proceedings under section 2001 of the California Corporations Code, each of which powers and duties may be executed and performed without further order by or authority from this Court, subject, however, to the power of this Court to make and issue such further orders, decrees, and injunctions as may be necessary or desirable.

Dated: _ _ _ _ _ _

_____
Judge

Comment: Involuntary proceedings for winding up are deemed to commence when the order requiring dissolution and winding up is entered. Corp C §§1804, 1805(a).

§7.79   3. Form: Notice of Commencement of Proceedings for Involuntary Winding Up and Dissolution

Form 7.79–1

[*Caption; see*   **No. _ _ _ _ _ _**
Form 7.77–1]
                                     NOTICE OF COMMENCEMENT OF PROCEEDINGS FOR INVOLUNTARY WINDING UP AND DISSOLUTION

TO ALL SHAREHOLDERS, CREDITORS, AND CLAIMANTS OF [*name of corporation*]:

NOTICE IS HEREBY GIVEN that in an action in the Superior Court of _ _ _ _ _ _ _ _ County, California, entitled "[*names of plaintiffs***], Plaintiffs v.** [*name of corporation*], **a Corporation, Defendant," which is a proceeding for the involuntary winding up and dissolution of** [*name of corporation*], **a California**

corporation, a court order was entered on _ _ _ _ _ _, 19_ _, ordering the winding up and dissolution of the corporation. The proceeding for winding up the corporation commenced on the date when that order was entered.

Dated: _ _ _ _ _ _

[*Name of corporation*]

By _____
[*Typed name and title*]

Comment: The directors are required to cause written notice to be mailed to all shareholders and all known creditors and claimants whose addresses appear on the records of the corporation, informing them that winding-up proceedings commenced as of the date the court order was entered. Corp C §1805.

§7.80   4. Form: Notice of Motion To Stay Proceedings and Ascertain Value of Plaintiffs' Shares

Form 7.80–1

[*Caption; see*   No. _ _ _ _ _ _
Form 7.77–1]

NOTICE OF MOTION TO
STAY PROCEEDINGS AND
ASCERTAIN VALUE OF
PLAINTIFFS' SHARES

To plaintiffs and their attorneys of record:

NOTICE IS HEREBY GIVEN that on _ _ _ _ _ _, 19_ _, at _ _ _.m., or as soon thereafter as the matter may be heard, in [*Department No._ _ of*] this Court, [*name of corporation*], defendant, will move for an order to stay the proceedings and to ascertain and fix the fair value of the shares owned by plaintiffs.

The motion will be made on the grounds that the holders of 50 percent or more of the outstanding shares of defendant corporation have elected to purchase plaintiffs' shares, are unable to agree with plaintiffs on the fair value of these shares, and will give bond with sufficient surety to pay the plaintiffs' reasonable expenses (including attorney fees) if payment for their shares is not made within the time required.

The motion will be based on this notice of motion, on the declaration of [*e.g., name of purchasing shareholder*] and the memorandum of points and authorities served and filed with this motion, on the papers and records on file, and on such oral and documentary evidence as may be presented at the hearing of the motion.

Dated: _ _ _ _ _ _

[*Attorney for defendant*]

Comment: A memorandum of points and authorities relied on must be served and filed with this notice. Cal Rules of Ct 313(a). See 4 Cal Points and Authorities, Corporations, Form 166 (1988) for a suggested memorandum.

§7.81   5. Form: Declaration in Support of Motion To Stay Proceedings

Form 7.81–1

[*Caption; see Form 7.77–1*]

No. _ _ _ _ _ _

DECLARATION IN SUPPORT
OF MOTION TO STAY
PROCEEDINGS AND
ASCERTAIN VALUE OF
PLAINTIFFS' SHARES

I, [*e.g., name of shareholder electing to purchase*], **declare:**

The total number of outstanding shares of defendant corporation is _ _ _ _ shares. The undersigned holds [*number*] shares of such stock, which holdings are 50 percent or more of the total outstanding shares.

On _ _ _ _ _ _, 19_ _, the undersigned elected to purchase plaintiffs' shares by written offer to purchase at $_ _ _ _ _ _ per share. A copy of the written offer is attached as Exhibit A. Plaintiffs did not accept the offer, and disagreed with the undersigned that the price offered represented the fair value for the shares. Therefore, plaintiffs and the undersigned do not agree on the fair value of plaintiffs' shares.

The undersigned will deposit with the Court a bond with sufficient surety in the amount fixed by the Court on granting the motion.

I declare under penalty of perjury that the foregoing is true and correct, and that this declaration was executed on _ _ _ _ _ _, 19_ _, at _ _ _ _ _ _ _ _, California.

[*Signature*]

_____
[*Typed name*]
Shareholder

§7.82　　6. Form: Order Staying Proceedings and Appointing Commissioners

Form 7.82–1

[*Caption; see*　　　　　　　**No. _ _ _ _ _ _**
Form 7.77–1]

ORDER STAYING PROCEEDINGS AND APPOINTING COMMISSIONERS TO ASCERTAIN FAIR VALUE OF PLAINTIFFS' STOCK

The motion of [*name of corporation*], a California corporation, to stay these proceedings and to ascertain the value of the shares held by plaintiffs came on regularly for hearing before this Court on _ _ _ _ _ _, 19_ _. Moving party appeared by counsel [*name*]; plaintiffs appeared by counsel [*name*].

On proof to the satisfaction of the Court that the motion should be granted,

IT IS ORDERED that:

1. The above-entitled proceeding for involuntary winding up and dissolution is stayed pending ascertainment by the Court of the fair value of plaintiffs' shares in accordance with this order.

2. [*Name of shareholder electing to purchase plaintiffs' stock*] shall deposit with the Court a bond in the amount of $_ _ _ _ _ _, with sufficient surety to pay the estimated reasonable expenses (including attorney fees) of plaintiffs if the petitioners herein fail to make payment for the plaintiffs' shares within the time required.

3. [*Names of three commissioners*], three impartial persons with no interest in this matter, are appointed commissioners and are directed to appraise the fair value of the shares owned by plaintiffs and to report this value to the Court within _ _ _ _ days from the date of this order.

Dated: _ _ _ _ _ _

_____
Judge

§7.83   7. Form: Order Confirming Award for Purchase of Plaintiffs' Shares

Form 7.83–1

[*Caption; see*   **No.** _ _ _ _ _ _
Form 7.77–1]
                         **ORDER CONFIRMING
                         AWARD FOR PURCHASE OF
                         PLAINTIFFS' SHARES**

The Court having appointed commissioners to ascertain the fair value of the shares of defendant corporation held by plaintiffs, and the commissioners having made their report to the Court, ascertaining the value of plaintiffs' shares to be $_ _ _ _ _ _ per share and awarding to plaintiffs the sum of $_ _ _ _ _ _ for [*number*] shares,

IT IS ORDERED that:

1. The award by the commissioners is confirmed.

2. The sum of $_ _ _ _ _ _ shall be paid to plaintiffs by [*name of shareholder electing to purchase shares*] **and** [*name of surety on bond*] **within** [*e.g., ten days*] **after entry of this decree; provided that if this payment is not made within that time, the involuntary winding up and dissolution of defendant corporation shall proceed immediately.**

3. On receipt of payment as ordered in this decree, plaintiffs shall transfer their [*number*] **shares to** [*name of shareholder electing to purchase*].

Dated: _ _ _ _ _ _

_____
Judge

Comment: This decree is in the alternative, providing for winding up and dissolution if payment is not made within the time specified in the decree.

VI. CONTINUED EXISTENCE OF DISSOLVED CORPORATION

§7.84   A. General Rule; Corp C §2010

After dissolution, whether or not the dissolution was supervised by a court, a corporation continues to exist for an indefinite period to wind up its affairs, prosecute and defend actions, collect and discharge obligations, dispose of and convey property, and collect and divide its assets. Corp C §2010(a). It may not, however, continue the normal corporate business except as necessary for winding it up. Title to assets inadvertently or otherwise omitted from winding up remains in the corporation after final dissolution. Later distribution of these assets must be made to the persons who would have been entitled to receive them at the time the corporation was dissolved. Corp C §2010(c).

Actions or proceedings to which a corporation is a party do not abate because of proceedings for dissolution and winding up. Corp C §2010(b).

An unresolved issue exists concerning whether Corp C §2010, which allows the survival of lawsuits by or against dissolved corporations for injuries arising out of predissolution activities, should be limited solely to domestic corporations. In *North American Asbestos Corp. v Superior Court* (1986) 180 CA3d 902, 255 CR 877, the court held that a foreign corporation licensed to do business in California fell within the scope of Corp C §2010, regardless of the law of its state of incorporation. Another California court has reached the opposite result. *Riley v Fitzgerald* (1986) 178 CA3d 871, 876, 223 CR 889, 892.

§7.85 B. Shareholder Liability for Future Claims

Under Corp C §2011, the shareholders of a dissolved corporation may be sued in the name of the corporation on any cause of action arising prior to its dissolution. The phrase "arising prior to its dissolution" has been considered by the court in *Allen v Southland Plumbing, Inc.* (1988) 201 CA3d 60, 246 CR 860, a case in which a condominium homeowners' association sued the general contractor for defects without naming the subcontractor. Shortly after the suit was filed, the subcontractor filed a certificate of corporate dissolution. The general contractor subsequently cross-complained against the subcontractor for equitable indemnity. The subcontractor argued that the claim for equitable indemnity arose after dissolution and therefore could not be maintained under Corp C §2011(a). Rejecting this argument, the appellate court held that the contractor's cause of action against the subcontractor arose no later than the date the association filed suit, which was before the subcontractor's dissolution.

As to causes of action arising after dissolution, however, Corp C §2011(a) has been strictly construed to bar suits against the shareholders of dissolved corporations if the claim arose after dissolution, even though such claims could formerly have been asserted under the equitable "trust fund" theory. In *Pacific Scene, Inc. v Penasquitos, Inc.* (1988) 46 C3d 407, 250 CR 651, the appellate court had held that while the plaintiffs could not bring suit under Corp C §2011 because the cause of action arose after the corporation's dissolution, they were entitled to sue the shareholders directly on an equitable "trust fund" theory. The Supreme Court reversed, holding that in enacting Corp C §2011 and related statutes, the legislature had preempted the field, superseding all former common law causes against the former shareholders of dissolved corporations. The Court noted the possibility, however, that a dissolved corporation or its shareholders might in appropriate cases be sued for the recovery of fraudulently transferred assets under the Uniform Fraudulent Transfer Act (Corp C §§3439–3439.12).

Because of the possibility of claims being brought against the shareholders of a dissolved corporation under Corp C §2011 or under the Uniform Fraudulent Transfer Act, consideration should be given to providing for potential claims through the purchase of insurance, or through contractual indemnification from the persons continuing the business of a dissolved corporation. See Comment, *Continuing Corporate Existence for Post-Dissolution Claims: The Defective Products Dilemma,* 13 Pac L Rev 1227 (1982).

Table of Statutes, Regulations, and Rules

Rules

FEDERAL RULES OF CIVIL PROCEDURE

ABA MODEL RULES OF PROFESSIONAL CONDUCT

SECURITIES AND EXCHANGE COMMISSION
Regulations

Rules

Rulings

REVENUE RULINGS

Miscellaneous Rulings, Releases, Policy Statements

Table of Cases

Bibliography

ADVISING CALIFORNIA EMPLOYERS (Cal CEB 1981).

ADVISING CALIFORNIA NONPROFIT CORPORATIONS (Cal CEB 1984).

ADVISING CALIFORNIA PARTNERSHIPS (2d ed Cal CEB 1988).

American Bar Association, Section of Antitrust Law. ANTITRUST LAW DEVELOPMENTS. 2d ed. New York: American Bar Association, Supplement, 1986.

ANTITRUST ADVISER. Edited by Carla A. Hills. New York: McGraw-Hill Book Co., 1971.

Aranow, Edward R., Einhorn, Herbert A. & Berlstein, G. DEVELOPMENTS IN TENDER OFFERS FOR CORPORATE CONTROL. New York: Columbia University Press, 1977.

_____ & Einhorn, Herbert A. TENDER OFFERS FOR CORPORATE CONTROL. New York: Columbia University Press, 1973.

ATTORNEY'S GUIDE TO CALIFORNIA PROFESSIONAL CORPORATIONS (Cal CEB 1987).

ATTORNEY'S GUIDE TO THE LAW OF COMPETITIVE BUSINESS PRACTICES (Cal CEB 1981).

ATTORNEY'S GUIDE TO PENSION AND PROFIT-SHARING PLANS (3d ed Cal CEB 1985).

Ballantine, Henry W. CALIFORNIA CORPORATION LAWS. Edited by Graham L. Sterling. 3 vols. 4th ed. Los Angeles: Ballantine & Sterling Publishers, 1977. Supplemented periodically.

Bittker, Boris I. & Eustice, James S. FEDERAL INCOME TAXATION OF CORPORATIONS AND SHAREHOLDERS. 5th ed. Boston: Warren, Gorham & Lamont, 1987. Supplemented regularly.

Bloomenthal. SECURITIES LAW HANDBOOK. New York: Clark Boardman Co., 1987–1988.

BUSINESS BUY-OUT AGREEMENTS (Cal CEB 1976).

CALIFORNIA ADMINISTRATIVE MANDAMUS (2d ed Cal CEB 1989).

CALIFORNIA ATTORNEY'S DAMAGES GUIDE (Cal CEB 1974).

CALIFORNIA CIVIL PROCEDURE BEFORE TRIAL. 2 vols. (Cal CEB 1977).

1, 2 CALIFORNIA TAXES (2d ed Cal CEB 1988, 1989).

Collier, William M. COLLIER ON BANKRUPTCY. Edited by James W. Moore. 26 vols. 15th ed. New York: Matthew Bender Co., 1979. Updated regularly.

Desmond, Glenn M. & Kelley, Richard E. Business Valuation Handbook. Rev. ed. Los Angeles: Valuation Press, 1988.

Drafting Agreements for the Sale of Businesses (2d ed Cal CEB 1988).

Financing California Businesses (Cal CEB 1976).

Fleischer, Arthur, Jr. Tender Offers: Defenses, Responses, and Planning. New York: Law & Business, Inc./Harcourt Brace Jovanovich, 1983.

Fletcher, William M. Cyclopedia of the Law of Private Corporations. 20 vols. Rev ed. Mundenlein, Ill.: Callaghan & Co., 1989.

Gadsby, Edward N. Business Organizations–Securities Regulations–Federal Securities Exchange Act. 2 vols. New York: Matthew Bender Co., 1977.

General Information Concerning Trademarks. Rev ed. Washington, D.C. G.P.O. (1984).

Gorman, Robert A. Basic Text on Labor Law. St. Paul: West Publishing Co., 1976.

Hicks, William J. Exempted Transactions Under the Securities Act of 1933. New York: C. Boardman Co., 1979.

Lattin, Norman D. The Law of Corporations. 2d ed. Minneola, N.Y.: Foundation Press, 1971.

Lipton, Martin & Steinberger. Takeovers and Freezeouts. New York: New York Law Publishing Co., 1978.

Loss, Louis. Fundamentals of Securities Regulation. 3 vols. 3d ed. Boston: Little, Brown & Co., 1988.

_____ & Seligman, Joel. Securities Regulation. 3d ed. Boston: Little, Brown & Co., 1989.

Marsh, Harold, Jr. California Corporation Law and Practice. 2d ed. St. Paul: West Publishing Co., 1977.

_____ & Volk, Robert H. Practice Under the California Securities Laws. 3 vols. Rev ed. New York: Matthew Bender Co., 1976.

Mertens, Jacob, Jr. The Law of Federal Income Taxation. Rev ed. Chicago: Callaghan & Co., 1987.

Morris, Charles J. The Developing Labor Law. 2d ed. Washington, D.C., BNA, 1985.

O'Neal, F. Hodge. Close Corporations. 2 vols. 3d ed. Chicago: Callaghan & Co., 1983. Supplemented periodically.

_____ & Thompson, Robert B. Oppression of Minority Shareholders. 2d ed. Wilmette, Ill.: Callaghan & Co., 1985.

Organizing Corporations in California (2d ed Cal CEB 1983).

Plant & Eager, CALIFORNIA TAXATION. New York: Matthew Bender, 1990.

Pratt, Shannon P. VALUING SMALL BUSINESSES AND PROFESSIONAL PRACTICES. Homewood, Ill.: Dow-Jones Irwin, 1986.

Schnepper, Jeff A. THE PROFESSIONAL HANDBOOK OF BUSINESS VALUATION. Reading, Mass.: Addison-Wesley Pub. Co., 1982.

SECURITIES LAW SERIES. New York: Clark Boardman Co., 1990.

SECURITIES LAW TECHNIQUES. Edited by A. A. Sommers, Jr. New York: Matthew Bender, 1985.

SHARK REPELLENTS AND GOLDEN PARACHUTES: A HANDBOOK FOR THE PRACTITIONER. Edited by Robert H. Winter, Mark H. Stumpf & Gerard L. Hawkins. New York: Law & Business, 1983.

Sommer, A.A., Jr. SECURITIES LAW TECHNIQUES. Looseleaf, 5 vols. New York: Matthew Bender.

Sowards, Hugh L. BUSINESS ORGANIZATION—SECURITIES REGULATIONS—FEDERAL SECURITIES ACT. Rev ed. New York: Matthew Bender Co., 1970; Supplement 1989 Vol. 11.

U.S. Patent & Trademark Office. GENERAL INFORMATION CONCERNING TRADEMARKS. Washington, D.C.: Government Printing Office, rev. 1976.

Witkin, CALIFORNIA PROCEDURE. 6 vols. 3d ed. San Francisco: Bancroft-Whitney Co., 1985. Supplemented periodically.

_____. SUMMARY OF CALIFORNIA LAW. 8 vols. 8th ed. San Francisco: Bancroft-Whitney Co., 1974, supplemented periodically.

WHAT CONSTITUTES DOING BUSINESS: New York: CT Corporation System, 1985.

WRONGFUL EMPLOYMENT TERMINATION PRACTICE (Cal CEB 1987).

Table of Forms

References are to chapter section numbers

Index

References are to chapter section numbers. Comments are designated by the abbreviation "com" in parentheses.